GIVING the SENSE

Understanding and Using Old Testament Historical Texts

David M. Howard Jr.
Michael A. Grisanti
editors

APOLLOS

Giving the Sense: Understanding and Using Old Testament Historical Texts

© 2003 by David M. Howard Jr. and Michael A. Grisanti

Published by Kregel Publications, a division of Kregel, Inc., P.O. Box 2607, Grand Rapids, MI 49501

and by Apollos (an imprint of Inter-Varsity Press), 38 De Montfort Street, Leicester, LE1 7GP, England; email: ivp@uccf.org.uk; website: www.ivpbooks.com.

All rights reserved. No part of this book may be reproduced, stored in a retrieval system, or transmitted in any form or by any means—electronic, mechanical, photocopy, recording, or otherwise—without written permission of the publisher, except for brief quotations in printed reviews.

Unless otherwise noted, Scripture quotations are from the *Holy Bible, New International Version®*. © 1973, 1978, 1984 by International Bible Society. Used by permission of Zondervan Publishing House. All rights reserved.

Scripture quotations marked KJV are from the King James Version of the Holy Bible.

Scripture quotations marked NASB are from the *New American Standard Bible*. © The Lockman Foundation 1960, 1962, 1963, 1968, 1971, 1972, 1973, 1975, 1977, 1995.

Scripture quotations marked NKJV are from *The New King James Version*. © 1979, 1980, 1982, Thomas Nelson, Inc., Publishers.

US ISBN 0-8254-2892-0

British Library Cataloguing in Publication Data
A catalogue record for this book is available from the British Library
UK ISBN 1-84474-016-1

Printed in the United States of America

03 04 05 06 07 / 5 4 3 2 1

Contents

Contributors 9
Preface 13
Abbreviations 17

Part 1: Methodological Issues in Studying Israel's History
1. History as History: The Search for Meaning 25
   David M. Howard Jr.
2. History or Story? The Literary Dimension in Narrative Texts .. 54
   Robert B. Chisholm Jr.
3. Archaeology and Biblical History: Its Uses and Abuses 74
   Eugene H. Merrill
4. History and Theology: The Tale of Two Histories 97
   C. Hassell Bullock

Part 2: Overview of Israel's History: Issues and Debates
5. Factors in Reading the Patriarchal Narratives: Literary, Historical, and Theological Dimensions 115
   Richard E. Averbeck
6. Conquest, Infiltration, Revolt, or Resettlement? What Really Happened During the Exodus–Judges Period? 138
   Carl G. Rasmussen
7. The United Monarchy: Archaeological and Literary Issues 160
   Hermann Austel
8. The Divided Monarchy: Sources, Approaches, and Historicity 179
   Richard D. Patterson

9. The Exilic and Postexilic Periods: Current Developments 201
   Edwin M. Yamauchi

Part 3: Historical and Archaeological Issues in Israel's History
10. Dating of the Patriarchal Age: The Contribution of
    Ancient Near Eastern Texts 217
    Mark F. Rooker
11. The Date of the Exodus 236
    William H. Shea
12. From Ramesses to Shiloh: Archaeological Discoveries
    Bearing on the Exodus–Judges Period 256
    Bryant G. Wood
13. The Incredible Numbers of the Hebrew Kings 283
    David Fouts
14. After the Exile: Haggai and History 300
    Byron G. Curtis

Part 4: Literary and Theological Issues in Israel's History
15. Did the Patriarchs Know the Name of the Lord? 323
    Allen P. Ross
16. The Challenge of Faith's Final Step: Israel's Journey Toward
    Victory in Numbers 33 340
    R. Dennis Cole
17. Authorial Intent and the Spoken Word: A Discourse-critical
    Analysis of Speech Acts in Accounts of Israel's United Monarchy
    (1 Sam. 1–1 Kings 11) 360
    Robert D. Bergen
18. A Funny Thing Happened on the Way to the Gallows! Irony,
    Humor, and Other Literary Features of the Book of Esther ... 380
    Gordon H. Johnston

Part 5: Preaching from Old Testament Historical Texts
19. Tell Me the Old, Old Story: Preaching the Message of
    Old Testament Narrative 409
    Daniel I. Block
20. Preaching from Historical Narrative Texts of the
    Old Testament 439
    Walter C. Kaiser Jr.

Eugene H. Merrill: A Brief Personal History 457
  Michael A. Grisanti

Subject Index 466
Author Index 472
Scripture Index 476

Contributors

Hermann Austel, Ph.D., University of California at Los Angeles
Distinguished Professor of Old Testament and Bible Exposition
Northwest Baptist Seminary, Tacoma, Washington

Richard E. Averbeck, Ph.D., Dropsie College
Associate Professor of Old Testament and Semitic Languages
Trinity Evangelical Divinity School, Deerfield, Illinois

Robert D. Bergen, Ph.D., Southwestern Baptist Theological Seminary
Professor of Old Testament and Biblical Languages
Hannibal-LaGrange College, Hannibal, Missouri

Daniel I. Block, D.Phil., University of Liverpool
John R. Sampey Professor of Old Testament Interpretation
The Southern Baptist Theological Seminary, Louisville, Kentucky

C. Hassell Bullock, Ph.D., Hebrew Union College
Franklin S. Dyrness Professor of Biblical Studies
Wheaton College, Wheaton, Illinois

Robert B. Chisholm Jr., Th.D., Dallas Theological Seminary
Professor of Old Testament Studies
Dallas Theological Seminary, Dallas, Texas

R. Dennis Cole, Th.D., New Orleans Baptist Theological Seminary
Professor of Old Testament and Archaeology, occupying the McFarland Chair of Old Testament and Archaeology
New Orleans Baptist Theological Seminary, New Orleans, Louisiana

Byron G. Curtis, Ph.D. candidate, Duke University
Assistant Professor of Biblical Studies
Geneva College, Beaver Falls, Pennsylvania

David Fouts, Th.D., Dallas Theological Seminary
Professor of Bible and Hebrew
Bryan College, Dayton, Tennessee

Michael A. Grisanti, Ph.D., Dallas Theological Seminary
Associate Professor of Old Testament
The Master's Seminary, Sun Valley, California

David M. Howard Jr., Ph.D., The University of Michigan
Professor of Old Testament
Bethel Theological Seminary, St. Paul, Minnesota

Gordon H. Johnston, Th.D., Dallas Theological Seminary
Associate Professor of Old Testament
Dallas Theological Seminary, Dallas, Texas

Walter C. Kaiser Jr., Ph.D., Brandeis University
President and Colman M. Mockler Distinguished Professor of Old Testament
Gordon-Conwell Theological Seminary, South Hamilton, Massachusetts

Eugene H. Merrill, Ph.D., Columbia University
Distinguished Professor of Old Testament Studies
Dallas Theological Seminary, Dallas, Texas

Richard D. Patterson, Ph.D., University of California at Los Angeles
Professor Emeritus of Old Testament
Liberty University, Lynchburg, Virginia

Carl G. Rasmussen, Ph.D., Dropsie University
Professor of Biblical and Theological Studies
Bethel College, St. Paul, Minnesota

Mark F. Rooker, Ph.D., Brandeis University
Professor of Old Testament and Hebrew
Southeastern Baptist Theological Seminary, Wake Forest, North Carolina

Allen P. Ross, Ph.D., University of Cambridge
Professor of Divinity
Beeson Divinity School, Birmingham, Alabama

William H. Shea, Ph.D., The University of Michigan
Former Professor of Old Testament, Andrews University; now Associate Director of the Biblical Research Institute, Silver Springs, Maryland

Bryant G. Wood, Ph.D., University of Toronto
Director
Associates for Biblical Research, Landisville, Pennsylvania

Edwin M. Yamauchi, Ph.D., Brandeis University
Professor of History
Miami University, Oxford, Ohio

Preface

It is a great pleasure and a privilege to present this collection of essays as an exemplar of the current state of evangelical scholarship on matters of history and the historical texts of the Old Testament. We think that these essays demonstrate something of the vitality, depth, and breadth of evangelical scholarship early in the twenty-first century.

This volume is intended for use in history-of-Israel courses in Christian Bible colleges, liberal-arts colleges, and seminaries, as well as Old Testament survey courses. It can be used as a stand-alone textbook in courses where the professor supplements readings of the Bible's history with lectures and other materials. It also can be used alongside such standards as Leon Wood's *A Survey of Israel's History,* Eugene Merrill's *Kingdom of Priests,* Walter Kaiser's *A History of Israel,* and John Bright's *A History of Israel.*[1] This volume does not survey Israel's history, but rather discusses issues arising from the historical texts. Such a scope allows much flexibility in its use.

In part 1, four chapters introduce different methodological issues involved in reading the historical texts. Part 2 surveys the state of scholarship in the different Old Testament eras, as the authors present their own views on the issues raised. Parts 3 and 4 present more narrowly conceived essays. Those in part 3 are written from historical or archaeological viewpoints, while those in part 4 work from literary or theological perspectives. Part 5 applies what has been learned to the practical tasks of preaching and teaching from Old Testament historical texts.

---

1. Leon Wood, *A Survey of Israel's History,* rev. David O'Brien (Grand Rapids: Zondervan, 1986); Eugene H. Merrill, *Kingdom of Priests: A History of Old Testament Israel* (Grand Rapids: Baker, 1987); Walter C. Kaiser Jr., *A History of Israel: From the Bronze Age through the Jewish Wars* (Nashville: Broadman & Holman, 1998); and John Bright, *A History of Israel,* 4th ed. (Louisville: Westminster/John Knox, 2000).

We have four objectives. The first is to acquaint the reader with the major methodological questions involved in reading historical texts of any type and specifically those in the Old Testament. Part 1 focuses on these, and other chapters add insights. Second, the reader will gain an understanding of the central issues arising from eras presented in the Old Testament.[2] These are presented in part 2. Third, parts 3 and 4 allow the reader to see ways in which historical texts can be read and used, from historical, archaeological, literary, or theological perspectives. Here, individual contributors were given freedom to write on anything they chose, and the results show how the texts can contribute valuable information on a number of levels. Fourth, part 5 enables the reader to appreciate the intensely practical value of Old Testament historical texts in their proclamation as God's Word.

The volume's title—*Giving the Sense: Understanding and Using Old Testament Historical Texts*—is taken from Nehemiah 8:8, which reads: "And they read from the book, from the law of God, translating to give the sense so that they understood the reading" (NASB). In this title, we highlight the interpretational activity involved in "to give the sense" (NASB), in "giving the meaning" (NIV). It is imperative for Christian leaders to be able to "give the sense," to explain clearly what the Word of God is saying. This is just as true for the Old Testament's historical texts as for the law or any other part of Scripture. Hence our title, *Giving the Sense*. We hope to do precisely that.

This project was the brainchild of Michael Grisanti, who desired to honor his teacher, Dr. Eugene H. Merrill, with a volume dedicated in his honor (i.e., a *"Festschrift"*). David Howard readily agreed to coedit the volume. After much discussion about the work's nature, we settled on a structure and purpose that departs from a classic *"Festschrift"* model—wherein one or two dozen unrelated essays are presented together in a rather haphazard manner. We opted for a more user-friendly, textbook model, as noted above. Nevertheless, we do present this work in honor of Dr. Merrill, our friend, colleague, and (Grisanti's) teacher. The topic of interpreting Old Testament historical texts is especially appropriate. Dr. Merrill has spent much

---

2. This volume does not include discussion of Genesis 1–11 as historical narrative, although the editors believe these chapters accurately describe events that took place in time and space. The style of Genesis 1–11 does not fit the "history" genre as readily as do the other corpora covered here.

of his professional career addressing such issues. For more of Dr. Merrill's insights, read his fine contribution (pp. 74–96) and see Michael Grisanti's biographical and bibliographical essay (pp. 457–65).

We are pleased that so many evangelical scholars agreed to write and have offered contributions that can be used with profit. All are original for this volume, except for the first one by Howard, which is adapted from his *An Introduction to the Old Testament Historical Books,* and his *Joshua.*[3] This has allowed Howard to revisit and refine this material, and we thank Moody Press and Broadman & Holman Publishers for granting permission to do so.

We also thank Kregel Publications for supporting this project. Jim Weaver, Director of Academic and Professional Books at Kregel, has been an encouraging supporter, and the project would not have seen the light of day without his efforts and those of his team.

If, in the end, this volume honors Dr. Eugene H. Merrill in some way, how much more is our desire that it should honor the God to whom Dr. Merrill has devoted his life and career. We are sure that Gene would have it this way, too. We write these words during the 2002 Advent season, and we are reminded again that this God has broken into history on our behalf. It is our prayer that the essays herein will glorify him and serve his church, in showing the many legitimate and helpful ways in which Old Testament historical texts can be used, in showing how problems can be approached, and in showing that, in the end, the Bible "makes sense."

---

3. David M. Howard Jr., *An Introduction to the Old Testament Historical Books* (Chicago: Moody, 1993), 29–44; idem, *Joshua,* NAC (Nashville: Broadman & Holman, 1999), 40–46.

ABBREVIATIONS

AASOR	Annual of the American Schools of Oriental Research
AB	Anchor Bible
ABD	Anchor Bible Dictionary, ed. D. N. Freedman et al., 6 vols. (New York: Doubleday, 1992)
ACEBT	Amsterdamse Cahiers voor Exegese in bijbelse Theologie
ADAJ	Annual of the Department of Antiquities of Jordan
AEL	Ancient Egyptian Literature, trans. M. Lichtheim, 3 vols. (Berkeley: University of California Press, 1971–1980)
AJA	American Journal of Archaeology
AJSL	American Journal of Semitic Languages and Literature
ANET	Ancient Near Eastern Texts Relating to the Old Testament, ed. J. B. Pritchard, 3d ed. with supplement (Princeton, N.J.: Princeton University Press, 1969)
AOOT	Ancient Orient and Old Testament, K. A. Kitchen (Downers Grove, Ill.: InterVarsity, 1966)
ARAB	Ancient Records of Assyria and Babylonia, D. D. Luckenbill, 2 vols. (Chicago: n.p., 1926–1927)
ARE	Ancient Records of Egypt, ed. J. H. Breasted, 5 vols. (1905–1907; reprint, New York: Russell and Russell, 1962)
ASAE	Annales du service des antiquités de l'Egypte
ASTI	Annual of the Swedish Theological Institute
AUSS	Andrews University Seminary Studies
BA	Biblical Archaeologist
BAR	Biblical Archaeology Review
BASOR	Bulletin of the American Schools of Oriental Research
BBR	Bulletin for Biblical Research

BDB	*The New Brown, Driver, Briggs Hebrew and English Lexicon of the Old Testament* (Oxford: Oxford University Press, 1907)
Bib	*Biblica*
BibInt	*Bible Interpretation*
BN	*Biblische Nötizen*
BR	*Biblical Research*
BRev	*Bible Review*
BSac	*Bibliotheca Sacra*
BTB	*Biblical Theology Bulletin*
BTS	*Bible et terre sainte*
BV	*Biblical Viewpoint*
BZAW	*Beihefte zur Zeitschrift für die alttestamentliche Wissenschaft*
CBQ	*Catholic Biblical Quarterly*
ConJ	*Concordia Journal*
COS	*Context of Scripture*, ed. W. W. Hallo and K. L. Younger Jr., 3 vols. (Leiden: Brill, 1997–2002)
CTR	*Criswell Theological Review*
CurBS	*Currents in Research: Biblical Studies*
EA	Tell el-Amarna tablets (cited from J. A. Knudtzon, O. Weber, and E. Ebeling, *Die El-Amarna Tafeln*, 2 vols., VAB 2, Leipzig, 1915; and A. F. Rainey, *El-Amarna Tablets 359–379: Supplement to J. A. Knudzton, Die El-Amarna Tafeln*, 2d rev. ed., AOAT 8, Kevelaer and Neukirchen-Vluyn, 1970)
EBC	Expositor's Bible Commentary
EcR	*The Ecumenical Review* (Geneva)
EncJud	*Encyclopaedia Judaica*
ErIsr	*Eretz Israel*
ESV	English Standard Version
FOTL	Forms of Old Testament Literature
FT	*Folia theologica*
GJT	*Grace Theological Journal*
HAR	*Hebrew Annual Review*
HS	*Hebrew Studies*
HTR	*Harvard Theological Review*
HUCA	*Hebrew Union College Annual*
IBC	Interpretation: A Bible Commentary for Teaching and Preaching

ICC	International Critical Commentary
IEJ	*Israel Exploration Journal*
ISBE	*International Standard Bible Encyclopedia*, ed. G. W. Bromiley, rev. ed., 4 vols. (Grand Rapids: Eerdmans, 1979–88)
JANES	*Journal of the Ancient Near Eastern Society of Columbia University*
JAOS	*Journal of the American Oriental Society*
JBL	*Journal of Biblical Literature*
JBQ	*Jewish Bible Quarterly*
JBR	*Journal of Bible and Religion*
JCS	*Journal of Cuneiform Studies*
JEA	*Journal of Egyptian Archaeology*
JES	*Journal of Ecumenical Studies*
JETS	*Journal of the Evangelical Theological Society*
JNES	*Journal of Near Eastern Studies*
JNSL	*Journal of Northwest Semitic Languages*
JPS	Jewish Publication Society
JQR	*Jewish Quarterly Review*
JR	*Journal of Religion*
JSOT	*Journal for the Study of the Old Testament*
JSOTSup	Journal for the Study of the Old Testament—Supplement Series
JSS	*Journal of Semitic Studies*
JSSEA	*Journal of the Society for the Study of Egyptian Antiquities*
JTS	*Journal of Theological Studies*
KAT	Kommentar zum Alten Testament
KJV	King James Version
NAC	New American Commentary
NASB	New American Standard Bible
NCBC	New Century Bible Commentary
NEA	*Near Eastern Archaeology*
NEAEHL	*The New Encyclopedia of Archaeological Excavations in the Holy Land*, ed. E. Stern, 4 vols. (Jerusalem: Israel Exploration Society; New York: Simon and Schuster, 1993)
NEASB	*Near Eastern Archaeological Society Bulletin*
NIBC	New International Biblical Commentary

NIDBA	*New International Dictionary of Biblical Archaeology,* ed. E. M. Blaiklock and R. K. Harrison (Grand Rapids, Zondervan, 1983)
NIDOTTE	*New International Dictionary of Old Testament Theology and Exegesis,* ed. W. VanGemeren, 5 vols. (Grand Rapids: Zondervan, 1997)
NIV	New International Version
NKJV	New King James Version
NRSV	New Revised Standard Version
OEAE	*The Oxford Encyclopedia of Ancient Egypt,* ed. Donald B. Redford (New York: Oxford University Press, 2001)
OEANE	*Oxford Encyclopedia of Archaeology in the Near East,* ed. E. M. Myers (New York: Oxford University Press, 1997)
OTE	*Old Testament Essays*
OTL	Old Testament Library
OTS	*Oudtestamentische Studiën*
PEFQS	*Palestine Exploration Fund Quarterly Statement*
PEQ	*Palestine Exploration Quarterly*
POTW	*Peoples of the Old Testament World,* ed. A. J. Hoerth et al. (Grand Rapids: Baker, 1999)
RB	*Revue biblique*
RelSRev	*Religious Studies Review*
ResQ	*Restoration Quarterly*
RQ	*Römische Quartalschrift für christliche Altertumskunde und Kirchengeschichte*
RTR	*Reformed Theological Review*
SBL	Society of Biblical Literature
SBT	Studies in Biblical Theology
SBTS	Sources for Biblical and Theological Study
SJOT	*Scandinavian Journal of the Old Testament*
SOTS	Society for Old Testament Study
SwJT	*Southwestern Journal of Theology*
TBT	*The Bible Today*
TOTC	Tyndale Old Testament Commentaries
TT	*Teologisk Tidsskrift*
TynBul	*Tyndale Bulletin*
TZ	*Theologische Zeitschrift*

VT	*Vetus Testamentum*
VTSup	Vetus Testamentum Supplements
WBC	Word Biblical Commentary
ZAW	*Zeitschrift für die alttestamentliche Wissenschaft*

PART 1
METHODOLOGICAL ISSUES IN STUDYING ISRAEL'S HISTORY

I

History as History

The Search for Meaning

David M. Howard Jr.

The term *history* has at least three general meanings in English.[1] First, it can refer to the "facts," i.e., the events, the happenings of history. Second, it can refer to the record or account of the facts or events. Third, it can refer to the *study* of the facts (events), or, more precisely, the study of the accounts of these facts (events).

In our title above, *history* is used in two different ways, referring in the one case to the facts or events, and in the other case to the record of the facts or events. The title makes sense regardless of which meaning is assigned to which occurrence of the term. That is, the title could mean something like "historical events as translated into historical records" or it could mean something like "historical records as they give account of historical events." In both cases, the emphasis is on the first element in the title. In the first understanding of our title—where the meaning is "historical events as translated into historical records"—the focus is on the events themselves (and their subsequent "translation" into records), whereas in the second understanding—where the meaning is "historical records as they give account of historical events"—the focus is more on the records and how they derive from the events.

In the discussion below, the focus will be primarily on the written records

---

[1]. Portions of this essay are adapted and updated from David M. Howard Jr., *An Introduction to the Old Testament Historical Books* (Chicago: Moody, 1993), 29–44; and idem, *Joshua,* NAC (Nashville: Broadman & Holman, 1999), 40–46, and are used with permission. I am pleased to acknowledge here an essay by Eugene Merrill that covers some of the same ground: "History," in *Cracking Old Testament Codes: A Guide to Interpreting the Literary Genres of the Old Testament,* ed. D. B. Sandy and R. L. Giese Jr. (Nashville: Broadman & Holman, 1995), 89–112.

and how they purport to give account of historical events, i.e., events that took place in time and space. So, the second version of the title should be understood as governing the discussion here: *"historical records as they give account of historical events."*

The Modern Study of History—General

Definitions

Historians have offered many and varied definitions of *history* as they have reflected upon the historian's task. Indeed, many do not even attempt a definition, or do so with only minimal precision or clarity.[2]

Four representative definitions define the second of the above meanings:

> [History is] the science which first investigates and then records, in their causal relations and development, such past human activities as are (a) definite in time and space, (b) social in nature, and (c) socially significant.[3]

> The story of experiences of men living in civilized societies.[4]

> History is the intellectual form in which a civilization renders account to itself of the past.[5]

> History is the undertaking of rendering an account of a particular, significant, and coherent sequence of past human events.[6]

---

2. M. Eisenberg cheerfully acknowledges this fact, and he refuses to define it himself, noting the many conflicting definitions in the process. See his section, "A Nondefinition" in Michael T. Eisenberg, *Puzzles of the Past: An Introduction to Thinking About History* (College Station, Tex.: Texas A & M University, 1985), 3–5.
3. Gilbert J. Garraghan, *A Guide to Historical Method* (New York: Fordham University, 1946), 10. Garraghan exegetes this definition on pages 7–10.
4. Gustaaf Johannes Renier, *History: Its Purpose and Method* (London: George Allen & Unwin, 1950; reprint, Macon, Ga.: Mercer University, 1982), 38. He unfolds this definition on pages 33–39.
5. Johan Huizinga, "A Definition of the Concept of History," in *Philosophy and History: Essays Presented to Ernst Cassirer*, ed. R. Klibansky and H. J. Paton (Cambridge: Cambridge University, 1936), 9 (also see pp. 1–10). The citation here of this oft-quoted definition comes from K. Lawson Younger Jr., *Ancient Conquest Accounts: A Study in Ancient Near Eastern and Biblical History Writing*, JSOTSup 98 (Sheffield: Sheffield Academic Press, 1990), 26.
6. Baruch Halpern, *The First Historians: The Hebrew Bible and History* (San Francisco: Harper & Row, 1988), 6.

We should note that almost every definition here speaks of history as a societal endeavor, one that records (mainly or only) those events that are *socially significant*. In this sense, not every event that ever occurred anywhere belongs in a "history" (even though they certainly did happen). A "history" records events that are significant to the author and to the group for or about which she/he is writing.

The last definition limits the genre significantly as well, since *any* account of the past is not "history" (such as an accounts book, a diary, or a shopping list). Rather, only that account is "history" that attempts to impose some coherence on the past. This limitation, while not expressed in the same way, is assumed in the first three definitions, as well.

History as "the Facts"

The notion of *history* in most people's minds usually refers to the events, the happenings of human endeavor. This is "what people have done and suffered," that is, the "historical process,"[7] or "past actuality."[8]

We should remember several things about such happenings. First, events are always out of reach, except at the moment of occurrence. Our access to such events is through records or accounts of them. Second, evidence for such events is always limited (i.e., it is not unlimited). Absence of evidence does not prove that the event did not happen; it merely means that no record or evidence of the event is available at hand. Third, such evidence as does exist must be interpreted, in order to understand it.

History as the Record of the Facts

History also refers to the writing of history or "historiography."[9] This is sometimes called by the Greek term ἱστορία, which has to do with inquiry. Its original use simply meant " investigation, research, inquiry," but it later came to refer to the record or narration of the results of such an

---

7. David W. Bebbington, *Patterns in History: A Christian View* (Downers Grove, Ill.: InterVarsity, 1979), 1.
8. Garraghan, *Guide to Historical Method*, 3.
9. "Historiography" can also refer to the third use of the term *history* mentioned at the outset—the study of the records of the facts—and thus some confusion occasionally exists. Here, we will primarily use the term to refer to the record of the facts, that is, to the history writing itself.

inquiry.[10] Herodotus, called "the father of history" by the Roman statesman Cicero (and most modern historians would agree), introduced his own work by this term, meaning an "inquiry" *(historia)*. Historical studies in this sense differ from stories, myths, chronicles, or memories, all of which also speak of the past. Histories "depend upon inquiry, the purpose of which is to establish the truth concerning particular events that did actually occur,"[11] in contrast to these other types of records, which do not try to establish such truth about events (or the relationships among events).

As we have noted, history writing is a record or representation of the events, not the events themselves. A picture of an apple, regardless of how realistically it presents the apple, is not an apple; it cannot be eaten. Rather, it is a representation of an apple. So it is with historical events and history writing. What we study are the records of the events.

Not just *any* record of the past can be considered "history." Checkbooks, tax returns, grocery-store receipts, personal diaries, and subway walls decorated by graffiti all contain records of the past, but they are not consciously written, coherent accounts of past, societally significant events, based on conscious inquiry.

In the Bible, we have evidence that several biblical writers wrote with a degree of historical self-consciousness. In the New Testament, we see this best in the Gospels of Luke (and the book of Acts) and John. Luke stated,

> Many have undertaken to draw up an account of the things that have been fulfilled among us, just as they were handed down to us by those who from the first were eyewitnessed and servants of the word. Therefore, since I myself have carefully investigated everything from the beginning, it seemed good also to me to write an orderly account for you, most excellent Theophilus, so that you may know the certainty of the things you have been taught. (Luke 1:1–4; all Scripture quotations in this chapter from NIV)

John acknowledged that his own record of Jesus' life was incomplete:

---

10. Garraghan, *Guide to Historical Method,* 3. Liddell and Scott define it as "inquiry" and as a "written account of one's inquiries, narrative, history." H. G. Liddell and R. Scott, comps., *A Greek-English Lexicon,* rev. H. S. Jones (Oxford: Clarendon, 1940), s.v. "ἱστορία."
11. Maurice Mandelbaum, *The Anatomy of Historical Knowledge* (Baltimore: Johns Hopkins University Press, 1977), 7.

Jesus did many other miraculous signs in the presence of his disciples, which are not recorded in this book. But these are written that you may believe that Jesus is the Christ, the Son of God, and that by believing you may have life in his name. (John 20:30–31)

Jesus did many other things as well. If every one of them were written down, I suppose that even the whole world would not have room for the books that would be written. (John 21:25)

In the Old Testament, the numerous references in the books of 1–2 Kings and 1–2 Chronicles to extrabiblical sources used by the authors to compose their works attest to this. These were sources to which the public had some sort of access, since the writers asked a rhetorical question, such as "And the deeds of [king's name], are they not written in the Books of the Chronicles of the Kings of Israel?" In the book of Ezra, numerous official letters and decrees are recorded in the language in which they were written (Aramaic), presumably verbatim.

Historical Method: The Study of the Facts

The Sources for History Writing: Written Texts

Written materials usually form the most important source for historians as they construct their histories. These come in two categories: (1) casual (or official) history, and (2) deliberative (or literary) history.

(1) Casual history consists of the "raw material" of history, of the records produced at all levels of society, from the individual to the international. Today, this consists of such things as checkbooks; appointment calendars; personal diaries; business receipts; courthouse records of births, marriages, and deaths; governmental rules, regulations, and laws; international treaties; and so forth. They consist of information presented in statement form, impersonal, with minimal analysis, if any at all.

In the ancient Near East, the raw materials include gravestone inscriptions, administrative and economic documents of the great empires, petty receipts, and letters. Modern biblical scholars use these alongside the Bible in attempting to reconstruct Israel's history.

We can also identify the raw materials of history writing in the Bible itself. These include songs, poems, genealogies, census lists, lists of clean and unclean animals, and king lists. Sometimes the Bible's sources are even named explicitly, such as "The Book of the Wars of the LORD" (Num. 21:14).

(2) Deliberative history represents true historiography. It is analytical, interpretive written history. It is the product of selection by an author, with specific purposes in mind, creatively arranging the final product. (In the Bible's case, we would affirm that it is by inspiration, as well as by "creativity.")

Deliberative history is built upon casual history. It uses the raw data as building blocks for its construct, which is the final written history.

In the Bible, we see much of this type of history writing. In the Old Testament, it includes most of the Pentateuch and Joshua-Esther. In the New Testament, it certainly includes Luke-Acts and also the other three Gospels.

The Sources for History Writing: Material Remains

Material remains are the objects and artifacts left behind by people and societies. These represent mute evidence and usually come into play after written sources are analyzed. For modern historians of Israelite history, the material remains are recovered archaeologically. These have included pottery, building remains, bones and tomb remains, tools and weapons, and jewelry. Archaeology is becoming increasingly sophisticated, and now such things as pollen, teeth, and even feces are studied for information about ancient diets; on Egyptian mummies, DNA studies are carried out and even "autopsies" performed.[12]

There is no evidence that the biblical historians studied material remains in writing their histories. The erection of memorial stones may, however, be an example of this (e.g., Gen. 31:44–53; Josh. 4).

The Sources for History Writing: Tradition

Many things are passed down (a) orally or (b) as customs in a society. The former are such things as genealogies, nursery rhymes, place names, and folk tales. The latter are the rituals and customs of a society.

---

12. See H. Darrell Lance, *The Old Testament and the Archaeologist* (Philadelphia: Fortress, 1981).

In modern times, historians and anthropologists can study these first-hand in contemporary societies. However, for societies such as ancient Israel, which is long dead, these can only be recovered if they have been committed to writing at some point. Once written down, the materials in this category would be studied as "casual" history. One way around this problem is taken up by emerging sociological and anthropological approaches to studies of ancient societies, and these are increasingly common in biblical studies.[13] These include the assumption that traditions and customs are very long-lived at the grass-roots level. Thus, by studying modern-day peasant or nomadic life in the lands of the Bible, we can get a fairly good picture of what life was like in biblical times. There is some justification for this approach, but it must be used with caution.

In the Bible, tradition and customs undoubtedly were among the biblical writers' building blocks. Many traditions were written down (casual history) and many undoubtedly came as oral tradition, as customs, or by direct revelation from God. Many etiologies, for example, could very well have been oral tradition passed down. However, today we only have access to these via the final written compositions now existing as the Scriptures.

The Intent of History Writing

Intent is an important element in understanding "history" in the sense in which the term is used here. Written histories intend to be accurate, coherent accounts of the past. As Baruch Halpern states, "histories purport to be true, or probable, representations of events and relationships in the past."[14] Meir Sternberg makes the point even more strongly.[15] In distinguishing between history and fiction, he argues that the truth claims of the two are different. Fictional works certainly may contain factual references to historical events—a novel set at the end of the Cold War might mention Ronald Reagan, Mikhail Gorbachev, and the fall of the Berlin Wall, for example, at the same time it traces the lives and actions of many fictional characters. But only history *claims* to be historically accurate.

---

13. See Robert R. Wilson, *Sociological Approaches to the Old Testament* (Philadelphia: Fortress, 1984); Norman K. Gottwald, "Sociology (Ancient Israel)," in *ABD,* ed. David N. Freedman (New York: Doubleday, 1992), 6:79–89.
14. Halpern, *First Historians,* 6.
15. Meir Sternberg, *The Poetics of Biblical Narrative* (Bloomington, Ind.: Indiana University, 1985), 24–26.

This does not mean that if a single factual error is found in a work, it is then automatically relegated to "fiction" as a literary category. Many historians are proven wrong in one or more of their facts, but their works are still "histories." Rather, we must treat histories in terms of what they claim to do, what their intent is.[16] Halpern again: "We call a narrative a history on the basis of its author's perceived intentions in writing, the author's *claim* that the account is accurate in its particulars, the author's sincerity."[17]

The dual questions of truth claims and truth value are of obvious importance in approaching the Bible's historical texts.[18] First we can ask, Do the Bible's texts claim (or presume) to be presenting historical events accurately? Second, If they claim (or presume) to be true, does the evidence support the claims? What is their truth value?

We can illustrate the distinctions between the truth claims of writings that intend to be historical and those that do not through two examples. First, Jesus' story of the "Good Samaritan" (Luke 10:30–36) is very "true to life." We could easily imagine such a series of events happening, based on our own everyday experiences or our knowledge of life in the New Testament era. But no truth claim is associated with this story. It is understood to be a parable, which is told to make a certain point (or set of points), not to "retell history."[19]

Second, we can consider the stories of Jesus' resurrection (Matt. 28:1–15 and parallels). These accounts are *not* "true to life" in that we cannot easily imagine such a series of events happening, based on our own everyday experiences or our knowledge of life in other eras. Yet the Bible presents these stories as true (i.e., as making truth claims and as having truth

---

16. A helpful discussion of the relations between truth and the Bible's different literary forms, including history, is Kevin J. Vanhoozer, "The Semantics of Biblical Literature: Truth and Scripture's Diverse Literary Forms," in *Hermeneutics, Authority, and Canon,* ed. D. A. Carson and J. D. Woodbridge (Grand Rapids: Zondervan, 1986), 53–104.
17. Halpern, *First Historians,* 8.
18. For a helpful discussion of this, see V. Philips Long, "What Is Truth?" in *The Art of Biblical History* (Grand Rapids: Zondervan, 1994), 91–93.
19. Robert Stein, for example, recognizes that parables are not "history," regardless of how "true to life" they might be. See Robert H. Stein, *An Introduction to the Parables of Jesus* (Philadelphia: Westminster, 1981), 39–41. Stein also argues the classic scholarly position that the parables make one point. See Craig L. Blomberg, *Interpreting the Parables* (Downers Grove, Ill.: InterVarsity, 1990), for the argument that parables are closer to allegories than often thought, with more than one point made.

value). Indeed, their factuality is the very foundation of our faith (1 Cor. 15).[20]

At the same time, histories are selective: "Historiography cannot—and should not—be infinitely detailed. All history is at best an abridgement—better or worse—of an originally fuller reality. . . . History is always the study of one thing, or several things, and the exclusion of many others."[21] The question of selectivity is thus also important in our study of the Bible's historical texts. We should not expect an account to be exhaustive. Note the Apostle John's admission of his own selectivity, for example, when he wrote that "Jesus did many other miraculous signs in the presence of his disciples, which are not recorded in this book" (John 20:30), or that "Jesus did many other things as well. If every one of them were written down, I suppose that even the whole world would not have room for the books that would be written" (John 21:25). A study of parallel texts in the Bible—for existence the parallels of 2 Samuel and 1–2 Kings with 1–2 Chronicles, or parallels within the Synoptic Gospels—will make this immediately obvious. Many individual stories are told just once in larger narratives that are otherwise parallel. Likewise, when certain stories *are* told twice (or more), certain details will be highlighted in one telling and not in another.

The Problem of Historical Distance

Much history writing is separated by "a great gulf fixed"[22] from the people about whom it is written because of the historical distance between the historian and the events he writes about.[23] This is certainly true in regard to much of the Old Testament's historical materials. A presumption often is made that such materials are necessarily less accurate than materials produced close to the time of the events described. Because of this, many evangelicals love to see evidence that seems to show

---

20. V. Philips Long discusses the issue of historical factuality of biblical events—in both Old and New Testaments—in an excellent discussion titled "If Jericho Was Not Razed, Is Our Faith in Vain?" in *Art of Biblical History,* 116–18. He also argues that, for Christians who take their cues from the Bible's self-understanding, "the Bible's truth claims . . . and its truth value . . . coincide" (29).
21. Halpern, *First Historians,* 7.
22. Bebbington, *Patterns in History,* 2.
23. See also the discussion in the next section of this essay titled "The Problem of Historical Evidence."

a narrow gap between when the events occurred and when they were set down in books.[24]

However, we should note that greater historical distance between the events and the writing does not, *in itself,* necessitate less accuracy. Records or traditions could have preserved an accurate account even of something that happened long before. Also, the divine Author of the Scriptures could have directly revealed the necessary information to the human authors—otherwise unknown and unrecorded—for certain portions of their works. Many evangelicals who affirm Mosaic authorship of the Pentateuch have little problem with a great historical distance between Moses and the events described in Genesis. By the same reasoning, there is no *necessary* compulsion to argue for early authorship of the anonymous works found in the historical corpus.

The Problem of Historical Evidence

Modern historians may have very little evidence with which to work.[25] The past is always mediated to us via the evidence.[26] We cannot recover or repeat it in the same way that mathematicians can recalculate an equation or scientists can rerun an experiment. Often the evidence is spotty, and there are large gaps in our knowledge of the past.[27]

In reconstructing Israel's history by using the Bible alongside written and nonwritten nonbiblical sources, the evidence must be evaluated. Mute evidence, recovered via archaeological methods, must be interpreted and evaluated. So too must written records. They can be so tendentious as to be useless, or they may even be forgeries. For example, almost no historian uses the apocryphal "Additions to Esther" to reconstruct history in Esther's day. These additions not only were written much later than the events, but they have different purposes from the canonical book. Nor do they use the

---

24. See, for example, C. F. Keil, "The Book of Joshua," *Biblical Commentary on the Old Testament,* trans. James Martin (n.p.; reprint, Grand Rapids: Eerdmans, 1976), 15–19; and R. K. Harrison, *Introduction to the Old Testament* (Grand Rapids: Eerdmans, 1969), 671–73.
25. Bebbington, *Patterns in History,* 3–5. See also the discussion above of "The Problem of Historical Distance."
26. This point is known by all historians. See, for example, Garraghan, *Guide to Historical Method,* 4–5; and Edward Hallett Carr, *What Is History?* (New York: Random House, 1961), 24.
27. Carr, *What Is History?* 12, states that "History has been called an enormous jig-saw with a lot of missing parts."

"Psalms of Joshua," written in the late intertestamental period, to reconstruct history in Joshua's day.

With the evidence problem an issue, the attitude of "inquiry" is important in reconstructing history.[28] The historian must have a curiosity about sources and facts. The great historians are almost universally praised for having had an insatiable curiosity, especially those who lived in early periods, or in periods when the prevailing mood of their day was not conducive to such inquiry. Examples are Herodotus and Thucydides among the Greeks, or Augustine and Eusebius among the early Christians. This curiosity gives their work value, whatever flaws modern historians might otherwise point out regarding their methods.

Probability and Historical Evidence

In the last analysis, modern historians usually deal with probabilities, not absolute certainties. They must rely on such sources as possess a certain reliability. In many cases, the sources are so reliable or the data so overwhelmingly clear that historians do deal with certainties. This is more often the case with well-verified dates or events. Otherwise, historians must sift and sort, and come to their own conclusions.

This dependence upon probabilities is important, because history cannot be repeated, and even its patterns are not capable of repetition. Indeed, the historian is interested precisely in unique events, *not* just repetitive patterns. R. J. Shafer notes that

> Both historians and social scientists are interested in regularities, tendencies, or repetitive elements in social behavior, but the former are also concerned with the unique event and person for their own sakes, and the latter are more uniformly dedicated to identifying "laws" of human conduct.[29]

Because historians so often deal with the unique, the extreme skepticism with which historians sometimes approach the possibility of final

---

28. Whether the extreme skepticism evidenced by many historians is altogether healthy is another question, one whose answer is usually "no." (See further below.)
29. R. J. Shafer, ed., *A Guide to Historical Method* (Homewood, Ill.: Dorsey, 1969), 5.

"truth" in historical knowledge should be tempered.[30] Early in the twentieth century, W. Dilthey insisted that, despite the limitations on knowledge, "one thing is still possible and necessary: true and adequate understanding of past history."[31] M. Mandelbaum devoted an entire treatise—which has become a classic—to the proposition that "the ideal of objective historical knowledge is in fact possible of at least partial attainment."[32] He expands on this idea in a later work, arguing that, "when one clears away the preceding misunderstandings, the interlocking connections among the data with which historians are concerned permit us to hold that the cumulative results achieved through their individual inquiries can, in most cases, be regarded as establishing knowledge that is objective."[33]

The Problem of the Historian

In modern historical study, the problems are not only about chronological historical distance between events and the writing about them, nor merely about spotty or suspect evidence. Another problem relates to the modern historian.[34] All history writing is "perspectival," even "subjective," in the sense that it owes its shape to its author's activity in selecting and communicating material. There is the inevitable picking and choosing among sources of information and a selectivity in what is reported.[35]

This is true even when there is no historical distance between the historian and the events or people, or when the source material is abundant. Each of the recent presidents of the U.S. has his own presidential library

---

30. See the discussion below on "Modern Challenges to Biblical Historicity" for an overview of skeptics in biblical studies.
31. Wilhelm Dilthey, cited in Paul Schubert, "The Twentieth-Century West and the Ancient Near East," in *The Idea of History in the Ancient Near East*, ed. R. C. Dentan (New Haven, Conn.: Yale University Press, 1955), 320. Despite Dilthey's own assertions that "universally valid synthetic judgments are possible in history," Maurice Mandelbaum argues that, in the end, Dilthey was a historical relativist who held that no historical account can faithfully depict the past. See Maurice Mandelbaum, *The Problem of Historical Knowledge: An Answer to Relativism* (New York: Liveright, 1938), 58–59.
32. Mandelbaum, *Problem of Historical Knowledge*, 177.
33. Mandelbaum, *Anatomy of Historical Knowledge*, 150. What he means by "objective" is that "a judgment can be said to be objective . . . because we regard its truth as excluding the possibility that its denial can also be true" (ibid., 149–50). His extended discussion of objectivity is on pages 143–94.
34. Bebbington, *Patterns in History*, 5–8; and Shafer, *Guide to Historical Method*, 4, 12.
35. That history can and should be "objective," in the sense that it points to truth, is a point well made by Maurice Mandelbaum in the works cited in notes 11 and 31.

with millions of documents. Yet, those who write about Ronald Reagan or Bill Clinton are clearly selective as to what they will write, and they will inevitably take a certain slant.

Historians in the past two or three centuries have been proud to speak of history as a "science." There are established rules of evidence, research, and documentation.[36] However, all historians are products of their own time and inclinations, and to pretend otherwise is merely to deny or hide one's "biases." As David Bebbington states: "Value-neutrality is impossible. The unconscious assumptions of the historian's own age are inescapable. The historian is part of the historical process, powerfully influenced by time and place.[37] This is not necessarily bad, however. As Bebbington further notes:

> If a historian's personal attitudes do not necessarily harm his history, it is equally true that they can enhance it. Great history is commonly a consequence of a historian's pursuit of evidence to vindicate his previously formed beliefs. [Edmund] Gibbon, for instance, wrote his masterpiece, *[History of] The Decline and Fall [of the Roman Empire (1776–88)]*, because he conceived himself to be a champion of civilization and rationalism who could point out that Rome succumbed to 'the triumph of barbarism and religion.' A pure love of scholarship is rare. Deeply held convictions are needed to drive people to major historical achievements.[38]

The modern historian should at least attempt to understand the values in the period under study, and not just his or her own values. Ferdinand Lot, a French historian at the turn of the twentieth century, made a similar point. When one writes a synthesis of history, Lot stressed that

> ... qualities other than the erudite skills come into play. There must be sympathy with the subjects under study, for without it there can be no imaginative insight into the past. Ideally, a historian must display capacities akin to those of a poet or an artist.

---

36. Two works that introduce the historical method in biblical studies are Edgar Krentz, *The Historical-Critical Method* (Philadelphia: Fortress, 1975); and J. Maxwell Miller, *The Old Testament and the Historian* (Philadelphia: Fortress, 1976).
37. Bebbington, *Patterns in History*, 6.
38. Ibid., 7.

Such a quality was, by and large, lacking in the work of the historians of the Enlightenment, who had been unable to achieve imaginative insight into civilizations very different from their own. The greatest shortcoming of Gibbon was his temperamental inability to appreciate religion.[39]

The modern writer's purpose in writing a history, then, is important, and it is usually inseparable from personal background, experience, and philosophy. The purpose may be reportorial, proclamative, didactic, nationalistic, hortatory, or polemic. Thus, in evaluating such modern histories of Israel as are mentioned below under "The Focus of Historical Study," the writers' purposes and presuppositions must be evaluated. Their inclinations to believe the scriptural accounts vary, and these inclinations must be understood.

We may apply this same insight into our evaluation of biblical writers. That is, our evaluations of them must include a sensitivity to their own purposes as expressed in their works, and to their own biographies and experiences, insofar as these may be identified as essential parts of their works' purposes.[40]

The Modern Study of History—Biblical

The Focus of Historical Study

Many modern scholars consider themselves to be "biblical historians" or historians of Israel's history. For them, the events of Israel's history are indeed their focus. Representative works by such scholars include, among nonevangelicals, Martin Noth's *The History of Israel*,[41] John Bright's *A History of Israel*,[42] John Hayes and Maxwell Miller's *Israelite and Judaean History*,[43] Miller and Hayes' *A History of Israel and Judah*,[44] and Alberto Soggin's

---

39. Edmund B. Fryde, et al., *Encyclopaedia Britannica: Macropaedia,* vol. 20 (Chicago: Encyclopaedia Britannica, 1998), s.v. "History of Historiography."
40. See also in this regard, Halpern, *First Historians,* 6–13; and John Sailhamer, "Exegesis of the Old Testament as a Text," in *A Tribute to Gleason Archer: Essays on the Old Testament,* ed. W. C. Kaiser Jr. and R. F. Youngblood (Chicago: Moody, 1986), 279–96.
41. Martin Noth, *The History of Israel,* 2d ed., trans. P. Ackroyd (New York: Harper & Row, 1960).
42. John Bright, *A History of Israel,* 4th ed. (Louisville: Westminster/John Knox, 2000).
43. John H. Hayes and J. Maxwell Miller, eds., *Israelite and Judaean History* (Philadelphia: Westminster, 1977).
44. J. Maxwell Miller and John H. Hayes, *A History of Ancient Israel and Judah* (Philadelphia: Westminster, 1986).

A History of Ancient Israel.[45] Evangelical "histories" include Leon Wood's *A Survey of Israel's History*,[46] Eugene Merrill's *Kingdom of Priests*,[47] and Walter Kaiser's *A History of Israel*.[48] All of these works, to a greater or lesser degree, use the Bible as one source among several by which to reconstruct Israel's history. The Bible itself is not—in the last analysis—the focus of study; the events or happenings of Israel's history are the focus.

This is an entirely legitimate pursuit for at least two reasons. First, humans have a natural curiosity to pursue knowledge in all fields, and the history of Israel is as legitimate a focus of study as the history of Imperial Rome or Victorian England. Second, since the study of Israel's history does indeed bring us much closer to the Scriptures than does the study of, say, Victorian England, it is legitimate to study Israel's history in order to arrive at conclusions concerning the Bible's reliability. More often than not, the study of Israel's history from this perspective points to the reliability of the Bible's accounts. We must admit that, in many cases, it does not do this, but we must also admit that the historical method does not deal with absolute certainties but only with probabilities (see below).

Many scholars would add a third reason for the study of Israel's history; namely, that it is essential to understanding the Bible itself. That is, without knowledge of extrabiblical materials that illuminate Israel's history, we cannot fully—or, in some cases, at all—understand many texts in the Scriptures. A certain modern arrogance sometimes creeps in here, however. It can be seen in approaches that would claim, for instance, that the writer of Genesis intentionally wrote his work against the backdrop of such extrabiblical works as the "Gilgamesh Epic," which tells of a great flood, in many ways reminiscent of Noah's flood, or other ancient creation epics, without leaving any clues as to this intent. This would suggest that the secrets to Genesis lay unavailable to students of the Bible for centuries, only to be revealed in the modern day when discovery of these epics was made.

Certainly extrabiblical discoveries have shed light on biblical texts and concepts, making many of them clearer or more vivid. However, it is one

---

45. J. Alberto Soggin, *A History of Ancient Israel*, trans. J. Bowden (Philadelphia: Westminster, 1984).
46. Leon Wood, *A Survey of Israel's History*, rev. David O'Brien (Grand Rapids: Zondervan, 1986).
47. Eugene H. Merrill, *Kingdom of Priests: A History of Old Testament Israel* (Grand Rapids: Baker, 1987).
48. Walter C. Kaiser Jr., *A History of Israel: From the Bronze Age through the Jewish Wars* (Nashville: Broadman & Holman, 1998).

thing to say this and another thing to say that they have uncovered secrets in the Bible previously unknown. What more properly may be said is that extrabiblical discoveries may highlight in bolder relief truths, assumptions, or patterns that already reside in the biblical texts. An example of this is the modern discovery that portions of biblical covenants—mainly in the Pentateuch—resemble the structure of Hittite covenant treaties of the late second millennium B.C.[49] The study of biblical covenants far antedated this modern discovery. The relationships described within the biblical covenants already were known (i.e., covenants between equals, covenants between overlords and vassals). However, the Hittite discoveries have helped to highlight aspects of biblical covenants already present in the biblical texts.

These discoveries have also shed light on matters of the Bible's reliability. Since the Hittite treaties date to the late second millennium B.C. and the Pentateuchal covenants resemble them so closely, this suggests that the Pentateuch was written during the same time period. This is one piece of evidence pointing to—though certainly not, by itself, proving—Mosaic authorship of the Pentateuch. However, knowledge of these extrabiblical covenants is not essential to understanding the *meaning* of the Pentateuch.

Revelation in History

The questions of whether the Bible accurately records the events of history, on the one hand, and whether and how God revealed himself directly through the events of history, on the other hand, are two separate questions. We will argue below that the answer to the first question is that the Bible does indeed accurately record the events it portrays.

The answer to the second question is that God did reveal himself directly through events of history, but this mode of revelation was somewhat limited, even to those living through or observing these events. The introduction of the book of Hebrews may provide insight into this: "In the past God spoke to our forefathers through the prophets at many times and in various ways, but in these last days he has spoken to us by his Son" (Heb. 1:1–2a). "Various ways" suggests that God's modes of revelation were not

---

49. See George E. Mendenhall, "Covenant Forms in Israelite Tradition," *BA* 15 (1954): 50–76; Meredith Kline, *The Structure of Biblical Authority* (Grand Rapids: Eerdmans, 1972); and John H. Walton, *Ancient Israelite Literature in Its Cultural Context* (Grand Rapids: Zondervan, 1989), 95–109.

limited to writings. However, it also suggests that the prophets and God's Son were necessary mediators of the nonwritten revelatory modes.[50]

Many have argued that God's revelation was *primarily* through historical events.[51] However, this overstates the case, and it does not properly account for the need for interpretation of such events (not to mention its deemphasis of the Bible's claims to be the Word of God). As V. Philips Long states, "Divine revelation should be located in both historical events and the interpretative word which mediates these events to us."[52]

God's revelation in historical events may be compared to his revelation in nature: Both communicate something of God, but both are incomplete without written revelation. When Psalm 19:1 states that "The heavens declare the glory of God; the skies proclaim the work of his hands," we understand that these natural elements reveal something about God to us. In an analogous way, historical events also can reveal something about God. However, in both of these cases, the revelatory information is limited.

With reference to historical events, we can take an example from Exodus 19. Here, the thunder and lightning, as well as the earth's shaking and the thick cloud that the people experienced at the foot of Mount Sinai, were clearly a communication of God's presence and power. However, these events needed to be interpreted by Moses to the people in order for them to have any clear comprehension of this revelation. To take another example, the stopping up of the waters of the Jordan River in Joshua 3 was also an instance of God's "speaking" through an historical event. However, it was interpreted by Joshua to the people so that its meaning was very clear, and they were to interpret it to their children in years to come (Josh. 4).

The Scriptures that record and interpret the God-directed events are not merely *testimonies to* God's revelatory activities.[53] They themselves *are* revelation. When Paul states that "All Scripture is God-breathed" (2 Tim. 3:16a), he uses the words πᾶσα γραφὴ, "All that is written [is God-breathed]." He is stating that the written words themselves are God's revelation, not merely witnesses to some "true" (or "truer") revelation in the events of history.

---

50. The NIV's renderings "through the prophets" and "by his Son" somewhat obscure the parallels between the revelation via the prophets and God's Son, since the prepositions in both cases are the same: *en* "by, through."
51. A classic statement of this position is G. Ernest Wright, *God Who Acts: Biblical Theology as Recital*, SBT 8 (London: SCM, 1952).
52. Long, *Art of Biblical History*, 105–6 (emphasis Long's).
53. This is contrary to the assertions of many, such as Wright, who asserts that the "Word of God" is *present* in Scripture but that the Scripture itself is not the "Word" (*God Who Acts*, 12, 107).

We must emphasize here that, even given that God's workings in history were revelatory in some limited way, we today only have access to these workings through the mediation of the written Scriptures.[54] This was true even in biblical times among those who experienced them first hand. Even then, these events were always interpreted. How much more is this true today. We only know of most of the events in the Scriptures through the Scriptures themselves. Even when we can gain independent knowledge of them, the vehicles of that knowledge are not "God-breathed"; only the Scriptures that interpret these events are God's revelation. Thus, the Scriptures themselves are the proper focus of our study, not the hypothetical re-creations of the events behind these Scriptures. The historical reconstructions can give us confidence in the reliability of the Scriptural texts, and can give us something of their essential purpose. But, we must remember that the events themselves were never sufficient at any time to communicate God's revelation fully, and today, they are accessible only through written interpretation in the Scriptures.

The Importance of Historicity

The modern focus upon the events or happenings of history that we have just noted is important in the Bible's case because the Bible makes numerous "truth claims"—explicitly and implicitly—concerning the factuality of the events it records.

At the core of Christian belief is the fact that Christ did indeed die for the sins of humanity and then did rise from the dead in a great victory over death. This forms the ground and basis of our faith. Paul makes this point forcefully in 1 Corinthians 15 concerning the Resurrection (see esp. vv. 12–19).

---

54. This latter point is the thrust of John Sailhamer's important essay, "Exegesis of the Old Testament as a Text," 279–96, as well as his comments in *The Pentateuch as Narrative* (Grand Rapids: Zondervan, 1992), 15–22. He states that "given the theological priority of an inspired text (2 Ti 3:16), one must see in the text of Scripture itself the locus of God's revelation today. Thus, on the question of God's revelation in history, the sense of *history* in a text-oriented approach would be that of the record of past events.... Even the formula 'revelation in history' then concerns the meaning of a text" (ibid., 17). However, he acknowledges the theoretical possibility of nonwritten modes of revelation in the past when he states that "There is no reason to discount the fact that God has made known his will *in other ways at other times*" (ibid., emphasis added). He expands on these thoughts in a more recent work, "Text or Event," in *Introduction to Old Testament Theology: A Canonical Approach* (Grand Rapids: Zondervan, 1995), 36–85.

Beyond this, in portions such as the Gospels and the historical books, most of what is recorded purports to be true.[55] This is illustrated by the explicit claims in Luke and John noted above, as well as by the way in which the authors of 1–2 Kings, 1–2 Chronicles, and Ezra–Nehemiah used their sources. This is also illustrated by the implicit claims of the historical materials in the Bible: They present themselves as historical and they are treated as historical elsewhere in the Scriptures.

If, in the last analysis, God is the "Author" of the Scriptures, then he who knows all things would have "written" an accurate record of those things. In this way, what the Scriptures claim to be true is indeed true.[56] As we noted above, we can often discover information that will confirm to us this reliability through the study of the events of history. Our trust in the Bible's reliability can be supported via this type of study.

The Bible's message is given to a large extent through historical writings, and not, for example, through abstract philosophical treatises. It is through historical writings about historical events that we learn much about God and his purposes for humans. As we have noted, the intent of these historical writings is to provide an accurate account of the history of God's people, and their message is undermined if their historical accuracy is compromised.

Walter Kaiser makes this point well:

> Will Herberg says that biblical faith is also historical, not because it *has* history, or deals *with* historical events (there's nothing particularly novel in that), but it is historical in a much more profound sense because *it is itself* history. The message that biblical faith proclaims, the judgments it pronounces, the salvation it promises, the teaching it communicates; these are all defined historically and are understood as historical realities. This does not make it offensive to us, since it helps to humanize it, to bring it

---

55. Exceptions include such literary forms as Jesus' parables (already noted above) or Jotham's fable (Judg. 9).
56. The best treatment of this issue is the extended discussion in Long, "History and Truth: Is Historicity Important?" in *The Art of Biblical History*, 88–119. See also Gordon Wenham, "History and the Old Testament," in *History, Criticism, and Faith*, ed. Colin Brown (Downers Grove, Ill.: InterVarsity, 1976), 13–75, esp. 22–34; and several essays in James K. Hoffmeier, ed., *Faith, Tradition, and History: Old Testament Historiography in Its Near Eastern Context* (Winona Lake, Ind.: Eisenbrauns, 1994).

down to our level where we can understand it and where we can (as we say today) "identify" with it. To de-historicize history or to de-historicize biblical faith is like trying to paraphrase poetry. You ruin it. You just take all that is good and meaningful out of it. It is no longer poetry.[57]

Modern Challenges to Biblical Historicity

For most believing Christians and Jews over the centuries, the Old Testament's historical texts, when they are correctly understood, give an accurate picture of the events of Israel's life as a nation, beginning with Abraham and ending with Ezra and Nehemiah. However, for many scholars in the past two hundred years, the Old Testament is almost worthless as a source of historical information. So, for example, Julius Wellhausen (1844–1918), an influential nineteenth-century critic, claimed that in Genesis "we attain no historical knowledge of the patriarchs, but only of the time when the stories about them arose in the Israelite people."[58] Wellhausen argued that all the Bible's historical texts were written many hundreds of years after the events, and they could only give us information about the times in which they were written, not the earlier periods that they discussed.

A reaction to the Wellhausen approach set in during the first part of the twentieth century in the "biblical archaeology" approach espoused by G. Ernest Wright, William F. Albright, and others. These scholars believed that the Bible was generally accurate historically, and archaeology when accurately interpreted usually confirmed its reliability. The so-called "biblical archaeology movement" thus provided a positive alternative to the negative conclusions of historical criticism that had been growing in influence through the nineteenth century.

---

57. Walter C. Kaiser Jr., *The Old Testament in Contemporary Preaching* (Grand Rapids: Baker, 1973), 73.
58. Julius Wellhausen, *Prolegomena to the History of Ancient Israel* (Edinburgh: A. & C. Black, 1885; reprint, New York: Meridian, 1957), 318–19. In a similar vein, William Dever quotes Wellhausen as stating that "the text tells us something only from the time when it was written down." Dever, "'Will the Real Israel Please Stand Up?' Archaeology and Israelite Historiography: Part I," *BASOR* 297 (February 1995): 64, although I cannot locate this quote directly in Wellhausen.

The Recent "Minimalist" Challenge

In the 1970s, a neo-Wellhausenian reaction to the biblical archaeology movement set in.[59] Especially in the last fifteen years, a thoroughgoing skepticism has infected influential scholars. Many of these would date the Old Testament's historical books very late, to the period of the Exile or later.[60] Indeed, the very idea that there was an entity called "Israel" during or at the end of the Late Bronze Age (ca. 1400–1200 B.C.) and in the Iron Age (ca. 1200–586 B.C.) is challenged. Even more radical, almost all minimalist scholars would dispense with the Old Testament entirely as a source for historical reconstruction.

The debate concerning whether any events took place as the Bible depicts them pits what are sometimes called "maximalists" against "minimalists." "Maximalists" differ among themselves concerning the Bible's reliability. Most evangelicals affirm it in its entirety, properly interpreted, whereas others trust its usefulness as a historical source more broadly. The latter question details, but they use Scripture alongside other written materials and archaeological evidence in helping reconstruct the story of this period. Most "minimalists" insist that archaeological evidence alone should be used in such reconstructions, because written texts—especially the Bible—are late, tendentious, and ideologically biased.

Thus, for example, Niels Peter Lemche states that "I propose that we decline to be led by the biblical account and instead regard it, like other legendary materials, as essentially ahistorical; that is, as a source which only exceptionally can be verified by other information."[61] Similarly, Robert B. Coote and Keith W. Whitelam employ an approach "which assigns priority to interpreting archaeological data within a broad interdisciplinary

---

59. Most especially represented by T. L. Thompson, *The Historicity of the Patriarchal Narratives: The Quest for the Historical Abraham,* BZAW 133 (Berlin: de Gruyter, 1974); and J. Van Seters, *Abraham in History and Tradition* (New Haven, Conn.: Yale University Press, 1975).
60. Philip R. Davies, for example, dates almost all of the Old Testament to the Persian period (fifth–third centuries B.C.) (*In Search of "Ancient Israel,"* JSOTSup 148 [Sheffield: Sheffield Academic Press, 1992], 76). John Strange dates the book of Joshua even later, to the second century B.C. See "The Book of Joshua: A Hasmonean Manifesto?" in *History and Traditions of Early Israel: Studies Presented to Eduard Nielsen, May 8th, 1993,* ed. A. Lemaire and B. Otzen, VTSup 50 (Leiden: Brill, 1993), 136–41. Giovanni Garbini agrees. See *History and Ideology in Ancient Israel* (New York: Crossroad, 1988), 132.
61. N. P. Lemche, *Early Israel: Anthropological and Historical Studies on Israelite Society Before the Monarchy,* VTSup 37 (Leiden: Brill, 1985), 415.

framework."⁶² Thomas Thompson puts it even more starkly: "It is . . . the independence of Syro-Palestinian archaeology that now makes it possible for the first time to begin to write a history of Israel's origins. Rather than in the bible *[sic]*, it is in the field of Syro-Palestinian archaeology, and the adjunct fields of ancient Near Eastern studies, that we find our primary sources for Israel's earliest history."⁶³

A profound skepticism toward the reliability of the biblical accounts is embedded in the work of minimalist scholars. Thus, John Strange states that "It goes without saying that the book [of Joshua] as such does not relate any actual conquest and division of the promised land to Joshua. Everybody agrees on that."⁶⁴ Similarly, Coote states that "The writers of the Hebrew Scriptures knew little or nothing about the origin of Israel, although the Scriptures can provide much information relevant to the investigation of early Israel. The period under discussion, therefore, does not include the periods of the patriarchs, exodus, conquest, or judges, as devised by the writers of the Scriptures. These periods never existed."⁶⁵ John Van Seters states that "there is no justification for trying to associate archaeological ruins of the end of the Late Bronze Age with a conquest narrative written six hundred to seven hundred years later. [The Deuteronomistic Historian] did not have any records from Israel's earliest period, nor did he follow old oral traditions. The invasion of the land of Canaan by Israel under Joshua was an invention of [the Deuteronomistic Historian]. The conquest narrative is a good example of ancient historiography but it cannot pass for historical by any modern criteria of historical evaluation."⁶⁶

Because of such skepticism, many of these scholars now attempt to reconstruct the history of the Late Bronze Age and Early Iron Age in Palestine primarily or entirely without reference to the Bible. These include

---

62. Robert B. Coote and Keith W. Whitelam, *The Emergence of Early Israel in Historical Perspective* (Sheffield: Almond, 1987), 8.
63. Thomas L. Thompson, *The Origin Tradition of Ancient Israel*, JSOTSup 55 (Sheffield: JSOT, 1987), 27.
64. Strange, "The Book of Joshua: A Hasmonean Manifesto?" 141.
65. Robert B. Coote, *Early Israel: A New Horizon* (Minneapolis: Fortress, 1990), 2–3.
66. John Van Seters, "Joshua's Campaign of Canaan and Near Eastern Historiography," *SJOT* 1 (1990): 12.

Coote and Whitelam,[67] Thompson,[68] Gösta W. Ahlström,[69] and Lemche,[70] among others.[71] For most of these scholars, "Israel" is a modern scholarly construct, and the product of the imaginations of late biblical writers. But no nation of "Israel" was actually to be found in Palestine at the end of the second millennium B.C., at least not in any form close to that described in the Bible. The outer limits of skepticism are reached in the work of Philip R. Davies, for whom a "historical Israel" as depicted in the Bible simply never existed,[72] or Whitelam, for whom "ancient Israel" is solely an invention of ideologically driven biblical writers, who have been followed in the modern day by biblical scholars, historians, and archaeologists with their own ideological (i.e., political) agendas in favor of the modern-day state of Israel (as over against the modern Palestinian cause).[73]

---

67. Coote and Whitelam, *Emergence of Early Israel in Historical Perspective;* Coote, *Early Israel;* and Keith W. Whitelam, *The Invention of Israel: The Silencing of Palestinian History* (London: Routledge, 1996).
68. Thomas L. Thompson, *Early History of the Israelite People from the Written and Archaeological Sources,* Studies in the History of the Ancient Near East 4 (Leiden: Brill, 1992).
69. Gösta W. Ahlström, *The History of Ancient Palestine from the Palaeolithic Period to Alexander's Conquest,* JSOTSup 146 (Sheffield: Sheffield Academic Press, 1993). He dismisses the historical value of the biblical records, stating that "the historiography of certain periods for which there are no other sources available than those of the biblical writers will rest on shaky ground because of the subjective presentation and religious *Tendenz* of the material" (ibid., 32).
70. Lemche, *Early Israel;* idem, *Ancient Israel: A New History of Israelite Society,* Biblical Seminar 5 (Sheffield: JSOT, 1988); and idem, *The Canaanites and Their Land: The Tradition of the Canaanites,* JSOTSup 110 (Sheffield: Sheffield Academic Press, 1991).
71. Two recent works with essays by some of these scholars, as well as others, are V. Fritz and P. R. Davies, eds., *The Origins of the Israelite States,* JSOTSup 228 (Sheffield: Sheffield Academic Press, 1996); Lester L. Grabbe, ed., *Can a "History of Israel" Be Written?* (Sheffield: Sheffield Academic Press, 1997).
72. For Davies, there are three "Israels": (1) "biblical Israel," which existed (and exists) *only* as a literary construct in the pages of the Bible; (2) the "historical Israel," which refers to "the inhabitants of the northern Palestinian highlands during part of the Iron Age" and "whose resemblance to biblical Israel is superficial and not substantive"; and (3) "ancient Israel," which is a modern scholarly construct built from the first two "Israels" (Davies, *In Search of "Ancient Israel,"* 11, 18).
73. For Whitelam, to search for an ancient Israel in Canaan (Palestine) is to commit a methodological sin, and it is at the expense of the search for other, equally valid histories, particularly Palestinian history. See Whitelam, *Invention of Israel.* Two critiques of Whitelam's work are Hershel Shanks, "Keith Whitelam Claims Bible Scholars Suppress Palestinian History in Favor of Israelites," *BAR* 22, no. 2 (March–April 1996): 54, 56, 69; and Iain W. Provan, "The End of (Israel's) History? K. W. Whitelam's *The Invention of Ancient Israel:* A Review Article," *JSS* 42 (1997): 283–300.

Responses to the "Minimalist" Challenge

It should be obvious that, where minimalist constructions are believed, the Bible has suffered greatly in terms of its reliability as a source of information for the periods covered by the historical books. Such minimalist constructions are profoundly skeptical. The biblical records are approached with what is often called "a hermeneutic of suspicion." They are assumed to be in error until they can be proven to be correct by some independent means of verification.

This skeptical approach is currently in vogue in some wings of biblical scholarship, but it has not gone unchallenged by evangelicals and by scholars who make no claim to be evangelicals. Most of these represent something closer to a "maximalist" approach to the Bible and the book of Joshua, where the book is treated as entirely or highly reliable as a source of historical information.

For example, J. Maxwell Miller points out the inconsistency of many of the minimalists' efforts to reconstruct a history of Israel, in that they rely on the Bible in much of what they do, notwithstanding their stated aims to the contrary. With reference to Coote and Whitelam, for example, he states that "either they assume information that can only have come from the Hebrew Bible, or they appeal to scholarly consensus, which itself rests on the Bible. In short, their study does not bypass the Hebrew Bible, it only bypasses any critical evaluation of it."[74] William G. Dever makes similar points, and has mounted the most sustained assault on minimalist positions. He offers his own, more positive reconstructions of Israel's life and society, using both the Bible and archaeological remains.[75]

A more serious flaw than their inconsistency in using the Bible is the minimalist assumption that written texts are necessarily corrupted by ideology or theology, so they must be worthless for true historical investigation. Not only do these scholars reject the Bible as a valid source, but they

---

74. J. Maxwell Miller, "Is It Possible to Write a History of Israel Without Relying on the Hebrew Bible?" in *The Fabric of History: Text, Artifact and Israel's Past*, ed. D. V. Edelman, JSOTSup 127 (Sheffield: Sheffield Academic Press, 1991), 93–102.
75. William G. Dever, *What Did the Biblical Writers Know and When Did They Know It? What Archaeology Can Tell Us About the Reality of Israel* (Grand Rapids: Eerdmans, 2001); and idem, *Who Were the Early Israelites and Where Did They Come From?* (Grand Rapids: Eerdmans, 2003). Dever takes great pains to distance himself from "fundamentalists." He states that "I am not a theist, and indeed remain a secular humanist" (*What Did the Biblical Writers Know*, x), but he nevertheless takes a much more positive view of the *reality* of ancient Israel than do minimalist scholars.

resist reading other extrabiblical texts that intersect with the Bible in any way that would reinforce the biblical picture. They go out of their way to reinterpret certain extrabiblical materials that most scholars understand to refer to people or events found in the Bible in ways that deny such connections. For example, the reference to "the house of David" found in an inscription discovered in 1993 at Tell Dan (the first extrabiblical mention of David discovered in the ancient Near East),[76] has been vigorously disputed by Davies.[77] His objections, however, fly in the face of the grammar and epigraphy of the inscription.[78] Likewise, Whitelam dismisses the Merenptah inscription's reference to Israel as ideologically tainted and thus worthless for historical inquiry. He argues that the inscription itself is ideological and, further, that modern-day attempts to equate the "Israel" of the inscription and the "Israel" of the Bible are themselves ideologically driven.[79] It appears that the objections of Davies and Whitelam are themselves driven primarily by ideological commitments to the *un*reliability of any text that lends support to the biblical picture.

The Importance of Written Texts

Indeed, one common thread among such skeptical scholars is a bias in favor of the supposedly untainted, "objective" data of archaeology. This stance ignores the fact that archaeological remains are mute and can give only so much information without written texts. For example, excavations at Tell Mardikh, a large site in northwestern Syria, began in 1964 with no knowledge as to the identity of the ancient site. In 1968, a statue was found identifying the site as ancient Ebla, a name known for more than 100 years from Mesopotamian documents. During the period 1964–1968, much was learned about the site, primarily in the way of buildings and pottery types and artifacts; even the physical size of the site gave clues as to its importance. With the identification of the site in 1968, knowledge was advanced

---

76. See A. Biran and J. Naveh, "An Aramaic Stele Fragment from Tel Dan," *IEJ* 43 (1993): 81–98; [H. Shanks,] "'David' Found at Dan," *BAR* 20, no. 2 (March–April 1994): 26–39.
77. P. R. Davies, "'House of David' Built on Sand: The Sin of the Biblical Maximizers," *BAR* 20, no. 4 (July–August 1994): 54–55.
78. Anson Rainey, "The 'House of David' and the House of the Deconstructionists: Davies Is an Amateur Who 'Can Safely Be Ignored,'" *BAR* 20, no. 6 (November–December 1994): 47; and D. N. Freedman and J. C. Geoghegan, "'House of David' is There!" *BAR* 21, no. 2 (March–April 1995): 78–79.
79. Whitelam, *Invention of Ancient Israel*, 206–10.

further. However, knowledge about the site was revolutionized in 1974, when the first of what turned out to be thousands of tablets were discovered. The earlier discoveries had given insights into social, administrative, political, economic, and religious life, and they fit the site into the context of known history in other areas. But, with the texts, the earlier picture was fleshed out, and vast amounts of new information became available about life in the third millennium B.C.[80]

Mute archaeological records must be interpreted. As soon as individuals begin the process of interpretation, the archaeological remains take on a voice, but only that voice supplied by the interpretation. It is certainly true that, in studying the written records of history, "value-neutrality is impossible. The unconscious assumptions of the historians' own age are inescapable. The historian himself is part of the historical process, powerfully influenced by his time and place."[81] However, the same is the case with the study of mute archaeological remains that must be interpreted. Modern-day interpretations sometimes cloud the issues, rather than clarify them.

Another assumption on the part of "minimalist" scholarship is that the Bible, as a theological or ideological document written many centuries after the events depicted, is less reliable than other written records from the ancient Near East. For example, Lemche states that "Ordinarily, such external sources [Assyrian and Babylonian royal inscriptions] are regarded as providing more reliable information than the Old Testament does, since they are contemporaneous with the events they depict."[82] Yet, as William F. Hallo notes, "The Biblical record must be . . . scrutinized like other historiographical traditions of the ancient Near East, neither exempted from the standards demanded of those other traditions, nor subjected to severer ones than they are."[83] Using such standards, Hallo concludes that "one can hardly deny the reality of a conquest from abroad, implying a previous period of wanderings, a dramatic escape from the prior place of residence and an oppression there that prompted the escape."[84]

---

80. Introductions to the excavations at Tell Mardikh (Ebla) may be found in W. S. LaSor, "Tell Mardikh," in *ISBE*, 4:750–58; R. D. Biggs, "Ebla Texts," *ABD*, 2:263–70.
81. Bebbington, *Patterns in History*, 6.
82. Lemche, *Ancient Israel*, 70.
83. William H. Hallo, "The Limits of Skepticism," *JAOS* 110 (1990): 193. This was the 1989 Presidential Address of the American Oriental Society.
84. Ibid., 194.

The intent here is not a thorough critique of historical minimalism. Suffice it to say that, not only are such approaches profoundly anti-biblical, but they flounder methodologically in their use and interpretation of biblical and extrabiblical evidence. Numerous rejoinders to minimalist approaches have pointed out many shortcomings. In addition to those already noted, see the responses of nonevangelicals Dever,[85] A. F. Rainey,[86] Avi Hurwitz,[87] and others,[88] as well as evangelicals such as Long,[89] Iain W. Provan,[90] James K. Hoffmeier,[91] Richard S. Hess,[92] and K. Lawson Younger Jr.[93] Note also the challenges in two recent volumes: *Faith, Tradition, and History* and *Windows*

---

85. William G. Dever, "'Will the Real Israel Please Stand Up?' Archaeology and Israelite Historiography: Part I," 61–80; idem, "'Will the Real Israel Please Stand Up?' Part II: Archaeology and the Religions of Ancient Israel," *BASOR* 298 (May 1995): 37–58; idem, "The Identity of Early Israel: A Rejoinder to Keith W. Whitelam," *JSOT* 72 (1996): 3–24; idem, "Revisionist Israel Revisited: A Rejoinder to Niels Peter Lemche," *CurBS* 4 (1996): 35–50; idem, "Philology, Theology, and Archaeology: What Kind of History Do We Want, and What Is Possible?" in *The Archaeology of Israel: Constructing the Past, Interpreting the Present,* ed. N. A. Silberman and D. Small, JSOTSup 237 (Sheffield: Sheffield Academic Press, 1997), 290–310. Dever's most important critique is to be found in his *What Did the Biblical Writers Know and When Did They Know It?* (cited above, n. 75).
86. A. F. Rainey, "Uncritical Criticism," *JAOS* 115 (1995): 101–4.
87. Avi Hurwitz, "The Historical Quest for 'Ancient Israel' and the Linguistic Evidence of the Hebrew Bible: Some Methodological Observations," *VT* 47 (1997): 301–15.
88. A collection of useful essays by scholars who are not minimalists is N. A. Silberman and D. Small, eds., *The Archaeology of Israel* (see n. 85).
89. V. Philips Long, *The Art of Biblical History* (Grand Rapids: Zondervan, 1994); and idem, "Historiography of the Old Testament," in *The Face of Old Testament Studies,* ed. B. T. Arnold and D. W. Baker (Grand Rapids: Baker, 1999), 145–75.
90. Iain W. Provan, "Ideologies, Literary and Critical: Reflections on Recent History Writing on the History of Israel," *JBL* 114 (1995): 585–606; idem, "The End of (Israel's) History?" 283–300; and Iain W. Provan, V. Philips Long, and Tremper Longman III, *A Biblical History of Israel* (Louisville: Westminster/John Knox, 2003). The latter work is a most welcome addition to the literature on Israel's history. In addition to providing a careful re-presentation of biblical history based on sensitive genre analysis and extrabiblical materials, it also is characterized by its thorough and sophisticated introduction to historiographical issues, including a further critique of minimalist historians.
91. James K. Hoffmeier, "The Evangelical Contribution to Understanding the (Early) History of Ancient Israel in Recent Scholarship," *BBR* 7 (1997): 77–90; and idem, *Israel in Egypt: The Evidence for the Authenticity of the Exodus Tradition* (New York: Oxford University Press, 1997), esp. chaps. 1–2.
92. Richard S. Hess, "Fallacies in the Study of Early Israel: An Onomastic Perspective," *TynBul* 45 (1994): 339–54; idem, "Non-Israelite Personal Names in the Book of Joshua," *CBQ* 58 (1996): 205–14; idem, "West Semitic Texts and the Book of Joshua," *BBR* 7 (1997): 63–76; and idem, "Getting Personal: What Names in the Bible Teach Us," *BR* 13, no. 6 (December 1997): 30–37.
93. Younger, *Ancient Conquest Accounts,* esp. chap. 1; and idem, "Early Israel in Recent Biblical Scholarship," in *The Face of Old Testament Studies,* ed. B. T. Arnold and D. W. Baker (Grand Rapids: Baker, 1999), 176–206.

into Old Testament History.[94] Both critique minimalist approaches and make positive contributions to the study of Israel's history.[95]

Conclusion

God has chosen to communicate much of his Word through writings about historical events, and we do well to attempt to understand historical narrative as fully as possible. In the end, however, we must remember that even the most historically oriented portions of the Bible, such as 1–2 Samuel or 1–2 Kings, are not written as history for history's sake. The apostle Paul states that "All Scripture is God-breathed and is useful for teaching, rebuking, correcting, and training in righteousness, so that the man of God may be thoroughly equipped for every good work" (2 Tim. 3:16–17). The Bible's ultimate intent in every literary genre, including the historical texts, is to change people's lives and point them to God.[96] As C. S. Lewis stated, the Bible is "not merely a sacred book but a book so remorselessly and continuously sacred that it does not invite, it excludes or repels, the merely aesthetic approach."[97] The same would apply to the "merely" historical approach.

Most importantly, the Bible is a "theological" work. In the end, God is

---

94. A. R. Millard, J. K. Hoffmeier, D. W. Baker, eds., *Faith, Tradition, and History: Old Testament Historiography in Its Near Eastern Context* (Winona Lake, Ind.: Eisenbrauns, 1994); and V. Philips Long, David W. Baker, and Gordon J. Wenham, eds., *Windows into Old Testament History: Evidence, Argument, and the Crisis of "Biblical Israel"* (Grand Rapids: Eerdmans, 2002). Edwin Yamauchi's lead essay in the first volume—"The Current State of Old Testament Historiography" (1–36)—represents another able critique of minimalist scholarship, as do several essays in the second volume: V. Philips Long, "Introduction" (1–22); Jens Bruun Kofoed, "Epistemology, Historiographical Method, and the 'Copenhagen' School" (23–43); and Iain W. Provan, "In the Stable with the Dwarves: Testimony, Interpretation, and the History of Israel" (161–97).
95. An invaluable resource for any study of Israel's history is the collection of essays in V. Philips Long, *Israel's Past in Present Research: Essays on Ancient Israelite Historiography,* SBTS 7 (Winona Lake, Ind.: Eisenbrauns, 1999). Long, who has written extensively on historiography, has now also produced the above-mentioned history, in conjunction with Iain W. Provan and Tremper Longman III, titled *A Biblical History of Israel* (see n. 90).
96. I have made this point in connection with the royal chronicles that may have formed the basis for the writing of the books of 1–2 Kings. The chronicles themselves were strictly historical and archival in nature, but when they were included in the writing of 1–2 Kings, evaluative comments about Israel's and Judah's kings were added, written from a spiritual perspective (e.g., "and so-and-so did evil in the LORD's eyes"). See Howard, *Introduction to the Old Testament Historical Books,* 177–78.
97. C. S. Lewis, *The Literary Impact of the Authorized Version* (Philadelphia: Fortress, 1963), 33; quoted in Leland Ryken, *Words of Delight: A Literary Introduction* (Grand Rapids: Zondervan, 1974), 30.

the subject and the hero of the Bible.[98] Even in texts that emphasize human individuals, such as David in 1–2 Samuel, the individuals are important only as they are instruments in God's plan.[99] In the end, God's dealings with humans in the historical narratives reveal much about himself. We are more than merely entertained or informed; we are taught and exhorted. To be sure, the Bible's historical texts have many characteristics that can impress us, entertain us, or move us, and they often teach or exhort only indirectly.[100] But, in the last analysis, these texts do point us to God and urge us to respond to him in specific ways. May all who read these words see beyond "history" as either events or accounts of events to the God behind that history.[101]

---

98. See Gerhard Hasel, "The Problem of the Center in the Old Testament Debate," ZAW 86 (1974): 65–82; and C. Hassell Bullock, "An Old Testament Center: A Re-evaluation and Proposition" (paper presented at the Midwest meeting of the Evangelical Theological Society, St. Paul, Minnesota, 17 March 1990).
99. David is much more important as a theological symbol in Scripture—a person whom God chose and blessed, and one who was attuned to God—than he ever was as a "historical" figure, one who was a great military leader, administrator, or musician.
100. I have briefly surveyed many of these in Howard, An Introduction to the Old Testament Historical Books, 44–49.
101. I thank my secretary (and Bethel Seminary student), Abigail C. Miller, and my colleague, William G. Travis, for reading this manuscript and making a number of trenchant comments.

2

HISTORY OR STORY?

The Literary Dimension in Narrative Texts

Robert B. Chisholm Jr.

IN 1895, G. F. MOORE WROTE IN THE preface to his commentary on the book of Judges: "The interest and importance of the Book of Judges lie chiefly in the knowledge which it gives us of the state of society and religion in Israel in the early centuries of its settlement in Palestine." He adds: "In the following commentary matters of history, antiquities, and especially the social and religious life of the people in this period, are properly given the largest place; not only for their intrinsic interest, but because the knowledge of these things is indispensable to any right understanding of the history of Israel and its religion."[1] For Moore, the main value of the biblical narrative is its contribution to the reconstruction of Israelite history.

How times have changed! A century later, following the rise of rhetorical criticism, literary analysis, and other synchronic methods of interpretation, many would reject Moore's view as mere historicism. Advocates of these recent approaches emphasize the literary dimension of Old Testament narrative. Some interpreters even prefer to characterize Old Testament narrative as story, rather than history.[2] Many view literary analysis of the text as a worthwhile endeavor in its own right, apart from any value the text might have for reconstructing Israel's history. Numerous studies have appeared in which authors isolate and analyze the basic elements of story (setting, characterization, and plot) within Old Testament narratives, as well as other liter-

---

1. George F. Moore, *Judges*, ICC (Edinburgh: T. & T. Clark, 1895), v.
2. See James Barr, "Story and History in Biblical Theology," *JR* 56 (1976), 1–17; as well as A. R. Millard, "Story, History, and Theology," in *Faith, Tradition, and History: Old Testament Historiography in Its Near Eastern Context,* ed. A. R. Millard, J. K. Hoffmeier, and D. W. Baker (Winona Lake, Ind.: Eisenbrauns, 1994), 37–64.

ary features.[3] This has been, for the most part, a healthy trend, because these approaches tend to treat texts as unified, at least in their final edited form. Nevertheless, many of these critics de-emphasize historicity and are aware of the difficulty of distinguishing between fiction and nonfiction.[4] Many would probably be content to characterize the narratives as "historicized fiction" or "fictionalized history," to use Robert Alter's terms.[5]

---

3. See, among many others, Robert Alter, *The Art of Biblical Narrative* (New York: Basic Books, 1981); Yairah Amit, *Reading Biblical Narratives* (Minneapolis: Fortress, 2001); Shimon Bar-Efrat, *Narrative Art in the Bible,* trans. D. Shefer-Vanson (Sheffield: Almond, 1989); Adele Berlin, *Poetics and Interpretation of Biblical Narrative* (Winona Lake, Ind.: Eisenbrauns, 1994); Herbert Chanan Brichto, *Toward a Grammar of Biblical Poetics: Tales of the Prophets* (New York: Oxford, 1992); Jan P. Fokkelman, *Reading Biblical Narrative,* trans. I. Smit (Louisville: Westminster/John Knox, 1999); David M. Gunn and Danna Nolan Fewell, *Narrative in the Hebrew Bible* (New York: Oxford, 1993); Meir Sternberg, *The Poetics of Biblical Narrative* (Bloomington, Ind.: Indiana University Press, 1987); and Phyllis Trible, *Rhetorical Criticism: Context, Method, and the Book of Jonah* (Minneapolis: Fortress, 1994). Evangelical scholars have contributed to the discussion. See, among others, Tremper Longman III, *Literary Approaches to Biblical Interpretation* (Grand Rapids: Zondervan, 1987); Richard L. Pratt Jr., *He Gave Us Stories* (Brentwood, Tenn.: Wolgemuth & Hyatt, 1990); and Leland Ryken, *How to Read the Bible as Literature* (Grand Rapids: Zondervan, 1984).

4. Robert Alter suggests that the distinction between fiction and nonfiction may be a modern, artificial one. He expresses skepticism about our ability to understand what was going on in the ancient narrators' minds as they constructed their narratives. He says "that we probably have no way of recovering what might have figured as a fact in the ancient Hebrew mind, whether the narrative data of centuries-old traditions were assumed to be facts, or to what extent the writers consciously exercised a license of invention." See his introduction to *The Literary Guide to the Bible,* ed. Robert Alter and Frank Kermode (Cambridge: Harvard University Press, 1987), 15. Commenting on Judges 10–11, he states: "Whether or not things happened precisely as reported here, and whether or not the ancient audience conceived this as a literally accurate account of historical events (both questions are unanswerable), it is clear from the way the text is organized that the writer has exercised considerable freedom in shaping his materials to exert subtle interpretive pressure on the figures and events. In such writing, it is increasingly difficult to distinguish sharply between history and fiction, whatever the historical intentions of the writers" (ibid., 18). Berlin states: "Above all, we must keep in mind that narrative is a *form of representation.* Abraham in Genesis is not a real person any more than a painting of an apple is a real fruit. This is not a judgment on the existence of a historical Abraham any more than it is a statement about the existence of apples. It is just that we should not confuse a historical individual with his narrative representation" (emphasis hers). See Berlin, *Poetics and Interpretation of Biblical Narrative,* 13. Brichto speaks of the "fictional" and "historical" ends of the "spectrum of narrative genres." He suggests that "the *showing* technique, featuring a high proportion of *dialogue,* would be one indication of imaginative and fictional intent; while the telling technique (featuring little or no dialogue) would be an indication of historiographic intent on the part of the narrator" (emphasis his). See Brichto, *Toward a Grammar of Biblical Poetics,* 25.

5. Drawing on the work of Herbert Schneidau, Alter suggests that we can speak of biblical narrative as *"historicized* prose fiction" (emphasis his). Yet he quickly qualifies this and observes that "it may often be more precise to describe what happens in biblical narrative as fictionalized history" (*The Art of Biblical Narrative,* 24–25). In commenting on the Ehud story, he suggests that this narrative "is perhaps less historicized fiction than fictionalized history—history in which the feeling and the meaning of events are concretely realized through the technical resources of prose fiction" (ibid., 41).

While generally applauding the trend toward synchronic readings, most evangelicals continue to affirm the text's historicity. Most agree that the biblical narratives contain stories, but they are quick to assert that they are true stories. This is easy to affirm at a presuppositional level, but it is more challenging to explain exactly how the literary dimension comes into play in these historical documents without diminishing the text's historicity. Though these are accounts of what happened, one quickly realizes that in most cases we are not talking about simple "just-the-facts" reports of events. Indeed, in many instances the narratives read more like the genre of the modern historical novel, as the narrator laces his story with quotations and tells us what characters are thinking or doing behind closed doors. Evangelicals attempt to balance the historicity of the biblical narratives and their literary dimension in such a way that both aspects are given their proper due.[6] This essay discusses some literary features of narrative. These features should be recognized by interpreters, but they can be overlooked by those preoccupied with the debate over historicity or hemmed in by inadequate notions of how the narrative genre works. Until these features are recognized, one cannot construct an adequate definition or description of the narrative genre or of biblical history writing.

Literary Conventions

Several scholars have demonstrated the importance of viewing Old Testament historiography and narrative in its ancient Near Eastern context.[7] Such analyses often identify literary conventions that were used in the culture and appear in the biblical narratives. Recognizing such conven-

---

6. See, for example, the fine study by V. Philips Long, *The Art of Biblical History* (Grand Rapids: Zondervan, 1994), the very title of which reflects a concern for both the text's historicity and its literary dimension. See as well (1) the observations of John Bimson, "Old Testament History and Sociology," in *Interpreting the Old Testament,* ed. Craig C. Broyles (Grand Rapids: Baker, 2001), 133–38; (2) the helpful remarks of Iain W. Provan, *1 and 2 Kings,* NIBC (Peabody, Mass.: Hendrickson, 1995), 1–10, who affirms that Kings is both narrative and historiographical in its scope; and (3) the insightful discussion of Tremper Longman III, "Storytellers and Poets in the Bible: Can Literary Artifice Be True?" in *Inerrancy and Hermeneutic,* ed. Harvie M. Conn (Grand Rapids: Baker, 1988), 137–49.
7. See, among others, various authors represented in *Faith, Tradition, and History: Old Testament Historiography in Its Near Eastern Context,* ed. A. R. Millard, J. K. Hoffmeier, and D. W. Baker (Winona Lake, Ind.: Eisenbrauns, 1994); Simon B. Parker, *Stories in Scripture and Inscriptions: Comparative Studies on Narratives in Northwest Semitic Inscriptions and the Hebrew Bible* (New York: Oxford, 1997); and William W. Hallo and K. L. Younger, eds., *COS,* 3 vols. (Leiden: Brill, 1997–2002).

tions enables one to read the biblical accounts as they were intended to be read and understood in their original context by their original audience. What this means, however, is that our modern, straightforward reading of the text sometimes proves to be simplistic and misleading. For example, K. Lawson Younger's comparison of ancient Near Eastern military accounts with the biblical conquest account in Joshua reveals the presence of certain literary conventions and syntagmatic constructions in the biblical text. Recognizing these features is essential if one is to appreciate how the narrative genre works in this case. Failure to recognize these conventions will cause one to misread the intention of the author and make wrong assumptions about what actually happened.[8] David Fouts has shown that large numbers were sometimes used hyperbolically in ancient Near Eastern texts and proposes that biblical narrative employs such inflated figures in a similar manner.[9] Taking such figures literally can result in a misreading of the biblical text and a misunderstanding of what actually transpired. Both Younger and Fouts have demonstrated that the description of "what happened" is couched in cultural idiom and must be qualified accordingly.

Contextualized Perspective

A comparison of biblical texts with ancient Near Eastern materials reveals that the biblical record is often contextualized by its divine Author to reflect the worldview of the culture. For example, one detects the presence of accommodated language in the very first chapter of Genesis. In the creation account we read how the Creator divided the waters of the great deep (vv. 2, 6) and placed an expanse (רָקִיעַ), later called "sky" (שָׁמַיִם) between the "waters below" and the "waters above" (vv. 7–8). The cosmological structure depicted here includes a heavenly ocean above the sky (see Pss. 104:3; 148:4; 2 Kings 7:2). There is, of course, no heavenly ocean in reality, but ancient Near Eastern conceptions of the cosmos include such

---

8. See K. Lawson Younger Jr., *Ancient Conquest Accounts: A Study in Ancient Near Eastern and Biblical History Writing* (Sheffield: JSOT, 1990).
9. See David M. Fouts, "Another Look at Large Numbers in Assyrian Royal Inscriptions," *JNES* 53 (1994): 205–11; and the same author's "A Defense of the Hyperbolic Interpretation of Large Numbers in the Old Testament," *JETS* 40 (1997): 377–87. See also his essay, "The Incredible Numbers of the Hebrew Kings," chapter 13 in this volume.

an ocean.[10] Since the biblical creation account reflects this cultural view of the cosmos, it should be regarded, at least in this respect, as a contextualized description of creation, rather than a scientifically precise account of "what happened."

It is possible that some references to direct divine involvement in events may reflect a view of divine pancausality that was popular in the ancient Near East. In the deterministic idiom of the culture, actions that were simply permitted by God, mediated through agents, or accomplished through the laws of nature, can be attributed directly to God. Bertil Albrektson observes that "the gods of the ancient Near East were supposed to reign over a realm which included the two spheres which we call nature and history."[11] In the context of such a worldview, it is possible and perhaps likely that references to Yahweh closing wombs (1 Sam. 1:6), creating handicapped babies (Exod. 4:11), giving Saul's wives to David (2 Sam. 12:8), and the like, are an accommodation to the mindset of the culture. As the sovereign king of the world and history, God is ultimately behind the situations and events in view, but his involvement may be more indirect than the language of the text suggests. The situations described may reflect his permissive will, rather than his ideal or his moral will.

Point of View

The narrator usually assumes an omniscient, divine perspective that transcends the event per se and exceeds what a mere observer would have perceived. However, this is not always the case. Occasionally, a narrator speaks from the limited point of view of one of the characters or of an observer of the event.[12] For example, in Ruth 3:8, as Boaz wakes up, we read: "Look! There was a woman lying at his legs." The statement is correct as far as it goes, but it is also much more vague than we might expect. After all, we

---

10. See Luis I. J. Stadelmann, *The Hebrew Conception of the World* (Rome: Pontifical Biblical Institute, 1970), 47; Othmar Keel, *The Symbolism of the Biblical World* (New York: Seabury Press, 1978; reprint, Winona Lake, Ind.: Eisenbrauns, 1997), 36; and Klaus Seybold, *Introducing the Psalms* (Edinburgh: T. & T. Clark, 1990), 182.
11. Bertil Albrektson, *History and the Gods* (Lund: CWK Gleerup, 1967), 23.
12. Narrators sometimes interrupt the mainline of the discourse with a clause beginning with וְהִנֵּה, "and look," signaling a shift from an external to an internal point of view. For a discussion of the literary use of וְהִנֵּה, see *BDB*, 244 (par. c), and Berlin, *Poetics and Interpretation of Biblical Narrative*, 91–95.

know the woman is Ruth, because the narrator has told us (vv. 6–7), but he heightens the dramatic effect by assuming Boaz's perspective and thereby inviting us to experience the event as Boaz did.[13]

Unfortunately for modern interpreters, biblical narrators do not routinely signal their use of a limited perspective. The interpreter must often rely on broader contextual clues to know when this literary device is being used. Failure to detect its use can lead to wrong historical conclusions. For example, according to Judges 1:19, the men of Judah, despite being accompanied and energized by the Lord himself, were unable to defeat the people of the plains, because the latter "had iron chariots" in their arsenal.[14] The statement begs us to ask, "Since when have chariots been able to thwart God's purposes and power!?" After all, the Lord destroyed the Egyptian chariots in the Red Sea (Exod. 14:23–28; 15:4). He promised to give the Canaanite chariots into Israel's hands and instructed Joshua to burn them (Josh. 11:4–6, 9). Later Joshua assured the tribe of Joseph that the Canaanite iron chariots would not prevent them from conquering the plains (Josh. 17:16–18). In Judges 4–5 we read how the Lord annihilated the iron chariots of Sisera. But according to Judges 1:19, the army of Judah was unable to overcome iron chariots, even though the Lord was with them! In its larger literary context the passage cannot mean what it appears to say. We soon discover there is more here than meets the eye. A few verses later the author explains that the people's failure was really due to spiritual compromise and idolatry (Judg. 2:1–5). Judges 1:19 must reflect the people's limited and warped perspective, not the author's own interpretation.[15] The author is toying with his

---

13. See Berlin, *Poetics and Interpretation of Biblical Narrative*, 91–92.
14. The Hebrew text has simply, "though not to conquer the residents of the plain." It is likely that the verb יָכֹל has been accidentally omitted after the negative particle (see Josh. 15:63; 17:12). In its original form the text may have read כִּי לֹא יָכְלוּ לְהוֹרִישׁ, "though they were not able to conquer . . ." or perhaps כִּי לֹא יָכֹל לְהוֹרִישׁ, "though he [Judah] was not able to conquer . . ." The use of the collective singular in verse 18–19a favors the latter. For discussion of the textual issues, see Barnabas Lindars, *Judges 1–5* (Edinburgh: T. & T. Clark, 1995), 45; and Robert H. O'Connell, *The Rhetoric of the Book of Judges* (Leiden: Brill, 1996), 447.
15. See Barry Webb, *The Book of Judges: An Integrated Reading* (Sheffield: JSOT, 1987), 90. Failing to detect the literary irony and obviously troubled by the apparent implications of the statement, the Targum reads here, "because they sinned, they were not able to drive out." See O'Connell, *Rhetoric of the Book of Judges,* 447. J. Marais fails to recognize the rhetorical role of perspective in this passage. He contends that Judges reflects various fields of reference. In the frame of reference exhibited in Judges 1:19: "Yahweh is not expected to overcome every stumbling block." He suggests that this text may represent "a human perspective on Yahweh and his influence on history, or it may be a perspective born from the human experience that Yahweh's presence does not guarantee an ideal history." He adds, "Whichever way one looks at it, it is clear that the premise of this text is not the logic of an almighty deity." See Jacobus Marais, *Representation in Old Testament Narrative Texts* (Leiden: Brill, 1998), 80.

audience here. With tongue-in-cheek, as it were, he raises our curiosity by giving us a signal that something is wrong. Expecting us to object, he prepares the way for the real explanation for Israel's partial success.

Sometimes it is difficult to know when the narrator is using a limited perspective. For example, 2 Chronicles 28:23 observes that Ahaz "offered sacrifices to the gods of Damascus, who had defeated him." Are we to take this statement at face value? The text may simply reflect Ahaz's polytheistic perspective; he thought these gods had defeated him. However, we should not rush to this conclusion. In the worldview of the narrator, these gods may actually exist and possess the capability of defeating God's people. Even if this is the case, the Chronicler qualifies this view by making it clear that these gods were able to defeat Judah only because Yahweh gave his rebellious people over to the enemy (see vv. 5, 19).[16] From a broader biblical perspective, one could argue that the reality behind the pagan gods was Satan and the evil spiritual forces referred to in Ephesians 6:12.[17]

Sometimes a character's point of view influences a narrator's word choice in even more subtle ways than we see in the examples cited above. One of

---

16. Second Kings 3:27 may provide an instructive parallel in this regard. In fulfillment of Elisha's prophecy, the Israelite-Judahite-Edomite coalition defeated Moab and surrounded Mesha, the Moabite king. In desperation Mesha sacrificed his firstborn son as a burnt offering. We are then told that there was a great outburst of anger against Israel, prompting the Israelite army to retreat. The text begs us to ask: "Who is the source of this angry outburst?" The language of the text suggests that divine wrath is in view. With the exception of two texts, one or both of which are relatively late (Esther 1:18; Eccl. 5:16), the noun, קֶצֶף "anger," is used in the Hebrew Bible of Yahweh's anger. See Numbers 1:53; 17:11 (Eng., 16:46); 18:5; Deuteronomy 29:17; Joshua 9:20; 22:20; 1 Chronicles 27:24; 2 Chronicles 19:2, 10; 24:18; 29:8; 32:25–26; Psalms 38:2 (Eng., v. 1); 102:11 (Eng., v. 10); Isaiah 34:2; 54:8; 60:10; Jeremiah 10:10; 21:5; 32:37; 50:13; Zechariah 1:2, 15; 7:12. The related verb קָצַף frequently refers to divine anger, but it is also used often of human anger. However, in 2 Kings 3:27 it is more likely that Mesha's god Chemosh is in view. The most natural explanation within the "world" of the story is that Chemosh responded to the offering and counterattacked the Israelite army, regardless of what was the true ultimate cause. Though Chemosh is not specifically named here, his name may have been suppressed by the author or by a later editor who was uncomfortable with the image of a pagan deity fighting and defeating the forces of Yahweh. See Parker, *Stories in Scripture and Inscriptions*, 125, as well as Gregory A. Boyd, *God at War: The Bible and Spiritual Conflict* (Downers Grove, Ill.: InterVarsity, 1997), 118. Many interpreters shy away from this conclusion and prefer to attribute the anger to Yahweh. See, for example, Brichto, *Toward a Grammar of Biblical Poetics*, 207–8.

17. It is common for modern Western readers to dismiss the pagan gods of the Hebrew Bible as a mere figment of their worshipers' imagination. However, in the broader context of the entire Bible, it might be more accurate to say that there was a spiritual reality behind these "gods," namely, the rebellious members of God's heavenly assembly led by Satan. Paul refers to them as "the spiritual forces of evil in the heavenly realms" (Eph. 6:12). This may be the group addressed in Psalm 82; Daniel 10 gives us a glimpse of their authority and activities.

the oddities of Judges 6:36–40 is the use of the divine name Elohim ("God"), rather than Yahweh ("Lord"). Though some see the shift as evidence of different literary sources,[18] a better explanation is available when one views the narrative from a literary and rhetorical angle. At this point in the story Gideon has regressed. His faith in Yahweh, the ever-present God who helps those whom he commissions (v. 16; cf. Exod. 3:12), is wavering. Gideon knows by now he is dealing with a deity, but he is not yet sure of this God's reliability. In light of Gideon's insufficient faith, the name Yahweh is not appropriate here. The use of the more general name for deity reflects Gideon's limited, partially developed perspective.[19]

If this proposal is valid for verses Judges 6:36–40, then we may be able to explain why Elohim, not Yahweh, is used back in verse 20. Yahweh, the covenant God of Israel, initiated a relationship with Gideon and promised to protect and enable him. Yet by the end of their initial encounter Gideon was doubtful. He used אֲדֹנָי, "Lord," but not Yahweh, in addressing the Lord (v. 15) and requested a sign (v. 17). Because Gideon's lack of faith is highlighted at the end of the first scene of the story's first episode, it is quite appropriate that the first reference to the deity in the episode's second scene is Elohim. The use of Elohim (see "angel of God") in verse 20 reflects Gideon's perspective. He was not yet convinced that he was speaking with Yahweh or that the angelic messenger came from Yahweh. However, once the Lord gave him a sign, he was willing to use the name Yahweh (vv. 22, 24). The name Yahweh is appropriate in verses 25–34, where Gideon obeys the Lord's command and is energized by his Spirit, but not in verses 36–40, where Gideon essentially questions whether Yahweh really has called him.

Selectivity of Material

Any historian has to exercise selectivity. With respect to biblical history, the choice of what to include or omit is often determined by the narrator's

---

18. See, for example, Moore, *Judges*, 198.
19. Daniel I. Block (see his *Judges, Ruth,* NAC [Nashville: Broadman & Holman, 1999], 273) also sees a rhetorical purpose in the narrator's choice of divine names. He observes: "The narrator apparently recognizes the incongruity of the situation by deliberately referring to God by the generic designation Elohim rather than his personal covenant name Yahweh." Block suggests that this rhetorical device reflects Gideon's confusion. He states, "Apparently Gideon has difficulty distinguishing between Yahweh, the God of the Israelites, and God in a general sense."

overall theological perspective and purpose. For example, the Chronicler's version of the Davidic–Solomonic era differs from that of Samuel–Kings. Dillard and Longman observe: "In Chronicles David and Solomon are portrayed as glorious, obedient, all conquering figures who enjoy not only divine blessing but also the support of all the nation."[20] They conclude that this "idealization of the reigns of David and Solomon," rather than being "a kind of glorification of the 'good old days,'" "reflects a 'messianic historiography'" in which David and Solomon embody an "eschatological hope."[21]

Another well-known example of authorial selectivity is the omission in Kings of any reference to Ahab's involvement in the Battle of Qarqar (853 B.C.), where a western coalition beat back the Assyrian army under Shalmaneser III.[22] Though his success at Qarqar might have been a feather in Ahab's cap, the biblical history of his reign omits reference to it, probably because the narrator prefers, apparently for theological reasons, to paint an exclusively negative picture of Ahab's reign.

Sometimes the selection of material reflects a literary purpose. A comparison of the prose account of Sisera's death in Judges 4 with the poetic version in Judges 5 is instructive. The poetic account abridges and streamlines the earlier narrative in some respects, but highlights Jael's cunning and effectiveness through additional information and the poetic device of repetition. In the poem, we read nothing of Sisera's arrival or of Jael's initial gestures of apparent concern. Instead the focus is on her offer of milk. The prose account tells how she gave him milk when he asked for water; the poem adds that she brought him curdled milk in a bowl fit for a noble, which he must have seen as an obvious gesture of loyalty. The poem mentions nothing of Jael's tucking Sisera into bed; instead it focuses on the deadly deed. The prose account uses only one verb to describe the murder stroke (see Judg. 4:21); the poem employs four synonyms, emphasizing the deadly force of the blow and forcing us to replay it in our minds.[23] The

---

20. See Raymond B. Dillard and Tremper Longman III, *An Introduction to the Old Testament* (Grand Rapids: Zondervan, 1994), 174.
21. Ibid., 174–75.
22. See Eugene H. Merrill, *Kingdom of Priests: A History of Old Testament Israel* (Grand Rapids: Baker, 1987), 348–49; and Wayne T. Pitard, *Ancient Damascus* (Winona Lake, Ind.: Eisenbrauns, 1987), 128–29.
23. There is rhyme in the Hebrew text of 5:26b: note the *ah-a'-ah-o* // *ah-ah-o* pattern. The third feminine singular verbs also have the same vocalic pattern. The final *mem* of the first verbal root is repeated in the second verbal root, the *mem-ḥet* combination appears at the beginning of the second and third verbal roots, and the *ḥet* of the second and third roots appears at the beginning of the fourth verbal root.

prose account, while describing how the peg went through his skull into the ground, notes simply that he died (vv. 21–22); the poem uses seven finite verbal forms (כָּרַע and נָפַל appear three times each, and שָׁכַב once) to emphasize the efficiency and finality of the deed. It also repeats the location of his death ("at her feet," lit. "between her legs") to set up an ironic connection with verses 28–30, and concludes with a resounding passive form, "dead" (שָׁדוּד, "violently destroyed, devastated").

Sensitivity to possible literary motives for authorial selectivity may explain features of a text that heretofore have puzzled interpreters. For example, in Judges 1:30–36 there is no reference to the tribe of Issachar. Most attempt to explain this "ellipsis" (as Younger calls it) on historical grounds.[24] For example, some theorize that Issachar was assimilated into Manasseh or Zebulun.[25]

Perhaps we should consider a literary explanation for the ellipsis. For the most part, the arrangement corresponds to Joshua 19:10–48, with the notable absence of Issachar:

Table 2.1

Zebulun	Joshua 19:10–16	Judges 1:30
Issachar	Joshua 19:17–23	—
Asher	Joshua 19:24–31	Judges 1:31–32
Naphtali	Joshua 19:32–39	Judges 1:33
Dan	Joshua 19:40–48	Judges 1:34–36

In Joshua, the tribes of Benjamin (18:11–28) and Simeon (19:1–9) are listed before the northern tribes, while Joshua himself appears at the end (vv. 49–51). The sevenfold (plus one) list has an aura of completeness about it.[26] In Judges 1:27–36 Manasseh and Ephraim appear with the northern tribes, reflecting their geographical proximity in Joshua's allotment.[27] The

---

24. See the works cited in K. Lawson Younger Jr., "The Configuring of Judicial Preliminaries: Judges 1.1–2.5 and Its Dependence on the Book of Joshua," *JSOT* 68 (1995): 84 n. 28; as well as Lindars, *Judges 1–5*, 63.
25. See, for example, Yairah Amit, *The Book of Judges: The Art of Editing* (Leiden: Brill, 1999), 149.
26. Judah and Joseph (Ephraim and Manasseh) appear in the preceding section (Josh. 15–17), which is separated from the second list by the narrative in 18:1–10. Judah's and Joseph's textual prominence in Joshua reflects their importance and size (see Num. 1–2.). The order of the Joseph tribes reflects the reversal that occurred during Jacob's blessing recorded in Genesis 48.
27. Judah, Simeon, and Benjamin appear together earlier in Judges 1, for Joshua's allotment made it clear that they would live closely together in the south.

omission of Issachar produces a list of six, suggesting incompleteness and signaling that reality has fallen short of the ideal.

Issachar's absence contributes powerfully to the rhetoric of Judges 1:27–33, which give a litany of Israel's failure to take its allotted land. A recurring statement dominates: "Neither did X (Israelite tribal group) drive out Y (Canaanite people group)." In verses 27–30 the Canaanites live among the Israelite tribes, but a significant shift occurs in verses 31–33, where the Israelites now live among the Canaanites, as if the latter are now the more dominant group. In verse 34, structural patterns break down entirely as we are told that the Amorites forced the Danites to the hill country.[28] As one considers "what's wrong with this picture," invisible Issachar becomes an important element. As the litany unfolds, one entire tribe seems to have disappeared. But given the tone and theme of the context, this development is by no means unexpected.

Arrangement of Material

We are accustomed to narrative texts proceeding in a linear "A-to-Z" fashion. However, sensitivity to the literary dimension of the text enables us to detect other patterns, such as *recapitulation* and *temporal overlay*. Failing to recognize these structures, higher critics have typically devised elaborate source critical theories to explain apparent inconsistencies and duplications of such texts. But such proposals seem unnecessary and obsolete when examined under the lens of more sophisticated, discourse-oriented approaches to Hebrew narrative.

Recapitulation

Like Hebrew poetry, Hebrew narrative sometimes utilizes a form of parallelism in which an earlier statement is both repeated and expanded.[29] For example, the account of Israel's civil war against the Benjaminites in Judges 20 contains a condensed account of the battle (vv. 29–36a) followed by a

---

28. Webb (*Book of Judges*, 99) develops this progression nicely.
29. For a brief discussion of the technique, see Brichto, *Toward a Grammar of Biblical Poetics*, 13–14. He refers to it as "synoptic-conclusive/resumptive-expansive."

supplemental version that recapitulates the earlier account while adding further details (vv. 36b–45).[30]

This stylistic device also characterizes the account of the Noahic Flood, which is typically attributed by higher critics to different, conflicting sources (viz., J and P). Examples include: (a) In Genesis 6:11–13 God announces divine judgment upon "all flesh" in general terms. Then in verse 17 he reveals the form the judgment will take and further identifies "all flesh" as possessing "the breath of life." (b) In verses 19–20 God instructs Noah to bring two of every kind of animal into the ark. In 7:2–3 Yahweh gives more specific details, explaining that Noah must bring seven pairs of every clean animal aboard ship. (c) The account in verses 7–12 is recapitulated and expanded in verses 13–24. Verse 13 names the three sons mentioned in verse 7. Verses 14–16 give a much more detailed description of the animals referred to in verses 8–9. Here we find the observation that Yahweh shut Noah in. Verses 17–24 expand on verse 12 by describing what transpired during the forty-day period and by noting that the flood waters covered the earth for 150 days. (d) In 8:2–5 the narrator expands on verse 1 by giving us more detail concerning how God ended the Flood (in addition to sending a wind, he also stopped up the deep and caused the rain to cease)[31] and by providing us with a timetable.

Temporal Overlay

The main story line of a narrative, built on a succession of *wayyiqtol* verbal forms, usually proceeds from "A-to-Z" in sequential fashion. However, this is not always the case.[32] For example, a parallel and/or supplemental

---

30. For a structural analysis of the text see Robert B. Chisholm Jr., *From Exegesis to Exposition* (Grand Rapids: Baker, 1998), 139–42; as well as the articles by E. J. Revell, "The Battle with Benjamin (Judges xx 29–48) and Hebrew Narrative Techniques," *VT* 35 (1985): 417–33; and P. E. Satterthwaite, "Narrative Artistry in the Composition of Judges xx 29ff," *VT* 42 (1992): 80–89.
31. He may refer to the wind first (v. 1) because he is drawing a parallel to Genesis 1:1–2. In this regard see Bruce K. Waltke, with Cathi J. Fredricks, *Genesis: A Commentary* (Grand Rapids: Zondervan, 2001), 128.
32. Grammarians disagree over the use of the *wayyiqtol* as a pluperfect in a narratival sequence. Driver argued against such temporal overlay unless the *wayyiqtol* was beginning a new section. See S. R. Driver, *A Treatise on the Use of the Tenses in Hebrew* (Oxford: Clarendon, 1892), 84–89. Randall Buth makes room for unmarked temporal overlay if "some lexical redundancy or reference specifically points back to a previous event" or "from common cultural experience an event can be interpreted as giving a reason for comment on the immediately preceding events" ("Methodological Collision Between Source Criticism and Discourse Analysis: The Problem of 'Unmarked Temporal Overlay' and the Pluperfect/ Nonsequential *wayyiqtol*," in *Biblical Hebrew*

account sometimes flashes back to a point prior to where the preceding account ended or even began (see Judg. 2:6–3:6 in relation to 1:1–2:5).[33]

Sometimes a cluster of verbs can appear in a logical/thematic, rather than chronological sequence. For example, Judges 3:15b–17 uses *wayyiqtol* forms to describe four actions. The initial clause in verse 16 (introduced with a *wayyiqtol* form) involves a flashback. At the end of verse 15 we are told that the Israelites sent their tribute to Eglon by the hand of Ehud. Verse 17a informs us that Ehud then brought the tribute to the king. However, verse 16a flashes back to a time when Ehud made his sword, presumably before he was actually sent off with the tribute. The chronological order of events was probably: (1) Ehud made his sword (v. 16a), (2) the Israelites commissioned Ehud to take the tribute to the king (v. 15b), (3) just prior to leaving on his mission, Ehud strapped on his sword (v. 16b), (4) Ehud brought the tribute to the king (v. 17). The text presents the first two actions in reverse order, perhaps for literary effect. The references to making and strapping on the sword naturally complement each other and, when combined, facilitate the presentation of Ehud as a man who is on a different mission (assassinating the king) than the one he appears to be on (delivering tribute to the king). By reversing the verb order, the narrator creates a structure in which the secret mission is embedded within the ostensible mission: (A) Israel sends Ehud to deliver tribute, (B) Ehud makes a murder weapon, (B') Ehud straps on the murder weapon, (A') Ehud arrives with the tribute.[34]

---

and Discourse Linguistics, ed. R. Bergen [Winona Lake, Ind.: Eisenbrauns, 1994], 147). John Collins, working with data accumulated by David W. Baker, combines, modifies, and expands the criteria offered by Driver and Buth. He concludes unmarked overlay can be present and a *wayyiqtol* understood as a pluperfect if (1) "some anaphoric reference explicitly points back to a previous event," (2) "the logic of the referent described requires that an event presented by a *wayyiqtol* verb form actually took place prior to the event presented by a previous verb," and (3) "the verb begins a section or paragraph." See C. John Collins, "The *Wayyiqtol* as 'Pluperfect': When and Why," *TynBul* 46 (1995): 127–28.

33. Judges 2:6–9 actually recapitulates Joshua 24:28–31 and resumes where that story left off. The statement "and Joshua dismissed the people" at the beginning of 2:6 is identical to Joshua 24:28a and introduces a paragraph that essentially repeats Joshua 24:28–31. Through this resumptive technique the narrator links this new narrative (Judg. 2:10–3:6) with Joshua 24. See Chisholm, *From Exegesis to Exposition,* 121–22. An instructive parallel use of the *wayyiqtol* construction appears in the Moabite Stone. See Buth, "Methodological Collision Between Source Criticism and Discourse Analysis," 146.

34. Another option is to understand verse 15b as a preliminary summary statement that is then filled out in more detail in the following verses (see, e.g., Ruth 2:3). However, the collocation "sent by the hand of" in Judges 3:15b need not encompass the arrival of the one sent (see 1 Sam. 16:20–21 and 2 Sam. 10:2 where the verb "sent" is followed by the verb "arrived, came").

Judges 16:1–3 provides another example of this device. After Samson arrived at the prostitute's house, the men of Gaza set an ambush for him "all night" long and made no move to capture him "during the night" (v. 2). The actions described extend from the time when they became aware of his presence until morning. However, using a *wayyiqtol* verbal form, verse 3 informs us that Samson stayed with the prostitute until the "middle of the night" and then arose and left the city, apparently without the guards noticing.[35] Verse 3 involves a flashback; the actions described occurred within the time frame depicted in verse 2b.

Genesis 22:3 may provide another example of successive *wayyiqtol* forms where the chronological order of events may very well be rearranged for literary effect. One would think that Abraham would have split the wood before saddling the donkey and taking the servants and Isaac. Assuming that the actions are listed in chronological order, interpreters propose that Abraham was not thinking straight, that he was trying to keep everyone in the dark about the purpose of the trip, or that he was putting off the inevitable as long as possible. But the order may be literary. The narrator includes the routine actions first (saddling the donkey, summoning the servants), setting the stage for the scene to follow and signaling that Abraham will obey. Then he mentions Isaac and puts the most ominous action (chopping the wood) last in the list of preparatory actions for dramatic effect. When he saddles the donkey, one thinks: It looks like he's going to do it. When he splits the wood, one thinks: Wow, he really is going to do it.

Recognizing how narrators deal with temporal overlay can sometimes clarify what actually happened. For example, according to 2 Kings 23:29–30, Neco killed Josiah at Megiddo. Josiah's servants transported his corpse from Megiddo to Jerusalem and then buried him in his tomb. The parallel account in 2 Chronicles 35:23–24 appears to give a different sequence of events. Neco's archers shoot Josiah, who orders his servants to remove him from the battlefield because of his serious wound. They transfer him to another chariot and take him to Jerusalem. We are then informed that he died and was buried in his ancestral tomb. The NIV ("where he died")

---

35. Amit (*Reading Biblical Narratives*, 7–8) recreates the scene as follows: "The Philistines 'kept whispering to each other' all night long, planning to capture and kill Samson, while he slipped out of the city at midnight right under their noses. This means that they were still plotting away in whispers when he was already gone with their city gate on his shoulders. Moreover, he must have performed this presumably noisy exploit . . . extremely quietly. . . . Thus we see how the author's irony and mockery of the Philistines are implicit in the story."

assumes that the verb "and he died" (the Hebrew form is simply a *wayyiqtol*) is in sequence with what precedes, thus creating a contradiction between the Chronicler's version of the story and the account in 2 Kings. Is it possible that the verbal sequence in 2 Chronicles 35:24 is not strictly chronological, but thematic? After all, the idiom "die and be buried" is a common one in the Hebrew Bible.[36] In this case, Josiah actually died on the battlefield, but the Chronicler decides to withhold that fact briefly and combine it with a reference to the king's burial.

Genesis 8:1 provides another example of the flashback technique. After a description of the devastating effects of the Flood and Noah's isolation (7:17–24), the theme shifts to God's concern for Noah and the removal of the waters (8:1). In 7:17–24 the waters are described as prevailing over the earth for 150 days, but in 8:1–5 the focus is on their receding between the fortieth and one hundred and fiftieth days. As the theme shifts from judgment to renewal, the scene shifts back to the fortieth day of the Flood, when God began the process whereby he caused the waters to recede.[37]

Perhaps the chronological problem raised by Genesis 2:19a can be solved if we recognize a flashback in the narrative at this point. The *wayyiqtol* form at the beginning of the verse ("and he formed") appears to be in chronological sequence with what precedes, but this creates an apparent contradiction with Genesis 1. There the creation of the birds on day five and the land animals on day six precedes the creation of both the man and the woman. Some solve the problem by translating the form in 2:19a as a pluperfect (see NIV), while others object to this solution on grounds that the criteria for temporal overlay are not present here.[38] After all, the discourse boundary for 2:19 appears to be 2:4. However, even if this is the case, it is still possible that 2:19a constitutes a flashback. The narrator had no reason to mention the creation of the animals earlier because it did not suit his

---

36. See Genesis 35:8, 19; Numbers 20:1; Deuteronomy 10:6; Judges 8:32; 10:2, 5; 12:7, 10, 12, 15; Ruth 1:17; 2 Samuel 17:23; Jeremiah 16:4; 20:6.
37. Some understand the flashback to occur at 8:2 (see NIV), but it is more likely that the shift takes place at verse 1, which signals a thematic shift and a renewed focus on God as the primary actor in the episode (cf. 7:16, the last place where God/the LORD is the stated subject of a verb). The statement in 8:1 also marks the central point in the chiastic structure of the Flood account. In this regard see Gordon J. Wenham, "The Coherence of the Flood Narrative," *VT* 28 (1978): 337–39. Verse 2 is not in precise chronological sequence with verse 1. As noted earlier in our discussion of recapitulation, verse 2 supplements verse 1.
38. See Driver, *Treatise on the Use of the Tenses in Hebrew,* 88, and Buth, "Methodological Collision Between Source Criticism and Discourse Analysis," 148–49. For a discussion of the problem and an attempt to refute Buth's position, see Collins, "The *Wayyiqtol* as 'Pluperfect,'" 135–40.

anthropocentric purpose. He saves a reference to their creation until they play a role in his story.[39] This is similar to what we see in Judges 3:15–17, where the narrator does not mention Ehud's making the sword until the time comes for him to strap it on and use it.

Creative Use of Repetition

As noted above in our discussion of recapitulation, Hebrew narrative sometimes appears to be unduly repetitive. However, closer inspection can reveal a literary and rhetorical purpose behind this stylistic device. In addition to recapitulation, narrators utilize repetition in other ways, including paneled structuring and echoing.[40]

Paneled Structuring

Some stories display paneled structures, where repetition in the earlier panels creates a dramatic mood that prepares the audience for the climax that occurs in the final panel. Second Kings 1:9–15 is a prime example. Only slight changes occur in the preliminary panels, setting the stage for more startling alterations as the story reaches its peak. The first two panels (vv. 9–10 and 11–12) are virtually identical, though the second captain's command to the prophet is more emphatic (note the addition of "this is what" and "at once" in v. 11, cf. v. 9), epitomizing the king's arrogant attitude and sense of superiority. The report of the second captain's demise (v. 12) is almost identical to the report of the first captain's death (v. 10), but note how the second report refers to "the fire of God" (cf. simply "fire" in v. 10). The text emphasizes that God is indeed responsive to the prophet's prayer, for Elijah is truly a "man of God." The repetition sets the stage for the final panel, while the alterations heighten the dramatic tension. This tension is resolved in the third panel as the king's representative finally

---

39. In this regard Collins ("The *Wayyiqtol* as 'Pluperfect,'" 139) observes: "Perhaps the simplest explanation comes from the fact that both accounts are strongly anthropocentric: they see man as the pinnacle of God's creative work, the one for whom the earth and its animals exist. Putting the animals' formation in 2:19 directly after 2:18, where God sets about making a helper sutiable for the man, reinforces this point: even though physically the animals were made *before* man, yet conceptually their creation was in anticipation of their subservience to his governance, and therefore in God's mind the animals were a logical consequence of the making of man."
40. For a useful discussion of the techniques of repetition in biblical narrative, see Alter, *Art of Biblical Narrative*, 88–113.

bows the knee before the prophet and gives him the respect he deserves. While repetition gives these stories a contrived appearance, a brief moment of reflection remind one that human beings are creatures of habit and that real life sometimes follows such patterns. Other classic examples of paneled structuring are found in Judges 16:4–21 and 1 Samuel 3.[41]

Echoing

This literary device is a sort of *déjà vu* technique that has been misunderstood by many source critics, who typically label it a "doublet" and usually attribute it to different and competing literary sources. In this case an episode within the macroplot echoes an earlier episode, inviting the reader to note the similarity, make comparisons and/or contrasts, and draw thematic and even theological correlations between the episodes. Once again this kind of repetition may appear to be contrived, but anyone who has seriously reflected on the old adage "history repeats itself" knows that history and the real life experiences of people are characterized by such repetition and patterns.[42]

A well-known example of this technique can be found in the two accounts in which Abram/Abraham lies about the identity of his wife (Gen. 12:10–20; 20:1–18). In the second episode we even learn that Abraham typically used this ploy during his travels (v. 13). Later, his son even resorted to the same technique (26:7–10). The narrator includes the second story to show that just prior to Isaac's birth Abraham's character was still flawed and his faith still incomplete, despite all that had transpired during the intervening twenty-four years. This heightens the tension of the story as we continue to wonder if Abraham will prove faithful to God's challenge and receive the covenant in its full form (see 17:1–8). It sets the stage for the ultimate test, which Abraham passes with flying colors (22:1–17).

One of the most sophisticated uses of echoing appears in the Jacob story.

---

41. According to H. van Dyke Parunak, this technique, which he labels "alternation," is especially well-suited to oral literature. This explains why it appears in modern literature "with a strong aural orientation." See his "Some Axioms for Literary Architecture," *Semitics* 8 (1982): 9–10; as well as his "Oral Typesetting: Some Uses of Biblical Structure," *Bib* 62 (1981): 154 n. 2. One must remember that in ancient Israel these stories would have been heard, not read, by most people.
42. Robert Alter discusses this literary phenomenon and postulates the concept of type scenes to explain at least some of the examples. See his *Art of Biblical Narrative*, 47–62

By the time Jacob returns to Bethel, he has committed himself wholeheartedly to the Lord. The Lord has fulfilled Jacob's condition (compare Gen. 35:3 with 28:20), and Jacob is more than ready to serve him. God again gives him a new name (compare 35:10 with 32:28) and once more makes Jacob the recipient of the Abrahamic promise (compare 35:11–12 with 28:13–15). Jacob once more sanctifies the site and names it Bethel (compare 35:14–15 with 28:18–19).

The repetition of earlier actions and statements in Genesis 35:10–15 might suggest that different sources/traditions have been merged in the narrative, but a more likely explanation is that earlier declarations are formalized (made official) and earlier events reactualized in chapter 35. When Jacob returns to Bethel his spiritual journey is complete. God reiterates the promise, linking it to Jacob's new name as if to remind him that dependence on the God who promises is the key to the divine blessing being realized. On his initial visit to Bethel, Jacob was not ready to accept the God who promises on God's terms. But now, after the wrestling match at Penuel, he is prepared to do so. How appropriate that the renaming at Penuel is reactualized as the promise is reiterated and that Jacob reactualizes his worship, this time without making a bargain with God.

Intertextuality and Macrostructure

The narratives of the Hebrew Bible, when viewed simply as history, are sometimes read as a simple "A-to-Z" chronological account, with little sensitivity to patterns at the macrostructural level. Recognizing that we are dealing with story as well as history enables us to detect the larger patterns around which the narrative's theological themes revolve.

Literary analysis reveals the presence of foreshadowing, a device that is well-known in modern literature and film. In Exodus 2:17–19 Moses rescues Reuel's daughters from some shepherds. This brief and apparently minor episode casts Moses in the role of deliverer and foreshadows how the Lord would use him to deliver oppressed Israel. In Judges 14, Samson, empowered by God's Spirit, kills a roaring lion (vv. 5–6) and later eats some honey from the lion's carcass (vv. 8–9). Both of these events reveal important features of Samson's character and have a foreshadowing function in the story. The killing of the lion shows what Samson is capable of accomplishing in God's strength. Later in the story (15:9–19) the Philistines attack Samson like a lion.[43] Their shouts correspond to the lion's roar. God's Spirit descends (צָלַח) upon Samson (v. 14) and he supernaturally defeats the Philistines, just as he supernaturally killed the lion. Samson's eating the honey shows he has difficulty controlling his physical desires and suggests that satisfying his appetites is more important to him than maintaining his status as a Nazirite. It also foreshadows his demise, which stems from his unbridled urge for sex. The sweet honey foreshadows the charms of Delilah, who uses her psychological hold over Samson to destroy him. Samson can resist and defeat lions, but not honey.[44]

Literary analysis also reveals the presence of parallelism at the macro-structural level. In Judges–1 Samuel the anonymous mothers of Samson (Judg. 13) and Micah (Judg. 17) serve as foils for Hannah (1 Sam. 1). In contrast to Samson's mother, whose miraculously conceived Nazirite son fails to understand his true role as the Lord's deliverer and never rises to the level of an effective leader, Hannah supernaturally gives birth to a Nazirite son through whom the Lord restores effective leadership to Israel. In contrast to Micah's mother, whose misguided actions and obsession with idols contributes to the Danites' unauthorized cult, Hannah's commitment to the Lord is the catalyst for the revival of genuine Yahweh worship through the spiritual leadership of her son Samuel.

The three accounts even begin the same way:

> Judges 13:2: "Now there was a certain man from Zorah . . . whose name was Manoah" [וַיְהִי אִישׁ אֶחָד מִצָּרְעָה . . . וּשְׁמוֹ מָנוֹחַ].

> Judges 17:1: "Now there was a man from the hill country of Ephraim whose name was Micaiah" [וַיְהִי אִישׁ מֵהַר־אֶפְרַיִם וּשְׁמוֹ מִיכָיְהוּ].

> 1 Samuel 1:1: "Now there was a certain man from Ramathaim . . . whose name was Elkanah" [וַיְהִי אִישׁ אֶחָד מִן־הָרָמָתַיִם . . . וּשְׁמוֹ אֶלְקָנָה].

The formula "now there was a certain man from *[geographical name]* . . . whose name was *[personal name]*" seems to be a stylized way of introducing a new story. However, in Judges–1 Samuel this formula appears only in these three passages and in 1 Samuel 9:1, where Saul's family background

---

43. Note Hebrew לִקְרָאתוֹ in both Judges 14:5 and 15:14.
44. See Chisholm, *From Exegesis to Exposition,* 165.

is introduced. This suggests that the introductory formula is a linking device at the macrostructural or larger discourse level.[45]

Literary parallelism sometimes involves narrative typology, where earlier characters supply the pattern for a later character in the story. This in turn enables the reader to discern the narrator's evaluation of the later character's career. For example, 1 Samuel 17 depicts a youthful David as a new giant killer in the mold of Joshua, Caleb, and Othniel. However, later, when he succumbs to lust,[46] he turns into a new Samson. Murder, rape, and civil war dominate the literary landscape of 2 Samuel from this point on. The account of the turmoil that takes over his household and kingdom resembles the Judges period as described in the epilogue to the book of Judges (Judg. 17–21), which ironically follows (literarily, though not chronologically) the story of Samson's demise.[47]

Summary

Old Testament narrative is both history and story. These historical accounts, which evangelicals presuppose are true, have a literary dimension. Recognizing their literary quality is essential to understanding how the narrative genre works. Interpreters of narrative literature must take into account literary conventions, contextualized perspective, point of view, authorial selectivity, discourse features (such as recapitulation, temporal overlay, paneled structuring, echoing), and intertextuality. Failure to do so has led to erroneous conclusions about the narratives. Some ignore literary factors and insist on reading the narratives in a straightforward manner. They often end up misunderstanding what actually happened. Others, by ignoring the literary dimension, have often been forced to postulate theories about the text's origin and composition that call its literary integrity into question and strip it of any real authority.

---

45. See Robert B. Chisholm Jr., "The Role of Women in the Rhetorical Strategy of the Book of Judges," in *Integrity of Heart, Skillfulness of Hands: Biblical and Leadership Studies in Honor of Donald K. Campbell,* ed. Charles H. Dyer and Roy B. Zuck (Grand Rapids: Baker, 1994), 46–49.
46. In the Hebrew Bible the statement "he saw a woman," appears in both 2 Samuel 11:2 and Judges 16:1, but nowhere in between.
47. Second Samuel 13 in particular contains echoes of Judges 17–21. See Robert Polzin, *David and the Deuteronomist* (Bloomington, Ind.: Indiana University, 1993), 136–38.

3

ARCHAEOLOGY AND BIBLICAL HISTORY

Its Uses and Abuses

Eugene H. Merrill

IN A RECENT INTERVIEW WITH GUSTAV NIEBUHR in the *New York Times,* William G. Dever, the American doyen of Palestinian archaeology, when asked the question, "What was biblical archaeology, and why did it die?" responded as follows:

> The movement collapsed somewhere in the 70s for a variety of reasons. It never proved the history of the patriarchs, for example. The movement failed to reach its agenda. Basically, the field became more professionalized and more secularized. No serious archaeologist today would attempt to prove the Bible in the old-fashioned sense.[1]

Scores of biblical archaeologists who still call themselves such would, of course, challenge his assertion that their discipline is dead and that they are not serious when at least some of them attempt to "prove" the Bible, though that might not be a stated objective.[2] However, Dever's generalization does

---

1. Gustav Niebuhr, "Balancing Biblical Faith and Archaeological Facts," *New York Times,* Saturday, 4 August 2001, A17. William G. Dever's attitude on the matter may be found greatly elaborated in his *What Did the Biblical Writers Know and When Did They Know It?* (Grand Rapids: Eerdmans, 2001), 59–65.
2. Dever, in fact, while still resisting the term *"biblical" archaeology,* has increasingly come to the defense of the view that archaeology can and does point to the credibility of the Old Testament

point to an indisputable crisis in the interface between archaeology and the Bible, namely, whether or not there is a legitimate role for archaeology in biblical research—particularly in terms of the Bible's historicity—and if so, what its form, extent, and limitations ought to be. The purpose of this paper is to address the relationship between archaeology and Old Testament history and to provide suggestions as to how to achieve a healthy symbiosis between the two.

The Recovery of the Old Testament Past

A hallmark of the Judeo-Christian tradition is its claim to be rooted in real historical settings and events and to derive much of its theological meaning from the interconnection of those events. Many who adhere to the tradition in this time-honored sense go so far as to say that the reality of those events and their proper interpretation are indispensable to authentic faith.[3] The study presented here will not attempt to address the theological implications of the Bible's historicity, though it is obvious that individual convictions about such matters will dictate to a great extent conclusions as to the nature of the Bible as well as the methodology to be employed in dealing with its relationship to history, science, and the like.[4]

Issues Relating to the Old Testament as History

The Nature of the Old Testament

Views of the essential character of the Old Testament range from its being a divinely inspired text dropped *in toto* from heaven without a scintilla of alteration or corruption at human hands to its being nothing but a

---

as a witness to Israel's early history. See William G. Dever "Archaeology, Ideology, and the Quest for an 'Ancient' or 'Biblical' Israel," *NEA* 61, no. 1 (1998): 39–52; idem, "Save Us from Postmodern Malarkey," *BAR* 26, no. 2 (March–April 2000): 28–35, 68–69; and especially idem, "Excavating the Hebrew Bible, or Burying It Again?" *BASOR* 322 (2001): 67–77 (a review of Israel Finkelstein and Neil Asher Silberman, *The Bible Unearthed: Archaeology's New Vision of Ancient Israel and the Origin of Its Sacred Texts* [New York: Free Press, 2001]); along with Dever, *What Did the Biblical Writers Know and When Did They Know It?*

3. V. Philips Long, *The Art of Biblical History* (Grand Rapids: Zondervan, 1994), 108.
4. See Eugene H. Merrill, "Old Testament History: A Theological Perspective," in *A Guide to Old Testament Theology and Exegesis,* ed. Willem H. VanGemeren (Grand Rapids: Zondervan, 1997), 65–82. Cf. C. Hassell Bullock, "History and Theology," chapter 4 in this volume.

hopelessly chaotic, contradictory, and virtually indecipherable concoction of the religious ideas of self-serving zealots of late pre-Christian times.[5] Evangelical faith, while adopting neither of these extremes, does recognize and confess that the Old (along with the New) Testament is divine revelation, a body of truth mediated to humankind through a process of inspiration which guarantees its inerrancy and, hence, its historical integrity and reliability. A corollary to this is the conviction that the Old Testament reflects factual reality whenever it presents itself as history. That is, the Old Testament, among other things, is a credible account of ancient Israel's past.[6]

The Old Testament as History

The reliability of the Old Testament as a record of the past does not, however, suggest that it is by authorial intention a history in the conventional sense of the term. It speaks accurately when it addresses historical events but the selection, interpretation, and relevance of these events must be seen as subsidiary to a more comprehensive purpose, namely, the disclosure of salvation history, the divine program for humanity from creation, through history, to the eschatological fulfillment of all things.[7] This nuanced way of looking at the matter helps to explain why many readers of the Old Testament—scholars included—perceive a disconnect between history writing of modern times and that of the Bible. However, the charge that the Old Testament lacks cohesion, balance, and objectivity in its presentation of Israel's history is undercut by the fact that this was never its purpose.

First, the authors and editors of Old Testament texts were highly selective in what they wrote and what they included (or excluded) in their final compositions. There is never a hint of any attempt to develop a compre-

---

5. A moderate view from a critical perspective is represented by Walter Brueggemann, who suggests that Old Testament "testimony" becomes revelation. "That is, the testimony that Israel bears to the character of God is taken by the ecclesial community of the text as a reliable disclosure about the true character of God. . . . When utterance in the Bible is taken as truthful, human testimony is taken as revelation that discloses the true reality of God" (*Theology of the Old Testament* [Minneapolis: Fortress, 1997], 121).
6. David M. Howard Jr., *An Introduction to the Old Testament Historical Books* (Chicago: Moody, 1993), 35–38; cf. idem, "History as History," chapter 1 in this volume.
7. Willem VanGemeren prefers the felicitous term *redemptive history* rather than the rather loaded German *Heilsgeschichte*. See his *The Progress of Redemption* (Grand Rapids: Zondervan, 1988), 31–34.

hensive narrative of Israel's past. Only those ideas and events crucial to the redemptive message were retained, even though glaring historical lacunae might result. It is unfair at the very least to judge the Old Testament's historicity by historiographical criteria it never sought to embrace.

Second, the numerous incompatibilities between the Old Testament and extrabiblical accounts noted by many scholars can be explained largely by lack of extensive documentation from both sources, although other factors also come into play. For example, the Bible's focus on Israel as a theological *topos* precludes its interest in the larger world unless that world impinges on Israel's sacred history. Thus the political, military, and cultural exploits of the nations—as significant as they might be to world history—receive notice in the sacred text only when it is pertinent to do so. Conversely, Israel, even at its apogee of size and influence under David and Solomon, was a minor player in the world of the tenth century. There would be little reason for the scribes of Mesopotamia, Egypt, and Anatolia to take note of such a comparatively insignificant state. Besides, as we have already suggested, there is scant literary documentation from these cultures of a historical nature, especially from the earlier periods. As more becomes available, the extrabiblical evidence for an Israelite state as described in the Bible is increasingly enhanced. Even where both biblical and secular texts recount events in common, there is oftentimes considerable difference in the narrating and interpretation of those events, for it is the nature of historiography that national pride, political ideology, and religious overtones color the way things are perceived and recorded.[8] This is true even of the Bible, and those who view the Bible as revelation recognize that the "spin" it puts on history serves theological interests but leaves unscathed an account that is historically as well as theologically accurate.

The Old Testament and Critical Method

The European Enlightenment, an intellectual and cultural heir to the Renaissance, fostered challenges first to ecclesiastical authority and then to the Scriptures upon which the magisterium of the Church was largely based.[9]

---

8. Iain W. Provan, "Ideologies, Literary and Critical: Reflections on Recent Writing on the History of Israel," *JBL* 114 (1995): 595–96.
9. For brief but helpful treatments of the impact of Enlightenment thought on biblical authority see R. K. Harrison, *Introduction to the Old Testament* (Grand Rapids: Eerdmans, 1969), 11–27; and Long, *Art of Biblical History*, 99–116.

Epistemology moved beyond revelation and history became subject to free and open reinvestigation. As to the former, the question was, How and what can we know? History's query became, What happened and what does it mean? When applied to the Bible, these questions set in motion a process of skeptical analysis that predictably culminated in the so-called "historical-critical method," an approach that can be traced seminally to the seventeenth century and that found its classic expression in Wellhausen's *Prolegomena* of the late nineteenth century. It is unnecessary to describe that method here,[10] but it may be helpful to recognize some of the positive aspects of the critical methodology as they relate to the Old Testament as history when that methodology is embraced in the ameliorating spirit of commitment to the Bible as the written Word of God. An evangelical critical approach to recovering the full history of Israel will be attentive to the location of pertinent sources necessary to its reconstruction, a rigorous evaluation of those sources, and the development of a sound methodology in making the best use of them.

The Old Testament itself is obviously the primary repository of historical data relative to Israel's history. Its character as sacred history—a notion that must never be ignored—does not in any way diminish its value as a source of "ordinary" historical information. In addition, one must make use of the extensive postbiblical Jewish literature such as the apocryphal, pseudepigraphical, and Mishnaic writings and traditions as well as distinctly historiographical works such as those of Philo and Josephus. The vast literatures of the ancient Near Eastern world also must be tapped for whatever light they can shed on Israel's life and times. Though of very limited value for the pre-monarchic period, they become critical for a full rendition of Israel's history later, especially in the late divided monarchy and exilic and postexilic eras. Numbered now by the scores, these texts either corroborate biblical accounts, provide alternative versions of them, or fill in the narrative where the Old Testament is lacking. In addition to such sources outside Israel there are several hundred written artifacts originating in Israel. Most, admittedly, are extremely brief, but others are able to add substantially to the information preserved in the Old Testament.

Not to be ignored is the historical insight to be gained from the recovery

---

10. For a history of such approaches see Edgar Krentz, *The Historical-Critical Method* (Philadelphia: Fortress, 1975), 6–32.

of nonliterary sources by means of archaeology. Traditionally these have consisted of specific artifacts and objects of an artistic or utilitarian nature such as tools, weapons, jewelry, architectural features, and above all, pottery. In recent times a host of physical and social sciences have been employed to shed light on such matters as ancient Palestinian climate, agriculture, ethnicity, economy, trade, migration, and the like.[11] When used judiciously, these can provide clues to the larger environment of which Old Testament Israel was a part, and therefore can shed light on Israel's historical experience.

An element in critical thinking about history is the evaluation of the sources upon which it depends. There is room for a healthy skepticism in assessing the meaning and credibility of texts (and even nonliterary artifacts), including the texts of the Bible. One may indeed come to the task with certain positive assumptions about the Bible—its divine nature and infallible pronouncements—but the Bible itself invites questions as to its origins, its setting, its hearers, its apparent lack of completeness and cohesion. A sanctified criticism devoted to hard questions by and about the Bible is perfectly in order. This is all the more true of nonbiblical sources, of course, for no truth claims can be made for them. They must submit to dispassionate, objective, and penetrating analysis to see to what extent they can contribute to a knowledge of the things and times to which they belong.

The following brief list offers suggestions as to how critical evaluation of historical data can be undertaken.[12]

1. Accept sources at face value unless and until they must, on the basis of objective contrary evidence, be viewed otherwise.
2. Do not rule anything in or out just because of its uniqueness.
3. Avoid begging the question.
4. Be aware of the fragmentary and possibly tendentious nature of sources.
5. Beware of historical positivism or patternism.

---

11. R. E. Clements, ed., *The World of Ancient Israel* (Cambridge: Cambridge University Press, 1989). See especially the articles in that volume by J. W. Rogerson ("Anthropology and the Old Testament," 7–37), A. D. H. Mayes ("Sociology and the Old Testament," 39–63), and F. S. Frick ("Ecology, agriculture and patterns of settlement," 67–93).
12. To these add what Kaiser describes as "some modern fallacies" derivative of Enlightenment thought, especially as regards the history of Israel. Walter C. Kaiser Jr., *A History of Israel* (Nashville: Broadman & Holman, 1998), 3–8.

6. Seek to establish literary and cultural parallels, mutual dependencies or connections, and chronological parameters.

Unfortunately, these and other principles of sound critical method are frequently violated by practitioners of the art and science of history writing. On the one hand are those who suppose that any kind of critical method applied to the Bible is irreverent if not heretical. On the other hand are others who not only fail to see any unique religious character and authority in Scripture, but, in fact, treat with dismissive contempt any claims to its having historical integrity. They may be quite willing to acknowledge and embrace Hammurabi as an authentic figure of history, but Moses is denied any connection to the writings associated with him and, with increasing frequency, any historical reality at all. This betrayal of objective historical method is not legitimate criticism, but a form of obscurantism.

Old Testament Historiography

One of the major issues in modern Old Testament scholarship is the relationship between history and revelation. More particularly the question, raised especially by Gerhard von Rad, is whether the history related by the Old Testament is a record of actual events or is merely an interpretation of events underlying Israel's ancient confessions. If it is the latter then one must accept von Rad's own well-known definition of historical investigation as one that "searches for a critically assured minimum" as opposed to the "kerygmatic picture" which "tends towards a theological maximum."[13] If it is a factual account, it is incumbent upon the serious student of the Bible to employ every appropriate exegetical, theological, literary, and critical tool available to ascertain and interpret those facts so that both the historical and the kerygmatic meanings might be disclosed. Ideally these two sets of data coincide, for to posit two readings of history, frequently in contradiction, is to move in a direction of intellectual schizophrenia.

We turn now to the question of the genre(s) of Old Testament history writing. If the Old Testament is to be taken seriously as history, what are the literary clues that indicate what is historical narrative? If a text has con-

---

13. Gerhard von Rad, *Old Testament Theology*, trans. D. M. G. Stalker (New York: Harper & Row, 1962), 1:108.

cerns beyond the historical record, how can this also be demonstrated? We must approach genre issues with a few assumptions in mind:

First, until the advent of postmodern approaches to literary composition, known by such terms as *poststructuralism* and *reader-response hermeneutics*, virtually all readers of the Bible understood the historical books to be presenting a work that was fundamentally historical in orientation.[14] Second, major blocks of legal, poetic, wisdom, and prophetic material intrude into the text and break the flow of the story line. Nonetheless, there remains a story, a narrative professing to recount the history of Israel. Third, ancient narrators employed historiographical genres, such as chronicles, lists, annals, biographies, and historical narratives. The styles of these writings in that period were not always in line with the expectations and practices of modern historians. Fourth, one may feel free to challenge the historical "facts" of the record, of course, but there can be no cogent argument against the self-evident fact that the Old Testament is cast in the form of history writing.

With these principles given, it may be useful to suggest a method of analyzing and interpreting historical texts, specifically the Old Testament.[15] The following is offered as a guideline:

1. Assume the sequence of narratives and their embedded or parenthetical texts to be chronological.
2. Study the narratives critically for evidence of apparent internal disharmony, inconsistency, or other kinds of difficulty.
3. Test the narratives against whatever other data may be found in extrabiblical sources.
4. Be prepared to reconstruct the account chronologically (if that seems important) and to go against the strategy of the narrative itself. On the other hand, it is important to understand that the shape of a text fulfills a purpose of the author(s) that transcends mere chronological

---

14. For a survey of postmodernism and biblical scholarship see Edgar V. McKnight, "Reader-Response Criticism," in *To Each Its Own Meaning: An Introduction to Biblical Criticisms and Their Application*, ed. Steven L. McKenzie and Stephen R. Haynes (Louisville: Westminster/John Knox, 1993), 230–52; William A. Beardslee, "Poststructuralist Criticism," in *To Each Its Own Meaning: An Introduction to Biblical Criticisms and Their Application*, ed. Steven L. McKenzie and Stephen R. Haynes (Louisville: Westminster/John Knox, 1993), 253–67; and A. K. M. Adam, *What Is Postmodern Biblical Criticism?* New Testament Guides (Minneapolis: Fortress, 1995).
15. Eugene H. Merrill, "History," in *Cracking Old Testament Codes,* ed. D. Brent Sandy and Ronald L. Giese Jr. (Nashville: Broadman & Holman, 1995), 89–112.

order. Each text must be taken at its own face value in the hermeneutical and theological process.

Sources

In addition to the Old Testament—the primary source—the history of Israel depends for the fullness of its presentation on extrabiblical data as well. These data take the form of cultural artifacts, especially for preliterate periods, and literary artifacts (texts), each of which must be subject to careful interpretive controls if their nature and meaning are properly to be understood. That is, they must be "read" as witnesses to the age from which they come. This is obviously much more difficult for noninscriptional materials. To "read" these it is important to give strict attention to such matters as stratigraphy, the cultural level yielding the artifact, and typology, the place occupied by the artifact in the course of its cultural and technological evolution.[16] Newer methods strive to gain a picture of the environment—such elements as climate, soils, and water—associated with the materials in question.

The social sciences seek to develop hypotheses about the density and distribution of population. Social scientists look at labor, economics, and trade by carefully comparing an ancient culture with later and even modern patterns about which more is known. They carefully study material objects to learn about their content and the skills required in their manufacture. This is done to determine, if possible, their places of origin, which reveal more about trade practices, travel, technology, and diversity of specialization.[17]

Even if all this is done and done well, no amount of scrutiny of silent witnesses can definitively reveal the identity of the culture responsible for them. Identification requires texts, for inscriptions provide verbal information about both the writers and those who were written about. Texts also are artifacts, whose provenience must be ascertained by proper archaeo-

---

16. Gösta W. Ahlström, "The Role of Archaeological and Literary Remains in Reconstructing Israel's History," in *The Fabric of History: Text, Artifact and Israel's Past*, ed. Diana Vikander Edelman, JSOTSup 127 (Sheffield: Sheffield Academic Press, 1991), 116–41.
17. Maria de Jong Ellis, "'Correlation of Archaeological and Written Evidence for the Study of Mesopotamian Institutions and Chronology," *AJA* 87 (1983): 497–507; Baruch Halpern, "Research Design in Archaeology: The Interdisciplinary Perspective," *NEA* 61, no. 1 (1998): 53–65; and Gloria London, "Ethnoarchaeology and Interpretation," *NEA* 63, no. 1 (2000): 2–8.

logical method. Moreover, such disciplines as paleography and decipherment must be enlisted, followed by translation and interpretation. Studies of genre, comparative languages, and literatures are important to the proper use of written artifacts, recognizing bias and propagandistic agendas. Only when inscriptions are correctly assessed can they make meaningful contributions to the study of history.

The Archaeology and Old Testament Controversy

The idea prevails that "biblical" archaeology is dead and has been moldering in its grave for thirty years. Those who believe this death has occurred, offer the pathology that those who work in Syro-Palestinian archaeology have tried to achieve academic respectability by disconnecting from the embarrassment associated with faith-based archaeological enterprises. Almost from its beginning 150 years ago, archaeology as conducted in Palestine was under the auspices of persons who were at least sympathetic to the Bible and the Christian faith. Often their unabashed intent was to prove the Bible to be historically believable. They worked from the assumption that archaeological research could document Scripture's statements regarding ancient persons and events.

Today "biblical archaeology" has become a sub-discipline of archaeology in general that is associated with the lands of the Bible, especially the Levant. Biblical archaeology generally remains self-conscious in its attempts to do its work with reference to the Bible. Now the discipline is frequently caricatured as the work of untrained fundamentalist zealots who lack scholarly credentials and sophistication of method. However, many pioneers and giants in Palestinian archaeology have often cheerfully—even proudly—borne the biblical archaeologist label, although their religious orientations were anything but fundamentalist and their technical qualifications were of the highest order.[18] Some of these biblical archaeologists were the teachers and models for most practitioners of the "new archaeology" who so vociferously denounce the label "biblical" and even repudiate the labors and conclusions of their mentors. Yet, contrary to the overblown claims of those who embrace the new archaeology, biblical archaeology survives beyond evangelical Christian circles. Israeli scholars, by and large, continue to employ it to define the thrust of their labors to elucidate the biblical

---

18. Dever, *What Did the Biblical Writers Know and When Did They Know It?* 56–59.

texts and reconstruct the history of their forebears.[19] This is true also of scholars who embrace no particular faith tradition, or who at least do not make faith a publicly proclaimed motivation for their scholarly efforts. One might cynically suspect that some professionals pay lip service to the adjective *biblical* because much of the funding for their enterprises comes from individuals and institutions who are motivated by the value of Palestinian archaeology to the Bible. Nonetheless, it is clear that rumors of the demise of biblical archaeology are, to paraphrase Mark Twain, greatly exaggerated.

The "New" Archaeology and Historical "Minimalism"

New Archaeology

The rather imprecise term *new archaeology* is not used here to describe newer methods of doing archaeological research, methods that, on the whole, are to be greatly applauded. Rather, *new archaeology* as a movement arose in reaction to so-called "biblical" archaeology over more than a century. Its proponents, as we have noted, wish to disassociate themselves from the onus implicit in the term *biblical* and to align themselves with the larger archaeological establishment. In doing so, however, some have discarded not only the pejorative label but also the very notion that archaeology and the Old Testament share much of anything in common.[20] The method, as commonly practiced, is to assemble the archaeological record, to interpret it on its own terms, and then to see if and how the biblical tradition comports with the evidence or fails to do so. Almost always the assumption is that archaeology holds pride of place and that the biblical record must be

---

19. For an overview of the Israeli situation *vis-à-vis* the "crisis" in Palestinian archaeology, see Ephraim Stern, "The Bible and Israeli Archaeology," in *Archaeology and Biblical Interpretation*, ed. Leo G. Perdue, Lawrence E. Toombs, and Gary L. Johnson (Atlanta: John Knox, 1987), 31–40; and Amihai Mazar, *Archaeology of the Land of the Bible: 10,000–586 B.C.E.* (New York: Doubleday, 1990), 31–33.
20. William Dever, as much as anyone else, had at one time shunned the label "biblical archaeologist." See conveniently his "Syro-Palestinian and Biblical Archaeology," in *The Hebrew Bible and Its Modern Interpreters*, ed. Douglas A. Knight and Gene M. Tucker (Philadelphia: Fortress, 1985), esp. 31–32, 53–61, 64–67. Of late, however, he has come to identify himself with a school of thought that accords to the Bible a great deal of historical credibility, a position that appears to have come about largely in reaction to minimalists' revisionists. See Dever's famous interview with Hershel Shanks titled "Is This Man a Biblical Archaeologist?" *BAR* 22, no. 4 (July–August 1996): 30–39, 62–63. See also Dever, *What Did the Biblical Writers Know and When Did They Know It?*

judged against it and either vindicated or vitiated. The Old Testament is thus secondary, without independent authority as source material in providing a picture of Israel's past. Such a method, ironically, is precisely as flawed as the use of archaeology to "prove" or at least support the historical version of the Old Testament. It seems as unsound to reject the witness of the Old Testament when it fails to square with archaeological interpretation as it is to manipulate the archaeological data to favor a high view of the Bible's historicity. Good scholarship should view the biblical tradition and the evidence from archaeology as twin voices, which are to be equally respected and intently heard to see if and how they are mutually informing.

Historical Minimalism

Concomitant with the development of the new archaeology is a school of thought characterized by a radical skepticism that denies any shred of historical credibility to the Old Testament. Championed primarily by British and Danish scholars, few of whom have solid archaeological experience and credentials, this movement of historical minimalists has triggered vigorous debate among Old Testament scholars. Minimalism especially has challenged those advocates of the new archaeology who earlier tried to distance themselves from biblical archaeology.[21] Many of the latter now find themselves in the uncomfortable and possibly inconsistent position. They have sought to relegate the Old Testament to a position almost extraneous to the archaeological ideology they have chosen to pursue, yet they must defend the Old Testament against the nihilism of iconoclastic extremists who view it as postexilic propaganda with no basis in genuine historical fact.[22] In rising to a limited defense of the

---

21. See notably Robert B. Coote and Keith W. Whitelam, eds., *The Emergence of Early Israel in Historical Perspective* (Sheffield: Sheffield Academic, 1987); Philip P. Davies, *In Search of "Ancient Israel,"* JSOTSup 148 (Sheffield: JSOT, 1992); Israel Finkelstein, *The Archaeology of the Israelite Settlement* (Jerusalem: Israel Exploration Society, 1988); Niels Peter Lemche, *Ancient Israel: A New History of Israelite Society* (Sheffield: JSOT, 1988); idem, *Prelude to Israel's Past* (Peabody, Mass.: Hendrickson, 1998); and Keith W. Whitelam, *The Invention of Ancient Israel* (London: Routledge, 1996). Important analyses and critiques of these and other so-called "minimalists" may be found in William G. Dever, "'Will the Real Israel Please Stand Up?' Archaeology and Israelite Historiography: Part I," *BASOR* 297 (1995): 61–80; David M. Howard Jr., *Joshua,* NAC 5 (Nashville: Broadman & Holman, 1998), 40–46; Magnus Ottosson, "Ideology, History and Archaeology in the Old Testament," *SJOT* 8 (1994): 206–22; K. Lawson Younger Jr., "Early Israel in Recent Biblical Scholarship," in *The Face of Old Testament Studies,* ed. David W. Baker and Bill T. Arnold (Grand Rapids: Baker, 1999), 185–91.
22. Dever, *What Did the Biblical Writers Know and When Did They Know It?* 23–52.

Old Testament, the new archaeologists have been subjected to the same *ad hominem* misrepresentations formerly reserved for biblical archaeologists. They are dubbed fundamentalists, traditionalists, and Zionists. The pages of such periodicals as *Biblical Archaeology Review* are replete with attack and counter-attack in this acrimonious debate.[23] One result has been an apparent movement by some critics of biblical archaeology toward a more sympathetic rapprochement with it.

The Old Testament and Archaeology

In the context of such controversies, the question remains, What is the role of archaeology in elucidating the Old Testament narrative and, more specifically, in defending its historicity? Perhaps the answer can be shown in a brief survey of the uses and abuses of archaeological research. First, however, attention to archaeology in providing source material may be helpful.

Archaeology as a Provider of Source Material

Nonliterary Artifacts

Most of the objects recovered in archaeological excavations are mute, that is they are nonliterary, without voice and without self-interpretation.[24] This does not mean, however, that they cannot be "read," like texts, with proper interpretational method. All ancient material remains say something to those who ask the right questions, especially when the questions are unfreighted with any dogmatic *a priori*. For example, a mere potsherd has shape, size, color, consistency, and density. A skilled ceramicist can reconstruct the vessel of which the shard is a fragment. Approximate age can be found by relating it to well-established pottery typologies. Its place and conditions of manufacture are found by comparing it to other, soundly determined examples. Sometimes the fragment can indicate what histori-

---

23. For just the latest issues see *BAR* 22, no. 4 (July–August 1996); 22, no. 5 (September–October 1996); 23, no. 2 (March–April 1997); 23, no. 4 (July–August 1997); 26, no. 2 (March–April 2000).
24. For a somewhat dated but still useful work on the interpretation of nonliterary artifacts see Stuart Piggott, *Approach to Archaeology* (New York: McGraw Hill, 1959). A brief but more recent treatment is Mazar, *Archaeology of the Land of the Bible*, 9–33.

cal circumstances are likely to have left it *in situ* and in its present shape (for example, heavy burning).

If, to continue the example, the shard was of Mycenaean origin, it was obviously an import from a period when trade of such commodities was prevalent. If it seems to have been exotic and rare, more decorative than utilitarian, its owner must have been a person of means, or perhaps a thief who stole it from such a person. If it lay in a stratum marked by destruction, its own surface blackened by catastrophic fires, a logical conclusion is that the site in which it is embedded was overrun in violent conquest.

This said, it is important to recognize the limitations in reading such artifacts. Mycenaean ware could have become a collector's item even in the ancient world, an antique hundreds of years older than the site of its location would indicate. It could have been carelessly tossed by a child into a cook fire and then broken to pieces by its frustrated owner. Or the evidence of massive conflagration by fire might be accounted for by a natural disaster, such as an earthquake or lightning strike. In other words, just as texts need contexts for proper interpretation, so nonliterary artifacts require unambiguous and indisputable environmental contexts before they can yield a clear and certain message.

Literary Artifacts

Even the best-preserved inscriptions need contexts against which they can be understood or, in some cases, even read. The shorter the text the more obviously this is true. Besides locating the stratigraphical horizon from which the artifact is derived, other disciplines must be brought to bear, including paleography; history, and concerns of grammar, syntax, and lexicography. Does the message of the text communicate any meaningful historical information? If so, can it be correlated to biblical events and persons or to other inscriptions whose historical locus is better understood? Reading texts, like "reading" nonliterary artifacts, requires attention, then, to contexts of many kinds.

Proper Use of Archaeology in Regard to Old Testament History

The purpose here is not to show how Old Testament historical accuracy is "proved" by archaeological discovery, but rather to show how the latter correlates to the Old Testament record, thus providing clarification, amplification, and sometimes correction of misinterpretation of its message. Since inscriptions obviously are less susceptible to ambiguity and subjectivity, most of the following examples are literary in nature.

The Merenptah Stele

Sometimes called the "Israel Stele," the Merenptah Stele inscription of Pharaoh Merenptah, son of Ramesses II, records his campaign to put down revolts in the Egypt-held territories of Syria and Palestine in his third year (ca. 1210 B.C.).[25] After speaking of his defeat of the Libyans, Merenptah boasts, "Hatti is pacified; Canaan is plundered with every evil; Ashkelon is taken; Gezer is captured; Yanoam is made nonexistent; Israel lies desolate; its seed is no more."[26] This earliest extrabiblical reference to Israel occurs with the grammatical determinative for "people," suggesting that Israel was not a small city-state but a large population group still lacking clearly-defined national borders. Historical minimalists argue that the reference to Israel has nothing to do with the fictitious Israel they allege was created by postexilic Jews, so they dismiss it out of hand.[27] Most scholars interpret the text to mean that Merenptah was dealing with Israel in its infancy, in line with the well-known explosive rise of early Iron Age highland villages thought to be Israelite.[28] It is more likely, however, that the campaign occurred in the chaotic times of the judges, particularly in the period of Deborah and Gideon (ca. 1240–1200 B.C.).[29] In any case, that there was a recognized entity known as "Israel" as early as the Late Bronze Age has been indisputably documented.

---

25. Miriam Lichtheim, trans., "The Merneptah Stela," *AEL* (Berkeley: University of California Press, 1971–1980), 2:73–78; and Itamar Singer, "Merneptah's Campaign to Canaan and the Egyptian Occupation of the Southern Coastal Plain of Palestine in the Ramesside Period," *BASOR* 269 (1988): 1–10.
26. R. J. Williams, "The 'Israel Stele' of Merenptah," in *Documents from Old Testament Times*, ed. D. Winton Thomas (London: Nelson, 1958), 139; James K. Hoffmeier, trans., "The (Israel) Stele of Merneptah (2.6)," in *COS*, ed. W. W. Hallo and K. L. Younger Jr. (Leiden: Brill, 1997–2002).
27. T. L. Thompson, *The Early History of the Israelite People: From the Written and Archaeological Sources* (Leiden: Brill, 1992), 310. Gösta Ahlström proposed that the name "Israel" referred not to a nation or people but to a geographic area that only later provided that name to indigenous Canaanite people. Cited by James K. Hoffmeier, *Israel in Egypt* (New York: Oxford University Press, 1997), 27.
28. Robert B. Coote, *Early Israel: A New Horizon* (Minneapolis: Fortress, 1990), 84–87.
29. Eugene H. Merrill, "The Late Bronze Early Iron Age Transition and the Emergence of Israel," *BSac* 152 (1995): 145–62.

Hazor, Megiddo, Gezer, and Solomon

First Kings 9:15 records the fact that Solomon had taken pains to establish certain cities as focal points for storage and defense, including Hazor, Megiddo, and Gezer. All three have been exhaustively excavated and have yielded evidence that they functioned in precisely the manner indicated by the biblical text. Though there is disagreement among scholars as to whether such features as the city gates were Solomonic or later, there is virtual consensus that the cities reached positions of importance in the latter tenth century, the period of Solomon, and that they served the purposes alleged in the Old Testament account.[30] Here nonliterary artifacts lack the inscriptional information one might wish for, but the concurrence of the artifactual data with the biblical account is too remarkable to deny a Solomonic connection.

The Assyrian Eponym Lists

One of the most perplexing historical problems in Old Testament scholarship has been the proper correlation and interpretation of the chronological data of the Divided Monarchy era. Efforts to solve it have ranged anywhere from ingenious but unconvincing harmonistic hypotheses to the assumption that the pertinent texts were hopelessly corrupt and incapable of resolution.

The recovery of cuneiform tablets known as the Eponym Chronicle now makes possible a list of years from 910–649 B.C.[31] The Neo-Assyrian scribes responsible for its compilation included not only the names of the years but significant events occurring in various years. On the basis of astronomical calculation the year 763 was determined, thus allowing all prior and subsequent years to be dated. Of importance to Old Testament history are those years associated with some person or event in Israel.[32] When compared to Assyrian royal inscriptions, the Eponym Chronicle makes possible the dating of the death of King Ahab (853 B.C.), the accession to the throne of Israel by Jehu (841), and, consequently, virtually every date of every king

---

30. Mazar, *Archaeology of the Land of the Bible*, 380–87.
31. Alan Millard, trans., "Assyrian Eponym Canon (1.136)," in *COS*, 1:465–66.
32. Edwin R. Thiele, *The Mysterious Numbers of the Hebrew Kings*, 3d ed. (Grand Rapids: Zondervan, 1983), 67–78; and Leslie McFall, "A Translation Guide to the Chronological Data in Kings and Chronicles," *BSac* 148 (1991): 3–45.

of Israel and Judah from David to Jehoiachin and Zedekiah. Though certain issues of chronology remain unresolved to everyone's satisfaction, the scheme of the biblical chronographers as a whole is clear and convincing.

The Tell Dan Inscription

One of the most remarkable finds of modern times has been an Aramaic inscription at Tell Dan in northern Israel.[33] This is the Dan known in the Old Testament as one of two places of semi-pagan Israelite worship (1 Kings 12:28–29). Although the text itself appears to date to the reign of King Joram of Israel (852–841 B.C.), it refers to the twin kingdoms of Israel and *bêt-David* ("house of David"), respectively. Despite some dissenting voices from the camp of the minimalists,[34] scholars of all persuasions are convinced that the *bêt-David* = Judah interpretation is correct and that the kingdom was named after King David, thus supporting his historical reality.[35]

The Mesha Inscription

Sometimes called the "Moabite Stone," the Mesha Inscription is dated to about 850 B.C. It provides an account by King Mesha of Moab of his conflicts with Israel in the latter years of the Omri dynasty.[36] It is one of a very few documents recounting events that are also narrated in the Old Testament (2 Kings 3:4–27), providing an alternative version of what took place. Though obviously each story is told from a different perspective and with self-serving, ideological overtones, the basic story line is the same, and the historical events they describe are common to both accounts. Of special interest in light of the Tell Dan inscription is the likelihood that Judah also was known by Mesha as "House of David," a reading that hith-

---

33. A. Millard, trans., "The Tell Dan Stele (2.39)," in *COS*, 2:161–62.
34. See, for example, P. R. Davies, "'House of David' Built on Sand: The Sin of the Biblical Maximizers," *BAR* 20, no. 4 (July–August 1994), 54–55; and Whitelam, *The Invention of Ancient Israel*, 166–68.
35. Abraham Biran and Joseph Naveh, "An Aramaic Stele Fragment from Tel Dan," *IEJ* 43 (1993): 81–98; Victor Sasson, "The Old Aramaic Inscription from Tell Dan: Philological, Literary, and Historical Aspects," *JSS* 40 (1995) 11–30; William M. Schniedewind, "Tel Dan Stela: New Light on Aramaic and Jehu's Revolt," *BASOR* 302 (1996) 75–90.
36. See W. F. Albright, trans., "The Moabite Stone," in *ANET*, 3d ed., ed. James B. Pritchard (Princeton, N.J.: Princeton University Press, 1969), 320–21; and K. A. D. Smelik, trans., "The Inscription of King Mesha (2.23)," in *COS*, 2:137–38.

erto had not been widely accepted.[37] The Mesha text, therefore, not only lends credence to the Old Testament narrative but provides an alternative way of reading it.

The Black Obelisk

The handsome and well-preserved Black Obelisk records a campaign into Syria-Palestine by Shalmaneser III of Assyria (who reigned 858–824 B.C.) in his eighteenth year of rule, 841–840. Among other exploits he said that "at that time I received the tribute of the people of Tyre, Sidon, and of Jehu, son of Omri."[38] Comparison of this to Shalmaneser's foray twelve years earlier against Ahab and his allies at Qarqar, as recounted on the so-called Kurkh Stele, makes it clear that Jehu capitulated in his very first year and that Ahab engaged Shalmaneser in Ahab's last year (853). The Old Testament allows for twelve years between Ahab's demise and Jehu's accession,[39] exactly the length of time between Shalmaneser's two campaigns according to the Eponym Chronicle. In addition to identifying Ahab and Jehu as historical figures, the Black Obelisk depicts Jehu prostrate before the Assyrian ruler, the only artistic representation of an Israelite king so far identified.

The Taylor Prism

The famous Taylor Prism recounts a number of military exploits of the Assyrian ruler Sennacherib (ruled 705–681 B.C.), the most important for our purpose being his siege of Jerusalem in 701 in the reign of Hezekiah of Judah. He boasts that "as for Hezekiah, the Jew, who did not bow in submission to my yoke, forty-six of his strong walled towns and innumerable smaller villages in their neighborhood I besieged and conquered. He [Hezekiah] himself I shut up like a caged bird within Jerusalem, his royal city."[40] The Old Testament also tells of the siege (2 Kings 18:13–19:37;

---

37. André Lemaire, "'House of David' Restored in Moabite Inscription," *BAR* 20, no. 3 (May–June 1994): 30–37.
38. A. L. Oppenheim, trans., "Babylonian and Assyrian Historical Texts," in *ANET*, 280; and K. Lawson Younger Jr., trans., "Black Obelisk (2.113F)," in *COS*, 2:269–70.
39. Thiele, *Mysterious Numbers of the Hebrew Kings*, 50–51.
40. D. J. Wiseman, "Sennacherib's Siege of Jerusalem," in *Documents from Old Testament Times*, ed. D. Winton Thomas (London: Nelson, 1958), 67; and Mordechai Cogan, trans., "Sennacherib's Siege of Jerusalem (2.119B)," in *COS*, 2:302–03.

Isa. 36:1–39:8), indicating that it was lifted after Yahweh destroyed the Assyrian army. By his own account, Sennacherib never claims to have taken Jerusalem, settling instead for a heavy ransom. He is also silent about his defeat, suggesting merely a return to his homeland. Skeptics will, of course, discount the Bible's claim that Yahweh destroyed 185,000 Assyrian troops, either denying such a possibility out of hand or offering other explanations.[41] One is not surprised, of course, at Sennacherib's historical cover-up since it was unthinkable for the Assyrians to suffer such a devastating loss. One is left, then, with a choice as to what to believe about the outcome, but the fact remains that the biblical episode is well documented by extrabiblical, Assyrian sources.

The Lachish Letters

The siege of Jerusalem in 701 was followed by other invasions a century later, this time by the Babylonians. One took place in 598 B.C., another in 587–586, and possibly another occurred in 605, though evidence is lacking. The final siege, the one that ended with the fall of the city, the destruction of the temple, and the deportation of much of the population to Babylon, is well documented in the Old Testament (2 Kings 24:20–25:12; 2 Chron. 36:17–21; Jer. 52:3–27). A number of ostraca (pottery shards) from Tell Ed-Duweir (Lachish) give it extrabiblical attestation.[42] In perfect agreement with the biblical account, but adding many details to it, these memoranda graphically describe the desperation of the Jews living not in the capital but in outlying places such as Beth-haraphid (not yet identified), Azekah, and Lachish. They are particularly interesting and important because they were not official, royal inscriptions but urgent messages from ordinary people. They thus fill in the historical account from the viewpoint of *hoi polloi*.

Abuse of Archaeology in Regard to Old Testament History

The above examples illustrate the value of archaeology to biblical history when archaeological method is properly employed. Unfortunately,

---

41. For various explanations see Mordechai Cogan and Hayim Tadmor, *II Kings*, AB (Garden City, N.Y.: Doubleday, 1988), 239.
42. W. F. Albright, trans., "The Lachish Ostraca," in *ANET*, 321–22; and Klaas A. D. Smelik, *Writings from Ancient Israel*, trans. G. I. Davies (Louisville: Westminster/John Knox, 1991), 116–31.

archaeology—or, rather, its interpreters—has not always been so heuristic to the task of providing insight into the biblical text. In fact, its misreading continues to have damaging consequences. Abuses come at the hands of (1) those who earnestly but misguidedly make the record say what it does not say, and (2) those who vitiate a discovery's meaning because they fear its potential to undergird the Bible's historicity. Here are a few representative examples of these sorts of abuses.

The Nuzi Texts

Unearthed in 1925 at Nuzu, the modern Iraqi site named Yorghan Tepe, the Nuzi Texts are hundreds of cuneiform tablets written in a peripheral Akkadian dialect. The tablets provide scores of examples of laws, customs, and traditions from the Late Bronze Age (ca. 1450–1250 B.C.).[43] Since many of these appear to be reflected in the patriarchal narratives of Genesis, scholars of every persuasion began to say the texts supported their positions. One side suggested that the patriarchs lived hundreds of years later than the traditional period (ca. 2100–1800).[44] Others tried to force the contents of the Nuzi texts to an earlier period in line with the standard chronology of the patriarchs.[45] There is at least some evidence for an element of truth in the second interpretation. Much of the Nuzi legal material finds precedent in Hammurabi (ca. 1750) and, it seems, in other early law codes and conventions to which there are references. However, a close scrutiny of the claims for direct connection has forced a retreat by those who at first vigorously advocated it. Now it is admitted that both Nuzi and the Old Testament shared a common cultural world, in which various legal and social practices were independently carried out.[46]

The Joshua Conquest

The classic model of the conquest of Canaan by Israel under Joshua is one of violent and nearly total decimation of the peoples and structures of the land. Archaeology has, indeed, demonstrated such devastation, but only

---

43. Theophile J. Meek, trans., "Mesopotamian Legal Documents," in *ANET*, 219–20.
44. Cyrus H. Gordon, "Biblical Customs and the Nuzu Tablets," *BA* 3, no. 1 (1940): 1–12.
45. J. A. Thompson, *The Bible and Archaeology* (Grand Rapids: Eerdmans, 1962), 25.
46. See the essays in A. R. Millard and D. J. Wiseman, eds., *Essays on the Patriarchal Narratives* (Leicester: Inter-Varsity, 1980).

in the thirteenth century. Scholars who adopted the model of violent conquest argued, therefore, that the conquest must have occurred at 1225–1200 or so, and, consequently, that the Exodus could be no earlier than 1250.[47] This is obviously at variance with the Bible's own testimony, which dates the Exodus at 1446 and the conquest in the first half of the fourteenth century. The problem with this is the lack of evidence of wholesale destruction in Canaan from 1400–1350, a conundrum that many conservatives sought to redress by redating or reinterpreting archaeological material.[48] The answer lies, however, in reading more closely the biblical narrative which makes it most clear that the conquest was accomplished *without* major damage to structures (Deut. 6:10–11; 19:1; Josh. 24:12–13), though populations themselves fell to the sword. Neither proponents nor opponents of an early conquest find support in the archaeological evidence. Most likely the carnage reflected by the archaeological record is to be dated to the days of Deborah and Gideon and the upheavals caused by Israel's enemies at that time.[49]

Ancient Near Eastern Treaty Texts

For fifty years scholars have drawn attention to the parallels between Hittite treaty texts of the Late Bronze age and the covenant texts of the Bible, especially Deuteronomy and the Book of the Covenant (Exod. 20:1–23:33). Conservatives, at least, have employed these compelling comparisons in defense of the early (Mosaic) date of the biblical material, as opposed to the historical-critical theory of a seventh-century origination.[50] To counteract the Hittite parallels, advocates of a late Deuteronomy draw attention to Neo-Assyrian treaty texts of the seventh century, which also exhibit striking resemblances to the form of Deuteronomy.[51] These similarities are, indeed, striking, but they are incomplete. Notable by omission are any examples that have historical prologue and blessing sections, both of which

---

47. John Bright, *A History of Israel*, 4th ed. (Philadelphia: Westminster/John Knox, 2000), 130–33.
48. John J. Bimson, *Redating the Exodus and Conquest*, JSOTSup 5 (Sheffield: University of Sheffield, 1978), 229–37.
49. Eugene H. Merrill, "Palestinian Archaeology and the Date of the Conquest," *GTJ* 3 (1982): 107–21.
50. See, for example, Meredith G. Kline, *Treaty of the Great King* (Grand Rapids: Eerdmans, 1963).
51. Thus R. Frankena, "The Vassal-Treaties of Esarhaddon and the Dating of Deuteronomy," *OTS* 14 (1965): 122–54.

are found in the Hittite and biblical texts. The twisted logic and tortured explanations offered by those who wish at any cost to salvage a late Deuteronomy betray the uselessness of these particular archaeological artifacts for making their case.

Kuntillet ʿAjrud

Of many cult sites discovered in Israel, this one some thirty miles south of Kadesh-Barnea is among the most celebrated, because of a brief inscription reading, "I bless you by Yahweh of Samaria and his Asherah."[52] This reference to a nonmonotheistic faith in Israel, dating to about 800 B.C., has been seized upon by some scholars who, apparently in the interest of "proving" a later development of monotheism, suggest that the practice at this site was more or less normative.[53] It was only with the rise of Deuteronomic and prophetic theology that a strict monotheism was hammered out. The assumption, of course, is that this was *not* an aberrant cult but one only to be expected at that time and place.[54] A different reading, one that sees the Law already in place long before 800, makes the case that the Kuntillet ʿAjrud shrine, much like the one at nearby Tell Arad, was a syncretistic worship center, one roundly condemned by both Moses and the prophets.[55] The very identification of the deity as "Yahweh of Samaria" in a place deep in the South argues presumptively in favor of this being a "foreign" god imported from Samaria, which was a hotbed of deviant Yahwism all through the ninth century. The burden of proof is clearly on the side of those who suggest any kind of orthodoxy in the Kuntillet ʿAjrud cultus. The archaeological data are clear; the interpretation is in the eye and heart of those who read them.

---

52. Mazar, *Archaeology of the Land of the Bible,* 448; and P. Kyle McCarter, trans., "Kuntillet ʿAjrud (2.47)," in *COS,* 2:171.
53. Niels Peter Lemche, *Ancient Israel: A New History of Israelite Society* (Sheffield: JSOT, 1988), 226–27; cf. J. A. Emerton, "New Light on Israelite Religion: The Implications of the Inscriptions from Kuntillet ʿAjrud," *ZAW* 94 (1982): 2–20.
54. Tilde Binger, "Ashera in Israel," *SJOT* 9, no. 1 (1995): 18.
55. Chang-Ho C. Jo, "Is Kuntillet ʿAjrud a Cultic Center? A Psychological and Archaeological Reassessment," *NEASB* NS 39–40 (1995): 17–18.

Conclusion

This cursory examination of the relationship between archaeology and biblical history evokes a number of concluding observations, only three of which can be considered here:

1. Both archaeology and the Bible are neutral; indeed, one might say they are objects of inquiry subject to the worldview assumptions, methodologies, and interpretations of those who address them. This is not to say that they do not try to communicate, but their effectiveness as speakers is subject to the skills and predispositions of their hearers. The degree to which archaeology is beneficial to an understanding of the Bible as history depends on the extent to which one is willing to forego preconceived ideas about either and to let each be considered innocent of charges of error or inauthenticity unless proven guilty.
2. Archaeology and the Bible must be mutually informing. The kind of bias practiced in some circles says that archaeological data are objective whereas the Bible is ideologically tendentious, so archaeology occupies the moral higher ground. This view has no place in serious scholarship. Artifacts are artifacts, texts are texts, data are data—they must be dealt with alike. Until some or all are disqualified by rigorous scholarly method as having no basis in fact, they should be allowed to stand.
3. Archaeology must not be pressed into the service of those who would enslave it to a particular preconceived point of view about the Bible. Nor should the Bible or a given interpretation of the Bible dictate how a particular datum of archaeological research should be understood. Each must be dealt with on its own terms, even if no harmonization or reconciliation of the two seems apparent or even possible.

4

HISTORY AND THEOLOGY
The Tale of Two Histories

C. Hassell Bullock

OF ALL THE ISSUES THAT HAVE EXERCISED Old Testament scholars since the rise of the historical-critical method, the question of the relationship between history and theology would take a place of prominence among them. Sometimes theology has not consciously been part of the discussion, but any time Old Testament history is discussed, theology is necessarily implied.

DEFINITION OF HISTORY AND THEOLOGY

Obviously we have two terms to define, *history* and *theology*. The simplest definition of history is "a study of the past," but that is really a modern view of the discipline. It is questionable whether the Old Testament writers studied the past in such an objective way as we do in our modern Western world, or at least as we attempt to do. They certainly reflected on the past, but not with the object of establishing the historical validity of an event. That was a given. John Goldingay suggests that the definition of history as "what happened" in the past tends to throw the discussion out of focus, since that was not the concern of the biblical writers. He would prefer the term *events* to the term *history*.[1] Elmer Martens has formulated a helpful definition of *history* that seeks to be more reflective of the Old Testament view: "History is a human enterprise of chronologically selecting

---

1. John Goldingay, "'That You May Know That Yahweh Is God': A Study of the Relationship Between Theology and Historical Truth in the Old Testament," *TynBul* 23 (1972): 60–61.

and recording events in time and space, and doing so interpretatively or with a particular perspective."[2]

Edmond Jacob reminds us that Old Testament history brings together "raw facts and their interpretation."[3] Any time we refer to events *and* interpretation, the objectivity/subjectivity issue naturally surfaces. Objectivity has come to be highly esteemed in our world, and so it should be. It is virtually synonymous with *science,* even though there is definitely a subjective element involved even in the scientific method. At the same time, our Western world often looks askance at subjectivity, assuming that it is biased and tilted in the direction of a particular worldview, or that it is necessarily quasi-historical. Yet, in order to gain a healthy appreciation for biblical history, we have to look more favorably and positively on subjectivity, representing the personal or the interpretive aspect of history. It is virtually a truism to say that there is no such thing as total objectivity. A subjective element is involved in every "objective" report because human beings, who have emotions and opinions, are the conductors and reporters of all objective data.

Yet, the way to gain a more favorable view of subjectivity is certainly not to frame objectivity in an unfavorable light. Perhaps we need to abandon the terms altogether as ways of describing Old Testament history. Some will, of course, immediately conclude that this suggests turning in the direction of the modern historical-critical method and accepting its assumptions about history. That is not at all what is intended. What we have to do, as biblical theologians, is to redefine the genre of historical narrative, and that is what we shall attempt to do below.

The *second* term that our dual topic requires us to define is *theology*. Within the confines of this article, *theology* refers to Old Testament theology. This is Old Testament theology distinguished from the New Testament and its theology. Certainly the relationship between the testaments is of critical value for all Christians, but the explication of that relationship has to be shared by both the Old Testament and the New Testament theologians. It is not a study that belongs exclusively to either.

Thus any definition of *Old Testament theology* must take into account the fact that the Old Testament is the object of study, and it has an inherent

---

2. Elmer A. Martens, "The Oscillating Fortunes of History Within Old Testament Theology" (paper read at Wheaton College, Wheaton, Ill., 5 December 1990).
3. Edmond Jacob, *Theology of the Old Testament* (London: Hodder & Stoughton, 1955), 184.

authority of its own, apart from the New Testament. We must see the Old Testament as a legitimate body of writings worthy of its own exegetical enterprise. Until the Old Testament is allowed to speak by its own authority, the exegete cannot hear the New Testament's affirmation, the "Amen" of the Apostles.

Old Testament theology, then, is *the explanation of the writings of the Old Testament in their biblical settings.* In those writings God has revealed his will for Israel and the world. The reader, therefore, seeks to know God's will as revealed in the Old Testament. John Sailhamer, embracing a strong canonical position, confines his definition to the canonical Scriptures, exclusive of, but not in ignorance of, the extracanonical dimensions of history and culture. According to him, *Old Testament theology* is "the study and presentation of what is revealed in the Old Testament."[4]

Our task in this essay is to speak to the interfacing of these two disciplines. It is the contention of this article that when we reference the historical writings we are essentially speaking about one phenomenon, or one genre, even though there is certainly justification to deal with the two terms *history* and *theology* separately.

THE OLD TESTAMENT AS HISTORY: THE MINIMALISTS, MEDIALISTS, AND MAXIMALISTS

With the development of the historical-critical method, the gap between history and theology began to appear. If anything, it has grown wider, until presently there are those who find little of historical value in the Old Testament prior to the time of David and Solomon, and others propounding a broad range of views, ranging all the way from the minimalists through the medialists to the maximalists.

Minimalists

The minimalist position is a reductionist approach to biblical history, holding that, for various reasons, the historical framework of the Old Testament, as well as the details attached to it, does not carry the weight of historicity. In an earlier time, Gerhard von Rad became the principal

---

4. John H. Sailhamer, *Introduction to Old Testament Theology: A Canonical Approach* (Grand Rapids: Zondervan, 1995), 17.

spokesman for the minimalist position in his *Old Testament Theology*. Troubled with the stalemate that had developed in Pentateuchal studies, his search for the core of Israelite tradition originated in the belief that it was "no longer possible to reconstruct the political history of Israel's ancestors before the Settlement."[5] He calls that prehistory "the impenetrable darkness,"[6] suggesting that the frame of history in the Pentateuch was a reconstruction by authors/schools of writers long after the events the narratives describe. Even the people of the story, *Israel,* only received this name after the settlement (conquest) of Canaan.[7] In fact, insisted von Rad, the story of Israel's history as told by the Pentateuch was the result of a coalescence of traditions that had existed in a confessional form, and celebrated in particular sanctuaries of pre-Israelite Canaan.

To help us understand von Rad's position, we might compare it to the Apostles' Creed, which, by the name itself, implies an apostolic composition, or at least a creed that the apostles endorsed, when in fact it is the result of the fourth-century Roman symbol. Looking at the creed from one angle, we would have to conclude that it represents the theological understanding of the Christian Church in the fourth century rather than the faith of the apostles. From another angle, however, we could say that the creed is a formulation of the faith of the apostles, even though it is formulated in the language of the later church. While the analogy is not perfect, we can see how one could extrapolate from the creed and weave a fabric of gospel history. This writer, confessedly, believes that the historical data in the Apostles' Creed is reliable and authentic, and that the confessors of the Church did not misunderstand and did not misrepresent the historical element. The analogy, nevertheless, should help us understand the assumptions of von Rad and the form-critical method.

Von Rad shifted the search for the historical core of Pentateuchal history from the four "documents" on which the source critics had concentrated, JEDP, to three brief historical creeds that had, insisted von Rad, left their mark on the formative process of this story: (1) Deuteronomy 26:5b–10 (the prayer for the presentation of the first fruits in the sanctuary); (2) Deuteronomy 6:12–24 (a formula of the facts of Israel's redemption); and

---

5. Gerhard von Rad, *Old Testament Theology,* trans. D. M. G. Stalker (Edinburgh: Oliver & Boyd, 1962), 1:8.
6. Ibid.
7. Ibid., 6.

(3) Joshua 24:2b–13 (Joshua's farewell address at Shechem). In his view, these were essentially cult legends that gradually coalesced into a composite "history" of Israel. Further, von Rad observed that neither of these creeds mentioned the events of Sinai, leading him to propose that the Sinaitic tradition had a separate origin and transmission, and that it was only later combined with the canonical pattern found in the three creeds.[8]

Von Rad therefore made a radical adjustment in the study of Old Testament theology: he urged that the proper object of Old Testament theology was *Israel's confessions,* or *what Israel believed about God.* This emphasis forced upon him the distinction between secular and sacred history—between *Historie* (secular history as event) and *Heilsgeschichte* (sacred history as faith). While he admitted the importance of *Historie,* he was preoccupied with *Heilsgeschichte,* and insisted that Old Testament theology should be based upon that, not upon *Historie,* the story of fact and event. Some scholars have questioned von Rad's assumption that the so-called creeds were a complete representation of Israel's self-understanding. In fact, G. Henton Davies has said that this was probably the fundamental error of von Rad's hypothesis.[9] They were rather intended "to be select summaries and not exhaustive agendas of the facts they record."[10] J. Muilenburg has given the following balanced assessment: "No one has really grappled with the difficulties of a biblical theology so well as he, but it is precisely his historical formulations which make his work unsatisfactory to those who are more 'theologically' minded."[11] As valiant as von Rad's hypothesis was, he turned the issue on its head. The creeds—if they can be called such—were the result of the historical tradition, not its source.[12]

More recently, the minimalist position has taken on new life in the work of scholars who, in contrast to von Rad, are not theologians. These include John Van Seters, Thomas L. Thompson, Robert B. Coote, Keith W. Whitelam, N. P. Lemche, Philip R. Davies, and others, and they are dealt with in several other essays in this volume.[13]

---

8. Ibid., 66.
9. G. Henton Davies, "Gerhard von Rad, *Old Testament Theology,*" in *Contemporary Old Testament Theologians,* ed. Robert B. Laurin (Valley Forge, Pa.: Judson, 1970), 70.
10. Ibid., 69.
11. J. Muilenburg, "Old Testament Scholarship," *JBR* 28 (1960): 180.
12. D. N. Freedman, review of *Genesis: A Commentary,* by Gerhard von Rad, trans. John Marks, *TT* 20 (1963): 115.
13. See, for example, the essays by David Howard (chap. 1), Eugene Merrill (chap. 3), Hermann Austel (chap. 7), and Richard Patterson (chap. 8).

Medialists

The medialist view is more charitable toward historical fact and event in its willingness to seek authentic human persons and events in the biblical narratives. While more than one theologian represents this position, Walther Eichrodt gave it a plausible form in his two-volume *Theology of the Old Testament*.[14] He viewed the Old Testament as possessing a large measure of historical value in its reconstruction of the life of ancient Israel. He could even discern the lines of a historical figure in Moses, sharply distinguishing himself from the Alt-Noth school of thought that believed Moses was a legendary figure. Even the Exodus and Sinai have historical value, although he believed that all Israel did not, contrary to the Pentateuchal narrative, participate in those events. Later Israelites came to claim them as their own, regardless of their historical connection, or lack of it, with the ancestors of the people.

Maximalists

The maximalist position is all the more charitable still toward history and event than the other two positions. Today this position is virtually a relic in the museum of biblical methodology and belief, except for conservative Christians and Jews who still believe in the divine inspiration of the Bible. Generally speaking, these scholars accept Old Testament events as authentic representations of what actually happened in history. Eugene E. Merrill, the revered teacher and scholar to whom this volume is dedicated, has done historical work with the integrity of one committed to both divine inspiration of Scripture and to serious scholarship. His *Kingdom of Priests,* among other works, combines both of those qualities and illustrates well the solid scholarship conservatives have contributed to historical studies.[15]

---

14. Walther Eichrodt, *Theology of the Old Testament,* 2 vols., trans. J. A. Baker (Philadelphia: Westminster, 1967).
15. Eugene H. Merrill, *Kingdom of Priests: A History of Old Testament Israel* (Grand Rapids: Baker, 1987); idem, "Old Testament History: A Theological Perspective," in *NIDOTTE,* ed. Willem VanGemeren (Grand Rapids: Zondervan, 1997), 1:68–85; idem, "History," in *Cracking Old Testament Codes,* ed. D. Brent Sandy and Ronald L. Giese Jr. (Nashville: Broadman & Holman, 1995), 89–112; idem, "The 'Accession Year' and Davidic Chronology," *JANES* 19 (1989): 101–12; and idem, "The Late Bronze/Early Iron Age Transition and the Emergence of Israel," *BSac* 152 (1995): 145–62.

For the most part, however, evangelical Christians have not dealt with the issues of biblical history as openly as those who represent the other two positions. Yet the scene is changing, thanks to Professor Merrill and others like him. An example is V. Philips Long's book *The Art of Biblical History*,[16] which represents a long stride in the direction of open and honest grappling with the issues.

While there are sufficient representatives of the maximalist position, Walter Kaiser is one who has incorporated his confidence in biblical history in a theology of the Old Testament.[17] He does not argue with the events of Old Testament history, nor does he try to reconstruct them. Rather he takes them at face value. In fact, Kaiser structures Old Testament theology along the lines of history, assuming that they are a fair representation of the facts of history.

John Sailhamer's canonical approach to the Old Testament also falls into the category, although he lays the burden of theology on the canonical text as it has come to us, and not on the event. Revelation, urges Sailhamer, is not to be found in the historical event but in the text of Scripture. Yet, at the same time he affirms that "the authors of the biblical narratives intended to write history and not fiction."[18]

Sailhamer is by no means alone in his canonical approach to Old Testament theology. He follows Brevard Childs and others who look at theology from the end result, from the text as it has come to us, rather than from the other end as the literature was developing. Recognizing the tendency of historical criticism to splinter theology into sub-theologies, Childs insists on standing at the end of the process and looking at the development from the vantage point of the final product. He, of course, and in contrast to Sailhamer, is much more dubious about the historicity of Israel's beginnings.[19] Old Testament theology is not a historical enterprise. Childs insists that:

> a canonical approach envisions the discipline of Old Testament theology as combining both descriptive and constructive features. It recognizes the descriptive task of correctly interpreting an ancient

---

16. V. Philips Long, *The Art of Biblical History* (Grand Rapids: Zondervan, 1994).
17. Walter A. Kaiser Jr., *Toward an Old Testament Theology* (Grand Rapids: Zondervan, 1978).
18. John H. Sailhamer, *Introduction to Old Testament Theology* (Grand Rapids: Zondervan, 1995), 54.
19. Brevard Childs, *Old Testament Theology in a Canonical Context* (London: SCM, 1985).

text which bars testimony to historic Israel's faith. Yet it also understands that the theological enterprise involves a construal by the modern interpreter, whose stance to the text affects its meaning. For this reason, Old Testament theology cannot be identified with describing a historical process in the past (*contra* Gese), but involves wrestling with the subject-matter to which scripture continues to bear testimony."[20]

By recognizing the primary importance of the text as it has come to us, however that process might have occurred, canonical criticism, especially as represented by Sailhamer, shifted attention away from the historical element to the textual, and in so doing, freed the text from both the tyranny of historical reconstructionism, on the one hand, and the claim of inauthenticity, on the other.

While differing with Childs on the matter of historical authenticity, Sailhamer's emphasis nevertheless shifts attention away from historical fact, or at least a fixation with it (although he does not question it), and moves it to interpretation. With this understanding, revelation is to be sought in the text and not in the event. One could, on that basis, say that the historical details of the event are not so important, but that the interpretation of the event carries the burden of theology. Yet, the effect of this position, in our view, is beneficial in two ways: (1) it takes the burden off the historicity argument, while assuming historicity, thus enabling the interpreter to deal with the theology of the text; and (2) it recognizes the nature of the historical narrative, that it is an interpretation of event, and that revelation is concentrated in the interpretation of the event (text) rather than the event itself. In effect, this view is probably more faithful to the nature of Old Testament historical narrative, which is a blending of history and theology, and which does not ask whether the event actually happened. It is taken for granted that it did.

The Biblical Genre of History: The Medium and the Message

As already suggested above, the biblical genre of history is different from the modern genre. In the latter case, factuality is uppermost, at least uppermost in reporting the authenticity of the event. Yet, at the same time, even

---

20. Ibid., 12.

a purist would be hard put to deny that interpretation is involved in the modern genre. In comparison, the biblical view of history is much more an intentional blending of fact and interpretation. In view of that blending, the historical-critical method has tried to sort out the two factors and has put a value assessment on each of them. In general, it has made the message (interpretation) more important than the medium (history). Perhaps on the other side of the spectrum, the maximalists have made the medium more important than the message. Either position falls short of an accurate representation of the biblical genre. It seems, in fact, that Sailhamer's emphasis upon the text, while not denying the authenticity of the event, but merely shifting the focus to the meaning rather than the historical fact, is beneficial. Did the event occur? Indeed it did, but that is not the issue. The issue is the meaning of the event. The biblical writer assumes its historical authenticity and endows the text with its meaning.

Historical Fact as Critical to Theology

We grant that Old Testament theology should not concern itself with the historicity of the event, or should not build its house on a reconstructed foundation of history. Yet, the issue of what happened, that is, whether the historical details fall in the category of historical fact, is an issue that enters into the discussion of the relationship between history and theology. Does reliable theology depend upon whether a historical event occurred, or is merely believing that it occurred, to cite von Rad again, enough to validate the event as a firm basis for theology? If the Exodus did not occur, does it merit the central position in Israel's theology that the Old Testament gives it? To say it another way, can anything be theologically significant if it did not actually happen? John Goldingay, who is willing to make some allowance for the interpretive factor in Old Testament history,[21] answers this

---

21. John Goldingay, for example, cites the Rabshakeh speeches in 2 Kings 18 as an example of a method that applied the imagination to reconstruct the speeches. See Goldingay, "That You May Know That Yahweh Is God," 83. While I am willing to make some allowance here also, I would insist that the writer of the speeches was working with the substance of the speeches as he had received it. A modern example may be the speeches of Abraham Lincoln as they are recorded later by certain individuals who actually heard them. We may assume that they are a very good representation of the actual substance of the speeches. However, the difference between the Rabshakeh's speeches and Abraham Lincoln's may be that a long time lapse falls between the speeches and the reconstruction. Yet, I would insist that the substance of the speeches had been preserved in some form, either written or oral, and perhaps both.

question thus: "If words mean anything, the answer must be No."[22] He is uneasy with the thought that God produced the *tradition* of the events but not the events: "If God was really active in the production of this tradition, then surely the events it describes must have happened."[23]

Assuming, as we do, that the authenticity of the events is a given for the biblical writers, then to construct another picture of the events is to introduce something that was foreign to the writer. Whatever attitude we take toward the historical-critical method, we have to acknowledge that the picture that this method draws is only available in the mind of the critic, not in the mind of the biblical writer. In fact, one wonders if the altered picture produced by the critical method would not have forced the writer to formulate a different message and thus a different theology of Israel's past. If an event such as the Exodus was so minor an occurrence and affected so few people, as some critics claim, would this modified picture not have radically changed the theological assessment of the writer? Gerhard Hasel strongly suggests that it would: "In my opinion it is methodologically not possible to abstract an actual event or fact from the confessional-kerygmatic tradition of Israel with the historical-critical method, and then to designate this 'factual happening' as the action of God, thereby making it theologically relevant."[24] In part, this is a denial of von Rad's hypothesis that there is an "assured minimum." This simply means that by the historical-critical method one might come to understand what the basic historical elements in Israel's history were. At the same time, the same method might lead to the conclusion that they did not happen like the Old Testament describes them. It is, in fact, a refutation that there is such a thing as *the* scientific picture of Israel's history, "for such a picture is just not available."[25]

Having acknowledged the substantive nature of historical fact in biblical theology, we insist again that this is not an issue of Old Testament theology, which assumes the factual nature of history. Then is it ever appropriate to ask the question, Did the event really happen? Or, Did it happen as described in the text? The answer is "yes," but not for the purpose of theology. Theology does not, or should not, question historicity. Yet, for apologetic

---

22. Ibid., 83.
23. Ibid., 88.
24. Gerhard Hasel, *Old Testament Theology: Current Issues in the Debate,* rev. ed. (Grand Rapids: Eerdmans, 1991), 120.
25. Ibid.

purposes the question is appropriate, and the full resources of the auxiliary disciplines, like archaeology, philology, and secular history, should be called into service.

History-Writing Illustrated

Let us take some examples of history-writing and the way the Old Testament uses historical event to illustrate our point that history and theology are blended into a single genre in the Old Testament.

History as Theological Explication

The first example may be taken from the parallel histories of the monarchy found in Samuel–Kings and the book of Chronicles. V. Philips Long compares these histories more to a painting than a photo. Samuel–Kings includes much that Chronicles omits, and Chronicles includes much that Samuel–Kings omits.[26] He compares the parallel accounts of the Davidic covenant (cf. 2 Sam. 7:1–17; 1 Chron. 17:1–15), and insists that Chronicles is a *"second* painting of Israel's monarchical history, not an *over*painting of Samuel–Kings."[27] He sees the Chronicler making *explicit* what was only *implicit* in 2 Samuel 7.[28] In the Chronicler's context, when the kingdom of David has fallen, he lays out a vision of the kingdom of God. The promise "your house and your kingdom will endure forever before me" (2 Sam. 7:16) becomes in Chronicles "I will set him over my house and my kingdom forever" (2 Chron. 17:14). The historian/artist of Chronicles basically makes this shift with the change of a pronoun from Samuel's "your" (David) to "my" (the Lord), and a change of subject from Samuel's *"your* house and *your* kingdom will endure forever before me" to the Chronicler's first person (the LORD)—*"I* will set him over *my* house and *my* kingdom forever." The composers of these narratives were "historians" in the sense that they had a grasp of the basic events of the past, but they were "artists" in the sense that they had a *vision* of the past and its *relevance* for the future.[29]

---

26. Long, *Art of Biblical History,* 76–87.
27. Ibid., 82.
28. Ibid., 83.
29. Ibid., 69.

History as Paradigm

The second example is the story of Abraham and Sarah's sojourn in Egypt (Gen. 12:10–13:2). The story takes the shape of a paradigm of Israel's Egyptian sojourn: going down into Egypt due to a famine (comparable to Jacob's sojourn in Egypt, also prompted by famine—Gen. 41:57–42:2), the abuse of Sarah (comparable to Israel's oppression—Exod. 1:8–22), the affliction of Pharaoh and his house (comparable to the plagues on Egypt—Exod. 7:8–11:10), coming out of Egypt (comparable to the exodus—Exod. 14:21–29), and the wealth which Abraham brought out of Egypt with him (comparable to the despoiling of the Egyptians—Exod. 3:22). This proleptic rehearsal of Israel's sojourn in Egypt and subsequent Exodus points in the direction of the Joseph narrative, where the groundwork of the sojourn and Exodus is laid. While one could see this story as no more than a preparatory stage for the Joseph narrative, it at the same time forms part of the backbone of the patriarchal story. The writer builds the substantive event of Israel's history into the lives of their patriarch and matriarch. If the latter are merely legendary, then Israel's future redemption hangs on a thin framework, or no substantive framework at all.

Then was it contrived? Was this a literary device to portend the central event (Exodus) of Israelite history? If the patriarchal experience in Egypt was of any significance to the generation of the Exodus—and we must assume it was—the factual nature of Abraham and Sarah's episode in that land was of great value and inspiration to the Exodus generation. Moses and his followers saw their own history reflected in the story of their past. But that was not all. They could take courage in the prospects of the future as they read about the exodus of their ancestors. Given the Hebrew respect for the patriarchs and matriarchs, the story of the sojourn and Exodus would have much more theological substance if Israel's ancestors had undergone a comparable experience. In a sense, history was repeating itself, except on a much broader scale. The life of their ancestors was re-actualized in the life of the nation, and re-actualization would have little significance apart from the authentic actions of the ancestors who were, in their own personal lives, sketching the lines of future history. We have called this a *paradigm*. Perhaps it could also fall under Goldingay's "propaganda" factor; but he rightly insists, in our view, that its "very propaganda validity depends on its being a veracious interpretation of what actually happened."[30] The national experience found its validation in the personal experience of the ancestors. If the story were merely fabricated to provide a patriarchal grid on which to relate the central episode of Israel's history, the loss of historical authenticity in the first story would prove to be a flimsy grid on which to build the national history.

History with Editorial Purpose

A third example is the historical appendix in Isaiah 36–39, with its parallel account in 2 Kings 18:13–20:19. The writer records three events: (1) Sennacherib's thwarted attempt to capture Jerusalem (chaps. 36–37); (2) Hezekiah's illness and restoration to health (chap. 38); and (3) the embassy from the Chaldean king, Merodach-Baladan, concluding with a prediction of the Babylonian exile (chap. 39). Our historical information puts Sennacherib's invasion in 701 B.C., and Hezekiah's illness about 704, while the delegation from Merodach-Baladan likely occurred in 703, when he had acceded to the Babylonian throne again for a brief reign. The chronology is obviously out of order. John H. Walton[31] has pointed to the redaction of this account in Isaiah, and attributed the reversed chronology to Isaiah's editorial interest. He wanted to interface the Babylonian delegation's visit and the prophecy of the Exile with the oracles on the end of the exile and Judah's return which become the major theme of Isaiah 40–66.[32] In view of the undeniable fact that chronology was not a major concern for the prophets, it should not surprise us to see Isaiah arranging the material to suit his editorial purpose. Yet, this should pose no problem for the historical facts of the story.

History as Midrashic Embellishment

A fourth example is the use of midrashic detail in the Psalms to enhance the picture of historical events. To illustrate, Psalm 105 views Joseph, as does the book of Genesis, as the link between the patriarchs and the Egyptian oppression. The psalmist picks up the basic details as they are recorded

---

30. Goldingay, "That You May Know That Yahweh Is God," 83.
31. John H. Walton, "New Observations on the Date of Isaiah," *JETS* 28 (1985): 129–32.
32. Ibid. Walton observes that, while chronology is not the criterion by which Isaiah generally ordered his book, chronology is an important factor for the writer of kings. Based on that observation, he submits that Kings borrows the Isaiah text.

in the Genesis narrative: Joseph was a slave; he was known for his predictions; he was released from prison by the king; he became ruler of the pharaoh's household and caretaker of all his possessions (Ps. 105:19–21; Gen. 41). Yet, call it poetic license or midrashic memory, the psalmist provides details of the story that are missing from Genesis. Yet those details should not surprise us, given the prison setting of the story and Joseph's subsequent rise to respect and influence in Pharaoh's kingdom: "They bruised his feet with shackles,/his neck was put in irons." Joseph became instructor in wisdom of the king's princes and elders (Ps. 105:18, 22).[33] The basic facts of the story and the historical connections correlate perfectly with the Genesis narrative, even though the psalmist embellishes the story a bit, a literary feature that obviously posed no problem for the poet.

We can see the literary freedom of the psalmists again in their citation of the plagues on Egypt. Exodus 7–11 introduces the plagues with the turning of water to blood (Exod. 7:17–21) and concludes with the death of the firstborn (Exod. 11:1–10). The two citations of the plagues occur in Psalms 78 and 105. The order of the plagues is different, with some of them omitted. In fact, the one consistent detail is that both psalms end the plagues with the death of the firstborn (Pss. 78:51; 105:36). The psalmists were obviously not concerned about giving the entire slate of the plagues, or with the Exodus order per se, even though the death of the firstborn merited mention as the last in both instances, fitting the critical role it has in the Exodus narrative. These two examples lead us to suggest that the history writers paid faithful allegiance to the fact and the order of the major events of Israel's history, like the sojourn in Egypt and the Exodus, while taking some liberty in the details.[34]

Conclusion

The historical narratives of the Old Testament are a genre of their own, combining historical detail and interpretation in an inextricable composition. To separate history and theology and pit them against one another is to disregard the nature of the genre. The biblical writers did not question whether an event happened. They assumed it did. When critical scholars

---

33. C. Hassell Bullock, *Encountering the Book of Psalms* (Grand Rapids: Baker, 2001), 101.
34. Ibid., 102.

attempt to reconstruct the picture of Israel's history, they introduce a framework into consideration that was foreign to the biblical writers. We do not know what a biblical theology based upon that picture would look like. Since biblical theology is based on how the biblical writers interpreted the events as they knew them, any attempt to interpret a story otherwise constructed is to take a sidetrack away from biblical theology.

While theology leans on historical factuality, it is not the role of Old Testament theology to raise the question of whether or not an event really occurred. Rather its factuality is assumed. Nevertheless, there is a time and occasion to ask the question of factuality for apologetic purposes, and thus draw upon the auxiliary disciplines of biblical studies; but that is not the role of Old Testament theology. Its practitioners are obligated to interpret the text of the Old Testament as it has come to us, and that includes historical narrative. Anything less than that, or anything more, will produce a paratheology that is neither biblical nor historical.

PART 2

OVERVIEW OF ISRAEL'S HISTORY: ISSUES AND DEBATES

5

Factors in Reading the Patriarchal Narratives

Literary, Historical, and Theological Dimensions

Richard E. Averbeck

At the beginning of the twenty-first century the field of Old Testament studies is in an unsettled state of methodological pluralism.[1] In some ways this is good and healthy. No single approach to the biblical text overrules all others in the academy—none controls the field. In this environment scholars are free to concern themselves with the various dimensions of the text, whether they be of the literary, historical, or theological variety. Some scholars focus on one or another of these, while others attempt to combine them. Unfortunately, in some circles of scholarship there is a tendency to isolate these three dimensions of the text and treat the study of them as competitive endeavors, sometimes even mutually exclusive.

One of our goals at the beginning of the twenty-first century should be to put our methodological "Humpty Dumpty" back together again. We have an opportunity to take another look at how the Bible was put together and fits together as divinely inspired *literature* written in particular *historical contexts* with *theological* concerns in mind. Among other things, this will involve rethinking some of the historical-critical issues and theories that have arisen over the past two hundred years in the scholarly study of the Hebrew Bible. Even though by the unsound use of various methods,

---

1. It is a delight to dedicate this essay to my colleague and friend, Gene Merrill, who has done so much for this generation of believing students and scholars. He himself is a stalwart "patriarch" in the present-day scholarly study of Old Testament history.

historical-critical scholars have sometimes seen or created problems where there are none, nevertheless they have also made some important and legitimate observations about the text as it stands and the compositional processes through which it passed.

It is time to take another look at some of these legitimate historical-critical issues in the composition of the Old Testament from a conservative evangelical point of view. That is the goal and perspective of the present essay. This essay is concerned mainly with the overall literary, historical, and theological dimensions of the patriarchal accounts in Genesis 12–50, with special emphasis on the historicity of the patriarchs themselves, the historical veracity of the narratives about them, and the distinctive historiographical features of those narratives.

The Bible in Three Dimensions

As noted above, the biblical text has three major dimensions: literary, historical, and theological. Within each of these there are several subcategories. The *literary* dimension includes not only the study of different genres, such as prose and poetry, and the relationships between the two as types of literature from a "Bible as literature" point of view, but also such things as the grammar of discourse and the new literary-critical hermeneutics of reading and meaning. It also includes the ongoing discussion of the literary processes involved in the history of the composition of the biblical text. The latter will occupy much of our attention here.

The *theological* dimension, in general, involves us in the foment over presuppositions and beliefs, ancient and modern, regarding the nature of God, people, the world, the Bible, and the relationships between them since the Renaissance and the rise of the historical-critical method. Many in the academy think of the Bible as primarily human reflection on God, life and the world, or ultimate reality. Nevertheless, there are a good number of us in the academy who believe it is God's authoritative, inspired revelation through the agency of human writers, multifaceted like a well-cut diamond, but consistent within itself and profoundly meaningful for life in the past, present, and future. For us the theological dimension draws us into the study of the various theological perspectives and arguments within the text as they developed historically and as they stand canonically.

The *historical* dimension of the study of the Bible in the academy involves one in the historical factuality of the events, people, and conditions described in the text, the study of the cultures in and around Israel in its ancient Near Eastern context, the history of the composition and transmission of the text through the Old Testament period, and the nature of history writing as a genre (i.e., historiography). These historical concerns are all interrelated. They are all integral parts of the historical-critical method.

We will focus our attention on one main issue that involves all three dimensions of the text and affects everything else in the study of the patriarchal narratives; namely, the patriarchal genealogies and their relationship to the patriarchal stories. From a *literary* point of view, the genealogies are the key to the literary structure of the book of Genesis, both the primeval texts (Gen. 1–11) and the patriarchal narratives (Gen. 12–50), and the relationships between them. From a *theological* point of view, the fact that these narratives put so much emphasis on the "seed" (i.e., the birth of the descendants) of the patriarchs—and the history and promises regarding that seed—is also particularly suited to the genealogical emphasis in the book. From a *historical and cultural* point of view, the fact that the patriarchal narratives are presented as genealogical history imbedded within this literary, genealogical framework corresponds to the kinship-based enclosed-nomadic pastoral culture reflected in the patriarchal narratives themselves.

Genealogy and Genealogical History in Genesis

It is well known that the book of Genesis as a whole is arranged within a literary framework of introductory "generations" (*tôlᵉdôt,* from the verb *yld* "to give birth") formulas strewn throughout the book, some of which introduce genealogies and others the main narrative sections of the book.

It is readily apparent that the overriding concern in the composition of the patriarchal narratives is the family lineage from which Israel originated as a people long before they became a nation, and which continued as a live history into their national existence as well.

Genealogies are oral or written expressions of the descent of persons from their parents and/or previous ancestors. There are two types of genealogies in the book of Genesis: linear and segmented. *Linear genealogies* follow a single line of descent from father to son (or later descendant) to a particular ancestor without including the names of the other sons (see, e.g.,

Table 5.1

Genesis 2:4	"This is the account of [lit. *"These* are the *generations* of"] the heavens and the earth when they were created." (NIV)	*NARRATIVE #1*
Genesis 5:1	"This is the written account of [lit. *"This is the book of* the generations of "] Adam's line."	*GENEALOGY*
Genesis 6:9	"This is the account of Noah."	*NARRATIVE #2*
Genesis 10:1	"This is the account of Shem, Ham and Japheth, Noah's sons, who themselves had sons after the flood."	*GENEALOGY*
Genesis 11:9	"This is the account of Shem."	*GENEALOGY*
Genesis 11:27	"This is the account of Terah."	*NARRATIVE #3*
Genesis 25:12	"This is the account of Abraham's son Ishmael, whom Sarah's maidservant, Hagar the Egyptian, bore to Abraham."	*GENEALOGY*
Genesis 25:19	"This is the account of Abraham's son Isaac."	*NARRATIVE #4*
Genesis 36:1	"This is the account of Esau [i.e., Edom]."	*GENEALOGY*
Genesis 36:9	"This is the account of Esau the father of the Edomites in the hill country of Seir."	*GENEALOGY*
Genesis 37:2	"This is the account of Jacob."	*NARRATIVE #5*

Gen. 5:1–32; 11:10–26; 36:31–39). They are concerned with showing the lineage of a particular individual back to the specific ancestor through a sequence of ancestors, usually for purposes of showing one's significance, status, or authority. *Segmented genealogies* follow more than one line of descent from an ancestor down through the generations, so that there are several branches of the lineage in each generation (see, e.g., Gen. 10; 25:12–18; 36:1–30, 40–43; cf. also 11:27–30; 22:20–24; 24:15; 38:29–30 with Ruth 4:12, 18–22; and Gen. 46:8–27 with 48:1 and then Exod. 1:1–7). The purpose of this kind of genealogy is to link a person into a web of defined relationships in the current generation. Based on this web of kinship relationships, a particular person has a certain status, as well as rights and privileges in such matters as authority, position, responsibilities, and inheritance.[2]

This overriding focus on genealogical history takes us beyond literary considerations into the major historical and cultural issues of the patriarchal narratives. It is well known that "genealogical history" is characteristic of "nonliterate societies" that "recount history" through specified "relations of blood and kin," which serve as "the basis for recounting stories about" the known individuals in the history of the lineage.[3] The narratives

---

2. Robert R. Wilson, *Genealogy and History in the Biblical World* (New Haven, Conn.: Yale University Press, 1977), 9, 18, 37–47, 133–135. The occurrence of the formula in Genesis 2:4a ("these are the generations of *the heavens and the earth*") is of special interest. There is some debate about whether it concludes Genesis 1:1–2:3 or introduces Genesis 2:4b–4:26. In general, these formulas introduce what follows, linking it to what precedes. This is probably also the case in Genesis 2:4. However, unlike the other occurrences in Genesis and in the rest of the Hebrew Bible, in the context of Genesis 1 and 2 it is metaphorical and even somewhat awkward (see pp. 127–28). It emphasized the overall kinship and genealogical focus of historical consciousness in ancient Israel as it is reflected in the remainder of the book of Genesis and beyond (see, e.g., Exod. 1:1–5; and then *tôlᵉdôt* ["generations"] again in Exod. 6:16, 19; Num. 3:1; Ruth 4:18–22; and 1 Chron. 1–9; esp. 1:28–29a). See, for example, the discussion and literature cited in T. D. Alexander, "Genealogies, Seed and the Compositional Unity of Genesis," *TynBul* 44 (1993): 258 n. 8; and Duane A. Garrett, *Rethinking Genesis: The Sources and Authorship of the First Book of the Pentateuch* (Grand Rapids: Baker, 1991), 98–99. The Hebrew term for "generations" *(tôlᵉdôt)* also occurs in Genesis 10:32 and 25:13, but not in the formulaic pattern "(these are/this is the book of) the generations of . . ." found in the other eleven passages cited above. At the end of the table of nations in Genesis 10:32 ("These are the clans of Noah's sons, according to their *lines of descent [tôlᵉdôt],*" NIV) it refers back to the formula in 10:1 and in 25:13 it introduces the names of the sons of Ishmael "in their *order of birth (tôlᵉdôt)*" (cf. NIV, NASB, NRSV).

3. See, for example, Chris Gosden and Gary Lock, "Prehistoric Histories," *World Archaeology* 30 (1998): 5. See also the helpful analysis and application of this anthropological information to the Israelites in their ancient Near Eastern context in Frank Moore Cross, "Kinship and Covenant in Ancient Israel," in *From Epic to Canon: History and Literature in Ancient Israel* (Baltimore: Johns Hopkins University, 1998), 3–11. I am deeply indebted to my colleague Dr. Robert Priest,

of Genesis 12–50 present the patriarchs as enclosed-nomadic pastoral sheikhs whose life and culture was based in family and clan kinship. "Enclosed nomads" were pastoralists constituted and organized on the basis of kinship, who lived and moved about, often as a powerful force, amid a regional network of urban centers with which they had various kinds of relationships: filial, political, residential, and otherwise.[4]

Consider the introductory lines of Abram's commission in Genesis 12:1 ("go forth from your homeland, your kin, and your father's house"), the description of the reflections of patriarchal lifestyle in Genesis 12–50 (see, e.g., the various elements of kinship, pastoralism, and relationships with urban centers in Gen. 12:6–8; 13:3, 18; 14:13–14; 18:1; 20:1; 21:22–34; 22:19; 23:1–6; 24:1–4; 26:26–33; 29:1–3; 31:17–24; 33:18–34:2; 35:1–8, 16–21; 37:1, 12–17; 46:5–7; 47:1–6), and the overall concern for having a legitimate heir and continuing posterity within the larger clan system from the beginning to the end of the patriarchal stories (with regard to Abraham, e.g., see the mention of Sarai's barrenness in Gen. 11:30 and his getting of a wife for Isaac from within his native kinship system in Gen. 24:4). The familial, cultural, social, national, and historical consciousness of ancient Israel was based in their genealogical history and the stories that fill out that history, especially the patriarchal narratives of Genesis 12–50. The promises to their patriarchal fathers were no small matter to the later people of Israel (see, e.g., Exod. 2:24; 3:6; 32:13–14; Lev. 26:42; Deut. 1:8; 7:7–11; 26:3–5; Josh. 24:2–4; 1 Kings 18:36; 2 Kings 13:22–23; 1 Chron. 29:17–19; 2 Chron. 30:6; Neh. 9:7–8).

Historical-Critical Scholarship and the Patriarchs

Although there were some precursors before and during medieval times, the history of the historical-critical method in Old Testament scholarship

---

professor of mission and anthropology at Trinity Evangelical Divinity School, for his help in collecting the most useful published materials about kinship, genealogy, and genealogical history from the field of cultural anthropology. For a review of the current state of kinship studies in cultural anthropology, see Michael G. Peletz, "Kinship Studies in Late Twentieth-Century Anthropology," *Annual Review of Anthropology* 24 (1995): 343–72.

4. With regard to "enclosed nomadism" and the patriarchs, see now the very helpful up-to-date summary of scholarly literature and current status of the discussion, and the proposal made in Daniel E. Fleming, "Mari and the Possibilities of Biblical Memory," *Revue d'Assyriologie* 92 (1998): 41–78, esp. 41–48, 56–59, 71–78.

is largely bound up with the development of Western thought since the "Renaissance." The Renaissance was a transitional movement in Europe that brought us from the medieval period into modern times. It consisted largely of a humanistic renewal of interest in the Greek classics, and was marked by rapid developments in the arts and literature, and even the beginnings of modern science. This movement began in Italy in the fourteenth century and spread throughout Europe into the seventeenth century.

Both the Reformation and the historical-critical method were, to a significant degree, children of the Renaissance. Both were radical, but in different ways. This included—but was not limited to—their respective views of the basic nature of the Bible, and the proper way to read and study it.[5] The Reformation principle of *sola scriptura* called for a sincere belief in the truth and reliability of the Bible in faith and practice. This included historical reliability. However, it was not long before the Reformation of the sixteenth century gave way to the Post-Reformation of the seventeenth century and the new challenges that came with it: the Catholic Counter-Reformation and the subjectivism, rationalism, new philosophies, new scientific discoveries, and radical skepticism that led to the eighteenth-century "Enlightenment."

The Tradition of Skepticism

Benedict de Spinoza (1632–1677) is one of the most well-known skeptics of the Renaissance period. He was Jewish and reacted primarily against Jewish attempts to reconcile the Bible, science, and philosophy. In his efforts he made use of works by Francis Bacon (1561–1626), Thomas Hobbes (1588–1679), and especially the extreme skepticism and subjectivism of René Descartes (1596–1650). He was also familiar with the writings of Isaac de La Peyrère (1596?–1676), who had a Calvinist background but eventually attached himself to a group of intellectual skeptics in Paris.[6] Among other things, Spinoza denied that Moses authored the Pentateuch. His two main passions in regard to the scholarly study of the Bible were to demonstrate convincingly: (1) the need to subject the Bible to historical-critical

---

5. John H. Hayes and Frederick C. Prussner, *Old Testament Theology: Its History and Development* (Atlanta: John Knox, 1985), 12–34.
6. Ibid., 26–27.

examination like any other ancient document, and (2) the need to recognize that the biblical account of history and its view of reality could no longer accommodate the growing body of knowledge in the sciences, history, and culture.[7]

From its beginning, therefore, the historical-critical method in the study of the Hebrew Bible was infected with what one might call a "tradition of skepticism." Over the course of time, skepticism about the historical reliability of the Bible led to a multitude of theories regarding the historicity of the patriarchs and the nature of the patriarchal narratives, as well as most of the rest of biblical history. The historical-critical method itself, in fact, "cut its teeth" on the book of Genesis. Unfortunately, the history of Old Testament scholarship since the rise of the historical-critical method includes periods of time during which the confidence of critical scholars in some kind of "scholarly consensus" far outstripped the evidence available to support it. The theoretical consensus of the day attained the status of established fact in the minds of many. In the current environment, however, we have numerous proposals about the composition of the patriarchal narratives adhered to by scholars who are equally convinced of their mutually contradictory views.

The Patriarchal Narratives from Wellhausen to Today

Julius Wellhausen (1844–1918) is well known for his careful articulation and popularization of the "New Documentary Hypothesis"—"new" in his day (the mid to late nineteenth century). Much of his theory holds to the same conclusions as the previous "Old Documentary Hypothesis." What is "new" is that he dated the "P" source as the latest rather than the earliest in the sequence. As is well known, according to this theory there are four major source documents that can be distinguished within the Pentateuch: (1) the ninth-century "J" document (= "Yahwist," called such for his use of the divine name *Yahweh* in the Genesis narratives; the German *J* is commonly pronounced Y), (2) the eighth-century "E" document (= "Elohist," for his use of the divine name *Elohim* in the Genesis

---

7. Julius Wellhausen (1844–1918), one of the most influential biblical critics of the nineteenth and early twentieth centuries, refers specifically to Spinoza as one of the early founders of the historical-critical method. See Julius Wellhausen, *Prolegomena to the History of Israel* (1885; reprint, Atlanta: Scholars Press, 1994), 9.

narratives, never *Yahweh*), (3) the seventh-century "D" document (= "Deuteronomist," for the early version of Deuteronomy, which was supposedly produced in association with the religious reforms of Hezekiah [ca. 715–686] and/or Josiah [ca. 641–609 B.C.], 2 Kings 18–23), and (4) the sixth through fifth-century "P" document (= "Priestly source," for its focus on matters that would have concerned the priesthood in the postexilic period of Israel's history, i.e., after the first return from the Babylonian exile in 536 B.C.). The D document really does not come into the discussion of the patriarchs for Wellhausen.

Wellhausen himself combined J and E into one "JE" source, because he was not confident that E was ever a separate document as opposed to a supplemental layer in J.[8] It is no exaggeration to say that Wellhausen's view dominated Old Testament historical-critical scholarship from the end of the nineteenth century through most of the twentieth century. Specifically in regard to the patriarchs and the patriarchal narratives, he writes the following:

> The materials here are not mythical but national, and therefore more transparent, and *in a certain sense more historical* [as opposed to the primeval narratives of Genesis 1–11, which are mythical in his view]. It is true, we attain to *no historical knowledge of the patriarchs,* but only of *the time when the stories about them arose in the Israelite people;* this later age is here unconsciously projected, in its inner and its outward features, into hoar antiquity, and is reflected there like a glorified mirage.[9]

In the next twenty pages or so he develops his view of the JE versus the P version of the patriarchal narratives. He recognizes that "The skeleton of the patriarchal history consists . . . of ethnographic genealogy," and argues that the groupings of the various elements of the genealogy depend "to some extent on the point of view of the genealogist, or even his likings and antipathies."[10] The writings, therefore, reflect the age of their writing, not that of the situation and events themselves.

---

8. Ibid., 8–10, esp. n. 2.
9. Ibid., 318–19 (emphasis mine).
10. Wellhausen, *Prolegomena to the History of Israel,* 319.

As a result, from a literary-compositional point of view, we have two major issues to deal with: (1) the separation of the P from the JE material, and (2) the later date of P as compared to JE in the patriarchal narratives. A review of scholarship in the study of Genesis will show that these two features of the historical-critical consensus have remained stable throughout the twentieth century, even up to the present day.[11] This is true even though there have been a number of fairly radical departures from the traditional historical-critical approach since the 1970s.[12]

Currently, John Van Seters refers to pre-Yahwistic units of patriarchal tradition that the Yahwist (J) brought together to create a unified and theologically motivated historiography of the patriarchs during the Babylonian exile. The Yahwist composed his work as a prologue to the Deuteronomistic history (Deuteronomy–2 Kings), which was already known to him. Moreover, following Frank Moore Cross, he takes P to be "a secondary supplement to that of J and not an independent composition" (similar to Wellhausen's view of E described above). Accordingly, "the Priestly corpus does not represent a different genre from that of J, but merely a later stage in the development of the Pentateuch's historiography."[13] Also, Rolf Rendtorff has initiated, and Erhard Blum has developed in some detail, the alternative view that someone close to the traditions of the Deuteronomist and his theology (i.e., one who already knew the Deuteronomistic history, Joshua through Kings) authored the first unified writing of the patriarchal narratives. The priestly reworking of this "Deuteronomistic Pentateuch" followed shortly thereafter, both of them in the early postexilic period, and was "authorized by the Persian government as the official law for the Jewish ethnos within the Persian empire."[14]

---

11. For example, see Hermann Gunkel (1862–1932), *Genesis,* trans. Mark E. Biddle (Macon, Ga.: Mercer University Press, 1997), xvii, esp. lxxvi–lxxxv, and 156, 258, 372, 465–66; Gerhard von Rad (1901–1971), *Old Testament Theology,* trans. D. M. G. Stalker (San Francisco: HarperCollins, 1962), 1:232–34; Martin Noth (1902–1968), *A History of Pentateuchal Traditions,* trans. Bernhard W. Anderson (Atlanta: Scholars Press, 1981), 10–11, and n. 20; and the discussion of the more recent works by John Van Seters and Rolf Rendtorff below.
12. See the helpful summary up through 1997 in Rolf Rendtorff, "Directions in Pentateuchal Studies," *CurBS* 5 (1997): 48–58.
13. John Van Seters, *Prologue to History: The Yahwist as Historian in Genesis* (Louisville: Westminster/John Knox, 1992), 4–5, 328 (and the discussion on pp. 330–33 as a whole). See also his helpful chart of literary sources in the Abraham traditions in John Van Seters, *Abraham in History and Tradition* (New Haven, Conn.: Yale University Press, 1975), 313.
14. See Rendtorff, "Directions in Pentateuchal Studies," 51–52, and the literature cited there. See also his earlier summary of the details in Rolf Rendtorff, *The Old Testament: An Introduction* (Philadelphia: Fortress, 1986), 134–39, 143–44, 157–63.

The situation at the beginning of the twenty-first century, therefore, is that there has been a definite turn to the final form of the text, that is, synchronic analysis of the canonical form of the text, even while the diachronic analysis of the history of the composition of the Pentateuch is also taken seriously.[15] The two main features of the historical-critical analysis of the patriarchal narratives continue to be maintained. First, it is taken for granted that the P element of the accounts can be distinguished and separated from the J narratives. Second, in spite of the progressively later dating of the first comprehensive writing of the patriarchal history in the scholarly tradition, whether, for example, by an exilic J (Van Seters) or a postexilic adherent to D (Rendtorff and Blum), it is virtually always assumed that P is a later reworking of that first comprehensive writing. This is true whether P is conceived of as another somewhat continuous documentary source that was combined by redaction to the earlier source, a redaction or historiographic extension of the earlier source based on traditional priestly lore (oral and/or written), or some combination of the two.

In the meantime, however, there are those scholars who take seriously the concept of longstanding oral tradition, a long-term compositional process, and the possibility of real historical memory in the patriarchal narratives. For example, in his magnificent three-volume commentary on Genesis, Claus Westermann accepts the standard historical-critical division between the JE and P materials in Genesis, as well as the relative dating of P later than JE.[16] However, he does not agree with the late date for the first comprehensive account of the patriarchs that is so prevalent these days (see table 5.1 on p. 118). Moreover, based on Robert R. Wilson's work with the biblical genealogies,[17] Westermann rejects the Wellhausenian view, accepted in various forms by later scholars, that the patriarchal genealogies were later literary creations written specifically as a means of binding the patriarchal narratives together. He points out that, from an anthropological point of view, genealogy is a standard part of oral tradition in nonwriting kinship groups, where family and clan lineage and the stories that go with it are central to the identity, historical consciousness, and functioning of the group. We must allow for the

---

15. See Rendtorff, "Directions in Pentateuchal Studies," 57–58, and the literature cited there.
16. Claus Westermann, *Genesis 12–36: A Commentary,* trans. John J. Scullion (Minneapolis: Augsburg, 1981), 35.
17. Wilson, *Genealogy and History.*

importance of oral tradition combined with genealogy in the kind of society reflected in the patriarchal narratives.[18]

Moses as the Historian of the Patriarchs

Those of us who accept the essentially Mosaic authorship of the Pentateuch, including the patriarchal accounts in Genesis 12–50, should take full account of the obvious fact that the Bible does not present Moses as an eyewitness to the times, people, and events of the patriarchal period.[19] According to the biblical account, he lived some centuries after the patriarchs. Moreover, as the author of the patriarchal narratives, he must have written them sometime during Israel's journeys from Egypt to their arrival on the shores of Moab (40 years later). It is not likely that he wrote them before he led Israel out of Egypt (Exod. 3–18), or even before the law was revealed to them at Sinai (Exod. 19–24), the giving of the instructions to build the tabernacle (Exod. 25–31), and the incident of the golden calf (Exod. 32–34).

It is just as unlikely that there were no traditions about the patriarchs known to Moses and to the descendants of the patriarchs who came out of Egypt under the leadership of Moses. Consider, for example, God's words to Moses at the burning bush: "I am the God of your father, the God of Abraham, the God of Isaac and the God of Jacob" (Exod. 3:6a), and then:

> God also said to Moses, "Say to the Israelites, 'The LORD, the God of your fathers—the God of Abraham, the God of Isaac and the God of Jacob—has sent me to you.'"(Exod. 3:15a)

---

18. Westermann, *Genesis 12–36*, 37, 44, 54–56.
19. For a helpful recent discussion of the Mosaic authorship of the Pentateuch, especially as it relates to the book of Deuteronomy, see Daniel I. Block, "Recovering the Voice of Moses: The Genesis of Deuteronomy," *JETS* 44 (2001): 385–408. Regarding the issue of "post-Mosaic" elements in the Pentateuch, see the careful study of Michael A. Grisanti, "Inspiration, Inerrancy, and the Old Testament Canon: The Place of Textual Updating in an Inerrant View of Scripture," *JETS* 44 (2001): 577–98. Although the Bible never comes right out and says that Moses was the original author of the patriarchal narratives in Genesis 12–50, it is clear that he and the people of Israel at large knew a great deal about the patriarchs, the promises to them, and their descent from them even while they were still in Egypt (see the discussion presently, and Exod. 3:6–9, 15–22; 4:5; 6:2–9, 14–27; 32:13; Deut. 9:5). In light of this familiarity with the patriarchs in Moses' day, and their importance to the nation of Israel, it is most unlikely that Moses would have left the people without a written record of the patriarchs. The history of the patriarchs and the promises to them were too pivotal to the national existence, deliverance, and destiny of Israel as it was understood even in the wilderness period. Moreover, the Mosaic origin of the patriarchal stories and the Lord's commands to the patriarchs is either assumed or asserted in certain places in the New Testament (see esp. John 7:21–24; Acts 15:1 [cf. 6:11–14]; 21:21).

Whether Moses knew the patriarchal stories in Genesis 12–50 from oral traditions or written records, a combination of the two, and perhaps direct revelation from God, is unknown to us. We simply have no clear indication of one or the other. We know that the use of written sources was a factor in the writing of Scripture in some instances, including the Pentateuch, as the reference to "the Book of the Wars of the LORD" in Numbers 21:14 makes clear.

We should also keep another factor in mind. Moses wrote from a priestly, Levitical point of view. He himself was a Levite, the brother of Aaron, who was to become the first high priest of Israel. Moses was the one through whom the instructions for the building the tabernacle were given (Exod. 25–31), he was the inspector who approved the construction (Exod. 39:32–43), he directed the erection of the tabernacle (Exod. 40), he functioned as a priest when he consecrated Aaron and his sons to the priesthood (Lev. 8), and he was the one who received the revelation of the sacrificial regulations (Lev. 1–7).

On the one hand, therefore, whatever "priestly" or national perspective comes through in Genesis 12–50 could easily be due to the fact that Moses himself was writing those narratives centuries later as one who both birthed the nation and wrote from a priestly point of view. On the other hand, however, the genealogies in the patriarchal accounts are probably neither priestly nor Mosaic in origin. Instead, they were most likely part of the traditional conceptual framework within which the carriers of the patriarchal traditions set their family, clan, and tribal kinship stories of family origins and clan and tribal relationships. In other words, the genealogies were most likely passed down to Moses along with their associated patriarchal stories.

There are perhaps some exceptions to this. The most important seems to be the *tôlᵉdôt* formula that shapes the book of Genesis by introducing the major genealogies and the main sections of narrative in the book (see table 5.1 on p. 118). Unlike the other occurrences of the *tôlᵉdôt* formula in Genesis and in the rest of the Hebrew Bible, its use in Genesis 2:4 is metaphorical and even somewhat awkward.[20] One wonders what *"generations of the heaven and earth"* could mean. Elsewhere the formula always refers to the "generations" of *people*. The writer apparently extended the use of the

---

20. See the remarks in note 2 above.

same formula back to Genesis 2:4 because it suited and emphasized the overall kinship and genealogical focus of historical consciousness in ancient Israel, but this is not likely to have been the work of oral carriers of family and tribal traditions (see the further remarks on oral genealogical history below). The extension of the use of the formula back to the primeval section of Genesis was mostly like the work of Moses himself, the goal of which was to link the patriarchal history with creation, cosmology, and world history. The God of Israel is the God of the universe who reigns over all the nations of the earth, not just Israel. In fact, "all the families of the earth (Gen. 10:32) will find blessing" in Abraham (Gen. 12:3b) and in his descendants.[21]

The point is that the data used to support the various historical-critical approaches to the patriarchal accounts does not require anything other than the distance of time, situation, and perspective that stands between the patriarchs and Moses. What the critics have referred to as the J (or D) patriarchal history consists largely of the patriarchal stories and promises as they were passed down or revealed to Moses. Since the patriarchs were heads of families (not yet heads of tribes or a nation), the traditions that Moses used as a basis for writing the patriarchal accounts would reflect their nature and situation as enclosed nomadic pastoralists. Moses, however, brought their stories into a theocratic nationalistic and priestly environment—Israel was to be "a kingdom of priests and a holy nation" (Exod. 19:6). The chart below illustrates the correspondences between the non-Mosaic historical-critical views of the composition of the Pentateuch by Wellhausen and most recently Van Seters, Rendtorff, and Blum discussed above versus the Mosaic authorship view presented in the following chart.

The patriarchal family had grown into a nation, so Moses naturally wrote their stories with that in mind. All history writing is both selective and written from a particular perspective. For example, expressions such as "to this day" are often reflections of the historical perspective in a certain general sort of way. They are "etiological," explaining the historical origin or cause of some current state of affairs. Sometimes that perspective is reflective of the day of the events (e.g., Gen. 48:15), but most often it is either a

---

21. For further discussion of the relationship between the primeval and patriarchal narratives in Genesis, see Richard E. Averbeck, "Sumer, the Bible, and Comparative Method: Historiography and Temple Building," in *Mesopotamia and the Bible: Comparative Explorations*, ed. Mark W. Chavalas and K. Lawson Younger Jr. (Grand Rapids: Baker, 2002), 107–13.

Table 5.2

Non-Mosaic Compositional Perspective	Mosaic Compositional Perspective
a. ninth-century "J" document (= "Yahwist") eighth-century "E" document (= "Elohist") = Wellhausen's JE See also: 1. Van Seters' exilic J 2. Rendtorff/Blum's early postexilic adherent to D	a. Moses *receives patriarchal traditions*—oral and/or written, genealogies plus narratives
b. sixth–fifth-century "P" document (= "Priestly source") = Wellhausen's P See also: 1. Van Seters' postexilic P reworking of exilic J 2. Rendtorff/Blum's early postexilic P reworking of postexilic adherent to D	b. Moses writes as the *leader of the nation* and a *Levite/priest*, e.g., the *tôlᵉdôt* formulas[22]

---

22. This is not the place to attempt to work out all the details of what was passed on to Moses from the earlier oral or written family and tribal traditions of the patriarchs (something like J) as opposed to what he added to the patriarchal narratives as the original author and literary historian of the patriarchs writing from his nationalistic and priestly perspective (something like P). The basic question is this: what would the carriers of the pastoral family, clan, and tribal patriarchal traditions have passed down to Moses in oral or written form, as opposed to what most likely derives from Moses' own hand as the historian of the patriarchs centuries later, who wrote as the one who gave birth to the nation and functioned as the original priest and mediator of God's law in Israel, selecting from and expanding on the received patriarchal traditions from his own point of view under the guidance of the Spirit of God?

For the standard historical-critical consensus regarding what belongs to P versus J (or D), see especially the convenient and easy-to-follow explanation of the P point of view and the content of P in the patriarchal narratives in Anthony F. Campbell and Mark O'Brien, *Sources of the Pentateuch: Texts, Introductions, and Annotations* (Minneapolis: Fortress, 1993), 21–22, 28–35. See also Wellhausen, *Prolegomena to the History of Israel*, 327–42; and for the Abraham narratives only, Van Seters, *Abraham in History and Tradition*, 313.

The discussion begins with the all-important *tôlᵉdôt* formula, which I have treated briefly above, suggesting that this structural framework of Genesis probably arose primarily from Moses' hand. This does not mean that Moses had no preexisting written *tôlᵉdôt* sources at all. On the

later reflection on the eventual and/or perpetual outcome of a particular (set of) historical event(s), or a memorial of it (or them; e.g., Gen. 19:37–38; 22:14; 26:33; 32:32; 35:20; 47:26).[23] Moses naturally selected the stories that were most important to his perspective and the purposes he had as the leader of the tribal confederacy that Israel had become in his own day. Similarly, even though it seems that the patriarchs may not have known the Lord by the name "Yahweh" (Exod. 6:2–8; cf. 3:14–15), Moses had no difficulty with putting that name into the mouth of the Lord when he spoke to the patriarchs, or into the mouth of the patriarchs and their family members (see, e.g., Gen. 14:22; 15:2, 7, 8; 16:2, 5, 11; 18:14). From his point of view and that of the nation to whom the Lord revealed himself as "Yahweh," the God of the covenant, the patriarchal God, was Yahweh even if the patriarchs did not know him by that name.[24]

Historicity, Genealogy, and Story in Genesis 12–50

From the point of view of historical factuality, if the Genesis accounts themselves are to be believed, the kind of life the patriarchs lived as "enclosed nomadic pastoralists" (see table 5.2 on p. 129) would not lend itself to the kind of record keeping that was prominent in the cities, city-states, and empires of the ancient Near East. It is not likely that we will ever find the biblical Abraham, Isaac, and/or Jacob in any ancient Near Eastern sources

---

contrary, Genesis 5:1, "This is *the book of* the generations of Adam," may suggest the use of a written source. Both conservatives and nonconservatives have sometimes extended this by arguing that the formula reflects a whole series of previously existing written sources, a kind of *"tôlᵉdôt* book" (see, e.g., the helpful summary and the proposal in Garrett, *Rethinking Genesis,* 91–106). This is perhaps possible, but the expression "the book of" in Genesis 5:1 is unparalleled in Genesis or anywhere else in the Hebrew Bible. Moreover, the awkward extension of the standard "these are the generations" formula back to Genesis 2:4 (see above) and forward to Numbers 3:1 for the genealogy of Moses and Aaron suggests, to me at least, that Moses himself established the formulaic pattern as a way of structuring his writing of Genesis. The genealogical nature of the patriarchal traditions that he received led him to treat all of Genesis in this way. See more on genealogy and story in family, clan, and tribal kinship societies below.

23. See the helpful although somewhat speculative remarks on "to this day" in the patriarchal narratives in Westermann, *Genesis 12–36,* 51–52. He suggests that they are from the period of the development of tribal tradition, after the development of the oldest layers of the patriarchal family stories, but before the formation of the state. According to the reasoning in the present essay, however, there is no good reason they could not come from Moses himself. Westermann, of course, does not suggest that possibility.

24. See the full treatment of this debated subject in R. W. L. Moberly, *The Old Testament of the Old Testament: Patriarchal Narratives and Mosaic Yahwism* (Minneapolis: Fortress, 1992). See also Allen P. Ross, "Did the Patriarchs Know the Name of the Lord?" chapter 15 of this work.

simply because it is unlikely that they would have ever been referred to in them or that they would have written any themselves. Moreover, the fact that this kind of pastoralist lifestyle was so widespread in the ancient Near East over so long a period of time admittedly makes it difficult to isolate the historical period of the patriarchs on that basis.[25] Therefore, it is not likely that we will ever "prove" the historicity of the patriarchs. We will need to be satisfied with showing the historical "plausibility" of the patriarchs, the patriarchal period, and the stories about them in Genesis 12–50.

Wellhausen developed, promulgated, and popularized his theory among scholars in the nineteenth century, before most of the results of modern archaeological research were available to biblical scholarship. Furthermore, most of the twentieth century was so dominated by the Wellhausenian position that even the advances made in form criticism and tradition history were imprisoned behind the iron curtain of Wellhausen's previous "scholarly consensus." All of this, of course, was done under the longstanding influence of the tradition of skepticism that gave rise to the historical-critical method in the first place. For those of us who are not committed to that tradition of skepticism about the biblical text, many of the associated arguments within historical-critical scholarship before and since Wellhausen have not been convincing.

What we have in the patriarchal narratives is the written form of what would have naturally been oral at least up until the time of Joseph and perhaps even until Moses. A simple survey of some of the major ways genealogy and story are related to each other in Genesis would yield some very interesting and important observations, but there is no space for that here. In general terms, the stories are imbedded within, suspended from, or framed by the genealogies. It is important to take special note of the fact that we really do not know a great deal for sure about this process of transmission. The text itself seems to assume it (e.g., recall the pointed references to the patriarchs in Exodus 2–3, cited above), without making it known to us in any detail.

However, in the twentieth century, cultural anthropologists performed extensive ethnographic research into the relationship between genealogy, history, and story in nonwriting kinship societies that still exist around the

---

25. For a helpful summary of pastoral nomadism in the ancient Near East, see Glenn M. Schwartz, "Pastoral Nomadism in Ancient Western Asia," in *Civilizations of the Ancient Near East,* ed. Jack M. Sasson (Farmington Hills, Mich.: Charles Scribner's Sons, 1995), 1:249–58.

world. In the late 1970s Robert R. Wilson drew much of that anthropological information together with studies that historians had done on genealogies in the ancient Near East in order to bring it all to bear on the issue of genealogy and history in the Hebrew Bible.[26]

Ancient Near Eastern Genealogies and the Patriarchal Narratives

Van Seters points out that the predominantly linear genealogies of the ancient Near Eastern texts are quite unlike the consistently segmented genealogies of the biblical patriarchs in Genesis. Wilson himself admits this.[27] Van Seters suggests that the reason is that the literary tradition out of which the form of the patriarchal traditions in Genesis arose was not an ancient Near Eastern form in the first place, but a late form in the Greek tradition. He refers specifically to the *Catalogue of Women,* where "segmented genealogies are interspersed with narrative." One of the many problems with his argument here, as he himself admits and as others have noted, is that the *Catalogue* ultimately rests "on a number of local oral genealogical traditions." Moreover, he then goes on to mention that "between such oral forms and the *Catalogue* there may have been written versions of the major *stemmata* that made up the basis of the final work."[28] Yet he will not allow this for the patriarchal narratives in Genesis. He wants Genesis to reflect only the final form of the *Catalogue* and thereby ignores the distinct possibility if not probability that for Genesis to take such form would be a natural result of the oral and literary traditional processes that would lead to it, as in the case of the *Catalogue.*

It is of special interest that there are two linear Mesopotamian king lists that begin with a series of ancestral tribal names followed by a list of known rulers, and that they both seem to reach back to the same basic set of West Semitic tribal ancestors. These are the Genealogy of the Hammurabi Dynasty and the Assyrian King Lists.[29] In the Assyrian King Lists this group of enclosed nomadic ancestors is set off from the following names by a line

---

26. Thus, the title of Wilson's book on this topic is *Genealogy and History in the Biblical World.*
27. Van Seters, *Prologue to History,* 197–98; and Wilson, *Genealogy and History,* 134–37.
28. Van Seters, *Prologue to History,* 198.
29. See the convenient translations, introductions, and notes in Alan Millard, trans., "Babylonian King Lists (1.134)," in *COS,* 1:461–63; and idem, trans. "Assyrian King Lists (1.135)," in *COS,* 1:463–65. See also the very helpful discussion of the meanings of these names and their cultural and historical significance in J. J. Finkelstein, "The Genealogy of the Hammurapi Dynasty," *JCS* 20 (1966): 95–118.

that refers to them as "17 kings who lived in tents." The Genealogy of the Hammurabi Dynasty attaches the kings of the Hammurabi dynasty (designated as the "dynasty of Amorites") to a list of nineteen names of previous ancestors who, according to the main editor of the text, J. J. Finkelstein, may have been conceived of as either kings or perhaps better "sheikhs or patriarchs." Moreover, as Finkelstein put it, "It is a phenomenon paralleled in biblical tradition about the origin of the Hebrew and Israelite tribes," and he then adds, "similar beliefs about their own origins are entertained by the modern Bedouin tribes of the Arabian peninsula."[30]

In general, the relevance of these king lists to our present study is limited to two main points. First, even though they are presented as linear royal genealogies, they also allow for a previous patriarchal and/or tribal history before that of the better-known historical dynasties. The kind of shift made from ancestral and tribal life to the dynastic life and history that we find in the Bible can be fruitfully compared to the nonsegmented linear genealogies of these king lists (see, for example, the link *from* Jacob/Israel as ancestral father *to* David as king in Ruth 4:11–12, 18–22). Second, the Assyrian King List "contains extra information, implying the existence of a more extensive record."[31] This "extra information" includes, for example, short accounts of important conquests and incidents about succession to the throne.[32] Thus, it is not beyond the reach of our evidence to propose that a genealogy could serve as the framework or skeleton within which stories could be remembered and sometimes even recorded, in spite of Wilson's remarks to the contrary.[33]

Anthropology, Genealogies, and the Patriarchal Narratives

Recently, several anthropologists have written studies that affirm the possibility of considerable accuracy in both oral genealogical history and its written forms, sometimes including critiques of old studies that were overly skeptical about the historicity of their material. By comparing current oral

---

30. Ibid., 97–98.
31. Millard, "Assyrian King Lists (1.135)," in *COS*, 1.463.
32. Ibid., 464–65. Cf. Mark W. Chavalas, "Genealogical History as 'Charter': A Study of Old Babylonian Period Historiography and the Old Testament," in *Faith, Tradition, and History: Old Testament Historiography in Its Near Eastern Context,* ed. A. R. Millard, James K. Hoffmeier, and David W. Baker (Winona Lake, Ind.: Eisenbrauns, 1994), 115–16.
33. Wilson, *Genealogy and History,* 135.

genealogical information with written records from the Dutch annals, James Fox has shown that Indonesian oral tribal genealogies and the oral royal narratives that are told in relation to them retain a great deal of historically accurate information over a period of four hundred years.[34] He raises a challenge, therefore, against the tradition of skepticism in anthropological circles regarding the historicity of genealogies and genealogical narratives. Judith Irvine does the same for the Wolof tribal genealogies in Senegal (Africa), although she argues that the emphasis on historical accuracy in that case is due to the importance of the caste system in Wolof society. Accurate genealogies are necessary for the function of the caste system.[35]

Most importantly, Andrew Shryock's recent study of genealogy in modern day Jordanian Bedouin culture includes a forceful attack on those who argue that "tribal historicity" is not to be taken seriously because it is oral and, therefore, by definition, not historically accurate. He found that the genealogies themselves as well as many of the genealogical stories that tribesmen told him in 1989–1990 were told in "roughly the same form" to other researchers since 1812, whose records he consulted. Thus, "tribal history was a *received* tradition [*not* an invented one], a rich canon of memorized stories and poems, most of them demonstrably old."[36] The "tribal mentality" of the Bedouin "is intrinsically historical" even though it has been maintained over the centuries in oral form. It is true that each oral performance of a genealogy will differ from all others, but this does not necessarily make them inaccurate. The same genealogy or story can be told from different points of view, depending on the make up of the audience, without becoming inaccurate.

There have been numerous well-founded and well-argued studies that, to one degree or another, have made a case for the historical accuracy of the patriarchal genealogies and narratives, and the historical reality of the patriarchal period in Israel's history. For example, Kenneth A. Kitchen has recently collected data and made arguments for the patriarchs and the patriarchal age in the early second millennium B.C. based on comparisons of

---

34. James J. Fox, "A Rotinese Dynastic Genealogy: Structure and Event," in *The Translation of Culture: Essays to E. E. Evens-Pritchard,* ed. T. O. Beidelman (London: Tavistock Publications, 1971), 37–77.
35. Judith Irvine, "When Is Genealogy History? Wolof Genealogies in Comparative Perspective," *American Ethnologist* 5 (1978): 651–74.
36. Andrew Shryock, *Nationalism and the Genealogical Imagination* (Berkeley: University of California Press, 1997), 23, 25, with the logic developed on pp. 20–25.

patriarchal practices with the Code of Hammurabi (1792–1750 B.C.), the historical structure and content of treaties and covenants through the centuries, references that indicate geo-political conditions in the ancient Near East that could have been current only in the early second millennium, Egyptian references in the patriarchal narratives that confirm the same date, the "Amorite imperfective" names of Isaac, Jacob, and Joseph that were most prevalent in the early second millennium, the social world of the patriarchs, and the kind of narratives that constitute the patriarchal stories of Genesis. He argues that the biblical chronology and narratives are, therefore, generally reliable historically.[37]

Others come at the subject differently, with a view toward establishing the *relative* historical foundation and usefulness of the patriarchal accounts in Genesis. There are many different variations of this. Abraham Malamat, for example, is a Mari scholar who concludes that "Mari is not the Patriarchs, but it is of their world and it is closer to them than any other extrabiblical source."[38] He conceives of the patriarchal account in Genesis as a "reflective, theorizing" account, not historically accurate in any specific detail, but also not "a deliberately fabricated tradition."[39] In essence, the Mari materials provide a helpful picture of the kind of world reflected in the patriarchal narratives. This includes various elements of the tribal enclosed nomadic pastoral lifestyle that they lived, among other things.

Daniel Fleming takes this a step further when he argues that the patriarchal way of life, combined with the name of "Benjamin" for one of the sons of Jacob (later a tribe), reflects a distant historical memory among the Israelites that at least part of their group had historical connections back to the "Yaminites" (i.e., the *Binû-Yamina*), a tribal group directly referred to in the Mari texts and associated with the region of Haran in upper Mesopotamia (cf. Gen. 11:31; 24:10; 29:4–5; etc.). He also observes that, although much of the population of the Mari Yaminites occupied villages, they called "their population of mobile pastoralists a *hibrum*," which he takes to be related to the biblical term ʿibrî "Hebrew" (see, e.g., Gen. 14:13).[40]

---

37. K. A. Kitchen, "The Patriarchal Age: Myth of History?" *BAR* 21, no. 2 (March–April 1995): 48–57, 88–95.
38. Abraham Malamat, *History of Biblical Israel: Major Problems and Minor Issues* (Leiden: Brill, 2001), 27.
39. Ibid., 14.
40. Fleming, "Mari and the Possibilities of Biblical Memory," 71–78.

Conclusion

What the nonconservative historical-critical scholar senses and articulates in various ways in the form of the two points of the historical-critical consensus that still survive today—a distinction between J and P, and the lateness of P as compared to J—is taken in this essay to reflect something else: the difference of perspective between Moses as the later writer of Genesis 12–50 and the patriarchal traditions that were passed down to him in oral and/or written form. However, what such scholars would see as P is not always from the hand of Moses. For example, the genealogies belong with the stories from the start. The *tôlᵉdôt* framework of the book of Genesis may have come from Moses as a way of shaping the entire book, but in light of the anthropological data described and applied above, it is hard to imagine such stories being passed down without the genealogical lineage being part of it.

Of course, this approach to the composition of the patriarchal narratives (and the Pentateuch as a whole) will not meet with the approval of those who are committed to skepticism about the historical existence of the patriarchs and Moses. Nevertheless, those of us who are committed to—or even those open to the possibility of—their historicity will do well to take seriously the historical, cultural, and theological distance between the patriarchs and Moses as the Hebrew Bible presents it. We should think through the significance of the fact that Moses received ancient traditions and shaped them into the essential form in which we have them now in Genesis 12–50. He is the author of the patriarchal accounts, but he most likely used sources in authoring them. This is part of history writing inside and outside of the Bible, Old Testament and New Testament alike (see, e.g., Luke 1:1–4).

We believe that the Holy Spirit of God guided the writers along in the composition of the literature we know as Scripture so that they wrote both accurately on the historical level and meaningfully on the theological level. This does not mean, however, that we should ignore the process through which this happened, as if God simply dropped it into their laps fully written. He took the writers and the compositions through a process that often included the use of sources, oral and/or written. Sometimes the text reflects or cites the materials, or even remarks on the process (see, e.g., Num. 21:14 and Prov. 25:1). If we take all these matters seriously, we will end up in a place where we can show that those observations and arguments based on historical-critical investigation that are legitimate can be incorporated into a theory of literary composition that depends on and makes much of the historical and theological integrity of the biblical text.

From a *literary* point of view, Moses was a collector of the patriarchal traditions (genealogies and their associated stories) and the author of the patriarchal accounts in Genesis 12–50. From a *historical* point of view, he wrote as the leader who God used to birth the nation of Israel, which had grown out of the pastoral enclosed nomadic patriarchal family, and continued as a fully developed network of clans and tribes. From a *theological* point of view he wrote as a levitical priest who was the mediator of the theocratic covenant and law in Israel and wrote the patriarchal narratives in Genesis 12–50 with these priestly legislative concerns in mind.

6

Conquest, Infiltration, Revolt, or Resettlement?

What Really Happened During the Exodus–Judges Period?

Carl G. Rasmussen

Over the years many evangelical Christians have grown up with the comfortable idea that during the last 150 years the massive results of archaeological research have basically confirmed their interpretations of the inerrant biblical text. Some have dozed their way through PBS, History Channel, and Discovery Channel specials that portray the Egyptian King Ramesses II as the pharaoh of the Exodus thinking all is well—the Bible and ancient history agree.

But then they may come across a reprint of a *New York Times* or *Los Angeles Times* article in their local newspaper that loudly proclaims that archaeologists and historians now do not believe that Solomon, David, Moses, Abraham, and so forth, ever existed; that the biblical stories are stories that were *created* to help explain the existence of the Israelite, or Jewish, people in a later period—and that at best there *may* be a kernel of truth in the biblical stories. Many Christians will instinctively ask themselves, If the Bible has it wrong with regard to historical facts, how can we trust its teachings about God? In this chapter, we will examine some of the theories that have been proposed about the "origins" of the people of Israel.

In the Old Testament, the saving event that Israel looked back on was the Exodus from Egypt.[1] In fact, this is described as a sequence of events

---

1. For example, Psalms 74:12–15; 114:1–14; Hosea 2:14–15; Jeremiah 2:1–6, along with many other references and allusions.

that includes the oppression of Israelites in Egypt, the Exodus led by Moses, the giving of the Law at Mount Sinai, and disobedience followed by some forty years of life in the wilderness (Exodus–Deuteronomy). After the death of Moses, Joshua was appointed as head of the tribes, and it was Joshua who led the Israelites across the Jordan River, into the land of Canaan, and proceeded to conquer portions of it before allotting it to the various tribes (book of Joshua). The careful reader will note that the biblical text is clear that not all the land of Canaan had been conquered, and that large important portions of the land remained in non-Israelite hands (see, e.g., Josh. 13:1–7; Judg. 1). It seems that Israel was basically confined to the central hill country and the hills of Galilee until the days of King David. During the period of the Judges, Israel continued to grow and settle the land. Probably during most of this period she lived side by side with non-Israelite population groups, but on occasions she was assaulted by, and fought against, a variety of her neighbors (Moabites, Canaanites, Midianites, etc.).

Scholarly approaches to this body of textual material, and the actual events (if any) that lay behind it, are many. John Barton has developed a diagram (see fig. 6.1) that is very helpful in sorting out the relationships between the text, author(s), audience(s), and the reality that the text purports to describe.[2]

Figure 6.1

Historical Events or
Theological Ideas
|
Text
/   \
Author(s)   Reader
Editor(s)   Audience

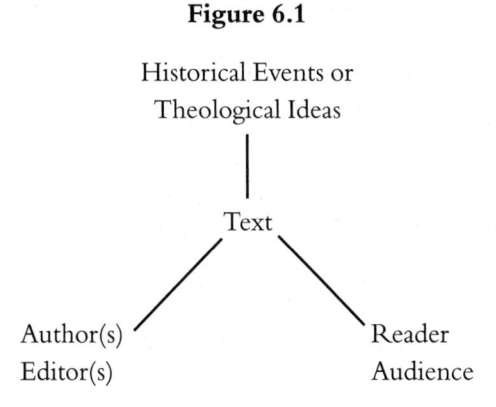

2. John Barton, *Reading the Old Testament: Method in Biblical Study*, rev. and enl. (Louisville: Westminster/John Knox, 1996), 240. Barton is actually adapting a diagram that was presented by M. H. Abrams in *The Mirror and the Lamp: Romantic Theory and the Critical Tradition* (New York: Oxford University Press, 1953).

The center of the diagram is the "Text." This could represent the whole Bible (say-T_{WB}), or a book of the Bible (e.g., Joshua could = T_J), or a portion of a book (Josh. 6–8 might = T_{J6-8}), or any other designated portion of Scripture (T_n). When reading and interpreting the text at hand (T_n)—and only the text—the interpreter is involved with topics such as literary genre, style, figures of speech, etc. The interpreter tries to take in all that the author(s) of the text was trying to say to the original audience(s).

In addition, the interpreter might be interested in investigating how the Text (T_n) under consideration came into existence. Was it composed at one sitting? Over a lifetime? Over several lifetimes? Did the author(s)/editor(s) make use of previously composed documents and/or oral traditions? Who was the original target audience of the Text (T_n)? Can anything be known of the author(s)/editor(s)/audience(s) of any documents or oral traditions that were used in the composition of the Text? At some point, the skilled interpreter will ask if ultimately such things can be known, and if they are important.

In historical studies, evangelical authors such as Merrill,[3] Wood,[4] Kaiser,[5] Hoerth,[6] and others have attempted to reconstruct a history of Israel based upon the biblical text. Because of their beliefs in the trustworthiness of the text (the Bible), they believe that it will convey actual truth about the reality it describes—if it has been interpreted properly. It is interesting to note that the historical narrative constructed by these authors is in essential and widespread agreement.

These authors expect that the historical narrative that they construct, derived from Scripture, will indeed match up with "reality"—what actually happened in the past (see fig. 6.2). But what do we know of ancient "reality" apart from the biblical text? This, of course, is where archaeology, and the discoveries of archaeology come into play.

During the past 150 years archaeologists, Egyptologists, Assyriologists, historians, etc., have been extremely active in their respective disciplines analyzing assemblages of artifacts, deciphering ancient Near Eastern texts

---

3. Eugene H. Merrill, *Kingdom of Priests: A History of Old Testament Israel* (Grand Rapids: Baker, 1987).
4. Leon J. Wood, *A Survey of Israel's History,* rev. ed., ed. by David O'Brien (Grand Rapids: Zondervan, 1986).
5. Walter C. Kaiser Jr., *A History of Israel: From the Bronze Age Through the Jewish Wars* (Nashville: Broadman & Holman, 1998).
6. Alfred J. Hoerth, *Archaeology and the Old Testament* (Grand Rapids: Baker, 1998).

and inscriptions and attempting to integrate all the available data into a coherent whole.

Figure 6.2

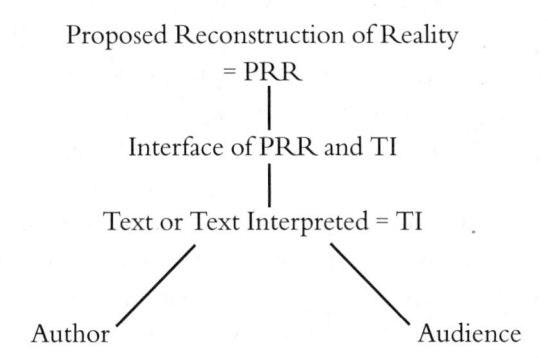

Proposed Reconstruction of Reality = PRR
|
Interface of PRR and TI
|
Text or Text Interpreted = TI
/ \
Author   Audience

The tricky part is that we do not really know what "the real Reality" was. But instead what we have is a "Proposed Reconstruction of Reality" (= PRR_1) of one researcher.[7] Unfortunately PRR_1 may differ considerably from the PRR_2 proposed by another researcher. For example, in reconstructing the contextual reality of the rectangular, basilica-like, pillared buildings discovered at Megiddo (and Beersheba, Hazor, etc.), the question arises as to whether they were used as stables, storerooms, warehouses, or as an ancient shopping mall.[8] Which is the true "real Reality"—$PRR_{stables}$, $PRR_{storerooms}$, $PRR_{warehouses}$, or PRR_{malls}? Do the buildings at Megiddo date to the days of Solomon (970–930 B.C. = $PRR_{Solomon}$) or to the days of Ahab (874–853 B.C. = PRR_{Ahab})? All of the above options have been proposed by serious and significant scholars. As Amihai Mazar has stated, in another but not unrelated context, the ". . . archaeological data lends itself to various interpretations."[9]

It should also be noted that what for one generation may be the "assured results of archaeology" may become completely revised by another generation. For example, Nelson Glueck pronounced that the copper mines of Timnah (in southern Israel) were a major source of wealth for Solomon,

---

7. Author's adaptation of Barton's diagram.
8. All of these ideas have been suggested.
9. Amihai Mazar, *Archaeology of the Land of the Bible: 10,000–586 B.C.E.* (New York: Doubleday, 1990), 328.

and he was enthusiastically followed by many in this belief. However, in the light of new discoveries he revised his opinion, and currently archaeologists maintain that during the days of Solomon no mining activity took place in the region.[10] Glueck's PRR$_{Solomonic}$ has now been replaced by PRR$_{non-Solomonic}$. The point is not to belittle the work of any of the above researchers, but to firmly note that one must really ask, With what "Proposed Reconstruction of Reality" am I, or the person whose work I am reading, attempting to correlate the biblical text? What if this Proposed Reconstruction of Reality changes? What does that do to my interpretive scheme?

In light of these initial observations it is worthwhile to try to describe and evaluate various models that claim to be accurate descriptions of how Israel came into existence in the land of Canaan, noting how they variously interface their respective interpretations of biblical data with their various views of their "Proposed Reconstructions of Reality."

One of the key pieces of biblical data that should be kept in mind in dating the Exodus from Egypt is 1 Kings 6:1, which states:

> Now it came about in the four hundred and eightieth year after the sons of Israel came out of the land of Egypt, in the fourth year of Solomon's reign over Israel, in the month of Ziv which is the second month, that he began to build the house of the LORD. (NASB)

Using Edwin Thiele's dating scheme, we can say that Solomon began to rule in 970 B.C.[11] Thus Solomon's fourth year would be 966 B.C. This would imply, that 480 years earlier, in 1446 B.C., or thereabouts, Israel exited Egypt and after forty years in the wilderness entered Canaan about 1406 B.C. This dating scheme is called the *"Early-Date* Exodus/Conquest Model."[12] If this is true, the "Conquest" took place at the junction of the archaeological eras known as Late Bronze I (1550–1400 B.C.) and Late Bronze II (1400–1200 B.C.).[13]

---

10. Nelson Glueck, "Ezion-geber," *BA* 28 (1965): 70–87.
11. See E. R. Thiele, *The Mysterious Numbers of the Hebrew Kings,* new rev. ed. (Grand Rapids: Zondervan, 1983); and K. A. Kitchen, "How We Know When Solomon Ruled," *BAR* 27, no. 5 (September–October 2001): 32–37, 58.
12. It is espoused by Merrill, Wood, Kaiser, and Hoerth, who are mentioned above.
13. The dates of these archaeological periods follow a widely (almost universally) accepted "Proposed Reconstruction of Reality."

Five Models

The *Late-Date* Exodus/Conquest Model

As modern archaeological excavations got underway in Palestine during the 1920s and 1930s, archaeologists such as John Garstang and William Foxwell Albright, based upon their knowledge of biblical (Textual) data, expected to find burn levels at sites such as Jericho, Ai, and Hazor, places said to have been destroyed by Joshua (Josh. 6:24; 8:28; 11:11).

It turned out that, contrary to expectations, relevant burn levels (ca. 1400 B.C.) were not found at sites such as Tell es-Sultan (= Jericho)[14] or at et-Tell (thought to be biblical Ai). However, burn levels dating later, to about 1250–1200 B.C. (e.g., at Tell Beit Mirsim, Beitin [= Bethel], etc.), were found. These destructions appeared to be concentrated at the end of the Late Bronze II period. In addition it was noticed that Exodus 1:11 states "So they appointed taskmasters over them to afflict them with hard labor. And they built for Pharaoh storage cities, Pithom and Raamses." Since the name Ramesses is not attested much before the beginning of the nineteenth Egyptian dynasty (which began ca. 1320 B.C.), various scholars posited that the enslaved Israelites were involved in construction projects forced upon them by the well-known nineteenth-dynasty pharaoh Ramesses II (1304–1237 B.C.). Further, Nelson Glueck's work east of the Rift Valley (Jordan River) led him to believe that that area lacked a settled population from roughly 1800–1200 B.C. This meant that there was no Sihon, king of the Amorites, nor Og, king of Bashan, for the Israelites to encounter if the Exodus took place around 1400 B.C. (e.g., Num. 21:21–35). One other important piece of data that came into play was the line from the stela of the Egyptian king Merenptah (dated to 1231 or 1207 B.C.), which said among other things that ". . . Israel is laid waste, his seed is not. . . ."[15]

All of this led Albright and many others[16] to conclude that the interface of their reading of the text ($T_{Albright}$) and their Proposed Reconstruction of Reality ($PRR_{Albright}$) implied that the Exodus from Egypt took place about

---

14. Kathleen Kenyon's correction of Garstang's work.
15. John A. Wilson, trans., "Hymn of Victory of Mer-ne-Ptah ('The Israel Stela')," in *ANET*, 378.
16. Names often associated with the theory include G. Ernest Wright, John Bright, Paul Lapp, and Yigal Yadin.

1290 B.C., during the reign of Ramesses II, and that the Conquest under Joshua occurred about forty years later, ca. 1250 B.C., just prior to the date of the mentioning of Israel in the Merenptah stela. This also meant that the period of the Judges was about 200 years long (1250–1050 B.C.). This view was, and still is, accepted by many scholars and is the view that most frequently has found its way into the popular media.[17]

On the textual side, the biblical narrative was interpreted as if the invading Israelites destroyed *numerous* cities—not merely Jericho, Ai, and Hazor.[18] When one attempts to interface this textual interpretation ($TI_{Albright}$) of Joshua 1–11 with the $PRR_{Albright}$, we find that the following biblical texts can not be read at face value and have to be massaged, reinterpreted, or even judged as fictional.

1. The conquest of Jericho (Josh. 6–8) did not happen—for the $PRR_{Albright}$ maintains that no one was living there in 1250 B.C.
2. The conquest of Ai (Josh. 9) did not happen—for the $PRR_{Albright}$ maintains that no one was living there in 1250 B.C. (assuming that Ai = et-Tell[19]).
3. First Kings 6:1 is not to be read at face value. Instead, the modern interpreter somehow gets into the mind of the writer (who lived at least 2500 years ago) and knows that he was really thinking of twelve generations but mistakenly thought that they each were forty years long. But in "reality," generations are only twenty-five years. Thus 12 x 20 = 300 years, getting back to the thirteenth century B.C.[20]
4. The statement of Jephthah, voiced near the end of the period of the Judges—"While Israel lived in Heshbon and its villages, and in Aroer and its villages, and in all the cities that are on the banks of the Arnon, three hundred years, why did you not recover them within that time?" (Judges 11:26 NASB)—is also inaccurate, for at most Israel had lived there 200, not 300 years.

---

17. Some PBS specials, History Channel, etc.
18. But a careful reading of the text does not even imply this—see Eugene H. Merrill, "Palestinian Archaeology and the Date of the Conquest: Do Tells Tell Tales?" *GTJ* 3:2 (1982): 107–21.
19. Cf. Bryant G. Wood, "From Rameses to Shiloh: Archaeological Discoveries Bearing on the Exodus–Judges Period," chapter 12 of this volume.
20. K. A. Kitchen, *AOOT*, 72–73; R. K. Harrison, *Introduction to the Old Testament* (Grand Rapids: Eerdmans, 1969), 316–17; and M. H. Woudstra, *The Book of Joshua* (Grand Rapids: Eerdmans, 1981), 23.

5. The internal chronology of the Bible regarding the life of Moses, the building of the storage city of Ramesses, etc., is inaccurate. For if you follow the internal biblical chronology, you end up with the Israelites constructing the city of Ramesses significantly *prior* to the beginning of the reign of Ramesses II—and the *Late-Date* Exodus/Conquest Model's point was that this work took place *during* his reign!
6. Finally, enough overlapping of Judges needs to be taken into account to compress 410 years into about 200, which is said to be from roughly 1250 to 1050 B.C.

Thus even in its classical form, the *Late-Date* Exodus/Conquest Model did not fit the Proposed Reconstruction of Reality proposed by Albright and others. In fact, this model may have created more problems than it solved. Please note carefully that this is the *Late-Date* Exodus/Conquest Model. Please also note, that when modern scholars jettison the "Conquest Model," in reality what they usually have in mind is jettisoning the *Late-Date* Exodus/Conquest Model—the *Early-Date* version of the theory is not even considered.[21]

The Peaceful-Infiltration Model (a.k.a. The Traditio-Historical Model)

About the same time that the *Late-Date* Exodus/Conquest Model was being developed, Albrecht Alt was proposing what today is sometimes called the Peaceful-Infiltration Model.[22] From Egyptian sources it was noted that during the Late Bronze Age the Egyptian rulers were primarily interested in maintaining control of the coastal plains and the Jezreel Valley of Canaan and that the central hill country—from Hebron in the south to the Jezreel Valley in the north—was sparsely settled. The only major population centers apparently were Hebron, Jerusalem, and especially Shechem. It was also noted that from 1400 to 1350 B.C. these "urban" centers in the central hill country were under military pressure from bands of discontents called *Habiru*.[23] It was also evident from the Bible (Joshua and Judges) that

---

21. See Wood, "From Ramesses to Shiloh," chapter 12 of this volume.
22. Albrecht Alt, "The Settlement of the Israelites in Palestine," in *Essays on Old Testament History and Religion* (Oxford: Blackwell, 1966), 133–69.
23. See the El Amarna letters, passim, W. F. Albright, trans., "The Amarna Letters," in *ANET*, 483–90.

according to these traditions the Israelite tribes were initially also centered in the central hill country and in the hills of Galilee, areas that, based upon the reading of the Egyptian materials, were not densely settled.

What Alt proposed was that instead of a "conquest" as described in Joshua 1–11, that there was a gradual, but growing, influx of nomads (or seminomads) with their flocks from the eastern deserts into the central hill country. These incursions were initially temporary, as the infiltrators searched for pasturage, but eventually they settled in the sparsely populated gaps between the urban centers—thus the "Peaceful-Infiltration Model." Despite its label, we should note that allowances are made for local tribal skirmishes, some of which may be reflected in the book of Judges. It was not until the late eleventh and tenth centuries, with the rise of David and Solomon, that Israelite expansion into the coastal plains and Jezreel Valley occurred.[24] So in a sense, this model argues that settlement was *followed* by conquest, contrary to the normal reading of the biblical text.

Martin Noth continued to develop this idea further and suggested that through time, various tribes formed alliances with one another and that these alliances eventually led to a twelve-tribe confederacy that worshiped at a central sanctuary—at Shiloh.[25] In this process, the various deities that the individual tribes had worshiped were sublimated, so that the worship of Yahweh became prominent.[26] In addition, various tribal traditions were adopted by other tribes, and eventually by the confederation as a whole. The study as to how these traditions developed and coalesced into what is now called the Pentateuch (or Hexateuch) is called "Tradition history." Note, that in Barton's diagram (fig. 6.1), this attempting to assign the origin of—and to trace the development of—these traditions falls under the rubric of "author/editor." However, the various traditions are not only associated with various tribes—for example, Joshua with Ephraim, Moses with Levi, and so forth—but also the tribes were associated with various localities (based primarily upon biblical data) and assigned a variety of roles. For example, some adherents of the Peaceful-Infiltration Model believe that one or more tribal groups may have come from Egypt, but not necessarily at the same time, nor under a unified leadership. Moses, for example, may have led a group of the tribe of Levi out of Egypt and then met Jethro, a

---

24. Even the expansion during the days of the United Monarchy was of relatively short duration.
25. This theory in part was based upon the analogy of the Greek *amphictyony*.
26. There are a number of theories to explain how this developed.

Midianite priest who introduced him to the worship of Yahweh in the desert. Moses, and his tribe, Levi, may have met the tribe of Judah in the Kadesh Barnea or Negev region and introduced them to the worship of Yahweh, etc. This is not the place to rehearse all of the almost infinite permutations of how various traditions developed and were adopted, but a reasonable, brief, "standard" presentation can be found in the work of Eugene Merrill.[27]

The Peaceful-Infiltration Model has a certain appeal to many researchers. Why bother with a 1250 B.C. Conquest as described by the *Late-Date Exodus/Conquest Model* if archaeology has conclusively shown that no one was even living at Tell es-Sultan (Jericho) and et-Tell (thought to be Ai) at that time? If two of the major stories of Joshua 1–11 have no basis in fact, then why believe any of it? As Fritz has stated: "the book of Joshua is of no historical value as far as the process of settlement is concerned. The stories in Joshua 1–11 are etiological sagas, composed during the time of the monarchy."[28] On a positive note, from the perspective of critical scholarship, this view helps to explain how the various "traditions" came to coalesce into what we know as the Pentateuch (or Hexateuch).

Since 1967 Israeli archaeologists have been busy surveying, and to a lesser extent excavating, territory and sites captured in the Six-Day War.[29] These territories are in fact the prime area where the Israelites are said to have settled—in the central hill country where the tribal territories of Judah, Benjamin, Ephraim, and Manasseh were located. Added impetus was given to this endeavor by the State of Israel's project to complete an archaeological survey of the whole country. As a result of these interrelated projects is it now generally accepted—note the new Proposed Reconstruction of Reality—that there are several hundred one-period Iron Age I (1220–1000 B.C.) sites in the central hill country: about one hundred in the tribal territory of Manasseh, one hundred in Ephraim, maybe fifteen in Benjamin, but fewer in the hill country of Judah south of Jerusalem or in the Shephelah.[30] Thus, these surveys have given added impetus to the idea that

---

27. Merrill, *Kingdom of Priests*, 122–26.
28. Volkmar Fritz, "Conquest or Settlement? The Early Iron Age in Palestine," *BA* 50 (1987): 98.
29. Variously called the "West Bank," "Occupied Territories," or "Judea and Samaria." The first of these published surveys was Moshe Kochavi, ed., *Judaea, Samaria and the Golan, Archaeological Survey 1967–1968 [Hebrew]* (Jerusalem: Israel Department of Antiquities, 1972).
30. Mazar, *Archaeology of the Land of the Bible*, 335–36.

some group(s) were settling down in the central hill country right at the time expected by the Peaceful-Infiltration Model.

Peasant-Revolt Model

Even prior to the extensive surface surveys just mentioned, George Mendenhall had proposed that the origin of Israel (ca. 1250–1100 B.C.) was not to be found in a major conquest nor in any movement from seminomadism from the south or the east to settled life in the central hill country, but that "Israel" was basically an outgrowth of the indigenous peasants, farmers, and shepherds who revolted against their Canaanite city-state overlords.[31] He believed that those at the top of the economic pyramid were oppressing those at the bottom, and finally those at the bottom revolted. The rebels eventually coalesced around the worship of the deity Yahweh, whose ethical demands led to a more just and egalitarian society. The hold of urban elite was thus broken, and the city states of the Late Bronze Age were either overthrown or they collapsed.

Norman Gottwald has built upon Mendenhall's work, but has put an even greater amount of stress on economic and social factors that led to the "peasant revolt."[32] In effect, he was filtering his Proposed Reconstruction of Reality and his selection and interpretation of biblical material through a Marxist grid.[33] As to the "whence?" of these rebels, Gottwald, in contrast to Mendenhall, believed that there was movement of disenfranchised peoples from the plains, valleys, and lowlands into the central hill country as they sought relief from the oppression of the urban elite. In addition, it was thought that recent technological developments such as the use of iron tools to aid in the cutting of cisterns, the common use of hydraulic plaster to seal them, and the willingness to terrace the hillsides assisted in this movement to, and settlement in, the central hill country.

Even though a possible "peasant revolt" analogy may be found in the antics of the *Habiru* mentioned in the El Amarna Letters, the complete lack of any biblical material supporting such a theory must bring it into ques-

---

31. George E. Mendenhall, "The Hebrew Conquest of Palestine," *BA* 25 (1962): 66–87.
32. Norman K. Gottwald, *The Tribes of Yahweh: A Sociology of the Religion of Liberated Israel, 1250–1050 B.C.E.* (Sheffield: Sheffield Academic Press, 1999).
33. It should be noted, at the time when Gottwald was writing—the 1970s—the intellectual elite in the U.S.A. was very enamored with Marxist liberation movements in Central and South America.

tion. In addition, from the purely archaeological point of view there is little or no evidence to support the idea of a "peasant revolt." Apart from the hints from the *Habiru,* were it not for certain modern social, economic, and political theories, it is difficult even to see why such a view would be proposed, and today it does not enjoy widespread support.

Agricultural-Resettlement Model

Since the results of modern Israeli surveys in the central hill country mentioned above have become available, all researchers have had to consider their implications. The surveys have located about 250 sites dating to the Iron I Age (1200–1000 B.C.). Most are one acre or less in size and exhibit very similar characteristics. They are not fortified. Many of the houses are "pillared-buildings," often "four-room" houses. The pottery assemblages found in these settlements are composed exclusively of domestic pieces: storage jars, cooking pots, oil lamps, etc. There are very few luxury or imported items. Stone-lined storage pits (for grain) are often located near the houses. The primary sources of water were small nearby springs—although some settlements made use of rock-hewn plastered cisterns. There are no large public buildings such as palaces or temples.[34]

Antecedents of the pottery forms, house styles, cistern building, and terrace farming can be found sporadically in the prior Late Bronze Age.[35] This seems to indicate that at this time (ca. 1200 B.C.) that there was not an influx of new people, whether by conquest or by peaceful infiltration. In addition, these characteristic items continue to grow in use throughout the subsequent period—Iron II (1000–586 B.C.)—by the population group living in exactly the same area, which was labeled as "Israelite."

Many Israelis have been involved in these surveys and in the analysis of the data, but one of the most active, and vocal of them has been Israel Finkelstein. Currently, he views these 250 Iron I settlements as reflecting the third of three waves of settlement in the central hill country that occurred in antiquity.[36] The first two waves were in the Early Bronze Age

---

34. For a concise description of the central hill country see Mazar, *Archaeology of the Land of the Bible*, 334–52; and for details on the whole country during the Iron Age I, see the comprehensive article by Elizabeth Bloch-Smith and Beth Alpert Nakhai, "A Landscape Comes to Life: The Iron I Period," *NEA* 62, no. 2 (June 1999): 62–92, 101–27.
35. Mazar, *Archaeology of the Land of the Bible*, 340, 345.
36. Israel Finkelstein and Neil Asher Silberman, *The Bible Unearthed: Archaeology's New Vision of Ancient Israel and the Origin of Its Sacred Texts* (New York: Free Press, 2001), 111–18.

(3500–2200 B.C.) and Middle Bronze Age II (2000–1550 B.C.) while this third wave began around 1200 B.C. and lasted until the destruction of the kingdom of Judah in 586 B.C.[37] Since there is some cultural continuity with the previous period, Late Bronze Age II, he does not believe that this "wave" is an intrusion of newcomers, but rather it was composed of pastoralists already in the country who began to construct farmsteads and began to grow their own grain crops. He speculates that the recent collapse—in some cases destruction—of the Late Bronze Age city-states triggered this, for with their collapse the pastoralists could no longer purchase needed grain from the economic network that had existed, but now they were forced to begin growing their own grain on a larger scale than previously. He believes that there are hints of this in the few excavated sites that seem to develop from a pattern of houses arranged in an oval shape, with a large open space in the middle for flocks (following a tent camp-like pattern of pastoralists), to a small village-like pattern.[38] Finkelstein writes that "the emergence of early Israel was an outcome of the collapse of the Canaanite culture, not its cause. And most of the Israelites did not come from outside Canaan—they emerged from within it."[39]

How does he know that these settlers were Israelites? First of all, there is the cultural continuity by which the Iron I culture continues and develops into the Iron II Age—a period that all acknowledge as "Israel." But another clue to the ethnicity of these settlers is the lack of pig bones at these central hill country sites. Pig bones are found at central hill country sites before this period, and pig bones are found in other regions of the country during this period, but not in the central hill country during the Iron Age. Thus even though the dietary laws of the Israelites were not written down in the biblical text until hundreds of years later (so Finkelstein believes) "the Israelites chose—for reasons that are not entirely clear—not to eat pork."[40]

In his most recent work Finkelstein continues to critique any and all

---

37. See the chart in Finkelstein and Silberman, *Bible Unearthed,* 114. Although Finkelstein's current viewpoint will be presented here, it should be noted that there are other theories about the origin of the peoples who built these Iron I sites. Adam Zertal, for example, believes that they originated from outside the country—from the east. See Adam Zertal, "The Trek of the Tribes as They Settled in Canaan," *BAR* 17, no. 5 (September–October 1991): 48–49, 75; and idem, "Israel Enters Canaan: Following the Pottery Trail," *BAR* 17, no. 5 (September–October 1991): 28–47. The point is that the same "facts" can be interpreted in a variety of ways.
38. Finkelstein and Silberman, *Bible Unearthed,* 111–13.
39. Ibid., 118.
40. Ibid., 119–20.

alternative theories thoroughly, the *Late-Date* Exodus/Conquest, the Peaceful-Infiltration, and the Peasant-Revolt models—upon primarily archaeological grounds, especially noting how their interpretations of the biblical texts do not fit the archaeological "facts" as now known. Finkelstein's own studies have led him to believe that "there was no mass Exodus from Egypt. There was no violent conquest of Canaan. Most of the people who formed early Israel were local people—the same people whom we see in the highlands throughout the Bronze and Iron Ages. The early Israelites were—irony of ironies—themselves originally Canaanites!"[41] He argues that these stories, and those found in the book of Judges, were basically tales composed in the seventh century, primarily as theological backing for the agenda of the Judean king Josiah (640–609 B.C.). What he says about Joshua basically fits his view for all of the materials recorded in Exodus–Judges, namely ". . . the book of Joshua is a classic literary expression of the yearnings and fantasies of a people at a certain time and place,"[42] namely the era of Josiah.[43]

Obviously Finkelstein does not pull any punches. At the beginning of his book he states,

> "[W]e will see how much of the biblical narrative is a product of the hopes, fears, and ambitions of the kingdom of Judah, culminating in the reign of King Josiah at the end of the seventh century B.C.E. We will argue that the historical core of the Bible arose from clear political, social, and spiritual conditions and was shaped by the creativity and vision of extraordinary women and men. Much of what is commonly taken for granted as accurate history—the stories of the patriarchs, the Exodus, the Conquest of Canaan, and even the saga of the glorious united monarchy of David and Solomon—are, rather, the creative expressions of a powerful religious reform movement that flourished in the kingdom of Judah in the Late Iron Age. Although these stories may have been based on certain historical kernels, they primarily reflect the ideology and the world-view of the writers. We will show how the narrative of the Bible was uniquely suited to further the religious reform and

---

41. Ibid., 118.
42. Ibid., 95.
43. See also ibid., 23.

territorial ambitions of Judah during the momentous concluding decades of the seventh century B.C.E."[44]

The *Early-Date* Exodus/Conquest Model

The *Early-Date* Exodus/Conquest Model has its roots in the biblical texts. Its starting point is an attempt to read/interpret the biblical texts as the original authors/editors intended them to be understood by their original audiences. There is a bias that the Bible does indeed convey true truth about reality—be it theological or historical reality.[45] It grants that the so-called historical books were not written as mere history, but that they have definite theological agendas that they expected their first hearers/readers to believe and act upon. However, even though the books were not written to merely transmit historical data, the data that is conveyed is assumed to be correct-unless conclusively proven otherwise.

It is not the purpose of this article to rehearse all of the features and nuances of the *Early-Date* Exodus/Conquest Model for these can be readily found in the histories of Wood (chaps. 5–9),[46] Merrill (chaps. 2–4),[47] Kaiser (parts 2–4),[48] and Hoerth (chaps. 7; 8; 10; 11).[49] Within the biblical text, the basis of the *Early-Date* Exodus/Conquest Model is 1 Kings 6:1,[50] which implies a date of about 1446 B.C. for the Exodus and a date of 1406 B.C. for the beginning of the Conquest of Canaan under Joshua. This means that the period of the Judges stretched from roughly 1375 B.C. to about 1050 B.C.—the beginning of Saul's rule.

As we have seen above, the *Early-Date* Exodus/Conquest Model was abandoned by many scholars in the 1920s and 1930s in favor of the *Late-Date* Exodus/Conquest Model because it was felt that the mentioning of Ramesses (Gen. 47:11, 27; Exod. 1:11; 12:37), the burn levels at a variety of Palestine tells (seemingly around 1250 B.C.) and the lack of Late Bronze Age remains in Transjordan (*à la* Nelson Glueck) mitigated against it, and

---

44. Ibid., 23.
45. See figure 6.2 above.
46. Leon J. Wood, *A Survey of Israel's History*, rev. David O'Brien (Grand Rapids: Zondervan, 1986).
47. Merrill, *Kingdom of Priests*.
48. Walter C. Kaiser Jr., *A History of Israel from the Bronze Age Through the Jewish Wars* (Nashville: Tenn.: Broadman & Holman, 1998).
49. Alfred J. Hoerth, *Archaeology and the Old Testament* (Grand Rapids: Baker, 1998). This view can also be found in numerous evangelical commentaries and handbooks.
50. See the discussion of this text above, p. 142.

many, including many evangelicals, felt that a *Late-Date* Exodus/Conquest Model fit the known archaeological and Egyptian data better. But as Finkelstein and many others have shown over the last twenty years, the *Late-Date* Exodus/Conquest Model is a terrible fit with the current Proposed Reconstruction of Reality for the Late Bronze Age II and Iron Age I (i.e., 1400–1000 B.C.). Thus the *Late-Date* Exodus/Conquest Model has been abandoned by many scholars in favor of the Peaceful-Infiltration, the Peasant-Revolt, or the Agriculturist-Resettlement Models. In fact, it seems that currently the major adherents to the *Late-Date* Exodus/Conquest Model are some evangelicals! The fact is, not only do the currently archaeological data not fit comfortably with the *Late-Date* Exodus/Conquest Model, but neither do the biblical data, unless major adjustments are made to the internal biblical chronology.

Indeed, none of the three major initial criticisms of the *Early-Date* Exodus/Conquest Model are valid today. The mentioning of Ramesses in the biblical texts has been more than adequately explained.[51] The supposed 1250 B.C. burn levels are really irrelevant as a fair reading of the biblical text will show—only Jericho, Ai, and Hazor are said to have been burned by Joshua.[52]

For Albright, the results of his excavations at Tell Beit Mirsim were among the key factors that led him to a 1250 B.C. date for the Conquest. Unfortunately, he identified Tell Beit Mirsim with biblical Debir. He did this through a contorted exegesis of Joshua 15:48–51, for according to the text, Debir was supposed to be located in the hill country, not in the lowland where Tell Beit Mirsim was located.[53] So one major factor of the "assured results" of archaeology that fed into the abandonment of the *Early-Date* Exodus/Conquest Model was based upon an inaccurate site identification, let along the fact that the Bible does not actually say that Joshua destroyed or burned Debir. And in addition, now Late Bronze Age sites are known in Transjordan—contrary to the pronouncements of Nelson Glueck and the many who have followed him—and contemporary Late Bronze Age Egyptian texts attest to the existence of at least few cites in that area during the Late Bronze Age.

---

51. See Wood, "From Ramesses to Shiloh," chapter 12 of this volume.
52. See Merrill, "Palestinian Archaeology and the Date of the Conquest," 107–21.
53. See Moshe Kochavi, "Khirbet Rabud," *Tel Aviv* 1, no. 1 (1974): 1–33, for a more reasonable identification of Debir—in the hill country of Judah!

We need to state clearly that the original reasons for the abandonment of the *Early-Date* Exodus/Conquest Model are simply not very persuasive today. So it must be asked of all who do not accept the *Early-Date* Exodus/Conquest Model, Why not reconsider it as a viable option? In the histories of Wood, Merrill, Kaiser, and Hoerth strong cases are made that this model—based upon a reasonable reading of the biblical texts—does interface well with a commonly accepted Proposed Reconstruction of Reality based upon archaeology and Egyptology. In this volume Bryant Wood has presented an up-to-date analysis of the interface of the biblical data with PRR, and on the Egyptological side, see the various works of James Hoffmeier.[54] Even all the survey data of the Iron I sites cited by Finkelstein can fit well with the *Early-Date* Exodus/Conquest Model—they are settlements of Israelites who arrived under Joshua and who were settling down during the period of the Judges.

Selected Issues

Modern-Day Models and Perspectives on the Biblical Text

In my view, three of the above views—the Peaceful-Infiltration Model, the Peasant-Revolt Model, and the Agricultural-Resettlement Model—can be considered as radical, for they basically abandon the biblical text as a significant source of information about the Late Bronze or the Iron I Ages, the purported setting of the Exodus, Conquest, and Settlement, or the text is twisted beyond recognition in order to make it fit a preconceived theory.

It is true that persons of faith and persons of no faith have worked—and are working—*side by side* in the archaeological trenches, have spent long hours together scouring the landscape doing surface surveys and processing finds in the dig laboratories, and have shared in the great human endeavor of reconstructing the ancient past based upon archaeological, Egyptological, Assyriological, and other studies. But when it comes to feeding the Bible into the mix of the ancient Near East, Long is right when he says that it is difficult to "continue to propagate the myth of personal ob-

---

54. See, for example, James K. Hoffmeier, *Israel in Egypt: The Evidence for the Authenticity of the Exodus Tradition* (New York: Oxford University Press, 1997), plus a variety of articles.

jectivity"[55]—whether by a person of faith, or a person of no faith. And evangelicals should heed well his comment that

> ... scholars should take some care to insure that harmony exists between the worldview that they themselves embrace and the worldview underlying the methods they employ. Where incompatibility is discovered (e.g., when theistic scholars find themselves using methods that are by definition atheistic), they should either adjust their own core beliefs, reject the incompatible method in favor a method more in keeping with what they believe to be the truth about 'God, the universe, and everything,' or make whatever modifications are necessary to bring the method into line with Reality as they understand it.[56]

These words should be kept in mind when reading and responding to the three radical views presented above. Or, as Eugene Merrill, in whose honor this book is dedicated, put it: "regarding the Old Testament as the Word of God radically alters the task of writing the history of Israel."[57] Thus while the disciplines of historical criticism, the social sciences, and literary criticism are useful in the task of the reconstruction of the historical reality of the past, they must be used from a theistic perspective.[58]

Tentative Proposed Reconstructions of Reality

When we attempt to interface our current interpretation of the biblical text with the currently Proposed Reconstruction of Reality,[59] we must recognize that the currently Proposed Reconstruction of Reality is a tentative reconstruction and not final. See the examples of "Solomon's Mines" and "Solomon's Stables" above. Thus, while current linkings of our current understanding of the biblical text with the current Proposed

---

55. V. Philips Long, "Historiography of the Old Testament," in *The Face of Old Testament Studies: A Survey of Contemporary Approaches,* ed. David W. Baker and Bill T. Arnold (Grand Rapids: Baker, 1999), 168.
56. Ibid., 168.
57. Merrill, *Kingdom of Priests,* 16.
58. See the judicious comments of Long on the proper use of these three disciplines ("Historiography of the Old Testament," 166–75).
59. See figure 6.2 above.

Reconstruction of Reality should be warmly applauded,[60] it must be remembered that the current Proposed Reconstruction of Reality may (probably will) change as new discoveries are made.

Tentative Interpretations of the Biblical Text

We also need to examine continually our reading and understanding of the biblical text. For example, some have interpreted Joshua 1–11 to indicate that "all the Canaanites and other indigenous peoples of Canaan had been utterly destroyed."[61] This, of course, is a caricature of the "Conquest," for the text only mentions the destruction of a limited number of cities,[62] and the text clearly indicates that significant portions of the land of Canaan had not been taken and remained in non-Israelite hands until the days of Solomon (1 Kings 4:7–19).[63] Many examples of inadequate interpretations of the biblical text could be cited but the point is that we should maintain a measured skepticism both towards the current Proposed Reconstruction of Reality and towards our current interpretation of the biblical text.[64]

Origin of Israel

When it comes to the "origins of Israel," we should be skeptical towards those views—the radical three again—that generally maintain that Israel originated (developed) as various disparate tribes came together and coalesced into a unified whole to become Israel. This flies in the face of the biblical genealogies which clearly indicate that Israel descended, in the main, from the ancestral pair of Abraham and Sarah. This is *not* to say that other families, clans, and/or tribes did not join themselves to "Israel"—they did! But to me these are exceptions to the norm, and to disregard the pervasive biblical picture seems unreasonable.

---

60. See the fine essay by Wood, "From Ramesses to Shiloh," chapter 12 of this volume.
61. Finkelstein and Silberman, *Bible Unearthed*, 98.
62. Merrill, "Palestinian Archaeology and the Date of the Conquest."
63. See, for example, Carl G. Rasmussen, *The Zondervan NIV Atlas of the Bible* (Grand Rapids: Zondervan, 1989), 104.
64. See Hoerth, *Archaeology and the Old Testament*, 18–22, on this matter.

Updating of the Biblical Text

In addition, as Bryant Wood maintains below in the case of the name "Ramesses,"[65] we do need to make allowances for the "updating" of the biblical text by later copyists and/or editors. For example, a quick count of the number of cities said to be located in the hill country of Judah totals 38 (Josh. 15:48–60). According to surface surveys of that same area, the first time that there were anywhere near enough settlements to attach 38 names to them was in the eighth or seventh centuries B.C.[66] This seems to imply that the "city list of Judah" dates to this time. Does this demand that Bible is wrong in stating that the allotment of territory to the tribes took place in the days of Joshua (ca. 1400 B.C.)? Not necessarily. Is it not possible that the original allotment to Judah by Joshua was described by the boundary description (Josh. 15:1–12) and that this outline was later "filled in" with the city list (15:13–62)? In other words, we could easily have a later updating of the text here.

Iron Age I Settlements

The recent advances in the number of surface surveys throughout Israel are certainly a welcome development for researchers. The study of the material remains of the Iron Age I (1200–1000 B.C.) and the prior Late Bronze Age (1550–1200 B.C.) have shown that items such as pillared houses,[67] lime-plastered cisterns, and collar-rim pithoi are not necessarily cultural markers exclusive to the Israelites. But does this discovery lead directly to the conclusion that the "people of Israel" developed from the Canaanites? An alternative explanation, more in keeping with the Conquest accounts of the Bible, would be that the Israelite newcomers, after 40 years of impoverished desert/wilderness living, adopted the material culture of the inhabitants of the land into which they were moving. Would

---

65. See the section titled "Twelfth Dynasty (Gen. 47:11, 27)" in the essay by Wood, "From Ramesses to Shiloh," pp. 260–62.
66. See, for example, Moshe Kochavi, "The Land of Judah," in *Judaea, Samaria and the Golan, Archaeological Survey 1967–1968 [Hebrew]*, ed. M. Kochavi (Jerusalem: Israel Department of Antiquities, 1972), 17–89.
67. See most recently Volkmar Fritz, "Israelites and Canaanites—You Can Tell Them Apart," *BAR* 28, no. 4 (July–August, 2002): 28–31, 63; and Shlomo Bunimovitz and Avraham Faust, "Ideology in Stone—Understanding the Four-Room House," *BAR* 28, no. 4 (July–August, 2002): 32–41, 59–60.

such people not learn agricultural techniques from the residents of the land? And if these techniques included the "worship" of Baal—in order to manipulate the weather, and hence the fertility of the land—is it no wonder that Israel was constantly pulled in the direction of Baal worship throughout its history prior to 586 B.C. (see, e.g., Judg. 2:10–23)? Thus the archaeological evidence that seems to point towards the conclusion that the Israelites are not all that distinguishable in the archaeological record (save for the lack of pig bones) is not contradictory to the biblical record.

In conjunction with the plethora of Iron Age I sites in the central hill country, it should be noted that the relationship between the shepherd and the farmer is probably more compatible than incompatible. In all probability a family/clan living on a farmstead was probably engaged in both activities. In the fall of the year, when the grain crops were planted and the rains began to fall, some family members would take the flocks out to the wilderness to the east of the central hill country to the winter pasturage. In average or above average years the vegetation in this area is adequate to pasture flocks. There the flocks would remain during the growing season and until the grain harvest was completed in the late spring or early summer. At that time the flocks would be brought back into the central hill country[68] for the animals to feed on the stubble in the recently harvested fields, and to fertilize them as well.

Conclusion

Given the interest by both scholars and laypersons in the relationship between the Bible and its ancient Near Eastern context, it is hoped that the interested layperson will be more attentive and aware of the view points and models that they are being confronted with. Our task is to look beyond the headlines, snappy book titles, and authoritative pronouncements and to evaluate what is actually being proposed. We must ask ourselves, What view of reality is being assumed or taught? What view of the biblical text is being espoused? What is at stake? And especially, What presuppositions are at the basis of this view point?

There is too much at stake to continue to doze through Sunday newspapers feature articles and TV specials that "trash" the Bible. Although

---

68. Finkelstein and Silberman's (*Bible Unearthed*, 330) description of the central hill country during the summer months as "the green pasture of the highlands" is a bit overstated.

this essay has focused on historical events (recounted in Exodus–Judges), note that in Barton's diagram (fig. 6.1), "Theological Ideas" are placed alongside of them. For many of us, the truth that we try to understand is not composed merely of physical reality, but also includes the unseen spiritual world. The Bible purports to be divine revelation, and many of us expect it to be correct in both areas.

7

THE UNITED MONARCHY

Archaeological and Literary Issues

Hermann Austel

THE ESTABLISHMENT OF THE MONARCHY represented the achievement of two major goals of the Exodus: (1) the establishment of God's people Israel in the land of promise with rest from their enemies; and (2) the establishment of a permanent residence for the glory of God among His people (Exod.6:6–8; 15:13–18). It represented the highest point in the development of Israel after their entrance into the land.

ARCHAEOLOGICAL ISSUES

Historicity of the United Monarchy

Until recent decades, the historicity of the United Monarchy was considered to be a "given," at least in the general outline of its description in Samuel/Kings. Now, however, there is a great crescendo of voices insisting that David and Solomon were no more real than King Arthur. These latter voices are the voices of scholars called "minimalists," "revisionists," or "deconstructionists." Their claim is (1) that there is no archaeological evidence, whether artifactual or textual, supporting the United Monarchy; that the evidence formerly cited in favor of this monarchy must be reinterpreted; and (2) that the biblical material is untrustworthy because of the late date of its writing (in the Persian period or as late as the Hellenistic period). The United Monarchy, by this view, is nothing more than a visionary construct of pious Jewish pseudo-historians who were attempting to provide historical roots for their nation.[1]

Archaeological Evidence for Jerusalem

Much has been made of the fact that there is very little archaeological evidence forthcoming from Jerusalem itself. The claim is that if Jerusalem had in actual fact been the capital of such a kingdom as described in the Bible, there would have to be some substantial on site verification

Nadav Na'aman addresses this problem,[2] showing why so little evidence is available from Jerusalem itself. The monuments and public buildings from the time of the United Monarchy are located under the Temple Mount, and are thus unavailable to archaeologists. Secondly, the ridge south of this area "was continuously settled from the tenth through the early sixth centuries B.C.E.," so that no destruction layers are available to the archaeologist. This area was, and is, built upon bedrock. "Each new city destroyed what was underneath, robbed and reused stones from the earlier buildings, and set its foundations on the solid rock."[3] Thus it is virtually impossible to "read" the archaeological record at this site.

---

1. See the report of the meeting between Thomas Thompson and Niels Lemche, representing the minimalists, and William Dever and Kyle McCarter, representing those who accept the historicity of the United Monarchy, in "Face to Face," *BAR* 23, no. 4 (July–August 1997): 26–42, 66. Some of the basic issues of both agreement and disagreement are stated here. Thompson (p. 28) states that what is represented in the historical books represents the "literary history, . . . the self-identity of peoples in Palestine in the second, first century B.C.E." For Dever (p. 28) these books were edited at this time, whereas Lemche (pp. 28–29) views them as being composed at this time, that the biblical writer "was not really writing history. He was making it up. He did not know the genre of history writing." The writers "were creating mythologies. It has nothing to do with history." Thompson puts the origin of the biblical books in the Persian period or later "when an Israel is possible, at least an Israel of the sort that we have in the Bible is possible." T. L. Thompson speaks of the writings of the biblical historians as providing tradition "in order to bring understanding: to evoke truth, not to recount it" ("W. G. Dever and Biblical Archaeology," in *The Origins of the Ancient Israelite States,* ed. Volkmar Fritz and Philip Davies [Sheffield: Sheffield Academic Press, 1996], 41). In other words, they were not writing true history at all, but a "story of the past that seeks to echo and evoke the truth of reality through metaphor (ibid., 41)." P. R. Davies (introduction to *The Origins of the Ancient Israelite States,* 13) asserts that archaeologists who support the historicity of the United Monarchy are motivated by biases in favor of the biblical narrative. In actual fact, it is the minimalists who have a closed mind with regard to the external verification, whether artifactual or textual, of the biblical record, refusing to admit corroborative evidence as it becomes available.
2. Nadav Na'aman, "Cow Town or Royal Capital?" *BAR* 23, no. 4 (July–August 1997): 43–45. See also Alan Millard, "King Solomon in His Ancient Context," in *The Age of Solomon,* ed. L. Handy (Leiden: Brill, 1997), 44.
3. Na'aman, "Cow Town or Royal Capital?" 44.

Amarna Letters

Na'aman also shows from the evidence of the Amarna letters (fourteenth century B.C.) that "it is dangerous to draw negative inferences from the lack of archaeological evidence."[4] These letters were written by rulers of various prominent cities to Akhenaton (1379–1362 B.C.) of Egypt.[5] Among these cities were the kingdoms of Urusalim (Jerusalem) and Shechem. The rulers of these cities considered themselves to be kings with continuing dynasties, and were so thought of by others (though under the hegemony of Egypt). These cities ruled considerable territory, and Shechem in particular was aggressive in enlarging its territory.[6] Yet, despite the importance of these cities as evidenced by the Amarna correspondence, there is scarcely any evidence whatsoever of their existence in LB II (1400–1200 B.C.) from archaeological considerations. With regard to the United Monarchy, though the archaeological evidence seems to be minimal, it is nonetheless there, and yet the minimalists seek to discredit and discount the evidence that does exist. Kenneth Kitchen has well stated that scholars in nonbiblical disciplines take ancient textual evidence seriously unless proven objectively to be unreliable, but when it comes to the Bible, it is treated with suspicion.[7]

---

4. Ibid.
5. This is according to the "high chronology" accepted by many. According to the "low" chronology (which Na'aman uses), the dates are 1353–1337 B.C.
6. Nadav Na'aman, "The Contribution of the Amarna Letters to the Debate on Jerusalem's Political Position in the Tenth Century B.C.E.," *BASOR* 304 (1996): 17–27. On the matter of the designation "kings," see Na'aman, "Contribution of the Amarna Letters," 21, 25. Modern sociological definitions and concepts may differ from those of the ancient world, but it is important to recognize the concepts of the times under consideration. The same is true with respect to the United Monarchy.

    In addition to the evidence of the Amarna letters, Na'aman adduces the evidence of Nehemiah's building activities. Na'aman ("Cow Town or Royal Capital?" 45) proposes: "The city of the Persian period, described so vividly in the books of Ezra and Nehemiah, is known only from fills and building fragments and is sandwiched between the debris of the Iron Age and the Hellenistic strata."
7. K. A. Kitchen, *AOOT* (Downers Grove, Ill.: InterVarsity, 1968), 29–34. William G. Dever, though ironically discounting the historicity of the Exodus and the conquest as depicted in the Pentateuch and in Joshua, makes the apt comment, in respect to the United Monarchy: "How is it that the biblical texts are always approached with postmodernism's typical 'hermeneutics of suspicion,' but the nonbiblical texts are taken at face value? It seems to be that the Bible is automatically held guilty unless proven innocent" (*What Did the Biblical Writers Know and When Did They Know It?* [Grand Rapids: Eerdmans, 2001], 128).

Areas of Dispute

One area of dispute is population levels.[8] Was there a sufficient population to warrant the concept of a centralized state in the tenth century B.C.? Surface surveys have shown that in the latter part of the Late Bronze Age (1550–1200 B.C.) some 300 small, unfortified, agricultural villages were founded in the central highlands of Israel where none had existed before.[9] These villages had characteristic houses surrounded by grain storage pits with hillside terracing. What is perhaps most remarkable about these villages is the "consistent absence of pig bones in excavated remains."[10] No monumental structures have been found. In the middle of the tenth century there was a sudden change. Holladay points out that the "burnt-out ruin heaps of Hazor, Megiddo, and Gezer . . . were radically transformed into roughly comparable complex fortified governmental centers, each with its own casemated wall system, six-chambered gateway (also called four-entryway gates), . . . and palace complex."[11] This development signals a sudden change from a loosely-knit tribal configuration to a strong centralized governmental system.[12]

Was there sufficient population to warrant the term *state*? Dever refers to numerous leading authorities on statehood, stating that the "most significant criterion for defining 'statehood' is centralization of power."[13] Neither size nor the degree of urbanization are the defining issue. The fortifications at the three cities mentioned above, as well as others, provide strong testimony to the military and political power of the United

---

8. Gary Knoppers, "The Vanishing Solomon: The Disappearance of the United Monarchy from Recent Histories of Ancient Israel," *JBL* 116, no. 1 (1997): 19–44, has given an excellent summary of the present state of inquiry into the matter of the United Monarchy. See also his "The Historical Study of the Monarchy: Developments and Detours," in *The Face of Old Testament Studies*, ed. D. Baker and B. Arnold (Grand Rapids: Baker, 1999), 207–305.
9. John Holladay Jr., "The Kingdoms of Israel and Judah: Political and Economic Centralization in the Iron IIA–B (ca. 1000–750 B.C.E)," in *The Archaeology of Society in the Holy Land*, ed. Thomas Levy (London: Leicester University Press, 1995), 370–71. Also William G. Dever, *What Did the Biblical Writers Know and When Did They Know It?* 110–24. For a more detailed discussion, see William G. Dever, "Archaeology and the 'Age of Solomon,'" in *The Age of Solomon*, ed. L. Handy (Leiden: Brill, 1997), 218–32. See also V. Fritz, "Monarchy and Re-urbanization: A New Look at Solomon's Kingdom," in *The Origins of the Ancient Israelite States*, 187–95.
10. Dever, *What Did the Biblical Writers Know and When Did They Know It?* 113.
11. Holladay, "The Kingdoms of Israel and Judah," 371.
12. See the comparison chart between the Iron I villages and the accounts in Judges and Samuel in Dever, *What Did the Biblical Writers Know and When Did They Know It?* 125.
13. Ibid., 126. He expands upon this theme in the following pages, pointing out that the Mayan state of Tikal had a population of only fifty thousand, and that several Andean states had only

Monarchy. "These were *political* actions designed to seize and hold the land."[14] As to the lack of domestic architecture in Jerusalem, Megiddo, and Hazor of this period, this is in actual fact evidence of a centralized government.[15]

Six-Chambered Gates

The understanding of the six-chambered gates at Gezer, Hazor, and Megiddo as providing evidence for the accuracy of the description of Solomon's building activities as found in 1 Kings 9:15–19 has recently been challenged on two fronts: (1) It is claimed that the discovery of similar gate systems outside the 3 cities undermines the correspondence to the Bible; (2) the dating of the gates is disputed, said by revisionists to be late tenth or early ninth century. As to (1), similar six-chambered gates have indeed been discovered at Ashdod and Lachish. If anything, this fact, as well as the finding of other fortified cities of this time period,[16] testifies to the strength of a centralized government. The reference in 1 Kings 9 concerns the most significant building projects, and certainly does not exclude other undertakings. As to (2), the downdating of these six-chambered entry gates is espoused (among archaeologists) primarily by Israel Finkelstein and David Ussishkin, current excavators at Megiddo. Their claim rests on Ussishkin's dating of pottery found at Jezreel (which is "somewhat similar" to that

---

fifteen to sixteen thousand. See also Holladay, "The Kingdoms of Israel and Judah," 373, for a table of archaeologically discernible characteristics of a state as seen in the material remains of tenth- and ninth-centuries Israel. Baruch Halpern, referring to the claim that the population of Jerusalem was too small to be the center of a real state, writes: "But a town of 5000 in Iron Age was a large one" ("Erasing History: The Minimalist Assault on Ancient Israel," *BR* 11, no. 6 [1995]: 33). Halpern makes note of the fact of the original small population of Washington, D.C., and Brasilia, cities that were likewise built away from traditional places of power so as to free the government from local pressures. See also I. Finkelstein, "State Formation in Israel and Judah: A Contrast in Context, a Contrast in Trajectory," *NEA* 62, no. 1 (1999): 39. A more extensive discussion is to be found in C. Schäfer-Lichtenberger, "Sociological and Biblical Views of the Early State," in *The Origins of the Ancient Israelite States*, 83–94; as well as Baruch Halpern, "The Construction of the Davidic State," in *The Origins of the Ancient Israelite States*, 72–75.

14. Holladay, "The Kingdoms of Israel and Judah," 372.
15. See the section titled "The Issue of Major Cities with Minimal Signs of Residences" below.
16. A. Mazar, *Archaeology of the Land of the Bible*, Anchor Bible Reference Library (New York: Doubleday, 1990), 384–90.

associated with the gate at Megiddo) to the ninth century.[17] Mazar reflects the view of the majority of archaeologists in his response, that "the resemblance of Jezreel to Megiddo has still to be proved, . . . (since) the small amount of pottery published so far from Jezreel . . . originated from several different stratigraphic contexts: some from constructional fills which might contain sherds originating from a pre-Omride settlement at that site."[18] Added to the nebulous nature of the evidence from Jezreel is the fact that the pottery associated with the gate at Gezer "included distinctive red-slipped and hand-burnished (polished) pottery characteristic of the early tenth century. *The equally distinctive wheel-burnished pottery characteristic of the early ninth century at all known sites was conspicuously absent.*"[19] The on-site evidence favors a tenth-century rather than a ninth-century date.

There is a well-documented synchronism between the biblical record of the invasion of Sheshonq (biblical Shishak) and Sheshonq's inscription in which he lists a number of cities he had defeated, including Megiddo and Taanach. Finkelstein downdates the destruction of the six-chambered gate at Megiddo to about 900 B.C., thus removing the synchronism between the Bible and the Sheshonq stele.[20] Most archaeologists, however, associate

---

17. I. Finkelstein, "The Archaeology of the United Monarchy: An Alternative View," *Levant* 28 (1996): 177–87, and in his response to Amihai Mazar's critique ("Iron Age Chronology: A Reply to I. Finkelstein," *Levant* 29 [1997]: 157–67) in "Bible Archaeology or Archaeology of Palestine in the Iron Age?" *Levant* 30 (1998): 167–74. See also Finkelstein's "Ethnicity and Origin of the Iron I settlers in the Highlands of Canaan: Can the Real Israel Stand Up?" *BA* 59, no. 4 (1996): 198–212, in which he takes issue with William Dever's article, "Ceramics, Ethnicity, and the Question of Israel's Origins," *BA* 58, no. 4 (1995): 200–13 (supporting the view that the "several hundred early Iron I hillside country settlements" are "proto-Israelite," precursors of the later United Monarchy). See also William G. Dever, "Archaeology, Ideology, and the Quest for an 'Ancient' or 'Biblical Israel,'" *NEA* 62, no. 1 (1999): 35–52. Ussishkin's dating of the pottery in question depends on his associating it with the Jezreel of Ahab's time (Ussishkin and Woodhead, "Excavations at Tel Jezreel," *Tel Aviv* 19 [1992]: 53). In his *Levant* and *NEA* articles, Finkelstein also argues for an "upper" terminus for Iron II of "mid-to-late tenth century rather than in the early tenth century" as proposed by almost all leading archaeologists (see Lawrence E. Stager, "Canaan, Israel, and the Formation of the Biblical World," in *The Archaeology of Society in the Holy Land*, ed. Thomas Levy [London: Leicester University Press, 1995], 334–44; and Mazar, "Iron Age Chronology," 158–60). Though this is relevant, Finkelstein's evidence rests on numerous unproven assumptions. The more definitive discussion revolves around the dating of the gates, as discussed in the text.
18. Mazar, "Iron Age Chronology," 161. In the same article and in idem, "Will Tel Rehov Save the United Monarchy?" *BAR* 26, no. 2 (March–April 2000) 38–48, 50–51, 75, he argues that there is frequently a continuation of pottery types from one period to another (as appears to be the case with the red-slipped hand-burnished pottery at Tell Rehov, which is found in both tenth century and ninth century contexts).
19. Dever, *What Did the Biblical Writers Know and When Did They Know It?* 132, emphasis mine.
20. Finkelstein, "The Archaeology of the United Monarchy," 182–83.

the Megiddo gate with Stratum VA–IVB, which in turn is contemporaneous with Taanach IIB. Taanach is on Sheshonq's list of cities conquered, and Stratum IIB is the only level that is a viable candidate for Sheshonq's destruction of 925,[21] thus strengthening the synchronism between Sheshonq's raid and the biblical statement in 1 Kings 14:25–28.

The Tell Dan Inscription

In 1993, after twenty-seven years of already fruitful excavations at Tell Dan, A. Biran's team discovered a broken stele with an inscription written in ancient Aramaic. The inscription, dated by Biran to the first half of the ninth century, includes the words "king of Israel," and in the next line "house of David."[22] Though the minimalists challenge the reading "David" here, they have nothing reasonable to suggest in its place.[23]

In 1994, André Lemaire reported his restoration of line 31 of the Mesha stele (also known as the Moabite stone) in which the same phrase, "house of David," appears.[24] This restoration is the result of years of study of the inscription and the squeeze made shortly after its discovery. It has been widely accepted, and provides further extrabiblical evidence from another ninth-century inscription for the historicity of David as dynastic head of the kingdom of Judah.

---

21. See Dever, *What Did the Biblical Writers Know and When Did They Know It?* 134–35; and idem, "Archaeology and the 'Age of Solomon,'" 239–42.
22. See the report by H. Shanks, "'David' Found at Dan," *BAR* 20, no. 2 (March–April 1994): 26–39. Subsequently, another piece of the stele was found. This matches the first piece, and lines 7–9 are read by Na'aman ("Cow Town or Royal Capital?" 46): "[I killed Jo]ram son of [Ahab] king of Israel, and [I] killed [Ahaz]iahu son of [Jehoram kin]g of *Beth David.*" He shows that such a dynastic designation was common in the northwest Semitic kingdoms of that time, and that it also designated a kingdom. Thus "the kingdom of Israel is called *Bit-Humri,* after the name of Omri. The name *Beth-David* for the kingdom of Judah fits perfectly into this ancient Near Eastern usage" (ibid.).
23. P. Davies, "The 'House of David' Built on Sand," *BAR* 20, no. 3 (May–June 1994): 54–55. See the response by A. Rainey, "The 'House of David' and the House of the Deconstructionists," *BAR* 20, no. 6 (November–December 1994): 47; and also Knoppers "Vanishing Solomon," 36. Halpern ("Erasing History," 32) describes the refusal on the part of the minimalists to accept the Tell Dan evidence as a matter of "fighting a rear-guard action for their original denials of the historical value of 2 Samuel and 1 Kings 1–11."
24. A. Lemaire, "'House of David' Restored in Moabite Inscription, " *BAR* 20, no. 3 (May–June 1994): 31–37. He reads 1.31: ". . . the sheep of the land. And *the house [of Da]vid* dwelt in Horonen."

The Stepped Stone Structure on the Eastern Slope of Jerusalem

This massive structure, preserved to a height of 50 feet, and which may at one time have been as high as 90 feet and as wide as 130 feet, was excavated most recently by Y. Shiloh. Its date is disputed, ranging from the tenth century B.C. to the twelfth or thirteenth.[25] If its date goes back to the thirteenth century, it would have been constructed by the Jebusites, then repaired and expanded by David (2 Sam. 5:9), and then again by Solomon (1 Kings 9:15, 24). If it dates to the tenth century, both David and Solomon would have been builders and expanders of the structure. In either case the work would have required extensive resources and governmental organization, thus providing evidence for the United Monarchy.

The Issue of Major Cities with Minimal Signs of Residences

It is charged that Jerusalem of the tenth century shows minimal signs of residential areas. This is thought to be an indication of low population size. Halpern responds to this by saying that the fact that the Megiddo and Hazor of that time were without domestic population[26] is in actuality "strong archaeological evidence for the presence of a central state."[27] It was a policy of the United Monarchy to distance the domestic population from state centers. The Bible frequently speaks of cities with their "daughters," that is, surrounding villages, where the bulk of the population lived (Num. 21:25; Neh. 11:25, 30; Ezek. 16:46–57).

The Presence or Absence of Synchronisms Between the Biblical Text and External Sources

B. Halpern has addressed this issue in a very convincing manner.[28] Though he accepts the widely-held view that Samuel/Kings were written in the Persian or Hellenistic periods, he demonstrates that the writer(s)

---

25. See *BAR* 24, no. 4 (July–August 1998), for several articles with contradictory views as to the dating of this structure. See also R. D. Patterson and H. J. Austel, *1, 2 Kings,* EBC, rev. ed. (Grand Rapids: Zondervan, forthcoming) at 1 Kings 9:15–24, for a discussion of the structure, and its possible connection with the "Millo."
26. Halpern, "Origins," 73; and idem, "Erasing History," 33. See also Dever, "Archaeology and the 'Age of Solomon,'" 227.
27. Halpern, "Erasing History," 33.
28. Ibid., 25–35, 47.

had access to accurate sources, and that the texts must not be dismissed out of hand as though they were mostly fictional. He provides an extensive table of synchronisms with external sources.[29] These synchronisms show that the writer, at whatever time he did his work, had access to sources contemporary with the events described.[30] Not only does the writer report accurately on Judean and Israelite kings, but on foreign kings as well. "There is not much doubt that the archaeological record of the eighth–sixth centuries comports in almost every particular with the general political picture we derive from the biblical record, critically regarded."[31] In regard to the United Monarchy, Halpern points to some of the corroborative evidence (as discussed earlier in this essay),[32] making a strong case for the historicity of the United Monarchy.

The Matter of Administrative Governors and Districts

Here Dever supplies some very helpful material, showing that the "compilers (of the list in 1 Kings 4), working at whatever date and for whatever reasons, had actual historical documents from which to draw."[33] He continues by saying that "some aspects of this list not only fit very well with what we know of the tenth century from extrabiblical sources, but they can scarcely be placed anywhere else."[34] Dever also identifies archaeologically some of the district capitals listed in 1 Kings 4.[35]

A New Methodology: The Application of Social Sciences

This methodology ignores the biblical text as irrelevant, with its emphases on the working of God in history and on the acts of leading individuals.

---

29. Ibid., 30.
30. Ibid., 31. He compares the numerous errors in the history of Herodotus (who wrote in the same period claimed by the minimalists for the writing of Kings) with the many accurate synchronisms in the biblical text.
31. Ibid.
32. Such as Shishak's raid, the population explosion in Iron I, the gates of Gezer, Megiddo, and Hazor; the indications of strong centralized government as shown by the large building projects of various kinds (Halpern, "Erasing History," 32–33). Halpern writes: "Moreover, the fact that Kings is so accurate about the history of the eighth–seventh centuries, *when the temple still stood*, suggests that our authors had both continuity and records on their side in naming the Temple's builder" (ibid., 33).
33. Dever, *What Did the Biblical Writers Know and When Did They Know It?* 139.
34. Ibid. See the list of archaeological correspondences Dever also provides (ibid., 140–44).
35. Ibid., 140–44.

This new methodology seeks to apply to the rise of Israel principles currently operating in newly emerging states in Africa and in some of the Pacific islands.[36] One major emphasis in this approach is the importance of "forces internal to a society."[37] This disregards factors such as the Philistine oppression and the guiding hand of God. Such an approach may be of some help in understanding ancient societies,[38] but it cannot claim to be an objective science in ignoring the testimony of the text.

All in all, the archaeological evidence for the United Monarchy is rather compelling when one is willing to accept the available facts. Only a persistent predilection against the veracity of Scripture can lead to any other conclusion.

Literary Issues

The "Deuteronomistic History" (DH)

In 1943 Martin Noth proposed that the writer of the books of Kings was also responsible for the books from Deuteronomy through Samuel.[39] This author (or collector and editor of previous materials) had a comprehensive plan, a clear theology, whereby he accounted for the demise of the Israelite and Judean kingdoms, namely, the lack of conformity to the provisions found in the book of Deuteronomy. He assigned the designation "Dtr." to this writer, and proposed that the most distinctive marks of Dtr. were to be found in discourses and prayers put in the mouth of the various central characters. The chief representatives of these deuteronomistic insertions are to be found in Joshua 23, 1 Samuel 12, and 1 Kings 8:14–53. In addition, he found personal historical reflections inserted by the author, such as Joshua 12; Judges 2:11–23; and 2 Kings 17:7–23.

---

36. See N. Gottwald, ed., "Social Scientific Criticism of the Hebrew Bible and Its Social World: The Israelite Monarchy," *Semeia* 37 (1986). This volume contains four essays on various aspects of the issue, authored, respectively, by F. Frick, M. Chaney, N. Gottwald, and Robert B. Coote and Keith W. Whitelam. See also I. Finkelstein ("The Emergence of the Monarchy in Israel: The Environmental and Socio-Economic Aspects," *JSOT* 44 [1989]: 43–47) who discusses the significance of settlement patterns as evidenced by surface surveys. V. P. Long ("Historiography of the Old Testament," in *Face of Old Testament Studies,* ed. D. Baker and B. Arnold [Grand Rapids: Baker, 1999], 156–61) provides an insightful critique.
37. F. Frick, "Methods for the Study of the Israelite Monarchy," *Semeia* 37 (1986): 13.
38. A rather positive picture is painted by Schäfer-Lichtenberger, "Sociological and Biblical Views of the Early State," in *The Origins of the Ancient Israelite States,* 78–105.
39. M. Noth, *Überlieferungsgeschichtliche Studien,* now available in English translation: M. Noth, *The Deuteronomistic History,* trans. J. Doull et al., 2d ed., JSOTSup 15 (Sheffield: JSOT, 1991).

Noth's contribution was significant in that his viewpoint was so widely accepted and virtually put to an end the atomizing attempts of scholars seeking to apply the principles of the Documentary theory to the historical books. On the other hand, his proposals have seen numerous modifications in attempting to reconcile all the evidence with the overarching theory. The chief challenge has been by F. M. Cross, who asserted that Noth's reason for the work of the "Dtr." was too negative, that he neglected entirely the element of hope in the narrative.[40] Thus he proposed a first edition, composed or compiled in Josiah's time, and another edition after the release of Jehoiachin from prison, as recorded in 2 Kings 25:27–30. Since that time there have been numerous modifications, including the addition of more and more layers of editorial activity.

Thomas Römer and Albert de Pury[41] provide an excellent review of the history and development of the theory of the DH, including the numerous difficulties encountered by the adherents of the DH in attempting to deal with the details of the composition, especially the matter of sources, and the differences of opinion among the various adherents.[42] They make the telling statement:

> Research on DH, even on Deuteronomism in general, finds itself today in a paradoxical situation. At first sight, we get the impression that the 'Deuteronomistic fact' is well established. But after a closer look, it turns out that the definitions of DH are legion and not always compatible with one another. How can we define what is Deuteronomic, Deuteronomistic and what is not?[43]

Despite these problems, the authors remain firmly committed to the theory of the DH, stating that it is "a touchstone for research on the formation of the Old Testament literature. If Israel was able to construct its history and through that to think of and choose its identity, it owes it to a great extent to the Deuteronomists."[44]

---

40. F. M. Cross, *Canaanite Myth and Epic* (Cambridge: Harvard University Press, 1973), 274–89.
41. A. de Pury and T. Römer, "Deuteronomistic Historiography (DH): History of Research and Debated Issues," in *Israel Constructs Its History*, ed. A. de Pury, T. Römer, and J-D. Macchi (Sheffield: Sheffield Academic Press, 2000), 24–141.
42. Ibid., esp. 106–33, on the question of sources.
43. Ibid., 134.
44. Ibid., 141.

Problems with Deuteronomic History

Though Noth's view that there is a consistent theological rationale that pervades the books from Deuteronomy through Kings is extremely insightful, his claim and that of his followers that these books are predominantly exilic poses severe problems.

(1) Not least of these is the severe lack of agreement on the part of its practitioners as is pointed out in *Israel Constructs Its History*.[45]

(2) This view does injustice to the internal witness of the Bible as a whole, and of Deuteronomy in particular with regard to the Mosaic authorship of the book.[46]

(3) It is illogical to claim that the actors in Israelite history should be held accountable for a theology of which they were unaware. If the book of Deuteronomy was not in existence, for example, in the time of the Judges, how would they be expected to know what God required of them?

(4) It seems preposterous for a work claiming to be historical to base its theological concepts on a work that the author himself had just created as the first in a series of documents. E. A. Knauf, in agreement with H. Donner, states that the DH "never consisted of more than the books of Joshua–2 Kings. It is Deuteronomy that is cited there as normative law. What other historiographic work would use its first volume as an authority? . . . Deuteronomy and the following books must be clearly separated."[47] Merrill remarks aptly: "One must concede, it seems, that a document made up of whole cloth from only the seventh century could hardly serve as a guideline for historical events that antedated it by several centuries."[48] He comments further: "To suggest that the deuteronomistic history can be based on Deuteronomy, can reflect the covenant expectations of that book,

---

45. Ibid., 24–141.
46. See G. L. Archer, *Survey of Old Testament Introduction*, rev. and expanded (Chicago: Moody, 1994), 274–83; and H. Wolf, *An Introduction to the Old Testament Pentateuch* (Chicago: Moody, 1990), 51–78, for a defense of the Mosaic authorship of Deuteronomy.
47. E. A. Knauf, "Does Deuteronomic Historiography Exist?" in *Israel Constructs Its History*, 394. As for Kings, he disassociates it from the prior books as an unsatisfactory conclusion to Israelite history, agreeing with R. Albertz in making it an introduction to the prophetic books, which speak of a great future yet for Israel (ibid., 397). He denies that there is any such thing as a unified DH (ibid., passim), and claims that the Old Testament represents a theological debate whose differences must neither be harmonized nor glossed over with "pious platitudes" (ibid., 397–99).
48. E. Merrill, *Deuteronomy*, NAC (Nashville: Broadman & Holman, 1994), 35.

and yet can consist essentially of a nonfactual record of Israel's actual historical experience is to border on the absurd."[49]

(5) The question of whether Deuteronomy more closely resembles the Hittite vassal treaty format (prior to the fourteenth century B.C.), or that of the Assyrian type (first millennium B.C.), has been much debated; but Kitchen's argument has not been effectively refuted.[50] Among the correspondences of Deuteronomy to the Hittite type is the presence of a historical prologue, consistently present in the Hittite treaty, but absent (so far as is now known) in the Assyrian treaty.[51]

There is another area in which Deuteronomy corresponds to the Hittite treaty type rather than to the Assyrian. This lies in the manner in which the stipulations are introduced. It is well known that what we know as the Ten Commandments is consistently referred to as "the words" of the Lord. Exodus 20:1 introduces the covenant with: "God spoke all these words." Moses, in his recapitulation of the covenant, says: "to declare to you the word of the Lord" (Deut. 5:5). In Deuteronomy 4:10 Moses, in referring to the same event, quotes God as saying: "Assemble the people to me, that I may let them hear my words." The Hittite treaty of Suppiluliumas begins with: "These are the words of the Sun, the great king. . . ."[52] So also in the treaty of Mursilis,[53] and that of Hattusilis with Raamses II,[54] even though the latter is a parity treaty. In all three instances the treaties begin with "These are the words. . . ."

By contrast the Aramaic treaties from Sefire use the word עדי "treaty," while the Assyrian treaties use the comparable word *adē*.[55] The word "treaty"

---

49. Ibid.
50. Kitchen, *AOOT*, 90–97. Those who hold to a late date for Deuteronomy seek confirmation of their views by asserting that the Assyrian treaty type is as good a model for the book as is the Hittite treaty. But fairness would suggest that even if the book matched both types equally (which is not the case), the matter ought to be decided by the internal claims of the book.
51. To the attempts to explain away the lack of such a prologue on the basis that the Assyrian types lack the beginnings, Kitchen responds that they "are hardly convincing," referring to the rather complete treaties of Sefire and Esarhaddon (ibid., 95 n. 34).
52. A. Goetze, trans., "Hittite Treaty," in *ANET*, 529.
53. A. Goetze, trans., "Treaty Between Mursilis and Duppi-Tessub of Amurru," in *ANET*, 203.
54. A. Goetze, trans., "Treaty Between Hattusilis and Ramses II," in *ANET*, 201–3.
55. Joseph Fitzmeyer, *The Aramaic Inscriptions of Sefire* (Rome: Pontifical Biblical Institute, 1967), 12 (lines 1, 2, 3, 4), 16 (lines 1, 3, 4, 5, 6, 7, 8, 11), 80 (Face B, lines 2, 9), 82 (line 18), 96 (line 4). See also the discussion of the word עדי, "treaty," in the Sefire inscriptions and the word *adē*, "treaty," used in the Assyrian inscriptions (ibid., 23–24).

is found frequently in the Vassal Treaties of Esarhaddon,[56] in the Treaty of Ashurnirari V,[57] and apparently in a broken text of the Treaty of Esarhaddon with Baal of Tyre.[58]

(6) To separate Deuteronomy from the rest of the Pentateuch is to leave a truncated work. D. M. Howard points out that "the resulting 'Tetrateuch' is most unsatisfactory—and unconvincing—as a literary unit.[59] He goes on to refer to scholars that have recognized this problem, causing them to "incorporate all of the material from Genesis to 2 Kings into one large, unified document . . . but it still begs the question of the authorship or composition of the smaller units."

(7) Related to the above is a grammatical feature that is peculiar to the five books of the Pentateuch. The third person singular pronoun is normally written הוּא for the masculine, and הִיא for the feminine. But in the Pentateuch, and only in the Pentateuch, the feminine is written הִוא. That is, without the Masoretic vowel pointing, the spelling is the same for the feminine as it is for the masculine. This rule holds true for Deuteronomy as it does for the other four books.[60] The same principle is true for the far demonstrative adjective.[61] This fact is overlooked or ignored by the proponents of a later composition or reworking of Deuteronomy. This point of grammar is rather unobtrusive, and one must ask why a late writer would use this rather unremarkable archaic spelling. As to a later editor or reworker of ancient material, it is inconceivable that he would not routinely update this rather insignificant matter without giving it a thought.[62]

(8) Another grammatical matter, which by itself may not furnish definitive

---

56. E. Reiner, trans., "Akkadian Treaties from Syria and Assyria," in *ANET*, 534–37, lines 1, 41, 283.
57. E. Reiner, trans., "Treaty between Ashurnirari V of Assyria and Mati'ilu of Arpad," in *ANET*, 532–33.
58. E. Reiner, trans., "Treaty of Esarhaddon with Baal of Tyre," in *ANET*, 533.
59. D. M. Howard Jr., *Introduction to the Old Testament Historical Books* (Chicago: Moody, 1993), 181.
60. The form הִוא occurs eight times in Deuteronomy (3:11; 4:3; 11:8; 24:4; 30:11 (2x), 12, 13). הִיא does not occur in Deut. (though it does occur rarely in Gen., Exod., and Lev.—Gen. 14:2; 26:7; Exod. 1:16; Lev. 5:11; 13:6; 16:31; 21:9).
61. The masculine is normally הַהוּא, and the feminine normally הַהִיא, but once again in the Pentateuch the "hybrid" form הַהִוא appears consistently; and it holds true for Deuteronomy as well—twenty-five times, spread throughout the book. The "normal" הַהִיא does not appear anywhere in the Pentateuch, including Deuteronomy.
62. See A. Kropat, *Die Syntax des Autors der Chronik Vergleichen mit der seiner Quellen*, BZAW 16 (Giessen: Töpelmann, 1909), 2 and passim, who shows how the postexilic Chronicler routinely updates the grammar of passages taken from Samuel–Kings.

evidence of the early authorship of Deuteronomy because the occurrences are too few for unqualified statistical validity, nevertheless is consistent with an early date for Deuteronomy. This has to do with the familiar phenomenon known as the "directive (or locative) *he.*" This means of designating the direction or goal of a movement is used far more extensively in the Pentateuch than elsewhere in the Old Testament. In those instances where it may optionally be employed, its rate of usage is 76 percent in the Pentateuch, dropping dramatically to 34 percent in the preexilic historical books, and dropping even more to 20 percent in the books of Chronicles and Ezra-Nehemiah.[63] While the possible occurrences in Deuteronomy are minimal, its rate of usage, nine times out of ten, or 90 percent, is consistent with an early date for the book. While it is true that a later editor might well include this device without change, since it was still in use (though to a considerably lesser degree) in the later pre- and postexilic times, it is consistent with early authorship.

(9) There are matters of content that are inconsistent with the concept of the DH. For example, why would the reference in Deuteronomy 17:14–15 appear necessary by a later writer or compiler, since by Josiah's time there had already been a long history of kings over Israel and Judah? More importantly, why would Deuteronomy 27, with its instructions regarding the building of an altar on Mount Ebal, be added or retained by a later writer or editor who wished to emphasize the concept of the single sanctuary?

(10) It is an accepted fact that the preexilic prophets spoke in a "deuteronomistic manner." Jeremiah is frequently mentioned in this regard. What seems to me to be beyond the bounds of credulity is to attempt to make a deuteronomist (or school of deuteronomists) responsible for all the "deuteronomistic" statements of the prophets. Virtually every part of the prophetic message is based on the Mosaic message as recorded in Deuteronomy, and applied to the situation in each prophet's life setting. This is particularly true in regard to Moses' frequent admonition to internalize the covenant, such as the matter of the circumcision of the heart (10:16; 30:6), and such characteristic passages as 6:4–5; 10:12; 11:1, 13, 18, 22 (all having to do with more than external obedience and ritual, and emphasizing a heartfelt devotion to God). Then there is as well the con-

---

63. H. Austel, "Prepositional and Non-Prepositional Complements with Verbs of Motion in Biblical Hebrew" (Ph.D. diss., UCLA, 1969), 349, app. A.

cern for one's fellow man and for the domestic animals as seen in Moses' comment on the Sabbath law (5:14–15, in the spirit of God's words in Exod. 23:10–12).

It is because of the theological accord between the prophets and the books Joshua—Kings that the ancient Rabbis referred to the latter as the "former prophets." Deuteronomy is the capstone of the Pentateuch, and at the same time forms the theological basis of the later books. It summarizes what is taught in the earlier books into a cohesive and practical theology for Israel to follow as they enter the land.

It seems appropriate at this juncture to state that the so-called DH is more than a reflection of the orthodox theology of post-Mosaic Israel, but in actual fact evidence for the guiding hand of God moving in the ancient writers of Israel as they measured the actions and motives of leaders and people by the standards set by God himself.

The Supposed Late Dating of Samuel/Kings

Though those who do research on the DH tend to date these books in the early preexilic period, archaeologists and textual critics tend to date them in the Persian period, or sometimes even as late as the Hellenistic period (the latter is particularly true of the minimalists). However, the evidence is very strong in favor of a clear linguistic distinction between Samuel/Kings on the one hand, and Ezra-Chronicles on the other.

Hurwitz's Critique

A. Hurwitz[64] takes P. R. Davies to task for one element of his many attacks on the historicity of Israel; namely, that the history of the biblical text is a late construct, artificially invented in the Persian period (so that the whole of the Old Testament is an invention in the Persian period, and therefore of no historical value whatsoever). Hurwitz shows that, contrary to Davies, there are external controls from the preexilic period that confirm the earlier dating (preexilic) of Kings: the Siloam inscription, the Lachish letters, the Yavneh Yam ostracon, the epitaph of the Royal Steward, the Arad Ostracon. The Hebrew of these documents matches that of

---

64. A. Hurwitz, "The Historical Quest for 'Ancient Israel' and Linguistic Evidence of the Hebrew Bible: Some Methodological Considerations," *VT* 47 (1997): 301–15.

Samuel/Kings. The Mesha inscription, though not Hebrew, "exhibits striking affinities with classical Hebrew prose." (and does have some value in this regard).[65] There are many more external controls for "postclassical" Hebrew.[66] He also gives one internal example of change: *iggeret* ("letter") replaces preexilic *sefer* ("letter," as used in the Lachish letters). In preexilic Hebrew it is used for any kind of writing, whether inscription, letter, or scroll). In postexilic Hebrew it was used exclusively for a scroll or book. In the Targums, the standard rendering for *sefer* ("letter") is *iggeret*. When *sefer* signifies "book," the rendering is *sipra*. *Iggeret* is a borrowing from Aramaic, affecting later Akkadian as well. It is thus an excellent indication of lateness, as opposed to *sefer*, which, when referring to a letter is a good indication of an earlier date. Thus there is solid evidence that there is development in the Hebrew of the Old Testament.

Kropat's Contribution

A. Kropat points out numerous distinctive characteristics that are consistently different in Chronicles from the preexilic books.[67] Once again, the indications are quite strong that Samuel/Kings were written in the classical era, i.e., before the Persian period.

Verbs of Motion

Research into the principles governing the manner in which a destination is introduced after verbs of motion shows that, when the goal of the

---

65. Ibid., 307–10.
66. Ibid., 310–11.
67. Kropat, *Die Syntax des Autors der Chronik Vergleichen*, 72–75. He ascribes this in part to the influence of Aramaic, such as the frequent use of ל, to designate a person in the accusative, as in Aramaic. See in this regard B. Waltke and M. O'Connor, *Biblical Hebrew Syntax* (Winona Lake, Ind.: Eisenbrauns, 1990), 184 n. 37. R. Polzin (*Late Biblical Hebrew: Toward an Historical Typology of Biblical Hebrew Prose*, Harvard Semitic Monographs, 12, ed. F. Cross Jr. [Missoula, Mont.: Scholars Press, 1976], 64–66) shows that this usage extends to accusatives generally. Just a few additional instances adduced by Kropat are: (1) the total lack of the use of the infinitive absolute in an imperatival sense. Where a passage in Kings uses the infinitive absolute, its parallel in Chronicles uses the imperative (*Die Syntax des Autors der Chronik Vergleichen*, 23); and (2) Chronicles has a greater tendency to put the subject first in verbal clauses, seen once again in parallel passages. Though a few isolated differences may be explained as accidental, their great number suggests a clear syntactic differentiation. This is just a small sampling of characteristics of the grammar of Ezra–Chronicles that are distinct from preexilic grammar, but consistent with later Hebrew literature.

movement is a simple place name, the place name is introduced without benefit of a preposition in 94 percent of the occurrences in the books Genesis–Kings. In Ezra–Chronicles the likelihood drops to 44 percent.[68]

Scribal Record-Keeping

It is often claimed that the putative small size of Jerusalem during the tenth century rules out the idea of there being any significant scribal activity. Thus it is argued that it would have been impossible for any formal records of this time to have been kept. Nadav Na'aman responds by referring to the accurate record of the invasion of Shishak. The author clearly had historical records of the time, thus inferring official scribal activity. It is difficult to imagine that scribal activity would have first been introduced by "a petty king like Rehoboam, but rather by one of his ancestors."[69]

Conclusion

The foregoing evidence lends support to the following conclusions.

(1) With regard to the historicity of the United Monarchy, the external support is quite strong. The lack of direct archaeological evidence from the period in question is readily explained, and is parallel to the lack of evidence for the Jerusalem of the Amarna Age. The sudden emergence of monumental structures (such as the six-chambered gates and fortified governmental centers) in the tenth century B.C. testify to a strong centralized government with a population sufficient to support it. The dating of these gates is supported by the Egyptian report of Shishak's invasion in 925 B.C. The Tell Dan inscription and the Moabite stone provide external textual support to the existence of the dynasty of David. The many synchronisms

---

68. H. Austel, *Verbs of Motion*, 324, 342, 378. In Ezra–Chronicles ל and אל encroach on the accusative. In a similar finding, ל, which is used to introduce simple place names only once in 328 occurrences in the former books, appears in 13 of 45 occurrences (29 percent) (ibid., 378, table 22, and nn. b and c).
69. Nadav Na'aman, "Sources and Composition in the History of David," in *The Origins of the Ancient Israelite States*, 170–71. Knoppers points out that "Jerusalem (in the Late Bronze Age) was fully capable of producing documents . . . and there is no good reason to believe that scribes under David and Solomon could not have written texts as well" ("Vanishing Solomon," 42). He also points to Nuzi, which had a population of only ca. 2000, but produced 6,500 texts. See also K. McCarter, "The Historical David," *Interpretation* 40 (1988): 118.

between later chapters of Kings and external sources indicate that the writers of these books had access to accurate historical sources.

(2) With regard to the Deuteronomic History, the book of Deuteronomy belongs with the rest of the Pentateuch, in the period of Moses and the Exodus. The following historical books do indeed evince a pervading theological theme, one that presupposes the content of Deuteronomy, but they are grammatically and logically distinct from it. The basic theological unity between these books and those of the writing prophets cannot be accounted for by the theory of the DH. If, on the other hand, the books in question are more than the work of human authors, but rather a product of divine-human cooperation, then a consistent and pervasive theology is to be expected. The same Spirit that moved and motivated the writing prophets was also at work in the writing of a history that is theologically motivated. Ezra's prayer of confession in Nehemiah 9 is in accord with this. The prophetic nature of this history was clearly recognized early on by the Jewish community. Because of this, it was carefully preserved, whereas other historical documents have not survived.

(3) Samuel/Kings were clearly written before the Persian period, and were based on historical documents written soon after the reported events took place. There is overwhelming evidence that the language of Samuel/Kings differs in many areas from that of the postexilic era. Aside from the clear linguistic evidence pointing in this direction, it must also be said that to claim (as "minimalist" scholars do) that a late writer would write an account of a fictitious "golden age" of great kings who ruled over a great kingdom, and to include in that account so much of a negative nature with reference to David and Solomon, is rather disingenuous. In actual fact, the biblical account demonstrates that God used real and imperfect people to accomplish His purpose for His people. The final achievement of that purpose awaits the coming of the Messiah, the Son of David.[70]

---

70. Since completing my essay, I have found the book by V. Philips Long, David W. Baker, and Gordon J. Wenham, eds., *Windows into Old Testament History: Evidence, Argument, and the Crisis of "Biblical Israel"* (Grand Rapids: Eerdmans, 2002). This book contains two chapters relating to the United Monarchy. The first is by Richard Hess, "Literacy in Iron Age Israel," 82–102. The second is by Kenneth Kitchen, "The Controlling Role of External Evidence in Assessing the Historical Status of the Israelite United Monarchy," 111–30.

8

THE DIVIDED MONARCHY

Sources, Approaches, and Historicity

Richard D. Patterson

STRETCHING FROM THE SCHISM IN THE Hebrew monarchy at the death of Solomon in 931 B.C. until the respective demises of the resultant kingdoms of Israel in the north (722 B.C.) and Judah in the south (586 B.C.) the era of the Divided Monarchy comprises nearly 350 years. This period forms one of the most eventful eras in the history of the ancient Near East. In addition to the political ebb and flow of many small states, this time witnessed the rise of such powerful kingdoms as the Neo-Assyrian (745–612 B.C.) and Neo-Babylonian (626–562 B.C.) empires, as well as the resurgence of Egypt with its twenty-sixth (or Saite) dynasty (664–525 B.C.).

Sandwiched between the expansionist kingdoms of Mesopotamia and Egypt, the prosperity of the Hebrew kingdoms depended upon the menacing presence of powerful foreign kings. Unfortunately, God's people were all too often led by leaders whose ineptitude was fostered by outright apostasy. Under such conditions the fortunes of the twin kingdoms were in constant flux. Therefore, both Israel's internal history and external relations with the surrounding nations are crucial to the understanding of the period.[1]

---

1. In addition to the standard general histories of the ancient Near East and a host of special studies of individual peoples, a particularly helpful source for studying texts relating to the Old Testament is W. W. Hallo and K. L. Younger Jr., *COS*, 3 vols. (Leiden: Brill, 1997–2002). A list of extrabiblical Hebrew texts bearing on 1 and 2 Kings can be found in D. M. Howard Jr., *An Introduction to the Old Testament Historical Books* (Chicago: Moody, 1993), 217–20. Most notable among these are the Siloam Tunnel Inscription commemorating the completion of a water conduit between the Gihon Spring and the Pool of Siloam; see W. F. Albright, trans., "The Siloam Inscription," in *ANET*, 321; K. L. Younger Jr., trans., "The Siloam Tunnel Inscription (2.28)," in *COS*, 2:145–46; the Lachish Ostraca detailing circumstances close to the fall of

Literary Sources

External Sources

Texts from Israel's near neighbors, the Egyptians,[2] Arameans,[3] Phoenicians,[4] and Moabites[5], yield valuable details concerning the earlier period of Israel's Divided Monarchy. The growing influence of Assyria is also noteworthy.[6] For the major part of the era, the literature of the Neo-Assyrian Empire is most important. Especially significant are annalistic reports of the Assyrian kings and texts of royal focus.[7] While Assyrian sources continued to play a significant role in the late period (seventh through sixth centuries B.C.), pride of place belongs to literature stemming from the Neo-Babylonian[8]

Jerusalem, in W. F. Albright, trans., "The Lachish Ostraca," in *ANET,* 321–22; and the ostracon from Arad; see V. H. Matthews and D. C. Benjamin, *Old Testament Parallels* (New York: Paulist, 1991), 137–38. Of interest also is the helpful excursus evaluating epigraphic evidence concerning the fall of Judah by Y. Avishur and M. Heltzer, *Studies on the Royal Administration* (Tel Aviv-Jaffa: Archaeological Center, 2000), 147–49.

2. For details see John A. Wilson, trans., "The Campaign of Sheshonk I," in *ANET,* 263–64; and J. H. Breasted, trans., "Reign of Sheshonk I," in *ARE,* 4:348–54.
3. Significant Aramaic inscriptions include those of Zakkur, King of Hamath (A. Millard, trans., "The Inscription of Zakkur, King of Hamath [2.35]," in *COS,* 2:155); Panamuwa (K. L. Younger Jr., trans., "Panamuwa Inscription [2.37]," in *COS,* 2:158–60); and Bar-Rakib, as well as the Tell Dan Stele (A. Millard, trans., "The Tell Dan Stele [2.39]," in *COS,* 2:161–62). For a thorough study of the Sefire Inscription, see J. A. Fitzmyer, *The Aramaic Inscriptions of Sefire* (Rome: Pontifical Biblical Institute, 1967).
4. Of special interest are the inscriptions of Kulamuwa (K. L. Younger Jr., trans., "The Kulamuwa Inscription [2.30]," in *COS,* 2:174–48); and Azatiwada (F. Rosenthal, trans., "Azitawadda of Adana," in *ANET,* 662; K. L. Younger Jr., trans. "The Azatiwada Inscription [2.31]," in *COS,* 1:148–50). For analysis of Phoenician literary features and their impact on the Bible, see Y. Avishur, *Phoenician Inscriptions and the Bible* (Tel Aviv-Jaffa: Archaeological Center, 2000).
5. Particularly significant is the well-known inscription of the Moabite King Mesha (W. F. Albright, trans. "The Moabite Stone," in *ANET,* 320–21; K. A. D. Smelik, trans., "The Inscription of King Mesha [2.23]," in *COS,* 2:137–38). See also A. Lemaire, "'House of David' Restored in Moabite Inscription," *BAR* 20, no. 3 (May–June 1994): 30–37.
6. See especially the annals of Shalmaneser III (D. D. Luckenbill, trans., "Shalmaneser III," in *ARAB,* 1:200–52; A. L. Oppenheim, trans., "Shalmaneser III [858–824]: The Fight Against the Aramean Coalition," in *ANET,* 276–81; K. L. Younger Jr., trans., "Shalmaneser III [2.113]," in *COS,* 2:261–72); and Adad-nirari III (D. D. Luckenbill, trans., "Adad-Nirâri III," in *ARAB,* 1:260–64; A. L. Oppenheim, "Adad-nirari III [810–783]: Expedition to Palestine," in *ANET,* 281–82; K. L. Younger Jr., trans., "Adad-nirari III [2.114]," in *COS,* 2:272–77).
7. For texts in translation, see *ARAB,* 1:269–97, 2:1–416; see also *ANET,* 282–301; and *COS,* 2:284–306.
8. See D. J. Wiseman, *Chronicles of the Chaldean Kings* (London: Trustees of the British Museum, 1956), 1–37, 50–74; A. L. Oppenheim, trans., "Nebuchadnezzar II (605–562)," in *ANET,* 307–08; and P-A Beaulieu, trans., "Neo-Babylonian Inscriptions," in *COS,* 2:306–10.

and Egyptian[9] archives for understanding the complex international situation of the time.

Internal Sources

The chief sources for the historical study of the divided kingdom are the biblical books of 1–2 Kings (1 Kings 12–2 Kings 25) and 2 Chronicles 10–36. The Chronicler's discussion of the divided kingdom provides a great deal of information that is not found in Kings. Of particular significance are those blocks of material dealing with the kings most noteworthy for their piety and reforms, such as Jehoshaphat (2 Chron. 17:1–18a; 19:1–20:30), Azariah (i.e., Uzziah—2 Chron. 26:6–15), Hezekiah (2 Chron. 29:3–32:8), and Josiah (2 Chron. 34:3–7; 35:1–25). The attention and detail given to these kings illustrate the distinctive theological purposes of the Chronicler's selection of historical events. Whereas the author of Kings was concerned to trace the covenantal violations (Mosaic and Davidic) and spiritual infidelity that culminated in the fall and exile of the twin kingdoms, the Chronicler writes from a postexilic perspective. The burning question of the time was whether God had abandoned his covenant people. "The Chronicler's answer . . . is affirmative: God still cares for his people and is bound to them in covenant."[10]

---

9. See J. Breasted, trans., "Reign of Psamtik I," in *ARE*, 4:477–79; idem, "Reign of Necho," in *ARE*, 4:497–508; M. Lichtheim, trans., "The Victory Stela of King Piye (Piankhy) (2.7)," in *COS*, 2:242–51; K. A. Kitchen, *The Third Intermediate Period in Egypt, 1100–650 B.C.* (Warminster, England: Aris & Phillips, 1973), 399–408; and M. Lichtheim, *AEL*, vol. 3 (Berkeley: University of California Press, 1980).

10. V. P. Long, "History and Fiction," in *Israel's Past in Present Research*, ed. V. P. Long (Winona Lake, Ind.: Eisenbrauns, 1999), 253. R. K. Harrison in *Introduction to the Old Testament* (Grand Rapids: Eerdmans, 1969), 1162, points out that the Chronicler's stress on the Davidic Covenant and Davidic succession as well as on the temple and it services served to "show that the Temple services and religious institutions of the postexilic theocracy were legitimate and valid adjuncts of community life"; see further, Howard, *Introduction to the Old Testament Historical Books*, 231–32, 253–69. The historical value of Chronicles has often been discussed. For a review of critical approaches to Chronicles, see S. Japhet, "The Historical Reliability of Chronicles," *JSOT* 33 (1985): 83–107. G. N. Knoppers, "History and Historiography: The Royal Reforms," in *Israel's Past in Present Research*, 578, observes that "Chronicles is not a treasure trove of information about preexilic history, but it does interact with preexilic history." Yet his consideration of the Chronicler's treatment of Judah's eighth century reformers Uzziah, Jotham, and Hezekiah in the light of archaeological evidence forces him to acknowledge that "the unique evidence of Chronicles . . . is occasionally of some value for historical reconstruction." See further, M. P. Graham, K. G. Hoglund and S. L. McKenzie, eds., *The Chronicler as Historian*, JSOTSup 238 (Sheffield: Sheffield Academic Press, 1997).

Other data can be gleaned from the prophetic books, whether in historical narratives (e.g., Isa. 7:1–16; 36–39; Jer. 7:1–8; 37–39; 52), or biographical sketches (Jer. 27–29), and small scraps of information providing historical settings (e.g., Ezek. 1:1–2; 24:1–2; Dan. 1:1–2) or tantalizing hints of possible activities (e.g., Hos. 10:14). This study will use as its basis data derived from Kings, while utilizing supplemental information from other biblical and extrabiblical sources.

Chronology

A basic problem concerns the use of the available sources for establishing a definitive chronology for the era of the Divided Monarchy. Final results have remained elusive. The vacillation between the observance of the beginning of the New Year between spring and fall, and the variation between the accession-year system and the nonaccession-year system of reckoning the years of a king's reign in the ancient Near East, have posed numerous difficulties.[11] Nevertheless, the use of the Greek geographer Ptolemy's Canon and the Assyrian *limmu* (or eponym) lists, giving names of the person who occupied the office of *limmu,* have provided helpful data for correlation with the biblical chronology. Thus Ptolemy's Canon provides the names of the rulers of Babylon from 747 B.C. down to his own time in the second century A.D. These lists often mention important historical or astronomical events. One such entry lists an eclipse of the sun, which has been accurately dated to June 15, 763 B.C. Using this as an anchor date, a rather firm series of dates for the period 892–648 B.C. has been determined. Further recourse to various Egyptian sources and Mesopotamian royal annals and king lists, such as synchronous histories listing specific contacts between Assyrian and Babylonian kings, has yielded a rather good external dating sequence for the era of the Divided Monarchy.[12]

The correlation of these data with the biblical record has proven to be a time-honored crux. Numerous schemes have been attempted, the most in-

---

11. In the accession-year system a king's first year began with the first day of the calendar year after his inauguration. The nonaccession-year system counted the remaining days in the calendar year in which the king was crowned as his first year.
12. Correlation between Ptolemy's Canon and the eponym lists provides the identical date for the accession of the Assyrian King Sargon II over Babylon (709 B.C.).

fluential being those by W. F. Albright[13] and E. Thiele.[14] In developing his system Thiele not only proposed certain calendrical changes but proposed variation in the use of the accession and nonaccession year systems and the existence of overlapping coregencies for the Hebrew kings. J. B. Payne modified several of Thiele's principles.[15] Thus he proposed that the nonaccession-year system was originally in vogue in the northern kingdom and that the New Year always began in the fall. The southern kingdom likewise used the fall as the time of the New Year and the accession year system was at first employed. However, with the reigns of Athaliah and Jotham a change to the nonaccession year system remained in place until the rise of the Neo-Assyrian Empire. At that time both kingdoms utilized the accession year system. As for coregencies, Payne affirmed that "the years of coregency are regularly included in the totals for the respective reigns."[16] With slight modification Payne's chronology and dating for the period of the Divided Monarchy are used in the discussion that follows.[17]

Approaches to the Study of the Divided Monarchy

The Deuteronomistic History

Departing from the critical analyses that found in the books of Kings traces of individual source documents that featured the divine names

---

13. Albright's developing views on the chronology of the monarchic period may be found in a series of articles in the *BASOR*. See W. F. Albright, "The Chronology of the Divided Monarchy of Israel," *BASOR* 100 (1945): 16–22; idem, "New Light from Egypt on the Chronology and History of Israel and Judah," *BASOR* 130 (1953): 4–11; and idem, "Further Light on Synchronisms between Egypt and Asia in the Period 935–685 B.C.," *BASOR* 141 (1956): 23–27.
14. E. R. Thiele, *The Mysterious Numbers of the Hebrew Kings,* 3d ed. (Grand Rapids: Zondervan, 1983). See also J. Finegan, *Handbook of Biblical Chronology: Principles of Time Reckoning in the Ancient World and Problems of Chronology in the Bible,* rev. ed. (Peabody, Mass.: Hendrickson, 1998).
15. J. B. Payne, "Chronology of the Old Testament," in *Zondervan Pictorial Encyclopedia of the Bible,* ed. Merrill Tenney (Grand Rapids: Zondervan, 1975), 1:829–45.
16. Ibid., 838.
17. Problems associated with biblical chronology and that of the ancient Near East have occasioned a vast literature on the subject. Among the many, see P. Van Der Meer, *The Chronology of Ancient Western Asia and Egypt,* 2d ed. (Leiden: Brill, 1963); J. H. Hayes and P. K. Hooker, *A New Chronology for the Kings of Israel and Judah* (Atlanta: John Knox, 1988); H. Tadmor, "The Chronology of the First Temple Period: A Presentation and Evaluation of the Sources," in *A History of Ancient Israel,* ed. J. A. Soggin (Philadelphia: Westminster, 1984), 368–83, 408–11; L. McFall, "A Translation Guide to the Chronological Data in Kings and Chronicles," *BSac* 148 (1991): 3–45; and G. Galil, *The Chronology of the Kings of Israel and Judah* (Leiden: Brill, 1996).

Yahweh (J) and Elohim (E) as well as postulating that Deuteronomy was a product of the Josianic age, M. Noth theorized that the biblical books from Deuteronomy to Kings were written by a single author living after the fall of Jerusalem in 586 B.C. This author, the Deuteronomist, believed that the collapse of the twin kingdoms was due to the people's failure to conform to the Deuteronomic standards of fidelity to God and the Mosaic Law.[18]

Although Noth's thesis won widespread approval, many refinements have been suggested. Several authors have challenged Noth's original ascription of the basic viewpoint of the Deuteronomist as being exilic. Thus S. L. McKenzie believes that the record of Israel's odyssey is chiefly that of a Deuteronomic editor living in the time of Josiah, whose interest was a "theological explanation of the history of Israel and Judah in the Divided Monarchy."[19] F. M. Cross suggested that the Deuteronomistic History was composed in two stages, the first in late preexilic times during reforms of Josiah (640–609 B.C.) and the second by an exilic author (ca. 550 B.C.).[20] The first edition laid stress upon the sins of Jeroboam I, while holding up God's promises in the Davidic Covenant (2 Sam. 7:1–16); the exilic writer augmented the Deuteronomistic History and emphasized the devastating effects of the sins of wicked Manasseh.[21] Some have suggested other themes that were important to the Deuteronomist.[22] Others opted for three editions of the Deuteronomistic History, a series of redactors/editors, or a

---

18. For details, see A. de Pury, and T. Römer, "Deuteronomistic Historiography (DH): History of Research and Debated Issues," in *Israel Constructs Its History*, ed. A. de Pury, T. Römer, and J-D. Macchi (Sheffield: Sheffield Academic Press, 2000), 46–53; Howard, *Introduction to the Old Testament Historical Books*, 179; and M. Noth, *The Deuteronomistic History*, 2d ed., JSOTSup 15 (Sheffield: JSOT, 1991).
19. S. L. McKenzie, "Dog Food and Bird Food: The Oracles Against the Dynasties," in *Reconsidering Israel and Judah*, ed. G. N. Knoppers and J. G. McConville (Winona Lake, Ind.: Eisenbrauns, 2000), 418. N. Na'aman, "Historiography, the Fashioning of the Collective Memory, and the Establishment of Historical Consciousness in Israel in the Late Monarchical Period," *Zion* 60 (1995): 449–72, finds the Deuteronomist's concentration on the sins of Jeroboam to be an excuse to justify the reforms of Josiah. M. Rose "Deuteronomistic Ideology and Theology of the Old Testament," in *Israel Constructs Its History*, 439–40, decides that the author of the Deuteronomistic History belonged to "the *first* deportation in 598, together with the young King Jehoiachin," for this deportation "would have been the most important."
20. F. M. Cross, "The Themes of the Book of Kings and the Structure of the Deuteronomistic History," in *Reconsidering Israel and Judah*, 79–94.
21. Ibid., 92.
22. See H. W. Wolff, "The Kerygma of the Deuteronomic Historical Work," *ZAW* 73 (1961): 171–86; H. Lohfink, "Kerygmata des Deuteronomischen Geshichtswerks," in *Die Botschaft und die Boten*, ed. J. Jeremias and L. Perlitt (Neukirchen-Vluyn: Neukirchener Verlag, 1981), 87–100; J. G. McConville, "Narrative and Meaning in the Books of Kings," *Bib* 70 (1989): 31–49.

veritable circle of Deuteronomic writers.[23] It would seem that the presuppositions, models, and methods of the proponents of the Deuteronomistic History, which have yielded widely varying results cast some doubt as to the value of the theory itself.[24]

Accordingly, several critical scholars have abandoned the concept of the Deuteronomistic History altogether. Thus E. A. Knauf remarks, "Noth's Dtr has been abandoned by everyone. We will see later that H . . . must be abandoned as well."[25] Conservatives have largely rejected the concept.[26] Nevertheless, in their tracing and evaluating the history of the rise and fall of the Divided Monarchy, they admit freely that the author of Kings is highly indebted to Deuteronomy and Mosaic Law. Thus the condemnation of idolatry (Deut. 4:15–20; 5:6–8; 27:15) together with the emphasis of unity of worship in the place of God's choosing (Deut. 12:5) are often cited as basic standards in Kings. Their violation is noted with regard to the sins of Jeroboam, which "he has committed and caused Israel to commit" (1 Kings 14:16). It was a crime that ultimately caused the demise of the northern kingdom (2 Kings 17:16–23).

Even the southern kingdom fell prey at times to the worship of other gods (1 Kings 15:11–13; 2 Kings 16:3–4; 17:19; 21:3–6) and the allowing of worship at various local altars (1 Kings 14:23; 15:14; 22:43; 2 Kings 12:3; 14:4; 15:4, 35; 16:4). The latter practice was strongly opposed only in the reforms of Hezekiah (2 Kings 18:4, 22) and Josiah (2 Kings 23:8–9, 13, 15, 19–20).

Other Deuteronomic standards such as the need to acknowledge and worship only Israel's sovereign God (Deut. 6:4–5), to be obedient to the

---

23. See B. Halpern, *The First Historians: The Hebrew Bible and History* (San Francisco: Harper & Row, 1988); A. LeMaire, "Toward a Redactional History of the Book of Kings," in *Reconsidering Israel and Judah,* 446–61; R. Smend, *Die Entstehung des Alten Testaments* (Stuttgart: Kohlhammer, 1978); and H. Weippert, "Die 'deuteronomistischen' Beurteilingen der Könige von Israel und Juda und das Problem der Redaktion der Königsbucher," *Bib* 53 (1972): 301–39.
24. G. N. Knoppers, introduction to *Reconsidering Israel and Judah,* 17–18, would consider such an assumption to be "too simplistic." Rather, he recommends an appreciation of the diversity and difficulties of the material in the text as well as the conclusions of those engaged in their study. Interestingly, M. Mills, *Historical Israel: Biblical Israel* (New York: Cassell, 1999), 53, acknowledges a similar problem in the application of archaeological data.
25. E. A. Knauf, "Does 'Deuteronomistic Historiography' (DTRH) Exist?" in *Israel Constructs Its History,* 388–98.
26. See W. C. Kaiser Jr., *Toward an Old Testament Theology* (Grand Rapids: Zondervan, 1978), 63–66; idem, *A History of Israel* (Nashville: Broadman & Holman, 1998), 131–33; K. A. Kitchen, "Ancient Orient, 'Deuteronomism,' and the Old Testament," in *New Perspectives on the Old Testament,* ed. J. B. Payne (Waco: Word, 1970), 17.

Law of Moses (Deut. 28), and to keep the obligations in the Mosaic Covenant (Deut. 26:16–19) are repeatedly felt throughout the books of Kings. In this regard the example of David, to whom God gave great promises conditioned upon personal faithfulness, is often held up as the model by which subsequent kings of the Divided Monarchy are evaluated (1 Kings 14:8; 15:3–5; 2 Kings 8:19; 14:3; 16:2; 18:3; 19:34; 20:5–6; 21:7–9; 22:2). Therefore, one may speak of the Deuteronomistic History yet "not succumb to the late dating of Deuteronomy to appreciate fully the impact which the Mosaic document had on the compiler of Kings."[27] D. Howard's conclusion is most apropos: "The term *Deuteronomistic* can thus be used in a more neutral descriptive way to refer to those books or ideas reflective of the distinctive viewpoints found in Deuteronomy—with no conclusions concerning authorship of Deuteronomy or the other books inherent in the use of the term."[28]

Additional Approaches

Numerous other methods of viewing the history of the Old Testament, which affect the understanding of the Divided Monarchy, have been put forward. Several have championed the use of socioeconomic models.[29] Thus D. M. Gunn and D. N. Fewell suggest that "history may be better thought of as an ideological and social construct, inevitably subjective and existing on a continuum with notions such as 'myth' and 'fiction.'"[30] J. M. Miller proposes that sociopolitical considerations concerning circumstances in the northern kingdom show that it was more powerful than the southern kingdom. In fact, "beginning with the Omride period, moreover, and until Israel's defeat and annexation by the Assyrians, Judah often was little more than an Israelite vassal."[31] While acknowledging the usefulness of the social

---

27. R. Dillard, "Kings, Books of First and Second," in *Baker Encyclopedia of the Bible,* ed. W. A. Elwell (Grand Rapids: Baker, 1988), 2:1282.
28. Howard, *Introduction to the Old Testament Historical Books,* 182.
29. For details on this approach and others, see J. H. Hayes, "The History of the Study of Israelite and Judaean History: From the Renaissance to the Present," in *Israel's Past in Present Research,* 38–42.
30. D. M. Gunn and D. N. Fewell, *Narrative in the Hebrew Bible* (Oxford: University Press, 1993), 11.
31. J. M. Miller, "Reading the Bible Historically: The Historian's Approach," in *To Each Its Own Meaning,* ed. S. L. McKenzie and S. R. Haynes (Louisville: Westminster/John Knox, 1993), 24; see also P. Dutcher-Walls, "The Social Location of the Deuteronomists: A Sociological Study of Factional Politics in Late Preexilic Judah," *JSOT* 52 (1991): 77–94.

sciences, especially where the biblical text lacks specific information, V. P. Long nevertheless asks, "Are we well advised to seek to escape the *constraints* of the text in matters that it *does* address? Should not the text at least be included among the available data?"[32]

Likewise the study of the Old Testament and the Divided Monarchy has been affected by the use of newer literary methods. J. C. Exum and David J. A. Clines survey such literary approaches as new criticism, rhetorical criticism, structuralism, feminist criticism, materialistic criticism, political criticism, psychoanalytic criticism, reader-response criticism, and deconstruction.[33] While each theory has its adherents, the last two have received increasingly wide recognition. The importance of the reader in the interpretive process has become a familiar tool for the study of the Old Testament. The reader is now viewed as having a significant, if not primary, role in the interpretative process. Such an approach recognizes "that texts are multivalent and their meanings radically contextual, inescapably bound up with their interpreters."[34] Deconstruction also has its advocates despite the possibility that absolute deconstruction leaves one on a sea of uncertainty. Thus T. Longman observes the dangers in deconstruction by noting that "nothing and no one, whether author, speaker, or God, is present out there to ground the meaning of a text. Literary texts have no determinate meaning, and one common feature of a deconstructive analysis is to undermine any attempts to provide a stable meaning for a text."[35] Nevertheless, the two theories continue to attract practitioners, many of whom blend the two together.[36]

---

32. V. P. Long, *The Art of Biblical History* (Grand Rapids: Zondervan, 1994), 139.
33. J. C. Exum and David J. A. Clines, "The New Literary Criticism," in *The New Literary Criticism and the Hebrew Bible,* ed. J. C. Exum and David J. A. Clines (Valley Forge, Pa.: Trinity Press, 1994), 11–25. The editors include a detailed bibliography. See also the collected articles in P. R. House, ed., *Beyond Form Criticism* (Winona Lake, Ind.: Eisenbrauns, 1992); K. Mathews, "Literary Criticism of the Bible," in *Foundations for Biblical Interpretation,* ed. D. Dockery, K. Mathews, and R. Sloan (Nashville: Broadman & Holman, 1994), 205–31; and T. L. Longman III, *Literary Approaches to Biblical Interpretation* (Grand Rapids: Zondervan, 1987), 13–45. Howard stresses the need for biblical interpreters employing rhetorical criticism to adhere to the classical definition of the subject with its emphasis on persuasion in spoken discourse. See D. M. Howard Jr., "Rhetorical Criticism in Old Testament Studies," *BBR* 4 (1994): 87–104.
34. Gunn and Fewell, *Narrative in the Hebrew Bible,* 9.
35. T. Longman III, "Literary Approaches to Old Testament Study," in *The Face of Old Testament Studies,* ed. D. W. Baker and B. T. Arnold (Grand Rapids: Baker, 1999), 108.
36. See David J. A. Clines, *What Does Eve Do to Help? And Other Readerly Questions to the Old Testament,* JSOTSup 94 (Sheffield: JSOT, 1990), 106–23; and P. Miscall, "The Workings of OT Narrative," Semeia Studies (Philadelphia: Fortress, 1983).

Their combination exemplifies the fact that current literary theory tends to be eclectic, using "a variety of approaches at the same time."[37]

The recognition of the usefulness of literary methods has led to a number of studies dealing with narrative literature in the Scriptures.[38] A literary reading of biblical narratives such as those detailing the history of the Divided Monarchy involves being acquainted with the basic features of narrative genre. These include formal distinctions between narrator, author (whether the real author or implied author, that is, what can be deduced of him through reading the text), and reader, whether the real reader (those who read the text) or implied reader (those to whom the author intended to communicate). Also, an understanding of such elements as structure, plot, characterization, and setting is essential.[39] Literary theories and historical approaches are increasingly being employed together, leading to a more balanced interpretation of the Scriptures, including the study of the Divided Monarchy.[40]

The Historicity of the Divided Monarchy

The Maximalist/Minimalist Debate

Current studies of the Old Testament including the Divided Monarchy reflect vast differences with regard to the perceived historical validity of the text. Often characterized as the maximalist/minimalist debate, it pits "maximalists," who consider the Bible to be historically reliable, or at least a useful source for examining Israel's history, against "minimalists," who insist that "archaeological evidence alone should be used in such reconstructions because written texts—most especially the Bible—are late, tendentious, and ideologically biased."[41] Prominent minimalists include P. R.

---

37. Longman, "Literary Approaches to Old Testament Study," 111.
38. See, for example, R. Alter, *The Art of Biblical Narrative* (New York: Basic Books, 1981).
39. See further, Howard, *Introduction to the Old Testament Historical Books,* 49–58.
40. See J. Barton, "Historical Criticism and Literary Interpretation," in *Israel's Past and Present Research,* 427–38. For the use of literary methods in the study of the Divided Monarchy, see J. T. Walsh, *1 Kings,* Berit Olam (Collegeville, Minn.: Liturgical, 1996); and R. L. Cohn, *2 Kings,* Berit Olam (Collegeville, Minn.: Liturgical, 2000). It is of interest to note that an advocate of the Deuteronomistic History like M. Mills, *Historical Israel,* 134–35, has developed a variety of methods including literary approaches, which she terms "ideological criticism."
41. D. M. Howard Jr., *Joshua,* NAC (Nashville: Broadman & Holman, 1998), 40.

Davies, N. P. Lemche, and T. L. Thompson, among others. Davies relegates most of the Old Testament books to composition in the Persian period and considers that their time framework, events, and people are unhistorical.[42] N. P. Lemche boldly asks whether a true history of Israel can actually be written.[43] His answer, though allowing the factuality of some events in the divided kingdom, is largely negative. Thus while acknowledging that the accounts of Senncherib's siege of Jerusalem in 701 B.C. and Nebuchadnezzar's capture of Jerusalem in 597 B.C. contain "historical information," clearly relying on the conclusions of biblical authors who "manipulated this history in their own interest" to produce a history of Israel "would be to continue in the tradition of these authors and to make their viewpoints one's own."[44] T. L. Thompson casts doubt upon the Old Testament as a reliable source of information, regarding it rather as "formally ahistorical . . . a source which only exceptionally can be verified by other information."[45] M. Z. Brettler observes that "while the positions of Lemche, Davies, and Thompson have not gained general assent, these three scholars have begun to make contemporary scholars who attempt to reconstruct ancient Israelite history much more aware of the fundamental problems involved in their task."[46]

Criticism of the minimalist position has come from all sides. R. N. Whybray rejects Davies' basic position on the Old Testament historical books and the Old Testament as a whole as astounding: "This astonishing theory, for which there appears to be no solid evidence, reduces the Old Testament in a lengthy and complex pastiche, whose authors successfully imitated a great variety of styles (but if they had no models, how could they do this?) in order to give a false impression of antiquity."[47] S. Herrmann insists that Lemche's historical reconstruction is nothing more than *"his* picture, and it remains to be asked whether all in all the biblical picture isn't better and more relevant than Lemche's construction based on

---

42. See P. R. Davies, "In Search of Ancient Israel," JSOTSup 148 (Sheffield: JSOT, 1992).
43. N. P. Lemche, "Is It Still Possible to Write a History of Israel?" in *Israel's Past in Present Research*, 391–414.
44. Ibid., 397, 413.
45. T. L. Thompson, *Early History of the Israelite People*, Studies in the History of the Ancient Near East (Leiden: Brill, 1992), 4:132.
46. M. Z. Brettler, "The New Biblical Historiography," in *Israel's Past in Present Research*, 48.
47. R. N Whybray, "What Do We Know about Ancient Israel?" in *Israel's Past in Present Research*, 186.

extrabiblical evidence that can be interpreted in various ways."[48] S. Norin also finds fault with Lemche's position by pointing out such matters as the verification of Old Testament data with external historical information gleaned from Israel's neighbors and the value of prophetic oracles describing preexilic conditions in Israel.[49] J. Goldingay observes that Thompson's position is also open to criticism. For "the way in which the biblical testimonies to faith refer us to past historical events for their explanation and justification makes it difficult to believe that they imply no claim for their story's factuality."[50] Y. Avishur and M. Heltzer also denounce the negative approach of "a certain number of scholars, such as Lemche, Thompson, Davies, Whitelam and a number of others" who "are simply denying the historicity of the biblical historic tradition."[51]

B. Halpern and H. Shanks condemn the general position of the minimalists. Concerning their view of the veracity of the Divided Monarchy Halpern laments, "What is particularly disturbing about the 'minimalists' is their willful failure to distinguish between Kings, with its synchronistic chronologies and distinctive Israelite and Judahite regnal formularies, and the Pentateuch."[52] Shanks observes, "The biblical minimalists very shrewdly build on some sound scholarship to reach unsound conclusions. Much of what they say is correct—until the 'therefore.' The infirmities in the biblical testimony mean not that the Bible should be entirely ignored but that it must be used with caution as a historical resource."[53]

---

48. S. Herrmann, The Devaluation of the Old Testament as a Historical Source," in *Israel's Past in Present Research*, 353. Herrmann also cites the criticism of F. H. Cryer, *Divination in Ancient Israel and Her Eastern Near Eastern Environment: A Socio-Historical Investigation* (Ph.D. diss., University of Arrhus [Denmark], 1989), 15–16, as proposing "for our consideration a narrative of his own devising."
49. S. Norin, "Respons zu Lemche, 'Ist es noch möglich die Geschichte des Alten Israels zu schreiben'?" *SJOT* 8 (1994): 191–97.
50. J. Goldingay, "The Patriarchs in Scripture and History," in *Israel's Past in Present Research*, 486.
51. Avishur and Heltzer, *Studies on the Royal Administration*, 10. Their own study of the biblical data and information supplied from epigraphic sources has enabled them to bring great clarity with regard to the officials and organization of the kings of Israel. In a similar vein, Mills, *Historical Israel*, 48, concludes that "it does, indeed, seem possible that such a centralised kingship existed in eighth-to seventh-century Israel and Judah." Her conclusion is somewhat tempered, however, by noting that the biblical record is not necessarily scientifically accurate in accordance with modern standards (ibid., 50).
52. B. Halpern, "Erasing History: The Minimalist Assault on Ancient Israel," in *Israel's Past in Present Research*, 425. Halpern caustically questions the historical abilities of some of the leading minimalist scholars, stating that they "are not *real* historians. Biblical scholars such as Philip Davies, John Van Seters, Niels Lemche, and their ilk have typically been trained in either theological seminaries or departments of Near Eastern studies or religion."
53. H. Shanks, "The Biblical Minimalists: Expunging Ancient Israel's Past," *BR* 13, no. 3 (1997): 32–39, 50–52.

Evangelicals who have full confidence in the Bible's historicity naturally reject the minimalist position. D. Howard points out that "not only do these scholars reject the Bible as a valid source, but they resist reading extrabiblical texts that intersect with the Bible in any way that would reinforce the biblical picture."[54] After a thorough study of current historiography, E. Yamauchi concludes, "Textual evidence must be primary even where the archaeological evidence is lacking."[55] Surely a similar courtesy should be accorded the biblical text.

It can readily be seen that Old Testament historiography is in a state of flux. Thus J. W. Flanagan remarks, "The historian then offers a holographic image, an interpretation of the past. The image is a hypothesis—one of many possible interpretations. . . . Thus, there can be no single, definitive history written, and not everyone will see the image as the historian does."[56] Yet for responsible historians one basic source of information must be the scriptural record itself. Even if one were to grant a late dating of the final form of the texts, it by no means follows that the sources the authors used were not contemporaneous with the events they describe or that they give inaccurate information. Nor should we who live millennia after those events and authors necessarily consider ourselves in a better position to evaluate those sources and produce a more accurate account however "scientific" our analyses may be.

Evangelical scholars, of course, are committed to the inspiration of the Scriptures.[57] Nevertheless, this does not excuse them from employing all due care in using all the data responsibly. Evangelicals increasingly are utilizing information gained from external sources in coordination with biblical data and a judicious use of literary approaches in order to arrive at a

---

54. Howard, *Joshua*, 43. It should be pointed out as well that many specialists in ancient Near Eastern history, such as W. W. Hallo, K. A. Kitchen, A. Malamat, and A. Millard maintain the validity of the biblical data as viewed in comparison with other extrabiblical texts. See, for example, W. W. Hallo, "Biblical History in Its Near Eastern Setting: The Contextual Approach," in *Israel's Past in Present Research,* 77–97.
55. E. Yamauchi, "The Current State of Old Testament Historiography," in *Faith, Tradition, and History: Old Testament Historiography in Its Ancient Near Eastern Context,* ed. A. R. Millard, J. K. Hoffmeier, and D. W. Baker (Winona Lake, Ind.: Eisenbrauns, 1994), 36.
56. J. W. Flanagan, "History as Hologram: Integrating Literary, Archaeological, and Comparative Sociological Evidence," in *Society of Biblical Literature 1985 Seminar Papers,* ed. K. H. Richards (Atlanta: Scholars Press, 1985), 309.
57. B. Halpern, *The First Historians,* 3–4, is no more charitable toward conservative scholars than to the minimalists (see above, n. 52). He cites their confessional commitments as precluding their ability to do true historical research.

proper interpretation of the biblical texts and thus achieve a reasonably accurate account of Israel's history.

An Examination of the Biblical Record

In light of the previous discussions, what can be said concerning the historical accuracy of the biblical presentation of the Divided Monarchy? Representative test cases from various periods that help to clarify the situation are presented in the discussion that follows. Selected examples are drawn from each of three historical stages: (1) the early period, represented by the era of the first three dynasties of Israel (Jeroboam to Jehoram, 931–841 B.C.) and kings Rehoboam through Ahaziah in Judah, in which the newly formed kingdoms attempted to establish and maintain their identities amid external pressures by Egyptians, Arameans, and Assyrians, (2) the middle period, comprising the time from the fourth dynasty in Israel until its collapse in 722 B.C. and the reigns of Athaliah through Amon in Judah (841–640 B.C.), in which a brief respite from external incursions allowed the twin kingdoms to experience their greatest heights since the days of Solomon but saw the formidable power of the Neo-Assyrian Empire launch invasions that brought about the fall of Samaria and placed Jerusalem under siege, and (3) the late period from Josiah to Zedekiah (640–586 B.C.), during which complex international events brought about the collapse and demise of the once mighty Neo-Assyrian Empire, the emergence of the Neo-Babylonian (or Chaldean) Empire, and a series of Babylonian invasions of Judah that led to several deportations of its people and the capture of Jerusalem in 586 B.C. Such a procedure approximates but does not exactly reproduce the overall literary design of Kings.

The essential historicity of the biblical record during this period can be illustrated by some key events. The author of Kings describes an invasion by Sheshonq I (biblical Shishak, 950–929 B.C.), the founder of Egypt's twenty-second dynasty, during the reign of Rehoboam (1 Kings 14:25–28; 2 Chron. 12:1–12). The event is also noted in a relief "on the outside of the south wall of the great Karnak temple, between the Bubastite gate and the south wall of the hypostyle."[58] Although the biblical writer's special focus is on Shishak's advance against Jerusalem (1 Kings 14:25; 2 Chron. 12:4), the inscription

---

58. J. H. Breasted, trans., "Reign of Sheshonk I," in *ARE*, 4:348.

accompanying the Egyptian relief gives the names of more than 150 cities that the Egyptian king defeated and despoiled. Accordingly, W. M. Petrie remarks that these cities "are so uniformly scattered over a large part of the country that, if actually visited by the army of Shishak, the clearance of the wealth of the land must have been very thorough."[59]

In recent years D. Rohl has given an interesting twist to the Shishak invasion.[60] Rohl suggests that biblical Shishak was not Sheshonq I, but the Nineteenth Dynasty pharaoh Ramses II (1301–1234 B.C.). Rohl links hypocoristic spellings found in accordance with Ramses family name *(ss, ssy, ssw, sysw)* and the fact that Ramses boasts of attacking Jerusalem. To underscore his argument Rohl emphasizes the absence of a name for Jerusalem in the Sheshonq Karnak inscription as supporting his thesis. Rohl's theory, however, founders on the rather firm and well-accepted Egyptian chronology and, therefore, has not met with wide acceptance among Egyptologists. In addition, his attempt to account for biblical spelling of Shishak (*Kethib*, שִׁוְשַׁק *[šiwšaq]*; *Qere*, שִׁישַׁק *[šîšaq]*) is scarcely convincing, and the MT need not be understood as demanding a full attack against Jerusalem by Shishak.[61]

Of special interest also is the intriguing question the limited space the author of Kings assigned to King Omri of Israel (1 Kings 16:21–28). Omri's accomplishments are listed as twofold: his prevailing over his rival Tibni and his founding of the city of Samaria. Otherwise he is dismissed with a typical formula of condemnation (1 Kings 16:26). Omri was better known than the scriptural record indicates. Thus Assyrian kings commonly referred to the northern kingdom as *Bīt-Ḥumri* ("The House of Omri"). For example, Sargon II claims to be the conqueror of Samaria "and the whole land of *Bit-Humria.*"[62] Detailed information concerning Omri also comes from the well-known Moabite Inscription, which tells of Omri's subjugation of northern Moab. Thus the Moabite king acknowledges that "Omri was the king of Israel, and he opposed Moab many days, for Chemosh was angry with his land."[63]

---

59. W. M. Petrie, *Egypt and Israel* (London: Society for Promoting Christian Knowledge, 1911), 74.
60. D. Rohl, *Pharaohs and Kings* (New York: Crown, 1995).
61. See my note on 1 Kings 14:25 in R. D. Patterson and H. J. Austel, *1, 2 Kings,* EBC, rev. ed. (Grand Rapids: Zondervan, forthcoming).
62. D. D. Luckenbill, trans., "Sargon: The Khorsabad Texts," in *ARAB,* 2:40.
63. K. A. D. Smelik, trans., "The Inscription of King Mesha," in *COS,* 2:137; see also the discussion in D. W. Thomas, *Documents from Old Testament Times* (New York: Harper & Row, 1961), 196–99.

His relation to Phoenicia may have further enlarged Omri's prestige, for Omri's son Ahab was married to the daughter of Ethbaal, king of Sidon (1 Kings 16:31). Since royal marriages were customarily affairs of international protocol arranged by the parents, E. Merrill may be correct in suggesting that Omri fostered the marriage as part of his hope for commercial and political gain. All of this may indicate that "Omri was in fact one of the most influential of Israel's early kings."[64]

Several events in the middle period are also mentioned in the extrabiblical records. Thus Jehu's capitulation to Shalmaneser III is duly recorded on the Assyrian king's Black Obelisk as "the tribute of Jehu, son of Omri" (*mâr Ḫumri;* i.e., a descendant of Israel's third dynasty founder).[65] Of prime interest is Sennacherib's invasion of Judah in 701 B.C., which is recorded both in the Old Testament (2 Kings 18:13–37; 2 Chron. 32:1–22; Isa. 36–37) and Sennacherib's own annals.[66] Some have suggested that Sennacherib actually launched two campaigns against Judah and Jerusalem, the first in 701 B.C. and the second assumedly occurring later.[67] Different biblical schema have been put forward with some deciding that 2 Kings 18:14–16 relates to the first campaign and 2 Kings 18:17–19:37, the second, while others place the first campaign in 1 Kings 18:13–19:7 and the second in 2 Kings 19:8–37.[68] The Assyrian account, however, reports only one campaign against Judah and Jerusalem. Although some details still remain unclear, a comparison of the biblical and Assyrian accounts can yield a good general grasp of the campaign.

Sennacherib swept down through Syria causing the capitulation of the cities of Phoenicia. Continuing down the coast, Sennacherib secured the submission and tribute of the various cities all the way into Philistia. Those who did not quickly submit were treated harshly by the fierce Assyrian king.[69] The campaign against the Philistines was especially important to

---

64. E. Merrill, *Kingdom of Priests* (Grand Rapids: Baker, 1987), 340. Halpern provides a helpful chart in "Erasing History: The Minimalist Assault on Ancient Israel," 419; he lists Omri among the names of the kings of Israel and Judah that appear in nonbiblical, non-Israelite inscriptions.
65. Oppenheim, "Shalmaneser III (858–824)," 281; see also Luckenbill, "Shalmaneser III," 1:211; and K. L. Younger Jr., trans., "Black Obelisk (2.113f)," in *COS*, 2:270.
66. See D. D. Luckenbill, trans., "Sennacherib: The Historical Texts," in *ARAB*, 2:118–21.
67. See, for example, J. Bright, *A History of Israel*, 4th ed. (Philadelphia: Westminster/John Knox Press, 2000), 298–309; W. H. Shea, "Sennacherib's Second Palestine Campaign," *JBL* 104 (1985): 401–18; and C. Begg, "Sennacherib's Second Palestinian Campaign: An Additional Indication," *JBL* 106 (1987): 685–86.
68. Other variations of relating the two accounts also occur. See, for example, the extensive comments of M. Cogan and H. Tadmor, *II Kings*, AB (New York: Doubleday, 2001), 228–51.
69. Luckenbill, "Sennacherib," *ARAB*, 2:119.

Sennacherib, for Hezekiah had rebelled against him and invaded the Philistine coast as far as Gaza (2 Kings 18:7–8). Apparently dividing his forces, Sennacherib sent a contingent toward Ekron while he himself led a sizeable force into Judah. When he reached Lachish, he received Hezekiah's tribute (2 Kings 18:13–16). The arrangements apparently included Hezekiah's surrender of Padi, the king of Ekron, to Sennacherib, for the Assyrian king reports that the officials of Ekron had previously delivered their king to Hezekiah.[70] When those officials learned of the advance of Sennacherib's forces, they petitioned the Egyptians for aid. This forced Sennacherib, who had completed the siege of Lachish[71] and moved on to Libnah,[72] to turn to meet the Egyptians. The battle took place at El Tekeh (2 Kings 19:9), where Sennacherib successfully routed the Egyptians, took the city, and despoiled it.[73]

With the Egyptian threat thwarted and affairs settled at Ekron, Sennacherib systematically reduced the cities of Judah and placed Jerusalem under siege.[74] At this point the biblical account provides additional details concerning the negotiations for Jerusalem, Isaiah's assurance that the Lord would deliver the city, and the great loss of life suffered by Sennacherib's forces (2 Kings 18:17–19:36).

Thus a coherent picture of the campaign can be achieved despite difficulties at several points without resorting to a second western campaign for Sennacherib.[75] Regardless of differences at minor points, the essential historicity of such an invasion is underscored by the full treatment in the Old

---

70. Ibid. When Ekron finally capitulated, Sennacherib reinstalled Padi as king and imposed tribute upon him (ibid., 2:120).
71. Sennacherib's successful siege of Lachish is noted in a relief found at Nineveh. See K. N. Schoville, *Biblical Archaeology in Focus* (Grand Rapids: Baker, 1978), 424.
72. During his campaigning Hezekiah apparently had regained Libnah, which had been lost to Judah in an earlier rebellion (2 Kings 8:22).
73. Luckenbill, "Sennacherib," *ARAB*, 2:120. Second Kings 19:9 records the name of the Cushite king who led the Egyptian forces as Tirhakah. It was formally thought the Tirhakah was a mere lad, too young to be involved with the 701 B.C. battle at El Tekeh, hence an indication of a second campaign by Sennacherib. Recent studies, however, have demonstrated that Tirhakah was at least twenty years old, hence well able to lead the Egyptian forces. Although he was not yet the king of Egypt, the narrator ascribes to him his eventual title. For full details, see Kitchen, *Third Intermediate Period*, 154–72, 383–86. See also my note in R. D. Patterson and H. J. Austel, *1, 2 Kings*, EBC (Grand Rapids: Zondervan, 1988), 4:263–64.
74. Sennacherib boasts of shutting up Hezekiah "like a caged bird" in Luckenbill, "Sennacherib," *ARAB*, 2:120, 143; and A. L. Oppenheim, trans., "Sennacherib, 704–681," in *ANET*, 288.
75. See also the arguments against the two-campaign hypothesis by Cogan and Tadmor, *II Kings*, 249–50.

Testament and the Assyrian account.[76] As for the divine deliverance of Jerusalem at this time, it is interesting to note that while Sennacherib provides graphic details of the capture and despoiling of many cities, he mentions only the tribute, not the fall, of Jerusalem.

One of the more interesting problems connected with the fall of the northern kingdom is the identity of "So, King of Egypt." According to 2 Kings 17:4, Israel's last king Hoshea hoped to find support against his Assyrian overlord from an Egyptian king. A difficulty arises, however, when one examines the names of the Egyptian kings in this period, for no So is listed as such. Some scholars have therefore suggested that the author of Kings has confused So with a later Egyptian king, such as the twenty-fifth-dynasty pharaoh Shabaku or a certain Sib'e, an Egyptian commander.[77]

Among the many suggestions for identifying the biblical So, three appear to have the most merit. First, K. A. Kitchen concludes that the best candidate is Osorkon IV, the last king of the twenty-third dynasty located in Tanis.[78] Kitchen points out that the biblical So may simply be an abbreviation of Osorkon. His rule in Egypt's northeastern delta, directly adjacent to Hebrew territory, would make him a natural candidate for help. Further, longstanding relations between Israel and the Tanite dynasty would make Hoshea's petition to Osorkon to be a natural one.[79]

A second suggestion was put forward by Hans Goedicke.[80] Goedicke builds upon the suggestion that Hebrew "So" would be pronounced Sâ in Akkadian, the *lingua franca* of the ancient Near East, and would designate the Egyptian Sais (lit., Saʾw), the capital of Egypt's twenty-fourth dynasty. Thus Hoshea sent messengers to Sais (Saʾw—Sā—Sôʾ), the capital city of Tef-nekht, king of Egypt's twenty-fourth dynasty.

Third, a recent proposal by A. R. Green combines Egyptian and

---

76. Partial resolution of the difficulties may lie in seeing that the Assyrian account is more thematic than chronological in order. For a literary appraisal of the biblical account, see D. N. Fewell, "Sennacherib's Defeat: Words of War in 2 Kings 18.13–19.37," *JSOT* 34 (1986): 79–90.
77. See G. H. Jones, *1 and 2 Kings*, NCBC (Grand Rapids: Eerdmans, 1984), 2:546–47; J. Gray, *I and II Kings*, 2d ed. (Philadelphia: Westminster, 1970), 643; and D. B. Redford, "Studies in Relations Between Palestine and Egypt During the First Millennium B.C.," *JAOS* 93 (1973): 3–17, decides for a general confusion of So with pharaohs of the Saite Dynasty.
78. Kitchen, *Third Intermediate Period*, 371–76.
79. See further G. W. Ahlström, "Kung So och Israels Undergang," *Svensk Exegetisk Årsbok* (1989): 5–19.
80. H. Goedicke, "The End of So, King of Egypt," *BASOR* 17 (1963): 64–66. See also J. Day, "The Problem of 'So, King of Egypt' in 2 Kings xvii 4," *VT* 42 (1992): 289–301.

Mesopotamian information with linguistic data to suggest that So be equated with the twenty-fifth-dynasty pharaoh Piankhy.[81] In his move northward this Egyptian pharaoh succeeded in defeating Tef-nekht in 727 B.C., thus establishing himself as a power to be reckoned with in the Nile Delta region. Accordingly, Hoshea may have viewed him as a likely champion for his cause to free himself of Assyrian rule.

All three proposals have merit. Although certainty may be lacking as to the precise identity of So, no need exists to attribute a blunder to the narrator of Kings.

The essential historicity of the scriptural record in the third period can also be demonstrated by the secular literature of the period. Thus Nebuchadnezzar's successful siege of Jerusalem in 597 B.C. is documented in the Babylonian Chronicles:

> In the seventh year, the month of Kislev, the king of Akkad mustered his troops, marched to the Ḫatti-land,
> and encamped against (i.e., besieged) the city of Judah and on the second day of the month of Adar he seized the city and captured the king.
> He appointed there a king of his own choice (lit. heart), received its heavy tribute and sent (them) to Babylon.[82]

Likewise, confirmation of the Babylonian advance that resulted in the fall of Jerusalem in 586 B.C. comes from the ostraca recovered at Lachish. Consisting of twenty-one letters detailing conditions in Judahite Lachish, they reveal circumstances in the city as it faced the coming Babylonian army. Ostracon IV is especially interesting: "And let (my lord) know that we are watching for the signals of Lachish, according to all the indications which my lord hath given, for we cannot see Azekah."[83] Although Jeremiah (Jer. 34:7) notes that the cities of Azekah and Lachish were still holding out while the Babylonians were besieging Jerusalem, this letter supplies details of a subsequent development. Written by an army officer as he watched for

---

81. A. R. Green, "The Identity of King So of Egypt: An Alternate Interpretation," *JNES* 52 (1993): 99–108.
82. Wiseman, *Chronicles of the Chaldean Kings,* 73.
83. W. F. Albright, trans., "Palestinian Inscriptions," in *ANET,* 322.

the signal fires from Azekah, the fact that none were seen may indicate that the city had fallen.[84]

One special problem concerns the failure of the author of Kings to mention a Babylonian siege of Jerusalem prior to those in the days of Jehoiachin (2 Kings 24:10–17) and Zedekiah (2 Kings 25:1–21). Those two sieges have been accurately dated to 598 and 586 B.C. respectfully. Yet, according to the book of Daniel (1:1–7) Nebuchadnezzar launched an earlier campaign against Jerusalem in the third year of Jehoiakim (605 B.C.). At that time Daniel and others were carried away captive to Babylon along with some of the temple furnishings. The omission of this event in Kings and the lack of clear confirmation in the Babylonian records for such a strike against Jerusalem in that year have cast some doubt as to such a siege.[85]

Historical light on Daniel's account may be found, however, in the Babylonian Chronicles, which record that in 605 B.C. Nebuchadnezzar led the successful Babylonian campaign against the Assyrians and Egyptians at Carchemish. Following the victory at Carchemish, Nebuchadnezzar mopped up the few enemy forces that escaped to Hamath and then proceeded to campaign in the west. The Chronicles record that "at that time Nebuchadnezzar conquered the whole area of the Hatti-country."[86] While campaigning there, Nebuchadnezzar's father Nabopolassar died and Nebuchadnezzar hastily returned home to claim the crown. Interestingly, the last two royal edicts of Nabopolassar are dated in April and May of 605 B.C., while Nebuchadnezzar's first two edicts are dated in April and September of that same year. Additional confirmation of this comes from Josephus who cites the priest and historian Berossus as reporting that when Nabopolassar died while Nebuchadnezzar was campaigning, Nebuchadnezzar

---

84. M. Mills *(Historical Israel,* 50) notes that stone panels depicting the Babylonian capture of Lachish are preserved in the British Museum in London. Mills cites this together with evidence from the Mesha Stele and the Black Obelisk of the Assyrian king Shalmaneser III showing Ahab's submission as evidence that "in the eighth to seventh centuries there were centralized kingdoms in Israel and Judah." See also the discussion in A. J. Hoerth, *Archaeology and the Old Testament* (Grand Rapids: Baker, 1998), 364–66.

85. See, for example, I. M. Price, *The Dramatic Story of History,* 2d ed. (New York: Revell, 1935), 358; and S. R. Driver, *Introduction to the Literature of the Old Testament* (New York: Scribner's, 1950), 498. The author of Kings also does not mention Jeremiah's recording (Jer. 52:30) of a later deportation of 745 citizens of Judah in Nebuchadnezzar's twenty-third year (i.e., 582 B.C.). F. B. Huey Jr., *Jeremiah Lamentations,* NAC (Nashville: Broadman & Holman, 1993), 438, suggests that "this group may have been taken in retaliation for the murder of the Babylonian-appointed governor, Gedaliah (41:1–2)."

86. Wiseman, *Chronicles of the Chaldean Kings,* 69.

... set the affairs of Egypt and the other countries in order, and committed the captives he had taken from the Jews and Phoenicians, and Syrians, and of the nations belonging to Egypt to some of his friends, that they might conduct that part of the forces that had on heavy armor, with the rest of the baggage to Babylonia, while he went in haste . . . over the desert to Babylon.[87]

Having secured the throne in this accession year (605 B.C.), Nebuchadnezzar rejoined his troops and campaigned for several months in the west. Marching "unopposed through the Ḫatti-land . . . he took the heavy tribute of the Ḫatti-territory to Babylon.[88] This may be reflected in the Chronicler's statement that Nebuchadnezzar attacked Jehoiakim "to take him to Babylon" (2 Chron. 36:6–7).[89]

In light of these data, Daniel's account can be seen to be trustworthy. What is uncertain is whether this deportation of Jerusalem after the victory at Carchemish was prior to Nebuchadnezzar's return to Babylon to solidify his claim on the throne or came after his return to the campaign in the west. In either case the year is 605 B.C.[90]

Conclusion

These specific cases noted in the above discussions of events narrated in the scriptural presentation of the Divided Monarchy illustrate well the contributions of extrabiblical historical data to the understanding of the biblical

---

87. Josephus, *Contra Apion,* 1:19.
88. Wiseman, *Chronicles of the Chaldean Kings,* 69.
89. See further, ibid., 28.
90. Interestingly, Jeremiah (46:2) records the battle of Carchemish that would have led to Daniel's captivity as taking place in Jehoiakim's fourth year rather than Daniel's report that it was his third. S. Miller, in his commentary, *Daniel,* NAC (Nashville: Broadman & Holman, 1994), 56–57, suggests that Jeremiah was using the Babylonian dating system and Daniel the system current in Judah. Others take the opposite view that Daniel, ministering in Babylon, used the Babylonian system whereas Jeremiah, who ministered in Judah, employed the system in vogue there. See G. L. Archer, *Encyclopedia of Bible Difficulties* (Grand Rapids: Zondervan, 1982), 284–85; J. Baldwin, *Daniel,* TOTC (Downers Grove, Ill.: InterVarsity, 1978), 77; J. Walvoord, *Daniel: The Key to Prophetic Revelation* (Chicago: Moody, 1971), 30–31; R. D. Wilson, *Studies in the Book of Daniel,* 2 vols. in 1 (Grand Rapids: Baker, 1972), 1:60–82; and E. J. Young, *The Prophecy of Daniel* (Grand Rapids: Eerdmans, 1949), 267–70. L. Wood, *A Commentary on Daniel* (Grand Rapids: Zondervan, 1973), 25–28, assumes that both Jeremiah and Daniel used the system current in Judah, with Daniel opting for the religious calendar, in which the New Year began in the spring, while Jeremiah employed the civil calendar, which began in the autumn.

text. In some instances the harmonization of the data of external history with the biblical record provides a fuller picture of the historical situation narrated by the biblical author (e.g., the respective campaigns against Judah and Jerusalem by Sheshonq I, Sennacherib, and Nebuchadnezzar). Here details from three different peoples (Egyptians, Assyrians, and Babylonians) in three different centuries (the tenth and eighth centuries, and the 598 B.C. Babylonian invasion in the sixth century B.C.) impinge upon the biblical record, providing confirmatory evidence for the essential reliability of the biblical record.

In some cases, external historical data supplement the scriptural record where sufficient information is lacking (e.g., the significance of Omri's rule in Israel). In other cases they can clarify or validate misunderstood or misjudged biblical data (e.g., "So, King of Egypt"). In still other situations knowledge of ancient Near Eastern history can supply information omitted by the biblical historian (e.g., the 605 B.C. deportation of Daniel and his friends). In all of this history proves to be the handmaiden of biblical exposition and a critical tool for balanced exegesis of the text.[91]

---

91. I have argued in *Nahum, Habakkuk, Zephaniah* (Chicago: Moody, 1991), xvi, that "the chair of proper exegesis rests upon the four evenly balanced legs of grammatical precision, historical accuracy, literary conventions, and proper theological conclusions."

It is my distinct privilege to have been asked to contribute this short study to a book honoring a dear friend and colleague who indeed has exemplified such balance throughout his long years as scholar, teacher, and role model to his students.

9

THE EXILIC AND POSTEXILIC PERIODS

Current Developments

Edwin M. Yamauchi

EVANGELICAL OLD TESTAMENT SCHOLARS, while they recognize the importance of placing the Scriptures in their proper historical and cultural contexts, have been understandably concerned primarily with the biblical texts themselves. It is difficult to keep up with the abundance of monographs and articles on the Exilic and Postexilic Period, that is the late seventh to the fifth centuries B.C., which saw the collapse of the Assyrian Empire, then the rise in succession of the Neo-Babylonian and the Persian Empires. It is the merit of Eugene H. Merrill that he has attempted to be well informed, but in writing his *Kingdom of Priests,* he was limited as to how much new material he could incorporate.[1]

SECOND-TEMPLE STUDIES

As many scholars have noted, the period of the second temple (that is, the Persian and Hellenistic eras [539–330 and 330–133 B.C.]) has received intense scholarly attention recently. Paolo Sacchi declares, "First of all I think it is worth emphasizing the fact that, unlike in the past, scholarly interest has come more and more to be focused on the history of the second

---

1. Eugene H. Merrill, *Kingdom of Priests: A History of Old Testament Israel* (Grand Rapids: Baker, 1987). In his shorter work, *An Historical Survey of the Old Testament,* 2d ed. (Grand Rapids: Baker, 1991), Merrill incorporates more recent references.

temple period instead of the history of Israel in general."[2] This is in part due to the conviction of scholars that many of the Old Testament texts came from or were redacted in this period.[3] But this is also the result of the claim of revisionist scholars, dubbed "minimalists" by their critics,[4] who credit this late period for the creation of all of the books of the Hebrew Bible, including the Torah.[5] Other scholars such as Peter Frei have argued for the authorization of the Torah by the Persian authorities, noting as a parallel the codification of Egyptian law by Darius I.[6]

New Approaches

Since the Scriptures do not present a comprehensive account of this period, scholars have attempted to use insights from the social sciences to read between the lines to gain a better insight into the social and political background of the biblical texts, as does Jon L. Berquist in his *Judaism in Persia's Shadow: A Social and Historical Approach*.[7] T. C. Eskenazi and E. P. Judd make some interesting comparisons between the problem of mixed

---

2. P. Sacchi, *The History of the Second Temple Period* (Sheffield: Sheffield Academic Press, 2000), 9.
3. J. Blenkinsopp: "Haggai, Zechariah 1–8, Malachi, Joel, much if not all of Isaiah 54–66, a good part of Isaiah 1–39, and a variably calculated percentage of the material in other prophetic books, depending on who is doing the calculating, are assigned to this period" ("The Social Role of the Prophets," *JSOT* 93 [2001]: 43). For an evangelical commentary that affirms a Persian date for the composition of Isaiah, see J. D. W. Watts, *Isaiah 1–33* (Waco: Word, 1985); idem, *Isaiah 34–66* (Waco: Word, 1987); cf. H. G. M. Williamson, *The Book Called Isaiah: Deutero-Isaiah's Role in Composition and Redaction* (Clarendon: Oxford University Press, 1994). For a commentary that defends the unity and the early date of Isaiah, see J. N. Oswalt, *The Book of Isaiah, Chapters 1–39* (Grand Rapids: Eerdmans, 1986); and idem, *The Book of Isaiah, Chapters 40–66* (Grand Rapids: Eerdmans, 1998).
4. For a sharp critique of minimalist approaches, see W. G. Dever, *What Did the Biblical Writers Know and When Did They Know It?* (Grand Rapids: Eerdmans, 2001).
5. P. R. Davies, *In Search of "Ancient Israel"* (Sheffield: Sheffield Academic Press, 1992), 95, places the birth of "biblical Israel" in the Persian period. E. Nodet, *A Search for the Origins of Judaism*, trans. E. Crowley (Sheffield: Sheffield Academic Press, 1997), 387, opts for the Hellenistic era as the time when the Torah was created.
6. See Frei's article and responses to his proposal in *Persia and Torah*, ed. J. W. Watts (Atlanta: Society of Biblical Literature, 2001).
7. Jon L. Berquist, *Judaism in Persia's Shadow: A Social and Historical Approach* (Minneapolis: Fortress, 1995). Cf. also D. L. Smith, *The Religion of the Landless: The Social Context of the Babylonian Exile* (Bloomington, Ind.: Meyer Stone Books, 1989). One problem with Smith's work is his dependence on the theories of J. P. Weinberg, *The Citizen-Temple Community*, trans. D. L. Smith-Christopher (Sheffield: Sheffield Academic Press, 1992), whose proposals are sharply criticized by H. G. M. Williamson, "Judah and the Jews," in *Studies in Persian History: Essays in Memory of David M. Lewis*, ed. M. Brosius and A. Kuhrt (Leiden: Nederlands Instituut voor het Nabije Oosten, 1998), 145–63.

marriages in Ezra and similar problems among population groups in modern Israel.[8] An excellent example of the helpful collaboration between a biblical scholar and a social scientist is the analysis of Nehemiah according to the paradigm of an anthropologist by K. D. Tollefson and H. G. M. Williamson.[9]

General References

An invaluable survey of current scholarship, including references to the many important contributions of the author himself, is H. G. M. Williamson, "Exile and After: Historical Study."[10] Also useful is Victor P. Hamilton's *Handbook on the Historical Books*.[11] Especially rich in bibliographical references is the second volume of R. Albertz's *A History of Israelite Religion in the Old Testament Period*.[12] Two collections of stimulating and provocative essays on this era are: *Second Temple Studies, 1: Persian Period*,[13] and *Second Temple Studies, 2: Temple and Community in the Persian Period*.[14]

For the Neo-Babylonian era we have no recent overall history devoted exclusively to this period.[15] We do have important monographs on individual rulers, most notably by D. J. Wiseman on Nebuchadnezzar.[16] As

---

8. T. C. Eskenazi and E. P. Judd, "Marriage to a Stranger in Ezra 9–10," in *Second Temple Studies, 1: Persian Period*, ed. P. R. Davies, JSOTSup 117 (Sheffield: Sheffield Academic Press, 1991), 2:266–85.
9. K. D. Tollefson and H. G. M. Williamson, "Nehemiah as Cultural Revitalization: An Anthropological Perspective," *JSOT* 56 (1992): 41–68.
10. H. G. M. Williamson, "Exile and After: Historical Study," in *The Face of Old Testament Studies: A Survey of Contemporary Approaches*, ed. D. W. Baker and B. T. Arnold (Grand Rapids: Baker, 1999), 236–65. Among his notable studies is H. G. M. Williamson, "Ezra and Nehemiah in the Light of the Texts from Persepolis," *BBR* 1 (1991): 50–54.
11. V. P. Hamilton, *Handbook on the Historical Books* (Grand Rapids: Baker, 2001).
12. R. Albertz, *A History of Israelite Religion in the Old Testament Period*, 2 vols., trans. J. Bowden (Louisville: Westminster/John Knox, 1994).
13. P. R. Davies, ed., *Second Temple Studies, 1: Persian Period*, JSOTSup 117 (Sheffield: Sheffield Academic Press, 1991).
14. T. C. Eskenazi and K. H. Richards, eds., *Second Temple Studies, 2: Temple and Community in the Persian Period*, JSOTSup 175 (Sheffield: Sheffield Academic Press, 1994).
15. See H. W. F. Saggs, *Babylonians* (Norman, Okla.: University of Oklahoma Press, 1995); B. Arnold, "Babylonians," in *POTW*, 43–76.
16. D. J. Wiseman, *Nebuchadnezzar and Babylon* (Oxford: Oxford University Press for the British Academy, 1985). Cf. also D. B. Weisberg, *Texts from the Time of Nebuchadnezzar*, Yale Oriental Studies, Babylonian Texts, no. 17 (New Haven, Conn.: Yale University Press, 1980); and R. H. Sack, *Image of Nebuchadnezzar: The Emergence of a Legend* (Cranbury, N.J.: Susquehanna University Press, 1991).

Williamson points out, we now have numerous treatments of the Persian Empire, which have superseded the classic *History of the Persian Empire* by A. T. Olmstead (1948). The most comprehensive treatment is now P. Briant's *From Cyrus to Alexander: A History of the Persian Empire*, followed by *The Cambridge History of Iran*, vol. 2, *The Median and Achaemenian Periods*, edited by E. Yarshater; see also M. Dandamaev, *A Political History of the Achaemenid Empire*.[17] Works which deal in particular with the Jews in the Persian Empire include *The Cambridge History of Judaism*, vol. 1, *Introduction: The Persian Period*, ed. W. D. Davies and L. Finkelstein,[18] and the first volume of L. L. Grabbe's *Judaism from Cyrus to Hadrian*.[19] See also R. Zadok's valuable study of the cuneiform evidence for the exiles.[20] The area of Syria, Lebanon, and Palestine which the Persians called "Beyond the River (i.e., the Euphrates)," is the focus of a new journal, *Transeuphratène*, and a series of essays by J. Elayi and J. Sapin, *Beyond the River*.[21] These scholars lament the earlier neglect of this area during the Persian period by scholars, who were either primarily interested in the earlier civilizations of the Egyptians and Mesopotamians or the later civilizations of the Greeks and Romans.

THE NEO-BABYLONIAN EMPIRE

The Medes

The overthrow of the fearsome Assyrian Empire in 612 was effected by an alliance of two disparate peoples, the Medes[22] in the Zagros Mountains to the east, and the Chaldeans in southern Mesopotamia.[23] The Medes

---

17. M. Dandamaev, *A Political History of the Achaemenid Empire* (Leiden: Brill, 1989). See my review in *Bibliotheca Orientalis* 49 (1992): 455–56. The English edition of P. Briant's massive *Histoire de l'empire perse* (Paris: Fayard, 1996) has now been issued: P. Briant, *From Cyrus to Alexander: A History of the Benson Empire* (Winona Lake, Ind.: Eisenbrauns, 2002).
18. W. D. Davies and L. Finkelstein, eds., *Introduction: The Persian Period*, vol. 1 of *The Cambridge History of Judaism* (Cambridge: Cambridge University Press, 1984). Cf. T. C. Mitchell, "The Babylonian Exile and the Restoration of the Jews in Palestine (586–c. 500 B.C.)," in *Cambridge Ancient History*, ed. J. Boardman et al., 2d ed. (Cambridge: Cambridge University Press, 1991), 3:2:410–60.
19. L. L. Grabbe, *Judaism from Cyrus to Hadrian* (Minneapolis: Fortress, 1992).
20. R. Zadok, *The Jews in Babylonia during the Chaldean and Achaemenian Periods in the Light of Babylonian Sources* (Haifa: Haifa University Press, 1979).
21. J. Elayi and J. Sapin, *Beyond the River: New Perspectives on Transeuphrates*, trans. J. E. Crowley (Sheffield: Sheffield Academic Press, 1998).
22. E. Yamauchi, *Persia and the Bible* (Grand Rapids: Baker, 1990), 31–63.
23. See E. Yamauchi, "Chaldea, Chaldeans," in *NIDBA*, 123–25.

were an Indo-European people, closely allied to the Persians; the Greeks, in fact, called the Persians "Medes."[24] Their capital, called Ecbatana, was located at the modern city of Hamadan.[25]

The Chaldeans

The Chaldean leader, Merodach-Baladan, is mentioned in the Bible (2 Kings 20:12–15; Isa. 39:1–4) as being solicitous about Hezekiah's health. From extrabiblical texts we learn that he was a thorn in the side of the last Assyrian kings, from Tiglath-pileser III to Sennacherib.

Nebuchadnezzar

It was the Chaldean ruler, Nabopolassar,[26] who began the Neo-Babylonian Empire, and who, in alliance with the Median king Cyaxares, overthrew the Assyrians. Nabopolassar's son, Nebuchadnezzar,[27] built the famous Hanging Gardens for his Median bride.[28] In 605 Nebuchadnezzar defeated an Egyptian army sent by Necho at the key Euphrates crossing site of Carchemish. It was in a futile attempt to stop Necho at Megiddo[29] four years earlier (609 B.C.) that Josiah lost his life (2 Kings 23:29–30). The excavators at Carchemish discovered a Gorgon shield, which had been used by a Greek mercenary. We now have abundant evidence of the presence of Greek mercenaries fighting for the Egyptians, the Babylonians, and the last kings of Judah.[30]

---

24. See E. Yamauchi, "Medes," in *NIDBA,* 304–6; and idem, *Persia and the Bible,* 31–63.
25. See Yamauchi, *Persia and the Bible,* 305–14. Recent excavations by the Iranians themselves have uncovered extensive ancient buildings, whose date has not yet been established. See M. R. Saraf, "Neue architektonische und städtebauliche Funde von Ekbatana-Tepe (Hamadan)," *Archäologische Mitteilungen aus Iran und Turan* 29 (1997): 321–39. I owe this reference to Professor David Stronach.
26. See E. Yamauchi, "Nabopolassar," in *NIDBA,* 326–27.
27. See E. Yamauchi, "Nebuchadnezzar," in *NIDBA,* 332–34.
28. D. W. W. Stevenson, "A Proposal for the Irrigation of the Hanging Gardens of Babylon," *Iraq* 54 (1992): 35–55.
29. See E. H. Cline, *The Battles of Armageddon* (Ann Arbor, Mich.: University of Michigan Press, 2000).
30. See E. Yamauchi, *Greece and Babylon* (Grand Rapids: Baker, 1967); and idem, *Persia and the Bible,* 379–94. On the site of Mezad Hashavyahu on the coast of Palestine, see E. Stern, *The Assyrian, Babylonian, and Persian Periods (732–332 B.C.E.),* vol. 2 of *Archaeology of the Land of the Bible* (New York: Doubleday, 2001), 140–42. Stern (ibid., 227) concludes: "From the combined evidence of both written documents and archaeological remains, it appears that, even before the arrival of the Assyrians, but mainly during and after their period of domination, there was Greek penetration into Palestine by traders and mercenaries."

The Capture of Jerusalem

The important *Chronicles of the Chaldean Kings* published by D. J. Wiseman cover only the earlier years of Nebuchadnezzar's reign (605–562).[31] They do refer to his attack upon Jerusalem in 597.[32] The question of whether he then destroyed the Jerusalem temple in 587 or in 586 has depended upon the calendars scholars have adopted.[33] Y. Shiloh declared that his 1978 "excavation found for the first time in Jerusalem a Persian-period ceramic layer within clear stratigraphical context—solid archeological evidence for that resettlement of the Babylonian exiles in the City of David."[34]

The Exile of the Judeans

The total number of Judeans the Babylonians deported can only be guessed.[35] One striking difference between the earlier Assyrian deportations and those of the Babylonians was that the former brought newcomers into the land of Israel, whereas the Babylonians did not. Surveys conclude that the Assyrians invested heavily in the economic development of Samaria, whereas the Babylonians neglected the area of Judah. The staggering dimensions of the devastation wrought upon the kingdoms of Israel and of Judah are revealed by excavations and surveys. Of 354 Judean sites only thirty-nine were reestablished after Sennacherib's invasion of 701. The invasions under Nebuchadnezzar wreaked havoc and left only small, poor villages in their wake. Archaeological evidence and inscriptions reveal that the Phoenicians[36] occupied the Philistine coast, and that the Edomites[37] occupied the area south of Hebron. The latter incursion served as the basis for Obadiah's condemnation of Edom.

---

31. D. J. Wiseman, *Chronicles of the Chaldean Kings* (London: Trustees of the British Museum, 1956).
32. W. W. Hallo, "Nebukadnezar Comes to Jerusalem," in *Through the Sound of Many Voices*, ed. J. V. Plaut (Toronto: Lester & Orpen Dennys, 1982), 40–57.
33. H. Cazelles, "587 ou 586?" in *The Word of the Lord Shall Go Forth: Essays in Honor of David Noel Freedman*, Carol L. Meyers and M. O'Connor (Winona Lake, Ind.: Eisenbrauns, 1983), 430, favors 587 B.C.
34. Y. Shiloh, "City of David: Excavation 1978," *BA* 42 (1979): 168.
35. On the exile of the Israelites, see K. L. Younger Jr., "The Deportations of the Israelites," *JBL* 117 (1998): 201–27.
36. See W. A. Ward, "Phoenicians," in *POTW*, 183–206.
37. See K. G. Hoglund, "Edomites," in *POTW*, 335–47. See R. Cohen and Y. Yisrael, *On the Road to Edom: Discoveries from ʿEn Ḥaṣeba* (Jerusalem: Israel Museum, 1995); and idem, "The Iron Age Fortress at ʿEn Ḥaṣeba," *BA* 58 (1995): 223–35.

Later Neo-Babylonian Kings

Nebuchadnezzar was succeeded by a number of ephemeral kings: Evil-Merodach (562–560),[38] Neriglissar (560–56),[39] and Labashi-Marduk (556). Nabonidus,[40] the last of the Neo-Babylonian kings, is not mentioned in the Hebrew Bible but his son Belshazzar is depicted as the king of Babylon when it fell to Cyrus. The "Prayer of Nabonidus" from Qumran[41] has been taken by a number of scholars as the basis for Nebuchadnezzar's madness in Daniel 4.[42] But there are numerous problems with such an assumption.[43]

Jeremiah

I have supported the earlier view that Jeremiah's "peoples from the north" may have been Scythians, some of whom may have aided the Babylonians.[44] It is significant that Scythian type arrowheads were found in the destruction level of Jerusalem. Extrabiblical data, including the bulla of Jeremiah's scribe, Baruch,[45] and many other names confirm "the essential reliability of the Jeremianic prose material."[46]

Ezekiel

Excellent two-volume commentaries on Ezekiel have been authored by L. Allen,[47] and D. I. Block.[48] Block has devoted a number of articles to a

---

38. See R. H. Sack, *An Economic, Historical Study of the Reign of Amel-Marduk, King of Babylon 562–560 B.C.* (Kevalaer: Neukirchen-Vluyn, 1972).
39. See R. H. Sack, *Neriglissar: King of Babylon* (Kevalaer: Neukirchen-Vluyn, 1994).
40. P.-A. Beaulieu, *The Reign of Nabonidus, King of Babylon, 556–539 B.C.* (New Haven, Conn.: Yale University Press, 1989).
41. F. G. Martínez, *The Dead Sea Scrolls Translated* (Leiden: Brill, 1994), 289.
42. For example, J. Collins, *Daniel* (Minneapolis: Fortress, 1993), 32.
43. See E. Yamauchi, "Nabonidus," in *ISBE*, 3:468–70. Cf. W. H. Shea, "Nabonidus, Belshazzar, and the Book of Daniel: An Update," *AUSS* 20 (1982): 133–50.
44. See E. Yamauchi, *Foes from the Northern Frontier* (Grand Rapids: Baker, 1982), esp. 87–107; and idem, "The Scythians: Invading Hordes from the Russian Steppes," *BA* 46 (1983): 90–99.
45. N. Avigad, *Bullae from the Time of Jeremiah* (Jerusalem: Israel Exploration Society, 1986); and H. Shanks, "Jeremiah's Scribe and Confidant Speaks from a Hoard of Clay Bullae," *BAR* 13, no. 5 (September–October 1987): 58–65.
46. D. A. Glatt-Gilad, "The Personal Names in Jeremiah as a Source for the History of the Period," *HS* 41 (2000): 31–45.
47. L. Allen, *Ezekiel 1–19* (Waco: Word, 1990); and idem, *Ezekiel 20–48* (Waco: Word, 1994).
48. D. I. Block, *Ezekiel, Chapters 1–24* (Grand Rapids: Eerdmans, 1997); and idem, *Ezekiel, Chapters 25–48* (Grand Rapids: Eerdmans, 1998).

subject of perennial interest, Gog in Ezekiel 38.[49] Cuneiform onomastic and topographical references of Jewish settlements in Mesopotamia as summarized in an important essay by B. Oded confirm descriptions of the dispersion of the exiles found in Ezekiel and in Ezra.[50]

Daniel

The reason for Aramaic portions in Daniel and in Ezra has been plausibly explained by D. C. Snell as attempts "to lend authenticity to reports about foreigners and to statements to them."[51] In the past, one of the strongest arguments adduced for the Hellenistic date for Daniel was the presence of three Greek words in the Aramaic of Daniel, all referring to musical instruments. T. C. Mitchell has recently reviewed the evidence for musical instruments in antiquity,[52] and in Nebuchadnezzar's band.[53]

I have long maintained that the abundant evidence of Greek interpenetration into the Near East antedated Alexander's conquest, and that such Greek loanwords cannot be used to date Daniel to the Hellenistic period.[54] A survey by J. C. Waldbaum lists early Greek contacts prior to 600 B.C.[55] A palimpsest indicates that thirty-six of forty-two ships arriving at an Egyptian port in 475 B.C. were Greek.[56]

Nonetheless other reasons, such as the close correspondence of Daniel 11 with the events of the rise of Antiochus IV, have persuaded even some evangelical scholars, such as J. Goldingay, to accept a Hellenistic date for

---

49. D. I. Block, "Gog and the Pouring Out of the Spirit," *VT* 37 (1987): 257–70; idem, "Gog in Prophetic Tradition," *VT* 42 (1992): 154–72; cf. B. P. Irwin, "Molek Imagery and the Slaughter of Gog in Ezekiel 38 and 39," *CBQ* 65 (1995): 93–112; J. P. Tanner, "Rethinking Ezekiel's Invasion by Gog," *JETS* 39 (1996): 29–46; cf. Yamauchi, *Foes from the Northern Frontier: Invading Hordes from the Russian Steppes* (Grand Rapids: Baker, 1982), 19–27.
50. B. Oded, "The Settlements of the Israelite and the Judean Exiles in Mesopotamia in the 8th–6th Centuries B.C.E.," in *Studies in Historical Geography and Biblical Historiography Presented to Zechariah Kallai*, ed. Z. Kalai, G. Galil, and M. Weinfeld (Leiden: Brill, 2000), 91–103.
51. D. C. Snell, "Why Is There Aramaic in the Bible?" *JSOT* 18 (1980): 43.
52. T. C. Mitchell, "The Music of the Old Testament Reconsidered," *PEQ* 124 (1992): 124–43.
53. T. C. Mitchell, "And the Band Played On . . . but What Did They Play on?: Identifying the Instruments in Nebuchadnezzar's Orchestra," *BRev* 15, no. 6 (1999): 32–39.
54. See Yamauchi, *Persia and the Bible*, 379–94. This linguistic argument for a Hellenistic date is abandoned by Collins, *Daniel*, 254 n. 121.
55. J. C. Waldbaum, "Early Greek Contacts with the Southern Levant, ca. 1000–600 B.C.: The Eastern Perspective," *BASOR* 293 (1994): 67–78. See also W.-D. Niemeier, "Archaic Greeks in the Orient: Textual and Archaeological Evidence,"*BASOR* 322 (2001): 11–32.
56. A. Yardeni, "Maritime Trade and Royal Accountancy in an Erased Customs Account from 475 B.C.E. on the Ahiqar Scroll from Elephantine," *BASOR* 293 (1994): 67–78.

Daniel's composition.[57] For a thorough exposition of Daniel on the basis of a Hellenistic background, we now have J. Goldstein's *Peoples of an Almighty God*.[58]

Life in the Diaspora

Onomastic evidence of Israelites deported by the Assyrians and of the Judeans deported by the Babylonians have been compiled in a comprehensive reference work by R. Zadok.[59] These data indicate that in a few cases the Israelites retained their identity for a century.

The Murashu Archives

Light on the Jews in Mesopotamia who did not return to the Holy Land is shed by the archive of the Murashu family, wealthy bankers and brokers, dated to the reigns of Artaxerxes I, Darius II and Artaxerxes (from 454–404 B.C.), whose clients included many Jews.[60]

The Elephantine Community

An important source of extrabiblical information on the Jewish community in Egypt during the Exilic period are the Aramaic and other documents from the mercenary garrison on the Elephantine Island near Aswan.[61] B. Porten has pointed out the syncretistic aspects of their religion.[62] M. Silverman argues that their religion was more assimilationist than syncretistic.[63]

---

57. J. Goldingay, *Daniel* (Waco: Word, 1989). Cf. J. Goldingay, "What Are the Characteristics of Evangelical Study of the Old Testament?" *EQ* 73 (2001): 99–117.
58. J. Goldstein, *Peoples of an Almighty God* (New York: Doubleday, 2002). Goldstein is the author of the Anchor Bible Commentaries on I and II Maccabees.
59. R. Zadok, *The Pre-Hellenistic Israelite Anthroponymy and Prosopography* (Leuven: Peeters, 1988).
60. M. W. Stolper, *Entrepreneurs and Empire* (Leiden: Nederlands Historisch-Archaeologisch Instituut te Istanbul, 1985). See E. Yamauchi, "The Eastern Jewish Diaspora under the Babylonians," in *Mesopotamia and the Bible,* ed. M. Chavalas and K. L. Younger Jr. (Grand Rapids: Baker, 2002), 356–77.
61. B. Porten, *Jews of Elephantine and Arameans of Syene: Aramaic Texts with Translation* (Jerusalem: Hebrew University, 1976); idem, *The Elephantine Papyri in English* (Leiden: Brill, 1996).
62. B. Porten, *Archives from Elephantine* (Berkeley, Calif.: University of California Press, 1968).
63. M. Silverman, "The Religion of the Elephantine Jews: A New Approach," in *The Proceedings of the Sixth World Congress of Jewish Studies, 1973,* ed. A. Shin'an (Jerusalem: World Congress of Jewish Studies, 1975), 377–88.

"The Empty Land"?

H. M. Barstad seeks to overturn the "Myth of the Empty Land"; that is, the impression given by the hyperbolic language of the Chronicler that the deportations had left Palestine essentially desolate.[64] Archaeological surveys of Galilee do indicate that the Assyrian attacks beginning with Tiglath-pileser III did desolate this area.[65] We now have an abundance of epigraphic as well as archaeological evidence for Palestine during the Persian period.[66]

THE PERSIAN EMPIRE

Cyrus

The antecedents and implications of the Cyrus Cylinder, which has been used to illustrate Persian policy in Ezra 1, have been studied by Amélie Kuhrt.[67] Stefan Timm has interpreted some cuneiform tablets as evidence for a deportation of Arameans from Neirab in northern Syria to southern Mesopotamia in the early reign of Nebuchadnezzar, and then their repatriation under Cyrus, providing a striking parallel to the experience of the Jews.[68]

Esther

The story of Esther has understandably attracted a great deal of attention from feminist scholars[69] and scholars interested in gender issues.[70] These scholars generally classify Esther as simply an entertaining tale, despite its

---

64. H. M. Barstad, *The Myth of the Empty Land: A Study in the History and Archaeology of Judah During the "Exilic" Period* (Oslo: Scandinavian University Press, 1996).
65. Z. Gal, "Israel in Exile," *BAR* 24, no. 3 (May–June 1998): 49–53.
66. I. Eph'al, "Changes in Palestine During the Persian Period in Light of Epigraphic Sources," *PEQ* 48 (1998): 106–19; S. C. Herbert and A. M. Berlin, "A New Administrative Center for Persian and Hellenistic Galilee," *BASOR* 329 (2003): 13–59.
67. A. Kuhrt, "The Cyrus Cylinder and Achaemenid Imperial Policy," *JSOT* 25 (1983): 83–94.
68. S. Timm, "Die Bedeutung der spätbabylonischen Texte aus Nērab für die Rückkehr der Judäer aus dem Exil," in *Meilenstein: Festgabe für Herbert Donner*, ed. M. Weippert and S. Timm (Wiesbaden: Harrassowitz, 1995), 276–88.
69. A. Brenner, *A Feminist Companion to Esther, Judith and Susanna* (Sheffield: Sheffield Academic Press, 1995).
70. T. K. Beal, *The Book of Hiding: Gender, Ethnicity, Annihilation, and Esther* (London: Routledge, 1997).

authentic Persian features,[71] which have been corroborated by archaeology, such as a gate at the palace of Susa,[72] and an official named Marduka,[73] who may possibly be identified with Mordecai. A detailed commentary which fully appreciates its authentic Persian background is that by Frederic W. Bush.[74] T. S. Laniak explores the anthropological themes of shame and honor in Esther.[75]

Haggai and Zechariah

An important monograph on the significance of the rebuilding of the temple and the roles of Haggai and Zechariah is P. R. Bedford's, *Temple Restoration in Early Achaemenid Judah*.[76] Bedford suggests that Haggai and Zechariah held out expectations that were not fully realized. The completion of the temple did not solve the issue of political autonomy. He believes that it was "in defence of the continuing eastern diaspora that Ezra–Nehemiah came to be written."[77]

Ezra

The mission of Ezra has been compared to the function of the Egyptian official Udjahorresnet, who played a key role in assisting Cambyses' conquest of Egypt.[78] K. Hoglund has clarified the mission of Ezra and the refortification of Jerusalem by Nehemiah as part of the imperial Achaemenid strategy against the dangers of Athenian imperialism, which included the coastal Palestinian city of Dor in its Delian League.[79]

The authenticity of the official documents cited in Ezra, including the

---

71. E. Yamauchi, "The Archaeological Background of Esther," *BSac* 137 (1980): 99–117.
72. See Yamauchi, *Persia and the Bible*, 279–303.
73. E. Yamauchi, "Mordecai, the Persepolis Tablets, and the Susa Excavations," *VT* 42 (1992): 272–75.
74. F. W. Bush, *Ruth/Esther* (Waco: Word, 1996); cf. idem, "The Book of Esther: *Opus non gratum* in the Christian Canon," *BBR* 9 (1998): 39–54.
75. T. S. Laniak, *Shame and Honor in the Book of Esther* (Atlanta: Scholars Press, 1998).
76. P. R. Bedford, *Temple Restoration in Early Achaemenid Judah* (Leiden: Brill, 2001).
77. Ibid., 309.
78. Cambyses is not mentioned in the Hebrew Bible. But the Persian invasion of Egypt in 525 no doubt caused the king to place demands on all provinces, including Judah, for men and supplies. See Yamauchi, *Persia and the Bible*, 93–128.
79. K. G. Hoglund, *Achaemenid Imperial Administration in Syria-Palestine and the Missions of Ezra and Nehemiah* (Atlanta: Scholars Press, 1992).

decree of Cyrus, has been validated by extrabiblical evidence.[80] The recent reexamination of a Babylonian legal text by M. W. Stolper has led him to conclude, "The parallel mention of the governor and the 'scribe-chancellors' in BM 74554 therefore, does not undermine the suggestion that Ezra 4:8f. and 17 were constructed from the subscript of an authentic administrative letter."[81] Against the criticisms of D. Janzen that the letter authorizing Ezra's mission (Ezra 7:12–26) is not authentic,[82] R. C. Steiner concludes that "In short, the legal component of Ezra's mission and even the term for it fit squarely into the fifth century B.C.E."[83]

On the basis of archaeological surveys, C. E. Carter has proposed a radically reduced province of Yehud,[84] which raises questions about the figures of about fifty thousand returning exiles listed in Ezra 2 and Nehemiah 7,[85] even if one accepts the view that these were cumulative totals. But Carter does note that some Jews did live outside the boundaries of the province. He would estimate the size of Jerusalem in the Persian period as between 130 and 140 dunams, with 80 dunams occupied by the Temple Mount.[86]

Nehemiah

The traditional order of Ezra coming before Nehemiah has been affirmed by most recent scholars,[87] including the important commentaries by

---

80. See C. Hensley, "The Official Persian Documents in the Book of Ezra" (Ph.D. diss., University of Liverpool (England), 1977); and A. R. Millard, "A Decree of a Persian Governor," *Buried History* 11, no. 2 (June 1975): 88.
81. M. W. Stolper, "The Governor of Babylon and Across-the-River in 486 B.C.," *JNES* 48 (1989): 300.
82. D. Janzen, "The 'Mission' of Ezra and the Persian-Period Temple Community," *JBL* 119 (2000): 619–43.
83. R. C. Steiner, "The *mbqr* at Qumran, the *episkopos* in the Athenian Empire, and the Meaning of *lbqr'* in Ezra 7:14: On the Relation of Ezra's Mission to the Persian Legal Project," *JBL* 120 (2001): 630. Cf. J. Fleishman, "The Investigating Commission of Tattenai: The Purpose of the Investigation and Its Results," *HUCA* 66 (1995): 81–102.
84. C. E. Carter, "The Province of Yehud in the Postexilic Period: Soundings in Site Distribution and Demography," in *Second Temple Studies, 1: Persian Period,* 2:108, suggests that "the population of Yehud ranged from a low of 11,000 in the late-sixth/early-fifth centuries B.C.E. to a high of 17,000 in the fifth/early-fourth centuries B.C.E."
85. On various population estimates, see E. Yamauchi, "The Archaeological Background of Ezra," *BSac* 137 (1980): 185–97.
86. Carter, "The Province of Yehud in the Postexilic Period," 129. A dunam = 1,000 square meters. Elsewhere on page 135, Carter estimates the population of Jerusalem at about 1500. See also C. E. Carter, *The Emergence of Yehud in the Persian Period* (Sheffield: Sheffield Academic Press, 1999).
87. See E. Yamauchi, "The Reverse Order of Ezra/Nehemiah Reconsidered," *Themelios* 5, no. 3 (1980): 7–13.

H. G. M. Williamson,[88] and J. Blenkinsopp.[89] An exception is the essay by L. Dequeker.[90] J. Bright on the basis of a textual emendation placed Ezra's arrival in 428 rather than in 458.[91]

Against the view of Albrecht Alt that Judah was only a sub-province of Samaria, despite Nehemiah's reference to previous governors (Neh. 5:15), we now have the evidence of bullae (seal impressions) which provide us with convincing evidence that there was a series of governors prior to Nehemiah.[92] Siegfried Mittmann makes the rather dubious suggestion that the enemies of Nehemiah, Tobiah and Sanballat, were members of families who had been repatriated with other exiles and then placed respectively by the Persian authorities over Amman and over Hauran, the latter on the basis of Sanballat's identification as a Horonite.[93]

Against other views, James C. VanderKam argues that the lists of the high priests in Nehemiah (and in Josephus) are complete, assuming that the six individuals had tenures averaging thirty-plus years for the two century span of time.[94]

Malachi

In his excellent commentary, A. E. Hill dates Malachi to the reign of Darius I, and provides a survey of scholarship on the postexilic period.[95] E. H. Merrill has also written well-informed commentaries on Malachi, Haggai and Zechariah.[96]

---

88. H. G. M. Williamson, *Ezra, Nehemiah* (Waco: Word, 1985).
89. J. Blenkinsopp, *Ezra–Nehemiah* (Philadelphia: Westminster, 1988).
90. L. Dequeker, "Nehemiah and the Restoration of the Temple After the Exile," in *Deuteronomy and Deuteronomic Literature: Festschrift C. H. W. Brekelmans,* ed. M. Vervenne and J. Lust (Leuven: Peeters, 1997), 547–68.
91. J. Bright, *A History of Israel,* 4th ed. (Philadelphia: Westminster/John Knox Press, 2000), 391–402.
92. See N. Avigad, *Bullae and Seals from a Postexilic Judean Archive* (Jerusalem: Hebrew University Press, 1976). In contrast to the rapacity of the earlier governors, Nehemiah acted with compassion at a time of economic and social crisis. See E. Yamauchi, "Two Reformers Compared: Solon of Athens and Nehemiah of Jerusalem," in *The Bible World: Essays in Honor of Cyrus H. Gordon,* ed. G. Rendsburg et al. (New York: KTAV, 1980), 269–92.
93. S. Mittmann, "Tobia, Sanballat und die persische Provinz Juda," *JNSL* 26 (2000) 1–50.
94. J. C. VanderKam, "Jewish High Priests of the Persian Period: Is the List Complete?" in *Priesthood and Cult in Ancient Israel,* ed. G. A. Anderson and S. M. Olyan (Sheffield: Sheffield Academic Press, 1991), 67–91.
95. A. E. Hill, *Malachi,* AB (New York: Doubleday, 1998), 51.
96. Eugene H. Merrill, *An Exegetical Commentary: Haggai, Zechariah, Malachi* (Chicago: Moody, 1994).

Conclusion

Unlike the fate of the members of the so-called "Ten Lost Tribes," who had already lapsed from the exclusive worship of Yahweh, the exiles from Judah who were transported to Mesopotamia, were apparently revulsed by the rampant idolatry they beheld in Babylon.[97] During the Assyrian period the recovery of over 800 idols, half from Jerusalem, indicate that idolatry persisted in Judah despite the fulminations of the prophets. What the prophets by their preaching could not achieve, the trauma of the Babylonian exile accomplished. As Stern observes, "Another difference is, perhaps, even more meaningful: Since the beginning of the Persian period, in all the territories of Judah and Samaria, there is not a single piece of evidence for any pagan cults!"[98]

---

97. See E. Yamauchi, "Babylon," in *Major Cities of the Biblical World*, ed. R. K. Harrison (Nashville: Nelson, 1985), 32–48.
98. Stern, *Assyrian, Babylonian, and Persian Periods (732–332 B.C.E.)*, 479.

PART 3

HISTORICAL AND ARCHAEOLOGICAL ISSUES IN ISRAEL'S HISTORY

10

DATING OF THE PATRIARCHAL AGE

The Contribution of Ancient Near Eastern Texts

Mark F. Rooker

THE DATING OF THE PATRIARCHS IS RELATED to the larger question of the historicity of the patriarchs. Since the time of Julius Wellhausen the position has been promoted that the patriarchal narratives do not reflect actual history, but rather were contemporary projections back into ancient time. While in most other types of world literature, written accounts are given the benefit of the doubt with regard to their historical reliability, the same cannot be said for many modern scholarly treatments of the patriarchal narratives.

GEOGRAPHICAL AND POLITICAL BACKGROUND TO THE PATRIARCHAL NARRATIVES

Toward the end of the fourth millennium B.C., the foundations of human civilization were laid in Mesopotamia and Egypt, the regions of the three great rivers. These two regions saw the rise of the first imperial kingdoms that succeeded in imposing an organized and unified government over their respective populations, and at various times spread their authority to areas beyond their natural borders. The situation was by no means the same in Syria-Palestine. In Syria and Palestine the geographical features tend to separate the land into smaller districts serving as serious obstacles to unification. As a consequence, Israel became much like a land bridge between the major civilizations of the ancient world and, as a result, the controllers of the region enjoyed an international influence over neighboring states.

Two tremendous waves of Semites into Palestine and the other lands had monumental impact on the culture and politics of the ancient Near East. The first was known as the Amorite wave at the end of the third millennium B.C. and the second was the Aramean wave in the last centuries of the second millennium B.C. Many scholars have argued that the wave of Amorites at the end of the third millennium B.C. supplied the context for Abraham's migration to Canaan along the Fertile Crescent. This paradigm has been subsequently criticized both for the lack of hard evidence as well as for following the romantic notion that human history is to be explained as a series of migrations.[1] Because the common explanation for Abraham's arrival in Canaan has now fallen out of favor, scholars such as Niels Lemche have concluded that no such migrations took place that would have contained the families of the patriarchs at the end of the third millennium B.C.[2]

If the Amorite wave hypothesis is to be abandoned, however, it does not follow that Abraham's personal migration to Haran and eventually to Canaan is thereby ruled out. The likelihood that we would find material remains of such a migration is not particularly strong. We should not hold out the hope that one day we will find an inscription on a domicile that reads: "Abraham slept here." Moreover, the text of Scripture does not say that Abraham made his way from Ur to Canaan with a large group (Gen. 11:27–32). He came only with his family members. The biblical narrative assumes that his migration was not in conjunction with other peoples or tribes but was, in fact, out of the ordinary. It was disruptive for Abraham and his family. Thus the absence of mass migration can just as easily be cited to support what is actually said in the biblical narrative. If the Amorite wave did take place it would only illustrate the free movement of the patriarchs into the region of Canaan.[3]

There is ample documentary evidence of travel by small groups from the beginning of the second millennium B.C. Commercial caravans are

---

1. For this approach to history, see Johannes V. Jensen, *The Long Journey,* trans. A. G. Charter, Nobel Prize ed. (New York: A. A. Knopf 1945).
2. Niels Peter Lemche, *Prelude to Israel's Past: Background and Beginnings of Israelite History and Identity,* trans. E. F. Mianiscalco (Peabody, Mass.: Hendrickson, 1998), 31.
3. See Eugene Merrill, *Kingdom of Priests: A History of Old Testament Israel* (Grand Rapids: Baker, 1987), 30 n. 21.

mentioned in Genesis 37:25 and the Amarna Documents refer to merchant caravans passing through the land of Canaan.[4] In addition, during Solomon's reign a tremendous amount of goods was being transported to Solomon's palace (2 Kings 4:21–34; 9:15–18). The *Via Maris* and the King's Highway were well-established caravan routes, along the Mediterranean Coast and in the Moabite highlands east of Jordan, respectively (1 Kings 4:24; 9:18; 2 Chron. 8:4).

Modern Approaches to the Historicity of the Patriarchal Narratives

From the middle of the last century, four competing approaches to the study of the patriarchal narratives emerged: the traditional or orthodox approach, the view of archaeological "maximalists," the tradition-historical approach, and the "minimalist" approach.

The Traditional or Orthodox View

The oldest view is clearly the traditional or orthodox position. In this position the Bible is taken at face value concerning the historicity and dating of the patriarchal narratives. If we examine the chronological data in the Old Testament we find that Abraham was one hundred years old when Isaac was born (Gen. 21:5); Isaac was sixty years old when Jacob and Esau were born (Gen. 25:26); and that Jacob was 130 years old when he went to Egypt (Gen. 47:9, 28). The period then from the birth of Abraham to Jacob's entry into Egypt is 290 years: 100 + 60 + 130. From Exodus 12:40 we learn that the Israelites lived in Egypt for a total of 430 years, and 480 years later Solomon's temple was completed in the fourth year of his reign (967 B.C.) (1 Kings 6:1). Adding these years to the date of the completion of the temple we derive the following formula: 290 + 430 + 480 + 967 = 2167. Thus, using these calculations, Abraham was born in 2167 B.C.[5]

---

4. EA 7:73; 8:13; 52:37; 226:15; 225:8. See Yohanan Aharoni, *The Land of the Bible: A Historical Geography*, rev. ed. (Philadelphia: Westminster Press, 1979), 16.
5. See Y. Kaufman, *The History of the Religion of Israel*, 4th ed. (Jerusalem: Bialik Institute & Dvir Co., 1937–56), 2:1 n. 1 (in Hebrew); cf. Merrill's date of 2166 B.C.: Merrill, *Kingdom of Priests*, 25, and n. 9.

Rejection of the Traditional Approach

Subsequent approaches rejected the traditional biblical chronology. During the 1950s a full-blown debate on early Israelite origins commenced between the "American school" represented by W. F. Albright, G. E. Wright, Cyrus Gordon, and John Bright, on the one side, and the "German school," represented by Albrecht Alt, Gerhard von Rad, and Martin Noth on the other side. Generally speaking, the American school approached what might be considered a "maximalist" view, believing archaeological discoveries verified the historical reality of what is recorded in the biblical narrative,[6] whereas the German school represented a "minimalist" approach to the biblical narrative, believing that little of the information in the narrative was historically valid. One of the critical issues in this discussion regarded the historicity of the patriarchal period and the role of archaeology in the discussion.

The Archaeological "Maximalist" View

The second approach was archaeological, best represented by W. F. Albright (1891–1971), who sought to collaborate biblical data with archaeological discoveries. Albright worked on the premise that the traditions reflected in the Old Testament narrative texts were generally reliable and that archaeological discoveries, whether of literary or artifactual nature, could provide external corroboration to the biblical traditions. Between the 1940s and 1960s scholars like Albright and Cyrus Gordon tried to show that the Patriarchal Age as described in the Bible could be compared to specific Near Eastern backgrounds, namely in the Middle Bronze Age, roughly 1800 B.C. Many like G. E. Wright maintained that there are historical elements of the Late Bronze and Early Iron I Ages embedded in the patriarchal narratives even if they did not accept the historicity of all the events and details.[7] Recently Kyle McCarter and Ronald Hendel, both of whom were trained by Frank Moore Cross, a prize student of Albright, argued that the personal names and geographical references in the patriarchal nar-

---

6. For a fuller treatment of the "maximalist" and "minimalist" approaches to the history of Israel, see David M. Howard Jr., *Joshua,* NAC (Nashville: Broadman & Holman, 1998), 40–46.
7. J. Maxwell Miller, "The Patriarchs and ExtraBiblical Sources: A Response," *JSOT* 2 (1977): 66.

ratives provide valid criteria for tracing the historical memories that do exist. For example, the divine name El, which is commonly found in Amorite personal names, is known to be the god of the Amorites who would have lived in the region of Haran.[8] This fits well with the Bronze Age, but it would not fit well at all later in the Iron Age. McCarter and Hendel also reason that no historical group would think of tracing its origin and ancestral homeland to the home of their traditional enemies (Syria and Mesopotamia) unless in fact it were not an incontrovertible memory in the national consciousness.[9]

In addition, there is good reason to believe that the patriarchal age preceded Moses in the middle of the second millennium B.C. From internal biblical evidence, certain Israelite customs found in the legal portion of the Pentateuch actually contradict what is recorded in the patriarchal narratives. For example, the inheritance law found in Deuteronomy 21:15–17 states that the first-born son is to be given a double portion of his father's inheritance. This was apparently not the practice prior to the Mosaic Law (Gen. 48–49). In the account of Jacob's deathbed blessing in Genesis 49 we find all of Jacob's sons by his wives Rachel and Leah and their handmaids sharing equally in the inheritance. This is harmonious with the pre-Mosaic time reflected earlier in the Laws of Hammurabi and the Laws of Lipit-Ishtar in the twentieth century B.C. but different from the Mosaic legislation reflected in the Pentateuch, as we have seen.[10]

Also, in the Mosaic legislation a man was prohibited from marrying his wife's sister (Lev. 18:18). This law was not part of the legal consciousness in the patriarchal period, as demonstrated by Jacob's marriages to Leah and her sister Rachel (Gen. 29:21–30). These examples indicate that the events described in these narratives reflect a time before the Law was given to Moses. The patriarchs had lived in a culture prior to and distinct from the Mosaic era.[11]

---

8. The name is also one of the names of the true God in the Old Testament.
9. P. Kyle McCarter and Ronald S. Hendel, "The Patriarchal Age: Abraham, Isaac and Jacob, in Ancient Israel," in *From Abraham to the Roman Destruction of the Temple,* ed. Hershel Shanks, rev. ed. (Washington D.C.: Biblical Archaeology Society, 1999), 20–21.
10. See Kenneth Kitchen, "The Patriarchal Age: Myth or History," *BAR* 21, no. 2 (March–April 1995): 92.
11. R. W. L. Moberley, *The Old Testament of the Old Testament* (Minneapolis: Fortress, 1992), 103.

The Tradition-Historical View

The third approach to the study of the patriarchal narratives has often been called the tradition-historical approach. This approach was popularized through the efforts of such scholars such as Albrecht Alt (1883–1956), Martin Noth (1902–1968), and Gerhard von Rad (1901–1971). But the real genius behind this approach was Hermann Gunkel (1862–1932), who played the major role in the development of form-critical studies. Gunkel operated on the premise that the writing of the historical narratives of the Bible was a long process spanning perhaps centuries and that the actual biblical writers were more like redactors than writers. In addition, the Old Testament accounts originally existed merely as oral accounts that had a long history before they were committed to writing.[12] In his monumental work on the history of Israel,[13] Noth not only followed Wellhausen's position that the pentateuchal narratives were virtually legendary material, but also assumed that the documents had been transmitted orally for centuries.

Once it is assumed that the biblical narratives were transmitted by oral transmission, the rationale for speaking of historical recollections is removed, even if the oral transmitters made efforts to be faithful and accurate.[14] It is thus not surprising that Noth believed the patriarchal narratives were fabricated materials reflecting the later time when the narratives were composed.[15] For Noth, the ancestors of Israel may have been seminomads who lived on the desert fringe of Canaan until they gradually infiltrated the land and took up an agricultural life. Noth responded to the claims of the American school that elevated the contribution of archaeological finds by advocating the severing of Syro-Palestinian archaeology from biblical studies. Similarly, von Rad expressed the view that the narratives of the Pentateuch were not based in historical reality but were merely an expression of the religious experience of Israel. He maintained that the fundamental expression of Israel's religious creed was expressed in Deuteronomy 26:5–10. The patriarchal stories are not historical, but what he called saga. While a

---

12. See John H. Hayes, "The History of the Study of Israelite and Judean History," in *Israelite and Judaean History*, ed. John H. Hayes and J. Maxwell Miller (Philadelphia: Westminster Press, 1977), 66–68.
13. Martin Noth, *The History of Israel*, 2d ed. (New York: Harper & Row, 1960).
14. Lemche, *Prelude to Israel's Past*, 21 n. 19.
15. Niels Peter Lemche has also recently argued that the Old Testament writers invented the ancient Israelites ("Is It Still Possible to Write a History of Ancient Israel?" *SJOT* 8 [1994]: 168).

saga may contain events which are indeed historical, it also reflects the historical experience of the time and community in which the account was written.

The "Minimalist" View

Since the 1970s a fourth approach has been advocated by many scholars, launched by the work of John Van Seters and Thomas L. Thompson.[16] These two scholars have been influential in the research of the patriarchal narratives. The popularity and dissemination of the approach advocated by Van Seters and Thompson warrant that it to be considered a fourth approach, although it has much in common with the "German school" discussed above. These scholars began to re-examine some of the conclusions made by Albright and Gordon and dismissed a variety of erroneous comparisons particularly regarding their use of the material from Nuzi (see below). In opposition to scholars of the Albright school, like G. E. Wright who generally assumed the factuality of Hebrew narratives, Thompson reverted back to the critical method promoted by Wellhausen that the narratives of Genesis are a reflection of the time in which they were written, not about the times they attempt to portray.[17] Thompson also raised great questions about the contribution of archaeology: "For not only has 'archaeology' not proven a single event of the patriarchal traditions to be historical, it has not shown any of the patriarchal traditions to be likely."[18]

Van Seters had a more favorable opinion about the use of archaeology but argued that the conclusions of those sympathetic to the American school were not consistent with the actual data. He argued that the archaeological

---

16. John Van Seters, *Abraham in History and Tradition* (New Haven, Conn.: Yale University Press, 1975); Thomas L. Thompson, *The Historicity of the Patriarchal Narratives* (Berlin: de Gruyter, 1974). Subsequent works that betray the same "minimalist" approaches advocated by Van Seters and Thompson include: Gösta Ahlström, *Who Were the Israelites?* (Winona Lake, Ind.: Eisenbrauns, 1988); Robert B. Coote, *Early Israel: A New Horizon* (Minneapolis: Fortress, 1990); Philip R. Davies, *In Search of "Ancient Israel,"* JSOTSup 148 (Sheffield: JSOT, 1992); Keither W. Whitelam, *The Invention of Ancient Israel: The Silencing of Palestinian History* (New York: Routledge, 1996); and many others.
17. Mark Noll has captured the thrust of this "minimalist" tenet: "The central argument underlying this view is that present circumstances and present realities so thoroughly define the vision of a historian that our supposed knowledge of the past is actually an expression of the historian's own longings, self-interest, ideology, or psychology. No path exists to the past which is not a disguised tour of the present" ("Traditional Christianity and the Possibility of Historical Knowledge," *Christian Scholar's Review* 19 [1990]: 397).
18. Thompson, *Historicity of the Patriarchal Narratives,* 328.

evidence does not support a second millennium backdrop for the patriarchal narratives but rather a first millennium context. The great popularity and dissemination of the studies of Van Seters and Thompson have had a profound effect on many Old Testament scholars. To many, the old consensus established by the Albright School lies now in ruins. William Dever illustrates this in the following statement:

> Today there is a growing realization that the formative period in the correlation of archaeological data with research on Israelite origins is over. . . . "Biblical archaeology" cannot claim independent status or authority; strictly speaking it is not a discipline at all in the academic sense, but rather an interdisciplinary inquiry in which biblical scholars and archaeologists engage in a dialogue.[19]

As a result, Dever began to revive Noth's position that archeology and biblical studies should be kept separate. Where these two disciplines do overlap only archaeology can be objective and thus more reliable.[20] What can be seen in the new analyses of Van Seters, Thompson, and to some extent Dever,[21] is a shift to the earlier German school approach rather than continuing the more maximalist approach with regard to the patriarchal narratives.

It may well be true that scholars such as Speiser,[22] Albright, and Gordon jumped to conclusions too early and thus opened themselves up to Van Seters' later criticism. Regardless, the pendulum has swung in the minimalist direction and there is now more skepticism towards the Old Testament. Presently, many "biblical" historians maintain that in order for an Old Testament text to be considered historical, it must be corroborated by information external to the actual biblical text. The approach is thus that

---

19. William G. Dever, "Palestine in the Second Millennium B.C.E.: The Archaeological Picture," in *Israelite and Judaean History*, 72.
20. William G. Dever, *What Did the Biblical Writers Know and When Did They Know It?* (Grand Rapids: Eerdmans, 2001), 46–48, 89, 105, 271, 281, 298. For a recent critique of the view that archaeology alone can apply objectivity in determining Israel's history, see Howard, *Joshua*, 44–46.
21. While it is clear from Dever's newly published book, *What Did the Biblical Writers Know and When Did They Know It?* that Dever would recoil at the thought of being linked with Van Seters and Thompson, it is still true that Dever is in agreement with these scholars on the subject of the nonhistoricity of the patriarchs.
22. E. A. Speiser, *Genesis,* AB (Garden City, N.Y.: Doubleday, 1964).

the text is "guilty until proven innocent."[23] We agree with Kenneth Kitchen that both Van Seters and Thompson are reactionaries rather than innovators trying to push the study of the extrabiblical support of the pentateuchal narratives back one hundred years.[24] Dever is critical of Thompson's methodological approach toward the understanding of the history of Israel: ". . . this is irresponsible scholarship—simply ideological rhetoric, with no attempt at documentation or a well-balanced presentation that might enlighten the reader."[25] Van Seters' conclusion that the chronological data of the social customs all point to the first millennium B.C. rather than the second millennium is an overstatement in correcting the positive enthusiasm of earlier studies.[26] Neither Van Seters' preference for the first millennium dating of inscriptional evidence nor Thompson's argument for the radical nonhistorical nature of the narratives can be supported from the evidence of the social customs of ancient Near Eastern inscriptions.[27]

These four distinct approaches to the patriarchal narratives have dominated discussions of the patriarchal narratives, particularly since the last half of the twentieth century. Given the distinctiveness of each approach, it is not surprising that each leads to separate conclusions on the question of the dating of the patriarchal narratives, although the orthodox view and the archaeological approach are not categorically different in the end. But as noted at the outset, one cannot actually deal with the dating of the narratives until grappling with the question of historicity. It is to this issue that we now turn.

---

23. James K. Hoffmeier, *Israel in Egypt: The Evidence for the Authenticity of the Exodus Tradition* (New York: Oxford University Press, 1997), 10–11.
24. Kenneth Kitchen, "Closing Remarks," in *Biblical Archaeology Today, 1990: Proceedings of the Second International Conference on Biblical Archaeology,* ed. Avraham Biran and Joseph Aviram (Jerusalem: Israel Exploration Society, 1993), 758.
25. Dever, *What Did the Biblical Writers Know and When Did They Know It?* 32. Dever does agree with Thompson, however, about the nonhistorical nature of the patriarchal narratives (ibid., 33, 97–98, 284).
26. M. J. Selman, "Comparative Customs and the Patriarchal Age," in *Essays on the Patriarchal Narratives,* ed. A. R. Millard and D. J. Wiseman (Leicester: Inter-Varsity, 1980; reprint, Winona Lake, Ind.: Eisenbrauns, 1983), 125.
27. See ibid., 125, 138.

What Is History?

Introduction

In his article titled, "Story and History in Biblical Theology," James Barr promoted the thesis that the long narrative corpus of the Old Testament should be called story rather than history,[28] echoing the presuppositions established by the German school. John J. Collins, while acknowledging Barr's influence on his own thinking, similarly argued that it was not necessary for the biblical historian to concern himself with the issue of whether the events described in the Bible actually happened. He argues that an imaginative, poetic or mythical description can capture the "real" character of an actual event more adequately than a purely factual account. In fact, according to Collins, the revelatory status of the narratives in the Bible in no way depends upon their historical reliability. As Collins argues, even when there may have been an historical event behind a story, it was still the story itself that lived on and influenced the religious community.[29]

Definition of History

According to Ferdinand Deist, history "is an explanation of the meaningful connectedness of a sequence of past events in the form of an interested and focused narrative."[30] The Old Testament narratives, including the patriarchal narratives, certainly fit this criterion.

If we approach the Old Testament narrative text with the slightest amount of objectivity, we must ask if the events described in the Genesis narrative are within the realm of plausibility, and then we must answer "yes." The events described in the pentateuchal narratives are plausible, because they are in harmony with all that is known about the culture of the first half of the second millennium B.C. As S. M. Warner states: "We know of no time during the second millennium when such a mode of existence could not have taken place on the fringes of Syria and Palestine."[31]

---

28. James Barr, "Story and History in Biblical Theology," *JR* 56 (1976): 5.
29. John J. Collins, "The 'Historical Character' of the Old Testament in Recent Biblical Theology," *CBQ* 41 (1979): 196–97.
30. Ferdinand Deist, "Contingency, Continuity and Integrity in Historical Understanding: An Old Testament Perspective," *Scriptura* 11 (1993): 106. For further definitions, see David M. Howard Jr.'s essay, "History as History," chapter 1 in this volume.
31. S. M. Warner, "The Patriarchs and ExtraBiblical Sources," *JSOT* 2 (1977): 58.

Genre and History

The Critical View

Since the time of Herman Gunkel, biblical scholars have often maintained that a rigid genre analysis could determine whether a body of literature was historical or fictional. Genre analysis alone could differentiate history from legendary writing. It was argued that certain constitutive elements were required in historical writing and where these were absent, the literature must be considered nonhistorical. This approach has now been discredited by modern literary critics.[32] Another commonly accepted feature of historical writing stemming from the nineteenth century was that a historian had to be completely unbiased and objective in order to be able to write history. But as A. R. Millard has stated:

> Undoubted bias, therefore, need not provoke the modern reader to a totally adverse attitude to a document, nor give rise to allegations that the accounts are untrue or imaginary. Recognition of the unconsealed standpoints of many ancient documents has resulted in fuller understanding of their contents, without any recourse to a devaluation or discrediting of them. The fact that the modern interpreter does not share the beliefs and aims of the writers does not prevent him from respecting and giving them their weight.[33]

Thus, if authors write from a particular perspective, say, a religious conviction, this does not make what they say invalid from a historical standpoint. Philosophers of history have noted that historical narrative is differentiated from fiction by its commitment to real rather than imaginary subject matter, not by an analysis of form.[34] Reference to a deity or

---

32. See Meir Sternberg, *The Poetics of Biblical Narrative: Ideological Literature and the Drama of Reading* (Bloomington: Indiana University Press, 1985), 26, 29–30; and K. L. Younger, *Ancient Conquest Accounts: A Study in Ancient Near Eastern and Biblical History Writing*, JSOTSup 98 (Sheffield: University of Sheffield Press, 1990), 27–31, 268–69.
33. A. R. Millard, "The Old Testament and History: Some Considerations," *FT* 110 (1983): 41. Hence, we disagree with Dever's generalization that "literature is largely fiction" (*What Did the Biblical Writers Know and When Did They Know It?* 18–19). See also V. Philips Long, *The Art of Biblical History* (Grand Rapids: Zondervan, 1994), 58–87.
34. See H. White, "The Question of Narrative in Contemporary Historical Theory," *History and Theory* 23 (1984), 21; cited by Younger, *Ancient Conquest Accounts*, 35–37.

deities is not evidence in itself that a narrative is dealing with imagined or fabricated events.

Because critical scholars assume that the social and historical context of the composition of the pentateuchal narratives is that of the exilic and postexilic periods, they then posit that this material must be considered fiction and not history. The composers of the Pentateuch anachronistically characterized their own religion as the beliefs of the patriarchs almost a millennium earlier. It is thus no surprise that Lemche proclaims:

> First impressions must be revised. We must question whether these texts do reflect history. The historical-critical analysis presented here eliminates any possible connection between these texts and the history of the ancient Near East as far as Israel's early history is concerned. In the final analysis, the pentateuchal narratives are of little use for the study of the history of ancient Palestine.[35]

Lemche, in fact, suggests that there should be an entirely new paradigm regarding the study of the history of Israel. We should no longer attempt to study the history of the people of Israel, but rather the history of the ideologies that persuaded the biblical writers to describe their past in the way they did.[36] To find more objective and historical information, it is argued, scholars are better served by examining other ancient Near Eastern sources.[37]

The Orthodox View

It should be beyond doubt that the recorders of the biblical narratives, including the pentateuchal narratives, believed that what they were writing was actual history, in straightforward prose.[38] With regard to the narratives we find in the book of Genesis, the *tôl^{e}dôt* structure and other chronological and geographical information prevent the narrative from being viewed as a mere fairy tale.[39]

---

35. Lemche, *Prelude to Israel's Past*, 227.
36. Ibid., 231.
37. Ibid., 65.
38. John Goldingay, "The Patriarchs in Scripture and History," in *Essays on the Patriarchal Narratives*, 39.
39. Acknowledged by Lemche, *Prelude to Israel's Past*, 25–26.

Egyptologist Kenneth Kitchen has classified the writings of ancient Near Eastern literature into three general categories: autobiographical/biographical, historical legends, and fictional writings.[40] The patriarchal narratives are admittedly somewhat unique, but clearly fit the category of autobiographical/biographical. The similarities between the historical narratives of the Pentateuch and the histories of the ancient Near East argue in favor of considering these documents as real history writing. The use of narrative writing is an effective way to recount genuine historical events.[41] Judged on this data the patriarchal traditions should be considered factual.[42] Imaginative fiction novels did not arise until relatively modern times, several millennia after the time of the patriarchal period.[43]

Thus the Old Testament should be read on its own terms. Again we cite Millard:

> The patriarchal narratives can be taken as products of the Israelite monarchy era, and interpreted as reflecting life in that time. Before anyone can assert that they can only derive from that period, a careful examination of them in an early second-millennium context needs to be made, and to be shown to be impossible. Is the earlier date really so unthinkable as some maintain? The narratives apparently assume that is their context, so they should be inspected on the assumption they make. There would be no hesitation in treating most texts that are excavated from ancient cities in this way.[44]

Where no overwhelming evidence exists to the contrary, we should treat a written document of any kind as a valuable and reliable record. It is to a few of these ancient records that we now turn to discern what light they may shed on the narratives of the patriarchs.

---

40. K. A. Kitchen, *The Bible in Its World: The Bible and Archaeology Today* (Downers Grove, Ill.: InterVarsity, 1977), 61–68.
41. See J. T. Luke, "Abraham and the Iron Age," *JSOT* 4 (1977): 37; L. Stone, "The Revival of Narrative: Reflections on a New Old History," *Past and Present* 85 (1979): 3–24; and Merrill, *Kingdom of Priests*, 36.
42. Kitchen, "Patriarchal Age," 92.
43. Kitchen, *The Bible in Its World*, 65.
44. A. R. Millard, "Methods of Studying the Patriarchal Narratives as Ancient Texts," in *Essays on the Patriarchal Narratives*, 44–45.

Ancient Near Eastern Inscriptions

Mesopotamian Sources

Nuzi

The town of Nuzi was excavated between 1925 and 1931. The tablets date to the fifteenth century B.C., but because of a generally static living environment they reflect living conditions before and after this time.[45] Yet, because they do not directly overlap with the patriarchal period and also because the people who were part of this civilization were not Semitic but Hurrian, an Indo-European people, caution should be exercised in making parallels.

One custom that does appear to parallel a practice in the patriarchal narratives is that of the barren wife providing a concubine to her husband for the purpose of producing a child. This parallels Sarah's gift of Hagar to Abraham in Genesis 16 as well as the gift of Rachel's handmaid Bilhah to Jacob in Genesis 30. According to the Nuzi law, the original wife maintained authority over any subsequent offspring. This may explain Abraham's statement, "Your maid is in your hand" (Gen. 16:6; cf. 21:10). This is a clear parallel, but the practice was not limited to the Nuzi documents or the patriarchal narratives. A similar law is found in the Law of Hammurabi (§§144–47)[46] as well as in Old Assyrian texts, and a twelfth century Egyptian document.[47] Nevertheless, the parallel indicates the acceptability of a practice that is foreign to Western readers.[48]

In the Nuzi documents, we also find an example of childless parents adopting a son. This adopted son would serve his parents as long as they lived and would be responsible for their burial upon their death. The adopted

---

45. Alfred J. Hoerth, *Archaeology and the Old Testament* (Grand Rapids: Baker, 1998), 102 n. 1.
46. Theophile J. Meek, trans., "The Code of Hammurabi," in *ANET,* 172, laws 144–147; see also Tikva Frymer-Kensky, "Patriarchal Family Relationships and Near Eastern Law," *BA* 44 (1981): 211.
47. For translations of the Assyrian text, see J. Lewy, "Old Assyrian Institutions," *HUCA* 27 (1956): 9–10; and for the Egyptian text, A. H. Gardiner, "Adoption Extraordinary," *JEA* 26 (1940): 23–29.
48. Related to this practice was the inclusion of the gift of a female slave as part of a dowry. This practice is also indicated in the Nuzi tablets (for translation, see E. A. Speiser, "New Kirkuk Documents Relating to Family Laws," *AASOR* 10 [1930]: 31–32; and the Laws of Hammurabi [Meek, "The Code of Hammurabi," 172, law 144]).

son was made an heir. This perfectly parallels Abraham's proposal to make Eliezer his heir (Gen. 15:3). This practice reflects a custom apparently practiced for generations. According to the Laws of Hammurabi, this adoptive son could be displaced as the eldest son if another son were born to the formerly barren wife. This explains why Isaac was legally considered the first-born even though he was younger than Ishmael.[49]

Martha Morrison has pointed out numerous parallels between the Nuzi documents and the Jacob and Laban narrative of the Pentateuch. She points out that gifts proffered in the marriage of Rebekah are reminiscent of marriage transactions at Nuzi.[50]

Other mutual agreements between Jacob and Laban are like those found in Nuzi texts. These agreements appear to be like those typical of sheep owners and shepherds in the ancient Near East. By these contracts free herdsmen agreed with the livestock owners to tend the flocks and herds for a share of the profits from the livestock and dairy products. As Morrison states:

> The agreements between Jacob and Laban bear a strong resemblance to Old Babylonian herding contracts. . . . A herding cycle similar to that of the Old Babylonian period and of Nuzi pervades the Jacob and Laban story. . . . By initiating the first herding contract shortly after Jacob's arrival at Haran, Laban intended to exclude Jacob from the family's holdings but to retain his services as a herdsman. . . . The practices and institutions of Nuzi presented here are not unlike those of other settled centers of the Near East in the second millennium B.C.E. such as Mari, Alalakh, and Ugarit.[51]

Similar contracts also exist in Old Babylonian texts. Jacob's agreement to serve seven years for Rachel is also close to the six-and-a-half-year turnover of flocks in the Nuzi arrangements.[52]

---

49. Meek, "The Code of Hammurabi," *ANET*, 173, law 171; see Frymer-Kensky, "Patriarchal Family Relationships," 213.
50. See M. Morrison, "Nuzi," in *ABD*, 4:1161.
51. M. Morrison, "The Jacob and Laban Narrative in Light of Near Eastern Sources," *BA* 46 (1983): 156, 158, 160, 163.
52. See Morrison, "The Jacob and Laban Narrative," 156; and John Walton, *Ancient Israelite Literature in Its Cultural Context* (Grand Rapids: Zondervan, 1989), 55.

Another custom shared between the patriarchal narrative and the Nuzi tablets is that of the "deathbed blessing" found in numerous passages such as Isaac's blessing on Jacob and Esau (Gen. 27), Jacob's blessing on his and Joseph's sons (Gen. 48–49), Moses' blessing on Israel (Deut. 33), and Joshua's blessing on the nation (Josh. 23–24). While it is true that at Nuzi this deathbed blessing is confined to property litigation, it was viewed as a legally recognized procedure to distribute an inheritance.

All in all it is clear from Nuzi that the culture of the patriarchs was not dramatically different from what was customary in the ancient Near East during the Middle Bronze Age (first half of the second millennium B.C.). Chronological support for a particular date should not be forced, but the Nuzi tablets satisfactorily place the patriarchs into the wider context of the ancient Near East.[53]

Mari

The archaeological evidence indicates that Mari was founded near the end of the fourth millennium B.C. and was particularly prominent at two different times in its history. The city was thriving during the first half of the third millennium B.C. until Sargon's conquest of the city around 2300 B.C. and returned to prominence later in the eighteenth century B.C. An enormous palace, one of the most remarkable in antiquity, was built on the ruins of the earlier civilization.

Over a thousand letters and two thousand economic, legal, and administrative texts have been published from Mari. Most of the texts come from a small time frame, from 1800 to 1760 B.C. making Mari one of the best-documented cities of ancient history. Although the Bible does not refer to the city of Mari, numerous Mari documents mention Hazor, Harran, and Nahor. The latter two cities were significant locations for the patriarchal history as they provided the ancestral home for Abraham's family before they made their final move to Canaan (Gen. 11:31–31). Nahor was also the name of Abraham's brother. The Mari texts mention these locations within a few centuries of Abraham's residence there.

Also important for the patriarchal narratives is the description of the

---

53. John Walton, "Cultural Background of the Old Testament," in *Foundations for Biblical Interpretation,* ed. David Dockery, K. A. Mathews, and Robert B. Sloan (Nashville: Broadman & Holman, 1994), 255–73; and idem, *Ancient Israelite Literature,* 58.

way of life in the Mari documents. The Mari texts speak of large-scale movements of herdsmen and far-reaching migrations of tribes between the Euphrates region and Syro-Palestine. This information furnishes a realistic backdrop for the patriarchal life, especially the experience of Abraham.[54] We also learn in the Mari texts of a seminomadic form of life where groups carried on a pastoral existence, pitching their tents from time to time outside of occupied cities (cf. Gen. 12:6; 13:18; 26:25).[55] Mari society like that reflected in Israelite society appears to have been a dimorphic society where inhabitants of the city clashed or merged with tribal elements.[56] As Dever states:

> If the biblical traditions are accorded any historical worth, and if their original milieu was a village-pastoral/urban society basically like that reflected in the Mari texts, then the nucleus of these traditions might go back to the MB IIA-early B period, from about the twentieth to the eighteenth century B.C.E.[57]

The personal names that occur in the Mari texts provide one of the most potent arguments for the second millennium B.C. dating of the patriarchs, for it is in these texts that we come across names cognate to the patriarchs in various lists. The form of the patriarchal names of Isaac, Jacob, Israel, Joseph, and Ishmael begin with the i/y prefix, which are common in the Mari archives of the early second millennium B.C.[58]

Egyptian Sources

Execration Texts

The documents from Egypt have more to say about Palestine than what is found in the Mesopotamian inscriptions in the Bronze Age. As the

---

54. See A. Malamat, "Mari," in *EncJud*, ed. Cecil Roth and Geoffrey Wigoder (Jerusalem: Keter Publishing, 1971), 11:981.
55. See A. Malamat, *Mari and the Bible: A Collection of Studies* (Jerusalem: Hebrew University, 1977), 48–49.
56. See André Lemaire, "Mari, the Bible, and the Northwest Semitic World," *BA* 47, no. 2 (1984): 103.
57. Dever, "Palestine in the Second Millennium B.C.E.," 118.
58. See J. M. Sasson, "Mari," *The Interpreter's Dictionary of the Bible, Supplementary Volume*, ed. Keith R. Crim (Nashville: Abingdon, 1976), 571; and Kitchen, "Patriarchal Age," 90.

documents come closer to the Middle Bronze Age references to Palestine become more frequent and detailed.

The Execration texts contain references to Palestinian cities such as Jerusalem, Shechem, Hazor, and Ashkelon. The life situation of Canaan described in the Execration texts is in harmony with what is described in the patriarchal narratives, but unlike Canaan in the middle of the second millennium B.C. when Canaan was under Egyptian control.[59]

The Tale of Sinuhe

The story of Sinuhe is an autobiographical narrative about an Egyptian official Sinuhe who, fearing for his life, fled to Syria-Palestine in the twentieth century B.C. The account records his movements from Egypt to Palestine and describes a high level of seminomadic activity between these regions. The account provides a glimpse of life in Canaan identical to what we find described in the patriarchal narratives.

Other Considerations

Genesis 14

Kenneth Kitchen has convincingly demonstrated that the international situation described in the patriarchal narratives at Genesis 14 fits only in the early second millennium B.C. Only in the early second millennium B.C. did Mesopotamia allow for shifting alliances, and only in that time period was Elam active in regional issues. Later, after the eighteenth century B.C., Hammurabi of Babylon and Shamsi-Adad I of Assyria dominated the areas of Assyria and Babylon, making such alliances described in Genesis 14 impossible. After the eighteenth century the Levant was controlled by successive imperial powers that would prevent alliances such as described in Genesis 14 from taking place. The Mesopotamian city-states had vanished.[60]

---

59. See Kitchen, *The Bible in Its World*, 73.
60. See Kitchen, "Patriarchal Age," 57; and W. C. Kaiser Jr., *A History of Israel: From the Bronze Age Through the Jewish Wars* (Nashville: Broadman & Holman, 1998), 62.

Cost of a Slave

Another issue of historical importance is the cost of a slave in the ancient world. In Genesis 37:28 Joseph was sold to the Ishmaelites for twenty silver shekels as the price of a slave. Twenty shekels was the same price of a slave in the first quarter of the second millennium B.C. in the Laws of Hammurabi and in the Mari texts. By the fourteenth and thirteenth centuries B.C. as represented at Nuzi and Ugarit the price of a slave had crept up to thirty shekels, consistent with the cost of a slave at the time of Moses (Exod. 21:32). Later, in the Assyrian period, near the beginning of the first millennium B.C., the price of a slave had gone up to 50 to 60 shekels, while even later in the Persian period the cost of slaves jumped from between 90 to 120 shekels.[61] Whereas the nation of Israel might share many customs with various ancient cultures over the centuries, the inflationary change of the cost of a slave precisely pinpoints the time of the patriarchs to the first quarter of the second millennium B.C.

Conclusion

The study of ancient Near Eastern texts provides the general historical background of the patriarchal narratives. The social customs represented in these documents legitimately illustrate and illuminate the events recorded in the patriarchal records. From the perspective of ancient Near Eastern and Palestinian archaeological evidence,[62] there is absolutely no reason to reject an early setting for the events of the patriarchs, somewhere between the twenty-first to the nineteenth centuries B.C. Because no overwhelming evidence exists to the contrary, the chronological data presented in the Bible should not be ignored. This is the position so assiduously championed by my friend and former professor and colleague Eugene Merrill throughout his academic career.

---

61. Kitchen, "Patriarchal Age," 52; and Kaiser, *History of Israel*, 63.
62. Eugene Merrill, "Ebla and Biblical Historical Inerrancy," *BSac* 140 (October–December 1983): 308.

II

THE DATE OF THE EXODUS

William H. Shea

THE DECIPHERMENT OF EGYPTIAN hieroglyphs in the nineteenth century A.D. opened up another avenue through which to explore and illuminate the historical record of the Bible. This source has provided evidence for various Egyptian features in Genesis and Exodus. However, it has not yet provided direct and firm evidence that would allow scholars to pinpoint a date for the Exodus with complete certainty. This is bound up with the identification of the pharaoh whom Moses confronted when he led the Israelites out of Egypt. Thus, that identification must be made on the basis of indirect evidence—how well the various pharaohs proposed fit with the evidence from the biblical record.

Two Major Proposals for Dating the Exodus

Two main proposals have been made. The first is that the pharaoh of the Exodus was Ramesses II of the Nineteenth Dynasty, who ruled in the thirteenth century B.C. The basis for this identification is the name of Ramesses as one of the store cities in Egypt that the Israelites built for pharaoh (Exod. 1:11). The other proposal is that the pharaoh mentioned in Exodus belonged to the Eighteenth Dynasty and ruled in the fifteenth century B.C. This proposal is derived from the chronological datum of 1 Kings 6:1, which indicates that the Exodus took place 480 years before Solomon began to build the temple in Jerusalem. These proposals are examined in detail below after a review of some of the literature that has been written on this subject.

A Late Date for the Exodus: The Nineteenth Dynasty (Thirteenth Century B.C.)

On September 22, 1822, Champollion sent and published his famous fifty-two-page work, *Lettre à M. Dacier*, in which he proposed his decipherment of Egyptian hieroglyphs. This turned out to be the major breakthrough needed to interpret that ancient scripture correctly. One week before that he deciphered the royal names of Thutmose and Ramesses in a text he was working on beside the trilingual decree of 196 B.C. from Ptolemy Epiphanus that is known as the Rosetta Stone.[1]

In 1828, before he visited Egypt in July of that year, he was working on a text that told of the battle between Ramesses II and the Hittites.[2] One of the highlights of his explorations in Egypt was his visit to the temple of Dendera where he again found the royal names of Thutmose and Ramesses.[3] The references to two kings by these names set the stage for the two main theories for locating the biblical Exodus within Egyptian history.

Since the name of Ramesses occurs in Exodus 1:11 as the name of one of the store cities that the Israelites built for pharaoh, it was natural to select the long-lived Ramesses II as the pharaoh of the Oppression. He has left many monuments and ruins of monumental buildings in Egypt, and it was easy to see the Israelites participating in the construction of those projects. That made his son Merenptah, who succeeded him to the throne, the pharaoh of the Exodus. Thus, throughout the nineteenth century A.D., the biblical Exodus was securely located by scholars within the confines of the nineteenth Egyptian Dynasty.

The picture described above changed with Petrie's discovery of Merenptah's Victory Stele in the ruins of his mortuary temple at Thebes in 1896.[4] Since Israel is mentioned in this text as a people living in Canaan by Merenptah's fifth year, the date of the inscription, this means that Israel was already settled there by the end of the thirteenth century B.C. While a minority of scholars have challenged that reading, it remains the dominant

---

1. F. Hintze, *Champollion: Entzifferer der Hieroglyphen* (Berlin: Berlin Museum, 1972), 14–15.
2. Ibid., 17.
3. C. W. Ceram, *Gods, Graves, and Scholars* (New York: Knopf, 1961), 112.
4. John A. Wilson, trans. "Hymn of Victory of Mer-ne-Ptah (The 'Israel Stela')," in *ANET*, 376–78.

and most direct interpretation of that reference to the present day.[5] Additional studies related to the text have supported that conclusion.[6]

This date for Israel in Canaan so early in the reign of Merenptah presented a direct challenge to his being identified as the pharaoh of the Exodus. That identification could only be maintained by drastically reducing the length of time that Israel spent wandering in the wilderness after the Exodus but before the entry into Canaan. Responses to this new datum went in two directions. The first of these came from scholars who continued to maintain that the Exodus occurred during the Nineteenth Dynasty. In order to sustain this connection, it became necessary to move the identifications of the pharaohs involved back by one generation each. Thus Seti I became the pharaoh of the Oppression, and Ramesses II became the pharaoh of the Exodus. In his research on this subject H. H. Rowley collected twenty-eight references to scholarly works published between 1928 and 1946 that continued to maintain the connection of the Exodus with the Nineteenth Dynasty.[7] The other alternative is an Eighteenth Dynasty setting for the Exodus from Egypt.

An Early Date for the Exodus: The Eighteenth Dynasty (Fifteenth Century B.C.)

The second major response to the mention of Israel on the Merenptah Stele was to look for the Exodus earlier in Egyptian history, more specifically in the fifteenth century B.C. during the Eighteenth Dynasty. This date was arrived at on the basis of 1 Kings 6:1, which gives the length of time between the Exodus and Solomon's commencement of construction of the temple as 480 years. Both Old Testament chronology and Egyptian chronology had been refined sufficiently by the early twentieth century A.D. that these correlations pointed to the middle of the fifteenth century B.C. during the Eighteenth Dynasty as the time of the Exodus. Solomon came to the throne around 970 B.C. and his fourth year (1 Kings 6:1) was

---

5. For the most recent and detailed study of the reference to Israel in this text see M. G. Hasel, "Israel in the Merneptah Stela," *BASOR* 296 (1994): 45–61.
6. F. J. Yurco, "3,200-Year-Old Picture of Israelites Found in Egypt," *BAR* 16, no. 5 (September–October 1990): 20–38.
7. H. H. Rowley, *From Joseph to Joshua* (London: British Academy, 1950), 11 n. 1.

967 or 966 B.C.[8] The Eighteenth Dynasty was now dated as extending from the middle of the sixteenth century B.C. to the middle of the fourteenth century B.C.[9] 480 years back from Solomon placed the Exodus squarely in the middle of the fifteenth century B.C. and the middle of the Eighteenth Dynasty, ca. 1446 B.C.

Support for this new date came quickly after the discovery of Merenptah's Stele. The same year that Petrie published the text, 1897, Orr adopted this new date and he was followed by Hommel in 1898 and by Miketta in 1903.[10] A dozen more scholars followed suit between 1922 and 1948.[11]

Pharaohs of the Exodus: Alternative Possibilities

Thus, two main theories concerning the date of the Exodus have emerged: (1) that it occurred during the Eighteenth Dynasty in the middle of the fifteenth century B.C., or (2) that it occurred during the Nineteenth Dynasty in the thirteenth century B.C. The first theory is based primarily upon chronological correlations with 1 Kings 6:1, and the second is based primarily upon the occurrence of the name of Ramesses in Exodus 1:11 as one of the store cities that the Israelites built for the pharaoh. We turn now to study specific pharaohs who come up for examination within the frameworks of those two theories.

Early-Date Possibilities: The Eighteenth Dynasty (Thutmose II, Thutmose III, Amenhotep II)

If the Exodus occurred in the fifteenth century B.C. as the chronological datum in 1 Kings 6:1 appears to indicate, there are three pharaohs in that

---

8. Ibid., 10 n. 4. Here Rowley surveyed sixteen scholars writing between 1911 and 1945 and found the dates for Solomon's accession ranged from 976 B.C. to 952 B.C. The most recent study of this problem concludes that Solomon died in 931/930 B.C. and thus his forty-year reign would have begun in 971. G. Galil, *The Chronology of the Kings of Israel and Judah* (Leiden: Brill, 1996), 24, 147.
9. For a standard chronology of the Eighteenth Dynasty, see A. Gardiner, *Egypt of the Pharaohs* (Oxford: Oxford University, 1964), 443. A more recent (revised) analysis is K. A. Kitchen, "The Basics of Egyptian Chronology in Relation to the Bronze Age," in *High, Middle, or Low? Acts of an International Colloquium on Absolute Chronology Held at the University of Gothenburg 20th–22nd August 1987*, ed. Paul Åstrom (Gothenburg: Paul Åstroms Förlag, 1987, 1989), pt. 1, 37–55, pt. 2, 152–59.
10. Rowley, *From Joseph to Joshua*, 10 n. 2.
11. Ibid., 10 n. 2, 11 n. 1.

century, any one of whom could be the pharaoh of the Exodus. In terms of chronology, one can think of the fifteenth century as a clock face. The pharaoh who died at three o'clock, at the end of the first quarter of that century, was Thutmose II. The pharaoh who died at the halfway mark in that century was Thutmose III. The pharaoh who died at the end of the third quarter of that century was Amenhotep II. Each of these rulers merits consideration in this context. They are taken in chronological order.

Thutmose II: An Exodus in 1479 B.C.

The Year of His Death. Three different chronologies have been suggested for the Eighteenth Dynasty on the basis of a Sothic Cycle observation and new moon dates.[12] The most recent and currently most popular is that which dates the death of Thutmose II in 1479 B.C.[13] The datum in 1 Kings 6:1 points to an Exodus at approximately 1450 B.C. Thus this date is slightly early for that datum. The chronology of the book of Judges probably points to an earlier date for the Exodus than 1 Kings 6:1, and that might be a way in which to reconcile these dates.

The Day of His Death. Information of this kind is provided by Thutmose III's record of his campaign against Megiddo in his twenty-third year. In the course of that campaign he celebrated the anniversary of his coronation on day four of the first month of the third season.[14] Tables are available with which to correlate ancient Egyptian dates with Julian dates B.C. When those correlations are carried out they indicate that Thutmose III came to the throne on April 25, and Thutmose II died just before that date.[15] This correlates well with the biblical date for the death of the pharaoh of the Exodus some days after Passover on the fourteenth of Abib, or Nisan. Since this date overlaps March and April in the Julian calendar Thutmose II died at the right time of year for this biblical pharaoh.

The Nature of His Reign. Thutmose II is an obscure pharaoh. His only dated inscription comes from his first year, and it tells of his dispatching troops to quell a revolt in Nubia. Beyond that, we do not know how long he reigned. Estimates commonly run to a decade or less. The most recent

---

12. R. A. Parker, "Calendars and Chronology," in *The Legacy of Egypt,* 2d ed., ed. J. R. Harris (Oxford: Oxford University, 1971), 13–26.
13. Åstrom, *High, Middle, or Low,* pt. 3.
14. John A. Wilson, trans., "The Asiatic Campaigns of Thut-mose III," in *ANET,* 235.
15. Ibid., n. 16.

and detailed study places the length of his reign at three years.[16] Perhaps this obscurity was intentional, produced by the pharaohs who followed him.

His Tomb. No tomb has been identified for Thutmose II in the Valley of the Kings. There is no tomb there in which his name was written. An anonymous tomb has been suggested as his. It is KV 42, described as, "unadorned and with an uninscribed sarcophagus, it is almost stark in its simplicity; it is matched by the relatively undistinguished mortuary temple set on the edge of the cultivation at Medinet Habu."[17] The conclusion drawn from this is that "This lack of elaborate funeral provision strongly suggests that the sudden death of the king had caught the royal stonemasons napping."[18] This is precisely the type of situation that one would expect from a pharaoh who reigned but a short time and then died suddenly at the time of the Exodus.

His Mummy. When Maspero unwrapped his mummy in 1886 he found that it was badly damaged. "The left arm had become detached. The right arm was severed from the elbow downward and the right leg had been completely amputated by a single axe-blow."[19] While the detached left arm could have resulted from normal movement or grave robbers, the other injuries go beyond what would normally have occurred in the process of searching for valuables. If the body of pharaoh washed up on the shore (Ps. 136:15, cf. Exod. 14:30) his body could have been desecrated by the Israelites or the enraged Egyptian search party that took his body back to Egypt.

The second aspect of his mummy that deserves attention is the nature of his skin lesions. From his examination of the body Maspero observed, "He had scarcely reached the age of thirty when he fell victim to a disease of which the process of embalming could not remove the traces. The skin is scabrous in patches and covered with scars."[20] From his examination of the body some years later, Smith concurred, "The skin of the thorax, shoulders and arms (excluding the hands), the whole of the back, the buttocks and the legs (excluding the feet) is studded with raised macules varying in size from minute points to patches a centimeter in diameter."[21] Ancient

---

16. L. Gabolde, "La chronolgie du règne de Thoutmosis II," *Studien zur Altaegyptischen Kultur* 14 (1987): 61–81.
17. J. Tyldesley, *Hatchepsut: The Female Pharaoh* (London: Viking, 1996), 94.
18. Ibid.
19. Ibid., 90.
20. Ibid.
21. Ibid., 90–91.

medical terminology is difficult to pin down exactly, but if pharaoh himself was also afflicted with the skin lesions described under the sixth plague (Exod. 9:8–12), then what has been found on the skin of Thutmose II would fit well with that plague. A photograph showing these patches is available in the volume with the x-rays of the pharaohs.[22]

Legal Fictions After His Death. When Hatshepsut took over the kingship during the minority of her stepson Thutmose III, she did so by the legal fiction that her father Thutmose I named her as coregent with him.[23] Not only was this coregency fictitious, but she completely skipped over the reign of her husband Thutmose II in her attempt to establish it.

Thutmose III did the same thing to vindicate his right to the throne by claiming that his father, Thutmose II, had installed him as coregent with himself. The falsity of this claim is supported by the fact that he did not make that claim until his forty-second regnal year.[24]

Thus both of the pharaohs who followed Thutmose II on the throne created legal fictions to justify their claims to the throne, leaving those claims as obscure, suspect, weak, and possibly dishonored.

The Campaigns of Thutmose III. Starting with his twenty-second year, Thutmose III conducted some sixteen campaigns into Asia. The last of these occurred in year forty-two. After the Israelites left Egypt, they spent one year at Sinai and forty more years wandering in the wilderness before they came into the Promised Land. This means that they came into Canaan in the forty-second year after the Exodus, the same year that Thutmose III stopped his campaigns there. If Thutmose II was the pharaoh of the Exodus, an incipient fear of the Israelites may have provided a hidden motive for the cessation of those campaigns.

Thutmose III: An Exodus in 1450 B.C.

The Year of His Death. The older interpretation of the new moon dates for Thutmose III located his fifty-four-year reign from 1504 B.C. to 1450

---

22. J. E. Harris and K. R. Weeks, *X-raying the Pharaohs* (New York: Scribners, 1973), 36.
23. Tyldesley, *Hatchepsut,* 105.
24. Ibid., 95.

B.C.[25] A variant of this view utilized the dates from 1501 B.C. to 1447 B.C.[26] This early date for his reign is still held by some modern scholars.[27] Using this high chronology for his reign makes him the pharaoh who died nearest the date approximated by 1 Kings 6:1, from 1450 B.C. to 1446 B.C.

The Day of His Death. The date of Thutmose III's death has come down to us through the "Biography of Amenemhab" who served in the Egyptian navy under several pharaohs.[28] The date is "the last day of the 3d month of the 2d season" or VII/30 of his last year. According to the tables referred to above under Thutmose II, this date equals March 17, 1450 B.C. This date is also in the Spring near the time of Passover. It is a little earlier than the death date of Thutmose II, but still within the range of possibility.

The Nature of His Reign. For the first twenty-two years of his reign he was the junior coregent to his stepmother Hatshepsut. When she passed off the scene of action, he launched a major series of Asiatic campaigns that brought a part of Western Asia under Egyptian control. Previous campaigns in that region had only been raids to collect booty. Now under Thutmose III some of that area was incorporated into the Egyptian empire. Thus he was one of the great empire builders in Egyptian history. The significance of this becomes evident in Exodus 14:18 where Yahweh said that he would get glory over pharaoh. If Thutmose III was the pharaoh of the Exodus, the Exodus occurred at a time of Egyptian strength, not a time of weakness, and this demonstrated who was the true God and who was only a human military conqueror parading as a god.

His Tomb. As a pharaoh who ruled for fifty-four years, he had plenty of time to execute his plans for his residence in the afterlife (KV 34).[29] One interesting aspect of this tomb is a scene in the wall paintings at the end of the last chamber which show some warriors falling into or drowning in a body of water.

---

25. L. Borchardt, *Die Mittel zur zeitlichen Festlegung von Punkten der ägyptischen Geschichte und ihre Anwendung* (Cairo: Selbstverlag, 1935); W. C. Hayes, "Egypt: Internal Affairs from Tuthmosis I to the Death of Amenophis III," *Cambridge Ancient History*, rev. ed., vol. 2, chap. 9, pt. 1 (Cambridge: Cambridge University, 1973), 315–22; W. S. LaSor, "Egypt," in *ISBE*, 2:41.
26. J. H. Breasted, *A History of Egypt* (New York: Bantam, 1964), 502.
27. E. F. Wente and C. C. Van Siclen, "A Chronology of the New Kingdom," in *Studies in Honor of George R. Hughes* (Chicago: University of Chicago, 1977), 217–61.
28. W. C. Hayes, "Egypt: Internal Affairs," 336–37; and J. H. Breasted, *ARE* (Chicago: University of Chicago, 1906), 2:234, §592.
29. Harris and Weeks, *X-raying the Pharaohs*, 137; Tyldesley, *Hatchepsut*, 215; and Gardiner, *Egypt of the Pharaohs*, 195.

His Mummy. The royal mummies in the Cairo Museum have been x-rayed.[30] The mummy labeled there as that of Thutmose III does not fit well with his inscriptions. On the basis of his x-rays, he is estimated to have been forty to forty-five years of age at the time of his death.[31] His inscriptions, however, run up toward the end of his fifty-third year, and he must have been a child of at least a few years when he came to the throne. This discrepancy could point to an occurrence of death at the time of the Exodus.

The pharaoh of the Exodus died in the sea. That is the logical inference from Exodus 14–15 and it is explicitly stated in Psalm 136:15. Some, but not all, of the bodies of the Egyptians washed ashore by the morning after the Israelite crossing. It may be that the body of pharaoh was not among those that washed ashore. What action would the search party sent out have taken if they found some of the drowned soldiers but they did not find the body of pharaoh? One possibility is that they might have taken a body of a soldier that did wash ashore back to Egypt and treated it as if it were the body of pharaoh.

Bases for Military Campaigns into Asia. From his conquests, the booty and tribute described in long lists of Thutmose III flowed into Egypt's treasuries. It was also necessary to establish a base north of Memphis as a point of departure for these campaigns. The location of the later Ramesses would have been a logical location for such a base. The cities of Pithom and Ramesses that the Israelites participated in building are described as "store cities." Elsewhere in the Old Testament this phrase refers to military bases with armories and supply depots, which were usually on the borders of the Hebrew kingdoms. This phrase should have a similar meaning in Exodus 1:11, and the Asiatic campaigns of Thutmose III provide an excellent explanation why construction of these delta projects would have been more pressing. They served both as bases from which his troops and their supplies were sent into Asia, and as sites for the temporary storage of the booty and tribute brought back from those campaigns.[32]

The Pharaoh After the Exodus. If Amenhotep II held the Hebrews responsible for the death of his father, Thutmose III, at the time of the Exodus, it would have been natural for him to seek revenge. The first contemporary

---

30. Harris and Weeks, *X-raying the Pharaohs,* 137.
31. Ibid., 138.
32. W. H. Shea, "Exodus, Date of," in *ISBE,* 2:235.

record of Habiru *outside* of Egypt comes from his Memphis Stele in which he claimed to have brought back 3,600 Habiru captives from his Syro-Palestinian campaigns.[33] While these would not have been the biblical Hebrews, who would still have been in the wilderness after an Exodus in 1450 B.C., they still belonged to the same social class. The loss of a sizeable number of Hebrew slaves also depleted the ranks of the Egyptian work force. Amenhotep's claim to have brought back a total of 90,000 captives from these campaigns could have been an attempt to replenish that depleted work force.[34]

From the end of Amenhotep's reign comes a text so unusual that some Egyptologists think that he may have been drunk while dictating it. Basically, it expresses a hatred of Semites.[35] The inscription is dated 14 years after the last of his Asiatic campaigns, but it shows that he still had Semites on his mind, even when he was as far away from them as Nubia. The Hebrews are not mentioned by name in the inscription but Takhsi, located in Syria, is, and that makes a connection with Semites in the general region from which the Hebrews had come.[36]

Amenhotep II: An Exodus in 1446 B.C.

The Year of His Death. The highest regnal year recorded for Amenhotep II comes from his twenty-third year.[37] If he came to the throne in 1450 B.C. when Thutmose III died, then he ruled until 1427 B.C., according to the high chronology for the reign of Thutmose III. The middle or low chronology would put his death date even later. This does not accord well with the date in 1 Kings 6:1, which would put his death, if he were the pharaoh of the Exodus, a quarter of a century earlier. It is not easy to condense the 480-year period of 1 Kings 6:1, because the time periods in the book of Judges seem to put that event even earlier, not later.

There is a way, however, in which to reconcile the date of the Exodus with the date for the death of Amenhotep II. This is to suggest that there were two kings that shared the same name and titles. The first of these would have been the pharaoh of the Exodus, and the second would have

---

33. John A. Wilson, trans., "The Asiatic Campaigning of Amen-Hotep II," in *ANET*, 247.
34. Shea, "Exodus, Date of," *ISBE*, 2:236.
35. Ibid.; and Gardiner, *Egypt of the Pharaohs*, 199.
36. Shea, "Exodus, Date of," *ISBE*, 2:236.
37. Wilson, "The Asiatic Campaigning of Amen-Hotep II," 247–48.

served as the pharaoh after the Exodus. The first would have died in 1446 B.C. while the second served later and died in 1427 B.C. While this suggestion may seem curious at first, there is some textual evidence that lends support to the idea.

The records of the military campaigns of Amenhotep II to Asia are described on four stelae that come in pairs. From Amada and Elephantine come the stelae that record the campaign of year 3.[38] From Karnak and Memphis come the stelae that record the campaigns of years 7 and 9.[39] The curious feature of these two pairs of texts is that they both describe their campaigns as Amenhotep's "first campaign of victory." This was a phrase that was commonly used by pharaohs to describe their very first military campaign.

It is not possible for Amenhotep to have had two "first campaigns of victory." One attempt to resolve this paradox has been to suggest that the first "first campaign" was conducted while Amenhotep was coregent with his father Thutmose III.[40] The second "first campaign of victory" then came from his first campaign of his sole reign after his father died. The problem with this theory is that there is no other reason to propose a coregency between Thutmose III and Amenhotep II.

If these texts really mean what they say, then there was not one pharaoh who had two "first" campaigns, but a "first" pharaoh who had one campaign and a second "first" pharaoh who had the other campaign. The first Amenhotep would have died between year 3 of the first campaign and year 7 of the second campaign. The second Amenhotep then conducted the campaigns of years 7 and 9. If Amenhotep II (A) died the year after his "first campaign of victory" that would date his death to 1446 B.C. Amenhotep II (B) would have come to the throne when he died and served the other 20 years of their combined reign.

This proposed date for the death of Amenhotep II (A) fits very closely with the date for the Exodus from 1 Kings 6:1. Solomon came to the throne in 972 B.C., and he began to build the temple in 967 B.C.[41] 480 years back from that comes to 1446 B.C., the year of the death of the hypothetical

---

38. Ibid.
39. Ibid., 245–47.
40. D. B. Redford, "The Coregency Between Tuthmosis III and Amenophis II," *JEA* 51 (1965): 121.
41. See the references found above in n. 8.

Amenhotep II (A). Amenhotep II (B) may have taken over his names and titles to hide the death of his predecessor from the Egyptian public.

His Military Campaigns. As discussed above under Thutmose III, the number of captives brought back to Egypt from Amenhotep's campaigns of years 7 and 9 totaled 90,000.[42] The number is so high that some Egyptologists do not believe it. On the other hand if Egypt had just lost a large amount of slave labor with the Exodus of the Israelites, this may have been an effort on the part of Amenhotep II (B) to make up for the losses under Amenhotep II (A).

Thirty-six hundred Habiru are listed as a part of the captives brought back to Egypt from these campaigns.[43] These could not be the biblical Hebrews if they were still wandering in the wilderness. To claim captives from the same social group, however, could have gone a ways towards assuaging the grief inflicted by the biblical Hebrews with the plagues and the Exodus.[44]

Hatred for Semites. In this case the same text that is mentioned above as coming from the end of the reign of Amenhotep II as the pharaoh after the Exodus in the time of Thutmose III also applies here. If Amenhotep II (A) was the pharaoh of the Exodus, Amenhotep II (B) would have had just as much reason to be angry at Semites like the Hebrews.

The Son of the Tenth Plague. The Dream Stele of Thutmose IV, son of Amenhotep II, records how as a prince he was hunting near the Sphinx. He lay to rest, fell asleep, and dreamed that the Sphinx told him that he would become pharaoh.[45] This was a surprise because he was not in line for the throne. Thus this text provides an unnamed crown prince who was in line for the throne before Thutmose IV. This could also be a reference to the eldest son of Amenhotep II who died in the tenth plague, thus giving a reason why Thutmose IV came to the throne instead.

His Tomb and Mummy. Unlike a number of pharaohs whose mummies were found elsewhere outside of their tombs, the mummy of Amenhotep II was found in place in his tomb (KV 35).[46] X-ray analysis of this mummy provides an age that corresponds well with the length of his reign. X-rays

---

42. Wilson, "The Asiatic Campaigning of Amen-Hotep II," 247.
43. Ibid.
44. The identification of "Habiru" = "Hebrew" is tenuous at best. See the discussion in David M. Howard Jr., *An Introduction to the Old Testament Historical Books* (Chicago: Moody, 1993), 73–74. See also Bryant G. Wood's essay, "From Ramesses to Shiloh: Archaeological Discoveries Bearing on the Exodus–Judges Period," chapter 12 in this volume.
45. J. H. Breasted, *ARE*, 2:320–24, §§810–15; and Gardiner, *Egypt of the Pharaohs,* 204.
46. Gardiner, *Egypt of the Pharaohs,* 205; and Harris and Weeks, *X-raying the Pharaohs,* 138.

show him to be about forty-five years of age.[47] If he came to the throne at twenty and ruled for approximately twenty-five years, that age is accurate. In the hypothesis presented here this should be the mummy of Amenhotep II (B). The corpse of Amenhotep II (A) may not have been recovered from the sea.

Late-Date Possibilities: The Nineteenth Dynasty (Ramesses II)

As pointed out above, the reference to Israel on Merenptah's Victory Stele rules out his identification as pharaoh of the Exodus. The fifth year of his reign in which this text was inscribed does not allow sufficient time for the Israelites to have left Egypt and wandered in the wilderness for forty years. That means that if the Exodus occurred during the Nineteenth Dynasty, Ramesses II, the father of Merenptah, is the most likely candidate. That would make Seti I the pharaoh of the Oppression. As a cruel military conqueror, he would fit that role well. That turns our attention to the reign of Ramesses II as the time of the Exodus.

Ramesses' Name

The name of Ramesses is used in Exodus 1:11 for one of the store cities that the Israelites worked on, and it occurs again in Exodus 12:37 as the name of the city from which they departed at the Exodus. This undoubtedly refers to the Egyptian city of Per-Ramesses which was given that name for its expansion under Ramesses II. Given these connections, it is logical to think of Ramesses II as the pharaoh of the Exodus.

This conclusion must be tempered, however, by the use of the same name for the "land of Ramesses" as the area assigned to the Israelites when they came to Egypt, according to Genesis 47:11. By no one's chronology can the entrance of Jacob and his family into Egypt be dated as late as the reign of Ramesses II. That would put the entry into Egypt and the Exodus as transpiring during the reign of the same king, and it would not allow any significant length of time for the lengthy sojourn in Egypt (Gen. 15:13–16; Exod. 12:40). In Genesis 47:11, therefore, this name represents an updating of an earlier name to a later time.

---

47. Harris and Weeks, *X-raying the Pharaohs*, 138.

Another example of this kind of phenomenon is found in the record of the pursuit of the four kings from the east by Abraham and his troops. He pursued them as far as Dan (Gen. 14:14). In Abraham's time the name of this city was Laish, and it was not renamed Dan until ca. 1100 B.C. when the site was taken over by the tribe of Dan (Judg. 18:7, 27). Given one such case with Ramesses already in Genesis, it could well be that the references in Exodus resulted from a similar phenomenon. Thus the name of Ramesses in Exodus is not the ultimate determinative for the identification of the pharaoh of the Exodus.

The Archaeology of Ramesses

Archaeological indicators were already present as early as the 1930s that Per-Ramesses was located at Qantir in the eastern Delta.[48] Subsequent investigations have confirmed that initial identification for the Hyksos capital of Avaris is now known to have been located at nearby Tell el-Dabᶜa.[49] Egyptian texts identify the location of earlier Avaris as also the location of later Per-Ramesses.[50] Thus there clearly was a capital city located in the eastern delta by the time of Ramesses II.

In some older works the archaeology of Per-Ramesses was used to argue against an Exodus as early as the fifteenth century B.C. by holding that there was no Eighteenth Dynasty occupation there. This criticism must now be laid to rest with the discovery of an Eighteenth Dynasty citadel at Tell el-Dabᶜa. As the excavator M. Bietak states, "It is now a major surprise to have firm evidence that the Hyksos citadel was re-occupied in the early Eighteenth Dynasty with palatial installations forming a new royal citadel."[51]

---

48. Significant work at this site recognizing it as Ramesses began with M. Hamza, "Excavation of the Department of Antiquities at Qantir (Faqus District)," *ASAE* 30 (1930): 31–68. It was followed up by W. C. Hayes, *Glazed Tiles from a Palace of Ramesses II at Kantir* (New York: Metropolitan Museum, 1937); and by L. Habachi, "Khata'na-Qantir, importance," *ASAE* 52 (1954): 443–559. See the works of M. Bietak, the excavator of Tell el-Dabᶜa, cited note 49.
49. See the works of M. Bietak, the excavator of Tell el-Dabᶜa: M. Bietak, *Avaris and PiRamesse: Archaeological Exploration in the Eastern Nile Delta,* Wheeler Lecture for 1979 (Oxford: Oxford University Press, 1981); idem, *Avaris: The Capital of the Hyksos* (London: British Museum, 1996). See also E. P. Uphill, "Pithom and Raamses: Their Location and Significance," *JNES* 27 (1968): 291–315; and idem, "Pithom and Raamses: Their Location and Significance," *JNES* 28 (1969): 15–39.
50. Uphill, "Pithom and Raamses," *JNES* 27 (1968): 291–316; and idem, "Pithom and Raamses," *JNES* 28 (1969): 15–39.
51. Bietak, *Avaris and PiRamesse,* 67.

This citadel sat upon a 70 x 50 meter platform and had a 6 meter wide ramp running up to it. To the southeast 150 meters, a large storage building has been found, and it contained a large cache of Late Bronze I pottery.[52] In the 1995 season, another Eighteenth Dynasty building, possibly a temple, was found west of the citadel. North of the citadel thousands of fragments from magnificent Minoan style frescoes were found and their remarkable presence here dates to the same period.[53]

Bietak dates the use of this complex from Ahmose to Amenhotep II.[54] Since Amenhotep II has been suggested above as a possible pharaoh of the Exodus, the abandonment of this site and the dismantling of the frescos could be related to the Exodus. The same point could also apply to either of the two pharaohs discussed above who preceded him, Thutmose II or Thutmose III.

Military Campaigns

The military campaigns of Ramesses II can be examined for a potential but indirect relationship to an Exodus during his reign. Ramesses II mounted most of his military campaigns to Asia during the first decade of his long reign.[55] The campaign of year 4 and probably the campaign from year 10 are recorded in inscriptions at the Dog River in Lebanon. It was during the campaign of year 5 that Ramesses II fought his major battle with the Hittites at Kadesh in Syria. The record of this battle was inscribed in at least seven locations in Egypt.[56] Seven or eight towns of Syro-Palestine were claimed as conquered during the campaign of year 8. With this much military activity going on, the first decade of his reign does not look like a very opportune time for the Exodus.

By way of contrast, the second decade of his reign was more peaceful. Only one campaign is known from this period, that of year 18. This probably was the expedition during which he campaigned through Edom and Moab

---

52. Ibid., 70.
53. Ibid., 73–79, and Plates III–VIII.
54. Ibid., 72.
55. For the chronological arrangement of the inscriptions of Ramesses II, including those of his military campaigns, see J. D. Schmidt, *Ramesses II: A Chronological Structure for His Reign* (Baltimore: Johns Hopkins, 1973).
56. Ibid., 28.

in Transjordan.[57] The northernmost extent of this campaign probably was represented by his stela at Beth-shan. This campaign shows more promise of a potential relationship to the Exodus. If the Exodus occurred between year 10 and year 18, then this campaign could be seen as a search and destroy mission looking for the escaped Israelites. On the other hand, if the Exodus occurred after year 18, then this campaign could be seen as a providential way of destroying or diminishing future opposition to the Israelites when they passed through that area.

Political Relations

The major achievement in foreign diplomacy during the reign of Ramesses II was his treaty with the Hittites in year 21.[58] The third of the four major stipulations in this treaty is of special interest here. The third stipulation incumbent upon the Hittite king was that, in the event that Ramesses' "own subjects" committed "another crime against him," the Hittite king would come to his aid in suppressing such a disorder.

In the case of the Egyptian king, that condition appears to have involved a recent "crime" committed by his subjects against him. The evident distinction between the foreign territories of the pharaoh in the second stipulation and "his own subjects" in Egypt in the third stipulation appears to be quite intentional. The use of the word "another," modifying the word for crime, also appears to be intentional.

In spite of the paucity of sources from this time, the situation presupposed by the third stipulation in Ramesses' treaty with the Hittites could be viewed as providing a veiled reference to the biblical Exodus. The departure of the Israelite slaves could have been viewed as just such a crime. The severity of the "crime" perpetrated by his subjects was of such severity that he was willing to appeal to a foreign ruler for assistance in suppressing another occurrence of a similar nature. The biblical description of the events surrounding the Exodus appears to reach this level of importance from an Egyptian point of view.[59]

---

57. For the Shashu in Edom see R. Giveon, *Les Bedouins Shosou des documents Egyptiens* (Leiden: Brill, 1971), 226–28, 235. For Moab see K. A. Kitchen, "New Light on the Asiatic Wars of Ramesses II," *JEA* 50 (1964): 47–50. For the Bethshan Stele of Ramesses II see Schmidt, *Ramesses II,* 36–37, 111–53.
58. Schmidt, *Ramesses II,* 111–53.
59. Shea, "Exodus, Date of," *ISBE,* 2:232.

Monumental Building

Ramesses II's sixty-seven-year long reign gave him ample opportunity to carry out many major building projects all over Egypt.[60] His palace at Qantir/Ramesses has already been mentioned above. He carried out extensive building operations at Abydos, including the completion of a magnificent temple begun there by his father. He also completed his father's mortuary temple at Thebes and built another for himself, the Ramesseum. In Nubia, he built six new temples, including the famous Abu Simbel. He was especially fond of producing great statues of himself, a number of which have survived in whole or in part. He produced dozens of obelisks, many of which have also survived. From this, J. H. Breasted concluded, "his own legitimate building was on a scale quite surpassing in size and extent anything that his ancestors had accomplished."[61] Obviously, slave labor like that which the Israelites could have provided would have been beneficial to carrying out these projects.

The Death of Ramesses II, His Mummy and the Royal Tombs

According to a tax document which Petrie found at Gurob, Ramesses died in his sixty-seventh year between day eighteen of the first month of the first season and day nineteen of the second month of the first season.[62] Correlations with the Julian calendar indicate that he died around September. Psalm 136:15 indicates that a pharaoh died at the time of the Exodus and that is the logical way in which to understand Exodus 14–15. If this is correct, then Ramesses II could not be the pharaoh of the Exodus who should have died in the Spring just after Passover.

It is also doubtful that a frail old man over seventy years of age could have led his chariot corps in pursuit of the Israelites (Exod. 14:6–7). Harris and Weeks affirm that "x-rays show severe degenerative arthritis in the hip joint and arteriosclerosis of all of the major arteries of the lower extremities. Such disorders often produce uncomfortable circulatory disorders and make movement painful."[63]

---

60. For a review of some of these building projects see Breasted, *History of Egypt*, 372–75.
61. Ibid., 372.
62. Cited in Schmidt, *Ramesses II*, 64.
63. Harris and Weeks, *X-raying the Pharaohs*, 155.

The tomb of Seti I, the father of Ramesses II, is one of the most magnificent of all the royal tombs in the Valley of the Kings. The tomb of Ramesses II is larger but more poorly decorated, and it was cut in a badly chosen and poorly engineered site, which has left it in a crumbling condition.[64] It is difficult to locate a son of Ramesses II as the victim of the tenth biblical plague. Because of his long reign, a series of chief royal wives and lesser wives produced a large number of children for him. Many of their names are registered in his temples. [65] Their total is estimated to be about one hundred. A dozen of Ramesses' sons died before he did. Merenptah, who came to the throne after his father's death, was thirteenth in line for the throne. This succession of sons who died has been borne out by recent excavations in the Valley of the Kings.

In 1989 Kent and Susan Weeks began working in KV 5 near the entrance to the Valley of the Kings.[66] This tomb was noted some time ago, but it had not been explored to any great extent. As a result of more than a decade of work there, the Weeks have demonstrated that this was the tomb that Ramesses II made for his sons who died before he did.

The tomb is about 50 meters long and it contains approximately 150 rooms. To the present time it is estimated that only about seven per cent of it has been cleared. Some canopic jars for the storage of bodily organs have been recovered, along with a statue of Ramesses II as the god Osiris, the judge for the afterlife. The tomb indicates that Ramesses named his eldest son as coregent with him, and then when he died his brothers who followed him were successively elevated to that status.

This makes it difficult to locate the son who died during the tenth plague if Ramesses II was the pharaoh of the Exodus. Some of these difficulties can be avoided, however, by dating the Exodus earlier during the reign of Ramesses, as has been suggested above. With an earlier Exodus, however, no pharaoh died at the time of the Exodus.

Summary and Conclusions

For most of the nineteenth century—from the time that Champollion discovered the name of Ramesses (II) in the hieroglyphs that he deciphered

---

64. Ibid.; and Gardiner, *Egypt of the Pharaohs*, 267.
65. Ibid.
66. As reported in a TV documentary on the Discovery Channel on May 28, 2001.

until the end of the century—the dominant view was that the Exodus took place in the thirteenth century B.C., that is, that Ramesses II was the pharaoh of the Oppression and his son Merenptah was pharaoh of the Exodus.

This picture changed in 1896 when Petrie discovered Merenptah's Victory Stele, which mentions Israel as a people settled in Canaan. Merenptah no longer fit as pharaoh of the Exodus, or the Exodus would have to have occurred during the first four years of his reign. This led back to Ramesses II as the pharaoh of the Exodus and Seti I as the pharaoh of the Oppression. For those who consider the Exodus a historical event, this probably is the most commonly held view on this subject. However, there are a number of problems that make it difficult to fit the Exodus into the reign of Ramesses II.

In spite of the large amount of work that has been done on the Ramesside period, however, the evidence for Ramesses II as the pharaoh of the Exodus has not improved. If one takes seriously the reference to the death of the first born of pharaoh during the tenth plague, the view of Ramesses II has faded somewhat with the excavation of Tomb number five in the Valley of the Kings. As many as a dozen of the sons of Ramesses may have been buried there before the king himself died.

By the beginning of the twentieth century, biblical and Egyptian chronologies had been refined to a sufficient degree to point back to the Eighteenth Dynasty on the basis of 1 Kings 6:1; i.e., a date in the fifteenth century B.C., ca. 1446 B.C. This period does appear to offer a better fit with Egyptian history in terms of circumstances elucidated from biblical history. Not one but three pharaohs during that century offer features from their reigns that make anyone of the three the potential pharaoh of the Exodus—Thutmose II, Thutmose III, and Amenhotep II.

Probably the most popular of these for scholars in the past has been Amenhotep II. In his case, however, one must posit another ruler by the same name who died early in their combined reign. Thutmose III is the ruler who died nearest the biblical date for the Exodus on the basis of the high Egyptian chronology, and this writer previously favored him.[67] Adopting the low Egyptian chronology for the Eighteenth Dynasty brings Thutmose II into view as the possible pharaoh of the Exodus. More features of his person and his reign currently favor him as the best candidate for the pharaoh of the Exodus. Although biblical chronology does not quite reach as far

---

67. Shea, "Exodus, Date of," *ISBE,* 2:230–38.

back as 1479 B.C. for the Exodus, some minor adjustments in either biblical chronology or Egyptian chronology may bring these two dates together.

Finally, it should be stressed here that from the Egyptian side of this question we are dealing with circumstantial evidence. In the 180 years since hieroglyphs were deciphered, no Egyptian text has ever been found that refers directly to the Israelite Exodus. It is unlikely that such a text will ever be found. The reason for this is not that the Exodus did not occur, but that the Egyptians did not want to admit that it occurred. From the point of view of their propaganda, they could not admit that such a defeat had occurred because it would have impugned the divinity of pharaoh.

All of the Old Testament, not just the book of Exodus, stands as the direct witness to that event. Egyptian texts and archaeology can fill in the background of that event, but it is the Bible that provides the direct witness to it.

12

From Ramesses to Shiloh

Archaeological Discoveries Bearing on the Exodus–Judges Period

Bryant G. Wood

WHO SAYS YOU CAN'T TEACH AN OLD dog new tricks? I take great pride in having lured Eugene H. Merrill from the comfort of the armchair to the rigors of the trenches. It was a distinct pleasure to have him as a staff member of the Kh. el-Maqatir Excavation Project during the 1997, 1999, and 2000 dig seasons. I am pleased to offer this overview of recent and not-so-recent archaeological discoveries that shed light on a crucial period in Israel's history, in celebration of the distinguished teaching and writing career of friend and colleague Eugene H. Merrill.

Introduction

Attempts to correlate the findings of archaeology with the biblical record for the period under review have seemingly met with insurmountable obstacles. Much of the scholarly community today has despaired of making any valid connections and has dismissed biblical history prior to the kingdom period as nothing more than myth and legend. When one probes these supposed difficulties, however, one finds that the problem lies not with the biblical narrative, but rather with a lack of scientific rigor in analyzing the archaeological data. In all cases, allegations made against the biblical text can be attributed to misrepresenting biblical chronology, arguments from silence (nonevidence), misinterpretation and/or lack of in-depth analysis of the archaeological evidence, or just plain bad scholarship. In this brief overview I hope to expose some of these misunderstandings. My methodology is to utilize the biblical model as a framework for understanding the early history of Israel. When the Bible is allowed to speak for itself and the archaeological data are properly understood, the archaeological evidence and the biblical record are in complete agreement.

Exodus

A King Who Did Not Know Joseph (Exod. 1:8)

There have been a number of suggestions as to the identity of the unnamed[1] Pharaoh in Exodus 1:8. Recent archaeological work in the eastern Delta of Egypt, I believe, has provided the evidence needed to place the identification on firmer ground. The only time when the Israelites could have worked at Pithom (Exod. 1:11) was during the Hyksos period (see below). Thus, it stands to reason, the new king who did not know Joseph was the first Hyksos king (Maaibre Sheshi?).[2] Since he was a foreigner,[3] he would have had an incomplete knowledge of Egyptian history and been unaware of Joseph's accomplishments over two hundred years earlier. The narrative of Exodus 1 supports this view.

Exodus 1:8–12 should be assigned to the Hyksos period. As Rea has pointed out, *wayyāqom melek-ḥādāš ʿal-miṣrāyim* in Exodus 1:8 is better translated "A new king rose up against Egypt," rather than "Now a new king arose over Egypt" (NASB).[4] The Hyksos forcefully took over Egypt in the mid-seventeenth century B.C. and ruled for 108 years according to the Turin king list.[5] They feared the Israelites would join forces with the Egyptians ("those who hate us") and "fight against us" (v. 10).[6] Thus, the Hyksos

---

1. Biblical references to the king of Egypt follow Egyptian scribal practice. Prior to the tenth century B.C. the title "Pharaoh" was used alone without a proper name. After the tenth century B.C. "Pharaoh" plus a proper name became common usage. K. A. Kitchen, "Pharaoh," in *ISBE*, 3:821.
2. James M. Weinstein, "Hyksos," in *OEANE*, 3:133.
3. Neutron activation analyses of pottery from Tell el-Dabʿa (= Avaris, the Hyksos capital) indicate that the Hyksos came from southern Palestine. Patrick E. McGovern, *The Foreign Relations of the "Hyksos": A Neutron Activation Study of Middle Bronze Age Pottery from the Eastern Mediterranean* (Oxford, England: Archaeopress, 2000).
4. John Rea, "The Time of the Oppression and the Exodus," *Grace Journal* 2 (1961): 7–8. All biblical quotations in this chapter are from the NASB.
5. Weinstein, "Hyksos," 3:133.
6. The use of the title "Pharaoh" for a Hyksos king (Exod. 1:11) is perfectly in keeping with the Hyksos practice of adopting Egyptian royal titularies (Weinstein, "Hyksos," 3:133).

placed the Israelites in harsh bondage constructing Pithom and Ramesses, major commercial centers of the Hyksos kingdom.[7] The names Pithom and Ramesses are both later names by which these places were known (see below). Since the earlier names were no longer in use, later copyists updated the biblical texts to the names by which the sites were known in their day.[8]

Under the leadership of Amosis, the Egyptians drove out the Hyksos in the mid-sixteenth century B.C. and reestablished Egyptian control of the Delta. Amosis then founded the mighty Eighteenth Dynasty. Exodus 1:13ff. is set in the early Eighteenth Dynasty period following the expulsion of the Hyksos.

Store City of Pithom (Exod. 1:11)

Textual and excavation evidence point to Tell el-Maskhuta in the eastern end of the Wadi Tumilat, 16 km. west of Ismaliya, as being Pithom of Exodus 1:11.[9] Excavations from 1978 to 1985, under the direction of John S. Holladay Jr., of the University of Toronto, have established the occupational history of the site. Prior to ca. 610 B.C. (Saite period), the only occupation was during the Hyksos period. The name Pithom was attached to the Saite town, with the name of the Hyksos settlement being unknown.[10] Thus, the only possible time period when the Israelites could have worked there as slaves was during the Hyksos period.

The Hyksos town was ca. 5 acres in size and unfortified. It was occupied

---

7. John S. Holladay Jr., "The Eastern Nile Delta During the Hyksos and Pre-Hyksos Periods: Toward a Systemic/Socioeconomic Understanding," in *The Hyksos: New Historical and Archaeological Perspectives*, ed. Eliezer Oren (Philadelphia: University of Pennsylvania, 1997), 198–209.
8. This was a known practice, as can be observed with such names as Bethel (named by Jacob in Gen. 28:19, but used retrospectively in Gen. 12:8 and 13:3), Dan (named by the Danites in Judg. 18:29, but used retrospectively in Gen. 14:14), and Samaria (named by Omri in 1 Kings 16:24, but used retrospectively in 1 Kings 13:32).
9. John Van Seters, "The Geography of the Exodus," in *The Land That I Will Show You: Essays on the History and Archaeology of the Ancient Near East in Honour of J. Maxwell Miller*, ed. David J. A. Clines and Philip R. Davies (Sheffield: Sheffield Academic Press, 2001), 256–64; John S. Holladay Jr., "Maskhuta, Tell el-," in *ABD*, 4:588; idem, "Maskhuta, Tell el-," in *OEANE*, 3:432; Donald B. Redford, "Exodus I 11," *VT* 13 (1963): 403–8; idem, "Pithom," in *Lexikon der Ägyptologie*, ed. Wolfgang Helck and Eberhard Otto (Wiesbaden: Otto Harrassowitz, 1982), 4:1054–58; and idem, *Egypt, Canaan, and Israel in Ancient Times* (Princeton, N.J.: Princeton University Press, 1992), 451 n. 92. Hans Goedicke ("Papyrus Anastasi VI 51–61," *Studien zur Altägyptischen Kultur* 14 [1987]: 93), and James Hoffmeier (*Israel in Egypt* [New York: Oxford University Press, 1997], 119–21), however, prefer Tell el-Retabeh (14 km. west of Tell el-Maskhuta) as Pithom.
10. See Holladay, "Maskhuta, Tell el-," and Redford, "Exodus I 11," in previous note.

for less than a century and then abandoned prior to the expulsion of the Hyksos.[11] Approximately 735 m² of the town and 100 m² of an adjacent cemetery from the same period were excavated.[12] Both public and private buildings made of mud bricks were in evidence, as well as boundary walls and storage silos.[13] Quantities of hand-made, flat-bottomed cooking pots common in Canaan were found at the site. Holladay believes these cook pots are evidence of pastoralists who "were recruited by the Asiatics [Hyksos] for building their new settlement."[14]

Fig. 12.1. Excavating the Hyksos phase at Tell el-Maskhuta, Egypt, thought to be biblical Pithom, 1983. (Credit: Bryant G. Wood)

---

11. John S. Holladay Jr., "Pithom," in *OEAE*, 3:50.
12. John S. Holladay Jr., *Cities of the Delta, Part III: Tell el-Maskhuta,* American Research Center in Egypt Reports; Malibu, Calif.: Undena, 1982), 44–47; Patricia Paice, John S. Holladay Jr., and Edwin C. Brock, "The Middle Bronze Age/Second Intermediate Period Houses at Tell el-Maskhuta," in *Hous und Palast im Alten Ägypten,* ed. Manfred Bietak (Vienna: Österreichischen Akademie der Wissenschaften, 1996), 159–73; and Holladay, "Eastern Nile Delta," 188–94. For summary reports, see Holladay, "Pithom," in *ABD,* 4:588–92; and idem, "Pithom," in *OEANE,* 3:432–37
13. The author was a staff member of the Tell el-Maskhuta excavation during the 1979, 1981, and 1983 seasons. During the 1983 season he supervised the excavation of the major portion of a large 11 x 13.6 m Hyksos workshop in Square R7 in which industrial activities involving high-temperature hearths and grinding stones were carried out.
14. Holladay, "Eastern Nile Delta," 190.

Holladay suggests that Tell el-Maskhuta was part of an international trading network operated by the Canaanite Hyksos, with its center at Tell el-Dabʿa, ancient Avaris, the capital of the Hyksos.[15]

City of Ramesses

Twelfth Dynasty (Gen. 47:11, 27)

When Jacob and his family migrated to Egypt, they were settled in "the land of Ramesses" and given their own land (Gen. 47:11, 27). Later, after being pressed into slavery, they were used to construct a store city at Ramesses (Exod. 1:11). When the Israelites left Egypt after 430 years (Exod. 12:40), they departed from Ramesses (Exod. 12:37). From these passages it is clear that the Israelites spent the years of the Sojourn in and around Ramesses. Excavations in 1966–1969 and 1975–present at Tell el-Dabʿa-Qantir in the eastern Nile delta, ca. 100 km northeast of Cairo, have demonstrated that this was the location of biblical Ramesses.[16] In antiquity, the Pelusiac branch of the Nile flowed past the site, giving access to the Mediterranean. In addition, the town was the starting point for the land route to Canaan, the famous Horus Road. Because it was at the crossroads of international maritime and overland routes, it was an important commercial and military center.

When the Israelites first arrived in the nineteenth century B.C., the name of the town was Rowaty, "the door of the two roads."[17] Toward the end of the eighteenth century B.C., the name was changed to Avaris, "the (royal) foundation of the district."[18] When the Hyksos established their capital at the site in the seventeenth century B.C., they retained the name Avaris. Amosis established a royal center there after he had driven the Hyksos out (see below). Undoubtedly he gave the town a new name at that time—possibly Peru-nefer, "happy journey," although this is not known for certain.[19] If Peru-nefer was indeed the name of the early Eighteenth Dynasty

---

15. Holladay, "Eastern Nile Delta," 209; and idem, "Pithom," in *OEAE*, 51.
16. Van Seters, "Geography of the Exodus," 264–67; and Manfred Bietak, *Avaris and Piramesse: Archaeological Exploration in the Eastern Nile Delta* (London: British Academy, 1986), 278–83.
17. Manfred Bietak, *Avaris, the Capital of the Hyksos: Recent Excavations at Tell el-Dabʿa* (London: British Museum, 1996) 9, 19.
18. Ibid., 40.
19. Ibid., 82.

town, then the Israelites left from a place called "happy journey"! Later, in the thirteenth century B.C., when Ramesses II built his royal city on the site, he renamed it "Ramesses."[20] We now know that when the Israelites were there the names of the town were Rowaty, Avaris and possibly Perunefer, not Ramesses, as some have theorized.[21]

Prior to the arrival of the Canaanite Hyksos, there was a settlement of nomadic pastoral Asiatics at Rowaty in the late Twelfth Dynasty (mid-nineteenth century B.C.) in Area F/I, Str. d/2, and Area A/II, Str. H.[22] About 82 acres in size,[23] it was unfortified, although there were many enclosure walls, most likely for keeping animals.[24] The living quarters consisted of small rectangular buildings built of sand bricks.[25] Neutron activation analysis indicates that Palestinian-type pottery from the village originated in southern Palestine, and Bietak notes that the presence of handmade cooking pots is evidence of a nomadic pastoral population. He further observes that these "foreigners" could not have settled there without Egyptian consent.[26]

Since the Bible places the Israelites at Ramesses at this very time, it is plausible that Bietak has discovered the initial Israelite settlement at Ramesses. Perhaps the most compelling connection with the Israelites is a four-room house.[27] It was the largest building in the community, 10 x 12 m in size, situated on one side of an enclosure measuring 12 x 19 m. The size and layout corresponds to later Iron Age four-room houses commonly associated with Israelites.[28] Moreover, a monumental tomb of an Asiatic

---

20. Edgar B. Pusch, "Piramesse," in *OEAE*, 3:48–50.
21. Eugene H. Merrill, *Kingdom of Priests: A History of Old Testament Israel* (Grand Rapids: Baker, 1987), 70–71.
22. Bietak, *Avaris and Piramesse,* 237–38; idem, "Egypt and Canaan During the Middle Bronze Age," *BASOR* 281 (1991): 27–72; idem, *Avaris, the Capital,* 10–21; idem, "The Center of Hyksos Rule: Avaris (Tell el-Dabʿa)," in *The Hyksos: New Historical and Archaeological Perspectives,* 97–100; and idem, "Dabʿa, Tell ed-," in *OEAE,* 1:351. The absolute dates of the Tell el-Dabʿa phases is somewhat controversial since Bietak has adopted an ultralow Egyptian chronology that is being challenged by a number of scholars. See James M. Weinstein, "Reflections on the Chronology of Tell el-Dabʿa," in *Egypt, the Aegean and the Levant,* ed. W. V. Davies and L. Schofield (London: British Museum Press, 1995), 84–90.
23. Bietak, "Center of Hyksos Rule," 97.
24. Bietak, "Egypt and Canaan During the Middle Bronze Age," 32.
25. Bietak, *Avaris and Piramesse,* 237; and idem, "Egypt and Canaan During the Middle Bronze Age," 32.
26. Bietak, "Center of Hyksos Rule," 98–99.
27. Bryant G. Wood, "The Sons of Jacob: New Evidence for the Presence of the Israelites in Egypt," *Bible and Spade* 10 (1997): 55–56.
28. John S. Holladay Jr., "House, Israelite," in *ABD,* 3:308–18.

dignitary in the village cemetery raises the possibility of a connection with Joseph. In contrast to surrounding tombs, this one had been broken into and the bones removed (cf. Exod. 13:19)![29]

Early Eighteenth Dynasty (Exod. 1:13–2:14, 4:29–12:36)

Bietak uncovered an early Eighteenth Dynasty royal citadel at Tell el-Dabʿa most likely constructed by Amosis following the expulsion of the Hyksos.[30] It consisted of a fortress and palace, and remained in use until at least the reign of Amenhotep II.[31] The fortress was constructed on a 70 x 47 m platform approximately 30 m from the riverbank. A ramp on the eastern side led to a gate in a fortification wall, giving access to the river. South of the fortress was a large palace with thick walls, storage magazines, corridors, and bathrooms. Both structures were within a walled compound that included a temple, workshops and a military camp. Minoan wall paintings lined the rooms of the palace and fortress, and possibly other buildings within the complex. It is quite possible that this royal compound was the scene of events described in Exodus 1:13–2:15 and chapters 5–12.

Conquest

Jericho (Josh. 2:1–21; 6)

The first city the Israelites conquered in the Promised Land was Jericho (Josh. 2; 6). Ever since the excavations of British archaeologist Kathleen Kenyon in the 1950s, Jericho has been considered by most scholars to be a primary example of the nonagreement between the findings of archaeol-

---

29. Wood, "Sons of Jacob," 56–58. David Rohl was the first to make this association in his book *Pharaohs and Kings: A Biblical Quest* (New York: Crown, 1995), 360–67. Although I do not agree with his revised Egyptian chronology (see my "David Rohl's Revised Egyptian Chronology: A View from Palestine," *NEASB* 45 [2000]: 41–47), his arguments relating the tomb to Joseph have merit.
30. Bietak, *Avaris, the Capital*, 67–83; idem, "Center of Hyksos Rule," 115–24; idem, *OEAE*, 1:353; Manfred Bietak, Josef Dorner, and Peter Jánosi, "Ausgrabungen in dem Palastbezirk von Avaris. Vorbericht Tell el-Dabʿa/ʿEzbet Helmi 1993–2000," *Egypt and the Levant* 11 (2001): 36–101; and Josef Dorner, "A Late Hyksos Water-Supply System at Ezbet Hilme," *Egyptian Archaeology* 16 (2000): 12–13.
31. Bietak, *Avaris, the Capital*, 72; idem, "Center of Hyksos Rule," 124; idem, *OEAE*, 1:353; and Bietak, Dorner, and Jánosi, "Ausgrabungen," 38.

ogy and the Bible with regard to the Conquest.[32] Based on her interpretation of the evidence, she believed that the city had been destroyed in the middle of the sixteenth century B.C. and that there was no occupation in the fifteenth century B.C., the time of the Exodus and Conquest according to biblical chronology.[33] A previous excavator, another British archaeologist, John Garstang, concluded from his work in the 1930s that Jericho had been destroyed at the end of the fifteenth century B.C.[34] Garstang based his conclusion on a detailed analysis of the pottery found in the destruction level.[35] Kenyon, on the other hand, never published a definitive study of the Jericho pottery. The basis for her dating was articulated in a few brief remarks in various publications.[36]

An examination of the destruction level pottery makes it clear that the event occurred in the latter part of the fifteenth century B.C., as Garstang maintained, and not in the mid-sixteenth century B.C.[37] When the dating is properly assessed, the archaeological findings correlate with the biblical record in a remarkable fashion. According to the biblical narrative, the city was heavily fortified (Josh. 2:5, 15; 6:5, 20). Kenyon's meticulous fieldwork revealed the details of the fortification system. The tell was surrounded by a great earthen rampart, or embankment, with a stone retaining wall some 4–5 m high at its base. On top of the retaining wall was a mud brick wall 2 m thick and ca. 6–8 m high. At the crest of the embankment was a similar mud brick wall whose base was roughly 14 m above the ground level outside the retaining wall.[38] Within the upper wall was an area of ca. 6 acres, with the total area of the upper city and fortification system about 9 acres.

---

32. Kathleen M. Kenyon, *Digging Up Jericho* (London: Ernest Benn, 1957), 261–62; and Thomas A. Holland, "Jericho," in *OEANE*, 3:223.
33. Kenyon, *Digging Up Jericho*, 262; idem, "Jericho," in *Archaeology and Old Testament Study*, ed. D. Winton Thomas (Oxford: Clarendon, 1967) 265–67; idem, "Jericho: Tell es-Sultan," in *NEAEHL*, 2:680; idem, *The Bible in Recent Archaeology* (Atlanta: John Knox, 1978) 33–37; and idem, *Archaeology in the Holy Land*, 4th ed. (London: Ernest Benn, 1979) 182.
34. John Garstang, "Jericho and the Biblical Story," in *Wonders of the Past*, ed. J. A. Hammerton (New York: Wise, 1937), 1222.
35. John Garstang, "Jericho: City and Necropolis, Fourth Report," *Liverpool Annals of Archaeology and Anthropology* 21 (1934): 118–30, plates 13–44.
36. Bryant G. Wood, "Did the Israelites Conquer Jericho? A New Look at the Archaeological Evidence," *BAR* 16, No. 2 (1990): 50.
37. Ibid., 51–52.
38. Kenyon, *Archaeology and Old Testament Study*, 162–64; and Ernst Sellin and Carl Watzinger, *Jericho: Die Ergebnisse der Ausgrabungen* (Leipzig, Germany: J. C. Hinrichs, 1913; reprint, Osnabruck, Germany: Otto Zeller, 1973), 58.

The citizens of Jericho were well prepared for a siege as a copious spring lay inside the city wall and jars full of grain found in their homes indicated the harvest recently had been taken in (Josh. 2:6; 3:16).[39] After the Israelites made seven trips around the city on the seventh day, the walls fell (Josh. 6:5, 20).[40] Kenyon found evidence that the mud brick city wall had indeed collapsed and was deposited at the base of the tell.[41] The jars full of grain testify that the siege was short—very little had been used before the end came—and also that the Israelites did not plunder the city (Josh. 6:17–18). An early German expedition found houses built against a preserved section of the lower city wall on the north side of the tell, reminiscent of Rahab's house (Josh. 2:15).[42]

After the Israelites went up into the city (surmounting the embankment! Josh. 6:5, 20), they set fire to the city (Josh. 6:24). Both Garstang and Kenyon found abundant evidence of a fierce fire.[43] Kenyon noted that the walls collapsed prior to the burning, the same sequence as recorded in the biblical account.[44]

Ai (Josh. 7–8)

Following the defeat of Jericho, the Israelites proceeded into the highlands of Canaan and attacked the small fortress of Ai (Josh. 7–8). Finding the correct location of Ai has been a major difficulty in Old Testament scholarship. The search got off to an unfortunate start at the very beginning of biblical research in Palestine. On May 5, 1838, the pioneer of historical geography in the Holy Land, Edward Robinson, made two tragic blunders that are still with us today.

---

39. John Garstang, "The Walls of Jericho: The Marston-Melchett Expedition of 1931," *PEFQS* 63 (1931): 193–94; idem, "Fourth Report," 123, 128, 129; idem, "The Fall of Bronze Age Jericho," *PEFQS* 67 (1935): 61–68; idem, "Jericho and the Biblical Story," 1218; Kenyon, *Archaeology and Old Testament Study,* 171; idem, *Excavations at Jericho,* vol. 3, *The Architecture and Stratigraphy of the Tell* (London: British School of Archaeology, 1981), 369–70; and idem, *Digging Up Jericho,* 230.
40. The word describing how the city wall fell, *taḥtêhā* in Joshua 6:5, 20, is more accurately translated "beneath itself" rather than "flat."
41. Kenyon, *Excavations at Jericho,* 3:110.
42. Sellin and Watzinger, *Jericho,* Blatt 13, Tafel III; the situation of Rahab's house, *bᵉqîr haḥômâ* in Joshua 2:15 is better translated "against the vertical surface of the (city) wall," rather than the variety of renderings found in modern translations.
43. Garstang, "Walls of Jericho," 192; idem, "Fourth Report," 122–23; idem, "Fall of Bronze Age Jericho," 68; idem "Jericho and the Biblical Story," 1218; Kenyon, *Excavations at Jericho,* 3:369–70; idem, *Archaeology and Old Testament Study,* 171.
44. Kenyon, *Excavations at Jericho,* 3:370.

Robinson arrived at the village of Beitin at 7:30 in the morning on that ill-fated day and identified it as biblical Bethel based on two considerations. First, according to Eusebius, Bethel was located approximately 12 Roman miles, equivalent to 11 English miles,[45] north of Jerusalem.[46] Since it took Robinson 3¾ hours to travel from Beitin to Jerusalem by horse, he calculated the distance to be 12 Roman miles [47] based on his rule-of-thumb of 3 miles per hour for his horse's rate of travel.[48] Secondly, the similarity between the names Beitin in Arabic and Bethel in Hebrew led him to equate the two.[49] Since the Bible states that Ai is east of Bethel (Josh. 7:2; 8:9, 12) and in the vicinity of Bethel (Josh. 12:9), finding the correct location of Bethel is crucial for finding Ai.

Looking east of Beitin, the only candidate with remains earlier than the Hellenistic period is et-Tell. In an influential 1924 article William F. Albright lent his support to this site as the location of Ai.[50] Later he stated,

> Since the writer has scoured the district in question in all directions, hunting for ancient sites, he can attest the fact that there is no other possible site for Ai than et-Tell.[51]

With such a strong endorsement from Albright, nearly all scholars accepted the et-Tell-Ai identification. This raised a major problem, however, in that there was a long occupational gap at et-Tell from the end of the Early Bronze Age, ca. 2400 B.C., until the beginning of the Iron Age, ca. 1200 B.C.,[52] and thus no city for the Israelites to attack. As with Jericho, this led scholars to dismiss the account of Ai as unhistorical.

---

45. John Wilkinson, *Jerusalem Pilgrims Before the Crusades* (Warminster, England: Aris & Phillips, 1977), table: Units of Measurement, v.
46. G.S.P. Freeman-Grenville, *Palestine in the Fourth Century A.D.: The Onomasticon by Eusebius of Caesarea* (Winona Lake, Ind.: Eisenbrauns, 2003) 4:27.
47. Edward Robinson, *Biblical Researches in Palestine and the Adjacent Regions: A Journal of Travels in the Years 1838 and 1852*, 3d ed. (London: John Murray, 1867; reprint, Jerusalem: Universitas Booksellers, 1970), 1:449.
48. Edward Robinson, *Later Biblical Researches in Palestine, and in the Adjacent Regions: A Journal of Travels in the Year 1852* (Boston: Crocker and Brewster, 1856), 635.
49. Robinson, *Biblical Researches in Palestine and the Adjacent Regions*, 449.
50. W. F. Albright, "Ai and Beth-Aven," in *Excavations and Results at Tell el-Ful (Gibeah of Saul)*, AASOR 4, ed. Benjamin W. Bacon (New Haven, Conn.: American Schools of Oriental Research, 1924), 141–49.
51. W. F. Albright, *The Biblical Period from Abraham to Ezra* (New York: Harper & Row, 1963), 29.
52. Robert E. Cooley, "Ai," in *OEANE*, 1:32–33.

Livingston has called into question the Beitin–Bethel equation, citing among other evidence the actual distance from Jerusalem to Beitin as 14 Roman miles rather than 12 as Robinson had supposed.[53] He provides convincing evidence that Bethel should be located at the modern town of El-Bireh, which is 12 Roman miles from Jerusalem.[54]

Shortly after his arrival at Beitin, Robinson continued on to nearby Kh. el-Maqatir, 1.5 km to the south-southeast, where he made his second major error of the day. Local inhabitants told him this was the location of Ai. After inspecting a Byzantine church on the summit, he concluded, "But there is not the slightest ground for any such hypothesis. There never was any thing here but a church; and Ai must have been further off from Bethel, and certainly not directly in sight of it."[55]

Had Robinson walked 200 m down the southeast slope of the site he might have changed the course of Palestinian archaeology. There, also missed by Albright, in clear view, is abundant evidence for early occupation, including ancient walls visible on the surface. When Ernest Sellin visited Kh. el-Maqatir in 1899 he also was told it was Ai: "Women of Ramallah, who were searching for snails, called it Khirbet Ai."[56] Investigators of the location of Ai have overlooked these notices, as well as the ruins at Kh. el-Maqatir. Excavations at the site since 1995, under the direction of the author, have provided the necessary evidence to identify the site as Joshua's Ai.[57]

---

53. David P. Livingston, "Further Considerations on the Location of Bethel at El-Bireh," *PEQ* 126 (1994): 154–59, and further references there.
54. Beitin is more likely Beth Aven. See Bryant G. Wood, "Beth Aven: A Scholarly Conundrum," *Bible and Spade* 12 (1999): 101–8.
55. Robinson, *Biblical Researches in Palestine and the Adjacent Regions*, 448.
56. E. Sellin, "Mittheilungen von meiner Palästinareise 1899," *Mittheilungen und Nachrichten des Deutschen Palaestina-Vereins* 6 (1900): 1.
57. The large Early Bronze Age ruin at et-Tell, on the other hand, should be identified as the landmark site of Ai in Abraham's day (Gen. 12:8). It is east of El-Bireh (Bethel) and the modern Arabic name "et-Tell" means "the ruin," as does the Hebrew rendering of the name, *hā‘ay*, which always includes the definite article. The name could have later migrated to Kh. el-Maqatir only 1 km to the west and then, following the destruction by the Israelites, been changed to Kh. el-Maqatir which means "the ruin of the place of the rising of sacrificial smoke." The rising of the smoke from the signal fire set by the ambush force was the signal for Joshua to begin the *ḥāram*: the offering up of the people of Ai as a sacrifice to *Yahweh* (Josh. 8:21–26). After Ai was plundered, there was further sacrificial smoke when Joshua set fire to the fortress (Josh. 8: 27–28).

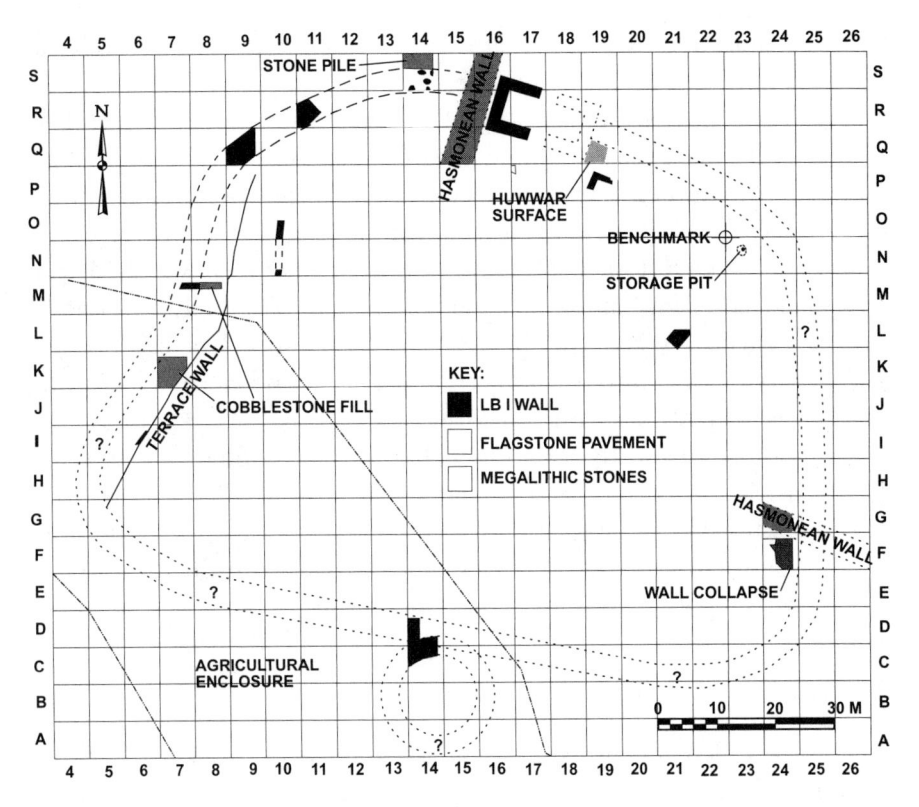

Fig. 12.2. The LBI Fortress at KH. El-Maqatir, 2000.

Joshua 7 and 8 contain many geographic and archaeological requirements that a candidate for the Ai of Joshua must meet. Kh. el-Maqatir meets these requirements as follows:[58]

- Near Beth-aven (Josh. 7:2)—Kh. el-Maqatir is 1.5 km southeast of Beitin, the most likely candidate for Beth-aven
- East of Bethel (Josh. 7:2)—Kh. el-Maqatir is 3.5 km northeast of El-Bireh, the most likely candidate for Bethel
- Ambush site between Bethel and Ai (Josh. 8:9)—between Kh. el-Maqatir and El-Bireh is a very deep valley, the Wadi Sheban, out of

---

58. For further details, see Bryant G. Wood, "The Search for Joshua's Ai: Excavations at Kh. el-Maqatir," *Bible and Spade* 12 (1999): 21–30; idem, "Kh. el-Maqatir 1999 Dig Report," *Bible and Spade* 12 (1999): 109–14; idem, "Khirbet el-Maqatir, 1995–1998," *IEJ* 50 (2000): 123–30; idem, "Khirbet el-Maqatir, 1999," *IEJ* 50 (2000): 249–54; idem, "Kh. el-Maqatir 2000 Dig Report," *Bible and Spade* 13 (2000): 67–72; and idem, "Khirbet el-Maqatir, 2000," *IEJ* 51 (2001): 246–52.

- sight of both Kh. el-Maqatir and El-Bireh, which could easily accommodate a large ambush force
- Hill north of Ai suitable for Joshua's command center (Josh. 8:11)—Jebel Abu Ammar 1.5 km north of Kh. el-Maqatir is the highest hill in the region and provides a commanding view of the battle area
- Shallow valley north of Ai such that the king of Ai could see Joshua and his men (Josh. 8:14)—the Wadi Gayeh between Kh. el-Maqatir and Jebel Abu Ammar is shallow and easily visible from Kh. el-Maqatir
- Small fortress dating to the time of Joshua (Josh. 7:3, 5; 8:29; 10:2)—a fortress about 3 acres in size has been found at Kh. el-Maqatir, with pottery from the fifteenth century B.C.
- Gate on the north side (Josh. 8:11)—the gate of the fortress at Kh. el-Maqatir is on the north side
- Destroyed by fire (Josh. 8:28)—abundant evidence for a destruction by fire has been found at Kh. el-Maqatir in the form of ash, burned pottery, burned stones, and burned bedrock

Hazor (Josh. 11:1–11)

Hazor is called "the head of all these kingdoms" (Josh. 11:10). This description is borne out by archaeology as Hazor has been shown to be the largest city in Canaan, comprising an area of 200 acres.[59] In addition, the only ruler to be referred to as "king" in the Amarna Letters (see below) was the king of Hazor, showing his importance relative to the other Canaanite rulers in the mid-fourteenth century B.C.[60]

As with Jericho and Ai, Hazor was put to the torch (Josh. 11:1). Abundant evidence has been found in the excavation of the fifteenth-century city (Stratum XV in the upper city and Stratum 2 in the lower city) that it was destroyed by fire. In the upper city, the Long Temple in Area A was destroyed and never rebuilt,[61] and in Area M evidence was found that Str.

---

59. Amnon Ben-Tor, "Hazor," in *NEAEHL*, 2:595.
60. William L. Moran, *The Amarna Letters* (Baltimore: Johns Hopkins University Press, 1992), 235, 289.
61. Yigael Yadin, "The Fifth Season of Excavations at Hazor, 1968–1969," *BA* 32 (1969): 52; idem, *Hazor the Head of All Those Kingdoms,* Schweich Lectures of the British Academy 1970 (London: Oxford University Press, 1972), 103, 125; idem, *Hazor: The Rediscovery of a Great Citadel of the Bible* (New York: Random House, 1975), 260, 261; Ben-Tor, "Hazor," in *NEAEHL*, 2:604; and Amnon Ben-Tor et al., *Hazor V: An Account of the Fifth Season of Excavation, 1968,* James A. de Rothschild Expedition at Hazor (Jerusalem: Israel Exploration Society, 1997), 102.

XV was brought to an end by a conflagration.[62] In the lower city, the Square Temple in Area F went out of use at the end of Str. 2,[63] and the Str. 2 Orthostat Temple in Area H was covered by a 15 cm thick layer of ash on the floor[64] and a 70 cm thick layer of mud brick debris above that.[65] Further evidence for the destruction of Str. 2 was found in Areas C, K and P.[66]

JUDGES

Amarna Letters

The diplomatic correspondence of the Amarna archive spanned ca. twenty years in the mid-fourteenth century B.C. 106 of the recovered 382 clay tablets are from vassals in Canaan.[67] These 106 documents provide unique insight into conditions in Canaan just a few decades after the Conquest. According to the biblical timeline, mid-fourteenth century B.C. was a time early in the Judges period when the tribes were engaged in consolidating their hold on their assigned allotments (Judg. 1). That is precisely the situation reflected in the Amarna tablets.

Native rulers complained bitterly to Pharaoh of incursions by a people called ʿapiru.[68] The term ʿapiru is known not only from the Amarna Letters, but also from other ancient Near Eastern texts spanning the period 1750–1150 B.C. A detailed study of the texts reveals that the term ʿapiru refers to nomadic peoples. Astour sums up the findings as follows:

> [T]hey were . . . semi-nomads in the process of sedentarization, who came from the semi-desert zone and entered civilized regions

---

62. Amnon Ben-Tor, "Tel Hazor, 2001," *IEJ* 51 (2001): 235–8, esp. 238.
63. Yadin, *Hazor the Head of All Those Kingdoms* 45, 100–1.
64. Yigael Yadin et al., *Hazor III–IV: An Account of the Third and Fourth Seasons of Excavation, 1957–1958, Text*, James A. de Rothschild Expedition at Hazor (Jerusalem: Israel Exploration Society, 1989) 228.
65. Yadin, *Hazor the Head of All Those Kingdoms*, 80; and Yadin et al., *Hazor III–IV*, 227.
66. Concerning Area C, see Yigael Yadin et al., *Hazor I: An Account of the First Season of Excavations, 1955*, James A. de Rothschild Expedition at Hazor (Jerusalem: Magnes, 1958), 73; and idem, *Hazor II: An Account of the Second Season of Excavations, 1956*, James A. de Rothschild Expedition at Hazor (Jerusalem: Magnes, 1960), 92. Concerning Area K, see Yadin et al., *Hazor III–IV*, 287. Concerning Area P, see Ben-Tor et al., *Hazor V*, 382.
67. For an introduction to the Amarna Letters, see William L. Moran, *The Amarna Letters*, xiii–xxxix; and Nadav Naʾaman, "Amarna Letters," in *ABD*, 1:174–81.
68. The letters are from cities the Israelites could not capture during the Conquest: Megiddo (Josh. 17:11–12; Judg. 1:27), Gezer (Josh. 16:10; Judg. 1:29), and Jerusalem (Josh. 15:63; Judg. 1:21).

as strangers . . . they were members of tightly knit tribal units whose allegiance was determined by kinship and who had their own system of law.[69]

One could not ask for a more accurate description of the Israelites shortly after entering the land of Canaan. At this juncture they were tribal entities that had not yet come together as a unified political body. The scribes employed by the highland rulers certainly would have referred to the Israelites as ʿapiru.

The ʿapiru described in the Amarna Letters, "acted in large armed units which were not only engaged in plundering raids but were also seizing for themselves towns and parts of the lands under Egyptian rule."[70] Furthermore, "History shows that whenever one finds independent armed bands, these were always ethnically homogeneous."[71]

The most striking theme of the letters is that the ʿapiru were taking over the highlands of Canaan. The king of Gezer wrote, "So may the king, my lord, save his land from the power of the ʿapiru" (EA271).[72] He also referred to the superiority of the ʿapiru forces (EA299, cf. EA305, 306). The king of Jerusalem was particularly distressed. He said, "the war against me is severe . . . ʿapiru has plundered all the lands of the king . . . if there are no archers, lost are the lands of the king" (EA286), "Milkilu and . . . the sons of Lab'ayu . . . have given the land of the king to the ʿapiru" (EA 287), "the land of the king is lost . . . the ʿapiru have taken the very cities of the king" (EA288), and "the land of the king deserted to the ʿapiru" (EA290).

By examining the historical records to see who was in control of the highlands after the mid-fourteenth century B.C., we can confirm the identity of these ʿapiru forces. Although the data are meager, nevertheless sufficient information is available to ascertain that it was the Israelites. In the latter part of the thirteenth century B.C.,[73] a coalition of Israelite tribes defeated Hazor, the largest city-state in Canaan (Judg. 4–5; see below). This feat demonstrated that the Israelite tribes were the dominant military force

---

69. Michael C. Astour, "The Hapiru in the Amarna Texts: Basic Points of Controversy," *UF* 31 (1999): 41.
70. Ibid., 31.
71. Ibid., 40.
72. The letters are referred to by the notation EA, for el-Amarna, followed by a number. Quotations are from Moran, *The Amarna Letters*.
73. Merrill, *Kingdom of Priests*, 164.

in the region in the thirteenth century B.C. The Merenptah Stele provides extrabiblical evidence that this was indeed the case (see below).[74]

Eglon's Palace at Jericho (Judg. 3:12–30)

Eglon, king of Moab built a residence at Jericho, "the city of the palm trees" (Deut. 34:3; 2 Chron. 28:15) and oppressed the Israelite tribes for eighteen years. The time frame for these events was the late fourteenth century B.C.[75] During the 1933 season at Jericho, Garstang discovered a large palatial-type structure he identified as the palace of Eglon.[76] He called it the "Middle Building," since it was sandwiched between Iron Age structures above and the destroyed Bronze Age city below. In 1954 Kenyon found a floor, oven and portions of walls from the same period just north of Garstang's Middle Building, her Phase 54.[77] Garstang,[78] Kenyon[79] and Bienkowski[80] date the Middle Building to the fourteenth, or possibly early thirteenth, century B.C, the biblical time frame for Eglon and his Jericho palace.

Garstang's Middle Building is an impressive structure ca. 14.5 x 12 m, with a large retaining wall on the downhill side. In addition to its size, the abundance of imported pottery found in and around the building, and an inscribed clay tablet found just outside the east wall, attest a well-to-do

---

74. For additional correlations between the Amarna Letters and the biblical record, see S. Douglas Waterhouse, "Who Were the Habiru of the Amarna Letters?" *Journal of the Adventist Theological Society* 12 (2001): 31–42.
75. Leon Wood, *Distressing Days of the Judges* (Grand Rapids: Zondervan, 1975), 410; John H. Walton, *Chronological and Background Charts of the Old Testament* (Grand Rapids: Zondervan, 1978), 48; cf. Merrill, *Kingdom of Priests*, 163.
76. Garstang, "Jericho: City and Necropolis," 106–10; idem, "The Story of Jericho: Further Light on the Biblical Narrative," *AJSL* 58 (1941): 368–72; idem, "The Story of Jericho: Further Light on the Biblical Narrative," *PEQ* 73 (1941): 168–71; and John Garstang and J. B. E. Garstang, *The Story of Jericho*, rev. ed. (London: Marshall, Morgan & Scott, 1948), 177–80.
77. Kenyon, *Digging Up Jericho*, 261–63; idem, *Archaeology and Old Testament Study*, 272–3; idem, *The Bible and Recent Archaeology*, 38–40; idem, *Archaeology in the Holy Land*, 208; idem, *Excavations at Jericho*, 3:371; idem, "Jericho," in *ISBE*, 2:993–94; and idem, "Jericho: Tell es-Sultan," in *NEAEHL*, 2:680.
78. Garstang, "Story of Jericho," *AJSL*, 371–72; idem, "Story of Jericho," *PEQ*, 73, 171; and Garstang and Garstang, *The Story of Jericho*, 180.
79. Kenyon, *Digging Up Jericho*, 261; idem, *Archaeology and Old Testament Study*, 273; idem, *The Bible and Recent Archaeology*, 39; idem, *Archaeology in the Holy Land*, 208; idem, *Excavations at Jericho*, 3:371; idem, "Jericho," in *ISBE*, 2:994; idem, "Jericho: Tell es-Sultan," in *NEAEHL*, 2:680.
80. Piotr Bienkowski, *Jericho in the Late Bronze Age* (Warminster, Wiltshire, England: Aris & Phillips, 1986), 120.

occupant involved in administrative activities. Yet, the building complex is isolated, with no evidence for a town to rule over. It was occupied for only a short period and then abandoned (Judg. 3:14, 29).[81]

Considerable detail is provided in Judges 3 concerning Eglon's palace. Based on the biblical text and Near Eastern examples, Halpern reconstructed Eglon's Jericho palace.[82] Although apparently unaware of Garstang's discovery, Halpern's reconstruction matched the plan of the Middle Building remarkably well.[83]

Destruction of Hazor by Deborah and Barak (Judg. 4–5)

Joshua and the Israelites burned Hazor in the course of the Conquest (see above). The city quickly recovered, however, as attested by the Amarna Letters, Judges 4–5 and excavations at Hazor. In the time of Deborah, Jabin, called "king of Canaan, who reigned in Hazor" (Judg. 4:2), oppressed the Israelite tribes for twenty years (Judg. 4:3).[84] Deborah and her general Barak rallied six of the Israelite tribes and defeated the army of Jabin at the Kishon River (Judg. 4:13–15). The Israelites continued their offensive, "until they had destroyed Jabin the king of Canaan" (Judg. 4:24). The destruction of the king implies the destruction of his city.

The chronology of the book of Judges places the offensive of Deborah and Barak in the late thirteenth century B.C.[85] Excavations at Hazor have revealed a massive destruction at about this time, so severe that the city was not rebuilt until the time of Solomon in the tenth century B.C.[86] Because of the intentional mutilation of statues of both Egyptian and Canaanite dei-

---

81. Ibid., 118.
82. Baruch Halpern, *The First Historians: The Hebrew Bible and History* (San Francisco: Harper & Row, 1998), 39–75; and idem, "The Assassination of Eglon," *BRev* 4, no. 6 (1998): 33–41, 44.
83. Garstang, "Jericho: City and Necropolis," pl. XIV; Halpern, *First Historians*, 53; and idem, "The Assassination of Eglon," 37.
84. Jabin was also the name of the king of Hazor in the time of Joshua (Josh. 11:1). Texts from Hazor, Mari, and Egypt attest that Jabin was a dynastic name at Hazor during the Middle and Late Bronze Ages. See Bryant G. Wood, "Jabin, King of Hazor," *Bible and Spade* 8 (1995): 83–85.
85. Merrill, *Kingdom of Priests,* 164.
86. Amnon Ben-Tor, "The Fall of Canaanite Hazor—The 'Who' and 'When' Questions," in *Mediterranean Peoples in Transition, Thirteenth to Early Tenth Centuries B.C.E.,* ed. Semour Gitin, Amihai Mazar, and Ephraim Stern (Jerusalem: Israel Exploration Society, 1998), 456–67; Amnon Ben-Tor and Maria Teresa Rubiato, "Excavating Hazor Part II: Did the Israelites Destroy the Canaanite City?" *BAR* 25, no. 3 (1999): 22–39.

ties and kings, Ben-Tor concludes that the destruction must have been the work of the Israelites.[87] Ben-Tor, like Yadin before him, wishes to ascribe the destruction to Joshua, following the thirteenth century B.C. Conquest model. This is not feasible on two counts. First, if the thirteenth century conquest is ascribed to Joshua, there would be no later city for Deborah and Barak to conquer. Secondly, the Joshua scenario presupposes the Israelites would have immediately settled on the ruins as part of the Iron Age I settlement process. Recent excavations at Hazor have demonstrated that there was a gap of as much as two hundred years between the destruction of the Late Bronze Age city and the subsequent poor, transient, Iron Age I settlement.[88]

If one follows the biblical model, the archaeological evidence makes perfect sense. The Israelites under Deborah and Barak destroyed Hazor in order to overthrow Jabin. They had no interest in settling there since they were already well established elsewhere in the land. Later, in the eleventh century, due to changing social-economic factors, the previously seminomadic Israelites were forced to become sedentary. As a result, they were looking for new places to live, such as the uninhabited mound of Hazor.[89]

Merenptah Stele

The Merenptah, or "Israel," Stele is the most important extrabiblical document relating to Israel's origins. Found in 1896 in Pharaoh Merenptah's mortuary temple at Thebes by Sir Flinders Petrie,[90] it records Merenptah's victories in Libya and a campaign to Canaan in which Israel is mentioned. The text is exceptional in that it is the only direct reference to Israel yet found in Egyptian records and the only reference to Israel outside the Bible prior to the divided kingdom. Marginalized, or totally ignored, by many scholars, its significance is far reaching.

---

87. Ben-Tor, "The Fall of Canaanite Hazor," 456, 465; Ben-Tor and Rubiato, "Excavating Hazor Part II," 38–39.
88. Doron Ben-Ami, "The Iron Age I at Tel Hazor in light of the Renewed Excavations," *IEJ* 51 (2001): 148–70.
89. Interestingly, the new occupants did not settle in the area of the Canaanite palace. Ben-Ami suggests this may have been the result of a "stigma" being attached to the structure that did not allow the new occupants to settle there (ibid., 167–68).
90. W. M. Flinders Petrie, *Six Temples at Thebes in 1896* (London: Quaritch, 1897), 13; pls. 13, 14.

The section relating to Israel reads as follows:

> The (foreign) chieftains lie prostrate, saying "Peace." Not one lifts his head among the Nine Bows.
> Libya is captured, while Hatti is pacified.
> Canaan is plundered, Ashkelon is carried off, and Gezer is captured.
> Yenoam is made into non-existence; Israel is wasted, its seed is not; and Hurru is become a widow because of Egypt.
> All lands united themselves in peace. Those who went about are subdued by the king of Upper and Lower Egypt . . . Merneptah.[91]

Merenptah's Canaanite campaign can be dated to the first few years of his reign, ca. 1210 B.C.[92] The record of the campaign is written in a poetic style and many analysts agree that it has a chiastic format, although there is lack of agreement as to the exact structure.[93] Apart from the format, however, there are a number of significant aspects of the poem on which most scholars agree. The word for Israel has the determinative for a people-group, as opposed to the other named nations and city-states that have the determinative for a political entity. This indicates that Israel was a tribal community at this time, with no fixed boundaries,[94] perfectly in keeping with the biblical depiction of Israel in the Judges period. It must be recognized that the Merenptah Stele is a eulogy and, as such, extols the great accomplishments of the Pharaoh. The fact that Israel is mentioned at all indicates that, by the end of the thirteenth century B.C., the Israelite tribes had achieved sufficient status to be deemed worthy of being defeated by the king of one of the most powerful nations on earth. Perhaps Deborah and Barak's defeat of Hazor about this time (see above) brought Israel onto the stage of international politics. Israel had progressed from being referred to as generic ʿapiru in the Amarna Letters (see above) in the previous century, to being known by their correct biblical name in Merenptah's day.

---

91. James K. Hoffmeier, trans., "The (Israel) Stela of Merneptah (2.6)," in *COS*, 2:41.
92. Ibid.
93. Ibid.
94. K. A. Kitchen, "The Physical Text of Merenptah's Victory Hymn (The 'Israel Stela')," *JSSEA* 24 (1994): 74–75. In more recent Egyptological studies, the more commonly known name, "Merneptah," is being replaced by "Merenptah."

Perhaps the most important feature of the stela is that Israel is presented in parallel with *Hurru*, the Egyptian term for Palestine. The implication is that since Egypt (theoretically) did away with Israel ("its seed is not"), all of Palestine was devastated ("Hurru is become a widow"). This indicates that Israel was the most powerful people group in Canaan at the end of the thirteenth century B.C.,[95] which has implications for the integrity of the biblical model. The idea that Israel emerged from the indigenous Canaanite population in the twelfth century B.C. has gained favor in recent years. However, since the Merenptah Stele testifies that Israel was well established and recognized by Egypt by the end of the previous century, such cannot be the case.[96]

Migration of the Danites (Judg. 17–18)

Judges 18 describes the migration of the tribe of Dan, or a portion of it, from their assigned allotment west of Benjamin to Laish, which they renamed Dan. The time of the migration can be bracketed within a narrow range. In the days of Deborah in the late thirteenth century, the Danites were still living in their coastal allotment as indicated by the reference to Dan staying in ships (Judg. 5:17). Judges 18:31 states that Micah's images were in use at Dan throughout the time the Tabernacle was at Shiloh. Since Shiloh fell to the Philistines ca. 1100 B.C. or a little later (see below), the migration must have taken place between the late thirteenth century and 1100 B.C. The most likely event that would have occasioned the displacement of Danites was the incursion of the Philistines into the southwest coastal plain in the eighth year of Ramesses III, ca. 1177 B.C.[97]

Laish/Dan has been identified as Tell el-Qadi, now called Tell Dan, at the foot of Mount Hermon, ca. 40 km north of the Sea of Galilee.

---

95. William F. Albright, "The Israelite Conquest of Canaan in the Light of Archaeology," *BASOR* 74 (1939): 22; Ronald J. Williams, "The Israel Stele of Merneptah," *Documents of Old Testament Times*, ed. D. W. Thomas (New York: Harper & Row, Publishers, 1958), 140–41; Lawrence E. Stager, "Merneptah, Israel and the Sea Peoples: New Light on an Old Relief," *ErIsr* 18 (1985): 61; John J. Bimson, "Merneptah's Israel and Recent Theories of Israelite Origins," *JSOT* 49 (1991): 22–24; Michael G. Hasel, "Israel in the Merneptah Stela," *BASOR* 296 (1994): 54, 56 n. 12; Hoffmeier, "The (Israel) Stela of Merneptah (2.6)," *COS*, 2:41; and Waterhouse, "Who Were the Habiru," 35.
96. Bimson, "Merneptah's Israel."
97. Bryant G. Wood, "The Philistines Enter Canaan," *BAR* 17, no. 6 (November–December 1991): 44–52, 89–92; and Paul W. Ferris Jr., "Sorek, Valley of," in *ABD*, 6:159.

Excavations since 1966 under the direction of Avraham Biran have revealed a prosperous Late Bronze Age culture, Str. VII, destroyed by fire early in the twelfth century B.C. This appears to be the city burned by the Danites (Judg. 18:27).[98] Laish had a connection, perhaps commercial, with the coastal city of Sidon, ca. 45 km to the northwest (Judg. 18:7, 28).[99] The most impressive discovery in Str. VII was a tomb containing imported Mycenaean pottery from Greece, including a unique "charioteer vase." Anthropological examination revealed that the individuals buried in the tomb did not belong to the local Canaanite population.[100] Moreover, neutron activation testing of plain ware vessels in the tomb indicates they came from the Phoenician coast.[101] It is possible that the inhabitants of Str. VII Laish were involved in an import trade business with Sidon.

A nomadic, or seminomadic, culture characterized by pits, some of which were stone-lined, next occupied the site in Str. VI.[102] Large pithoi called "collared-rim store jars," well known from the highlands where they are associated with Israelite settlement, were found in the pits.[103] Ten of 11 of the pithoi tested by neutron activation analysis were made from clay not native to the Tell Dan area, indicating the new settlers brought them from elsewhere.[104] The newcomers soon became urbanized, as Str. V was a dense array of domestic and industrial architecture across the tell.[105] This stratum was destroyed in a fierce conflagration in the mid-eleventh century B.C.,

---

98. Avraham Biran, *Biblical Dan* (Jerusalem: Israel Exploration Society/Hebrew Union College-Jewish Institute of Religion, 1994), 126.
99. Avraham Malamat, "'. . . After the Manner of the Sidonians . . . and How They Were far from the Sidonians . . .' (Judges 18:7)," *ErIsr* 23 (1992): 194–95 (Hebrew), English summary 153.
100. Biran, *Biblical Dan*, 114; and Avraham Biran and Rachel Ben-Dov, *Dan II: A Chronicle of the Excavations and the Late Bronze Age "Mycenaean" Tomb* (Jerusalem: Nelson Glueck School of Biblical Archaeology/Hebrew Union College-Jewish Institute of Religion, n.d.), 228.
101. J. Gunneweg et al., "On the Origin of a Mycenaean IIIA Chariot Krater and Other Related Mycenaean Pottery from Tomb 387 at Laish/Dan (By Neutron Analysis)," *ErIsr* 23 (1992): 59–62; and Biran, *Biblical Dan*, 116.
102. Biran, *Biblical Dan*, 126–35; A. Biran, "Tel Dan: Biblical Texts and Archaeological Data," in *Scripture and Other Artifacts*, ed. Michael D. Coogan, J. Cheryl Exum, and Lawrence E. Stager (Louisville: Westminster/John Knox, 1994), 4–5.
103. A. Biran, "The Collared-rim Jars and the Settlement of the Tribe of Dan," in *Recent Excavations in Israel: Studies in Iron Age Archaeology*, ed. Seymour Gitin and William G. Dever (Winona Lake, Ind.: Eisenbrauns, 1989), 71–96.
104. Joseph Yellin and Jan Gunneweg, "Instrumental Neutron Activation Analysis and the Origin of the Iron Age I Collared-rim Jars and Pithoi from Tel Dan," in *Recent Excavations in Israel: Studies in Iron Age Archaeology*, 133–41.
105. Biran, *Biblical Dan*, 135–42; and David Ilan, "Dan," in *OEANE*, 2:109.

possibly at the hands of the Philistines at the same time Shiloh was destroyed (Judg. 18:31, see below).[106]

This evidence once again counters the twelfth century emergence theory. Clearly, the tribe of Dan was a preexisting entity with a prior history when it arrived at Laish early in the twelfth century. It was in existence well before the appearance of the twelfth century Iron I villages that presumably mark the beginning of Israelite culture according to the emergence theory.[107]

Abimelech at Shechem (Judg. 9)

For some eight hundred years, from the Middle Bronze through the Iron Age I periods, Shechem was an important highland urban center controlling the area from Megiddo to Jerusalem.[108] It is no surprise, then, that Gideon's son Abimelech went to the leaders of Shechem to gain support for his failed attempt to become king of the Israelite tribes.[109] Three archaeological discoveries at Shechem relate to the narrative of Judg. 9.

Temple of Baal-Berith

References to the "house of Baal-berith" (v. 4), "Beth-millo" (vv. 6, 20), "house of their god" (v. 27), "tower of Shechem" (vv. 46, 47, 49), and "temple of El-berith" (v. 46), all appear to be the same structure at Shechem.[110] *Berit* is the Hebrew word for covenant, so the temple was for "Baal of the covenant."

---

106. Biran, *Biblical Dan,* 138; and idem, "Tel Dan," 6.
107. Bimson, "Merneptah's Israel," 3–13.
108. For the significance of Shechem at the time of the Conquest, see Bryant G. Wood, "The Role of Shechem in the Conquest of Canaan," in *To Understand the Scriptures: Essays in Honor of William H. Shea,* ed. David Merling (Berrien Springs, Mich.: Institute of Archaeology/Siegfried H. Horn Archaeological Museum, 1997), 245–56.
109. The word used in Judges 9 for the rulers of 'Shechem, *ba'al,* is also found in the Amarna Letters. See Moran, *The Amarna Letters,* 175 n. 5.
110. Edward F. Campbell Jr., "Judges 9 and Biblical Archaeology," in *The Word of the Lord Shall Go Forth: Essays in Honor of David Noel Freedman in Celebration of His Sixtieth Birthday,* ed. Carol L. Meyers and M. O'Connor (Winona Lake, Ind.: Eisenbrauns, 1983), 269; Lawrence E. Toombs, "Shechem (Place)," in *ABD,* 5:1184; Lawrence E. Stager, "The Fortress-Temple at Shechem and the 'House of El, Lord of the Covenant,'" in *Realia Dei: Essays in Archaeology and Biblical Interpretation in Honor of Edward F. Campbell Jr., at His Retirement,* ed. Prescott H. Williams and Theodore Hiebert (Atlanta: Scholars Press, 1999), 242, 245; idem, "The Shechem Temple Where Abimelech Massacred a Thousand," *BAR* 29, no. 4 (2003): 26–35, 66, 68–69; and Edward F. Campbell Jr. and James F. Ross, "The Excavation of Shechem and the Biblical Tradition," *BA* 26 (1963): 16.

A large fortress (or *migdāl*) temple discovered on the acropolis of Shechem has been identified as the temple of Judges 9.[111] It was constructed in the seventeenth century B.C. and lasted until the destruction of the city by Abimelech in the twelfth century B.C. (see below). The largest temple yet found in Canaan, it measures 21.2 x 26.3 m, and has foundations 5.1 m thick that supported a multistoried superstructure of mud bricks and timber. On the east, two towers containing stairwells to the upper stories flanked the entrance. Inside, two rows of columns, three in each row, divided the space into a nave and two side aisles (cf. vv. 46–49).[112]

Fig. 12.3. The "Migdol" fortress-temple at Shechem, with a courtyard and sacred stone in front. The largest temple found in Canaan, it was most likely here that Joshua erected a sacred stone as a reminder of the covenant between *Yahweh* and the people of Israel (Josh. 24:26–7), and Abimelech became the self-appointed king of Israel (Judg. 9:6). (Credit: Bryant G. Wood)

In front of the temple was a courtyard with a large earthen and stone altar, 2.2 x 1.65 m and 35 cm high, 6.5 m from the temple entrance. An enormous limestone stela, or *maṣṣēbâ*, stood 2 m further to the southeast. It is 1.48 m wide, 42 cm thick, and, although broken, 1.45 m high. Since

---
111. Stager, "Fortress-Temple at Shechem"; idem, "The Shechem Temple."
112. Stager, "Fortress-Temple at Shechem," 229, 243–45; idem, "The Shechem Temple," 29–31.

the temple existed in Joshua's day, it is possible this was the "large stone" which he set up "under the oak that was by the sanctuary of the Lord" at Shechem (Josh. 24:26).[113] The stela is undoubtedly the "pillar" where Abimelech was made king (v. 6).[114]

East Gate

The city gate from the time of Abimelech (vv. 35–40) was excavated on the east side of the site,[115] where it faced the agricultural fields of the Plain of Askar. It is a two-entryway gate, with an 8.0 x 6.55 m paved courtyard between the two entryways. On either side of the courtyard are guardrooms with stairways leading to upper stories. To enter, one approached from the south along a cobbled street, turned left, and passed through the two entryways 3.4 m wide, ca. 6.5 m apart.

Destruction Level

Abimelech "razed the city and sowed it with salt" (v. 45). Abundant evidence was found throughout the site that a violent destruction had occurred at the time of Abimelech.[116] Lawrence Toombs, one of the excavators of Shechem, described the devastation as follows:

> The Iron I city underwent violent destruction, which obliterated its buildings and left the site a wilderness of ruins. At the time of its

---

113. Stager, "Fortress-Temple at Shechem," 242; and Campbell and Ross, "The Excavation of Shechem," 11.
114. Stager, "Fortress-Temple at Shechem," 242; idem, "The Shechem Temple," 31, 33; and Campbell and Ross, "The Excavation of Shechem," 11.
115. G. Ernest Wright, *Shechem: The Biography of a Biblical City* (London: Gerald Duckworth, 1965), 71–76; Robert G. Boling, *Judges*, AB (Garden City, N.Y.: 1975), 179; Campbell, "Judges 9," 265–8; Toombs, "Shechem (Place)," 5:1183–84; Joe Seger, "Shechem," in *OEANE*, 5:22; and Campbell and Ross, "The Excavation of Shechem," 16.
116. Wright, *Shechem: Biography*, 101–2; idem, "Shechem," in *Archaeology and Old Testament Study*, ed. D. Winton Thomas (Oxford, England: Clarendon, 1967), 364; Lawrence E. Toombs, "The Stratigraphy of Tell Balatah (Ancient Shechem)," *ADAJ* 17 (1972): 106; idem, "The Stratification of Tell Balâtah (Shechem)," *BASOR* 223 (1976): 58, 59; idem, "Shechem: Problems of the Early Israelite Era," in *Symposia: Celebrating the Seventy-Fifth Anniversary of the Founding of the American Schools of Oriental Research (1900–1975)*, ed. Frank Moore Cross (Cambridge, Mass.: American Schools of Oriental Research, 1979), 70–73, 78; idem, "Shechem (Place)," in *ABD*, 5:1178, 1184; idem, "Shechem: Tell Balâtah," in *NEAEHL*, 4:1347, 1352; and Seger, "Shechem," in *OEANE*, 5:22.

destruction, the culture of the city was fully-developed Iron I. The end of the Iron I city is almost certainly to be attributed to its capture by Abimelek (Judges 9).[117]

The excavators date the destruction to ca. 1125 B.C.,[118] in excellent agreement with Merrill's approximation of ca. 1117 B.C. based on biblical data.[119]

Fall of Shiloh (1 Sam. 1–4)

Significant architecture from the Iron Age I, the time of Eli, has been excavated at Khirbet Seilun, ancient Shiloh, 17 km south of Shechem. All traces of Iron Age and earlier occupation on the summit of the site unfortunately were removed by later building activity. On the slopes, however, enough material from the Iron Age I period has been found to determine that the settlement at that time was 2½ to 3 acres in size.[120]

The best-preserved remains from the time of Eli are on the west slope of the site. There, a three-room structure 27 x 11 m, containing a rich assemblage of pottery, was uncovered. Over 20 pithoi in the complex suggests it functioned as a storage facility. Sophisticated building techniques were employed, such as slope terracing to provide two levels, well-made floors, stone-drum columns, and a rock-cut plastered cistern.[121] Israel Finkelstein, the excavator, concluded, "In their plan, constructional method and adaptation to the slope these structures represent the peak of early Israelite architecture."[122] Because of the advanced technology, Finkelstein believes the structure could not have been built prior to the mid-twelfth century

---

117. Toombs, "Shechem: Problems," 73.
118. Seger, "Shechem," in *OEANE*, 5:22.
119. Merrill, *Kingdom of Priests*, 170.
120. Israel Finkelstein, ed., "Excavation at Shiloh 1981–1984," *Tel Aviv* 12 (1985): 168; idem, "Shiloh Yields Some, but Not All, of Its Secrets," *BAR* 12, no. 1 (January–February 1986): 40; idem, "Seilun, Khirbet," in *ABD*, 5:1072; idem, "Shiloh: Renewed Excavations," in *NEAEHL*, 4:1369; Israel Finkelstein, Shlomo Bunimovitz, and Zvi Lederman, *Shiloh: The Archaeology of a Biblical Site*, Tel Aviv University Sonia and Marco Nadler Institute of Archaeology Monograph Series 10 (Tel Aviv: Institute of Archaeology of Tel Aviv University, 1993), 384.
121. Finkelstein, "Excavation at Shiloh," 131–38; idem, "Shiloh Yields Some . . . of Its Secrets," 37–39; Finkelstein, Bunimovitz, and Lederman, *Shiloh: The Archaeology of a Biblical Site*, 20–31.
122. Finkelstein, "Excavation at Shiloh 1981–1984," 169; cf. Finkelstein, Bunimovitz, and Lederman, *Shiloh: The Archaeology of a Biblical Site*, 385.

B.C.,[123] approximately the beginning of Eli's judgeship.[124] He theorizes it was an auxiliary building for the Tabernacle that originally stood on the summit.[125]

Psalm 78:60 and Jeremiah 7:12–14; 26:6, 9 indicate that Shiloh was destroyed and abandoned as a result of God's judgment. The archaeological findings dramatically demonstrate that Iron Age I Shiloh was terminated in a fiery destruction:

> These buildings were destroyed in a fierce conflagration. Burnt floors were found all over. Collapsed burnt bricks accumulated on these floors to a height of more than three feet. Some of the bricks had been baked by the blaze that had raged here. Roof collapse was discernible in many places. All this dramatic evidence of fire must be associated with the destruction of Shiloh by the Philistines after they defeated the Israelites near Ebenezer in the mid-eleventh century B.C.[126]

The published date for the destruction, ca. 1050 B.C., is based on pottery chronology, which is very imprecise, particularly for the Iron Age I period. A date anywhere from ca. 1104 B.C., Merrill's estimated date for the battle of Ebenezer,[127] to ca. 1050 B.C. would accommodate the pottery types found in the destruction level.

Conclusion

Scholars many times raise the issue of the lack of extra biblical literary evidence to support this or that person or event in Israel's early history. Complete verification of every biblical text will never be achieved.

---

123. Finkelstein, "Excavation at Shiloh," 168; cf. Finkelstein, Bunimovitz, and Lederman, *Shiloh: The Archaeology of a Biblical Site,* 383.
124. Merrill estimates the battle of Ebenezer and the death of Eli took place ca. 1104 B.C. (*Kingdom of Priests,* 176). Since Eli judged Israel forty years (1 Sam. 4:18), he began his judgeship ca. 1144 B.C.
125. Finkelstein, "Excavation at Shiloh," 169; idem, "Shiloh Yields Some . . . of Its Secrets," 41; idem, "Seilun, Khirbet," in *ABD,* 5:1072; cf. Finkelstein, Bunimovitz, and Lederman, *Shiloh: The Archaeology of a Biblical Site,* 384–85.
126. Finkelstein "Shiloh Yields Some, but Not All, of Its Secrets," *BAR* 12, no. 1 (January–February 1986), 39; and idem, "Shiloh: Renewed Excavations," in *NEAEHL,* 4:1368.
127. Cf. Merrill, *Kingdom of Priests,* 176 n. 83.

Documentary evidence relating to early Israel is rare, so the expectation of finding epigraphic evidence to substantiate the activities of specific individuals, families, or tribes prior to the monarchy is unrealistic.[128] However, when we examine the archaeological evidence that we do have that bears on events in the early history of Israel, and utilize the internally self-consistent chronology of the Old Testament, the findings of archaeology and the biblical record harmonize extremely well.

---

128. K. A. Kitchen, "The Patriarchs Revisited: A Reply to Dr. Ronald S. Hendel," *NEASB* 43 (1998): 55–56.

13

THE INCREDIBLE NUMBERS OF THE HEBREW KINGS

David Fouts

EUGENE MERRILL WAS THE ONE WHO first alerted me to the problem of large numbers in the Old Testament, particularly relating to the figures of the Exodus and Conquest.[1] My first year of doctoral work at Dallas Seminary juxtaposed this enormous conundrum with a challenge from Allen Ross to select a dissertation topic as early in my studies as possible.

As I researched the topic over the course of my work, I was faced with the reality that large numbers present many problems, not only in the Pentateuch, but in almost every historical context in which they are found.[2] The books of Samuel, Kings and Chronicles are not exempt. In fact, thirty-five of the fifty-five largest of the numbers in Scripture (those in excess of 100,000) are found in these books that deal with the kings of the Monarchy, both United and Divided. At times the large numbers conflict with demographic data of Iron Age Palestine now available. At other times, as with the parallel accounts in Samuel and Chronicles of the census taken by David, the numbers themselves conflict. It is the purpose of this essay to explore the contexts of some of these numbers in order to inform our study of this very significant time frame. An evaluation of population demographics is in order to lay first a foundation for the biblical data.

---

1. I offer the title of this essay with apologies to Edwin R. Thiele, *The Mysterious Numbers of the Hebrew Kings* (Grand Rapids: Zondervan, 1983). The present article differs from the work of Thiele, in that it deals not with the lengths of reign, but rather with the enormous numbers associated with military campaigns and building projects of the kings of Israel.
2. The results of my research may be found in David M. Fouts, "The Use of Large Numbers in the Old Testament with Particular Emphasis on the Use of *'elep*" (Th.D. diss., Dallas Theological Seminary, 1992). A very condensed version occurs in David M. Fouts, "A Defense of the Hyperbolic Interpretation of Large Numbers in the Old Testament," *JETS* 40 (1997): 377–87.

Demographic Methodology

Demographic studies based on archaeological discoveries in Israel have been conducted primarily over the past three decades.[3] While the results of such pursuits are certainly open to debate, inasmuch as the data may be interpreted variously (and the authors of the studies are quick to point this out), those results may not be far from the actual circumstances that existed in ancient Israel. I hasten to mention that not all the archaeological data are in (most of the studies to date have been limited either chronologically and/or geographically), and that subsequent discoveries may produce conclusions that differ from the results of this article. However, two factors mitigate this position. First, one doubts that the demographers involved hold a hidden agenda against biblical teaching on the subject, though that might be at least possible.[4] Second, the physical evidence that does remain is overwhelmingly supportive of a population considerably smaller than that suggested by taking the biblical census numbers at face value.

Numerous methods to estimate the populations of ancient cities and nations have been proposed by scholars involved in archaeological and demographic research in the ancient Near East. The methods discussed below differ, and any given proponent at times finds fault with differing methods. However, it is noteworthy that the totals of all modern demographic studies are consistently lower for all periods of Israel's history than that which is suggested by accepting the census figures of the Old Testament as actual value. The primary methods are discussed below.

Available Water Supplies

The premier study in English that concentrates on measuring the population of ancient Jerusalem alone on the basis of available water supplies is that of Wilkinson.[5] One must agree that available water supply does indeed

---

3. For information concerning earlier population analyses conducted prior to the last three decades, see Israel Finkelstein, "A Few Notes on Demographic Data from Recent Generations and Ethnoarchaeology," *PEQ* 122 (1990): 47–52.
4. It seems as though, whereas most overt minimalists simply ignore archaeological data, especially when it supports the scriptural record, most archaeological demographers seem not to be so skeptical.
5. John Wilkinson, "Ancient Jerusalem: Its Water Supply and Population," *PEQ* 106 (1974): 33–51. A similar but shorter study has been conducted by N. Rosenan for the city of Arad ("A Note on the Water Storage and Size of Population," in *Early Arad,* ed. Ruth Amiran [Jerusalem: Israel Exploration Society, 1978], 14).

play an important part in sustaining a certain population over lengthy periods of time. By a thorough study of the archaeological data concerning various spring-fed pools and aqueducts, he concludes that the population of ancient Jerusalem ranged from 2,500 in David's time to a high of 76,130 in the time of Herod Agrippa.[6] Wilkinson bases his population figures on an average water consumption of twenty liters per person per day, a figure based in part on the amount of water from the systems he studied.[7] He qualifies this by suggesting that cisterns could have stored up to perhaps 50 percent of the rain-water, providing a more reasonable daily consumption.[8] One may assume for the sake of argument that his estimate is wrong and that total consumption was less than his suggested 20 liters per person per day, say only 10 liters. This would allow for a doubling of his figures from a low of about 5,000 in David's time to a high of about 152,000 in Agrippa's.[9] On the other hand, raising the estimated daily consumption would reduce the feasible population figures proportionately. Broshi has questioned the estimating of population size by this method for these reasons:

> The principal inconvenience of this method is that it is not able to give the approximate maximum number of inhabitants and therefore the conditions by which one may know the average daily consumption of water or the total quantity of water available. It goes without saying that these two conditions are very difficult to realize. The first given is almost impossible to obtain, for one cannot by any means arrive at a knowledge of the daily consumption of water, even approximately, since the parameters are too great, from 3 liters per person in certain localities in Libya to 363 in the United States.[10]

It is because of these problems that Broshi offers a differing method to determine population figures. This method is discussed below.

---

6. Wilkinson, "Ancient Jerusalem," 50.
7. Ibid., 47.
8. Ibid., 48–49.
9. These figures are still too small to support the large numbers of population suggested by the census of David.
10. Magen Broshi, "La population de l'ancienne Jérusalem," *RB* 82 (1975): 7. Translated by the present writer.

Urban Areas and Population Densities

Broshi offers what he considers to be the most viable method of estimating past populations of Jerusalem by calculating a *density coefficient,* which is to be multiplied by the surface area of the city at a given time in its history.[11] Density factors include the size of dwellings, the average size of families, the number of slaves, and urban area devoted to public usages. Broshi observed this density coefficient in other ancient cities as 40 persons per dunam,[12] and later applied to Palestine as 250 persons per hectare.[13] Though he is skeptical of the methodology of Wilkinson (see above), his results are surprisingly similar to Wilkinson's at several points.[14] This fact may actually serve to validate each of the two methods above as adequate estimators of early populations.

The method of Broshi has proven to be one of the most widely used methods, and was selected by Shiloh for his study of Iron Age Palestine.[15] Making the assumption that there were 60 Iron Age settlements in Palestine with an average area of 50 dunams each, Shiloh suggests that the urban population of the Iron Age era was 150,000, with the rural population somewhat larger.[16] The total would have been less than the 1 million that may have existed in the Roman era.[17] If this figure is correct, or even close to correct, then the numbers recorded in the census of King David (2 Sam. 24; 1 Chron. 21) may have a significance other than an actual accounting of the mustered army alone.

---

11. Ibid., 6.
12. Ibid. One dunam is 1,000 m^2 = $^1/_{10}$ hectare. Forty persons per dunam would therefore equate 400 persons per hectare. Two hundred fifty persons per hectare would equate 25 persons per dunam.
13. Magen Broshi and Ram Gophna, "The Settlements and Population of Palestine During the Early Bronze Age II–III," *BASOR* 253 (1984): 42.
14. For instance, he estimates the population of Jerusalem under David to be 2,000 and under Herod Agrippa to be 82,500 (Broshi, "La population de l'ancienne Jérusalem," 13).
15. Yigal Shiloh, "The Population of Iron Age Palestine in the Light of a Sample Analysis of Urban Plans, Areas, and Population Density," *BASOR* 239 (1980): 25–35. Shiloh adopts this method despite the pitfalls he mentions on p. 26.
16. Ibid., 32.
17. Ibid.

Other Methods

Other methods to estimate the populations of ancient cities and nations include the use of tax lists,[18] refugee lists,[19] available roof space,[20] analogy with present population,[21] and the maximum agricultural production of a given region,[22] among others. These methods all have their proponents and opponents, and all may be less reliable than the area/density coefficient method described above.[23]

Demographics of Iron-Age Palestine

This also may be referred to as the era extending from the middle of the period of the Judges to the Exile (1200–586 B.C.). It therefore includes the period of biblical literature that covers both the United and the Divided Monarchies and is therefore useful in comparing the large numbers of that body of literature with the data from demographic surveys. Though Yigal Shiloh discusses the issue at length in his 1980 article dealing with Iron-Age Palestine, he does not clearly state his opinion for the population as a whole. As stated above, he instead estimates the urban population at 150,000, with the rural population being somewhat higher.[24] He then compares it to Palestine of the Roman era, wherein the population did not exceed 1 million and states that Iron-Age Palestine held fewer inhabitants.[25] Indeed, this is supported by Broshi and Finkelstein who

---

18. J. E. Packer, "Housing and Population in Imperial Ostia and Rome," *JRS* 57 (1967): 80–89.
19. Cf. J. T. Milik, "La topographie de Jerusalem vers la fin de l'epoque Byzantine," in *Mélanges offerts au Père René Mouterde pour son 80e anniversaire,* ed. M. Dunand (Beirut: Imprimerie Catholique, 1961), 133.
20. R. Naroll, "Floor Area and Settlement Population," *American Antiquity* 27 (1962): 587–89. This method is confirmed as viable by Finkelstein, "A Few Notes on Demographic Data," 47–52.
21. A. Lucas, "The Number of Israelites at the Exodus," *PEQ* 76 (1944): 164–68. For this method in other lands, see William M. Sumner, "Estimating Population by Analogy: An Example," in *Ethnoarchaeology: Implications of Ethnography for Archaeology,* ed. Carol Kramer (New York: Columbia University Press, 1979), 164–74.
22. Magen Broshi, "The Population of Western Palestine in the Roman–Byzantine Period," *BASOR* 236 (1979): 6–7.
23. Shiloh, "The Population of Iron Age Palestine," 26–27, discusses reasons for not accepting these other methods.
24. Ibid., 32.
25. Ibid., 33; cf. Broshi, "The Population of Western Palestine," 7.

posit a total populace in 1000 B.C. to be about 150,000 for all of Western Palestine.[26] By the middle of the eighth century B.C. there were 400,000 in western Palestine, and by the end of that same century, 460,000 for Israel and Judah, together with 50,000 in Philistia.[27] These figures may be contrasted with a total population of 5 million, an extrapolation demanded by accepting the earlier census totals of David at face value (1.3 million in 2 Sam. 24 and 1.57 million in 1 Chron. 21). Shiloh writes about the Davidic Census at this point: "The historical reliability of these figures is open to doubt, both on historiographic grounds and in the light of the statistical-demographical analysis outlined above."[28] I take issue with Shiloh at this point. If the numbers have some meaning other than an accounting of actual value, historical reliability is not the issue with regard to those numbers. Instead, it becomes an issue of interpretation of the military accounts in a royal-inscription genre.[29]

In a diachronic demographic analysis for Jerusalem alone, Broshi suggests that the population of that city in the time of David was 2,000; in the time of Solomon, it was 5,200; in the time of Josiah, it was 20,000.[30] This may be contrasted to Nineveh, which became a much larger city of from 206,000 to 256,000,[31] figures which are somewhat in line with Jonah 4:11. The Lord God himself testifies in that verse to the presence in Nineveh of more than 120,000[32] who did not know their right from their left hand.[33] According to Broshi, much of the growth in Jerusalem between the time of Solomon and that of Josiah was attributable in part to the influx of refu-

---

26. Magen Broshi and Israel Finkelstein, "The Population of Palestine in the Iron Age II," *BASOR* 287 (1992): 55.
27. Ibid., 53–54.
28. Shiloh, "The Population of Iron Age Palestine," 32.
29. For further development of this idea, see below and Fouts, "A Defense of the Hyperbolic Interpretation," 377–87.
30. Broshi, "La population de l'ancienne Jérusalem," 13.
31. Shiloh, "The Population," 32. Simo Parpola estimates the population of Nineveh in the 620 B.C. era to exceed 300,000 including suburbs (quoted in Jack M. Sasson, *Jonah*, AB [New York: Doubleday, 1990], 312).
32. "More than twelve ten-thousands of persons." It is interesting to note that this phrase does not include the term *ʾelep*, but rather *ribbô*. One also notes the unusual use of the term *ʾādām* here instead of the usual and expected *ʾîš*. Also, in this case, the number is not seen in a military context nor in a royal-inscriptional genre.
33. For a discussion of whether or not these were children, see Hans Walter Wolff, *Obadiah and Jonah: A Commentary*, trans. Margaret Kohl (Minneapolis: Augsburg, 1986), 175.

gees following the destruction of Samaria and those who soon after were abandoning various Philistine areas.[34]

Scriptural Testimony

I have already noted that the demographic data present difficulties in light of the testimony of Scripture. As noted previously, the census by David of the standing army of Israel and Judah mentioned in 2 Samuel 24 and 1 Chronicles 21 may reflect (by extrapolation) a total population for the nation approximating 5 million.[35] Let us assume for the moment that Shiloh's estimate for the total population would be the stated 150,000 of the urban areas plus perhaps 180,000 in the rural areas, or a total of 330,000. This figure for a total population is actually smaller than the standing army of Judah alone (500,000) in the 2 Samuel 24:9 passage and far less than a third of that of the standing army of Israel and Judah combined in the 1 Chronicles 21:5 passage (1.57 million). The seeming difficulty is exacerbated if we assume that Shiloh's estimates are close to the actual situation that existed at that time, since the total population was far smaller than the total of the mustered army alone. This seems untenable.

Also untenable would be the results of Broshi and Finkelstein. Their totals of 460,000 at the end of the eighth century, then, are likewise far from the extrapolated 5 million of David's time, and still far below the census totals actually postulated for the mustered army at that time. One could conjecture a severe decline in the population from David's time to the end of the eighth century, but demographic analyses seem to indicate that the numbers were increasing rather than decreasing during that interval. The scriptural record and demographic analyses are mutually exclusive. Both cannot be true. Either the biblical figures are in error, or they are to be interpreted differently, or the demographers are wrong by a factor of at least 90 percent.[36] The first and third options seem unlikely, leaving the second the only viable option.

---

34. Broshi, "La population de l'ancienne Jérusalem," 9. Broshi had developed this premise earlier in "The Expansion of Jerusalem in the Reigns of Hezekiah and Manasseh," *IEJ* 24 (1974): 21–26, and reconfirmed it (as coauthor with Israel Finkelstein) in the more recent "The Population of Palestine in Iron Age II," *BASOR* 287 (1992): 47.
35. This extrapolation allows for roughly 3.3 persons per family, but the extrapolated total does not take into account that Levi and Benjamin were not numbered by Joab (1 Chron. 21:6).

Proposals to Resolve the Problem

How does one address this seeming difficulty? Many explanations have been presented in recent years that attempt to reconcile the enormous numbers of Scripture with archaeological and demographic data, and to reconcile the intra-biblical problems as well. These methods have been reviewed elsewhere.[37] However, evangelical scholars have gravitated toward one of two proposals as the best way of handling the problem. The earlier of the two hypotheses, that which was initially popularized by George Mendenhall, involves an early scribal conflation of differing meanings of *ʾelep* that putatively occurred in numerous contexts. The second of the theories, published initially by Ronald Allen,[38] was also my own position, developed simultaneously in my doctoral dissertation. It is the hypothesis that the largest numbers appearing in historical contexts in Scripture very likely may reflect numerical hyperbole, a common ancient Near Eastern literary convention appearing in royal inscriptions. This hypothesis will be further developed here, particularly as it informs the issue of large numbers in the accounts of the kings of Israel and Judah.[39] Following this discussion, a short analysis of the Mendenhall hypothesis will conclude this article.

The Royal-Inscription Genre in the Bible

Of the numerous passages detailing the kings of Israel and Judah, two stand out as primary examples of the royal-inscription genre seen in other ancient Near Eastern literature, particularly in Neo-Assyrian documents.[40] Together, these two passages reflect the greatness of the two kings of the Golden Era in Israel, David and Solomon.

The first passage, 2 Samuel 8:1–18 (paralleled by 1 Chron. 18:1–17), contains four large numbers, three of which are in excess of 10,000. In the first three examples, the exploits of David as a warrior are being honored.

---

36. By this I mean that if the demographers were wrong by 90 percent, their estimates could be enlarged by a factor of 10. One doubts that they are that far in error.
37. Fouts, "The Use of Large Numbers," 154–70.
38. Ronald B. Allen, *Numbers,* EBC, ed. Frank E. Gaebelein (Grand Rapids: Zondervan, 1990), 2:655–1008.
39. The following discussion is distilled in part from my earlier dissertation. The application to the royal inscriptions of David and Solomon, while observed earlier, is being developed here for the first time.
40. Fouts, "A Defense of the Hyperbolic Interpretation," 387.

Besides defeating the Philistines and the Moabites, he is reported to have captured 1,700 horsemen and 20,000 foot soldiers from the Zobahites of Aram, and to have killed 22,000 of the Arameans who had come to their aid (2 Sam. 8:4–5).[41] In the same context, David is lauded as a builder in 8:13–14, where it is told that after killing another 18,000 Arameans[42] in the valley of Salt, he put garrisons in Edom and subjugated all the Edomites.[43] This was in keeping with making "a name" for himself. We are also told in this chapter of his administrative decisions.

The second passage, 1 Kings 4:21–5:16,[44] lauds the greatness of Solomon. Besides expanding the kingdom of his father David, Solomon also had 40,000 stalls of horses to pull the chariots and 12,000 horsemen (1 Kings 4:26).[45] In his great wisdom, he spoke 3,000 proverbs and 5,000 songs (1 Kings 4:32).[46] In the 2 Chronicles parallel, we are told in hyperbolic simile that Solomon made silver as stones and cedars as plentiful as sycamores (9:27).[47] In addition to these things, Solomon employed 30,000 forced laborers (1 Kings 5:13), 70,000 transporters and 80,000 stone cutters (both 1 Kings 5:15).

In viewing these passages, one is struck by the affinities they share with the royal inscriptions of Assyria. It seems that the royal-inscription genre, originally only in small building inscriptions in Sumer, had developed considerably by the time of the Neo-Assyrians. The genre, which early on had

---

41. The parallel passage in 1 Chronicles 18:4 reads that he captured 1,000 chariots, 7,000 horsemen, and 20,000 foot soldiers. This is supported in part by 4QSam[a] that witnessed the presence of *rekeb* in its fragment (see David M. Fouts, "The Use of Large Numbers," 35).
42. More likely these were Edomites; cf. 1 Chronicles 18:12; Psalm 60 superscription, and the location of the placed garrisons.
43. He had also established garrisons in Aram near Damascus (2 Sam. 8:6).
44. First Kings 5:1–30 in the Hebrew text of *Biblia Hebraica Stuttgartensia*. The expansive parallel passage is 2 Chronicles 8:1–18 and 9:13–28. A near parallel exists in 1 Kings 9–10 which repeats many of the details of 4:21–5:16 and supplements other inscriptional material of Solomon's greatness. One could probably argue that the entire account of Solomon's life from 1 Kings 4:21–10:29 should be considered under the rubric of royal inscription (with the pericope of the visit of the Queen of Sheba excepted).
45. The 2 Chronicles 9:25 passage offers 4,000 for the number of stalls. The near parallel in 1 Kings 10:26 claims only 1,400 horse stalls. For discussion of the textual analysis, see Fouts, "The Use of Large Numbers," 36–37.
46. The reading 5,000 against the MT's 1,005 is supported by LXX, Irenaeus, and somewhat from the Vulgate. A number over 1,000 in the Deuteronomistic historical narratives that is not rounded off to the nearest 1,000 is extremely rare, a fact that calls the MT reading into question. Also, the order of the digit five before the 1,000 is suspect. Since there are numerous *waws* present in the immediate environment, it appears that the *waw* before the *'elep* is perhaps a late addition and that the variant reading is the better choice.
47. See also the near parallel in 1 Kings 10:27.

been "subject to strict rules of composition . . . typical for each of the various categories of Mesopotamian literature,"[48] had by the Assyrian era evolved into the recording of the military exploits of a given king primarily, though domestic feats might also be mentioned. Hyperbolic numbers became the norm, ostensibly to glorify the then reigning monarch.[49] Grayson lists characteristics of the Neo-Assyrian royal inscriptions as containing the following features:

1. The inscriptions are literary works of prose, as opposed to oral works.[50]
2. The inscriptions are primarily in the first person, though there are some texts that fluctuate between first and third person.[51]
3. The inscriptions employ rich imagery in describing the king.[52]
4. The inscriptions employ numerous similes and metaphors.[53]
5. Hyperbole regarding numbers of booty taken and enemy slain is "fully exploited."[54]

---

48. W. W. Hallo, "The Royal Inscriptions of Ur: A Typology," *HUCA* 33 (1962): 1.
49. A. Kirk Grayson, "Assyrian Royal Inscriptions: Literary Characteristics," in *Assyrian Royal Inscriptions: New Horizons,* ed. F. M. Fales (Roma: Istituto per L'Oriente, 1982), 41.
50. Ibid., 42, 44.
51. Ibid., 37, 42.
52. Ibid., 45.
53. Ibid. A good example of this comes slightly before the Neo-Assyrian period during the reign of Tiglath-Pileser I (ca. 1115–1077 B.C.) who claimed:

  With the support of the god Ashur, my lord, I put my chariotry and army in readiness (and), not bothering about the rear guard, I traversed the rough terrain of Mount Kashiyari. I fought with their 20,000 men-at-arms and five kings in the land Kadmuhu. I brought about their defeat. Like a storm demon I piled up the corpses of their warriors on the battle-field (and) made their blood flow into the hollows and plains of the mountains. I cut off their heads (and) stacked them like grain piles around their cities. I brought out their booty, property (and) possessions without number. I took the remaining 6,000 of their troops who had fled from my weapons and submitted to me and regarded them as people of my land.

  Quoted in A. K. Grayson, *Assyrian Royal Inscriptions* (Wiesbaden: Otto Harrassowitz, 1976), 2:6–7.
54. Ibid. Millard has recently argued that in many cases such numbers in Assyrian royal inscriptions are to be regarded as historically reliable. Though the present writer does not agree with all of his conclusions, it is interesting to note that Millard does allow for hyperbole in certain examples. Cf. Alan R. Millard, "Large Numbers in Assyrian Royal Inscriptions," in *Ah, Assyria . . . Studies in Assyrian History and Ancient Near Eastern Historiography Presented to Hayim Tadmor,* ed. Mordechai Cogan and Israel Eph'al, Scripta Hierosolymitana 33 (Jerusalem: Magnes, 1991), 213–22, with the response by David M. Fouts, "Another Look at Large Numbers in Assyrian Royal Inscriptions," *JNES* 53 (1994): 205–11. Even Millard allowed for the possibility of nu-

6. Often, the inscriptions include the motif that the current ruler had accomplished what none of his predecessors had accomplished.[55]

Using these six features as criteria, one may notice how close the two biblical passages come to meeting the characteristics of this genre.

1. Both passages have come down to us as literary prose, apparently taken from the written records of Samuel, Gad, and Nathan for David (1 Chron. 29:29), and from written records of Nathan, Ahijah and Iddo for Solomon (2 Chron. 9:29).[56]
2. Both of the biblical passages are in the third person, rather than the first, but this is an acceptable form even in the Assyrian models. The use of the third person here perhaps simply reflects the normal style of the historical literature of the Bible.
3. Regarding imagery, it is worthy to note here that straightforward divine approval of David is present where figurative self-praise is lacking. It is said twice that the Lord gave him victory wherever he went (2 Sam. 8:6, 8:14) and that he did what was just and right (2 Sam. 8:15). For Solomon on the other hand imagery is abundant, particularly hyperbole. Hiram brought him all the building supplies that he wanted (1 Kings 5:10). The Lord gave him wisdom that was greater than anyone's to the east or to the west (1 Kings 4:29), such that the world's kings sent men to listen to his wisdom (1 Kings 4:34). Nothing lacked from his table or from his horse's feeding

---

merical hyperbole in the inscriptions of Shalmaneser III (ca. 859–824 B.C.; Millard, "Large Numbers," 219). Shalmaneser had claimed in his Monolith inscription:

> Karkar, his royal city, I destroyed, I devastated, I burned with fire. 1,200 chariots, 1,200 cavalry, 20,000 soldiers, of Hadad-ezer, of Aram [? Damascus]; 700 chariots, 700 cavalry, 10,000 soldiers of Irhulêni of Hamath; 2,000 chariots, 10,000 soldiers of Ahab, the Israelites, 500 soldiers of the Gueans, 1,000 soldiers of the Mureans, 10 chariots, 10,000 soldiers of the Irkanateans . . . these twelve kings he brought to his support; to offer battle and to fight, they came against me. . . . From Karkar, as far as the city of Gilzau, I routed them. 14,000 of their warriors I slew with the sword.

Quoted in D. Luckenbill, *ARAB*, 1:§611. From the later Black Obelisk inscription concerning the same battle, the total killed was 20,500 (Luckenbill, *ARAB*, 1:§563). From a bull inscription, again about the same battle, the total was 25,000 (Luckenbill, *ARAB*, 1:§647).

55. Grayson, "Assyrian Royal Inscriptions," 45.
56. One perhaps should assume these sources served at least in part for the books of Samuel and Kings as well (cf. 1 Sam. 10:25).

troughs (1 Kings 4:27).[57] In the near parallel of 1 Kings 10, he received gold, gems, and spices from the Queen of Sheba, the latter of which there had never been before nor since in abundance (1 Kings 10:10), and he imported record amounts of almugwood (1 Kings 10:12). He had made an incomparable throne: "it was not made thusly for any kingdom" (1 Kings 10:20).

4. Though simile and metaphor are notably absent in the passages concerning David, one notes the hyperbolic simile describing Solomon's wisdom in 1 Kings 4:29, where it is said to have been "like the sand that is on the seashore." Of particular interest is that the passage concerning Solomon in 1 Kings 4–5 is prefaced by the seemingly extraneous 4:20, which claims that together Judah and Israel were "as numerous as the sand that is on the seashore in abundance."[58] As noted above, there is also the reference to silver being as *(numerous as)* stones in Jerusalem and cedars being as plentiful as sycamores in both 1 Kings 10:27 and 2 Chronicles 9:27.

5. Without arbitrarily declaring the numbers listed in these two passages to be numerical hyperbole, one does note that some of the figures do seem large given the demographic analysis offered above. They are, however, in keeping with the figures offered by the earlier census of David (at least in the amount of laborers Solomon employed). On the other hand, if the census figures of David are hyperbolic, then these would most likely also be hyperbolic. It is also interesting to note that most of the figures are all rounded off the nearest 1,000.

6. One does not find in David's records an explicit claim that he accomplished what his predecessor could not. There may be implications of this motif in his defeat of the Philistines (2 Sam. 8:1), a perennial opponent of Saul and the army that brought about his

---

57. The supply and provisions of one's table is a frequent motif from the earliest of royal inscriptions. Of Sargon I of Akkad (ca. 2350 B.C.) it was recorded: "5,400 warriors ate daily before him" (Samuel Noah Kramer, *The Sumerians* [Chicago: University of Chicago Press, 1963], 324). Of Assur-Nasir-Pal II (883–859 B.C.), it was written: ". . . all of them—altogether 69,574 (including) those summoned from all lands and the people of Kalach—for ten days I gave them food, I gave them drink, I had them bathed, I had them anointed" (Grayson, *Assryian Royal Inscriptions,* 2:176).

58. This is an interesting statement in view of the numbers offered in the census of David in 2 Samuel 24 and 1 Chronicles 21, since it seems to reflect a literary hyperbole relating to very large numbers. It may simply be an echo of God's promise to Abraham, however.

final defeat (1 Sam. 14:52; 31:1–13), and in the subjugation of the Edomites, Moabites, and Arameans (2 Sam. 8:2–14), peoples against whom Saul could only exact some punishment (1 Sam. 14:47). Of Solomon, on the other hand, it is recorded in 1 Kings 5:3 that he intended to build the Temple that David could not. This motif is also strongly implied in the other kudos for Solomon in territory expansion, subjugation of peoples, amount of sacrifices offered, etc. It may also be implied in the statement that in his time there was peace (cf. 1 Kings 4:24–25; 5:4, 12), whereas in David's there was warfare (1 Kings 5:3).

Are there therefore any intra-biblical clues of original numbers? The song sung at David's victory over Goliath, obviously a variant (x // 10x?) of the x // x + 1 pattern of numerical parallelism widespread in the ancient Near East may offer a hint: "Saul has slain his thousands, and David his ten-thousands" (1 Sam. 18:7). Other ancient Near Eastern cultures, operating on a sexagesimal system, often displayed larger numbers that are perfectly divisible by 6, 60, and/or 600, and this may indicate the original number served as a base for the embellished number. Israel employed a decimal system, so it is not surprising to find the vast majority of the larger numbers of Scripture ending in one or more zeroes. If this tenfold factor was used in the census lists of Numbers 2 and 26, for instance, the original numbers would have been 60,355 and 60,177 respectively. This could extrapolate into a national count of roughly 250,000–300,000, allowing the count of the Levites versus Israelite first born to be taken as actual value, for instance (Num. 3). It would allow two midwives to match the birth needs adequately. It would allow a population in Palestine for seven nations more numerous than Israel to run just under 2 million, more in line with demographic data for the Late Bronze Age (Deut. 7:1, 7). It would account for normal population growth during the Egyptian sojourn from seventy individuals (Gen. 46:27; 75 people—Acts 7:14).

Given that these two accounts of the exploits of David and Solomon do seem to fit the criteria for the royal-inscription genre, what conclusions can be drawn? It may be that the large numbers recorded in these accounts were also to be understood as numerical hyperbole, in keeping with the normally expected literary convention of glorifying a reigning monarch. In fact, to record instead actual smaller number totals within the genre would be to run counter to the literary milieu of the ancient Near Eastern world. The irony seems to be that, though some would question the veracity of an account with numerically hyperbolic numbers, such hyperbole may be more likely to reflect actual events than if less inflated numbers had been employed.

Though the census of David and that of the book of Numbers do not share as many affinities with the royal-inscription genre as the above passages do, they may also reflect numerical hyperbole in a military context that glorify King YHWH, who in fulfillment of the Abrahamic Covenant has caused his people to multiply to the point of being as numerous as the stars of heaven (cf. Gen. 15:5) or as the sand on the seashore for number (cf. Gen. 22:17).[59] Certainly the highest numbers in Scripture are found in these two censuses, ostensibly glorifying the King of Kings and Lord of Lords.

Large Numbers in the Accounts of Kings of the Divided Monarchy

There are more than 450 occurrences of numbers in excess of 1,000 in the Old Testament. The largest of these are in excess of 100,000. Of these fifty-five occurrences, fifty-four are found in military contexts, either of the census type[60] or of the royal-inscription type.[61] Eighteen of this num-

---

59. One may compare these hyperbolic promises of God to Abraham and the census figures of Numbers 1 and 2 Samuel 24; 1 Chronicles 21 with the Ugaritic Kirtu inscription:

> Let a multitude by provisioned
> And let it go out.
> Let the mightiest army be provisioned.
> Yea, let a multitude go out.
> Let your strong army be numerous,
> Three hundred ten-thousands.
> Conscripts without number,
> Soldiers beyond counting.

Andrée Herdner, *Corpus des tablettes en cunéiforms alphabétiques* (Paris: Paul Geuthner, 1963), 63 (my translation). The language of this epic literature, while not royal-inscription genre, is of course hyperbolic. One notes the hyperbolic terms "without number" and "beyond counting" in synonymous parallelism to the specific three hundred ten-thousands (3 million). It may inform us as to how large numbers were perceived in the ancient Near East.

60. It may be that the census figures offered in Scripture should also be considered to be of the royal-inscription genre, since they are related to military activity of a king (either divine or earthly).

61. The exception, found in Jonah 4:11 (120,000), does not employ the Hebrew term *ʾelep* and is not of the royal-inscription genre.

ber find no human king in Israel to glorify; YHWH alone is king. Of the remainder, eleven seem to glorify David as king, three glorify Solomon and three glorify Asa; five are in the records of Jehoshaphat; two each with Rehoboam, Jehoram, Hezekiah, Amaziah, and Pekah; and one each for Ahab and Uzziah.[62] Of these kings, it is said that Asa, Jehoshaphat, and Hezekiah were righteous according to the standard set by David.[63] Amaziah and Uzziah, David's descendants, did right before the LORD, but did not attain the righteous standard set by David. Rehoboam and Jehoram, though of the house of David, did not do right before the Lord. The Israelite kings Pekah and Ahab are anomalies in this group, since the vast majority of the largest numbers employed in the Old Testament (fifty-one of fifty-four) are used in conjunction with God as king or with David and his dynasty as the theocratic rulers over an united Israel and a separate Judah. If the purpose of numerical hyperbole in ancient Near Eastern royal inscriptions was to glorify a given king, it makes sense that the Scriptures employing the same genre would likewise give glory to YHWH and to his elected dynasty. In all other ancient Near Eastern historical literature of the royal-inscription genre, there are only twenty-five known occurrences of numbers in excess of 100,000; in Scripture there are fifty-four. Might it be that numerical hyperbole in royal inscriptional genre in the Old Testament not only should be understood as expected and proper, but may also be present as a polemic against the gods of other nations whose kings could not exceed the work of YHWH?

THE MENDENHALL HYPOTHESIS OF SCRIBAL CONFUSION

Some scholars have rejected the historicity of the Scriptures because of the very high numbers.[64] I do not choose to do so. Still others adopt the

---

62. There were two occurrences of numbers exceeding 100,000 during Saul's reign.
63. First Kings 15:11; 2 Chronicles 17:3; and 2 Kings 18:3 respectively. Josiah, the only other Judean king with this approval, recorded no large numbers.
64. J. W. Colenso, *The Pentateuch and the Book of Joshua Critically Examined*, 7 vols. (London: D. Appleton and Co., 1862–1879). Colenso devotes a great deal of the first volume to mocking the scriptural accounts that employ such large numbers. More recently, Clark claims that the incredibly high numbers were added in the process of the transmission of the text. See R. E. D. Clark, "The Large Numbers of the Old Testament—Especially in Connexion with the Exodus," *Journal of the Transactions of the Victoria Institute* 87 (1955): 83.

Mendenhall hypothesis,[65] or a variation of it. The theory popularized by George Mendenhall claims that many of the passages that include large numbers originally contained homonyms for "thousand" (ʾelep) and perhaps for "hundred" (mēʾâ). The former of these meant "tent-group"[66] or "officer,"[67] "troop"[68] or "platoon" of about ten men,[69] and the latter meant "small military unit."[70] Thus presented with a text containing both usages, the scribe accidentally conflated the two to mean enormously large multiple "thousands" or "hundreds" or both. Apparently to those who value this theory, this happened on a number of occasions (read: wherever the numbers seem implausible).

In my opinion, the hypothesis offered by Mendenhall may be challenged on several points. First, Mendenhall's position is critiqued by Scolnic, who claims that the burden of proof is on Mendenhall and that the term ʾelep with the meaning of "thousand" existed so early in poetry that a later misunderstanding of the type necessary would have been impossible.[71] For example, there are at least two passages of Scripture where ʾelep as a "clan" or "family" occurs in the very near context with ʾelep as a "thousand" (Judg. 6–9 and Mic. 5–6). Their own language does not confuse the scribes in these cases! Most recently, Heinzerling has stated: "I think that this extended variant of the solution proposal is rather improbable and that no solution will be found using two meanings of ʾlp as starting point."[72] Secondly, that scribes consistently misread and confused and conflated the text containing putative homonyms has no parallel of which I am aware.

---

65. George E. Mendenhall, "The Census Lists of Numbers 1 and 26," *JBL* 77 (1958): 52–66. Others adopting this theory, at least in part, include: J. B. Payne, "The Validity of the Numbers in Chronicles," *BSac* 136 (1979): 109–28; 206–20; C. J. Humphreys, "The Number of People in the Exodus from Egypt: Decoding Mathematically the Very Large Numbers in Numbers i and xxvi," *VT* 48 (1998): 196–213; and idem, "The Numbers in the Exodus from Egypt : A Further Appraisal," *VT* 50 (2000): 323–28. Most recently, David Merling has also adopted a form of this view in "Large Numbers at the Time of the Exodus," *NEASB* 44 (1999): 15–27. Unfortunately, Merling's criticism of my numerical hyperbole theory is based in part on a misreading of my dissertation.
66. W. M. Flinders Petrie, *Egypt and Israel* (London: SPCK, 1931), 40–46.
67. Clark, "The Large Numbers of the Old Testament," 84.
68. Humphreys, "The Number of People in the Exodus from Egypt," 203.
69. W. W. Hallo, *The Book of the People* (Atlanta: Scholars Press, 1991), 82.
70. J. W. Wenham, "Large Numbers in the Old Testament," *TynBul* 18 (1967): 19–53.
71. Benjamin E. Scolnic, "Theme and Context in Biblical Lists" (Ph.D. diss., Jewish Theological Seminary of America, 1987), 54–59.
72. Rüdinger Heinzerling, "On the Interpretation of the Census Lists by C. J. Humphreys and G. E. Mendenhall," *VT* 50 (2000): 251.

Thirdly, there is absolutely no external textual evidence to support their theory.

Conclusion

Perusing the available ancient Near Eastern literature that contains large numbers helps one understand the large number issue more clearly. For my part, seeing the literature of Israel consistently within the ancient Near Eastern literary convention of numerical hyperbole is far easier than thinking that Hebrew scribes consistently made the same type of mistake with large numbers in every case those large numbers now appear. In other words, numerical hyperbole is a natural expectation of the cultural milieu in which Israel existed. The Mendenhall hypothesis is based on systematic scribal error—not on a few isolated examples, but consistently nearly every time numbers reach into the multiple thousands (well over 200 times for numbers that now read in excess of 10,000). That would mean that one mistaken scribe would have been copying every passage where these numbers occurred, or that there were many confused scribes in Israel. Neither scenario is acceptable in my thinking. Furthermore, there is no known parallel to this type of scribal error occurring in any other text (i.e., a confusion of homonyms), and there is no evidence textually whatsoever of any variant reading where large numbers occur from which one could posit such an error.

When one considers these factors, the well-attested ancient Near Eastern literary convention of numerical hyperbole in military contexts appears the most reasonable explanation of the Bible's use of large numbers.

14

AFTER THE EXILE

Haggai and History

Byron G. Curtis

IN A TIME OF UNCERTAINTY FOR JUDAH, a prophet named Haggai arose to guide the people of God. The biblical book that now bears his name is a bit odd compared to most of the other books in the Minor Prophets, the collection known to the ancient rabbis as "the Book of the Twelve." Haggai's book is essentially a historical narrative, complete with the names of Judean dignitaries and references to a Persian monarch. Strung along within this historical narrative framework we find the collected oracles of this postexilic prophet.[1]

THE EXILIC ERA: 587–538 B.C.

To understand his role in Judean life, we must go back two generations before his time to 588–587 B.C., the time of Judah's second revolt against her Babylonian overlords. The revolt failed, with disastrous consequences. The Babylonian destruction of Jerusalem in 587 created a crisis of almost limitless proportions for Judeans. The city's destruction meant not only the loss of the Davidic dynasty's kingdom and historic capital city, but also the loss of Yahweh's chosen dwelling place, the temple of God on Mount Zion. The loss of city and temple struck at the very heart of Judah's identity.

---

1. On the narrative framework of Haggai, see Peter Ackroyd, "Studies in the Book of Haggai," *Journal of Jewish Studies* 2 (1951): 163–76; and Rex A. Mason, "The Purpose of the 'Editorial Framework' of the Book of Haggai," *VT* 27 (1977): 413–21.

That loss is well expressed by the grief-filled poetry of the book of Lamentations:

> How deserted lies the city,
>   once so full of people!
> How like a widow is she,
>   who once was great among the nations!
> She who was queen among the provinces
>   has now become a slave. (Lamentations 1:1)[2]

By the end of the failed revolt, no major city in Judah remained standing. All fortifications and buildings of any size were systematically reduced to rubble. The first temple lay in ruins. Once-forested hillsides had been denuded of their trees. Desolation swept the landscape.

At that time the Babylonians deported virtually all the remaining people of social rank (2 Kings 25:11–12). These people were resettled in Babylonia, in farming villages comprised of Judeans, where they joined still other Judean elites taken into exile after the first revolt in 597, among whom we find the priest-and-prophet Ezekiel. The deportees of 597 and 587 included members of the royal family and other aristocrats, members of the priesthood, landowners, educated people, craftsmen, and wealthy people of every kind (2 Kings 24:14–16).

Many other Judeans remained behind in the desolated land (2 Kings 25:12; Jer. 39:10). There they were ruled by the short-lived Babylonian provincial administration of the Judean governor, Gedaliah. Among these Palestinian Judeans we likely find the unnamed author of the book of Lamentations, whose melancholy voice represents the experience of those left behind in Judah with its ruined cities.

The Babylonian policy of deportation aimed at controlling the elites of rebellious people groups. In the Babylonian view, it was the elites who fomented rebellion, not the peasants. Deporting elite groups removed them from their natural bases of power, and made them dependent upon the empire. Peasant classes, who comprised the majority, were left to their usual hard labor of subsistence farming. The Judeans were not the only people to suffer exile at the hands of the Babylonians.

Some time after the capture of King Zedekiah and the execution of his

---

2. Unless otherwise noted, all Bible quotations in this essay are the author's translation.

sons, Gedaliah the Judean governor, with his officials and his Babylonian garrison, set up headquarters at Mizpah, a few miles to the north of Jerusalem. But Gedaliah was soon assassinated by Ishmael, a Judean aristocrat and military man who likely regarded himself as a freedom-fighter. Ishmael's Judean guerillas killed nearly the entire Judean-Babylonian administration of the new province; they then fled (Jer. 41). Survivors, under the leadership of an army officer named Johanan, kidnapped Jeremiah and fled with him to Egypt (Jer. 43), out of fear of the Babylonians.

A Babylonian raid in 581, followed by yet a third deportation of captives (Jer. 52:30), seems to have been a belated reprisal against Ishmael's revolt. Afterwards, the Babylonians neglected Judah. There is little extant literary evidence for a continuing Babylonian military or political presence in the ruined land. The archaeological record likewise reveals virtually no new building projects of any kind in the land of Judah for the period from Jerusalem's destruction in 587 to the time of the first return around 537.[3]

The probable situation for Judah on the eve of the first return is one of poor, illiterate peasant farmers eking out a subsistence-level living from the land amid a depressed economy without leadership, without fortified cities or other forms of protection, and without ready access to major markets. It is into this situation that we see the first returnees arrive in about 537.

Turning now to the exiles, we know of sizeable exilic communities of Judeans, foremost in Babylonia, but also in the broader Mesopotamian world, in Elam and in Egypt. Jeremiah's well-known letter to the exiles of 597 counseled them by Yahweh's word to "build houses and settle down, plant gardens and eat what they produce. Marry and have sons and daughters . . . [and] seek the peace and prosperity of the city to which I have carried you into exile" (Jer. 29:5–7).

It is clear that the Judeans obeyed this message. Babylonia became the spiritual and cultural center for the people who would soon become known to the world as Jews. Two generations of Judeans lived under enforced exile in Babylonia. Many more generations would continue to live in Babylonia and elsewhere outside Judah, even when the exile was no longer in force.

---

3. Ephraim Stern, *The Material Culture of the Land of the Bible in the Persian Period 538–322 B.C.* (Warminster, England: Aris & Phillips, 1982); and idem, *Archaeology of the Land of the Bible* (New York: Doubleday, 2001), 2:348–50.

The Restoration Era, 538–432 B.C.

The Bible's accounts of the restoration era focus our attention upon the decrees of Persian monarchs and upon efforts of exilic Jews for the restoration of Jerusalem and Judah. The works of restoration, the Bible reports, took place under the command of God, and at the urging of his prophets. The books of Haggai, Zechariah, Ezra and Nehemiah are our primary biblical sources for the history of the restoration era.

It was King Cyrus (559–530 B.C.), the founder of the Persian Empire, who conquered Babylon in 539 and who in the following year issued his famous decree ordering the return of the exiled peoples and the rebuilding of their ancestral temples. Cyrus's decree of 538 thus ended the Babylonian exile for Judeans and provided support for the first efforts to restore Jerusalem's altar and temple. Hebrew versions of this decree are found in 2 Chronicles 36:23 and Ezra 1:2–4. An Aramaic version appears in Ezra 6:3–5. A later decree issued by King Darius (522–486 B.C.) helped silence local opposition to Jerusalem's temple-reconstruction (Ezra 6:2–12). Still another decree from King Artaxerxes (486–465 B.C.) provided for the further maintenance or repair of the completed temple (Ezra 7:11–26).

Accordingly, the book of Ezra reports:

> The elders of the Jews continued to build and prosper under the preaching of Haggai the prophet and Zechariah, a descendent of Iddo. They finished building the temple according to the command of the God of Israel and the decrees of Cyrus, Darius and Artaxerxes,[4] kings of Persia. The temple was completed on the third day of the month of Adar, in the sixth year of the reign of King Darius.[5] (Ezra 6:14–15)

The efforts of exilic Jews also are highlighted by the biblical accounts. Sheshbazzar the prince, Zerubbabel the governor, Joshua the high priest, Zechariah the prophet, and Ezra the priest and scribe all came to Judah from Babylonia; Nehemiah, the cupbearer to the king, came from Susa,

---

4. The inclusion of the name of Artaxerxes I, who came to the throne in 465 B.C., fifty-one years after temple-completion, pertains to the *maintenance* of the temple building rather than to its construction. The name is included on the basis of Artaxerxes' decree in Ezra 4:17–23.
5. That is, March 12, 515 B.C.

the Persian capital. All of these individuals either initiated important works of restoration in Judah, or significantly aided such works.

Sheshbazzar and Zerubbabel and the Books of Ezra and Haggai

The book of Ezra is not altogether clear about the chronological order of some of the events that it narrates. The book abounds in historical puzzles and difficulties of interpretation. Obviously its author had other priorities to engage and different questions to answer than the ones modern historians bring to his book.[6] One of these murky matters is the historical relationship between Sheshbazzar and Zerubbabel. Since Sheshbazzar is named as governor of Judah in Ezra, and Zerubbabel is named as governor of Judah in the book of Haggai, and the two names appear in close proximity in Ezra 1:11 and 2:2, our investigation of the latter book leads us to raise the question, "Just what is the relationship between Sheshbazzar and Zerubbabel?"

Sheshbazzar, a mysterious figure in the Bible's account, is the named leader of the first return in about 537. He is identified as a "prince" *(nāśîʾ)* of Judah in Ezra 1:8, to whom was entrusted the more than five thousand articles of gold and silver taken by Nebuchadnezzar from Solomon's temple in 587. Sheshbazzar is credited with success in the difficult task of bringing these precious objects safely from Babylon to Jerusalem at the time of the first return (Ezra 1:11; 5:14–15). Ezra 5:14 also gives him the title "governor" *(peḥâ,* cognate to the Persian *pasha).* The probable meaning of the term here refers to the leader of a subprovince within the larger Persian province of Trans-Euphrates. Thus Sheshbazzar was answerable directly to the governor of Trans-Euphrates, an administrator over the region which encompassed all of Syria-Palestine, and which was governed under the satrapy of Babylon and Trans-Euphrates. Perhaps it was at this time that Judah was renamed "Yehud," an Aramaic form of the same name, to reflect its new status as a subprovince of the Persian Empire.[7]

The book of Ezra also credits Sheshbazzar with laying the foundations

---

6. The commentary of H. G. M. Williamson provides excellent help for understanding these difficulties: *Ezra, Nehemiah,* WBC (Waco: Word, 1985). For a briefer guide, see David M. Howard Jr., *An Introduction to the Old Testament Historical Books* (Chicago: Moody, 1993), 273–313.
7. Following Carol L. Meyers and Eric M. Meyers, *Haggai, Zechariah 1–8,* AB (Garden City, N.Y.: Doubleday, 1987), 13–16; but see the views of Sean McEvenue, "The Political Structure of Judah from Cyrus to Nehemiah, *CBQ* 43 (1981): 353–64; and Ephraim Stern, *Material Culture,* 213, who hold that Judah was governed from Samaria until the time of Nehemiah.

for the new temple (5:16), an action that may not be identical to the temple-founding narrated in Ezra 3:8–13. It is widely assumed that Sheshbazzar died not long after his return to Jerusalem. After Ezra 1:11 he does not appear at all, except for the historical reminiscence found in 5:14–16, where he is clearly a figure of the past.

Identifying Sheshbazzar with Shenazzar, a grandson of King Jehoiachin mentioned in 1 Chronicles 3:18, cannot be done with certainty. No genealogy or patronym is given for Sheshbazzar, and the Hebrew title "prince" *(nāśî')* need not be taken as a royal title. However, his prominence as the leader of the first return, and the Persian practice of appointing Davidites as governors of Yehud lend some credence to the theory, despite the difficulty of accounting for the different spellings of the two names.[8]

Zerubbabel, on the other hand, is well attested in the books of Ezra and Haggai as the "son of Shealtiel," and Shealtiel, according to the royal genealogies of 1 Chronicles 3, was a son of King Jehoiachin in the Babylonian exile (3:17). First Chronicles 3:19 lists Pedaiah, another son of King Jehoiachin, as Zerubbabel's father. It may have been that Pedaiah died young, and that Shealtiel became head of the family and the adoptive father of Zerubbabel. In any case, it is certain that Zerubbabel was a descendent of Jehoiachin in the line of David, and thus a likely choice as a leader for Yehud.

If Sheshbazzar is to be identified as the "Shenazzar" of 1 Chronicles 3:18, then Zerubbabel would be his nephew. It is to Zerubbabel that Haggai and Zechariah address some of their oracles; and the book of Haggai clearly identifies him as "governor" *(peḥâ)* of Yehud (Hag. 1:1; 2:2, 21).

Some interpreters of Ezra believe that the book narrates the story of a single return in chapters 1–6; others believe that two returns are involved. Most of those who hold to one return believe that Sheshbazzar, governor-prince of Judah, accompanied by Zerubbabel, as well as by the high priest Joshua, arrived in Jerusalem in about 537 B.C., ruled for a time, and, upon his death, was replaced by Zerubbabel.[9] Others hold that Sheshbazzar and Zerubbabel were the same person.[10]

---

8. Eugene H. Merrill, *A Kingdom of Priests: A History of Old Testament Israel* (Grand Rapids: Baker, 1996), 493, also supports this view.
9. So the notes for the book of Ezra in the NIV *Study Bible,* ed. Kenneth Barker (Grand Rapids: Zondervan, 1995), 673.
10. So C. F. Keil, *The Books of Ezra, Nehemiah and Esther,* Biblical Commentary on the Old Testament, trans. S. Taylor (n.d.; reprint, Grand Rapids: Eerdmans, 1976), 27.

Still others hold that there are two returns narrated in Ezra 1–6. The first, in about 537, was led by Sheshbazzar and resulted in an abortive attempt at temple-restoration in 536, as told in Ezra 1 and summarized in Ezra 5:14–16. The second, in about 521, led by Zerubbabel, resulted in successful temple completion in 515, as told in Ezra 2–6. This view suggests that the list in Ezra 2 of those who returned "in company with Zerubbabel" (2:2) represents a separate event than the return narrated in Ezra 1. An important observation supporting this view is the absence of Sheshbazzar's name anywhere else in the story, except for the reminiscence of his arrival in Ezra 5.14–16. Throughout Ezra 2–6, Zerubbabel is clearly the political leader. His absence in Ezra 1 and his prominence in Ezra 2–6 suggest that he was the leader of a second returning group.

This second view, the theory of two returns, seems to make more sense of the biblical data. The evidence of the book of Haggai is relevant here, since in the year 520 house-construction had been speedily proceeding, while the ruined temple lay dormant.[11] In that year the prophet Haggai rebuked the returnees by asking, "Is it a time for you yourselves to be living in your paneled houses, while this house [the temple] remains a ruin? . . . My house . . . remains a ruin, while each of you is busy with his own house" (1:4, 9). The construction of many houses is best understood as the activity of a newly-arrived group, rather than the work of a well-settled people.

Accordingly, Zerubbabel's Persian commission as governor likely began in approximately 521.[12] Together with the high priest Joshua, he led a new group of returnees to Yehud in a second return. The story of Haggai begins with this second return.

---

11. First Esdras 5:1–6 likewise presents Zerubbabel as newly commissioned to lead a return in the second year of Darius. Josephus, on the other hand, presents Zerubbabel as "governor of the Jews who had been in captivity," who, returning *from* Jerusalem to see his good friend the king, is commissioned to return and rebuild city and temple (*Antiquities* 11.3.1).

12. During Zerubbabel's governorship in Yehud, Tattenai was the administrative official over Trans-Euphrates (as mentioned in Ezra 5.3, 5.6; 6.13), and Hystanes *(Ushtannu)* was the satrap over the satrapy of Babylon and Trans-Euphrates. Cf. A. T. Olmstead, *History of the Persian Empire* (Chicago: University of Chicago Press, 1948), 139; and Edwin M. Yamauchi, *Persia and the Bible* (Grand Rapids: Baker, 1990), 156. Olmstead places the beginning of Zerubbabel's governorship in 520 B.C. (*History of the Persian Empire,* 136).

Haggai the Prophet

Of the prophets Haggai and Zechariah, only Zechariah can be said with confidence to have arrived from exile; Haggai's origins are uncertain. Aside from the contents of his preaching in his book, virtually nothing is known about Haggai. The very limited evidence regarding him seems to indicate that he may have been a native-born Judean, a member of the community of Jews who never experienced exile.

Studies of names provide important evidence about the identity of many persons in the Old Testament. It is the form of Haggai's name in the Bible that gives us some reason to think that he may have been born in the land of promise itself.

Haggai's name appears eleven times in the Old Testament: nine times in the book of Haggai, and twice in the book of Ezra. Five times in the book of Haggai it appears as "Haggai the prophet" *(ḥaggay hannābî)*. Four of these appear in the messenger formulae that introduce oracles in the book as coming "by the hand of Haggai the prophet" (*bᵉyad ḥaggay hannābî*, 1:1, 3; 2:1, 10). The historical narrative passage in Haggai 1:12–15 likewise once refers to him as "Haggai the prophet" (1:12) and once more as "Haggai, the messenger of Yahweh" *(ḥaggay malʾāk yhwh,* in 1:13). Then the reported conversation of Haggai with the Jerusalem priests in 2:11–14 merely refers to him as "Haggai," without further description (2:13 and 14), as does the messenger formula that introduces the final oracle of the book (2:20).

This pattern displays a strategy of establishing and reinforcing Haggai's identity as *prophet (nābî)* and *messenger (malʾāk)* of the Lord for the outset of the book. Having established Haggai's credentials as a true prophet, the name then stands by itself for the remainder of the prophet's book.

This survey accounts for nine of the eleven uses of the name Haggai. The remaining two occurrences appear in the book of Ezra, where in 5:1 and 6:14 both Haggai and Zechariah are credited with getting the second temple built. In the Aramaic of Ezra 5:1 the name forms appear as "Haggai the prophet and Zechariah the prophet, a descendent of Iddo" *(ḥaggay nᵉbîyyāʾ[h] ûzᵉkaryâ bar-ʿiddôʾ nᵉbîyyaʾ[yyāʾ])*. Ezra 6:14 is similar.

A great many of the personal names in the Old Testament appear in what is called *patronymic* form. The form is "personal name 1" + "son of" + "personal name 2" (PN1 *ben-* PN2), such as "Jeremiah, son of Hilkiah (*yirmᵉyāhû ben ḥilqîyyāhû,* Jer. 1:1). Patronyms identify an individual as the son or descendent of a father or prominent ancestor. One of the main narrative strategies for the use of Israelite masculine names in the Old Testament is to introduce a character into the narrative by citing his name and patronym; further uses of the name in the narrative will often omit the patronym.

For exilic and postexilic Judeans, the use of patronyms and genealogies helped the community to maintain clear lines of lineage back to preexilic times. Continuity of lineage guaranteed that these people were the true descendents of Israel, the true inheritors of Yahweh's promises to the patriarchs. For a people living far away from their native land, patronyms and genealogy provided boundaries and borders for a nation without territory.

The fact that Haggai's name never appears with a patronym may indicate that he came from the group of Judeans who had never been severed from their land. This group of Judeans, as noted above, were largely the poor and illiterate classes. In Haggai's time, the fact that they and their families had been living in Judah and claimed Judean identity was proof enough of their status as true Israelites. Such persons were perhaps less likely than the exiled Jews to use patronyms. Haggai may have come from such a family. However, Haggai, as his speeches indicate, was a well-educated man.

His appeal to "the people of the land" in Haggai 2:4 seems suited to address both the long-time residents of the land of Judah as well as the recently-returned exiles. There is no sense of any social conflict between the two groups: Haggai addresses the entire citizenry of the people.[13]

The name Haggai derives from the Hebrew word *ḥag*, meaning "festival." The name itself then means either "festival"[14] or "my feast"[15] Perhaps Haggai had been born during the week of an Old Testament feast. We do not know his age at the time of his preaching.

More significant to us are the titles ascribed to Haggai as we have noted. In the book of Haggai he is called both "prophet" (*nābî*, five times) and "messenger" (*malʾāk*, once). As a *prophet*, Haggai was called by God to speak or otherwise demonstrate the will of God. A prophet's main function was to

---

13. Meyers and Meyers, *Haggai, Zechariah 1–8*, 50–51. *Contra* Morton Smith, *Palestinian Parties and Politics That Shaped the Old Testament* (New York: Columbia University Press, 1971), 113–14; and Paul D. Hanson, *The Dawn of Apocalyptic*, rev. ed. (Philadelphia: Fortress, 1979), 240–46.
14. Translation from Eugene H. Merrill, *An Exegetical Commentary: Haggai, Zechariah and Malachi* (Chicago: Moody, 1994), 19.
15. Marvin A. Sweeney, *The Twelve Prophets* (Collegeville, Minnesota: Liturgical, 2000), 2:529.

transmit messages from the deity. It is this *messenger* function that Haggai's other given title emphasizes, in a phrase that is unique in the Old Testament:

> Then Haggai, Yahweh's messenger *[mal'āk yhwh]*, said in Yahweh's message *[mal'ªkût yhwh]* to the people, "I am with you"—oracle of Yahweh. (Hag. 1:13)

The word "messenger," *mal'āk* in Hebrew, is usually translated "angel" elsewhere in the Old Testament. The word for "message," *mal'ªkût*, derives from the same Hebrew root. Both terms together underscore the divinely authenticated character of the man Haggai and of his words. The point is made yet again by the final phrase, "oracle of Yahweh" *(nᵊʾûm yhwh)*, an oracular formula phrase more familiar in its King James Version rendering, "saith the Lord."

The book of Haggai places great emphasis upon the fact that Haggai is a true prophet speaking Yahweh's true word to his people. There are no less than 26 prophetic-word formulas, messenger formulas and oracular formulas in this book of thirty-eight verses. This is an unusually high number for such a brief book. We may surmise from this fact that the prophetic word had likely been absent for some time. The book's strong insistence on Haggai's validity as divine messenger serves as a historical clue that his claims came at a time when apparently no prophet had yet spoken in restoration-era Jerusalem.

Haggai's Messages

The book of Haggai contains five distinct oracles all given within the span of four months in the second year of Darius, the Persian king who ruled from 522 to 486 B.C. Darius had come to the throne amidst much intrigue. His predecessor King Cambyses was busy consolidating his control over Egypt when news reached him of a palace coup at home in Susa, the Persian capital. But Cambyses never made it back to Susa. According to the ancient historian Herodotus, he died in Syria-Palestine from an infection of a leg wound, caused by his own sword when he leaped onto his horse.[16] He left no heir to his throne. Instead, a usurper held sway, posing as the dead king's brother.

---

16. Herodotus, *Histories* 3:64.

Darius, a distant kinsman and spear-bearer to the dead king, sped home in a successful attempt to overthrow the usurper. In taking the throne, it is apparent that Darius, too, was widely regarded as a usurper. Rebellions broke out in far-flung places as well as in the heartlands of his empire. Darius, with his allies, conducted the first twelve months of the reign with near-constant warfare in one place or another, putting down revolt after revolt. His own account in the famous Behistun Inscription speaks of nineteen battles that he fought, and nine kings that he defeated.[17] Among the rebellious provinces was Egypt, Yehud's powerful southwestern neighbor. Darius invaded Egypt through Palestine in 519.

This historical context of revolt may provide the reason why the Jews of Haggai's time believed that "the time has not yet come for Yahweh's house to be rebuilt" (Hag. 1:2). Perhaps they feared that construction efforts would be misinterpreted as fortifications for a new revolt. Yehud, however, was a loyal subprovince, despite the insinuations to the contrary expressed in Tattenai's letter-report to the king, now found in Ezra 5:7–17.

It is this conviction—that the time to rebuild the temple had not yet come—that Haggai confronted in his first oracle, delivered on the first day of the sixth month, the month Elul, in the second year of Darius (August 29, 520 B.C.): "This people says, 'The time has not yet come for Yahweh's house to be rebuilt.' Is it time for you yourselves to be living in your paneled houses while this house remains a ruin?" (Hag. 1:2, 4).

The people erred in assessing their times. Their false assessment led to spiritual sloth. Instead of doing God's kingdom-work, they focused on building their own kingdoms, their own "paneled houses." That is why God had cursed their harvests:

> Give careful thought to your ways!
> You have sown much, but harvested little.
> You eat, but never have enough.
> You drink, but never have your fill.
> You put on clothes, but no one is warm.
> You earn wages, only to put them into a purse with holes in it! . . .
> You expected much, but see, it turned out to be little,

---

17. For a description and photograph of the Behistun Inscription, see Yamauchi, *Persia and the Bible*, 131–34. For the Old Persian text and translation, see Roland G. Kent, *Old Persian: Grammar, Texts, Lexicon*, 2d ed. (New Haven, Conn.: American Oriental Society, 1953), 116–34.

and what you brought home, I blew away.
Why?"—asks Yahweh of the heavenly armies—[18]
"because of my house which lies in ruins,
while each of you is busy with his own house!"
(Hag. 1:5–6, 9)

Now is the time to act! Start rebuilding the temple and blessing will come:

"Go up to the mountains and bring back timber, and build the house so that I may take pleasure in it, and be honored," says Yahweh. (Hag. 1:8)

The response to Haggai's first message was everything the prophet could have hoped. Having addressed his message to Zerubbabel the governor, to Joshua the high priest, and to the people at large, Haggai found himself received as a genuine prophet by the governing authorities of both state and temple and by the popular consensus, and obeyed (Hag. 1:12).

Rarely had a prophet succeeded so well and so quickly! Such favorable response elicited a second oracle, one that no longer spoke of divine displeasure and poor harvests. Now the message gave reassurance of their standing with God: "'I am with you!'—oracle of Yahweh" (Hag. 1:13, author's translation). After a brief time of preparations and gathering materials, reconstruction recommenced on the temple, according to the book's account, "on the twenty-fourth day of the sixth month," the month Elul (September 21, 520 B.C.; Hag. 1:15), just a little over three weeks after Haggai's initial message. God was indeed with them.

Haggai's third oracle, coming on the twenty-first day of Tishri, the seventh month (October 17, 520 B.C.), once again addressed Zerubbabel the governor, Joshua the high priest, and the people at large. The date, the seventh day of the Feast of Tabernacles, marked the time when, every seven years, the Torah was to be publicly read to the people of Israel (Deut. 31:9–13). That same week marked the time, according to 1 Kings 8:2, when

---

18. The phrase "Yahweh of the heavenly armies" ("LORD of hosts," KJV) paints a vivid picture of the power of Judah's God suitable for a time when Judah was relatively powerless; the phrase is characteristic of the oracular formulae in both Haggai and Zechariah, and appears there more than in any other biblical books. For fuller discussion, see Meyers and Meyers, *Haggai, Zechariah 1–8*, 18–19.

Solomon dedicated the first temple.[19] Hence, the date had historical and theological significance for Haggai's community regarding the Torah and the temple.

His message now was one of further reassurance and exhortation:

> "Now be strong, O Zerubbabel"—oracle of Yahweh—
> "be strong, O Joshua son of Jehozadak, the high priest,
> be strong, all you people of the land"—oracle of Yahweh—
> "and do the word that I covenanted with you when you came
>   out of Egypt;
> for I am with you"—oracle of Yahweh of the heavenly armies.
> "My Spirit stands in your midst; do not fear!"
>
> (Hag. 2:4–5)

Appropriately for the date, several parts of this exhortation reflect upon the early years of Israel's life, the time of Moses and Joshua, when Israel's basic institutions were being established. The triple command of Haggai 2:4, "be strong," hearkens back to the days of Joshua, son of Nun, who led Israel into the Promised Land and who received a similar triple command to "be strong" (Josh. 1:6–9).

The reference to "the word I covenanted with you when you came out of Egypt" emphasizes the revelations given at Mount Sinai through Moses. The assurance that "My Spirit stands in your midst" reasserts the presence of God in Yehud, just as he had been present in the glory-cloud and pillar of fire associated with Israel's tabernacle in the wilderness. Thus Yahweh was now reconstituting Israel under her sacred institutions, under the leadership of Zerubbabel the governor and Joshua the High Priest. It was a time of a New Exodus, out of Babylon; a time of a new entry out of the Wilderness into the Promised Land.

Reestablishing the temple in Jerusalem not only hearkened back to Israel's foundational events, it also entailed proper preparation for Yahweh's future work, a work of cosmic moment:

---

19. Marvin A. Sweeney, *The Twelve Prophets*, 2:544; Eugene H. Merrill, *Haggai, Zechariah, Malachi*, 36.

> This is what Yahweh of the heavenly armies says:
> "In a little while I will once more shake the heavens,
> the earth, the sea and the dry land,
> and I will shake all the nations,
> and the treasure of all the nations will arrive.
> Thus I will fill this house with glory!"
>
> (Hag. 2:6–9)

The cosmic shaking of Haggai's oracle speaks of the great eschatological day, the Day of Yahweh, when evil shall be conquered and all things set right. At that time, this temple's glory shall surpass the glory of Solomon's temple (Hag. 2:9). On that day, the temple will stand at the center of God's plan for the world, God will be glorified among the nations, and God will grant everlasting *shalom*.

The paltry fortunes of impoverished Yehud for temple construction could hardly hope to rival the resources of Solomon's empire. No wonder the prophet Haggai had asked, "Who of you is left who saw this house in its former glory? How does it look to you now? Does it not seem to you like nothing? (Hag. 2:3)."

In course of time, Haggai's prediction of "greater glory" would come true quite literally for Zerubbabel's temple. In 20 B.C. King Herod the Great (37–4 B.C.) began work on the massive reconstruction of the five hundred-year-old structure. The dimensions and outward opulence of that temple complex far surpassed that of Solomon. As told by the first-century Jewish historian, Josephus, Herod "restored the existing Sanctuary and round it enclosed an area double the former size, keeping no account of the cost and achieving a magnificence beyond compare."[20] The completed temple stood for a mere seven years before the Romans destroyed it during the Jewish War, in A.D. 70.

It is doubtful, however, that Herod's temple's passing magnificence fulfills the full spirit of Haggai's words. In Haggai's day God was busy re-establishing his covenant with the remnant of his people. God was building his kingdom. Just as the old temple represented God's heavenly dwelling on earth, the very existence of the new temple reasserted Yahweh's claim over the entire world. The temple thus stands as the symbol of the ultimate

---

20. Josephus, *The Jewish War*, rev. ed., trans. G. A. Williamson (New York: Penguin, 1979), 75 (= §1.21.1).

community, the city "with foundations, whose architect and builder is God" (Heb. 11:10), the "kingdom that cannot be shaken" (12:28). The latter glory of God's kingdom does not consist of gold and silver, or of an opulence that is only physical. It consists of the renewal of heaven and earth, where the dwelling of God is with human beings (Rev. 21:3) and where there is no temple, "because the Lord God Almighty and the Lamb are its temple" (v. 22). Zerubbabel's temple is a way-station along the road that leads to that latter-day glory.

That ultimate fulfillment is itself anticipated with greater power than mere architecture could convey when Jesus arrived at Herod's temple, and indirectly declared himself to be the temple of the Lord. When asked by certain Jewish leaders what miraculous sign he would perform to prove his authority, he answered, "Destroy this temple, and I will raise it again in three days!" (John 2:19). John's narration adds the cogent explanation, "the temple he had spoken of was his body" (v. 21). Thus the crucifixion and resurrection of Jesus achieve what architecture and opulence could never do: they establish the glory of the Lord.

Haggai's fourth message came on the twenty-fourth day of Kislev, the ninth month (December 18, 520 B.C.).[21] Yahweh directed the prophet to ask the priests for rulings regarding two issues of ritual defilement.[22]

> "If a person carries consecrated meat in the fold of his garment, and that fold touches some bread or stew, some wine, oil or other food, does it become consecrated?"
>
> The priests answered, "No."
>
> Then Haggai said, "If a person defiled by contact with a dead body touches one of these things, does it become defiled?"
>
> "Yes," the priests replied, "it becomes defiled."
>
> (Hag. 2:12–13)

---

21. Sweeney suggests that "the Maccabean rededication of the Temple altar on the twenty-fifth of Kislev" may have been understood "as a fulfillment of Haggai's prophecy" *(The Twelve Prophets,* 2:550).

22. The NIV is in error in 2:11, where it translates "Ask the priests what the law says." The correct interpretation of the phrase š^eal-nā ʾet-hakkōh^anîm tôrâ is that the prophet asks for a priestly *ruling* on a question not explicitly addressed in the Torah. See Eric M. Meyers, "The Use of *tôrâ* in Haggai 2:11 and the Role of the Prophet in the Restoration Community," in *The Word of the Lord Shall Go Forth: Essays in Honor of David Noel Freedman in Celebration of His Sixtieth Birthday,* ed. Carol L. Meyers and M. O'Connor (Winona Lake, Ind.: Eisenbrauns, 1983), 71.

The form of the questions is rhetorical: Haggai already knows the answers. Contact between the pure and the impure destroys purity. Ritual defilement is more contagious than ritual purity. The two questions with their priestly-ruling answers provide Haggai a public occasion. In that public occasion he pointedly applies the two priestly rulings to the people of Yehud:

> So it is with this people,
> and so it is with this nation before me—Yahweh's oracle—
> and so it is with all the work of their hands
> and whatever they offer there;
> it is unclean!
>
> (Hag. 2:14)

"This people" and "this nation" refer not to Samaritans or other local foreign groups, but to the Judean community.[23] "The work of their hands" refers to agricultural produce such as grain offerings and the sacrifice of livestock, since they "offer" such things "there," that is, at the altar of the ruinous temple. Those offerings of grain and animal sacrifice are unclean, declares the prophet.

If all their offerings are unclean, the questions asked of the priests in Haggai 2:12–13 now force Haggai's original hearers to consider what rendered these offerings unclean. Commentators are divided on the question. Some favor the view that some kind of contact with Samaritans or other foreigners is the source of the defilement. Others think that the problem lies within the Judean community itself. Some of these latter scholars suggest that the problem lies in the unfinished state of the temple: Haggai "regards the people as 'unclean' or 'defiled' because the Temple is not yet completed and because the uncleanness that abounds cannot yet be restrained."[24]

This is a good answer, but it seems there is a more specific solution to the exegetical problem.[25] It is clear from the book of Ezra that the altar of the temple was already functioning as a site for sacrifice and offerings before

---

23. *Contra* H. W. Wolff, *Haggai: A Commentary* (Minneapolis: Augsburg, 1988), 92–94, representing a long tradition of German scholarship. The same view is also found in Olmstead, *History of the Persian Empire*, 137–38.
24. Meyers and Meyers, *Haggai, Zechariah 1–8*, 57. So also Sweeney, *The Twelve Prophets*, 2:351.
25. Here I am following David L. Petersen's excellent exposition in his *Haggai and Zechariah 1–8*, OTL (Philadelphia: Westminster, 1984), 80–85.

the temple was completed. It is not that the temple is unfinished, or else the curse of nonproductivity mentioned already in Haggai 1:6 and reiterated in 2:16–17 could not be lifted until the time of temple completion, which would not take place until 515 B.C. In Haggai 2:10–19, relief from the curse is much more immediate. The solution lies in a close consideration of the end of verse 14 (author's translation): "So it is with all the work of their hands and whatever they offer there; it is unclean!"

It is not so much that the people are defiled, but that their offerings are defiled. The defilement seems to stem from the circumstance that their offerings are being offered *"there,"* that is, at the altar site of the still-ruined temple. It must be that the altar has not been properly purified. The temple site thus also remained defiled, thereby defiling all the offerings which were brought and offered "there." A word play using the assonance of the *-ah* (â) vowel plus the *m*-consonant *(mem)* in Hebrew helps bring the point home: "whatever they offer šām ("there"), it is ṭāmēʾ ("unclean").[26]

The day on which this oracle was delivered, the twenty-fourth day of Tishri (December 18, 520 B.C.), must have been an auspicious occasion in Jerusalem. So far the experience of Haggai's people has been one of hunger and deprivation. But Yahweh now says, "from this day on, I will bless you" (Hag. 2:19). What took place on that day to change their circumstances? If the solution to the problem of uncleanness suggested above is the correct one, then the twenty-fourth day of Tishri is very likely the day of the ritual solution to the problem.

That day would be marked by the proper purification of the altar, and very likely included a special ritual for the now-rising temple. Such a ceremony may well have involved a foundation deposit ceremony with the laying of a special stone, one that had been hollowed out and filled with dedicatory objects, accompanied by dedicatory inscriptions, a common ancient Near Eastern practice for public buildings, especially temples and palaces.[27]

---

26. Petersen, *Haggai and Zechariah 1–8*, 84.
27. Such a stone seems to be in mind in the parallel passage in Zechariah 4:7–10. For exposition of the passage as a foundation deposit ceremony, see David L. Petersen, *Haggai and Zechariah 1–8*, 240–44; and Meyers and Meyers, *Haggai, Zechariah 1–8*, 244–54. Both expositions are influenced by the archaeology of temple and foundation deposits discussed in R. Ellis, *Foundation Deposits in Ancient Mesopotamia* (New Haven, Conn.: Yale University Press, 1968).

Such a ceremony seems likely for this auspicious day, since it is the day when Yahweh promised to turn their fortunes from curse to blessing:

> From this day on, from this twenty-fourth day of the ninth month, give careful thought to the day when the foundation of the Lord's temple was laid. Give careful thought: Is there yet any seed left in the barn? Until now, the vine and the fig tree, the pomegranate and the olive tree have not borne fruit. From this day on I will bless you. (Hag. 2:18–19)

Haggai's fifth and final message comes as a second word from Yahweh on that auspicious day, the twenty-fourth of Tishri (December 18, 520 B.C.), thus highlighting the importance of the day even more. The word reprises the theme of cosmic shaking found in Haggai's third oracle. Only now the message adds a reference to Zerubbabel himself, Yehud's Davidic governor. The oracle is unique in the Old Testament: it is the only prophetic oracle that links traditional eschatological language to a named historical personage.[28] Thus, on the day of cosmic shaking, the same occasion as that envisaged in the temple oracle of 2:1–9,

> "On that day"—oracle of Yahweh of the heavenly armies—
> "I will take you, Zerubbabel, son of Shealtiel, my servant,
> —oracle of Yahweh—
> and I will make you like a signet ring, for I have chosen you,"
> —oracle of Yahweh of the heavenly armies.
>
> (Hag. 2:23)

In a time when the Davidic Zerubbabel was sworn as a vassal in loyalty to the Persian monarchy, when monarchy was thus denied him, God nonetheless granted extraordinary privilege to him and a crucial role in the future of redemption. Those interpreters who see Haggai's words as inciting insurrection against Persia misconstrue the eschatological language of the passage as well as the Persian-loyalist politics of Yehud's leaders and prophets. It is not that Yahweh is going to overthrow Persia and reestablish Israelite kingship in Zerubbabel's immediate future, nor is it

---

28. Meyers and Meyers, *Haggai, Zechariah 1–8*, 68.

that Zerubbabel is to take up arms to overthrow Persia and reign as the new Davidic king.[29]

After all, Zerubbabel had just been addressed in 2:21 not by his patronym, but by his official Persian title of "governor." Moreover, the entire set of oracles is dated to the second year of Darius, using a system of scribal dates expressing loyalty to the named royal figure as legitimate king. The oracle therefore does not rescind Zerubbabel's vassalage to Persia; rather, it affirms it. It is not an oracle of palace-building for a new earthly kingdom. Rather, "the rebuilding of the temple meant the reestablishment of the kingdom of God and not of man."[30]

The clue to Zerubbabel's role comes with the word *signet ring (ḥôtām)*. A signet ring has an engraved seal identifying the possessor. When stamped in clay or wax, the signet's seal authenticates that person's approval of the clay tablet or wax-sealed document. In light of Jeremiah 22:24, where King Jehioachin, Zerubbabel's grandfather, is compared to *a signet ring discarded by Yahweh,* this fifth oracle reverses the rejection of the Davidic line. The symbolism of the signet ring is both executive and promissory: Zerubbabel is Yahweh's chosen servant in whom the Davidic line is reclaimed for messianic service in the eschaton, the undisclosed time of the future when all earthly kingdoms shall fall and Yahweh's kingdom shall reign supreme.

It should come as no surprise, then, that Zerubbabel's name is listed in Matthew's and Luke's genealogies of Jesus Christ (Matt. 1:12; Luke 3:27). In Zerubbabel, God reasserted the messianic promise to his Old Testament people.

Aftermath

What happened to Haggai after he delivered his five oracles? We do not know. At the outset of his book he arose, so it seems, from the dust of Jerusalem, a man without patronym or genealogy. He preached to the

---

29. *Contra* Olmstead, *History of the Persian Empire,* 135–41, who takes Haggai as a "wild-eyed" prophet, preaching insurrection to a sober-minded and pragmatic Zerubbabel who is well-apprised of Persian might. See also L. Waterman, "The Camouflaged Purge of Three Messianic Conspirators," *JNES* 13 (1954): 73–78. More recently, Sweeney has taken Haggai's message to mean that once the Persian Empire fell, Yahweh would place Zerubbabel on the throne of world empire. See his *The Twelve Prophets,* 2:553–55.
30. Meyers and Meyers, *Haggai, Zechariah 1–8,* 82.

restoration community over the space of less than four months. Then he vanished from the historical record.

As we have seen, the book of Ezra reports that "the elders of the Jews continued to build and prosper under the preaching of Haggai the prophet and Zechariah, a descendent of Iddo. They finished building the temple . . ." (Ezra 6:14). At first glance the Ezra text seems to say that Haggai continued to preach until the second temple was completed in 515. A closer look at the text shows that the note in Ezra contains no new information about Haggai than that already known from the book that bears his name. It only affirms that Haggai preached for a time, that his preaching was accompanied by Zechariah's preaching, and that the work of both prophets contributed to the completion of the second temple. Indeed, the books of Haggai and Zechariah are in all likelihood the source of the information about the prophets now found in Ezra 6:14.

Despite this paucity of information and sources, it seems that we can say a little more about Haggai. This prospect arises from connections between his work and the work of Zechariah. Zechariah 1:1 tells us that "in the eighth month of the second year of Darius, Yahweh's word came to Zechariah son of Berechiah, the son of Iddo." Elsewhere, the book of Ezra identifies him as "Zechariah, a son [=descendent] of Iddo" (Ezra 5:1; 6:14). Thus we have two different patronym forms for Zechariah's name.

As we know from Nehemiah 12:4, Iddo was one of the chief priests who returned with Zerubbabel and with Joshua, the high priest, in the early Persian era. The difference between the two patronym forms for Zechariah suggests that Berechiah died young. Perhaps Zechariah was raised by his grandfather, Iddo. This surmise comports well with the information about Zechariah given in the lists of priests in Nehemiah 12:12–21 where the next generation of chief priests appears. There in 12:16 we find Zechariah, not Berechiah, listed as the priestly successor of Iddo.

Since the grandfather Iddo was alive and functioning as a chief priest at the time of the return of Zerubbabel and Joshua, Zechariah was a young man when he began to prophecy in the second year of Darius, in 520. Perhaps he is even the "young man" mentioned in the night-vision of Zechariah 2:4.[31]

It was Haggai who first preached about the rebuilding of the temple,

---

31. Alternatively, the "young man" is one of the angels in the vision.

starting in the sixth month of Darius's second year. Two months later, in the eighth month, Zechariah joined him in preaching the same cause. The two prophetic ministries thus overlapped for a time. These facts lead us to suppose that Haggai founded a new prophetic movement in Jerusalem, a movement in which young Zechariah was enlisted and in which he became Haggai's prophetic successor.

The very close connection between the two prophets is now displayed in the way that the book of Haggai and Zechariah 1–8 are woven together by a narrative framework marked by the series of date-formulae that generally introduce the various temple-related oracles of the two books.[32] These date formulas, all dated to the regnal years of Darius the Great, appear in Haggai (1:1, 15; 2:1, 10, 20) and Zechariah (1:1, 7; 7:1). Taken together, they serve to unite the literary remains of these two prophets, perhaps in token of the way their personal careers intersected in the streets of Jerusalem so long ago.

---

32. Meyers and Meyers, *Haggai, Zechariah 1–8,* lxii.

PART 4

LITERARY AND THEOLOGICAL ISSUES IN ISRAEL'S HISTORY

15

DID THE PATRIARCHS KNOW THE NAME OF THE LORD?

Allen P. Ross

FOR THOSE WHO ARE FAMILIAR WITH THE book of Genesis, the question of whether or not the patriarchs knew the holy name *Yahweh* might seem unnecessary. After all, the chapters are filled with the use of the name of the LORD.[1]

But biblical scholars have raised the question, and necessarily so, because of the statement in the revelation to Moses:

> (2) God said to Moses, 'I am the LORD *[Yahweh]*. (3) I appeared to Abraham, to Isaac, and to Jacob as *'El Shadday,* but by my name *Yahweh* I did not make myself known to them. (4) I also established my covenant with them to give them the land of Canaan, where they lived as aliens. (5) Moreover, I have heard the groaning of the Israelites, whom the Egyptians were enslaving, and I have remembered my covenant." (Exodus 6:2–5, author's translation)

YAHWEH IS A NEW NAME

Most biblical theologians and commentators have tried to explain this passage in the light of the use of the name *Yahweh* throughout Genesis. The most widely held view is that because Exodus clearly says that the name *Yahweh* was a new name for God, people living before Moses could not have known the name. Instead, in the religion of the patriarchs, and that of

---

1. English translations render the holy name *Yahweh* as "the LORD."

their Canaanite rivals, the common designation for God was ʾēl (or in the Hebrew records more often ʾĕlōhîm), and this term with its various epithets (ʾēl šadday, "almighty God," or ʾēl ʿelyôn, "the most high God") was well known, but the name *Yahweh* was not.

The immediate difficulty for this view is that there are a number of passages in Genesis that seem to provide evidence to the contrary. For example, Genesis 4:26 states that at the very dawn of human history people "began to call upon the name of Yahweh" (הוּחַל לִקְרֹא בְּשֵׁם יְהוָה *[hûḥal liqrōʾ bĕšēm YHWH]*). The natural way to interpret this expression is to say that it means people invoked God by the name *Yahweh*. But this interpretation is not acceptable to many because it would mean that the name *Yahweh* was known from the beginning.

For a long time the tension between passages like these was attributed to different sources for the Pentateuch, which for the most part were considered irreconcilable. Accordingly, the writer (or source), labeled "J" by scholars, preferred to use the name *Yahweh;* but the sources scholars called E, and then P, had a different point to make than J and so preferred the older, more general name *God*. But scholars who accepted this hypothesis were quick to point out that the different sections were written down long after the time of Moses, and so they all would be familiar with the holy name and would have used it in telling the stories, thus accounting for passages where both the names appear.[2] Therefore, Exodus 6, which was classified by scholars as P, reported the name *Yahweh* as a new revelation. Today the critical explanation of the compiling and editing of the source materials shows a far more complex development than this old theory proposed. And yet the division into sources remains as the working hypothesis, tensions and all, in most critical scholarship.

Among those who work with sources, the tension between them remains. G. H. Parke-Taylor, for example, in his study of the holy name, concludes that Genesis 4:26 (J) cannot be reconciled with Exodus 6:2–4 (P). But in spite of Exodus 6, he allows that Genesis 4:26 does seem to reflect a genuinely historical reminiscence of the fact that the divine name goes back to pre-Mosaic times.[3] Others have also acknowledged that there

---

2. Alan Cole, *Exodus: An Introduction and Commentary* (Downers Grove, Ill.: InterVarsity, 1973), 85.
3. G. H. Parke-Taylor, *Yahweh: The Divine Name in the Bible* (Waterloo, Ontario: Wilfred Laurier University Press, 1975), 30.

is evidence for the antiquity of the name in spite of the statement in Exodus 6. Herbert Ryle, for one, concluded on the basis of Genesis 4:26 and 12:8 that people worshiped God, using in the invocation the name *Jehovah*, for the name was the symbol of all the divine attributes.[4] He said, "it is not unreasonable to suppose that the name belongs to prehistoric antiquity," or at least that J taught that a form of the name was known in that age. And Gerhard von Rad, admitting that Genesis 4:26 cannot easily be reconciled with the "dominant primary tradition of the Old Testament" found in Exodus 6, allowed that the Yahweh cult had roots reaching further back than Moses, for the note in Genesis indicates that Yahweh worship was the primeval religion of humanity.[5] E. A. Speiser also concludes that Genesis 4:26 ascribes the use of the divine name to a very ancient practice, in contrast to the clear statement of Exodus 3:14 (E) and 6:3 (P). But he thinks there is a "plausible solution" that would justify both views based on their individual points of vantage. He explains: the worship of Yahweh was confined to a small body of searchers under the aegis of the patriarchs, and this movement was recorded by J; but when Moses had to fashion the religion for the nation and tie it to the faith of the ancestors, a personal revelation of Yahweh to him was necessary, and it is that which E and P celebrate.[6] But this does not entirely harmonize the passages.

Although there have been many similar attempts to resolve the tension, the prevailing view has been that the dominant tradition of the Old Testament is that the name *Yahweh* was a new revelation at the time of Moses, and that passages in Genesis have to be explained in that light. Brevard Childs says that in Exodus 6 Yahweh was revealing himself to Moses as the same God who had made the promises to the Fathers as *El Shadday* (the use of *El Shadday* making the immediate connection to Genesis 17). But, he explains, the revelation to Moses sharply contrasts with the revelation to the fathers, because a new element now entered history, the name *Yahweh*.[7]

Claus Westermann tried to resolve the tension by directing the question away from the knowledge of the meaning of the name. For him J could have no contradiction between Genesis 4:26 and what was in Exodus 3 and 6. The cult had to begin in the primeval period, but the beginning of Yahweh

---

4. Herbert E. Ryle, *The Book of Genesis* (Cambridge: Harvard University Press, 1914), 83.
5. Gerhard von Rad, *Genesis: A Commentary*, trans. John H. Marks (Philadelphia: Westminster, 1961), 109.
6. E. A. Speiser, *Genesis* (Garden City, N.J.: Doubleday, 1978), 37–38.
7. Brevard S. Childs, *The Book of Exodus* (Philadelphia: Westminster, 1974), 115.

worship for the people of Israel was clearly in Egypt. Therefore he reasoned that in writing Genesis 4:26, J could not have meant that a Yahweh cult began in antiquity, but simply that worship belonged to all people and to every epoch. So when J wanted to say that the worship of the one true creator began, he could only say that people "began to call on the name of Yahweh."[8] By this explanation, the expression is interpreted as a general or formulaic description of true worship.

The Meaning of *Yahweh* Revealed in Exodus Events

On the other hand, unconvinced that the division into sources provides a satisfactory explanation of the texts, a good number of traditional scholars have sought to harmonize the texts by offering a slightly different reading of the words given to Moses in Exodus 6. Although there are a number of variations in the explanations, in general they all conclude that the name was known by the patriarchs, but with Moses it was to have a new significance, meaning that the people would now come to know what the name *Yahweh* truly meant.

This approach is not new. Targum Pseudo-Jonathan rendered the passage this way: "I revealed myself to Abraham, Isaac, and Jacob as El Shadday, but with the face of my Shekainah I did not make myself known to them."[9] The use of "face" indicates a higher level of revelation that now came through Moses. In other words, they knew the word *Yahweh*, but did not experience the glory of the Shekainah associated with it.[10] Rashi made a similar distinction by connecting the Mosaic revelation to the fulfillment of the promises, meaning that Abraham received the covenant promises, but did not see the fulfillment of them, and not seeing that he did not know the full meaning of the divine revelation of Yahweh.[11] This explanation has been refined by other scholars more recently, including Alec Motyer[12] and Walter Kaiser.[13] Kaiser, for example, asserts that it was the

---

8. Claus Westermann, *Genesis 1–11*, trans. John J. Scullion (Minneapolis: Augsburg, 1984), 339.
9. See Israel Drazin, *Targum Onkelos to Exodus* (New York: KTAV, 1990), 81 n. 3.
10. G. J. Wenham, "The Religion of the Patriarchs," in *Essays in the Patriarchal Narratives*, ed. A. R. Millard and D. J. Wiseman (Leicester: Inter-Varsity, 1980), 178.
11. M. Rosenbaum and A. M. Silbermann, eds., *The Pentateuch with the Commentary of Rashi: Exodus* (Jerusalem: Silbermann, 1972), 24.
12. J. A. Motyer, *The Revelation of the Divine Name* (London: Tyndale Press, 1959), 11–17.
13. Walter C. Kaiser Jr., *Exodus*, EBC, 2:339–43.

character or capacity of the name that was not known in pre-Mosaic times, not the bare knowledge of the name.[14] Likewise, Roland de Vaux concludes that the name Yahweh was a pre-Israelite name known in various circles, and that in the revelation in the book of Exodus a new understanding of the name was given.[15] Several Jewish scholars such as M. H. Segal,[16] U. Cassuto,[17] B. Jacob,[18] and N. Leibowitz[19] have also explained that what was revealed to Moses was the full meaning or significance of the name, and not simply that the name was unheard of prior to Exodus 6.

Then other scholars translate Exodus 6:3 differently. Rather than rendering it "I did not make myself known to them" (לֹא נוֹדַעְתִּי לָהֶם *[lōʾ nôdaʿtî lāhem]*), some have interpreted the negative *lōʾ* as an orthographic error for an original *lû*, "indeed,"[20] or even translated the line as an implied question without the interrogative particle: "Did I not let myself be known to them by my own name Yahweh?"[21] These translations are certainly possible, but they lack compelling supportive evidence.

THE NAME IS THE INTERPRETATION OF LATER WRITERS

Finally, a more recent and rather attractive argument has been developed in which the name *Yahweh* in Genesis is explained as a literary convention. In other words, the use of the name in Genesis reflects the view of the writer and should not be taken to mean that the subjects in the stories knew the holy name. Gordon Wenham, accepting the view that in Exodus 6 the name *Yahweh* was revealed for the first time, analyzes the data from

---

14. Ibid., 342.
15. Roland de Vaux, "The Revelation of the Divine Name YHWH," in *Proclamation and Presence: Old Testament Essays in Honour of Gwynne Henton Davies,* ed. John I. Durham and J. R. Porter (London: SCM, 1970), 56.
16. M. H. Segal, *The Pentateuch, Its Composition and Its Authorship and Other Biblical Studies* (Jerusalem: Magnes, 1967), 4–8.
17. Umberto Cassuto, *A Commentary on the Book of Exodus,* trans. Israel Abrahams (Jerusalem: Magnes, 1967), 77–79.
18. Benno Jacob, *The Second Book of the Bible: Exodus,* trans. Walter Jacob (New York: KTAV, 1992), 142–56.
19. N. Leibowitz, *Studies in Shemot: Exodus* (Jerusalem: World Zionist Organization, 1976), 132–40.
20. W. J. Martin, *Stylistic Criteria and the Analysis of the Pentateuch* (London: Tyndale, 1955), 17; and F. I. Andersen, *The Sentence in Biblical Hebrew* (The Hague: Mouton, 1974), 102.
21. In addition to Martin, see L. A. Herrboth, "Exodus 6:3b: Was God Known to the Patriarchs as Jehovah?" *Concordia Theological Monthly* 4 (1931): 345–49; F. C. Smith, "Observations on the Use of the Names and Titles of God in Genesis," *Evangelical Quarterly* 40 (1968): 103–9; and G. R. Driver, "Affirmation by Exclamatory Negation," *JANES* 5 (1973): 109. See also the footnote in the NIV.

the book of Genesis and concludes that none of the uses of *Yahweh* in the text imply that the name *Yahweh* was actually known before Moses.[22] All of the uses of the name, he argues, can be explained as the interpretation of the writer or writers. In other words, when the text of Genesis 4:26 says that people began to call on the name of *Yahweh,* it means that the writer was telling us that the God they worshiped was in fact Yahweh, and not that they were worshiping him with the name *Yahweh.*

Moberly argues this case more thoroughly.[23] Challenging the "consistent minority report"[24] that attempts to reinterpret Exodus 6, he sets out to prove that the ancient traditions of the pre-Yahwistic era were being told by a Mosaic Yahwist, and so whenever the name *Yahweh* appears in the text it was the narrator's wording and therefore cannot be used as evidence that the name was known in antiquity. But Moberly, following Westermann, goes to great lengths to show that Exodus 6 had a different purpose than inquiries into historical critical questions have recognized. To him, offering new explanations of the name to harmonize Exodus with Genesis misses the point, for Exodus 6 was a later theological treatise and requires a different approach. In Genesis we have the universalist view, he explains, which presents Yahweh as the one true God that the ancients actually were worshiping; but in Exodus we have a particularist view that only to Moses and Israel did God reveal himself as Yahweh.

If this theory of the name's use in Genesis can be substantiated, it would go a long way toward solving this difficulty in a systematic way. But the question that must be asked is whether or not all the uses of the name in Genesis can be so easily explained. That is, are there any uses in Genesis that attest to a knowledge of the name *Yahweh* after all? A view like this requires a thorough investigation of the critical passages and their interpretation.

The study of the relevant passages is the immediate concern. But it cannot be forgotten that another consideration is the archaeological evidence that the name may have been ancient. Giovanni Pettinato believes that the element *Yah (-ia)* is present in a number of names from Ebla, centuries

---

22. Wenham, "The Religion of the Patriarchs," 157–88. The survey is necessarily selective, but some critical passages were not discussed that perhaps should have been.
23. R. W. L. Moberly, *The Old Testament of the Old Testament: Patriarchal Narratives and Mosaic Yahwism* (Minneapolis: Fortress, 1992), 53–78, in particular.
24. Ibid., 63.

before the patriarchs.[25] Kitchen allows that this element may be an abbreviation for the name Yahweh: "If the form *Yaw* was actually an early form of YHWH, then of course the common misconception about Exodus 6:3, that the name YHWH was unknown before Moses, would be eliminated at a stroke."[26] But he cautions that since the use of *-ia* in ancient names could have other interpretations, more evidence is needed.[27]

If the divine element *Yah* did exist in ancient names, it does not seem to have been used with patriarchal names in the pre-Mosaic period. However, it may have existed in biblical names prior to Moses! The name (יוֹכֶבֶד [*yôkebed*]) is the name of Moses' own mother (Exod. 6:20; Num. 26:59). On the etymology of this name, J. F. Ross writes that, "The most natural suggestion would be that it signifies 'Yahweh is glory'; this would mean, however, that the name *Yahweh* was known prior to the time of Moses. Thus the Priestly writer probably did not understand it in this sense."[28] But if this presupposition proves false, then this "natural" explanation of the name need not be discarded.

---

25. Giovanni Pettinato, *The Archives of Ebla* (Garden City, N.J.: Doubleday, 1981), 248–49; and idem, "Ebla and the Bible: Observations of the New Epigrapher's Analysis," *BAR* 6, no. 6 (November–December 1980): 39. Eugene H. Merrill also surveys the data in some detail, and adds further data that the divine element *Yah* is attested as early as the archives of Mari (ca. 1750–1700 B.C.) and even Fara (ca. 2600 B.C.). "Ebla and Biblical Historical Inerrancy," *BSac* 140 (October–December 1983): 313–14; cf. Mitchell Dahood, "The God Yå at Ebla?" *JBL* 100 (1981): 607 n. 1. Not all scholars agree with this conclusion, however. Alfonso Archi and others have argued against this conclusion in several publications: A. Archi, "The Epigraphic Evidence from Ebla and the Old Testament," *Bib* 60 (1979): 556–66; idem, "Ebla and Eblaite," in *Eblaitica: Essays on the Ebla Archives and Eblaite Language*, ed. C. H. Gordon, G. A. Rendsburg, and N. H. Winter (Winona Lake, Ind.: Eisenbrauns, 1987), 1:10–11; idem, "Further Concerning Ebla and the Bible," *BA* 44 (1988): 145–44; H. P. Müller, "Der Jahwename und seine Deutung, Ex 3:14 im Licht der Textpublikationen aus Ebla," *Bib* 62 (1981): 322–23; idem, "Eblaitische Konjugation in Kontexten und Personennamen: Bemerkungen zur Lautlehre, Morphologie und Morphosyntax," in *Eblaite Personal Names and Semitic Name-giving*, Archivi reali di Ebla, Studi 1 (Rome: Missione Archeologica Italiana in Siria, 1988), 71–87; and Lorenzo Viganò, "Literary Sources for the History of Palestine and Syria: The Ebla Tablets," *BA* 47 (1984): 12. Scholars who oppose the identification of the *Yah (-ia)* element found in certain Ebla texts with the divine name *Yahweh* contend that this element serves as a hypocoristicon (a short form for the name God *[-Il]*, found in the same tablet (Archi, "Further Concerning Ebla and the Bible," 146). Scholars who make a connection between the *-ia* element in various Ebla texts point to the similar way that a form of the "to be" verb serves as a conceptual motif underlying a divine name. Müller, "Der Jahwename und seine Deutung, Ex 3:14 im Licht der Textpublikationen aus Ebla," 322–23; cf. Tryggve N. D. Mettinger, *In Search of God: The Meaning and Message of the Everlasting Names*, trans. F. Cryer (Philadelphia: Fortress, 1988), 38–39.

26. K. A. Kitchen, *The Bible in Its World* (Downers Grove, Ill.: InterVarsity, 1977), 47.

27. Ibid. Kitchen suggests that it is more prudent to regard the *-ia* element as an abbreviation rather than the occurrence of the name *Yah* in Ebla texts until more information becomes available.

28. J. F. Ross, "Jochebed," in *Interpreter's Dictionary of the Bible,* ed. G. A. Buttrick et al. (Nashville: Abingdon, 1962), 2:925.

The Name *Yahweh* in Genesis

It is not possible here to look at all the passages in Genesis where the name occurs. Therefore, the following survey will select passages from three categories of usage.

Passages Where *Yahweh* Is Used as Part of the Narrative Report

It is easy to see how most of the occurrences of the name *Yahweh* in Genesis could be attributed to the narrator or writer and not the subjects in the narratives. The clearest example is the Joseph story. In its chapters the holy name is used in the framing paragraphs and explanatory clauses, but not in the words of Joseph or the other people. In Genesis 39, for instance, we are told by the narrator at the outset that Yahweh was with Joseph (v. 2) and that Yahweh blessed him (v. 5); and then this use of the name is repeated at the end of the chapter (vv. 21, 23). But the subjects in the story use the designation *God*. One could easily conclude that the people did not know the name, and that the writer was telling the story with his "Mosaic Yahwism" to make sure that the reader knew that Yahweh was this God at work through Joseph.

Likewise, beginning with Genesis 2:4 the name *Yahweh* is added to the title *God* to form *Yahweh God* for the subsequent passages. The section is clearly designed to say that the sovereign God of creation (Gen. 1) is Yahweh, the God of Israel. In Genesis 3 the serpent and Eve use only the word *God*.[29] In Genesis 4, however, the pattern is broken because Eve uses the name *Yahweh* in her naming of her son. Genesis 4:1, therefore, would require further explanation, namely that the writer has edited her words. But that will be considered in the next section.

The assumption that goes with this theory is that the "writer," whether a Moses or a Mosaic Yahwist, was reporting the traditions with this new revelation of the name in mind. The theory is certainly possible. And yet, would it not also be possible, at least in theory, to say that the narratives had been shaped to a certain extent prior to the time of Moses, perhaps in the family records preserved by Joseph. If that were the case, then the use of the name *Yahweh* would have been the work of pre-Mosaic narrators in the

---

29. But could this also be explained thematically, that the serpent would not use the covenant name Yahweh, and in the temptation manages to get the woman to refer to God as he does?

family of Israel, people who knew the name and used it carefully in the traditions.

Passages Where the Name *Yahweh* Is Part of the Speeches

But we now must consider cases like the one with Eve where the name occurs in the words of the subjects themselves and not merely in the narrative reports. Those who argue that the holy name was not known by the patriarchs say that the writer has replaced the speakers' designation of God with the name *Yahweh* when recording the traditions for the people of Israel. This literary license would find support in other places in the Bible, including the Gospels, where the writers may have put the speeches or dialogues in their own words. Whether they recorded statements carefully and changed only a particular word is a related consideration.

In Genesis, then, we first must consider passages where the LORD himself speaks. According to Genesis 15:7 he said, "I am Yahweh (אֲנִי יְהוָה [*pʰanî YHWH*]) who brought you out from Ur of the Chaldees." The self-revelation with the words "I am Yahweh" occurs so frequently in the Pentateuch that it has been called a stock phrase, that its presence is merely stylistic. Of course, it is possible that the narrator substituted the word for *God* in the text with the holy name *Yahweh* in order to anticipate the wording of the revelation at Sinai (Exod. 20:2). But that change alone might be enough to make some conservative uncomfortable, especially in such an important passage as this. So if the suggestion were broadened to say that the whole line was supplied by the narrator to link the call of Abraham with the call of Israel, then the proposal would certainly be opposed. It is one thing to say God said this to Abram, essentially; but it would be another thing altogether to say the statement was simply narrative art. Where should the line be drawn?

Another example we may consider is in Genesis 18:14, in the incident where Sarah laughs in her heart. The text records the words of Yahweh, saying, "Is anything too hard for Yahweh?" (הֲיִפָּלֵא מֵיְהוָה דָּבָר *[hʰayippāleʔ mê-YHWH dābār]*). Wenham discounts the use of the divine name as incidental to the thrust of the question.[30] But that dismissal is too easy. It would be better said that the introduction of the name by the writer was to make a

---

30. Wenham, "The Religion of the Patriarchs," 182.

theological interpretation for Israel. Likewise, in verse 19 Yahweh uses the holy name in his soliloquy about telling Abraham what is about to happen. Here too the passage is explained by Wenham as a divine soliloquy that Abraham would not have heard. The point of the text, at the least in its final form, is that it was Yahweh who was revealing to Abraham his plan for Sodom because there was a covenant obligation involved. And a covenant name would have been appropriate to such a text.

Then we have to consider passages where the patriarchs used the name. Genesis 15:2 is a somewhat complicated case. Abram responded to the revelation of the word of Yahweh by saying, "O Lord Yahweh" (אֲדֹנָי יֱהוִה [*ʾadōnāy YHWH]*). When *ʾadōnāy* was read in place of the holy name, a problem arose in passages like this. Here, because *ʾadōnāy* was in the text already, the holy name had to be pointed with the vowels for "God," to avoid reading *ʾadōnāy ʾadōnāy*. One very legitimate conclusion would be that Abram said, "[my] Lord Yahweh." But in this place too the theory is that the writer added (or changed) the name to clarify who this Lord was. In 14:22 we have the words of Abram's oath in which he raised his hand and swore "to Yahweh, the Most High God" (אֵל־יְהוָה אֵל עֶלְיוֹן [*ʾēl YHWH ʾēl ʿelyôn]*). Because Melchizedek had only referred to "the Most High God," we are told that the writer added the holy name to Abram's oath to clarify who the Most High God was. But why would that be added to Abram's speech alone unless it was meant to indicate that Abram knew the Most High God was Yahweh? At any rate, because the name is not found in all the versions of this verse, the reading is in question and should be set aside in this discussion.

Another example is the story of Hagar (Gen. 16:1–16). The angel of Yahweh told Hagar to name the child Ishmael ("God hears"), saying, "for Yahweh has heard of your misery" (v. 11). Then, in verse 16 Hagar gave a name to Yahweh who spoke to her: "the God who sees me." On the one hand, it may look as though an editor has inserted the holy name for clarity, but on the other hand, the story reads easily and naturally with the angel identifying Yahweh as the God who heard.

The same can be said of the account of Jacob's dream and the naming of Bethel in Genesis 28. In verse 16 Jacob said, "Surely Yahweh is in this place and I knew it not." The theory is that the editor supplied the name Yahweh to Jacob's speech to clarify who the God of Bethel was. But it is also possible that Jacob named the place Bethel to affirm that Yahweh was God.

So in these kinds of passages the presence of the divine name could be the writer's addition or substitution. But there is no compelling reason why it could not have been part of the original tradition—if the name was known before Moses.

Passages That Say That People Used the Name *Yahweh*

There are a couple of places where the evidence in Genesis is harder to set aside, and these are the critical passages. The first to consider is in the commemorative naming in Genesis 22, the story of the sacrificing of Isaac. At the end of the account (v. 14) when God provided a ram for the sacrifice, Abraham called the place, "Yahweh will provide" (יְהוָה יִרְאֶה *[YHWH Yirʾeh]*). In the narrative the motive for the naming used the word *God* ("God will provide" in v. 8), indicating to some that the name of the place originally might have been *ʾelōhîm Yirʾeh,* but that it was changed by the Mosaic Yahwist to *YHWH Yirʾeh.* But this is a commemorative naming; it is far more likely that a story would be worded to explain the name than that the name would be changed. But in this case the title God is left in the dialogue and Yahweh is part of the name.

Here we must consider for a moment the question of the nature of Scripture. The text says that Abraham named the place *YHWH Yirʾeh* (Gen. 22:14). That is either a true statement or it is not. If Abraham did not name it that, but some editor has inserted the name *Yahweh* to replace the word *God,* then we have to harmonize that kind of editing with our theological understanding of narrative reports in the text. Apart from the fact that there is no evidence that an editor did this, the interpretation calls into question the reliability of not only this statement but others in the text that say that people used the name. And this has been the age-old debate for the Pentateuch, namely, what actually was the original tradition as opposed to what later writers introduced into the text, and, how would one determine such things? In this case, if Abraham actually called the place *YHWH Yirʾeh,* as the text says, then he clearly knew the name.

While it still may be argued here that the editor simply changed the name of the place, as unlikely as that might be, the case in Genesis 4:26 introduces a greater problem for the theory. The text reports that "At that time men began to call on the name of Yahweh." As mentioned earlier in this essay, for this verse not to contradict the interpretation of Exodus 6:3

that the name Yahweh was not known before Moses, it has to be given a very general interpretation about the beginnings of organized worship in antiquity.[31] And that theory is essentially that the writer was explaining whom in fact they worshiped, and to do that he used a set expression about calling on the name of Yahweh. The verse, therefore, is said to mean only that people practiced the cult.

But such a general interpretation does not do justice to the words in the text. The expression states clearly that something specific was taking place, i.e., that the name Yahweh was being proclaimed or invoked. BDB says that the expression means "to use the name of *Yahweh* in worship."[32] The verb "called" (קָרָא *[qārāʾ]*) would indicate that the name was called or proclaimed, that is, the name was used in public worship.[33] The fact that the expression is used elsewhere in Scripture does not prove it was a general, formulaic expression; it proves that what was going on in antiquity was also going on elsewhere, later.

Rather than give the wording a general interpretation, we need to look at how the expression is used in the Pentateuch. The same expression occurs in Genesis 12:8, although with a different form of the verb, where we are told that Abram built an altar to Yahweh and there he "called on the name of Yahweh" (וַיִּקְרָא בְּשֵׁם יְהוָה *[wayyiqrāʾ bešēm YHWH]*). And this precise expression is used again in the narratives, but most significantly in Exodus 34:5–7. There we have the record of Yahweh's coming down to Sinai and making proclamation of Yahweh by name to Moses. The text reads:

> (5) Then Yahweh came down in the cloud and stood there with him and proclaimed the name of Yahweh (וַיִּקְרָא בְּשֵׁם יְהוָה *[wayyiqrāʾ bešēm YHWH]*).[34] (6) And he passed in front of Moses, and pro-

---

31. Moberly, *The Old Testament of the Old Testament,* 68.
32. BDB, s.v. "שֵׁם."
33. Moberly (*The Old Testament of the Old Testament,* 68) observes that Genesis 4 reports that Cain and Abel brought gifts to Yahweh. He argues that if the name "Yahweh" was known to them, why would there then be a beginning of the use of the name? But Genesis 4:26 would be saying that worship that included the invocation or proclamation of the name was new.
34. Although some commentators take the view that it was Moses who proclaimed the name of Yahweh, it is more likely that "he" refers to Yahweh who came down. Moses was prostrate before Yahweh receiving the revelation.

claimed (וַיִּקְרָא [*wayyiqrāʾ*]), 'Yahweh, Yahweh, the compassionate and gracious God, slow to anger, abounding in loyal love and faithfulness, (7) maintaining love to thousands, and forgiving wickedness, rebellion and sin. Yet he does not leave the guilty unpunished; he visits the children and their children for the sin of the fathers to the third and fourth generation.'" (author's translation)

This is the exact same expression found in Genesis 12:8, and essentially the same as that in 4:26. And its meaning is clear because the content of the proclamation is recorded: it is a proclamation of the attributes and actions of God, in short, it is a proclamation of the "Name."[35] To "make proclamation of Yahweh by name," then, means to declare the character of Yahweh to others. There is no reason to doubt that this exact meaning found in Exodus 34 is the intended meaning in Genesis.

The substance of the proclamation in Exodus 34 is found in eight other passages as a confession of the faith: Psalms 86:15; 103:8; 145:8; Numbers 14:18; Joel 2:13; Nahum 1:3; Nehemiah 9:17; and Jonah 4:2.[36] The critical thinking is that the later confession formula has been inserted into the Exodus story. Moberly, however, argues for the reverse, that Exodus 34:6–7 is so obviously a development of its context one must assume a narrative origin and a borrowing of it then for the later cultic use.[37] As Durham says, in this context when Yahweh proclaimed the meaning of his name, that is, his true nature, he made it clear how bad their rebellion was and what the next steps were to renew commitment.[38]

The clear content of the proclamation in this passage in Exodus strongly indicates that in Genesis the faithful proclaimed the name and nature of God at the altar in a similar way. Thus, when Genesis 12 says that Abram made an altar to Yahweh, and then proclaimed the name of Yahweh, it makes more sense to say that he knew and used the name of Yahweh and understood his nature. This interpretation does justice to the precise expression based on its use in the Pentateuch.

---

35. Cassuto explains that in proclaiming the name, he did this in accordance with the literary method of first making a general statement and subsequently giving the details, the attributes. *A Commentary on the Book of Exodus,* 439.
36. See R. C. Denton, "The Literary Affinities of Exodus xxxiv 6f," *VT* 13 (1963): 34–51.
37. R. W. L. Moberly, *At the Mountain of God* (Sheffield: JSOT, 1983) 128–31; see also John Durham, *Exodus* (Waco: Word, 1987), 453–54.
38. Moberly, *At the Mountain of God,* 128–31; Durham, *Exodus,* 454.

The Meaning of אֶהְיֶה

Although the theory that the use of the name in Genesis was the work of the writer is plausible, it is not convincing for some of the passages that indicate that the name was used. Therefore, the interpretation of Exodus 3 and 6 demands reconsideration.

There are a few general observations to be made when studying Exodus 3 and 6. First, when God appeared to Moses, Moses' concern was what he was going to tell the people when they asked, "What is his name?" But the fact is that God did not answer that question directly—he did not give a name. Rather, he explained the name[39] in anticipation of what lay ahead: "I am that I am" (אֶהְיֶה אֲשֶׁר אֶהְיֶה, *ʾehyeh ʾᵃšer ʾehyeh*). He said to tell Israel "I AM has sent me to you" (Exod. 3:13–14). The detailed analysis of this explanation must be left for another discussion, but it is sufficient to observe here that if God had revealed a new name *Yahweh* here, the answer to Moses would have been different.

Secondly, it would not do to have a new name revealed on this occasion anyway, given the fact that Moses had to convince the Israelites that the God of their Fathers had called him to deliver them. A new name would be suspect. But a name that was known, although not fully appreciated, would be convincing. The Israelites and their ancestors would not have worshiped a no-name God; the name of their God was *Yahweh*.[40] But they like their ancestors were living with the promises of the covenant, and not their fulfillment.

And third, God subsequently explained to Moses that he appeared *"as* El Shadday" (the preposition being a *bêt* of essence).[41] He did not say that that was his name, as in "I am El Shadday." The designation *El Shadday* appears in Genesis in connection with speeches of promise (Gen. 17:1; 28:3; 35:11, 47; 48:3; 49:25).[42] Now the Lord was going to reveal himself as

---

39. Segal, *The Pentateuch*, 4. The use of מָה (*mâh*) can carry the sense of "what is the meaning of" (see Exod. 12:26 and 13:14; Deut. 6:20).
40. Moberly thinks that if a new meaning was given here that that would mean that the ancestors had a meaningless name (*The Old Testament of the Old Testament*, 65). But that is not the case. A new significance for the name provided in the word play on the name does not mean the name had no meaning beforehand.
41. The *bêt* of essence (*bêth essentiae*) or *bêt* of identity marks the capacity in which an actor behaves and is to be translated "as, serving as, in the capacity of." See Bruce K. Waltke and M. O'Connor, *Introduction to Biblical Hebrew Syntax* (Winona Lake, Ind.: Eisenbrauns, 1990), 198.
42. Benno Jacob goes to great length to show that the text says he "appeared" as El Shadday, but does not say that that was his name. *The Second Book of the Bible: Exodus*, 146.

Yahweh because he was about to fulfill the promises. That is why in Exodus 6:4 he reminds Moses that he established his covenant with his people. Terence Fretheim suggests that he was saying, "I am Yahweh, even though I have not yet allowed myself to be experienced by this attribute, by what this name means, but that would now occur."[43]

The key to the interpretation of Exodus 6:3 is the verb translated "to know." The verb may be translated "I was not known" or "I did not let myself be known," or the like. But there are different levels of meaning for the verb "to know."[44] For example, in Isaiah 52:6 God says, "My people shall know my name." They already knew the name. But, they were awaiting a deliverance from exile and a fulfillment of the promise that they would return to the land. When that occurred, then they would know his name—his attributes—by experience.

It is the same with the Israelites in Egypt. Benno Jacob explains in some detail what is intended in this passage is that the people of Israel would now be allowed to experience the attribute of Yahweh through the great liberation.[45] When the people cried out to their God for deliverance, he provided the deliverer for them. But that deliverer, concerned that the people would not think their God had sent him, was given an explanation of the significance of the name that anticipated what God was about to do. The text then explains that this Yahweh was going to fulfill the promises that he had made to the ancestors by delivering them from Egypt and bringing them to the land he had promised to Abraham, Isaac, and Jacob. But even here, after he revealed himself to Moses, he said, "Then you will know that I am Yahweh your God" (Exod. 6:7). To know the name in conjunction with the fulfillment of the promises is to experience the fullness of that name, or to realize the divine attributes. The text is not giving a new meaning to the actual name, and it is not adding new attributes to the list. Rather, it

---

43. Terence E. Fretheim, *Exodus* (Louisville: John Knox, 1991), 147. We could say that the disciples knew the name "Jesus" and probably knew it had a meaning like "salvation," but after the crucifixion and resurrection they *knew* the name in a very different way.

44. Kikawada offers an analogy. *Elohim* and *Yahweh* were different for ancient Hebrews much as *God* and *Trinity* would have been for medieval Christians. Thomas Aquinas could use pagan philosophy to prove, or try to prove, many things about God. The Trinity, in contrast, was something revealed only to Christians, and ultimately only a mystery even to them. There is the God of the *Summa Contra Gentiles* and the Trinity of the *Summa Theologica*. Isaac M. Kikawada and Arthur Quinn, *Before Abraham Was: The Unity of Genesis 1–11* (Nashville: Abingdon, 1985), 18.

45. Jacob, *The Second Book of the Bible: Exodus,* 145–56.

is expressly linking the name with the fulfillment of the covenant promises. When Israel would experience the fulfillment of the promises, then they would truly know Yahweh.

M. H. Segal summarizes the revelation in this way:

> I was manifested to the patriarchs as El Shadday (making promises to them) but by my name Yahweh I was not made known to them (my promises were not fulfilled in their lifetime). Say I am Yahweh, who possesses the power and the faithfulness to perform my covenant. Then you will know that I am Yahweh your God who brings salvation.[46]

In this way the verse is interpreted more appropriately in its context, and not wrenched from it to support a critical approach to the Pentateuch.

Thus, we can see that there is no reason to conclude from Exodus 6:3 that the name *Yahweh* was unheard of before Moses' day. The wording of the explanation of the name to Moses and the dramatic movement of God to fulfill the covenant promises indicate that the full meaning of the holy name would now be realized by the covenant people.

Conclusion

For any given difficulty in the Bible there are numerous approaches that have been taken by scholars; but for those who believe in divine revelation as truth, then apparent difficulties cannot be left as irreconcilable views of different writers. They must be studied carefully to see how they may be harmonized. In this case, because the straightforward reading of Exodus 6 seems to indicate that the name *Yahweh* was not known before Moses, the use of that name in Genesis has to be accounted for.

The view that this usage was a literary convention, the wording of the writer of the biblical narratives and not the subjects themselves, would resolve the tension if it could be sustained. However, in passages where the name forms part of the dialogue, or is used in naming narratives, or is part of a report that people used the name in worship, the view is not very convincing, and may introduce other tensions about the nature of Scripture.

---

46. Segal, *The Pentateuch*, 7. Jacob addresses this question of why the critical view has been so entrenched in scholarly thinking. *The Second Book of the Bible: Exodus,* 154–55.

It still seems more likely that the solution to the difficulty is in the understanding of the verb meaning "to know" in the Exodus passage, rather than in reinterpreting a number of passages in Genesis to deny what seems so obvious, that they knew and used the name *Yahweh*. The explanation of how the name was used in Genesis and Exodus seems more tightly connected to the contents and themes of the individual passages, but that is another study.

16

THE CHALLENGE OF FAITH'S FINAL STEP

Israel's Journey Toward Victory in Numbers 33

R. Dennis Cole

AS THE NATION OF ISRAEL WAS POISED ON the doorstep of the final realization of the Lord's promise of a land inheritance, the experience of her wilderness journeys demanded that she consider carefully her walk of faith before she embarked on the last step of that journey. The nation needed to recall the dramatic victories that Yahweh her God had wrought for her against numerous enemies, from the Egyptians to the Amorites. The people were to remember the provisions of water and food during their wilderness experience as God demonstrated his faithfulness on numerous occasions. They also were wont to recall the struggles that resulted in the loss of a generation in the wilderness, so that they might not repeat the pattern of rebellion and judgment as they prepared to enter the Promised Land.

Within the literary and theological structure of the book of Numbers, I have previously delineated that chapter 33 stands in the center of the seventh and final cycle of the book (chaps. 31–36), which focuses on matters of "Preparation for War and Entry into the Promised Land."[1] Following the presentation of the Midianite campaign of chapter 31, which serves as a model for the conquest motif in the book of Joshua, the narrator outlines the potential rebellion of two and one-half tribes of Israel in their desire for land east of the Jordan River. The narrative tension is resolved when the

---

1. R. Dennis Cole, *Numbers,* in NAC (Nashville: Broadman & Holman, 2000), 50–51, 518.

Transjordan tribes commit themselves to the military campaign. Chapter 33 then stands conspicuously between (1) the granting of tribal inheritance in Transjordan for the people of Reuben, Gad, and half of Manasseh and (2) the defining of the boundaries of the Promised Land, which will be divided among the other nine and one-half tribes. Remarkable in the border delineations of 34:1–12 is the fact that the Transjordan territories are not included within the circumscribed inheritance. The inclusive commentaries on the itinerary in 33:3–4 and 33:50–56 serve to remind the people of their God's victory over the Egyptians in the Exodus and to challenge them to possess the land that he had given to them as an inheritance. Faithful obedience to God would be the key to their success; rebellion could result in disastrous consequences.

Literary Genre

The toponymic list of the stages of Israel's journeys and encampments from Ramses in Egypt to the plains of Moab stands in the tradition the of the itineraries of ancient kings in their travels and conquests across the ancient Near East. On the basis of his form-critical analysis, G. W. Coats demonstrates that the list in Numbers 33 is a genuine ancient Near Eastern itinerary.[2] D. Redford and J. Hoffmeier further confirm this identity by comparative analysis with the Late Bronze Age itineraries of Thutmose III from Karnak, which were both military and economic expeditions that included topographical and geographical features as well as place names.[3]

Source-Critical Division

Source-critical scholars have traditionally assigned the final composition of Numbers 33 to the postexilic Priestly source, who supposedly utilized traditions from the earlier Yahwistic, Elohistic, and Deuteronomistic

---

2. G. W. Coats, "The Wilderness Itinerary," *CBQ* 34 (1972): 135–52. See also G. I. Davies, *The Way of the Wilderness: A Geographical Analysis of the Wilderness Itineraries in the Old Testament*, SOTS Monograph Series 5 (Cambridge: Cambridge University Press, 1979); idem, "The Wilderness Itineraries: A Comparative Approach," *TynBul* 25 (1974): 46–81; and idem, "The Wilderness Itineraries and the Composition of the Pentateuch, *VT* 33 (1983): 1–13.
3. Cf. D. Redford, "A Bronze Age Itinerary in Transjordan (Nos. 89–101 of Thutmose III's List of Asiatic Toponyms)," *JSSEA* 9 (1982): 55–74; and J. Hoffmeier, *Israel in Egypt: The Evidence for the Authenticity of the Exodus Tradition* (New York: Oxford University Press, 1997), 176–98.

sources. The interpretation of Numbers 33 and its composition has varied widely, even among source-critical and literary scholars. J. de Vaulx, as an example of a source-critical approach, subdivides the itinerary into the following source-based divisions:[4]

Table 16.1

Verses	Source	Verses	Source
1–4	JE or Editorial Gloss	30–33	Deuteronomist
5–8	Priestly	34–35	Separate Document
8–9	Yahwist / Gloss	36–37	Priestly
10–11	Priestly	38–40	Editorial Gloss
12–14	E,P,R or Separate Document	41–42	Separate Document
15–17	Priestly	43–44	Priestly
17–18	JE—Yahwist/Elohist	45–49	Conflation of Ps
18–30	Separate Document	50–51a	Priestly

However, such positing of divisions between groups of verses, such as between verses 10–11 and verses 12–14, or between verses 18–30 and verses 30–33, seems extremely arbitrary when viewed from the context of literary structure, and it is based on very hypothetical source theory. These verses are structured exactly alike, and divisions by source seem to be based solely on the mention of names in Exodus (some Yahwist, but primarily Priestly). A. Dillmann counters this type of approach with the theory that Numbers 33 represents a master list for the other itinerary portions in the various narratives rather than a conflation of sources.[5] Y. Aharoni categorizes the latter portion of the Numbers 33 itinerary as a composition from ancient historical sources, "which describes a direct line from Kadesh-barnea through the Arabah, Edom and Moab to the 'plains of Moab' that are op-

---

4. The table reflects a combination of the approaches of J. de Vaulx, *Les Nombres,* Sources Biblique (Paris: J. Gabalda, 1972), 372–81; and G. B. Gray, *Numbers,* in ICC (Edinburgh: T. & T. Clark, 1903), 442–52.
5. A. Dillmann, *Das Bücher Numerii, Deuteronomium, und Josua* (Leipzig: Hirzel, 1897); cf. J. Milgrom, "Excursus 72: The Integrity of the Wilderness Itinerary," in *Numbers,* JPS Torah Commentary (Philadelphia: Jewish Publication Society, 1990), 497–99.

posite Jericho."[6] Yet the master list does not contain all of the collective sites mentioned in those narratives, such as the encampments in the Wadi Zered and Nahal Arnon, and those of Mattanah, Nahaliel, and Bamoth, mentioned in Numbers 21:12–20, and more than one-third of the sites are never mentioned elsewhere. It may have served a number of texts as a master list, but this was not its primary function.

Literary Unity

Each of these approaches has neglected the internal literary evidence of this section and its homogeneity as a literary unit, which probably functioned as an example of what T. Ashley calls the "journey-of-life" motif in the Bible.[7] Moses recorded this wilderness itinerary for the second generation of Israel as a recitation. This recitation was for remembering the stages of God's leading his people from the point of great deliverance in Egypt to the staging point of a new victory campaign in the land of Canaan. The critical approaches also have overlooked the literary and thematic ties with the marching song included in Numbers 9:15–23, which contains the pattern:[8]

9:18   At the Lord's command they departed [עַל־פִּי יְהוָה יִסְעוּ]
and at the Lord's command they encamped [וְעַל־פִּי יְהוָה יַחֲנוּ]

In the introduction to this chapter (vv. 1–2), similar phraseology is employed to draw the reader's attention to the role of Israel's God in directing them on this victory march to the land of Canaan. The stages of the Israelite itinerary were recorded by Moses using the similar terminology, and the record begins with similar phraseology for divine instruction ("at the Lord's command," עַל־פִּי יְהוָה), with Moses writing down the sequential itinerary. Thus we see the following:[9]

---

6. Y. Aharoni, *The Land of the Bible: A Historical Geography,* rev. ed., trans. A. Rainey (Philadelphia: Westminster, 1979), 84–85, 195–201.
7. Timothy R. Ashley, *The Book of Numbers* (Grand Rapids: Eerdmans, 1993), 625. Ashley suggests that this kind of journey motif is later paralleled in the book of Hebrews in 3:7–4:16. The exemplars of the faithful in Hebrews 11 represents another form of this motif using people rather than places.
8. Cole, *Numbers,* 158–59.
9. Note the simple chiasm in the structure of the terms for departures and beginnings.

(33:2) A their beginnings, [אֶת־מוֹצָאֵיהֶם]
B of their departures at the LORD's command
[לְמַסְעֵיהֶם עַל־פִּי יְהוָה]
B' and these are their departures [וְאֵלֶּה מַסְעֵיהֶם]
A' by their beginnings [לְמוֹצָאֵיהֶם:]

Some of the cities delineated are among those recounted in the lists of cities brought under the dominion of Egypt, following the victorious campaigns of pharaohs such as Thutmose III, Amenhotep III, Seti I, Ramses II, and Shishak (Sheshonq).[10] J. Milgrom followed closely the suggestion of G. I. Davies in citing parallels with the itinerary listed in a letter by Shamshi-Adad I of Assyria (eighteenth century B.C.), and even more striking parallels in the later annals of Ashurnasirpal II (883–859 B.C.). Milgrom concluded that

> Numbers 33 is part of a widely attested itinerary genre. In particular, it exhibits the same form and style as the ninth-century campaign records of the Assyrian monarchs: it repeats the names of the campsites and adds pertinent information regarding military exploits, the availability of water and provisions, and the crossing of rivers, but it does not indicate dates or distances covered. Israel's wilderness trek—also a military campaign—was, therefore, written down according to the prevailing ancient Near Eastern style of recording itineraries of military campaigns.[11]

However, the pattern need not be necessarily dated to the first millennium B.C. based simply upon the repetition of the site names. As noted above the pattern of the stages delineated in Numbers 33 derive from the pattern of the song of the march that is imbedded in the narrative of 9:18–23.

---

10. See the combined lists of these and other Egyptian kings in *ANET*, 242–43. The records of the campaigns of these pharaohs (ibid., 234–58) focus upon the military prowess of the given leader and the granting of dominion and power to them by the combined deities of the Horus, Amon, Re, and the Apis Bull. Note also J. Hoffmeier, "The Structure of Joshua 1–11 and the Annals of Thutmose III," in *Faith, Tradition, and History: Old Testament Historiography in Its Ancient Near Eastern Context*, ed. A. R. Millard, J. K. Hoffmeier, and D. W. Baker (Winona Lake, Ind.: Eisenbrauns, 1994), 167.
11. J. Milgrom, *Numbers*, JPS Torah Commentary (Philadelphia: Jewish Publication Society, 1990), 497–98.

With the literary genre of Numbers 33 firmly established in the tradition of ancient Near Eastern military conquest itineraries, the following section will examine the internal literary structure of the passage with the purpose of determining its function in the book of Numbers.

Literary Structure

The biblical text of Numbers 33 recounts the sequence of the Israelites' breaking camp some forty-one times along their forty-two-station journey from Ramses in Egypt to the edge of the Promised Land, just across the Jordan River from Jericho (see charts below). As noted above, ancient kings recorded in geographical sequence the towns, villages, and cities that they conquered in expanding their territorial dominion. Here Moses recounts the steps by which Yahweh God of Israel has led his people victoriously, even in light of their rebellious tendencies, from bondage and oppression in Egypt to freedom and prosperity, given them victory over the Canaanites, Amorites, and Midianites, and has now guided them to the brink of great blessing in the fulfillment of his ancient promise to Abraham, "To your offspring I will give this land."[12]

Gordon Wenham has rightly observed that the departure/encampment sites are organized into six groups or stages of seven sites. Each stage is delineated with the following pattern, as exemplified by 33:13:

> They departed from Dophkah [וַיִּסְעוּ מִדָּפְקָה]
> And they encamped at Alush [וַיַּחֲנוּ בְּאָלוּשׁ]

Wenham has also noted a number of parallels between various cycles in the book. First, he observed that often "similar events occur at the same point in the cycle. Second, some of the events occur at stations whose number may be symbolically significant."[13] The first and second cycles closely parallel one another.

---

12. Genesis 12:7; 13:14–17; 15:7, 18–21; 17:8; 24:7, et al.
13. Gordon J. Wenham, *Numbers: An Introduction and Commentary* (Leicester, England/Downers Grove, Ill.: InterVarsity), 218.

Table 16.2[14]
Parallels Between the First and Second Cycles of Numbers 33:3–17

Cycle I Stations	Content Description	Cycle II Stations	Content Description
1	Miracle: Firstborn death (Exod. 12:29–36)	8	Miracle: Manna and Quail Provided (Exod. 16:1–36)
2–3	Unknown	9–10	Unknown
4	Victory over Egyptians (Exod. 14:13–31)	11	Victory over the Amalekites (Exod. 17:8–16)
5	Statutes, ordinances, and commandments (Exod. 15:23–26); note also complaints and rebellion (Exod. 15:24)	12	Statutes, ordinances, and commandments (Exod. 19:1–20:21); note also complaints and rebellion (Exod. 32:1–35)
6	Abundant water (Exod. 15:27)	13	Abundant water and food (Num. 11:4–34)
7	Miriam's Song (Exod. 15:20)	14	Miriam's Rebellion (Num. 12:1–15)

Wenham highlights the significance of the numbers 1, 3, 4, 7, and 12 in biblical literature and in these cycles. He remarks that "epoch-making events, the exodus and the manna, are associated with the first and eighth (1 + 7) stations (Exod. 12:2; 16:35). One wonders whether it is just coincidence that after the fourth station the Red Sea was crossed, and that at the twelfth station the law was given."[15] Wenham further notes the parallel experiences in Numbers 11–12 and 20–21, on the journeys from Sinai to

---

14. This chart is an adaptation of Wenham's charts (*Numbers*, 217–18).
15. Ibid., 218–19.

Kadesh and Kadesh to the plains of Moab, and those of the journey from the Red Sea to Sinai in Exodus 13–19.

With the understanding that Numbers 33 is a literary construct, it need not be considered an exhaustive master listing of sites encountered on the lengthy journey. Note, in the charts below on Cycle VI, the number of sites from other biblical passages that do not occur in Numbers 33:42–49. The chapter organization and content have their own historical and theological import in the book of Numbers.

First, note the points of major literary expansion in the text. Following the introduction in verse 1, which highlights the leadership roles of Moses and Aaron, the narrative then focuses on the role of Moses faithfully recording ("at the command of the LORD," עַל־פִּי יְהוָה) the stages of the journey, beginning with the Lord's dramatic and miraculous work in the Exodus from Egypt (Num. 33:2–40). The narrator emphasizes that it is the Lord who brought judgment and destruction against the Egyptians and their gods. In verses 5–37, there are only minor expansions, usually commentary on certain geographical features encountered at several sites along the way. These include (1) "on the edge of the wilderness" (v. 6), (2) the "passing through the sea" (v. 8), (3) the "twelve springs of water and seventy palms" (v. 9), (4) the lack of water at Rephidim where "the people had no water to drink" (v. 14), and (5) "on the edge of the land of Edom" (v. 37). Note also the minor expansions in the setting of "the border of Moab" in verse 44, and finally "in the plains of Moab by the Jordan opposite Jericho in verse 49. The second major expansion occurs in verses 38–39, in which the narrator focuses upon the faithfulness of Aaron ("at the command of the LORD" עַל־פִּי יְהוָה) in going up on Mount Hor, where he died.

These two major expansions also include the only chronological markers in the chapter, the beginning of the journey and the end of the forty years of punishment in the wilderness. No mention is made of the numerous rebellions of the Israelites recounted in Exodus, Leviticus, and Numbers, nor of the rebellion of Moses and Aaron at the waters of Meribah (Num. 20:2–13). The purpose of the chapter is to set forth the victory march from Egypt to the edge of the Promised Land. For the early reader/audience, the background history of Israel's rebellion in the wilderness would have been ominously resonant. That part of the lesson would come forth in the concluding section.

But, another major expansion immediately follows that of the account of Aaron's death, namely, the remembrance of the victorious battle against the Canaanite king of Arad (Num. 21:1–3). There the Lord heard the voice of Israel who promised to utterly destroy the Canaanites and their cities. In verse 3 the victory is recounted, as well as the naming of the place as "Hormah" ("dedicate for destruction"). But wait! This is not the only Hormah mentioned in the account of Israel's wilderness journey. In 14:3–45, the Israelites were repulsed down to Hormah by the combined Canaanite and Amalekite forces following their rejection of the Promised Land (13:25–14:38). Perhaps there was a deliberate omission of the mention of the victory in 33:40 in order to create narrative tension (or conflict) in the mind of the reader for the challenge which lay ahead in the final section of the chapter.

Following the seven-cycle organization of the book of Numbers[16] and the Hebrew preference for the utilization of the number "seven" for denoting completeness and fulfillment, a seventh cycle would be anticipated by the reader/audience. Furthermore, chapter 33 stands at the center of the seventh cycle of the book of Numbers, which itself anticipates the entrance and conquest of the Promised Land. This anticipated conclusion to the itinerary recitation is found in the instructions for the conquest of the land of Canaan in 33:50–56. This challenge to assume ownership of their inheritance is the open-ended seventh stage of the journey motif, that which remains to be written under the leadership of Joshua in the coming months and years.

---

16. See Cole, "Introduction: 3. Structure and Outline of the Book of Numbers," in *Numbers*, 36–52.

The Israelite Victory March

Table 16.3
Cycle 1: From Rameses to the Red Sea

Numbers 33	Exodus 12–17; Numbers 1–21; Deuteronomy 1–4, 10
Rameses (vv. 3, 5)	Rameses (Exod. 12:37)
Sukoth (vv. 5–6)	Sukkoth (Exod. 12:37; 13:20)
Etham Wilderness (vv. 6–7)	Etham (Exod. 13:20)
(Pi-)Hahiroth (vv. 7–8)	Pi-Hahiroth (Exod. 14:2); between Migdol and Sea, opposite Baal-Zephon /Yam Suph crossing (Exod. 14:21–31) into Shur Wilderness (Exod. 15:22)
Marah (vv. 8–9)	Marah (Exod. 15:23); bitter waters made sweet
Elim (vv. 9–10); with 12 springs, 70 palms	Elim (Exod. 15:27); 12 springs, 70 palms, water
Yam Suph (vv. 10–11); Israelites camp by Yam Suph	Yam (Suph) "Sea" crossing site (Exod. 14:21–31; 15:4)

Table 16.4
Cycle 2: The Deserts of Sinai: Sin, Sinai, and Paran

Numbers 33	Exodus 12–17; Numbers 1–21; Deuteronomy 1–4, 10
Sin Wilderness (vv. 11–12)	Sin Wilderness (Exod. 16:1–15)—between Elim and Sinai on fifteenth day of second month. Complaint of food, God gives manna and quail.
Dophkah (vv. 12–13)	Lacking
Alush (vv. 13–14)	Lacking
Rephidim (vv. 14–15); "no water for people to drink"	Rephidim (Exod. 17:1)—No water quarrel; Massah and Meribah; Amalekite attack, Israel's victory
Sinai Wilderness (vv. 15–16)	Sinai Wilderness (Exod. 19:1f.—Moses with God on Mount Sinai)
Kibroth-Hatta'avah (vv. 16–17)	Paran Desert (Num. 10:12); Kibroth-Hatta'avah (Num. 11:34)
Hazeroth (vv. 17–18)	Hazeroth (Num. 11:35); Paran Desert (Num. 12:16)

EXCURSUS: THE LOCATION OF MOUNT SINAI

One of the key issues for locating sites in the second through fifth cycles is the location of Mount Sinai. No less than twenty different suggestions have been tendered through the centuries, including Jebel Helal and Har Karkom in the northeast Sinai peninsula, Jebel Sin Bisher in the western central region, Jebel Serbal and Jebel Musa in the southern Sinai region, mountains in the southern Negev region, and several mountains in the northwest Arabian peninsula, southeast of Aqaba. If the request of Moses before the pharaoh for permission to journey three days into the wilderness to celebrate a festival to the Lord (Exod. 3:18; 5:3; 8:27) is to be applied to the quest for the mountain's locale, then the sacred summit must be relatively close—approximately 45–50 miles—to the Egyptian border fortresses. Most of the proposed mountains range from 30 to 100-plus miles farther away, with the exception of Jebel Sin Bisher or another mountain in its vicinity in the western Sinai peninsula.

M. Harel has argued convincingly for the Jebel Sin Bisher location, noting that it most conforms to all the available biblical geographical criteria

Table 16.5
Cycle 3: Spies Sent from Desert Paran (Num. 13:3), Return to Kadesh in Desert Paran (Num. 13:26)

Numbers 33	Exodus 12–17; Numbers 1–21; Deuteronomy 1–4, 10
Rithmah (vv. 18–19)	Lacking
Rimmon-Perez (vv. 19–20)	Lacking
Libnah (vv. 20–21)	Lacking
Rissah (vv. 21–22)	Lacking
Kehelathah (vv. 22–23)	Lacking
Mount Shepher (vv. 23–24)	Lacking
Haradah (vv. 24–25)	Lacking

for identifying the mountain.[17] The most explicit passage bearing on this question is the statement in Deuteronomy 1:2 that the distance from Horeb (=Sinai) to Kadesh-barnea, via Mount Seir (southern Edom in the Ezion-geber area) is a distance of eleven-days journey or about 150 to 165 miles.

Table 16.6
Cycle 4: Kadesh to the Arabah

Numbers 33	Exodus 12–17; Numbers 1–21; Deuteronomy 1–4, 10
Makheloth (vv. 25–26)	Kadesh in Zin Wilderness; also Meribah
Tahath (vv. 26–27)	Lacking
Terah (vv. 27–28)	Lacking
Mithkah (vv. 28–29)	Lacking
Hashmonah (vv. 29–30)	Lacking
Moseroth (vv. 30–31)	Moserah in Deuteronomy 10:6
Bene-Yaʾakan (vv. 31–32)	Deuteronomy 10:6

---

17. M. Harel, "The Route of the Exodus of the Israelites from Egypt" (Ph.D. dissertation, New York University, 1964); idem, "The Wilderness of Sinai and the Negev and the Location of Kadesh-barnea," in *B.Z. Luria Volume* (Jerusalem: Kiriat Sepher, 1979), 287–97 (Heb). Note also G. Kelm, "The Route of the Exodus," *Biblical Illustrator* 7 (1979): 11–32. The more recent endeavor by R. Cornuke and D. Halbrook to identify Mount Sinai in northwest Saudi Arabia (the third such attempt in the recent decades) has similar shortcomings (*In Search of the Mountain of God: The Discovery of the Real Mt. Sinai* [Nashville: Broadman & Holman, 2000]; see also Web page, www.baseinstitute.org). The rationale that Midian refers only to the area east of the Gulf of Aqaba is faulty on several biblical counts. Milgrom notes that Hobab's wish to return to his homeland (Num. 10:29) would have been absurd had he already been there (*Numbers,* 280). Paul's reference to Arabia in Galatians 1:17; 4:25 (cf. Acts 9:2–10; 2 Cor. 11:32) refers to the Nabatean region whose borders were in constant flux, depending upon the compliance with the *pax Romana.* For brief periods it included Transjordanian territory as far north as Damascus and Sinai and Negev regions as far west as Gaza. The Midianite shrine from the twelfth and eleventh centuries B.C. at Timnah, located 15 miles north of Elat, is well-documented. See B. Rothenberg, "Timna," in *NEAEHL,* 4:1475–86. Thus the "Midianite" territory often included lands that were beyond the northwest region of modern Saudia Arabia.

Table 16.7
Cycle 5: Desert Journeys to Edom and the Death of Aaron

Numbers 33	Exodus 12–17; Numbers 1–21; Deuteronomy 1–4, 10
Hor-Haggidgad (vv. 32–33)	Gudgodah in Deuteronomy 10:7
Yotbathah (vv. 33–34)	Deuteronomy 10:7
Abronah (vv. 34–35)	Lacking
Ezion-Geber (vv. 35–36)	Lacking, but Way of Red Sea mentioned in Numbers 21:4
Kadesh (vv. 36–37) in Zin Wilderness	Kadesh (Num. 20:1)—Miriam dies; waters of Meribah
Mount Hor (vv. 37–41)	Mount Hor (Num. 20:22) near border of Edom; Aaron dies at age 123, 40 years after Exodus
Zalmonah (vv. 41–42)	Lacking

Table 16.8
Cycle 6: Punon to the Plains of Moab

Numbers 33	Exodus 12–17; Numbers 1–21; Deuteronomy 1–4, 10
Punon (vv. 42–43)	Lacking
Oboth (vv. 43–44)	Oboth (Num. 21:10)
Iye Abarim (v. 44); Iyim (v. 45)	Iye Abarim—E of Moab, then to Zered, Mattanah, Nahaliel, Bamoth, Pisgah (Num. 21:11)

Dibon-Gad (vv. 45–46)	Dibon in Numbers 21:30 proverb
Almon-Diblathaim (vv. 46–47)	Lacking
Abarim Mountains (vv. 47–48) before Nebo	Cf. Iye Abarim above (Num. 21:11); Mount Nebo in Abarim Mountains. (Deut. 32:49)
Plains of Moab (vv. 48–49) by Jordan from Beth Jeshimoth up to Abel Shittim	Plains of Moab (22:1); Balaam encounters

For the completion of the victory march, Cycle VII lay ahead for the Israelites as the challenge of verses 50–56 implies.

Instructions for the Conquest of the Land (33:50–56)

The seventh and final cycle of the victory march from Egypt to the land of Canaan comes in the form of a challenge, the list that remains to be written by Joshua, Moses' successor. The chiastic structure of the future and final stage of the Israelite victory march from Egypt to the Promised Land has been duly noted by J. Milgrom.[18] As they departed the plains of Moab, led by the Lord and the symbol of his presence in the ark of the covenant in crossing the Jordan River, they would make their encampment at Gilgal, from which their task would be to carry out their assigned instructions for taking possession of their inheritance. The following outline is based upon Milgrom, with my own modifications:

---

18. J. Milgrom, "Excursus 72: The Literary Structure of 33:50–56," in *Numbers*, 500–1.

The Structure of Numbers 33:50–56

Introduction: Instructions from the Lord for the Israelites (vv. 50–51)
Setting Protasis: "When you cross over the Jordan into the Land of Canaan"

A **Possession** of the Promised Land (two apodoses with וְהוֹרַשְׁתֶּם) (vv. 52–53)
   1 Possessing by Dispossessing (וְהוֹרַשְׁתֶּם) the Inhabitants of the Land (v. 52)
      a   Dispossess all the inhabitants of the land from before you
          b   Destroy all their carved images
          b' All their molten images you shall destroy
      a' All their high places you shall demolish
   2 Possessing (וְהוֹרַשְׁתֶּם) by Inhabiting the Land (v. 53)
      a   You shall possess the land and dwell in it
      b   For You I have given the land to possess it.

      B **Inheritance** To Be Divided Among the Tribes (v. 54)
         1 You shall receive the inheritance of the land by lot for your clans
             a   For the large you shall make large its inheritance
             a' For the small you shall make small its inheritance
         1' Toward whatever comes out to him there by lot is his
            By your patriarchal tribes you shall inherit.

A' **Dispossession** Warning (two apodoses with וְהָיָה) (vv. 55–56)
   Protasis: If you do not dispossess the inhabitants of the land from before you
      a   Then it will be (וְהָיָה) that those you allow to remain from them [will be]
          Splinters in your eyes and thorns in your sides
          They shall trouble you in the land where you dwell
      b   Then it will be (וְהָיָה)
          According to what I intended to do to them
          I will do to you!

Numbers 33:50–51: Introduction

In the standard introduction to didactic material throughout the book of Numbers, this pericope begins with the full Hebrew version of the familiar revelatory phraseology:

(v. 50) וַיְדַבֵּר יְהוָה אֶל־מֹשֶׁה . . . לֵאמֹר:

(v. 51) דַּבֵּר אֶל־בְּנֵי יִשְׂרָאֵל וְאָמַרְתָּ אֲלֵהֶם

"Then Yahweh instructed Moses . . . saying: . . . 'Instruct the children of Israel, and thus you shall say to them.'"[19] Typically, this extended formal introduction is found in specific priestly legislation,[20] though it also occurs in the introductions to the two challenges to enter the Promised Land and drive out its inhabitants.[21] The proper conclusion to the Israelites' following these instructions faithfully would be the phraseology of obedience found throughout the book of Numbers, that Israel did according to all that the Lord commanded Moses.[22] This would be recorded in Joshua 11:20 and 23, "that he (the Lord) might destroy them as the Lord had commanded Moses. . . . So Joshua took the whole land according to all that the Lord had said to Moses, and Joshua gave it as an inheritance to Israel according to their divisions by their tribes" (NKJV). The introduction also includes reference to the geographical setting of the receiving of the instructions from the Lord, "on the plains of Moab by the Jordan across from Jericho," Jericho being the place where the conquest would begin in the near future.

Numbers 33:52–53: Possession

The instructions of the Lord are set forth using the two parallel meanings of the hifil form of the Hebrew verb ירש which can mean either "possess" or "dispossess," depending on one's perspective. For the Israelites to possess the land would mean dispossessing the Canaanite inhabitants, driving them out of the land. The instructions concerning the dispossessing of the Canaanites were deliberately expanded to include that which would be the

---

19. Cf. the three sections of Leviticus 6:1–11, 12–16, and 17–23, in which each section begins with וַיְדַבֵּר יְהוָה אֶל־מֹשֶׁה לֵּאמֹר: ("And the Lord spoke to Moses, saying") and Numbers 15:1, 17, 37. For further discussion of this phraseology and its use in the book of Numbers, see Cole, "Introduction: Structure and Outline of the Book of Numbers," in *Numbers*, 38–40.
20. Numbers 5:11–12; 6:1–2; 8:1–2; 9:9–10; 16:23–24; 18:25–26; 29:1–2; 35:9–10.
21. Here and in Numbers 34:1–2.
22. The phrase וַיַּעֲשׂוּ בְּנֵי יִשְׂרָאֵל כְּכֹל אֲשֶׁר צִוָּה יְהוָה אֶת־מֹשֶׁה כֵּן עָשׂוּ, "And the children of Israel did according to all that the LORD commanded Moses" (Num. 1:54), is found in 1:19, 54; 2:33–34; 3:16, 39, 42, 51; 4:37, 41, 45, 49 (2x); 5:4; 8:3–4, 20–22; 9:5, 8, 18, 20, 23. Only in 10:13; 17:11 (Matt. 17:26), and 20:9, 27 does this phraseology occur in the three rebellion cycles. Then in the advent cycles, the theme recurs in 26:4; 27:11, 22–23; 31:7, 31, 41, 47; 32:25; 36:5, 10.

most problematic aspect of the Canaanite culture to Israel, the various forms of aberrant worship practiced by the land's inhabitants. They were to eradicate totally—"you shall demolish"—their sculpted or carved images and their molten images, and they were to obliterate all their high places throughout the land. In the Ten Commandments, the Israelites had been explicitly prohibited from making any form of image of Yahweh her God or worshiping any other gods (Exod. 20:3–5), and now they were commanded to demolish all forms and locales where the idolatrous activities took place. Pluralism in the form of peaceful coexistence with idolatry would be impossible, both for the well-being of the people and the sanctity of the land that Yahweh had given as a gift to his people. That gift was to be purified by the expurgation of idolatry and remain pure and holy before the Lord. Otherwise those various forms and accompanying practices would ensnare Israel and turn her heart from her God. The tragedy of Israel's history was that she failed to follow faithfully these commands from the Lord, and her demise at the hands of the Assyrians and Babylonians was largely due to her tendency toward idolatry.[23]

Numbers 33:54: Inheritance

The land belonged to the Lord, and it was his to grant to whom he desired. By his love, grace, and mercy he had promised and was now presenting the gift of the land to his people Israel. The distribution of the land among the tribes was to be proportionate, based upon the size of the tribe and through the casting of lots (Num. 33:54).[24] Lots were cast with the

---

23. The prophetic voices of Isaiah and Hosea of the eighth century B.C., and Jeremiah, Ezekiel, and Zephaniah of the seventh–sixth centuries B.C. all echoed the refrain that Israel's exile was due largely to her stubbornness of heart and persistence of spirit in pursuing the other gods of the nations which surrounded Israel. Cf. Isaiah 2:5–22; Jeremiah 7:1–34; 9:12–16; 10:11–18; Ezekiel 5:5–6:14; Hosea 4:11–5:15; Zephaniah 1:2–18.
24. The two terms for referring to the familial subgroups within Israel, "your clans" (לְמִשְׁפְּחֹתֵיכֶם) and "your ancestral tribes" (לְמַטּוֹת אֲבֹתֵיכֶם) are used synonymously in Num. 33:54. In the Hebrew structure, these two phrases and a Hithpael form of the verb נחל provide a chiastically structured inclusio to the verse, providing a literary artistry to the verse's emphases. See below:

Thus you shall apportion the land by lot to your families.	וְהִתְנַחַלְתֶּם אֶת־הָאָרֶץ בְּגוֹרָל לְמִשְׁפְּחֹתֵיכֶם
To the greater you shall allot a greater inheritance.	לָרַב תַּרְבּוּ אֶת־נַחֲלָתוֹ
To the lesser you shall allot a lesser inheritance.	וְלַמְעַט תַּמְעִיט אֶת־נַחֲלָתוֹ
In the way that the lot comes out to each.	אֶל אֲשֶׁר־יֵצֵא לוֹ שָׁמָּה הַגּוֹרָל
To each it shall be.	לוֹ יִהְיֶה
To the tribes of your forefathers you shall apportion it.	לְמַטּוֹת אֲבֹתֵיכֶם תִּתְנֶחָלוּ

confidence in the providence of God to apportion justly and fairly among the tribal components of the people of Israel.[25]

Numbers 33:55–56: Dispossession

The words of blessing in verse 24 that would result from the Israelites faithfully following the commands of the Lord are now contrasted with a stern warning and potential curse that would accrue to the nation if it were not steadfast in cleaving to Yahweh alone. The antithesis to the Israelites dispossessing the inhabitants of the land would be that they themselves would be dispossessed by the hand of the one who had given it to them. A similar warning to Israel was issued by Joshua in his farewell address to the nation before his death (Josh. 23:11–13):

> (11) Therefore take diligent heed to yourselves, that you love the Lord your God. (12) Or else, if indeed you do go back, and cling to the remnant among you and make marriages with them, and go in to them and they to you, (13) Know for certain that the Lord your God will no longer drive out these nations from before you. But they shall be snares and traps to you, and scourges on your sides, and thorns in your eyes, until you perish from this good land which the Lord your God has given you.

The language of the curse was very foreboding. Allowing the peoples of the land who were the source of idolatry to remain in the land would eventually lead to an infectious disease that would gradually consume the nation like leprosy. What lay ahead for the nation on this last stage of journey on the victory march to the Promised Land was a challenge of faith. Faithfulness like that depicted of the nation in Numbers 1–10 would result in their experiencing the fullness of God's blessing in the land flowing with milk and honey. Unity and harmony, celebration and worship, would be theirs. But if they rebelled against God like that first generation did in Numbers 11–25, then discord and disparagement would be the woeful conclusion to their story. The words were ominously prophetic.

---

25. Cf. Proverbs 16:33.

Conclusion

The literary structure and content of Numbers 33 reflect the structure and content of the entire book of Numbers. The literary genre of Numbers 33 has been firmly established in the tradition of ancient Near Eastern military conquest itineraries. The repetition pattern of the stages delineated in the chapter derives from the pattern of the song of the march that is imbedded in the narrative of Numbers 9:18–23.

The seven-cycle outline of the book, which couches the challenge to the Israelites faithfully to fulfill its goal of inheriting the Promised Land, is mirrored in the open-ended seven-cycle structure of chapter 33. The stages of the seventh cycle of the victory march lay unwritten at the point of Israel's encampment along the Jordan River across from Jericho. Narrative tension is created is several ways. First, chapter 33 stands at the center of the seventh cycle of Numbers, which has as its focus matters pertaining to the land and its yet unfulfilled inheritance by the Israelites. Second, bracketing chapter 33 are two chapters that each contain internal dissonance. Chapter 32 depicts the dissension between the tribes created by the decision of the Gadites, Reubenites, and half of Manasseh to take for their inheritance lands on the side of the Jordan where they were encamped. Though the tension is resolved somewhat by the promise of the Transjordanian tribes to assist in the conquest of the regions west of the Jordan, the tension re-emerges in chapter 34, in that the territory of the Transjordan lay outside the boundaries of the Promised Land as delineated in verses 1–15. Hence, the didactic intent of Numbers 33 is to challenge each generation of God's people toward living faithfully according to that which he has revealed in his Word. His abiding presence and power are available in fullness to those who accept the challenge with vision and hope.

17

AUTHORIAL INTENT AND THE SPOKEN WORD

A Discourse-critical Analysis of Speech Acts in Accounts of Israel's United Monarchy (1 Sam. 1–1 Kings 11)

Robert D. Bergen

DISCOURSE CRITICISM[1] ASSUMES THAT AUTHORS put meaning into texts and that the responsibility and challenge of readers is to find and understand that implanted meaning. Yet identifying the primary ideas biblical authors intended to convey within Old Testament narratives can be tricky business. There is a chasm between the sociological and technological world of ancient Israel and that of contemporary Euro-American society. Nevertheless, discourse criticism suggests that modern readers can accurately re-

---

1. The term *discourse criticism* was coined in connection with the publication of my first work, *Discourse Criticism* (selfpublished, 1982) and relates to an approach to analyzing texts developed from insights gained through interacting with discourse linguists at the Summer Institute of Linguistics. Discourse criticism as I practice it attempts to perform five foundational tasks: (1) identifying quantifiable features of biblical Hebrew texts, (2) creating electronic databases of these features, (3) producing statistical analyses of these features, (4) correlating the quantifiable features of a text with the text's semantic features, and (5) clarifying how authors manipulate variables in a text to encode their communicative intentions. The ultimate task of discourse criticism is to identify authorial intentions within a given text through the examination of the author's use of textual variables. Discourse criticism is related to "discourse analysis" only in the sense that it uses some operative assumptions from discourse analysis regarding the existence and function of post-sentence-level language features. For further reading on discourse criticism, see my "Text as a Guide to Authorial Intention: An Introduction to Discourse Criticism," *JETS* 30 (1987): 327–36. For a kind of discourse-critical study that examines a set of textual features different from those considered in the present study, see my "Evil Spirits and Eccentric Grammar," in *Biblical Hebrew and Discourse Linguistics,* ed. R. Bergen (Dallas: Summer Institute of Linguistics, 1994), 320–35.

trieve meaning from these ancient texts. This is possible because the biblical writers utilized techniques that are both predictable and identifiable to convey and rank the themes they wished to convey to their readers. It is the purpose of discourse criticism to employ strategies that help discern and rank the thematically significant propositions expressed by writers.

Couched in the language of traditional evangelicalism, discourse criticism assumes that the Holy Spirit guided biblical authors to embed clues into the structure of their texts so as to guide readers to God-intended conclusions. This approach to texts is aided by insights gleaned from discourse analysis, a relatively new branch of linguistics that focuses on identifying post-sentence-level language features and determining their functions within a text.[2] By determining the order, amount, types, and distribution of features within a biblical passage, discourse criticism assumes that it is possible to draw accurate, if not comprehensive, conclusions regarding an author's intended function for that passage. This is true because these Scriptural texts employ strategies for meaning production that are consistent with those that discourse analysts have found in languages throughout the world.

Within narrative texts, discourse criticism assumes that two different kinds of semantic features are given prominence: events and propositions. Though actions and ideas are highlighted in slightly different ways, both

---

2. A growing body of literature is available for the study of discourse analysis. See especially Robert E. Longacre, *The Grammar of Discourse,* 2d ed. (Lisse: Plenum, 1996). Other works include: Gillian Brown and George Yule, *Discourse Analysis* (Cambridge: University Press, 1983); James P. Gee, *An Introduction to Discourse Analysis: Theory and Method* (London: Routledge, 1999); and Deborah Schiffrin, *Approaches to Discourse* (London: Blackwell, 1994). Various biblical text analysts have utilized insights from discourse analysis. Preeminent among these is Robert E. Longacre (*Joseph: A Story of Divine Providence* [Winona Lake, Ind.: Eisenbrauns, 1989]). Other biblical studies that have a basis in discourse analysis include: W. Bodine, ed., *Linguistics and Biblical Hebrew* (Winona Lake, Ind.: Eisenbrauns, 1992); R. Bergen, ed. *Biblical Hebrew and Discourse Linguistics* (Dallas: Summer Institute of Linguistics, 1994); W. Bodine, ed., *Discourse Analysis of Biblical Literature: What It Is and What It Offers* (Atlanta: Society of Biblical Literature, 1995); and N. Winther-Nielsen, *A Functional Discourse Grammar of Joshua: A Computer-Assisted Rhetorical Structure Analysis* (Stockholm: Almqvist & Wiksell, 1995). Recent dissertations that apply aspects of discourse analysis to Old Testament studies include: R. Bouchoc, "An Analysis of Disjunctive *waw* Verbal Clauses in the Biblical Hebrew Narrative of the Pentateuch" (Ph.D. diss., Southeastern Baptist Theological Seminary, 2001); C. Douglas, "To Know and Not to Know: Hosea's Knowledge in Discourse Perspective" (Ph.D. diss., Trinity Evangelical Divinity School, 2000); and D. Stabnow, "A Discourse Analysis Perspective on the Syntax of Clauses Negated by *lo'* in the Primary History (Hebrew Text)" (Ph.D. diss., Westminster Theological Seminary, 2000). Two journals that regularly publish discourse-sensitive studies of Old Testament passages are *Journal of Translation and Textlinguistics* and *Journal of Northwest Semitic Languages.*

may be given special emphasis through the author's skillful use of the variables within a narrative text. Authors have large numbers of variables that can be used to mark information as especially significant. These variables exist at every level of the text: at the level of the word, the clause, the sentence, the paragraph, the episode, the story, and the story cycle. In addition, at every level of textual organization two different categories of variables may be manipulated; those that are structural in nature, and those that are semantic.

For narrative analysis, a complete discourse-critical investigation of an author's intended themes requires examination of all aspects of the author's highlighting of events and ideas. A thoroughgoing investigation of both these aspects for the monarchical narratives of 1 Samuel 8–1 Kings 11 would be massive in scope and is obviously outside the parameters established for writing this essay. Instead, the focus will be on direct quotations attributed to characters within the narrative.

Quote Prominence Analysis as a Technique for Determining Thematic Propositions

Narratives are usually thought of as texts that tell stories. Biblical narratives certainly describe events, but they perform the added task of expressing theological, moral, social, and political propositions as well. The author's values and ideological concerns are expressed through the medium of biblical narrative in three primary ways: (1) implicitly, through the narrative *Gestalt,* or overall storyline;[3] (2) indirectly, through statements made by characters in the narrative; and (3) directly, through nonnarrative comments embedded into the story.[4] Of these three means, it is through the voices of the *dramatis personae* that the author's own voice is most commonly heard.

Out of the millions of words that biblical personages must have spoken throughout their lifetimes, the authors/final editors of canonical narrative texts selectively included only those words that most suited their narrative

---

3. An instance of this in the United Monarchy accounts is 1 Samuel 9:1–20. In this section the author subtly conveys the proposition that Saul was unfit to rule over Israel by demonstrating him to be an incompetent shepherd.
4. The clearest instance of authorial use of nonnarrative comments to convey theological propositions within the monarchical accounts is found in 2 Kings 17:7–23.

intentions, and, quite frequently, those words that most clearly reflected their own deeply held beliefs or central concerns.[5] Thus, in an effort to identify the primary theological and political theses expressed by the canonical writer in the accounts of the United Monarchy, the present study focuses on the quotative material found within this section of Scripture.

The approach I have chosen for carrying out this task is the discourse-critical methodology known as Quote Prominence Analysis. This methodology is designed to identify the quotations that the canonical author highlighted the most, and in so doing to pinpoint the quotes most likely to contain thematically central propositions. After these quotations are identified, I will provide a brief summary and discussion of the content of those quotes. In the conclusion I will then propose a ranking of the most prominent propositions expressed by the author.

Though this study is highly limited in scope, it is likely to lead to valid conclusions because effective writers typically employ multiple devices—some structural and some semantic—at many different levels of textual organization to convey their intended conclusions to readers. Careful study of this one especially important feature within a narrative, therefore, should point to author-intended conclusions to which other devices within the same narrative also point.

The section of text stretching from 1 Samuel 8–1 Kings 11 contains 630 attributed quotes; the task of identifying the handful of most significant ones among them can be a daunting one. Since it is safe to assume that not all of them are of equal importance, the question must be asked, What exactly is it that makes one quote in a narrative account more important than another? Discourse criticism suggests that skillful authors use the semantic and structural variables available to them to highlight the quotes they deem to be most significant.

To gain a sense of how important a particular quotation was to the biblical author, one must first determine the significance of the character whom the author used to express it. The more important the speaker—as viewed from the perspective of the author and the community to which he wrote—the more thematically central the ideas contained in his/her speech are likely

---

5. Biblical text analysts outside of the conservative evangelical tradition would suggest that the producers of canonical texts formulated comments that they then placed within the mouths of their characters. Conservative evangelical commentators deny that this inventive kind of authorial activity occurred within biblical narrative, but are willing to concede that activities such as editing, summation, and encapsulation of characters' comments did take place.

to be. For the purposes of this study, only three different character classes need to be ranked: Israel's deity, spokesmen for Israel's deity, and kings.[6]

Determining the relative significance of characters within biblical narratives requires an understanding of the biblical writer's worldview. While the task of clarifying an ancient writer's worldview in its completeness is not possible, it is safe to assume that the writer of 1 Samuel 8–1 Kings 11 was an orthodox Yahwist who thoroughly understood the social power structure of preexilic Israel. As such, Yahweh, the creator and supreme-being of the universe, would always rank as the most significant character in a narrative that portrays him acting and speaking. Furthermore, characters in the narrative who speak as Yahweh's authorized representatives—the true prophets—would be second only to Yahweh in significance. Thus, among quotes placed within the mouths of humans, those attributed to true prophets of Yahweh would be the ones most likely to contain propositions of central significance to the biblical writer.[7] Third in rank would be quotations attributed to kings; authors could be expected to place ideas deemed by the writer as significant within royal mouths, since kings were the capstone of the societal pyramid in ancient Israel.

Thus, for the purposes of determining which quotations contain propositions of central significance to the biblical writer, discourse criticism sug-

---

6. Though many other characters speak within 1 Samuel 8–1 Kings 11—generals, princes, wives, and others—these are obviously lower on the social hierarchy of ancient Israel and therefore do not need to be ranked for the purposes of this study. The most prominent general is Joab (subject of eighty-eight verbs outside of quotations, twenty-two quotes; longest—seventy-five words [2 Sam. 19:6–8]; topics of longest quote—chiding David for failing to appreciate his soldiers, warning him he must acknowledge his soldiers' efforts). The most prominent prince is Jonathan (subject of sixty-four verbs outside of quotations; twenty-two quotes; longest—seventy-seven words [1 Sam. 20:18–23]; topics of longest quote—plan to inform David of Saul's disposition toward David, reminder of covenant relationship between David and Jonathan). The most prominent wife is Abigail (subject of twenty-nine verbs outside of quotations; three quotes; longest—153 words [1 Sam. 25:24–31]; topics of longest quote—plea to spare Nabal's life and avoid bloodguilt, recognition that Yahweh had selected David to be Israel's king and the founder of a lasting dynasty, recognition that Yahweh would protect David, plea for David to remember Abigail). Of the quotations placed in these individuals' mouths, clearly the most thematically significant is Abigail's. The unusual length of her quotation (longest by a woman, eighth longest in the United Monarchy accounts) as well as the occasion (a tense moment—while David is attempting to kill someone without just cause) and the addressee (David) suggests that the statements included in it are significant. Indeed they are, especially as they relate to Yahweh's plans for David. Nevertheless, Abigail's words merely underscore themes presented elsewhere by more authoritative characters in the narrative.

7. It is worth noting that the Hebrew Bible's monarchical accounts are found in the section known as the "Former Prophets," not the "Former Monarchs."

gests that one should first examine the quotes attributed directly to Yahweh, then those that come from Yahweh's true prophets, and third, those attributed to the Israelite kings. As propositions are ranked in terms of significance, those gleaned from Yahweh's direct statements would be considered to be more thematically central than those attributed to human beings. Similarly, prophets' statements, especially as they spoke in the name of Yahweh, would rank higher than the word of kings.

Within the monarchical narratives several different kings and prophets are portrayed as speaking. This does not suggest, however, that the writer necessarily put important propositions in each of their mouths. In attempting to identify author-intended centers of significance within a text, it is necessary to determine which of the kings and prophets a given author depicted as the most prominent. By considering the number of times each prophet and king spoke, as well as the total number of words placed within their mouths, it possible to draw a reasonable conclusion concerning which characters the author wanted us to listen to most attentively.[8]

Discourse criticism also assumes that quotations placed within the mouths of individuals within the same class—for example, prophets—will not all be equally weighted by the author. The quotes attributed to the prophet who spoke the greatest number of words are more likely to contain the propositions central to the author's theme than those placed within the quotations of less prominent prophets. Thus, characters should be categorized according to their social rank, and then compared for prominence among the members of that rank.

In the narratives extending from 1 Samuel 8–1 Kings 11, Yahweh is portrayed as an active participant and speaker. He is recorded as speaking 781 words[9] in a total of twenty-nine quotes. Following the criteria of discourse criticism, a text analyst is obligated to investigate the most prominent of Yahweh's quotations first in a search for most central thematic material.

Among human characters within the same stretch of narrative, the three

---

8. Another discourse-critical technique for determining the relative importance of the *dramatis personae* within a narrative is to count the number of verbs of which each character is the subject, with the character with the highest count being considered the most prominent. Counting the number of pronouns or nouns that refer to the particular character is another gauge for determining the degree of significance the author attributed to a character.
9. This and all other word counts in this essay are based on the Hebrew text as printed in the *Biblia Hebraica Stuttgartensia*. It does not take into account any of the variant readings mentioned in the textual apparatus.

most prominent prophets are Samuel (1103 words in forty-five quotes), Ahijah (360 words in two quotes), and Nathan (317 words in six quotes). According to the tenets of discourse criticism, Samuel's prominent quotations should contain propositions more central to the author's message than those of lesser prophets. Among the kings of the United Monarchy David is clearly the most prominent, with 3284 words in 161 quotes; Solomon is second, with 1255 words in twenty-one quotes; and Saul follows with 968 words in eighty-four quotes. Thus, among the kings, David's prominent quotations would be expected to contain materials most reflective of the author's central communicative intentions.

Quotation length is a second factor authors use to mark statements—and therefore the ideas contained in them, as significant. The longer the quotation, the more prominent it is. Within biblical Hebrew narrative the median quote length is twelve words—that is, half of all quotations are that length or less. Less than ten percent of quotations in biblical Hebrew exceed fifty words, less than five percent of all quotations exceed one hundred words, and less than three percent of all quotations exceed 130 words. For the purposes of this investigation, an attributed statement will be considered statistically significant if it has a size greater than one hundred words.

Using this criterion, the biblical author portrays six of the seven characters named above as uttering statements that were of a statistically significant length; only Saul lacked a sufficiently long quote.[10] The table below lists these six characters with the length and location of each statistically significant quote. Both of Yahweh's longest quotations, as well as the longest quotation attributed to each of the three prophets and two kings will be examined within this study.

---

10. Saul's longest quotation (2 Sam. 24:18–21) is a mere sixty-seven words. According to the guidelines established for the present study, this is too short for consideration. Nonetheless, the statement is marked as important in several ways: it is the longest uttered by that particular king, its addressee is a future king (David), and it is spoken on a battlefield during a time of conflict. The content is clearly significant: David is declared to be more righteous than Saul; Saul declares that David will become Israel's king; Saul states that Israel will be established in David's hands; and Saul appeals to David to spare his descendants. Saul's words play an important role in developing the theme of legitimacy for David's rule, but they are ultimately secondary. Saul's recognition of David's inevitable kingship and the success that will attend it prepare the way for Yahweh's later statements in 2 Samuel 7, but are much less authoritative than the deity's words.

Table 17.1

Character Role	Character	Quote Length	Location
Deity	Yahweh	197	2 Sam. 7:4–16
		152	1 Kings 9:3–9
Prophet (Spokesman for the Deity)	Samuel	205	1 Sam. 12:6–17
		147	1 Sam. 10:1–8
	Nathan	112	2 Sam. 12:7–12
	Ahijah	165	1 Kings 11:31–39
Israelite King	David	365	2 Sam. 22:2–51
		198	2 Sam. 7:18–29
		165	1 Kings 2:1–9
		114	1 Sam. 24:10–16
		110	2 Sam. 1:19–27
	Solomon	565	1 Kings 8:23–53

Other factors that affect quote prominence include addressee, geographic and temporal setting, and placement within the overall narrative. Words spoken to Yahweh within a biblical Hebrew narrative possess more gravity than those spoken to an unnamed slave. Words spoken in a palace or sacred site possess a higher degree of atmospheric highlighting than those spoken in a marketplace; similarly, statements made during national crises, holy convocations, and at night possess a subtle but real form of highlighting that authors employ to indicate the presence of propositions significant to the author. Quotations located at the beginning, peak, or conclusion of a narrative unit likewise stand out more than others.

Additional factors also affect quote prominence. Their expression in a highly stylized format, such as a poem, are evidence of an author's attempt to highlight material in a quotation. The author's inclusion of statistically rare speech acts—prayers and prophetic oracles, for example—suggests that the author intended to highlight the ideas contained in them. Furthermore, the inclusion of rare lexical items within a proposition, the presence of lexical items relating to sociologically significant categories (e.g., cultic terms), or the employment of statistically infrequent clause, sentence, or paragraph structures to convey a proposition also make that proposition stand out more prominently. Phonological devices such as alliteration and assonance can also add to the prominence of a statement. In the search for quotations intended by the author as central, one could profitably investigate these variables as well.

Examining all of these highlighting techniques as part of this study in an effort to determine authorial intentions would prove enlightening, but impractical. Since the authors of biblical narratives regularly supplied enough of the more obvious hints, the presence of some of these more subtle features only reinforce conclusions that could be drawn otherwise.

Presentation of Results

According to the tenets of discourse criticism's Quote Prominence Analysis, propositions the author intended to be taken as thematically central should be found in the quotes of statistically significant length attributed to the highest ranking cast member. Following this principle, the two quotes that should contain the author's most important propositions are those attributed to Yahweh in 2 Samuel 7:4–16 and 1 Kings 9:3–9. Other significant passages should include the longest quotations by Samuel, Nathan, and Ahijah, David, and Solomon. These seven will be briefly discussed below (2 Sam. 7:4–16; 1 Kings 9:3–9; 1 Sam. 12:6–17; 2 Sam. 12:7–12; 1 Kings 11:31–39; 2 Sam. 22:2–51; 1 Kings 8:23–53).

The Yahweh Quotes

2 Samuel 7:4–16

This is the longest quote by the highest-ranking character within the United Monarchy narratives. Discourse criticism suggests that among the propositions expressed through the medium of attributed quotations, those most central to the author's concerns are found here.

Additional features associated with this passage reinforce the conclusion that the author marked this quotation as especially significant. Besides other subtle evidences of authorial attempts to bring focus to this material, the following can be noted: the temporal setting for the quotation is both explicit (an unusual fact in itself) and unusual. It comes at night. The addressee is Nathan, one of the highest-ranking characters in the cast of the United Monarchy narratives, and the quotation is introduced in a manner unique among the 630 quotes recorded in the United Monarchy accounts, employing a finite form of *hyh* with *lēʾmōr*. In addition, this is the only statement attributed to Yahweh in the United Monarchy accounts that in its introduction is specifically termed *dᵉbar yhwh*, "the word of Yahweh."

Contemporary expositors, working quite apart from discourse criticism, have regularly noted the importance of this quotation. R. Youngblood considers this passage to be "the center and focus of the Deuteronomistic history itself."[11] W. Brueggemann suggests that it is "the dramatic and theological center of the entire Samuel corpus" and "the most crucial theological statement in the Old Testament."[12]

A full exegesis of Yahweh's 197-word quote is not possible here, but a brief summary of the ideas can be given:

1. Yahweh forbade David to build a temple dedicated to him.
2. Yahweh was responsible for David's rise to kingship.
3. Yahweh was responsible for all of David's military victories.
4. Yahweh would make David one of the most famous men in the world.
5. Yahweh would provide Israel with a safe and secure homeland.
6. Yahweh would give David rest from his enemies.
7. Yahweh would establish David as the founder of a dynasty.
8. David's offspring would build a temple for Yahweh.
9. Yahweh would establish the throne of David's offspring forever.
10. Yahweh would be the father of David's offspring.
11. While Yahweh would punish wrongdoing by David's offspring, he would never take away his love.
12. David's dynasty, kingdom, and throne would endure forever.

---

11. R. Youngblood, *1, 2 Samuel*, EBC, ed. F. E. Gaebelein (Grand Rapids: Zondervan, 1992), 3:880.
12. W. Brueggemann, *First and Second Samuel*, IBC (Louisville: John Knox, 1990), 253, 259. I have noted elsewhere that the "words recorded here arguably play the single most significant role of any Scripture found in the Old Testament in shaping the Christian understanding of Jesus"; see R. Bergen, *1, 2 Samuel*, NAC (Nashville: Broadman & Holman, 1996), 337.

This quotation by Yahweh is important within the canon for several reasons. The propositions contained in it demonstrate the fulfillment of the Torah prophecy regarding the presence of a scepter in Judah (Gen. 49:10). More precisely, they establish the fundamental justification for the House of David's dynastic claim. They also provide the basis for prophetic words of later generations in Israel (Isa. 9:1–7; 11:1–16; 16:5; 55:3; Jer. 23:5–6; 30:8; 33:15–26; Ezek. 34:23–24; 37:24–25; Hos. 3:5; Amos 9:11; Zech. 12:7–8), and they lay the foundation for understanding Jesus Christ as the messianic Son of God in the New Testament (Matt. 1:1; Luke 1:32; Acts 13:22–23; Rom. 1:3; 2 Tim. 2:8; Rev. 22:16 et al.). The sheer number of allusions to propositions within this quotation suggest that numerous biblical writers considered 2 Samuel 7:4–16 to be of central significance.

1 Kings 9:3–9

This passage contains the second-longest quotation (152 words) attributed to Yahweh during the United Monarchy period. As such, discourse criticism suggests that the author has designated the materials in it as thematically central, but slightly less important than those in 2 Samuel 7:4–16.

Two other factors associated with 1 Kings 9:3–9 also suggest that the author intended the materials in this quotation to be thematically dominant: (1) the statement was made in association with one of the most important events in Israelite religious history, the completion of the first temple built for Yahweh in Jerusalem; and (2) it was addressed to King Solomon, Israel's most prominent citizen at that time. Collectively, the employment of these four marking devices sets this quotation on a plane well above others in the Solomonic accounts.

Propositions contained within the quotation include the following:

1. In answer to Solomon's prayers, Yahweh sanctified the temple as a place for his name to dwell eternally.
2. Yahweh's eyes and heart would always be at the temple.
3. If Solomon was obedient to the Lord and lived righteously as David had done, Yahweh would establish his family line's right to rule Israel forever.
4. If Solomon and his descendants apostasized, Yahweh would remove Israel from the land he had given them, and would destroy the temple.

5. If Israel apostasized, they would become an object of ridicule.

The propositions in this quotation are both bright and ominous. On the one hand they demonstrate the fulfillment of Torah prophecies regarding the establishment of a place for Yahweh's name to dwell (Deut. 12:5, 11, 14, 18, 21, 26; 14:23–25; 15:20; 16:2, 6–7, 11). On the other hand, they threaten national disaster on an almost unimaginable scale as punishment for rejecting Yahweh. As such, these words simultaneously link up with additional Torah words (Lev. 26:33; Deut. 28:63–64) and set the stage for understanding the tragic events of the divided monarchy period (2 Kings 17:23; 25:8–21).

The Prophetic Quotes

1 Samuel 12:6–17

The author of 1 Samuel 8–1 Kings 11 clearly establishes Samuel as the most prominent prophet during the United Monarchy.[13] Thus, among the quotations placed in the mouths of the prophets, Samuel's longest quote must be considered first.

Besides speaker and length, other features that mark 1 Samuel 12:6–17 as significant include its cultically significant geographic setting (Gilgal, 11:15), its temporal setting (during a celebration marking Saul's first victory over an Israelite oppressor), and the addressees (*all* Israel).

Within this quotation the following ideas have been highlighted:

1. In response to the Israelites' plea, Yahweh had sent them Moses and Aaron to free them from Egypt.
2. In response to the people's apostasy, Yahweh had sold Israel into the hands of enemies.
3. In response to Israel's promise to return to Yahweh, he had sent them capable leaders and delivered Israel from their enemies.
4. In response to Nahash's threat, Israel had requested a human king to rule over them.

---

13. Besides having the greatest number of spoken words among the prophets, Samuel is the subject of more verbs found outside of the quotative material within the narrative framework than any other prophet (142 times). Nathan, who is the subject of thirteen narrative-framework verbs, had the second-highest count among the prophets.

5. Yahweh granted Israel's request for a king.
6. Good would come to Israel if they and their king followed God.
7. Yahweh would bring disaster upon Israel if they apostatized.
8. Israel had done evil by asking for a king.
9. God would express his displeasure with Israel by sending a sign of judgment.

This passage serves as a stern indictment of Israel by Samuel. In his recitation of Israel's history, the prophet noted that in the past when Israel had been oppressed by an enemy they cried out to Yahweh, who in turn raised up a deliverer for them. By contrast, Samuel noted that in the Ammonite crisis Israel had demanded help from an earthly king, not from Yahweh. In doing this Israel had done evil and angered God. To avoid disasters such as Israel had experienced in the past, the people and their king would have to follow God. As with the Yahweh quotations, Samuel's longest statement makes connections with the Torah and foreshadows the disastrous events presented in the final chapters of the Former Prophets. These words would have been relevant to an exilic-period audience,[14] since Israel was at that time without an earthly king, but—as subtly suggested by the narrator—could still look to Yahweh as their true king.

2 Samuel 12:7–12

The prophet Nathan's longest and most prominent quotation, like Samuel's, possesses a condemnatory tone. This statement exhibits supplemental highlighting by being addressed to King David within the royal palace in Jerusalem on the day of or soon after the festive occasion of the birth of a child to David and Bathsheba.

Within the prophet's statement the following ideas are expressed:

1. Yahweh had made David king over Israel.
2. Yahweh had protected David from Saul.

---

14. The question of when the books of Samuel attained their final canonical form is certainly a debatable one. My personal conviction is that an exilic-period editor/writer took accurate accounts dating to the period of the United Monarchy and created a document that retained historical accuracy while at the same time addressed theological and political issues relevant to his contemporary orthodox Yahwistic community. For further discussion see Bergen, *1, 2 Samuel*, 18–24.

3. Yahweh had given David Saul's house and wives, as well as Israel and Judah, and would have given David even more if David had asked for it.
4. By bringing about Uriah's death and taking his wife, David had shown contempt for the word of the Yahweh.
5. Because David had shown contempt for Yahweh and had taken Uriah's wife as his own, the sword would perpetually be in David's house.
6. Yahweh would henceforth raise up evil against David from his own household.
7. Yahweh would take David's wives and give them to one who would publicly lie with them.

This well-known prophetic message serves as a sorrowful tempering, though not elimination of, Yahweh's promises to David in 2 Samuel 7:4–16. Besides reinforcing the truth that David's success and prosperity were God's doing, this passage suggests that when even one so mighty as a king shows contempt for Yahweh's word, disaster of overwhelming magnitude results. Nathan's words speak of David's displacement of a previous regime and his enrichment at its expense, as well as the disasters that would come upon David and his descendants because of his sin.

These words prepare the reader for the tragic events that immediately follow in David's life. But they also possess a larger significance in that they reinforce the overarching narrative plotline of the Former Prophets. Like David, Israel displaced a former regime in the land, became possessors of the previous group's wealth, sinned against Yahweh, and would experience loss and humiliation as a result. The narrator's words expressed through Nathan thus would have spoken poignantly to those Israelites who themselves had experienced catastrophic loss and humiliation.

1 Kings 11:31–39

The prophet Ahijah's longest quote (165 words) continues the pattern of censure and judgment found in the most prominent quotations of Samuel and Nathan. Several factors suggest that this quotation is less important than others that have been discussed up to this point: it is attributed to the third most prominent prophet (one who had only two quotations in the narrative), the addressee was Jeroboam, who at the time was only a higher-level official in Solomon's court; and its setting was in a field outside Jerusalem.

Nevertheless, discourse criticism suggests that the words must be treated as significant. As a genuine prophet of Yahweh, Ahijah was a member of the second-highest-ranking category. In addition, the bulk of Ahijah's statement is an embedded quotation attributed to Yahweh, and the addressee Jeroboam would become a significant man in the history of Northern Israel as both a person of promise and shame.

Several key propositions are present within Ahijah's words to Jeroboam:

1. Yahweh had decided to tear the kingdom out of Solomon's hands because of the king's apostasy and general disobedience.
2. For David's sake Yahweh would give the Davidic dynasty permanent control over Jerusalem.
3. Because of Solomon's sins, Jeroboam would be made king over ten Israelite tribes.
4. If Jeroboam diligently obeyed Yahweh as David had done, Yahweh would establish a dynasty for Jeroboam over Israel that was as enduring as David's.
5. Yahweh's punishment of the Davidic dynasty because of Solomon's sins would not be permanent.

As Nathan's most prominent words do, so also do Ahijah's further trim the sails of the Davidic promise expressed in 2 Samuel 7:4–16. For the sake of righteous David, Yahweh would retain key elements of his gracious endowment to David, but at a level more suggestive of symbolism than substance.

The Royal Quotes

2 Samuel 22:2–51

According to the guidelines established in Quote Prominence Analysis, this quotation qualifies as the most prominent quotation attributed to a king. Its placement in the mouth of David, the central human figure of the narrative accounts of the United Monarchy, and its length (365 words) are sufficient to suggest its author-intended centrality. Additional highlighting is found in the fact that it is cast as poetry and not prose. The unique nature of its temporal setting—"when Yahweh delivered [David] from the hand of all his enemies and from the hand of Saul" (v. 1)—and its lack of an addressee have the effect of separating this quotation from its narrative context, thus creating the literary equivalent of a solitaire-diamond mounting for a ring.

This extensive quote is a virtual duplicate of Psalm 18, though its context-related function differs significantly. H. W. Hertzberg describes it as "a theological commentary on the history of David."[15] I have previously described it as a "showcase [of] the pious core of David's being."[16] Structurally, the material is understood to be a symmetrical chiasmus consisting of five sections, to which is appended a one-verse postscript. Its structure can be displayed as follows:

    A   Praise for Yahweh (vv. 2–4)
       B   Yahweh's deliverance of David (vv. 5–20)
          C   Reasons for David's deliverance (vv. 21–29)
       B' Yahweh's deliverance of David (vv. 30–46)
    A' Praise for Yahweh (vv. 47–50)
D Postscript: Yahweh's enduring support for the house of David (v. 51)

The central, and therefore most prominent, element in the chiastic structure[17] expresses reasons for David's great success within his career. Among the propositions found in this section are the following: (1) Yahweh had rewarded David according to David's righteousness (v. 21); (2) David had followed Yahweh's laws blamelessly, keeping himself from sin; and (3) Yahweh was David's lamp, providing him with guidance. These statements collectively reinforce the author's thesis that David embodied the Israelite ideal of kingship. As such, the central propositions in this quotation prepare the reader for the author's later use of David as the yardstick by which later kings would be evaluated.[18] The flanking layers of propositions within

---

15. H. W. Hertzberg, *I and II Samuel*, trans. J. S. Bowden (Philadelphia: Westminster, 1964), 393.
16. Bergen, *1, 2 Samuel*, 452.
17. I am indebted to the fine linguist L. F. Bliese for this insight (cf. "Structural and Metrical Parameters in Hebrew Poetry" [unpublished paper, Seminar on Discourse Linguistics and Biblical Hebrew, Dallas, June 1993]).
18. Cf.1 Kings 3:14; 11:4, 6, 33, 38; 15:3, 5, 11; 2 Kings 16:2; 18:3; 22:2.

David's speech (vv. 2–20, 30–50) contain propositions supportive of the theses found in verses 21–29: (1) Yahweh was David's protector; (2) Yahweh's multifaceted provisions enabled David to win great victories.

Of particular prominence within David's longest speech is its conclusion in verse 51: "[Yahweh] gives his king great victories; he shows unfailing kindness to his anointed, to David and his descendants forever." Because of their placement as the final words within the most prominent king's longest quote, these participial clauses occupy a position of special prominence, and should be understood as ones intentionally highlighted by the author.

Among the concepts contained in verse 51 are the following: (1) David's successes are the result of Yahweh's active involvement in his life; (2) David is Yahweh's divinely selected *(māšîaḥ)* king over Israel; and (3) the Davidic dynasty is the recipient of Yahweh's eternal, unfailing kindness *(ḥesed)*. Though these ideas are placed in David's mouth and can be legitimately understood as David's actual words, they are included in the Bible because they express core aspects of the writer's own understanding of David and the Davidic dynasty. While they are brought into focus through a technique regularly employed to highlight information, they are ideas that repeated elsewhere in various ways.[19]

1 Kings 8:23–53

Solomon's 565-word quotation recorded here stands as the longest quotation within the United Monarchy accounts. The magnificent length of the quotation—two hundred words (55 percent) longer than the second-longest quote, added to the fact that it was spoken by a particularly prominent king—is enough to mark this as one of the most important attributed statements of 1 Samuel 8–1 Kings 11, and therefore a likely center for statements particularly significant to the author. Other details supplied by the author ensure that this section is given special attention: its temporal setting is during a momentous occasion in Israelite history, the time of the dedication of the temple, shortly after Yahweh's glory had filled the build-

---

19. Yahweh's presence in David's life and the attendant successes that were reflected in it can be seen in 1 Samuel 16:13; 17:37, 46; 18:12, 14, 28; 19:5; 23:4; 24:4, 18; 25:29–31, 38–39; 26:24; 30:23; 2 Samuel 4:9; 5:10, 19–20, 24; 8:6, 14; 18:31; 22:1, 19; 1 Kings 1:29; David as Yahweh's chosen Messiah for Israel is seen in 2 Samuel 5:3, 12; 7:8; 12:7; the eternal dimension of the Davidic dynasty is seen in 1 Kings 2:45.

ing (v. 11); its geographic setting is that of one of the holiest sites in Israel—in front of the altar of burnt offerings located in the temple courtyard in Jerusalem (v. 22); and its addressee is Yahweh. Furthermore, the statement is specifically identified as both a prayer and supplication (v. 54), the only quotation in the United Monarchy accounts to be labeled in this way.

An abbreviated summary of the statements contained in this prayer includes the following:

1. Yahweh is a peerless and merciful God.
2. Yahweh, the faithful God of the covenant, has fulfilled terms of the Davidic covenant.
3. Yahweh had promised to maintain the Davidic dynasty as long as his descendants followed David's godly example.
4. Yahweh is too great to be contained in an earthly temple
5. Yahweh is asked to dispense justice.
6. Yahweh is asked to forgive and restore his people when they repent following divinely dispensed punishment, particularly the punishment of exile.

Thus, in the longest quotation present in the United Monarchy accounts are found the themes of Yahweh's mercy, his commitment to the Davidic covenant, his lack of need for any earthly temple, and prominent interest in having Yahweh restore his people to the land of Israel following their deportation. Solomon's prayer is thus an almost prophetic expression of themes and concerns characteristic of an orthodox Yahwistic Judahite living during the exilic period. This is not to say that the words were not authentically a part of Solomon's original prayer, only that the author of the final text may have included only those portions of Solomon's words that spoke most relevantly to the exilic community to whom the published work was originally addressed.

Summary and Conclusions

According to the results of the preceding Quote Prominence Analysis of 1 Samuel 8–1 Kings 11, the author's primary thesis in the United Monarchy accounts is located in 2 Samuel 7:4–16. In summary it is this: Yahweh, who was responsible for David's rise to power and for his success as king, permanently established the House of David as the family line from which legitimate rulers over the people of Israel would come.

Discourse criticism suggests that the second most important theme established by the biblical author is found in 1 Kings 9:3–9. It may be briefly stated as follows: although Yahweh accepted the temple built by Solomon as a place for his name to dwell, he would destroy that temple and exile the Israelites if they or their Davidic kings apostatized.

Discourse criticism understands these two theses to be central because the biblical author placed them in the longest quotations attributed to Yahweh, the highest-ranking character within the author's hierarchy of beings. Secondary highlighting features associated with these quotations underscore the impression that the biblical writer intended readers to look to these quotations for the author's major ideas.

Prominent ideas are also expressed in the statistically significant quotations attributed to the genuine prophets of Yahweh of the United Monarchy period. The words of Samuel, Nathan, and Ahijah all express warnings and judgments that would have been consistent with those of an orthodox Yahwist of the exilic period.

In their order of prominence, the key themes expressed through quotations attributed to prophets are the following. First, Israel had sinned by demanding an earthly king to deliver them instead of relying upon Yahweh for deliverance; nevertheless the Israelites could avoid judgment if they and their king recognized Yahweh as their true king. Second, the Davidic dynasty would experience severe judgment because of the sins of David and Solomon: consequences of their sins would include deadly family strife; reduction of the territory ruled by the House of David; and the breakup of the nation of Israel, with a non-Davidic king ruling over the bulk of the Israelite tribes. However, the judgment against the House of David would not be permanent.

Long quotations by kings also contained thematically significant material. Though David and Solomon played exceptionally prominent roles in the narrative action of the United Monarchy accounts, Quote Prominence Analysis suggests that the propositions contained within their quotations are less thematically central than those attributed to the Israelite deity and his spokesmen. Accordingly, David's most prominent speech is an eloquent psalm of praise to Yahweh in which the king credits the successes of his career to Yahweh and his obedience to Yahweh. In a different vein,

Solomon's longest quotation is a heartfelt prayer to Yahweh, prophetically requesting forgiveness and restoration for Israelites who would sin and be punished with exile.

While biblical authors can and do convey theological and political postulates in various ways, their preferred method is through the speech acts of the most significant characters within their narratives. Quote Prominence Analysis functions as a useful tool for identifying the most likely repositories of the main ideas the biblical writers were attempting to convey through the medium of narrative.

18

A FUNNY THING HAPPENED ON THE WAY TO THE GALLOWS!

Irony, Humor, and Other Literary Features of the Book of Esther

Gordon H. Johnston

THE BOOK OF ESTHER REPRESENTS AN ideal test case for the value of a literary approach to Scripture. Since the nineteenth century, nonconservatives have pointed to historical and chronological problems that seem to undercut its historicity.[1] However, recent archaeological and historical discoveries have answered many of these questions,[2] even showing that many details in the book accurately reflect the story's historical-cultural background.[3]

This essay is dedicated to my former teacher, present colleague, and esteemed friend, Dr. Eugene H. Merrill, who has made a profound impact on the conservative approach to the history of ancient Israel and its contribution to the study of Scripture.

1. For detailed discussion, see Carey A. Moore, *Esther,* AB (Garden City, N.Y.: Doubleday, 1971), xxx–liv; David J. A. Clines, *Ezra, Nehemiah, Esther,* NCBC (Grand Rapids: Eerdmans, 1984), 256–61; and Michael V. Fox, *Character and Ideology in the Book of Esther* (Columbia: University of South Carolina Press, 1991), 131–40.
2. J. Stafford Wright, "The Historicity of the Book of Esther," in *New Perspectives on the Old Testament,* ed. J. Barton Payne (Waco, Tex.: Word, 1970), 37–47; Carey A. Moore, "Archaeology and the Book of Esther," *BA* 38, no. 3 (1975): 62–79; William Shea, "Esther and History," *AUSS* 14 (1976): 227–46; Alan R. Millard, "The Persian Names in Esther and the Reliability of the Hebrew Text," *JBL* 96 (1977): 481–88; Edwin M. Yamauchi, "The Archaeological Background of Esther," *BSac* 137 (1980): 99–117; "Mordecai, the Persepolis Tablets, and the Susa Excavations," *VT* 42 (1992): 272–75; and idem, *Persia and the Bible* (Grand Rapids: Baker, 1990), 226–39.
3. A. Barucq, "Esther et la cour de Susa," *BTS* 39 (1961): 3; A. Leo Oppenheim, "On Royal Gardens in Mesopotamia," *JNES* 24 (1965): 328–33; W. F. Albright, "The Lachish Cosmetic Burner and Esther 2:12," in *A Light unto My Path,* ed. H. N. Bream et al. (Philadelphia: Temple University Press, 1974), 25–32; H. Shanks, "Albright, The Beautician Reveals Secrets of Queen Esther's Cosmetic Aids," *BAR* 2, No. 1 (1976): 1–6; Robert Gordis, "Studies in the Esther Narrative," *JBL* 95 (1976): 47–48; Ran Zadok, "On the Historical Background of Esther," *BN*

Nevertheless, archaeological and historical research has failed to document the historicity of the actual events narrated,[4] and due to their inherent limitations it is probably unrealistic to hope that the historicity of the scroll can ever be fully verified.[5] So many historical questions probably will remain unsolved.[6]

Consequently, contemporary scholars have focused more and more attention on the literary study of the book.[7] Here we will summarize some of the recent literary studies of the book of Esther and show how a literary approach can help solve some perennial exegetical/theological questions.

Literary Structure of the Book of Esther

Critical scholars often suggest that the book is composed of three independent sources (Mordecai story, Esther story, Purim story) and that the epilogue (9:6–10:3) is a late addition.[8] However, recent literary studies

---

24 (1984): 18–23; idem, "The Historical Background of Esther," *Beth Mikra* 30 (1984–85): 186–89 [Hebrew]; Yishaq Avishur, "Toward the Historical Background of the Scroll of Esther," *Beth Mikra* 32 (1986–87): 290–91 [Hebrew]; G. A. Klingbeil, "*r-k-s* and Esther 8,10–14: A Semantic Note," *ZAW* 107, no. 2 (1995): 301–3; Zefira Gitay, "Esther and the Queen's Throne," in *A Feminist Companion to Esther, Judith and Susanna*, Feminist Companion to the Bible, ed. Athalya Brenner (Sheffield: Sheffield Academic Press, 1995), 7:136–48.

4. For example, see David J. A. Clines, "In Quest of the Historical Mordecai," *VT* 41 (1991): 129–36; and Michael Hertzler, "The Book of Esther—Where Does Fiction Start and History End?" *BRev* 8, no. 1 (1992): 24–30, 41.

5. For example, see Alfred J. Hoerth, *Archaeology and the Old Testament* (Grand Rapids: Baker, 1998), 13–22.

6. Carey A. Moore, "Eight Questions Most Frequently Asked About the Book of Esther," *BRev* 3:1 (1987): 16–31; and Joshua J. Adler, "The Book of Esther: Some Questions and Responses," *JBQ* 19 (1990–1991): 186–90.

7. For example, Werner Dommershausen, *Die Estherrolle: Stil und Ziel einer alttestamentlichen Schrift* (Stuttgart: Katholisches Bibelwerk, 1968); W. Lee Humphreys, "The Story of Esther and Mordecai: An Early Jewish Novella," in *Saga, Legend, Tale, Novella, Fable*, ed. George W. Coats (Sheffield: JSOT, 1985), 97–113; Arye Bartal, "The Art of Narration in the Scroll of Esther," *Dor le Dor* 14, no. 3 (1986): 152–56; Mark Lehman, "The Literary Study of Esther," *BV* 26, no. 2 (1992): 85–95; Adele Berlin, "The Book of Esther and Ancient Storytelling," *JBL* 120 (2001): 3–14. Also see Carey A. Moore, *Studies in the Book of Esther* (New York: KTAV, 1982); idem, "Esther Revisited Again: A Further Examination of Certain Esther Studies of the Past Ten Years," *HAR* 7 (1983): 169–86; "Esther Revisited: An Examination of Esther Studies over the Past Decade," in *Biblical and Related Studies Presented to Samuel Iwry*, ed. A. Kort and S. Morschauser (Winona Lake, Ind.: Eisenbrauns, 1985), 163–72; Benjamin E. Scolnic, "Thinking Seriously About Purim: An Annotated Bibliography on the Book of Esther," *CJ* 47, no. 2 (1995): 37–45; Katerina J. A. Larkin, *Ruth and Esther*, Old Testament Guides (Sheffield: Sheffield Academic Press, 1996); and W. Lee Humphreys, "The Story of Esther in Several Forms: Recent Studies," *RelSRev* 24 (1998): 335–42.

8. For example, see David J. A. Clines, *The Esther Scroll: The Story of the Story*, JSOTSup 30 (Sheffield: JSOT, 1984), 9–68, 93–138; Michael V. Fox, *The Redaction of the Book of Esther*, SBL Monograph

reveal greater literary unity than is often assumed.[9] Every episode is crucial to the plot; no scene is superfluous.[10] Sections often alleged to be late additions are actually necessary for the integrity of the overall structure.

Plot Structure

The story features a carefully arranged plot structure.[11] It is divided into a prologue (1:1–2:23), plot proper (3:1–9:19) and epilogue (9:20–10:3).[12] These are marked by shifts in topic and time-frame. The prologue, which encompasses more than six years, proceeds at a leisurely pace. The plot proper encompasses one year, when the crisis breaks out and is resolved. At the height of its drama, the action rushes forward breathlessly, with the events of eighteen days squeezed into five chapters. The epilogue begins after the threat to the Jews has been resolved: Purim is established and Mordecai uses his political position to benefit his Jewish brethren henceforth. The plot structure is displayed below:

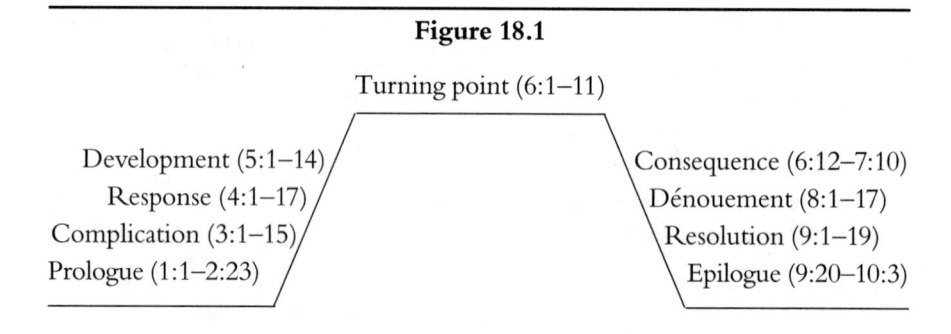

Figure 18.1

Turning point (6:1–11)

Development (5:1–14)
Response (4:1–17)
Complication (3:1–15)
Prologue (1:1–2:23)

Consequence (6:12–7:10)
Dénouement (8:1–17)
Resolution (9:1–19)
Epilogue (9:20–10:3)

Series 40 (Atlanta: Scholars Press, 1991), 96–102; and Ruth Kossmann, *Die Esthernovelle* (Leiden: E. J. Brill, 2000), 70–212. Also see the earlier studies of Bruce William Jones, "The So-Called Appendix to the Book of Esther," *Semitics* 6 (1978): 36–43; Samuel E. Loewenstamm, "Esther 9:29–32: The Genesis of a Late Addition," *HUCA* 42 (1971): 117–24; D. Daube, "The Last Chapter of Esther," *JQR* 37 (1946–47): 139–47; and Charles C. Torrey, "The Older Book of Esther," *HTR* 37 (1944): 1–40.

9. Jack M. Sasson, "Esther," in *The Literary Guide to the Bible*, ed. Robert Alter and Frank Kermode (Cambridge, Mass: Harvard University Press, 1987), 335–42; Frederic W. Bush, *Ruth/Esther*, WBC (Dallas: Word, 1996), 297–309; and Charles V. Dorothy, *The Books of Esther: Structure, Genre and Textual Integrity*, JSOTSup 187 (Sheffield: Sheffield Academic Press, 1997), 24, 226–75.
10. Bush, *Ruth/Esther*, 297–309, 336–37; and Dorothy, *The Books of Esther*, 24.
11. Adele Berlin, "The Book of Esther and Ancient Storytelling," *JBL* 120 (2001): 3–14.
12. Bush, *Ruth/Esther*, 297–309; and Dorothy, *The Books of Esther*, 226–75.

Symmetrical Structure

The plot structure is remarkably symmetrical. The nine episodes (displayed above) each consist of two scenes each, with the exception of the first, middle, and last episodes which contain three scenes each (see following chart). The plot structure is also arranged chiastically.[13] This is not surprising, because narrative plots in general tend to be somewhat symmetrical. The epilogue generally corresponds to the prologue; the resolution typically reverses the complication; and the turning point is often the hinge between rising and falling action. So *chiasmus* is the *vertical* counterpart to the *horizontal* display of a plot structure. The symmetrical structure of Esther is displayed in figure 18.2 on the next page.

This symmetrical structure highlights two features. First, the turning point in a chiasm is often theologically significant or literarily dramatic.[14] Here a seemingly insignificant event—the insomnia of the king—plays an extraordinarily dramatic role in the plot. The ironic scene that ensues—Haman unwittingly volunteers the very method by which his archenemy Mordecai is honored—signals a dramatic turn of events in favor of the Jews. Second, this symmetrical structure also highlights the theme of reversal.[15] The events in the first half describe situations portending disaster for the Jews, events that could be expected to lead, in the natural course of events, to their destruction. But the second half of the book reveals that the exact opposite of what was expected actually occurred. Haman's plot was foiled, and the Jews triumphed over their enemies.

---

13. Yehuda T. Radday, "Chiasm in Joshua, Judges and Others," *LB* 27–28 (1973): 9–10; Sandra Berg, *The Book of Esther: Motifs, Themes and Structure,* SBL Diss. Series 44 (Missoula, Mont.: Scholars Press, 1979), 106–13; Michael V. Fox, "The Structure of the Book of Esther," in *Isac Leo Seligmann Volume: Essays on the Bible and the Ancient World,* ed. A. Rofe and Y. Zakovitch (Jerusalem: Rubinstein, 1983), 3:291–303; W. T. McBride, "Esther Passes: Chiasm, Lex Talio and Money in the Book of Esther," in *Not in Heaven: Coherence and Complexity in Biblical Narrative,* ed. J. Rosenblatt and J. Sitterson (Bloomington, Ind.: Indiana University Press, 1991), 211–23; David A. Dorsey, *The Literary Structure of the Old Testament* (Grand Rapids: Baker, 1999), 162–64.
14. See Craig Blomberg, "The Structure of 2 Corinthians 1–7," *CTR* 4 (1989): 4–7. Also David N. Freedman, preface to *Chiasm in Antiquity,* ed. John W. Welch (Hildesheim: Gerstenberg, 1981), 7; H. van Dyke Parunak, "Oral Typesetting: Some Uses of Biblical Structure," *Bib* 62 (1981): 165–66; Ernst R. Wendland, "The Discourse Analysis of Hebrew Poetry: A Procedural Outline," in *Discourse Perspectives on Hebrew Poetry in the Scriptures,* ed. Ernst R. Wendland (New York: United Bible Societies, 1994), 15–16; and Dorsey, *The Literary Structure of the Old Testament,* 40–41.
15. Fox, "Structure of the Book of Esther," 291–303; and Berg, *The Book of Esther,* 93–110.

Figure 18.2

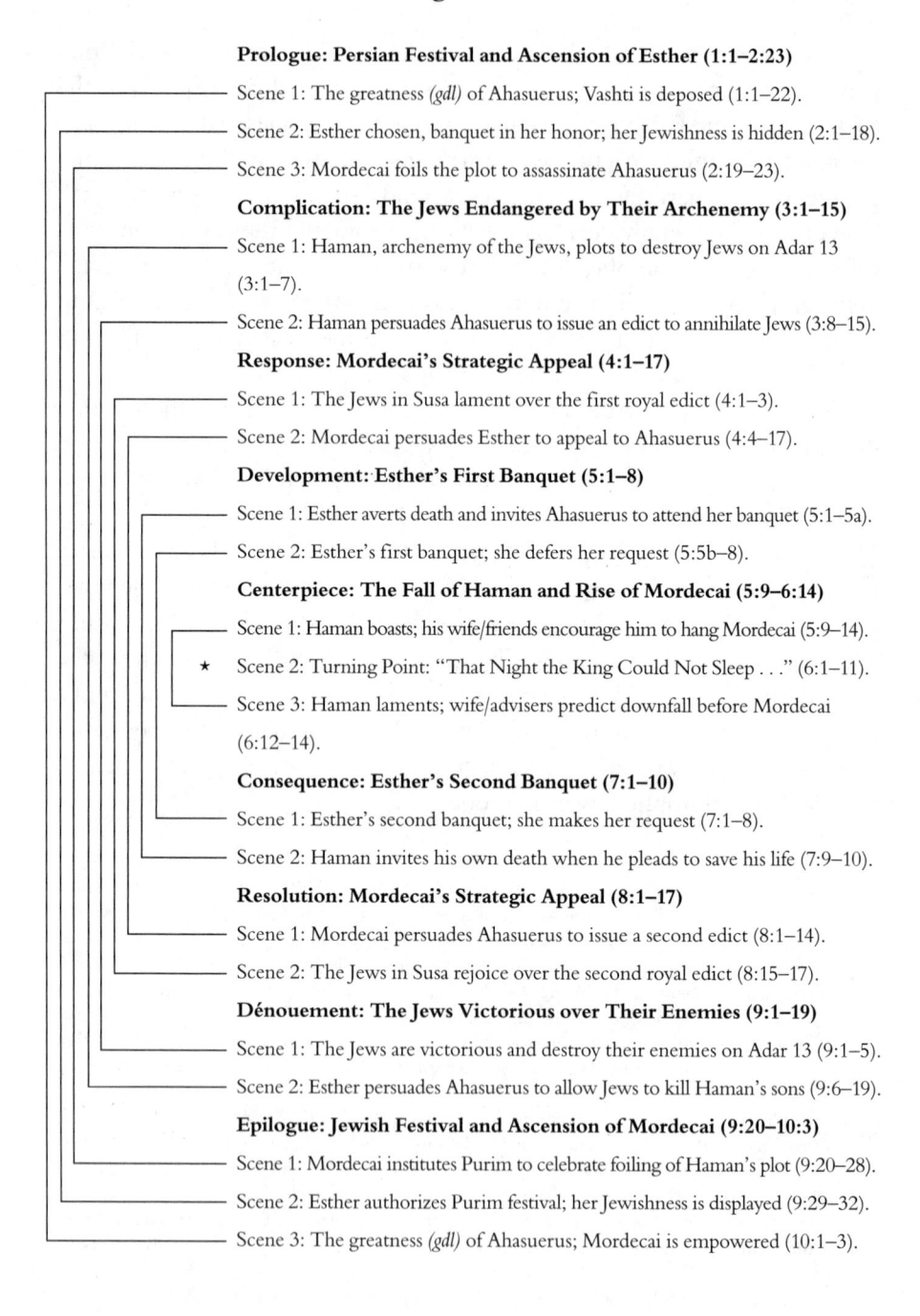

Prologue: Persian Festival and Ascension of Esther (1:1–2:23)
Scene 1: The greatness *(gdl)* of Ahasuerus; Vashti is deposed (1:1–22).
Scene 2: Esther chosen, banquet in her honor; her Jewishness is hidden (2:1–18).
Scene 3: Mordecai foils the plot to assassinate Ahasuerus (2:19–23).

Complication: The Jews Endangered by Their Archenemy (3:1–15)
Scene 1: Haman, archenemy of the Jews, plots to destroy Jews on Adar 13 (3:1–7).
Scene 2: Haman persuades Ahasuerus to issue an edict to annihilate Jews (3:8–15).

Response: Mordecai's Strategic Appeal (4:1–17)
Scene 1: The Jews in Susa lament over the first royal edict (4:1–3).
Scene 2: Mordecai persuades Esther to appeal to Ahasuerus (4:4–17).

Development: Esther's First Banquet (5:1–8)
Scene 1: Esther averts death and invites Ahasuerus to attend her banquet (5:1–5a).
Scene 2: Esther's first banquet; she defers her request (5:5b–8).

Centerpiece: The Fall of Haman and Rise of Mordecai (5:9–6:14)
Scene 1: Haman boasts; his wife/friends encourage him to hang Mordecai (5:9–14).
★ Scene 2: Turning Point: "That Night the King Could Not Sleep . . ." (6:1–11).
Scene 3: Haman laments; wife/advisers predict downfall before Mordecai (6:12–14).

Consequence: Esther's Second Banquet (7:1–10)
Scene 1: Esther's second banquet; she makes her request (7:1–8).
Scene 2: Haman invites his own death when he pleads to save his life (7:9–10).

Resolution: Mordecai's Strategic Appeal (8:1–17)
Scene 1: Mordecai persuades Ahasuerus to issue a second edict (8:1–14).
Scene 2: The Jews in Susa rejoice over the second royal edict (8:15–17).

Dénouement: The Jews Victorious over Their Enemies (9:1–19)
Scene 1: The Jews are victorious and destroy their enemies on Adar 13 (9:1–5).
Scene 2: Esther persuades Ahasuerus to allow Jews to kill Haman's sons (9:6–19).

Epilogue: Jewish Festival and Ascension of Mordecai (9:20–10:3)
Scene 1: Mordecai institutes Purim to celebrate foiling of Haman's plot (9:20–28).
Scene 2: Esther authorizes Purim festival; her Jewishness is displayed (9:29–32).
Scene 3: The greatness *(gdl)* of Ahasuerus; Mordecai is empowered (10:1–3).

Parallel Panels

The corresponding elements in the *chiasmus* appear in a series of parallel panels.[16] For example, Esther's first banquet (5:5b–8) is paired with her second banquet (7:1–8). Haman's first conversation with his wife and friends (5:9–14) is paired with his second conversation with the same (6:12–14). Mordecai's appeal to Esther to intervene on behalf of her Jewish brethren (4:4–17) is paired with his appeal to Ahasuerus to intervene on behalf of his Jewish citizens (8:1–14). The Jews in Susa lament over the first edict (4:1–3) and in the parallel panel they rejoice over the second edict (8:15–17). Haman's plot to annihilate the Jews on Adar 13 (3:1–7) is paired with the Jews defeating their enemies on that day (9:1–5). Haman persuades Ahasuerus to decree the Jews' destruction on Adar 13 (3:7–15), while Esther persuades him to certify a counter decree on Adar 13–14 (9:6–19). Esther's banquet and Mordecai's foiling the plot of Teresh and Bigthana (2:19–23) is paired with the Jewish festival celebrating the failure of Haman's plot (9:20–28). Esther averts expected death when she approaches the king (5:1–5a), while Haman unexpectedly invites death because he throws himself upon the queen (7:9–10). The chiasm also highlights parallels between the prologue (1:1–2:23) and epilogue (9:20–10:3): the Persian festival in the prologue is paired with the Jewish festival of Purim in the epilogue, and Esther's earlier ascent to queenship is paired with Mordecai's later ascent to political power.

To ensure that his readers do not miss these mirror relationships, the narrator often uses identical or nearly identical terms in the corresponding parallel panels.[17] For example, a remarkable 78 percent of the Hebrew terms in 3:12–15 are repeated in the parallel panel in 8:9–14:[18]

---

16. Fox, *Character and Ideology in the Book of Esther*, 159–62; Berg, *The Book of Esther*, 106–7; and Athalya Brenner, "Esther in the Looking Glass: On Symmetry and Duplication in the Scroll of Esther," *BN* 86 (1981): 267–78.
17. Berg, *Book of Esther*, 106–7; Fox, "Structure of the Book of Esther," 294–96; and Bush, *Ruth/Esther*, 323.
18. For convenience, the parallels are displayed in the author's translation. All Scripture quotations in this chapter are the author's translations.

Figure 18.3

First Royal Edict: Jews Endangered (3:12–15)

On the thirteenth day of the first month, the royal scribes were summoned. It was written in accordance with all Haman commanded the king's satraps and governors of each and every province, as well as the princes of each and every people—to each and every province in its own script and to each and every people in its own language. It was written in King Ahasuerus's name, and sealed with the king's signet ring. Then letters were sent by the hand of courtiers to slaughter, to slay, and to destroy all the Jews—both young and old, together with children and women, with their property as spoil—on a single day, the thirteenth day of the twelfth month, the month of Adar—with a copy of the edict to be issued as law in each and every province, made public to all the peoples, that they prepare for that day. Then the courtiers went out swiftly at the king's command. The edict was also issued in the Fortress of Susa. Then the king and Haman sat down to feast, but Susa was thrown into dismay.

Second Royal Edict: Jews Delivered (8:9–14)

On the twenty-third day of the third month, the royal scribes were summoned. It was written in accordance with all Mordecai commanded the Jews as well as the king's satraps and governors, as well as the princes of the provinces from India to Nubia, 127 provinces—to each and every province in its own script and to each and every people in its own language. He wrote it in King Ahasuerus's name, and sealed it with the king's signet ring. Then he sent letters by the hand of courtiers to slaughter, to slay and to destroy all their foes—together with children and women, with their property as spoil—on a single day, the thirteenth day of the twelfth month, the month of Adar—with a copy of the edict to be issued as law in each and every province, made public to all the peoples, that the Jews prepare for that day. . . . Then the courtiers went out swiftly at the king's command. The edict was also issued in the Fortress of Susa. Then Mordecai went out, and Susa rejoiced and was merry.

The parallels between 4:1–3 and 8:15–17, the Jews' response to the first and second edicts, are equally striking. For example, Mordecai's rending his clothes and putting on sackcloth and ashes (4:1) is reversed by his putting on royal robes and a golden crown (8:15). The Jews' mourning and fasting (4:3) is reversed by their rejoicing and feasting (8:17). The reversal is highlighted by the repetition of identical wording between the two panels: "And in every province wherever the king's command and his edict came, there was [mourning and weeping/gladness and rejoicing] among the Jews, with [fasting and lamenting/feasting and rejoicing]" (4:3a and 8:17a). This is seen as follows:

Figure 18.4

Response to the First Royal Edict (4:1–3)	**Response to the Second Royal Edict (8:15–17)**
Then Mordecai went out into the city when he learned what happened. Mordecai rent his clothes and put on sackcloth and ashes, wailing with a loud and bitter cry. Then he went to the entrance of the king's gate for no one could enter the king's gate clothed with sackcloth. And in every province, wherever the king's command and his edict came, there was mourning and weeping among the Jews, with fasting and lamenting. And many of the Jews laid down in sackcloth and ashes.	Then Mordecai went out from the presence of the king in royal robes of blue and white, with a great golden crown and a mantle of fine linen and purple, while the city of Susa shouted and rejoiced. The Jews had light and gladness and joy and honor. And in every province and in every city, wherever the king's command and his edict came, there was gladness and joy among the Jews, with feasting and rejoicing. And many people of the land claimed to be Jews out of fear of the Jews.

Turning Point in the Plot Structure

Scholars generally agree that 6:1–11 is the turning point in the plot structure.[19] The parallel panels are structured around this pivotal episode. The

---

19. Radday, "Chiasm," 9–10; Fox, "Structure of the Book of Esther," 302; and idem, *Character and Ideology in the Book of Esther*, 162.

preceding episodes describe the endangerment of the Jews; those that follow depict their deliverance. This pivotal episode is formally bracketed between Esther's two banquets, which play a crucial role in the plot development (5:1–8; 7:1–10). This episode also functions as the thematic turning point: the dramatic and unexpected reversal in the status of Haman and Mordecai in 6:1–11 foreshadows the eventual reversal in the fate of the Jews: it moves from their being endangered by their enemies to their emerging triumphant over their enemies. This pivotal episode is appropriately filled with irony and reversals of its own, depicting the most comical scene in the book: Assuming Ahasuerus is speaking about him, Haman unwittingly volunteers the method by which his archenemy, Mordecai, is honored by the king.

Characterization in the Book of Esther

Recent literary studies also focus on characterization in the book,[20] particularly the characterization of Esther herself.[21] Initially portrayed as a flat character who carries no weight in Persian politics, she becomes increasingly significant as the story unfolds. In fact, the plot is structured to highlight her progressively complex role.[22] From a dependent orphan, completely submissive to her uncle's manipulations and the king's whims, she emerges at plot's end in control of her own life—and the life of a nation.

---

20. For example, see Fox, *Character and Ideology in the Book of Esther,* 164–95; André Lacocque, "Haman in the Book of Esther," *HAR* 11 (1987): 207–22; Marshall A. Portnoy, "Ahasuerus is the Villain," *Dor le Dor* 18 (1989): 187–89; Robert K. Russell, "Reply to 'Ahasuerus is the Villain,'" *Dor le Dor* 19 (1990): 34–39; Robert T. Hyman, "Who Is the Villain?" *JBQ* 20 (1991–1992): 155–58; Jeffrey M. Cohen, "Vashti—An Unsung Heroine," *JBQ* 24 (1996): 103–6; and Romen Ahituv, "The Book of Vashti," *Beth Mikra* 158 (1999): 252–55 [Hebrew].
21. See Fox, *Character and Ideology in the Book of Esther,* 196–211; Katheryn Darr, "More Than Just a Pretty Face: Critical, Rabbinical, and Feminist Perspectives on Esther," in *Far More Precious Than Jewels: Perspectives on Biblical Women* (Louisville: Westminster/John Knox, 1991), 164–202; Linda Day, *Three Faces of a Queen: Characterization in the Books of Esther,* JSOTSup 186 (Sheffield: Sheffield Academic Press, 1995); John F. Craghan, "Esther: A Fully Liberated Woman," *TBT* 24 (1986): 6–11; Ronald T. Hyman, "Esther 3:3—the Question with No Response," *JBQ* 22 (1994): 103–9; Agnethe Siquans, "Die Rolle Esters im Esterbuch in Verhältnis zu Mordechai: Fürbitterin und Vorbild ihres Volkes," *BN* 86 (1997): 77–89; Leila L. Bronner, "Reclaiming Esther: From Sex Object to Sage," *JBQ* 26 (1998): 3–10; and Athlaya Brenner, "Looking at Esther Through the Looking Glass," in *A Feminist Companion to Esther, Judith and Susanna,* 71–80.
22. Wilma McClarty, "Esther," in *A Complete Literary Guide to the Bible,* ed. Leland Ryken and Tremper Longman III (Grand Rapids: Zondervan, 1993), 218.

Although 6:1–11 is the formal hinge-point in the plot structure (as noted above), 4:12–17 is the crucial turning point in the development of Esther's character.[23] Up to this point Esther has been the obedient niece of Mordecai, silently and willingly following his instructions, e.g., "Esther continually did whatever Mordecai said, just as she had done when he was raising her" (2:20). However, once he convinces her to aid her people (4:12–14), we witness a dramatic transformation in her entire demeanor (vv. 15–16). The once-submissive maiden suddenly issues her own commands to Mordecai, who "did everything which Esther commanded him" (v. 17). From this point, Esther becomes the initiator of events, reversing the roles of these two protagonists. She is now on her own, making astute decisions, planning strategy, handling crises, even risking her life. Indeed, she becomes the pivotal character in the rest of the story, functioning as the celebrated agent of the Jews' deliverance.[24]

The Prominent Role of Reversal in the Book of Esther

One of the main themes in the book is reversal.[25] This theme is explicitly stated in the story's climactic moment: "Now on the thirteenth day of the twelfth month, the month of Adar, when the king's word and his law were due to be carried out—on the very day when the enemies of the Jews had expected to gain control over them, *the reverse occurred:* The Jews gained control over their enemies" (9:1).[26] In several cases, reversals are explicitly marked by the repetition of identical or nearly identical wording.

---

23. Sandra B. Berg, "After the Exile: God and History in the Books of Chronicles and Esther," in *The Divine Helmsman: Studies on God's Control of Human Events, Presented to Lou H. Silberman*, ed. James L. Crenshaw and Samuel Sandmel (New York: KTAV, 1980), 115–16.
24. For feminist studies of the characterization of Esther, see Itumeleng J. Mosala, "The Implications of the Text of Esther for African Women's Struggle for Liberation in South America," *Semeia* 59 (1992): 129–39; Rikvah Lubitch, "A Feminist's Look at Esther," *Judaism* 42 (1993): 438–46; Susan Niditch, "Esther: Folklore, Wisdom, Feminism and Authority," in *A Feminist Companion to Esther, Judith and Susanna*, 26–46; Bea Wyler, "Esther: The Incomplete Emancipation of a Queen," in *A Feminist Companion to Esther, Judith and Susanna*, 111–35; and Klara Butting, "Esther: A New Interpretation of the Joseph Story in the Fight against Anti-Semitism and Sexism," in *Ruth and Esther*, A Feminist Companion to the Bible, 2d series, ed. Athalya Brenner (Sheffield: Sheffield Academic Press, 1999), 239–48.
25. Zdravko Stefanovic, "'Go at Once!' Thematic Reversals in the Book of Esther," *AJT* 8 (1994): 163–71; and Timothy S. Laniak, *Shame and Honor in the Book of Esther*, SBL Diss. Series 165 (Atlanta: Scholars Press, 1998), 2–7.
26. Berg, *The Book of Esther*, 105, 108.

For example, *"The king took his signet ring from his hand and gave it to Haman the Agagite, the son of Hammedatha, the enemy of the Jews"* (3:10) corresponds to *"The king took his signet ring, which he had taken from Haman, and gave it to Mordecai"* (8:2). When Ahasuerus granted permission to Haman to issue the first edict that endangered the Jews, he said, "Do *as you please* with the people" (3:11). Similarly, when granting permission to Mordecai to compose a second edict to deliver the Jews, he uttered similar words, "Write *as you please* with regard to the Jews" (8:8). In other cases the reversal is thematic. The month Adar was turned "from a time of grief to one of joy, from an occasion of mourning to a holiday" (9:22). The people to be annihilated end up a people to be feared (8:17). The reversal theme reaches its apogee when the Jews imitate the Persian manner of celebration (1:1–22): they too enjoy days of merriment and drinking (9:20–32).[27]

According to several scholars, many reversals in Esther are examples of peripety, sudden and unexpected reversals of circumstance or situations whereby intended actions produce the opposite results.[28] The occurrences of peripety in Esther are not incidental but form the very fabric of the story and the development of the plot: "Instead of a linear sequences of events, the Esther plot unfolds by reversals—not changes or breakdowns, but specific 180-degree turns. The force of evil is not merely overcome; it turns back on itself."[29] For example, Haman unwittingly volunteers the method by which his archenemy, Mordecai, is honored by the king (6:6–11). Haman's best-laid plans produce the opposite of what he hoped: he is hanged on the gallows he had built for Mordecai (7:9–10). Haman's master plan for Adar 13 backfires: the Jews are not only not annihilated but are given permission to kill all their enemies, including all ten of Haman's sons (9:1–19). Peripety is also highlighted by the climactic declaration, "Let the evil plan that [Haman] formed against the Jews recoil back upon his own head" (v. 25b).

---

27. Fox, *Character and Ideology in the Book of Esther,* 157.
28. Ibid., 153; Fox, "Structure of the Book of Esther," 296, 299; Berg, *The Book of Esther,* 103–110; idem, "After the Exile," 115–116; and Bush, *Ruth/Esther,* 323.
29. Kenneth M. Craig Jr., *Reading Esther* (Louisville: Westminster/John Knox, 1995), 81.

The Role of Irony in the Book of Esther

Irony permeates the story.[30] It adds to the literary quality of the book and enhances the reader's enjoyment.[31] Its humorous aspects were certainly well suited to the reading of the Scroll during the celebration of the Festival of Purim.

The narrator often gives his readers "inside" information so that they know more than the characters and thereby can discern the full significance of a situation. For example, unawares to Ahasuerus, the maiden he selects is a Jew—a critical development in the story. She is not only a member of the race against which Haman plots, but also the only person in the empire in a position to intervene.

The story is also filled with several cases in which what is least expected by one of the characters (usually Haman) occurs as a surprising plot twist. Haman attends Esther's second banquet assuming that he is the object of the queen's favor, only to become the object of the king's wrath. This shrewd politician becomes a hapless buffoon when he stumbles into a trap of his own making. Haman's intentions backfire when, falling before Esther to beg mercy, Ahasuerus mistakenly concludes that he is trying to rape the queen. Although he built the gallows to execute Mordecai, Haman ends up killed on his own device. Haman's plot to exterminate the Jews in the empire backfired: Those exterminated in the end are the enemies of the Jews, including all of Haman's sons.[32]

As previously noted, several forms of irony occur in the pivotal scene in 6:1–11. A seemingly mundane event plays a pivotal role in the resolution of the plot: Ahasuerus suffers from insomnia—which leads to his reading the royal chronicles and his discovery that Mordecai had gone unrewarded

---

30. B. W. Jones, "Two Misconceptions About the Book of Esther," *CBQ* 39 (1977): 171–81; Stan Goldman, "Narrative and Ethical Ironies in Esther," *JSOT* 47 (1990): 15–31; F. B. Huey, "Irony as the Key to Understanding the Book of Esther," *SwJT* 32:3 (1990): 36–39; Josiah Derby, "The Funniest Word in the Bible: Purim Torah," *JBQ* 22 (1994): 115–19; "The Paradox in the Book of Esther," *JBQ* 23 (1995): 116–19; M. D. Simon, "Many Thoughts in the Heart of Man: Irony and Theology in the Book of Esther," *Tradition* 31, no. 4 (1997): 5–27; and F. W. Bush, "The Book of Esther: *Opus non gratum* in the Christian Canon," *BBR* 8 (1998): 39–54.
31. Craig, *Reading Esther*, 120–46; Yehuda T. Radday, "Esther with Humour," in *On Humour and the Comic in the Hebrew Bible*, ed. Yehuda T. Radday and Athalya Brenner (Sheffield: Almond, 1990), 295–314; and Hershey H. Friedman, "Humor in the Hebrew Bible," *Humor* 13, no. 3 (2000): 258–85.
32. Haim M. I. Gevaryahu, "Esther Is a Story of Jewish Defense, Not a Story of Jewish Revenge," *JBQ* 21 (1993): 3–12.

for his good deed (6:1–3). Second, the omniscient narrator informs his audience about the events leading up to the king's desire to reward Mordecai (6:1–5). Although the question that Ahasuerus poses to Haman is fraught with ambiguity, the audience understands its meaning, while Haman clearly does not: "What should be done for the man whom the king wants to honor?" (6:6a). The narrator highlights the irony of the situation in the only occurrence of inner speech in the book: "Haman said to himself, 'Whom would the king want to honor more than me?'" (6:6b). Third, what Haman least expects occurs as a surprise development. Haman unwittingly initiates his own downfall by pronouncing the reward that, to his surprise, is bestowed upon Mordecai. The ultimate irony is that Haman is forced to honor the very man whom he himself loathed (6:7–10). Whereas he had originally gone to the royal quarters to seek permission to hang Mordecai (5:9–14), he is ultimately sent out with instructions to honor Mordecai (6:11). Finally, this reversal in status of Haman and Mordecai foreshadows the ultimate reversal in the fate of the Jews and their enemies, which the rest of the book narrates with delight.

The Pivotal Role of Coincidences in the Book of Esther

One of the most unique features in Esther is the remarkable series of extraordinary coincidences that ultimately led to the Jews' deliverance. These coincidences are not incidental but crucial to the plot development. The story moves forward from one coincidental event to the next.

Biblical narratives sometimes highlight an unexpected turn of events. While most narrators attribute the protagonist's good fortune to God's direct intervention, some adopt a viewpoint that seems to suggest the protagonist was the benefactor of good luck or a remarkable series of coincidences. Narrators often describe such seemingly chance coincidences with the noun מִקְרֶה (*miqreh*, "chance") or the related verb קָרָה (*qārâ*, "to happen [by chance]").[33] For example, "Ruth *happened to chance* upon (*wayyiqer*

---

33. See *BDB*, s.v. "קרה," 899; L. Koehler, W. Baumgartner, and J. J. Stamm, "קרה," in *The Hebrew and Aramaic Lexicon of the Old Testament,* trans. and ed. under the supervision of M. E. J. Richardson (Leiden: Brill, 1994–1999), 3:1137–38; Michael A. Grisanti, "קרה," in *NIDOTTE,* 3:984–86; S. Amsler, s.v. "קרה," in *Theological Lexicon of the Old Testament,* ed. C. Westermann and E. Jenni (Peabody, Mass.: Hendrickson, 1997), 3:1169–71; Helmer Ringgren, "קרה," in

miqrehā [וַיִּקֶר מִקְרֶהָ]) the field of Boaz" (Ruth 2:3). The young Israelite reported, "By *chance* I *happened* (*niqrōʾ niqrêtî* [נִקְרֹא נִקְרֵיתִי]) to be on Mount Gilboa, and there was Saul leaning on his spear!" (2 Sam 1:6). The Philistines, trying to determine whether or not divine providence was directing current events, said, "If [the cart] goes on the road to its own land to Beth-Shemesh, then it is He who has done us this great harm; but if not, we will know that it is not his hand that struck but it happened to us by *chance* (*miqreh* [מִקְרֶה])" (1 Sam 6:9). And Qoheleth observed, "The race does not always belong to the swift, the battle to the strong, bread to the wise, riches to the astute, nor favor to the skilled, for time and *chance* (*pegaʿ* [פֶּגַע]) *happen* (*yiqreh* [יִקְרֶה]) to them all" (Eccl. 9:11). Similarly, the narrator of Esther uses this standard idiom to depict two critical events as seemingly coincidental by the verb *qārâ* (קָרָה) "to happen (by chance)" (Esther 4:7; 6:13). Readers accustomed to attributing every event in life and human history to the direct control of God are often surprised when biblical authors seem to describe some events as chance events. Like Jacob, we often explain life's seeming chance events as being under divine control: "The Lord your God caused it to happen (*hiqrâ* [הִקְרָה])" (Gen. 27:20).

More often the narrator simply describes the coincidental events. Vashti disenfranchised herself, providing an unexpected opening for a new queen. Esther unexpectedly finds herself in the king's harem. Somehow she happens to find favor with Hegai, who gives Esther an advantage over the other women. Mordecai chances to overhear the plot to assassinate the king. The king unexpectedly departs from custom when Esther dares approach the throne uninvited, then promises to grant her any request. On the very night Haman is building the gallows on which to hang Mordecai, the king has insomnia. By chance he is read the section in the royal chronicles describing Mordecai's loyalty. Through a series of coincidental events, Haman enters the court at the very moment the king ponders how to reward Mordecai. Haman unwittingly suggests the method by which Mordecai is honored, yet Haman had come to court to seek the death of this very man. By chance Haman falls upon Esther to beg for his life just as the king walks into the chamber and mistakenly assumes the worst. Haman's inopportune

---

Theologisches Wörterbuch zum Altes Testament, ed. G. Johannes Botterweck, Helmer Ringgren, and Heinz-Josef Farby (Stuttgart: Verlag W. Kohlhammer Drucherei, 1990), 7:172–75; L. J. Coppes, "קָרָה," in *Theological Wordbook of the Old Testament*, ed. R. L. Harris, G. L. Archer Jr., and Bruce K. Waltke (Chicago: Moody, 1980), 2:813–14.

plea for his own life ironically seals his fate and leads to his unexpected death on the very gallows he built for Mordecai.

If the book is read outside its present canonical context, this extraordinary series of coincidences might be viewed as nothing more than mere chance and remarkable good luck.[34] However, the canonical context of the book of Esther begs the question of whether we should attribute them to mere chance or divine providence.[35] Weiland notes:

> If the book of Esther were entirely divorced from the Old Testament canon, a reader might attribute the occurrences in the story to mere coincidence.... Since it is part of the canon, the story should not ultimately be read in isolation from the rest of the Old Testament in which the person and work of the God of the Jews is central. The canonical context of the book of Esther allows for and even suggests a theme which includes God (though his name is not mentioned).[36]

While the remarkable series of extraordinary coincidences falls within the realm of possibility, the manner in which they work perfectly together—always in favor of the Jews—seems to strain the limits of probability or mere chance. Indeed, when considered in a canonical context, these coincidences seem (1) to portray God's hidden providence,[37] and (2) to emphasize the inviolability of the Jewish people.[38] Berg suggests:

> The coincidences of the plot demonstrate the truth of Mordecai's assurance: assistance of the Jews indeed would appear [4:14]. The author of the story thereby affirms his own belief that, despite the great dangers that threaten the diaspora Jewish communities, the Jews are inviolable.... These coincidences [also] point to the divine activity which lies beneath the surface of events.... That

---

34. Clines, *Esther Scroll*, 155.
35. B. Webb, "Reading Esther as Holy Scripture," *RTR* 52 (1993): 23–35.
36. Forrest S. Weiland, "The Contribution of Literary Analysis to the Understanding of Genre, Unity, and Message in the Book of Esther," (Ph.D. dissertation, Dallas Theological Seminary, 2001), 234.
37. Bush, *Ruth/Esther*, 323; Fox, *Redaction of Esther*, 75–76; and Laniak, *Shame and Honor*, 99–100. Also see Forrest S. Weiland, "Literary Clues to God's Providence in the Book of Esther," *BSac* 160 (2003): 34–47.
38. Berg, *The Book of Esther*, 103–6.

this series of coincidences in Esther point in a certain direction, viz., that of reversal, indicates that they cannot be attributed to mere chance.[39]

The Enigma of the Book of Esther

The most puzzling element in the book of Esther is the conspicuous absence of any direct mention of God, or of related theological concepts (covenant, law) and religious practices (prayer, dietary regulations, intermarriage). This is one reason that Esther was once listed among the *Antilegomena* (disputed books of the canon).[40] Jewish and Christian communities have responded to this enigma in one of several ways.

Early Jewish scholars were so exercised about this that when the Greek and Aramaic versions of Esther were produced, they added direct mention of God and introduced supernatural elements not found in the original Hebrew version. The Greek versions add six large blocks of material that directly mention God and attribute the Jews' deliverance to divine intervention (Additions A–F comprise more than 100 verses not present in any Hebrew manuscript).[41] The Aramaic Targums supplement the story with theologically oriented paraphrase and numerous legendary additions highlighting God's direct intervention.[42]

---

39. Ibid., 104–5.
40. For discussion of the Jewish controversy over the status of Esther in the Hebrew canon, see Roger Beckwith, *The Old Testament Canon of the New Testament Church* (Grand Rapids: Eerdmans, 1985), 283–95.
41. For the two Greek versions of Esther (LXX, AT), see Clines, *Esther Scroll,* 69–92; W. H. Brownlee, "Le Livre Grec d'Esther et la Royauté Divine," *RB* 63 (1966): 161–85; Carey A. Moore, "On the Origins of the LXX Additions to the Book of Esther," *JBL* 92 (1973): 382–93; Louis A. Brighton, "The Book of Esther: Textual and Canonical Considerations," *ConJ* 13 (1987): 200–18; Karen H. Jobes, *The Alpha-Text of Esther: Its Character and Relationship to the Masoretic Text,* SBL Diss. Series 153 (Atlanta: Scholars Press, 1996); André LaCocque, "The Different Versions of Esther," *BibInt* 7 (1999): 301–22; Kristin de Troyer, *The End of the Alpha Text of Esther,* SBL Diss. Series 48 (Atlanta: SBL Press, 2000); and Lisbeth S. Fried, "Towards an UR-Text of Esther," *JSOT* 88 (2000): 49–57.
42. For discussion of Targum Rishon (ca. 500–700 A.D.) and Targum Sheni (ca. 675–725 BC), see Beate Ego, "Targumization as Theologization: Aggadic Additions in the Targum Sheni of Esther," in *The Aramaic Bible: Targums in their Historical Context,* JSOTSup 166, ed. D. R. G. Beattie and M. J. McNamara (Sheffield: JSOT, 1994), 354–59; Bernard Grossfeld, *The First Targum to Esther* (New York: Sepher-Hermon, 1983), iv–vi; and Alexander Sperber, *The Bible in Aramaic: The Hagiographa* (Leiden: E. J. Brill, 1968), 4a:171–205.

Does the Book Contain Indirect References to God?

Some scholars claim to find hidden references to God in the book. Traditional Jewish scholars, using midrashic and haggadic methods of interpretation, claim to find the divine name in hidden acrostics and anagrams.[43] Likewise, some Christians have used allegorical and typological methods to find hidden Christological themes.[44] However, it is doubtful that the narrator intended his story to be used in this manner.[45]

Using a more conventional historical-literal method of interpretation, many suggest that the mention of fasting is an implicit reference to praying to God (4:3, 16). However, several prominent Esther scholars suggest that the mention of fasting in 4:3, 16 is not an intentional allusion to God but the development of the "feasting/fasting motif" that runs through the book.[46] For example, in contrast to Haman and Ahasuerus who celebrate the edict against the Jews with feasting and drinking (3:7–15), the Jews respond by fasting and lament (4:3, 16). Also, the turning point revolves around Esther's two feasts (5:1–8; 7:1–10) as the Jews fast all the while. And when the crisis is finally resolved, the Jews imitate the Persian manner of celebration that introduces the story (1:3–22): they too enjoy days of merriment and feasting (9:20–32).[47] Indeed, the very fabric of the story seems to be structured around six different feasts and several fasts.[48]

Many scholars also suggest that Mordecai alludes to God by circumlocution when he exhorts Esther, "If you keep silent at this time, relief and deliverance will arise for the Jews from *another place*, but you and your father's

---

43. David R. Blumenthal, "Where God Is Not: The Book of Esther and Song of Songs," *Judaism* 44 (1995): 80–93; Rachel B. K. Sabua, "The Hidden Hand of God," *BibRev* 8:1 (1992): 31–33; and Eliezer Segal, "Human Anger and Divine Intervention," *Proof* 9 (1989): 247–56.
44. For example, Michael Wechsler, "Shadow and Fulfillment in the Book of Esther," *BSac* 154 (1997): 275–84; T. Thornton, "The Crucifixion of Haman and the Shadow of the Cross," *JTS* 37 (1986): 419–26.
45. For this broader hermeneutical discussion, see Walter C. Kaiser Jr., "The Single Intent of Scripture," in *Rightly Divided: Readings in Biblical Hermeneutics*, ed. Roy B. Zuck (Grand Rapids: Kregel, 1996), 158–70; and Elliott E. Johnson, "Dual Authorship and the Single Intended Meaning of Scripture," in *Rightly Divided: Readings in Biblical Hermeneutics*, ed. Roy B. Zuck (Grand Rapids: Kregel, 1996), 171–79.
46. Fox, *Character and Ideology*, 156–58; Berg, *The Book of Esther*, 31–58; and Arndt Meinhold, "Zu Aufbau und Mitte des Estherbuches," *VT* 33 (1983): 435–45.
47. Fox, *Character and Ideology*, 157; and Jon D. Levenson, *Esther*, OTL (Louisville: Westminster/John Knox, 1995), 1–6.
48. Fox, "Structure of the Book of Esther," 291–303; and Levenson, *Esther*, 7–9.

house will perish" (4:14).[49] However, not all scholars agree that this is an allusion to deity.[50] Michael V. Fox and Robert Gordis suggest the expression "another place" refers to another human agent, not God.[51] And John Wiebe provides linguistic and contextual evidence that the apodasis functions, not as an indicative, but as a rhetorical question expecting a negative answer, "If you keep silent at this time, *will relief or deliverance arise for the Jews from another place?* [Implied answer: No!] And you and your father's house will also perish!"[52] According to Wiebe, Mordecai was urging Esther to intervene because she was the only possible source of human deliverance in this situation. If Wiebe is correct, 4:14 is not an indirect allusion to the certainty of divine help but a direct plea to Esther emphasizing her crucial role.

Why Is God Not Mentioned Directly?

Even if 4:3, 14, 16 give indirect allusions to God, this only begs the question of why the narrator does not refer *directly* to God anywhere in the book. A survey of scholarship reveals ten different approaches, which may be grouped into three major categories. The following discussion summarizes each view.

View #1: The Absence of God's Mention Reflects a Secular Viewpoint

Secular Narrator. Many nonconservatives suggest the narrator does not mention God because he had a secular viewpoint.[53] He was a skeptic indifferent to Jewish religion and did not attribute the Jews' deliverance to God but to the machinations of Esther and Mordecai.

Jewish Secularism. Some conservative expositors suggest the book reflects the secularism of the Jews in Persia living outside the will of God by not

---

49. Meshullam Margalit, "From Another Place—Esther 4:14," *Beth Mikra* 31 (1985–86): 6–9 [Hebrew].
50. For example, Hans Bardtke, *Das Buch Esther*, KAT 17, no. 5 (Gutersloh: Gutersloher Verlagshaus Gerd Mohn, 1963), 333; and Peter R. Ackroyd, "Two Hebrew Notes," *ASTI* 5 (1967): 82–86.
51. Fox, "Structure of the Book of Esther," 298; Robert Gordis, "Religion, Wisdom and History in the Book of Esther: A New Solution to an Ancient Crux," *JBL* 700 (1981): 360–61.
52. John M. Wiebe, "Esther 4:14: Will Relief and Deliverance Arise for the Jews from Another Place?" *CBQ* 53 (1991): 409–15.
53. For a concise summary and list of representatives of this approach, see Lewis Bayles Paton, *The Book of Esther*, ICC (Edinburgh: T. & T. Clark, 1908), 94–95.

returning to Jerusalem.[54] Not only did they not seek help from God, but they did not see his hand in the remarkable series of coincidences leading to their deliverance.[55] Accordingly, the narrator adopted the secular viewpoint of the Jews, portraying God as hidden yet faithful to his secular people.[56]

Non-Jewish Secularism. Another view is that the narrator composed Esther with a secular, non-Jewish viewpoint because of its Persian provenance.[57] Writing in Persia with the potential of heathen readers and threat of censure by a heathen ruler, he avoided references to Yahweh and Jewish religion to avoid offending the Persians.

View #2: The Absence of God's Mention Reflects the Book's Genre[58]

Wisdom Literature Genre. According to Shemaryahu Talmon, the book does not mention God because it belongs to the genre of wisdom literature, which sometimes veils divine causality.[59] For example, while some proverbs say that God blesses the righteous and punishes the wicked, others simply say that a person reaps the consequences of his own actions. Likewise, the book of Esther veils divine causality but it is nevertheless implied.

Persian Court Chronicle. Gordis suggests that a Jewish narrator cast the book in the form of a Persian court chronicle.[60] To create the impression of Gentile authorship, he deliberately omitted any mention of God or Jewish religious beliefs and practices.

Purim Lectionary Text. Lewis Bayles Paton and others suggest the divine name was deliberately suppressed (by the original author or later scribes) because the book was written as a lectionary text for the festival of Purim,

---

54. For example, Charles Edward Smith, "The Book of Esther," *BSac* 82 (1925): 397–402.
55. Huey, "Irony as the Key to the Book of Esther," 36–39.
56. Ronald W. Pierce, "The Politics of Esther and Mordecai: Courage or Compromise?" *BBR* 2 (1992): 75–89.
57. See Paton, *Esther,* 94.
58. For an overview of various views of the genre, see Fox, *Character and Ideology in the Book of Esther,* 141–52.
59. Shemaryahu Talmon, "'Wisdom' in the Book of Esther," *VT* 13 (1963): 419–55; J. A. Loader, "Esther as a Novel with Different Levels of Meaning," *ZAW* 90 (1978): 417–21. For a negative critique, see James L. Crenshaw, "Methods in Determining Wisdom Influence upon Historical Literature," *JBL* 88 (1969): 129–42.
60. Robert Gordis, "Religion, Wisdom and History in the Book of Esther," 359–88.

which often was celebrated in frivolity and drunkenness.[61] Paton writes: "Esther was meant to be read at the annual merrymaking of Purim, for which the Mishnah lays down the rule that people are to drink until they are unable to distinguish between 'Blessed be Mordecai!' and 'Cursed be Haman!' (*Megillah* 7b) (cf. Esther 9:19, 22). On such occasions the name of God might be profaned if it occurred in the reading, therefore it was deemed best to omit it altogether."[62]

View #3: The Absence of God's Mention Reflects the Narrator's Emphasis

Ironic Emphasis. Most scholars suggest that the narrator deliberately avoided any direct reference to God in order to ironically emphasize divine providence working behind the scenes.[63] Although God is not mentioned, his hand is recognizable in (a) the remarkable series of unlikely circumstances and extraordinary coincidences, which all work together in the resolution of the plot, and (b) the dramatic reversals that all work out in favor of the Jews and lead to their ultimate deliverance.[64] Moreover, the presence of God in the story is implied by its canonical context and historical setting.[65] Although God's name is absent, the person of faith can discern his hand behind every event and see his fingerprints on every page. Thus the narrator's avoidance of direct mention of God is ironic. It rhetorically emphasizes his sovereign control all the more.[66] The absence of the divine

---

61. Paton, *The Book of Esther,* 54–56, 96; Edward L. Greenstein, "A Jewish Reading of Esther," in *Judaic Perspectives on Ancient Israel,* ed. Jacob Neusner (Philadelphia: Fortress, 1987), 225–43; and Adele Berlin, *Esther,* JPS Bible Commentary (Philadelphia: Jewish Publication Society, 2001), xvi.
62. Paton, *Book of Esther,* 96.
63. Harald Martin Wahl, "'Jahwe, Wo bist Du?' Gott, Glaube und Gemeinde in Esther," *JSJ* 31 (2000): 1–22; Charles R. Swindoll, *Esther* (Nashville: Word, 1997), 1–20, 123–36; K. A. D. Smelik, "Het plan dat niet doorging... Gods verborgenheid in het boek Esther," *ACEBT* 15 (1996): 98–105; Angel Rodriguez, *Esther: A Theological Approach* (Berrien Springs, Mich.: Andrews University Press, 1995), 98–113; Nils S. Fox, "The Hidden Hand of God," *Dor le Dor* 18 (1989–90): 183–87; N. Ararat, "On the Book of Esther's 'Secularity' and 'Contrariness,'" *Tarbiz* 49 (1980): 223–36 [Hebrew]; John C. Whitcomb, *Esther: The Triumph of God's Sovereignty* (Chicago: Moody, 1979), 20–28; Meshullam Margaliot, "The Hidden Struggle Between Haman and the God of Israel," *Beth Mikra* 23 (1978): 292–300 [Hebrew]; Abraham D. Cohen, "'Hu Ha-goral': The Religious Significance of Esther," *Judaism* 23 (1974): 87–94; and William Grasham, "The Theology of the Book of Esther," *RQ* 16 (1973): 99–111.
64. Bush, *Ruth/Esther,* 323.
65. Clines, *Esther Scroll,* 156, 269.
66. Weiland, "Literary Analysis of Esther," 230–33; Huey, "Irony as the Key to Esther," 36–39.

name only serves to emphasize the transcendent quality of God's actions: God's transcendence is revealed through his hiddenness, and his immanence is revealed through his care of the chosen people.[67] The book thus points the reader to a God, who while remaining anonymous, is ever active behind the scenes.

Carefully Crafted Indeterminacy. Others suggest the narrator's omission of God's mention reflects a carefully crafted indeterminacy designed to convey his own uncertainty about God's role in the narrated events.[68] God's work in history is often inscrutable. According to Fox, this ambiguity is not a sign of unbelief or skepticism but reflects the limitations of human knowledge.[69] David Howard Jr. argues that "the author is intentionally vague about God's presence in events. He affirms, on the one hand, that God is indeed involved with his people, but on the other hand, he admits that it is sometimes difficult to perceive God's involvement. . . . His presence is not always clear in the experience of life."[70] Sandra Berg suggests that God continues to control history and its direction even though his presence remains hidden.[71] She states that:

> The book of Esther does not ignore the presence of divine activity; rather, it points to the hiddenness of Yahweh's presence. . . . Yahweh's control of history is neither overt nor easily discerned. . . . Yahweh remains active in human history, although we may not discern God's hand in everyday events. The narrator therefore refrains from any indication of Yahweh's overt activity in human affairs.[72]

Accordingly, the Scroll conveys the message that the people of God should not lose faith if they are uncertain where He is in a crisis.[73] The

---

67. Eugene H. Merrill, "A Theology of Ezra–Nehemiah and Esther," in *A Biblical Theology of the Old Testament,* ed. Roy B. Zuck (Chicago: Moody, 1991), 201.
68. Fox, "The Religion of the Book of Esther," *Judaism* 39, no. 2 (1990): 135–47; idem, *Character and Ideology,* 235–47; and Gerrie Snyman, "Bybelless en wedestrewigheid—leserreaksie op God en Esther," *Koers* 61 (1996): 37–55.
69. Fox, "Religion of Esther," 135–47; and idem, *Character and Ideology,* 235–47.
70. David M. Howard Jr., "Theology of Esther," in *NIDOTTE,* ed. Willem VanGemeren (Grand Rapids: Zondervan, 1997), 4:583–84.
71. Berg, *The Book of Esther,* 173–87.
72. Ibid., 178.
73. Fox, "Religion of Esther," 146–47.

book was designed to strengthen the faith of those who live in a world in which God seems to be absent. As such, the book may also mark the transition from the age of divine revelation to the present age of silence. Thus the lack of explicit mention of God gives the book a particular relevance for our time in which God might seem to have vanished from the scene and when uncertainty abounds about his role in human history, particularly in crises that confront his people.

Hidden Providence and Human Initiative. According to several prominent Esther scholars, the narrator's nonmention of God does not *emphasize* God's hidden providence but simply *assumes* it.[74] Thus its lack of direct mention of God shifts the emphasis to the crucial role of the human protagonists in the Jews' deliverance.[75] The narrator wants the reader to detect God's intervention, but he also wants to emphasize the crucial role of human initiative and action.[76] While the book assumes that the sovereign God is faithful to intervene on behalf of his people, it emphasizes the complementary truth that humans are also responsible to exploit the opportunities divine providence provides.[77] Howard suggests that:

> It is clear that God has been kept out of the book deliberately, since there are numerous occasions where the author could easily have mentioned God's intervention but did not.... The author also could easily have mentioned God as being behind any of the numerous "coincidences" in the book.... To say that the author deliberately suppressed references to God is not to say that the author did not believe in God or in his control over the affairs of the world.... One logical deduction from God's absence is that human action is important. Time and again, Esther's and Mordecai's initiatives are what make the difference for the Jews.[78]

---

74. Clines, *Ezra, Nehemiah, Esther,* 268–71; and Berg, "After the Exile," 115–16.
75. Berg, *The Book of Esther,* 106, 173–87; idem, "After the Exile," 107–27; Fox, "Structure of the Book of Esther," 291–303; idem, "Religion of Esther," 135–47; *Character and Ideology,* 235–47; Clines, *Ezra, Nehemiah, Esther,* 268–71; J. A. Loader, "Esther as a Novel with Different Levels of Meaning," *ZAW* 90 (1978): 417–21; C. H. Miller, "Esther's Level of Meanings," *ZAW* 92 (1980): 145–48; Horace Hummel, "Theological and Pastoral Perspectives in the Book of Esther," *ConJ* 13 (1987): 192–99; and David Beller, "A Theology of the Book of Esther," *ResQ* 39 (1997): 1–15.
76. Loader, "Esther as a Novel with Different Levels of Meaning," 417–21.
77. Beller, "A Theology of the Book of Esther," 1–15.
78. Howard, "Theology of Esther," 582–84.

Similarly, Berg suggests that the Scroll highlights the twin themes of the hidden sovereignty of God and the cruciality of human initiative.[79] Because divine providence is often hidden and inscrutable, the narrator emphasizes the importance of human initiative.[80]

> In Esther, human actions attain their importance precisely because Yahweh's control of history is not overt. The narrator stresses the importance of human response to history in his tale. Yet despite the stress which human actions receive in Esther, they remain only one part of a dialectic and in creative tension with the ordering principle at work behind the surface of events. . . . Yahweh's assistance in times of trial could *always* be relied upon. However, the book of Esther reveals that the Jewish people, too, must take every necessary action to secure its own salvation and to retain its place in history.[81]

Rhetorical Use of Limited Point of View. In a creative synthesis of several of the aforementioned views, Robert B. Chisholm Jr. has recently suggested that the absence of God's name in the book reflects a rhetorical use of point of view to emphasize the dual themes of hidden divine providence and the cruciality of human responsibility:

> In the Book of Esther the narrator utilized the point-of-view technique on a [large] scale. In fact this technique dominates the book. Despite this omission many contend that God's providence is a central theme of the book. Yet if this is the case, one would expect some reference to His guiding hand. At this point a consideration of literary point of view proves helpful. Likely the author deliberately suppressed the divine presence because he wanted to use a literary technique that reflected the limited perspective of the exiles, who lived in an environment where God seemed to be absent. By making God invisible and focusing on the characters' role in the deliverance of the exilic community, the author also empha-

---

79. Berg, *The Book of Esther,* 173–87; and idem, "After the Exile," 107–27.
80. Berg, "After the Exile," 107–27.
81. Berg, *The Book of Esther,* 183.

sized the importance of human responsibility in the outworking of God's purposes.[82]

Unique Emphasis: Synergism of Divine/Human Activity

Clearly, if the narrator had wanted to emphasize God's complete and meticulous control of history, he could have done so. Yet he carefully avoided any direct reference to God's role in the narrated events. As a result, the roles of Mordecai and Esther seem to take center stage. Although the series of extraordinary coincidences and dramatic reversals in the story can only be explained in the light of divine providence, it is also clear that the dramatic reversals in the second half of the book occur only *after* Esther agrees to risk her life (4:13–14) and dares to approach the king (5:1–8).

The book of Esther emphasizes that deliverance of the Jews depended not only on divine intervention but also on the initiative of the human protagonists.[83] Although providence was working behind the scenes to open doors for Esther and Mordecai, it was up to them to exploit these God-given opportunities (4:13–14).[84] According to David J. A. Clines, the book presents a divine/human synergism: "There is in reality no tension or conflict between the divine and human roles in the narrative. . . . Without the craft and courage of the Jewish characters the divinely inspired coincidences would have fallen to the ground; and without the [divinely orchestrated] coincidences, all the wit in the world would not have saved the Jewish people."[85] Likewise, Jonathon Partlow suggests that this twofold emphasis on the hiddenness of God and the cruciality of human initiative is a call to action.[86] When God is silent, his people must express their faith by taking courageous initiative.

Even more bold is Berg, who suggests that the narrator's emphasis on the cruciality of human action hints at "the conditional nature of divine assistance and the importance of Israel's own actions in securing its future."[87] According to Berg, the Jewish people share with Yahweh the responsibility

---

82. Robert B. Chisholm Jr., "A Rhetorical Use of Point of View in Old Testament Narrative," *BSac* 159 (2002): 413.
83. Berg, *The Book of Esther*, 173–87; idem, "After the Exile," 107–27; and Fox, *Character and Ideology*, 235–47.
84. Judith Rosenheim, "Fate and Freedom in the Scroll of Esther," *Proof* 12 (1992): 125–49.
85. Clines, *Ezra, Nehemiah, Esther*, 268–71.
86. Jonathon Partlow, "Tough Decisions in the Silence of God: Esther 4:13–14," *RQ* 35 (1993): 240–44.
87. Berg, *The Book of Esther*, 180.

for its fate; the shape and direction of history depends as much upon human action as divine providence:

> The events at Susa indicate that Yahweh continues to act, in some sense, in history for the benefit of His chosen people. In the Book of Esther, however, the assurance that history will prove beneficial to the people of Israel is not total; it is conditional. Only when each individual Jew is willing to assume responsibility for the fate of his/her people is Israel's place in history assured. Each Jew thereby shares with God the responsibility for the successful outcome of events.[88]

Elsewhere Berg argues that:

> The book of Esther offers an interesting contrast to the typical biblical portrait of the divine-human encounter. The Scroll focuses upon the actions of its human protagonists.... Esther points to a reliance upon human agencies, and appears antithetical to an alternate biblical tradition that one should depend only upon Yahweh.... While Yahweh ultimately shapes events, humans share in the determination of their fate.... Esther thereby presents a dialectical theology where Yahweh's ultimate but hidden control of history stands in creative tension with human responsibility. The future of the Jewish community resides not only with God, but with both God and humanity.[89]

This twofold emphasis on divine providence and human responsibility harmonizes with Yehezkel Kaufmann's observation that a dual causality of events (a natural cause is guided by divine providence) often characterizes the biblical worldview.[90] Horace Hummel said that this unique emphasis on the importance of human initiative is the often-overlooked complement to divine providence.[91] While the book of Esther implicitly assumes that God ultimately is responsible for the favorable turn of events, it also emphatically affirms that the Jews' survival hinged upon the acts of Esther and Mordecai.

---

88. Ibid., 183.
89. Berg, "After the Exile," 116.
90. Yehezkel Kaufmann, *The Religion of Israel* (Jerusalem: Bialik Institute and Dvir, 1956), 8:445–47 [Hebrew].
91. Hummel, "Perspectives in the Book of Esther," 192–99.

As a *Diasporanovelle,* the book of Esther shows that Jewish life in the Diaspora is fraught with anxiety.[92] At any moment and for no apparent cause, Gentile rulers might carry out vendettas against Jews under the pretense of serving the public. The narrator emphasizes that in such a potentially hostile world, survival of the Jewish community depends on a commitment to the community and willingness to undertake courageous action necessary for its preservation. As Berg states:

> In the book of Esther the survival of the Jews, even their successful accommodation to diaspora life, results from their own actions. The responsibility for saving the Jewish people rests with the queen who must decide whether to risk her own life. The Scroll suggests that each individual Jew who is in a position to do so must use his/her power and authority to assist the people of Israel.[93]

So the book of Esther celebrates the historical deliverance of the Jews from the threat of Gentile genocide. Unfortunately, such has not been the case throughout the whole of Jewish history. The rampant destruction of European Jewish communities in the Holocaust is not entirely dissimilar to the threat described but not fulfilled in the book of Esther. Tragically, Haman's spiritual descendants proved more successful in attaining their goal. Haman's plot reminds us of not only what could have happened during the exile, but also what did happen in the Holocaust. While the book of Esther affirms that the God who appears hidden nevertheless remains present, it emphasizes that the survival of the people of God also depends on the actions of individuals willing to take decisive steps on behalf of their brethren—even at great personal risk.[94]

---

92. W. L. Humphreys, "A Life-Style for Diaspora: A Study of the Tales of Esther and Daniel," *JBL* 92 (1973): 211–23; Jon D. Levenson, "The Scroll of Esther in Ecumenical Perspective," *JES* 13 (1976): 440–52; Arndt Meinhold, "Die Gattung der Josephgeschichte und des Esterbuches: Diasporanovelle," pt. 1, *ZAW* 87 (1975): 306–24; and idem, "Die Gattung der Josephgeschichte und des Esterbuches: Diasporanovelle," pt. 2, *ZAW* 88 (1976): 79–93; and idem, "Theologische Erwagungen zum Buch Esther," *TZ* 34 (1978): 321–33.
93. Berg, *The Book of Esther,* 176.
94. For sociological-political perspectives on the book of Esther, see John F. Craghan, "Esther, Judith, and Ruth: Paradigms for Human Liberation," *BTB* 12 (1982): 11–19; Orlando E. Costas, "The Subversiveness of Faith: Esther as a Paradigm for a Liberating Theology," *EcR* 40 (1988): 66–78; Karol Jackowski, "Holy Disobedience in Esther," *TT* 45, no. 4 (1989): 403–14; Yoram Hazony, *The Dawn: Political Teachings of the Book of Esther* (Jerusalem: Genesis Press, 1995); and David G. Firth, "The Book of Esther: A Neglected Paradigm for Dealing with the State," *OTE* 10 (1997): 18–26.

Conclusion

This essay has attempted to sketch the value of a literary approach to the Scriptures as illustrated in the book of Esther. Contrary to the opinion of some, the book of Esther is neither the black sheep of the Hebrew canon nor an embarrassment to the biblical historian. Rather, it is a treasure to the reader who appreciates its literary features. While many historical-critical issues remain unresolved, a literary approach reveals the central concern of the biblical narrator: the unique message of this unusual Scroll.

PART 5

PREACHING FROM OLD TESTAMENT HISTORICAL TEXTS

19

TELL ME THE OLD, OLD STORY

Preaching the Message of Old Testament Narrative

Daniel I. Block

FOR BETTER OR FOR WORSE, THE FACT THAT most congregations depend on their preachers for their spiritual diet lays a heavy burden on those who bear the pastoral mantle. If we would seek to recover for the church "the whole counsel of God" (Acts 20:27), the sheer bulk of narrative in the Old Testament makes this a good place to start. By biblical "narrative" we mean texts that recount events, whether real or imagined. According to this definition, narrative is the most common genre of material in the Bible,[1] accounting for most of Genesis; Exodus 1–19; 32–34; Numbers 10–17; 22–24; Deuteronomy 1–3; much of 4; 5; 8; 9:7–10:11; Joshua–Esther; Isaiah 6; 36–39; much of Jeremiah 1; 26–28; 36–43; 51:59–52:34; Ezekiel 1–3; 33:21–22; Daniel 1–8; Hosea 1; 3; Amos 7:10–17; Jonah; and, in the New Testament, the Gospels and Acts. While we reserve a closer look at the nature of Hebrew narrative until later, preliminarily we may classify most of this material more specifically as "historical narrative," because it purports to describe events that the respective authors deemed to have happened in history.[2] Most handbooks based on the Protestant version of the

---

1. Similarly W. C. Kaiser Jr., "'I Will Remember the Deeds of the Lord': The Meaning of Narrative," in *An Introduction to Biblical Hermeneutics: The Search for Meaning*, ed. W. C. Kaiser Jr. and M. Silva (Grand Rapids: Zondervan, 1994), 69.
2. As opposed to "myth," or "fiction," B. O. Long defines the former as "a narrative form set in a fantasy world designed to account for the real world by reference to activities of the gods in the divine world (Gen. 6:1–4)" (*Genesis: With an Introduction to Narrative Literature*, FOTL [Grand Rapids: Eerdmans, 1983], 318–19). R. Alter classifies most Old Testament narrative as "historicized fiction." See his discussion, "Sacred History and the Beginnings of Prose Fiction,"

Bible divide the Old Testament into four sections: Law (Genesis–Deuteronomy), History (Joshua–Esther), Poetry (Job–Song of Songs), Prophets (Isaiah–Malachi). Although each of these generic classifications is open to question and demands considerable qualification,[3] the limitation of historical writings to the second section obscures the fact that the Bible in its entirety is driven by a narrative framework: fundamentally it recounts the history of God's relationship with humanity beginning with the latter's creation and climaxing in the cross of Christ, which secures humanity's redemption. So when we speak about interpreting and preaching from biblical narrative, the principles we spell out apply far beyond what we commonly refer to as "the historical books" of the Old Testament.

The question we are trying to address in this paper is essentially a homiletical issue: How does one preach from biblical narratives? Contemporary homileticians are understandably concerned with *effective* preaching, but this is often measured primarily by one's ability to hold an audience, or to gather a following. However, a prior and even more important question is, How does one preach *authoritatively* from biblical narrative? In the final analysis this is what matters: grasping the biblical message and translating it into forms that result in the kinds of transformation called for by the biblical texts. The postexilic author of Ezra 7:10 presents Ezra as a paradigm for

---

in *The Art of Biblical Narrative* (New York: Basic Books, 1981), 23–46. However, S. Lasine ("Fiction, Falsehood, and Reality in Hebrew Scripture," *HS* 25 [1984]: 24–40) has argued convincingly that the Israelite authors who wrote these accounts perceived what they wrote to be historically based and not merely fiction.

3. To call the first five books of the Bible "Law" is not only to adopt a term that is too legalistic, but also to overlook the fact that large portions of the Pentateuch are not law at all: Genesis; Exodus 1–18; 32–34; Numbers 10–17; 22–24; Deuteronomy 1–4; 32–33. In fact, the book of Deuteronomy in its entirety is presented to us as Mosaic preaching, rather than Mosaic law. A general term like *Torah,* which means "instruction," is much more appropriate not only because this is how the book of Deuteronomy classifies itself (1:5), but also because this expression encompasses the wide range of materials contained in the Pentateuch: story, poetry, law, prayers, prophetic oracles, etc. The designation "poetic books" offers a relatively accurate description of the contents of Job–Song of Songs. However, the label is still somewhat misleading because it overlooks the fact that more than one half of Old Testament poetic writings are found outside this section (in the narrative and prophetic books). The classification of the last sixteen books as "the prophets" appears on first sight to be accurate. But even then it should be qualified on several counts. On the one hand, inasmuch as many other prophets ministered in Israel during the Iron Age (Samuel, Elijah, Nathan, etc.) without leaving their books of their sermons for posterity, a designation like "the writing prophets" or "prophetic writings" is preferable. On the other hand, not all the figures whose works are included in "the prophets" functioned primarily as professional prophets. Daniel was a statesman, a government official, whose position resembles that of Joseph and Nehemiah rather than Isaiah or Ezekiel, and the first eight chapters of the book are basically narrative rather than oracular in genre.

preachers today: "Ezra set his heart/mind to study the Torah of Yahweh, to put [it] into practice, and to teach law and justice in Israel." Study, application, teaching—these are the three keys to authoritative preaching. And they must operate in this order. Without study, the application may actually run counter to biblical ethics, and the teaching may be heretical. Without personal application, the study remains hypothetical and theoretical, disconnected from life, and the teaching lacks both authenticity and integrity. Without teaching, the study remains personal and the application private. We shall look at these three elements in closer detail, applying them particularly to biblical narrative.

Discovering the Message of Narrative Texts

The key to authoritative preaching from narrative texts is responsible study. A sound hermeneutical basis for such study has been laid by Eugene Merrill, to whom this book and this essay are dedicated;[4] David Howard, one of the editors of this volume;[5] and Walter Kaiser Jr., in the present volume and elsewhere.[6] These scholars have reminded us of the essential elements of Hebrew narrative and offered helpful guidance for the analysis of this genre of writing. My present discussion here builds on these works, and seeks to offer additional specific and practical guidance in the study of Old Testament narrative with the view to preaching the eternal message it bears.

As in the case of any biblical text, it is possible to be deflected from the actual message of a narrative passage by approaching it with a "homiletical hermeneutic." By "homiletical hermeneutic" I mean an approach to the biblical text that is driven by the need to preach a sermon from the text, rather than a thirst for understanding its message in its original context. A

---

4. E. H. Merrill, "History," in *Cracking the Old Testament Codes: A Guide to Interpreting the Literary Genres of the Old Testament,* ed. B. Sandy and R. L. Giese Jr. (Nashville: Broadman & Holman, 1995), 89–112. See also Merrill's own historical interpretation of the biblical texts in *Kingdom of Priests: A History of Old Testament Israel* (Grand Rapids: Baker, 1987).
5. D. Howard Jr., *An Introduction to the Old Testament Historical Books* (Chicago: Moody, 1993), 23–58.
6. Walter C. Kaiser Jr., "Preaching from Historical Narrative Texts of the Old Testament," chap. 20 in this volume; idem, "'I Will Remember the Deeds of the Lord': The Meaning of Narrative," in *An Introduction to Biblical Hermeneutics,* 69–84; idem, "Narrative," in *Cracking the Old Testament Codes,* 69–88; idem, "The Use of Narrative in Expository Preaching," in *Toward an Exegetical Theology* (Grand Rapids: Baker, 1981), 197–210.

"homiletical heremeneutic" displays at least six typical features. First, it begins by identifying a "bite-sized," sermon text, which in narrative genre is typically an episode in the life of a character or a people (usually Israel). The passage must be long enough to create an image in the mind of the reader/hearer, but not too long to be read from the pulpit without the audience getting impatient with the reading. Second, a "homiletical hermeneutic" is propelled by notions of efficiency and economy of time. It admits that preachers have only a limited amount of time for sermon preparation, and within that allotment, only a limited amount of time for actually wrestling with the text. A skillful preacher learns to spot the preaching points of a text quickly. Third, with a "homiletical hermeneutic," the primary question to be asked of a text is not, "What does the text mean?" but "What does this text mean *to me?*" It is driven by the preacher's need to be relevant and practical, rather than authoritative. Fourth, a "homiletical hermeneutic" looks at every text through the lens of modern Western definitions of sermon form and structure. Not only does it enable the interpreter to identify three or four preaching points even from a cursory reading of the passage; it also dictates that the passage be interpreted in accordance with those points. A "homiletical hermeneutic" has little patience for wrestling with the text, or for letting the text speak for itself. Fifth, a "homiletical hermeneutic" tends to place a higher value on secondary literature, especially commentaries that predigest for them the theological and practical lessons of the text, than on the primary biblical text itself. Rather than wrestling with the text of Scripture itself, it moves quickly to what reputed authorities (whether fellow preachers or biblical scholars) have said about the text. Sixth, in extreme forms, a "homiletical hermeneutic" is driven by the need for rhetorical novelty and homiletical memorability. Accordingly, the theological points of a passage are often forced into alliterative and assonantal grids. In the end the hearer leaves the sermonic event more impressed with the preacher's creativity than the text's message.

Although each of these features has its place, in the end, the need to preach a sermon from a biblical text may actually inhibit responsible interpretation and blind the preacher and audience to the authoritative meaning of the passage. How can these pitfalls be avoided, particularly with reference to narrative texts? Here are a few suggestions.

First, the preacher must recognize the purpose of Old Testament narrative. Most Old Testament narrative texts are historiographic in aim, that is, they represent accounts of real historical events. However, historiography is to be distinguished from history. "History" (German *Historie*) deals with the facts of history as events. It seeks to answer the questions, "What happened?" "When did it happen?" "Where did it happen?" "Who were the primary participants in the event?" It may even answer "Why?" questions, provided cause and effect are objectively identifiable. Indeed, according to modern Western conventions, good historical writing is objective, analytical, concerned with precision and order. Many readers of Scripture read the "historical" books as if they were "history," concentrating on the names, times, and places of events, often with the view to reconstructing what actually happened.

But few narrative texts in the Old Testament are intended to be read this way. Like virtually all ancient Near Eastern historiography, Old Testament narratives are anything but "objective" reports. For one thing, they always and intentionally reflect biases of the authors. And, even where God is not explicitly said to be operative (as in Esther), they are always driven by theological agendas. For this reason the Jewish Bible refers to Joshua–Kings as the "Former Prophets," and modern scholars designate these books the as "Deuteronomistic History." According to the first classification, the events of Israel's history provide the raw materials from which to craft prophetic appeals to covenant fidelity and loyalty to Yahweh. According to the second, the stages of Israel's history as a nation are evaluated according to the covenant ideals preached by Moses in the book of Deuteronomy.

The key to authoritative preaching from Old Testament narratives is to discover the theology that is reflected and expressed in the text. Since the theology that informs biblical authors derives from antecedent revelation and/or biblical texts, it is especially important to relate the theology arising out of narrative passages to earlier texts.

Biblical narrators were concerned not only to describe historical events, but also to interpret them. Indeed, it is in the authors' interpretation that we find the permanent message. Although God did in fact reveal himself and speak through the events of history and the experiences of Israel (see the purpose of the miracles in the Exodus narratives and the events prophesied by Ezekiel), it is difficult (if not impossible) for us to reconstruct the events and thereby recover the message of God in the original event. Indeed, our only access to that historical revelation is through the interpretation offered by the inspired writers of the texts of Scripture. The message we preach must accord with the message proclaimed by the inspired narrator and interpreter of those events.[7] That message may be retrieved only by carefully studying what the authors have written. While we recognize the value of the history of interpretation of biblical texts, and of interpretations given by contemporary commentators, only the meaning of the original author, not that of later interpreters, offers the normative message of God.

Although some preachers tend to treat Old Testament narratives as "objective" records of historical facts, an even greater danger in evangelical circles is to treat Old Testament narratives as case studies for psychological analyses. Much of what goes by the label "biographical preaching" is little more than the imposition of contemporary psychological theory or the latest thinking on leadership styles upon biblical texts. Analyzing the personalities of Ruth and Naomi and Boaz on the basis of the Myers-Briggs Inventory of Personality Types, or the patriarchs according to Jay Adams' personality categories yields some fascinating results. However, such approaches tend, on the one hand, to lead interpreters to find what they are looking for, rather than what is actually there,[8] and on the other to yield overly optimistic perceptions of the characters that appear in biblical texts.[9] Furthermore, they tend to focus on the human characters in the narrative, rather than on God. As in virtually all ancient Near Eastern historiography, in the Old Testament the perspective is always theological. The narrative texts are accounts of divine involvement in human affairs and human response to God/the gods. To us this is a matter of faith, not history. To the ancients it was both. The presupposition in Israel was that Yahweh was sovereign over history: he initiates it, he controls it, he determines its out-

---

7. Cf. the consequences for Old Testament theology summarized by J. H. Sailhamer in *Introduction to Old Testament Theology: A Canonical Approach* (Grand Rapids: Zondervan, 1995), 83–85.
8. I once heard a seminary chapel address on "The Qualifications for Effective Leadership" based on the portrait of David in 1 Samuel 16. The preacher completely missed one of the obvious points of this text, namely that David had so little going for him that even his father dismissed him as a candidate for leadership, and even Samuel seems surprised. The issue in the call of David is not his personal qualifications (Saul seems to have had these in even greater measure) but the sovereign hand of God in the election of his agents.
9. Thus, Gideon's fleece in Judges 6:36–40 becomes a symbol for the honest search for the will of God, when in reality it was the very opposite. Gideon knew perfectly well what the will of God was; the fleece was a symbol of his rebellion and his determination to get out of doing the will of God.

come. Therefore, historical events are fundamentally his acts—even when he is not explicitly named.[10]

Within this picture, humans play a secondary role in historical events. As the images of God, humans' function is to rule the world on God's behalf; they are accountable to him. Furthermore, while they are free to follow their own courses, God is able to integrate their free actions into his own agenda in such a way that his purposes are always met. In the narratives, human history is exploited to preach the truth of God (cf. John 20:31). Furthermore, within this picture Israel has a unique role to play, not because of her native genius (Deut. 4:6–7; 7:7–8) or spiritual superiority (9:1–24), but because of her election by God and his concern for the entire world. All of Israel's history must be interpreted in the light of this missiological agenda.[11]

Second, the preacher must recognize the nature of Old Testament narrative. In order to grasp a biblical narrator's intended meaning, the interpreter must be sensitive to several elements that play extremely important roles in Hebrew narrative style. Although laypersons tend to have a fairly mechanical view of inspiration (God dictated to biblical authors what they should write), upon closer analysis we discover that biblical narrators followed universal literary conventions in their selection, arrangement, and shaping, of materials. We shall explore each of these briefly in turn.

Selection

All artists make choices. The literary artist must choose which details to take up in his/her composition and which to leave out. Furthermore, he/she must choose to which ones to give full treatment and which to deal with only summarily. That this was true of the biblical narrators is clear as well. The author of John's gospel acknowledges outright that the episodes

---

10. As in the book of Esther, which never explicitly refers to Yahweh/God, or the opening paragraph of Ruth, which speaks of a famine in the dark days of the Judges. Whereas the book of Judges refers explicitly to the hand of God in sending in outside oppressors as punishment for Israel's apostasy, the narrator of Ruth leaves it to the reader to link the famine with the covenant curses of Leviticus 26:19–20 and Deuteronomy 28:23–24. Compare the accounts of the death of Saul in 1 Samuel 31:4 and 1 Chronicles 10:13–14 (the latter text interprets Saul's death in light of his sin against God), or the cause of the exile of the Northern Kingdom in 2 Kings 17, where a similar analysis of Israel's fall is found.
11. Cf. Genesis 12:1–3; Exodus 19:5–6; Deuteronomy 4:5–8; 2 Samuel 7:19; Isaiah 42:6; 49:6; Psalm 2.

from Jesus' life with which he deals have been carefully selected to develop a single thesis (20:30–31). We may also expect this in the Old Testament narratives. Seldom do biblical authors attempt to be exhaustive. They pick and choose material that will support their theses. In this they are quite conscious of what they are doing. The following represent some of the more obvious examples.

Genealogies. Frequently the author will pass over large amounts of material and long periods of time with a genealogy (e.g., Gen. 5, 10, 11, 36; Ruth 4:18–22; Matt. 1).[12] Genealogies represent a telescoped form of historiography. Sometimes (as in Exod. 6:14–27) the author's real purpose even interferes with his recounting of a genealogy.

The Wilderness Narratives. The events singled out for detailed description during the forty years in the desert (Exod. 16–17; Num. 10–21) are deliberately selected to develop the recurring motif of human ingratitude and faithlessness, on the one hand, and divine grace and patience, on the other. But the journey log in Numbers 33 demonstrates that the author was well aware that there were many other "pit-stops" along the way.[13]

The Conquest Narratives. From Joshua 12 we learn that literally dozens of Canaanite kings were defeated by the Israelites. Yet the author only selects a few for detailed treatment elsewhere in the book.

The Narratives of the Judges. From Judges 3:31; 10:1–5; and 12:8–15, we learn that there were several leading figures in Israel's early settlement days who receive only passing comment. The author is aware of their existence, but because they do not contribute to his primary thesis he does not structure his treatment of them according to his stereotypical pattern used elsewhere.

The Story of Solomon (1 Kings 4–11). The account of Solomon's forty-year reign is selective in the extreme. In Kings, the focus begins on his wisdom, then turns to his temple construction, and concludes with his

---

12. The artificial and conventional nature of Genesis 5, 11, and Ruth 4:18–22 is reflected in the fact that all three are linear genealogies consisting of ten generations and in each case a significant turning point occurs at generation seven. Genesis 10 (the Table of Nations) is an extremely unbalanced segmented genealogy, which (excluding the inserted notes) identifies exactly seventy nations descended from Noah's three sons. Matthew 1 divides the history of Israel's royal genealogy into three historical periods, each consisting of fourteen generations (the numerical value of the name "David") and climaxing in the birth of the Messiah: Abraham to David; David to the exile of the Davidic king; the exile to Christ.
13. See the essay by R. D. Cole, chapter 16 in this volume, which treats this chapter in depth.

folly. The Chronicler is even more discriminating. Apart from the activity related to the temple, he has little to say about Solomon at all.

Arrangement and Sequence

The narrators worked deliberately at both the macroscopic and the microscopic levels. Because of the Gospels' differences in chronology, it is extremely difficult to reconstruct the life of Jesus chronologically, for example. In truth, ancient authors were interested less in chronology than in making theological statements. Consequently, events are often reordered in accordance with their theological purposes. For example, how is David introduced to Saul and how does he land up in the latter's court? First Samuel 16 and 17 seem to present two different answers. The author is obviously more interested in other issues than presenting a chronological account of David's life. While many accounts follow a simple pattern of causes and consequences, others are structured after the following simple conventional pattern of plot development:[14]

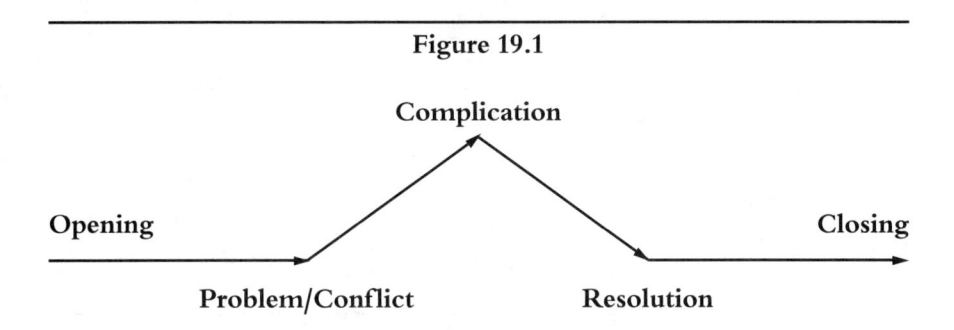

Figure 19.1

Opening — Problem/Conflict — Complication — Resolution — Closing

This pattern may be observed at the grand level of the composition, as in the cycle of narratives concerning Abraham:

Problem:	Sarah is barren (Gen. 11:30).
Complication:	God tells Abraham that his seed will be like the sand of the seashore and the stars of the sky (13:16; 15:5).
Resolution:	Isaac is born (chap. 21).

---

14. Cf. the more complex representation by T. Longman III, *Literary Approaches to Biblical Interpretation*, vol. 3 of Foundations of Contemporary Interpretation (Grand Rapids: Zondervan, 1987), 92–93.

Many texts illustrate this structure at the level of the smaller literary unit as well:

Genesis 22

Problem:	Abraham is commanded to sacrifice his special son, the one on whom the promise rests.
Complication:	Abraham proceeds to obey, although it jeopardizes the divine promise and his own life-long dream.
Resolution:	In the nick of time, the LORD provides a substitute ram and reconfirms the promise.

Exodus 14

Problem:	Israel is hemmed in between the sea and the desert.
Complication:	Pharaoh sees this, regrets that he has let the Israelites go, and sends his best military forces after the "easy pickings."
Resolution:	Yahweh opens a way of escape for Israel and deals a staggering blow to the Egyptian forces.

Judges 6

Problem:	Gideon is charged to destroy the altar of Baal.
Complication:	The whole village is baalist and seeks his life.
Resolution:	His father gives a "lame" defense of Gideon.

2 Kings 4:1–7

Problem:	A woman loses her husband and is left destitute.
Complication:	The creditor threatens to claim her sons.
Resolution:	Miraculously God provides for her.

Shaping

Even though human bodies typically share the same arrangement and sequence of parts, they are distinguishable by a host of features, such as skin, eye, and hair color; muscular development; the amount and distribution of body fat; and size. So it is with Hebrew narrative. Even when elements relating to plot are arranged similarly, the author's intent is communicated through a host of literary devices, such as repetition, the use of key words or concepts, point of view, characterization, reticence and omission, and dialogue. In order to grasp the point the author is trying to make, the way each of these is used demands careful attention. In this paper we have space to give only an example or two of some of these.[15]

Repetition. Biblical narrators use repetition in a variety of ways. One of the most common is the use of a key word *(Leitwort)* or leading idea *(Leitmotif)*. The former is "a word or word root that recurs significantly in a text, a continuum of texts, or in a configuration of texts."[16] Unfortunately, these are often lost in translation because it is considered poor English style to repeat the same word in a single context. We use different equivalents for the sake of felicity. But these lead-words are often the key to grasping the author's point of emphasis and/or the theme of a text.[17] A leading idea *(Leitmotif)* functions similarly, except that synonyms and correlatives are used in the original in place of the same root.[18]

However, repetition is not restricted to lead-words and motifs. Frequently phrases and entire statements are repeated. When this occurs, the interpreter should note how exact is the repetition, and, if deviations occur, ask why. The reshaping is always intentional. Ehud's statement to Eglon in Judges 3:19–20 provides an intriguing example in which a change in a single word transforms the theological significance of a statement:

v. 19: "I have a secret message for you" [דְּבַר־סֵתֶר לִי אֵלֶיךָ].
v. 20: "I have a divine message for you" [דְּבַר־אֱלֹהִים לִי אֵלֶיךָ].

---

15. For a fuller discussion see Alter, *The Art of Biblical Narrative;* A. Berlin, *Poetics and Interpretation of Biblical Narrative* (Sheffield: Almond, 1983); and M. Sternberg, *The Poetics of Biblical Narrative* (Bloomington, Ind.: Indiana University Press, 1985).
16. Alter, *Art of Biblical Narrative,* 93.
17. For example, in Exodus 33:11–13 Hebrew פָּנִים *(pānîm),* "face," occurs nine times; רָאָה *(rāʾâ),* "to see," six times; יָדַע *(yādaʿ),* "to know," six times; מָצָא חֵן *(māṣāʾ ḥēn),* "to find grace in the eyes," five times.
18. Note for example expressions for the noun "word," and terms for the verb "to speak" in Judges 11:29–40; and expressions for "knowing," "learning," "perceiving," and the motif of ignorance in Judges 13.

The fact that דָּבָר *(dābār)* is capable of a wide range of meanings ("word," "message," "act," "object") renders Ehud's statement all the more intriguing. Obviously he is talking about the special sword he has made and is hiding under his cloak, but did he really think it was a divine sword *(Excalibur)*? Whatever Ehud's disposition toward his instrument of death, Eglon is seduced by the words, which at first are introduced as a revelation of a secret (perhaps a plot against him), but then are transformed into a divine oracle (perhaps of divine favor).[19]

Point of View. With the exception of Ezra 7:27–9:15 and Nehemiah 1–7 and 12:31–13:31, which are cast in first-person autobiographical form, Old Testament narratives are generally composed in the third person. This means that the theological, ethical, and political perspectives represented in the accounts are fundamentally those of the narrator. However, inspired by the Holy Spirit of God, the writer looks out upon the world and especially on Israel's history and interprets it through God's eyes. So when the author of Judges declares repeatedly (seven times!), "The Israelites did evil in the

---

19. Judges 6:25–32 presents another intriguing case of repetition and modification.

In verses 25–26 Yahweh orders Gideon:	Pull down the altar; Cut down the Asherah, which is beside it; Offer a bull.
In verse 28 the narrator reports what the townspeople saw:	The altar was torn down; The Asherah, which was beside it, was cut down; The bull was offered.
In verse 30 the people demand Gideon's death:	For he has torn down the altar of Baal; He has cut down the Asherah, which was beside it.
In verse 31 Joash exposes the impotence of Baal:	Someone has torn down the altar.
In verse 32 Gideon's name is changed, with the explanation:	He has torn down his altar.

Observations: (1) The correspondence between the command in verses 25–26 and the action in verse 28 reflects the completeness of Gideon's obedience; (2) The omissions in verses 31–32 highlight the narrator's primary interest, which is in Baal, not the Asherah. The latter was an auxiliary part of the cult installation. (3) The simple statement, "Gideon did as he was commanded," in verse 27, without a repetition of the details, emphasizes the haste of his actions. It speeds up the pace of the narrative—lest he get caught—and is in keeping with his nocturnal acts.

sight of Yahweh,"[20] this is not a personal or private interpretation. This represents God's evaluation.

But who are these persons, these narrators and authors of Scripture? Like most literary documents from the ancient Near East, the narrative writings of the Old Testament are all anonymous.[21] Most of the Old Testament narratives seem to reflect prophetic perspectives, especially that of Moses, though footnotes in the books of Chronicles suggest that the authors had access to authoritative court records that Nathan, Gad, Iddo, and other prophets provided,[22] alongside the official record kept by the king's secretary. But who composed the documents that we now have as discrete books? The Chronicler seems to have had priestly connections. The author of Kings seems to have had some connection with Jeremiah, and betrays on every page the theology and style of Deuteronomy. But the identity of the authors of most biblical narrative texts remains a mystery. Fortunately, determining the meaning of these texts is not dependent on the precise identification of the authors.

Biblical narratives also reflect the viewpoints of the characters within them. At the macroscopic level, the entire narrative of Saul (1 Sam. 9–31) betrays an obviously anti-Saul and pro-David stance. And, at the level of a specific narrative unit, as in the case of the widow and her sons in 2 Kings 4:1–7, the narrator's sympathies are obviously with this destitute family. When we are preaching from narrative texts, determining the point of view of the author is critical.

Characterization. The development of characters and personalities is an extremely important part of Hebrew narrative. By a series of literary techniques, biblical narrators paint these figures as if they were real people doing real things, and relating to one another as people actually do. Scholars conventionally distinguish between two types of characters in biblical narratives. "Flat" characters appear as unidimensional figures. They are often nameless and their characters remain largely undeveloped in the account. They perform supporting roles; as *agents* they facilitate the actions of the major characters. "Round" characters appear as multidimensional and dynamic figures. They represent the narrator's focus of attention, and their

---

20. Judges 2:11; 3:7,12; 4:1; 6:1; 10:6; 13:1.
21. See D. I. Block, "Recovering the Voice of Moses: The Genesis of Deuteronomy," *JETS* 44 (2001): 386–87.
22. See for example, 2 Chronicles 9:29; 12:15; 13:22.

actions carry the plot.[23] A curious convention of Hebrew narrative is to avoid overt characterization. Rarely does the author describe a character explicitly as righteous or wicked, as wise or stupid, as good or bad. Generally a person's character must be deduced from a variety of features in the account: names and titular epithets; the narrator's report of a person's actions; the person's appearance, costume, gestures; one character's comments about another; direct speech by the character; inward speech, which amounts to interior monologue (Gen. 27:42; Deut. 8:17); the narrator's editorial comments about the attitudes, motives, intentions of a character; and flat narratorial explanations of someone's actions. The absence of explicit comments about a person's character often results in ambiguity, forcing the reader to consider whether a person functions positively or negatively.

The account of Yahweh's deliverance of Israel from the Moabite oppressor Eglon in Judges 3:12–30 illustrates these features well. In this account, the people who carried the tribute for Ehud (v. 18) and Eglon's attendants (vv. 19, 24–25) are obviously "flat" characters, without names or individual significance. But from the latter's actions—they leave their master alone in a room with an enemy Israelite, and then delay to help him when they suspect trouble (vv. 19b, 25)—and their internal speech (v. 24b) we conclude that they were both irresponsible and stupid. Ehud and Eglon are obviously "round" characters (the latter in both a literal corpulent sense [vv. 17, 22] and a literary sense). But the narrator does not make overt comments about their characters. From Ehud's actions we conclude that he was an extremely shrewd person, able to transform his left-handedness, which normally was considered a physical handicap, into a strategic asset (vv. 15–16, 20–22), and capitalize on the physical features of Eglon's palace to escape (v. 23); from his speech we conclude he was both devious (vv. 19–20) and bold (v. 28). From Eglon's name ("calf"), and the narrator's observation of his corpulence (vv. 17, 22) we are invited to expect a character who is also mentally fat/obtuse, and by his actions he does not disappoint. In fact, this entire pericope is constructed as a literary cartoon, intentionally humorous. But how should we evaluate Ehud? Was he a good man or a bad man? Since the author does not say, how one answers the question will depend upon one's point of view. Obviously from the perspective of

---

23. See further, Berlin, *Poetics and Interpretation*, 23–24.

Eglon and his attendants Ehud was a bad man, a treacherous rebel against the king. But to the oppressed Israelites he must have been a hero, for after eighteen years of oppression he threw off the Moabite yoke (v. 14).

Although as readers we are fascinated by the narrator's clever characterization of these human characters, read within the context of the entire book, especially chapters 3–16, it is clear that in the narrator's mind the primary actor in this series of scenes is Yahweh. Yahweh is the one offended by Israel's conduct (v. 12a); Yahweh raises up a foreign oppressor as an agent of punishment (v. 12b); when the Israelites cry out to him, despite any sign of repentance, Yahweh raises up Ehud as his agent of deliverance (v. 15); from Ehud's rallying cry we learn (albeit indirectly) that he was the one who actually delivered the Israelites (v. 28). From Yahweh's actions we learn that the formula, "Sin yields punishment; obedience brings blessing," is too simplistic. Sometimes Yahweh acts in mercy, in spite of rather than because of what people deserve.

Dialogue. One of the unique features of Hebrew narrative is its heavy reliance on direct speech. Actual narration is often relegated to the role of either tying speeches together or confirming assertions made in the dialogue.[24] Direct speech is used as the chief instrument for revealing varied nuances of ideas, and the relationships among the characters. If the direct speech is crossed out, often very little remains of the stories.[25] The conversations recorded in Hebrew narratives are generally true dialogues. Rarely will more than two parties get involved in a conversation, which explains why a problem like the matter of the patriarchal birthright in Genesis 27 is not resolved. The pattern of conversations runs as follows:

- verses 1–4, Isaac and Esau
- verses 5–17, Rebekah and Jacob
- verses 18–29, Isaac and Jacob
- verses 30–40, Isaac and Esau
- verse 41, Esau and his heart
- verses 42–45, Rebekah and Jacob
- verse 46, Rebekah and Isaac

---

24. Cf. Alter, *Art of Biblical Narrative*, 63–87.
25. The book of Ruth consists of ca. 1260 words. Without the dialogue it is reduced to ca. 520 words (in Hebrew).

No wonder there is tension in this family! People are forever skirting each other. The real protagonists never meet face to face to settle the dispute.

Third, the preacher must read each narrative text within its larger literary context. A major problem with much preaching from the Old Testament is that it is often based upon fragmentary texts, selected arbitrarily or simply according to the whim of the preacher, and interpreted in isolation from the surrounding narrative. Wise interpreters will spend more time, rather than less, on the texts surrounding the selected passage for development in the sermon.

Two specific exercises are recommended, especially if one is planning an expository preaching series.[26] First, one should read the entire composition[27] aloud several times from different versions, preferably a rigorously idiomatic translation like the *New Living Translation* to grasp the broad sweep of the account, and a formal-equivalence translation like the *English Standard Version* to see recurring patterns of thought and expression. Having read through the text several times, one should establish an overall theme for the composition, in the light of which each literary unit will be interpreted. For example, it is clear that the central issue in the patriarchal narratives (Gen. 11:27–50) is God's covenant with Abraham and the promises that attend that covenant. Every experience of Israel's ancestors reported within these chapters has implications for the covenant/promise. With regard to the Elijah-Elisha cycle of narratives (1 Kings 17–2 Kings 13), the key issue is Israel's covenant relationship with Yahweh: Will the Israelites be true to him, or will they go after the gods of the nations? Every literary unit contributes to the narrator's presentation of the conflict between Yahweh and the gods of Canaan.[28]

Second, if one takes the authorially intended meaning of biblical narratives seriously, one should create a coherent outline, demonstrating how all the parts contribute to the message as a whole.[29] One begins by identi-

---

26. Expository series on narrative texts (as opposed to epistolary or didactic texts) have the distinct advantage of seizing people's interest immediately. Most people love stories, and the stories in the Old Testament cry out for interpretation in extended expository series.
27. By "composition" we mean either an entire book like Joshua, or Judges, or Ruth, or a coherent portion of a larger book, like the story of Abraham (Gen. 11:27–25:11), or the Joseph narrative (Gen. 37–50), or the Elijah-Elisha cycle of narratives (1 Kings 17–2 Kings 13).
28. For example, 2 Kings 4:1–7 reflects not only the social disintegration that attended Israel's increasingly pagan culture (no one is caring for the widows and the fatherless), but also Yahweh's care for all who will trust in him (not to mention the remarkable power of those whom he calls as his prophetic agents).
29. Doing the work oneself is admittedly time-consuming, but the dividends that attend original discoveries are immeasurable, both for one's own understanding and excitement concerning the Scriptures, and the excitement this will generate in the congregation.

fying the boundaries of the major sections of the composition, and ascribing titles to each section relating to the central theme. For example, after repeated careful reading I concluded that the theme of the book of Judges is *The LORD's response to the Canaanization of Israelite society during the period of settlement*. The problem of Canaanization is formally described in 2:11–3:6, the preamble to the central part of the book (3:7–16:31); it is repeated seven times in the refrain, "The sons of Israel did evil in the sight of the LORD" (2:11; 3:7,12; 4:1; 6:1; 10:6; 13:1); and four times with the refrain, "In those days there was no king in Israel; [everyone did what was right in his own eyes]" (17:6; 18:1; 19:1; 21:25). The problem is demonstrated in the incomplete conquest of tribal lands in chapter 1, the repeated references to idolatry and the unethical conduct of individuals, including the judges, in chapters 2–16, and the utter degeneration of the Danites and Benjamites described in the last five chapters.[30] The evil of the Israelites provokes the wrath of God, who responds by sending in foreign enemies to oppress them in accordance with the covenant curses recorded in Leviticus 26 and Deuteronomy 28. When they cry out to God (generally without repentance) he *graciously* raises a deliverer and then provides miraculous deliverance from the enemy. Given this theme, the message of the book of Judges is one of the most relevant in all the Old Testament for the church today. Like Israel, we are being squeezed into the mold of the world and it is only by the grace of God that we are not consumed. The major sections of the book may be isolated as follows:

A. The Background to the Canaanization of Israel: Their Failure in the War of Conquest (1:1–3:6)
B. The LORD's Response to the Canaanization of Israel: The Cycles of Apostasy and Deliverance (3:7–16:31)
C. The Depths of the Canaanization of Israel: The Religious and Social Dimensions (17:1–21:25)

Having identified the major sections of the book, one examines each part in order to see where the major breaks occur within it. The stories of the deliverers obviously represent the center of gravity of the book of Judges.

---

30. For further discussion see D. I. Block, *Judges, Ruth*, NAC (Nashville: Broadman & Holman, 1999), 57–59.

Based upon recurring formulas and patterns of description,[31] chapters 3:7–16:31 subdivide as follows:

1. The Aram-Naharaim and Othniel Cycle (3:7–11)
2. The Moab and Ehud Cycle (3:12–30)
    Parenthesis #1: The Governorship of Shamgar (3:31)
3. The Canaanite and Barak Cycle (4:1–5:31)
4. The Midianite and Gideon Cycle (6:1–9:57)
    Parenthesis #2: The Governorships of Tola and Jair (10:1–5)
5. The Ammonite and Jephthah Cycle (10:6–12:7)
    Parenthesis #3: The Governorships of Ibzan, Elon, and Abdon (12:8–15)
6. The Philistine and Samson Cycle (13:1–16:31)

The narrator tells the reader in advance that with each cycle Israel sinks lower into apostasy (2:19). He thereby invites us also to interpret each of the judges accordingly. Thus he begins with Othniel, whose rulership is paradigmatic and who has already been presented as a genuine hero (1:11–15), and ends with Samson, who embodies all that is wrong with Israel. This sequencing is critical for interpreting each part. Thus if one is preaching on the account of Ehud and Eglon, we need to note that the author perceives Ehud's character more favorably than he does Gideon or Jephthah or Samson, though not as favorably as Othniel.

Fourth, the preacher must carefully analyze the specific passage selected as the basis for the sermon. Having broken the text down into its constituent literary units and having seen how they relate to one another, one may then proceed to analyze the text that has been selected for the sermon of the morning or evening. It may be helpful to begin by asking whether or not the passage fits the conventional model of crisis, complication, resolution. However, it is even more helpful if we inductively analyze the passage according to its grammar and syntax to remove our own biases as much as possible, and let the

---

31. Though the narratives become progressively more complex, each of these cycles is structured more or less on the paradigm established by the first cycle (3:7–11)
    a. The Marks of Israel's Canaanization (3:7)
    b. God's Agent of Punishment (3:8)
    c. Israel's Response to the Oppression (3:9a)
    d. God's Agent of Deliverance (3:9b–10a)
    e. God's Gift of Deliverance (3:10b)
    f. God's Gift of Security (3:11)

author speak for himself. I have found the grammatical-syntactical model illustrated in the following diagrams of 2 Kings 4:1–7 to be the most helpful.[32] The procedure assumes on the one hand that the grammar and syntax in a sentence or paragraph reflect the ideas and the relationships among ideas that the author intended to convey, and on the other that by grammatically and syntactically analyzing a sentence (in conjunction with the study of specific vocabulary employed, as well as the historical and cultural background of the text), it is possible to retrieve the intention and emphases of the biblical authors with a high degree of reliability.

The procedure is simpler than it first appears. Ideally, sermon preparation should be based on the original-language text. If one lacks facility with Hebrew, then the use of a formal translation such as the new *English Standard Version* or the traditional *New American Standard Bible* is essential. One begins by isolating all the independent/principal clauses and sending them to the left margin (right if one is working from Hebrew text).[33] Then one identifies all adjectival and adverbial modifiers, placing them under the word they modify and inserting an arrow in the direction of the modification. Direct speeches are framed and treated as semi-independent grammatical units. By visually diagramming texts in this way, one may not only spot repetitions, exceptional turns of phrases, and other features that one would not notice by simply reading the text,[34] but also gain a deeper appreciation for the syntax of the literary unit and the structural skeleton of the account, which helps produce the exegetical outline on the right.

To flesh out the skeleton, one explores the meanings of specific materially, culturally, and theologically significant terms. In the passage from 2 Kings 4:1–7 materially significant expressions include "jar" (אָסוּךְ) and "vessels" (כֵּלִים). These may seem like insignificant details, until one learns that the former refers to a small "juglet, dipper," and the latter is a generic

---

32. My methodology has its roots in and represents an adaptation of that proposed by W. C. Kaiser Jr. in *Toward an Exegetical Theology*, 87–104, 165–81.
33. An independent clause consists of a specified or implied (in the case of imperatives) subject, verb, and direct object or predicate adjective/nominative.
34. Note, for example, the preponderance of direct speech, confirming our earlier observations. If one removes the direct speech, the following [nonsensical] narrative gristle is all that remains:
    Now the wife of one of the sons of the prophets cried to Elisha. . . . And Elisha said to her. . . . And she said. . . . Then he said. . . . So she went from him and shut the door behind herself and her sons. And as she poured they brought the vessels to her. When the vessels were full, she said to her son. . . . And he said to her. . . . Then the oil stopped flowing. She came and told the man of God, and he said. . . .

Figure 19.2

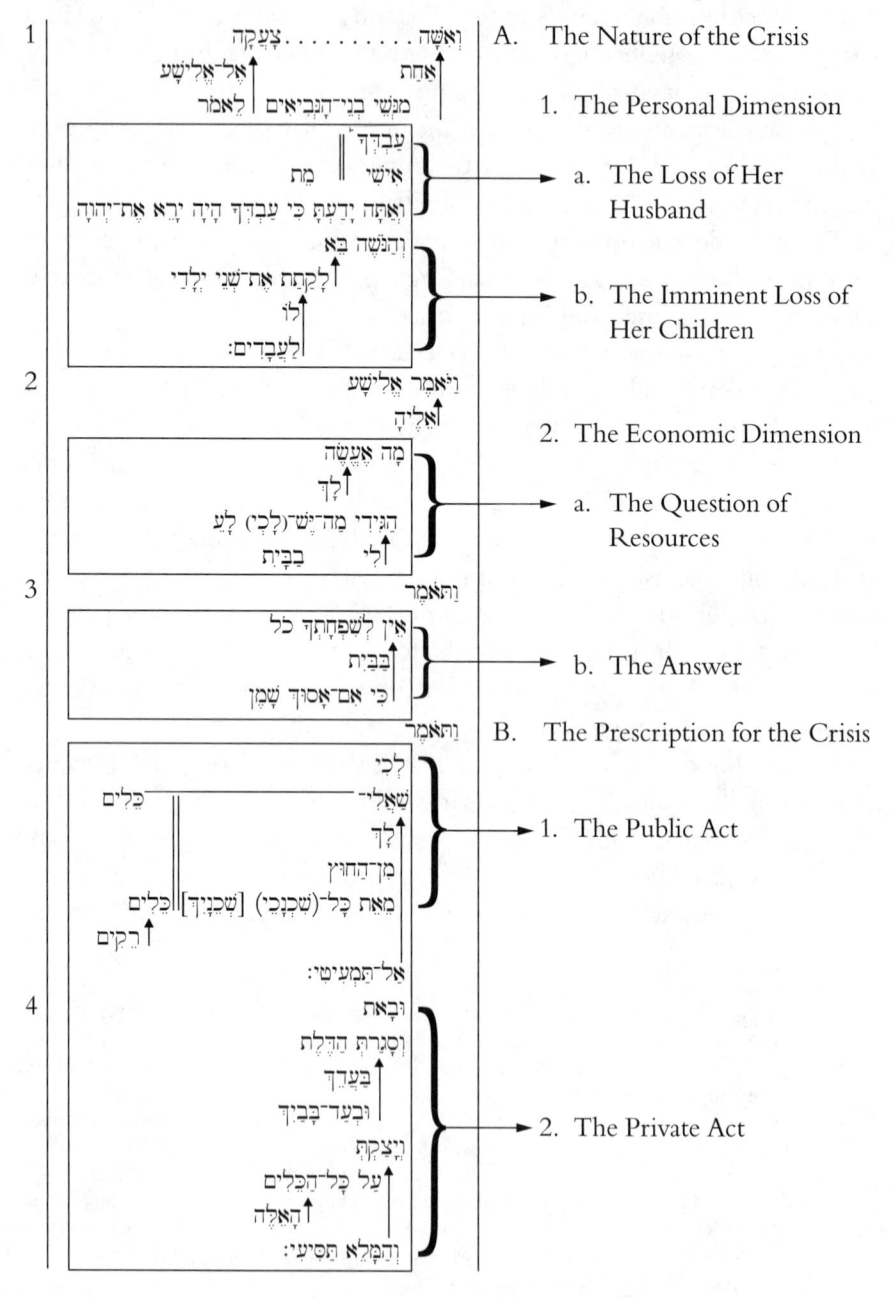

2 Kings 4:1–7: The Lord's Miraculous Provision in Desperate Times

1) וְאִשָּׁה .... צָעֲקָה | A. The Nature of the Crisis
אַחַת ↑ אֶל־אֱלִישָׁע
מִנְּשֵׁי בְנֵי־הַנְּבִיאִים | לֵאמֹר

    1. The Personal Dimension

עַבְדְּךָ
אִישִׁי ‖ מֵת
וְאַתָּה יָדַעְתָּ כִּי עַבְדְּךָ הָיָה יָרֵא אֶת־יְהוָה

       a. The Loss of Her Husband

וְהַנֹּשֶׁה בָּא
↑ לָקַחַת אֶת־שְׁנֵי יְלָדַי
לוֹ
לַעֲבָדִים:

       b. The Imminent Loss of Her Children

2) וַיֹּאמֶר אֱלִישָׁע
↑ אֵלֶיהָ

    2. The Economic Dimension

מָה אֶעֱשֶׂה
↑ לָּךְ
הַגִּידִי מַה־יֶּשׁ־(לָכִי) לָע
↑ לִי
בַּבָּיִת

       a. The Question of Resources

3) וַתֹּאמֶר

אֵין לְשִׁפְחָתְךָ כֹל
↑ בַּבַּיִת
כִּי אִם־אָסוּךְ שָׁמֶן

       b. The Answer

וַתֹּאמֶר | B. The Prescription for the Crisis

לְכִי
שַׁאֲלִי־ כֵּלִים
↑ לָךְ
מִן־הַחוּץ
מֵאֵת כָּל־(שְׁכֵנָכִי) [שְׁכֵנָיִךְ] ‖ כֵּלִים
↑ רֵקִים

    1. The Public Act

אַל־תַּמְעִיטִי:

4) וּבָאת
וְסָגַרְתְּ הַדֶּלֶת
↑ בַּעֲדֵךְ
וּבְעַד־בָּנַיִךְ
וְיָצַקְתְּ
↑ עַל כָּל־הַכֵּלִים
↑ הָאֵלֶּה
וְהַמָּלֵא תַּסִּיעִי:

    2. The Private Act

Figure 19.2—*continued*

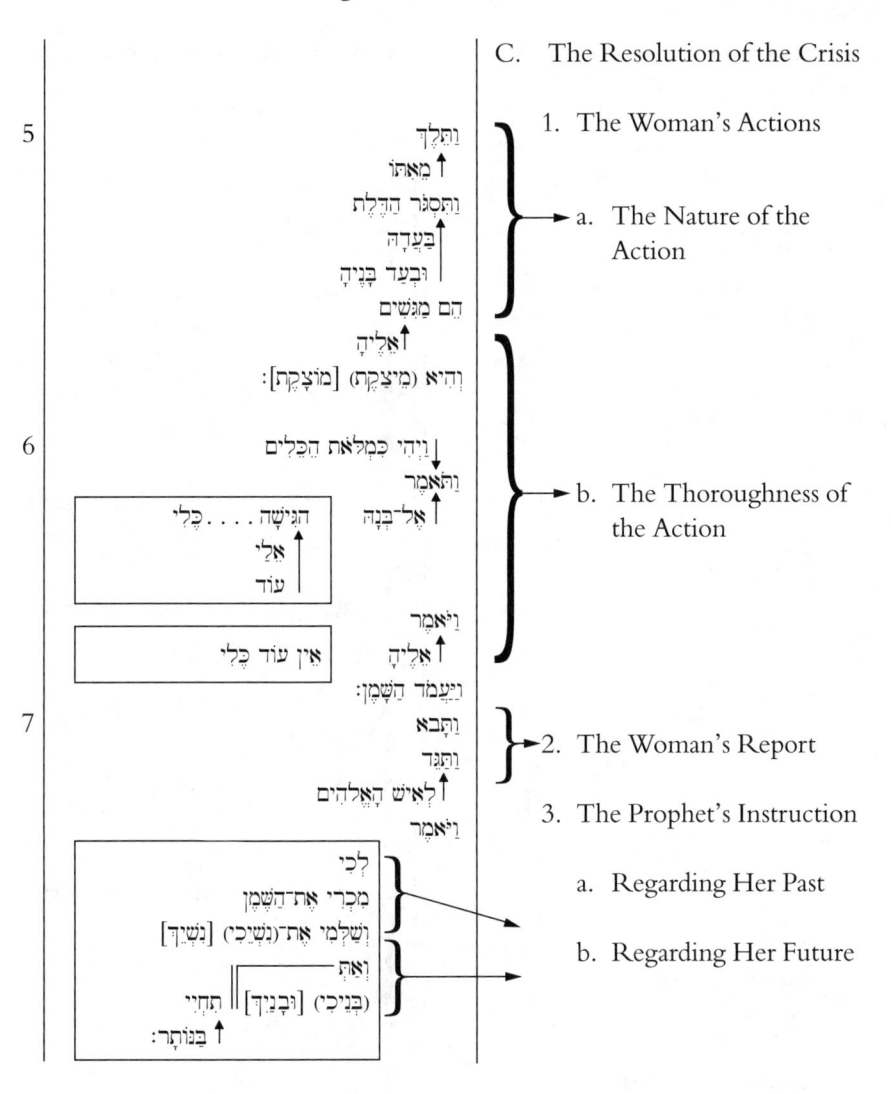

C. The Resolution of the Crisis

1. The Woman's Actions

5   וַתֵּלֶךְ
     ↑ מֵאִתּוֹ
     וַתִּסְגֹּר הַדֶּלֶת
     ↑ בַּעֲדָהּ
     וּבְעַד בָּנֶיהָ
     הֵם מַגִּשִׁים

a. The Nature of the Action

     ↑ אֵלֶיהָ
     וְהִיא (מֵיצֶקֶת) [מוֹצָקֶת]:

6   וַיְהִי כִּמְלֹאת הַכֵּלִים
     וַתֹּאמֶר
     ↑ אֶל־בְּנָהּ   הַגִּישָׁה . . . . כֶּלִי
               ↑ אֵלַי
               עוֹד

b. The Thoroughness of the Action

     וַיֹּאמֶר
     ↑ אֵלֶיהָ   אֵין עוֹד כֶּלִי
     וַיַּעֲמֹד הַשָּׁמֶן:

7   וַתָּבֹא
     וַתַּגֵּד
     ↑ לְאִישׁ הָאֱלֹהִים

2. The Woman's Report

     וַיֹּאמֶר

3. The Prophet's Instruction

         לְכִי
         מִכְרִי אֶת־הַשֶּׁמֶן
         וְשַׁלְּמִי אֶת־(נִשְׁיְכִי) [נִשְׁיֵךְ]

a. Regarding Her Past

         וְאַתְּ
         (בְּנֵיכִי) [וּבָנַיִךְ] ‖ תִחְיִי
         ↑ בַּנּוֹתָר:

b. Regarding Her Future

Figure 19.3

2 Kings 4:1–7: The Lord's Miraculous Provision in Desperate Times

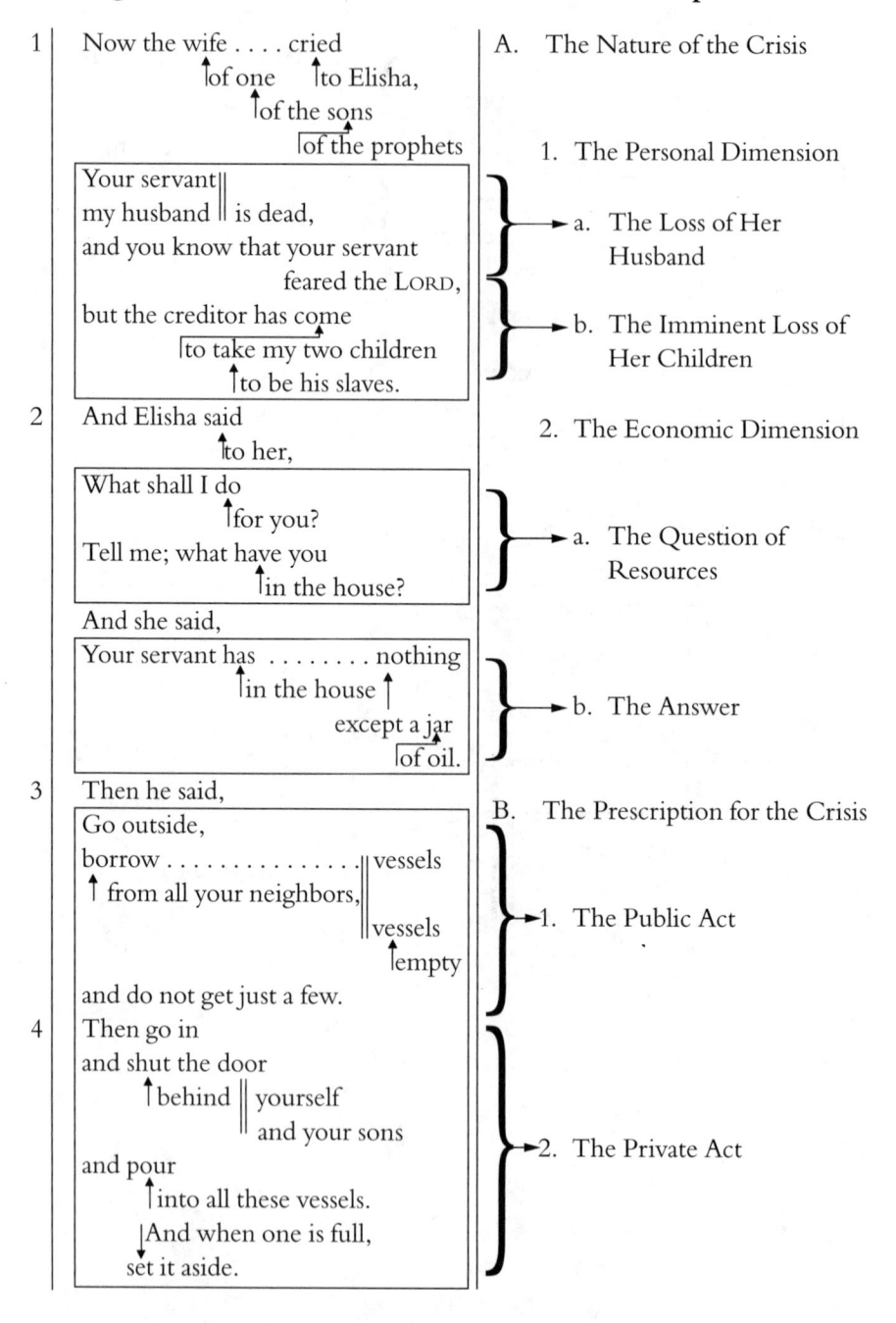

1	Now the wife . . . . . cried	A. The Nature of the Crisis
	↑of one ↑to Elisha,	
	↑of the sons	
	↑of the prophets	1. The Personal Dimension
	Your servant ‖	
	my husband ‖ is dead,	→ a. The Loss of Her
	and you know that your servant	Husband
	feared the LORD,	
	but the creditor has come	→ b. The Imminent Loss of
	↑to take my two children	Her Children
	↑to be his slaves.	
2	And Elisha said	2. The Economic Dimension
	↑to her,	
	What shall I do	
	↑for you?	→ a. The Question of
	Tell me; what have you	Resources
	↑in the house?	
	And she said,	
	Your servant has . . . . nothing	
	↑in the house ↑	→ b. The Answer
	except a jar	
	↑of oil.	
3	Then he said,	B. The Prescription for the Crisis
	Go outside,	
	borrow . . . . ‖vessels	
	↑ from all your neighbors, ‖	
	‖vessels	→ 1. The Public Act
	↑empty	
	and do not get just a few.	
4	Then go in	
	and shut the door	
	↑behind ‖ yourself	
	‖ and your sons	
	and pour	→ 2. The Private Act
	↑into all these vessels.	
	↓And when one is full,	
	set it aside.	

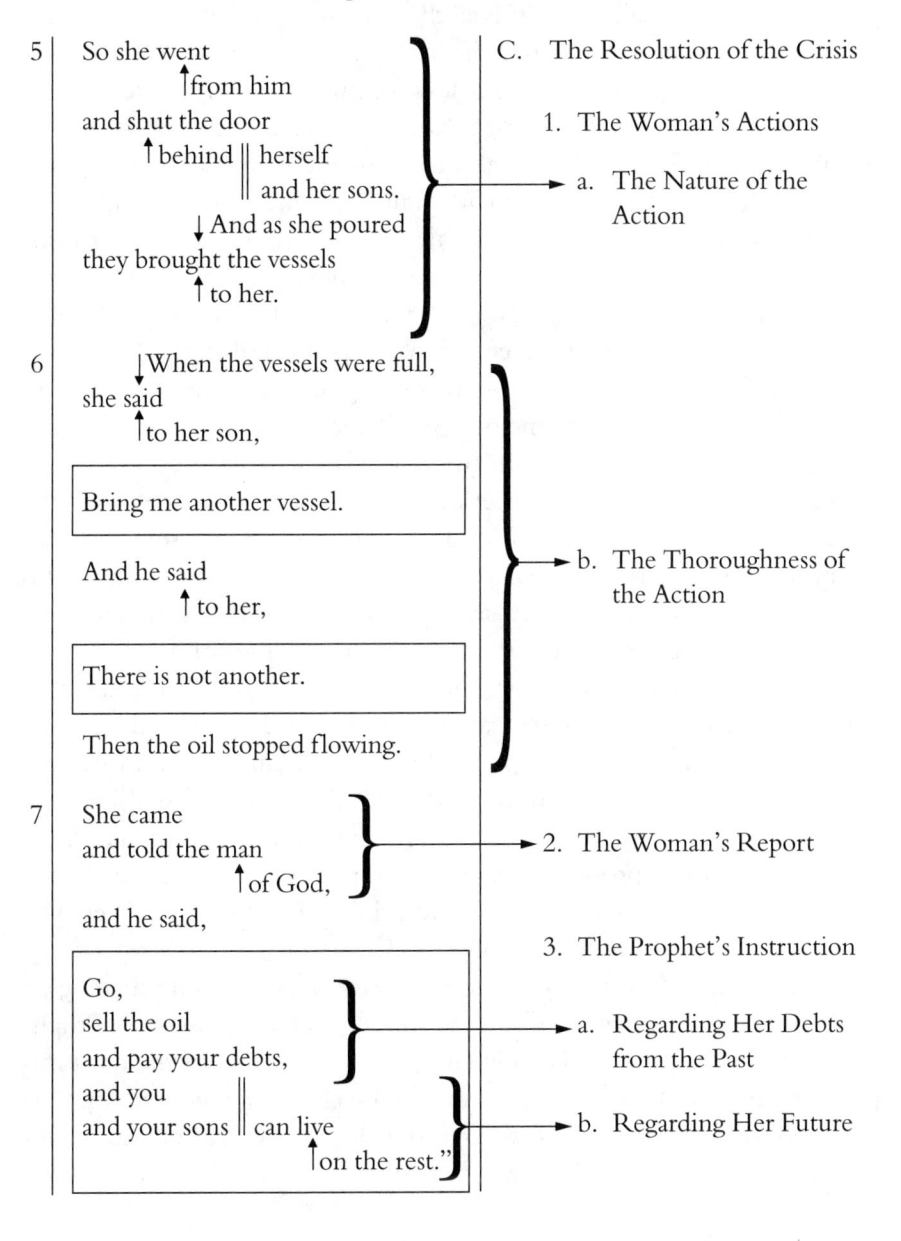

Figure 19.3—*continued*

5	So she went ↑from him and shut the door ↑behind ‖ herself ‖ and her sons. ↓And as she poured they brought the vessels ↑to her.	C. The Resolution of the Crisis 1. The Woman's Actions a. The Nature of the Action
6	↓When the vessels were full, she said ↑to her son, Bring me another vessel. And he said ↑to her, There is not another. Then the oil stopped flowing.	b. The Thoroughness of the Action
7	She came and told the man ↑of God,	2. The Woman's Report

	and he said,
	
	Go,
	sell the oil
	and pay your debts,
	and you
	and your sons ‖ can live
	↑on the rest."
		3. The Prophet's Instruction
		
		  a. Regarding Her Debts from the Past
		
		  b. Regarding Her Future

term for storage crocks and pots of all kinds and sizes. The fact that oil poured from one small dipper fills all the containers available in the village heightens the magnitude of the miracle.[35] Significant also is the reference to oil (שֶׁמֶן). In the ancient economy few commodities were more valuable than olive oil, which was used for cooking, as medicine and salve, as a lubricant, as fuel for lamps, for ritual anointings and sacrificial offerings, as a base in perfumes. In short, along with grain and wine, olive oil symbolized a land's fertility.[36] The significance of this fact extends far beyond the resolution of a poor widow's problem. As already noted, the entire Elijah-Elisha series of narratives reflect the conflict between Yahweh and the fertility deities of Canaan. In this instance, Yahweh defeats Baal at his own game.

Culturally significant concepts to be explored include the status of widowhood in ancient Israel, and the legal (if not moral) rights of the creditor to take the widow's children. In the face of Pentateuchal provisions for caring for widows and the fatherless, the crisis suggests that with the degeneration of Israelite faith came a degeneration of Israelite society. Elisha the prophet plays a crucial role in this episode. To grasp the meaning of this account it will be essential to determine the significance of the designations for prophet used by the narrator (2 Kings 4:1): נָבִיא, the common Hebrew expression usually translated "prophet" (after the Septuagint), and הָאֱלֹהִים אִישׁ, literally "man of God," but meaning "agent of God." To find the answer, one must go beyond etymology and dictionary definitions to investigate how these and other terms were used in the Elijah and Elisha stories in particular and in Samuel–Kings as a whole, and to study the roles of those who were labeled as prophets. Of specific importance in this passage is the expression "sons of the prophets." Determining who these men were will be crucial for understanding the plight of the woman.

Hebrew narrative often lacks the concentration of weighty theological terms that are found in books like Deuteronomy or the Psalms or the Prophets. However they are rarely absent all together. In our text the most important theological notion is "the fear of Yahweh," using the weighty term יָרֵא, "to fear" (2 Kings 4:1). Although this disposition is explicitly attributed to the deceased prophetic apprentice, by addressing her cry to Elisha,

---

35. Like Jesus' feeding of the five thousand with five loaves and two fish in Matthew 14:13–21. The expression אָסוּךְ שֶׁמֶן, "oil juglet," raises questions whether or not there was any oil in the jar at all. If there was no oil in the jar to begin with, the miracle is heightened.
36. Cf. Deuteronomy 7:13; 11:14; 12:17; 14:23; 18:4; 28:51; 32:13; 33:24.

the "agent of God," the widow demonstrates that she shared her husband's faith. Elisha's instructions to close the door behind her and her sons suggests that God's miracles are not there for the entertainment or even indulgence of the ungodly/carnal. The only witnesses to the miracle are those with faith, though the entire village will soon know about it.

Fifth, the preacher must interpret the passage theologically, identifying the timeless doctrinal and ethical truths the author is seeking to communicate.[37] After all, he is not simply telling stories to entertain; even biblical narrators write for transformation (cf. 2 Tim. 3:16–17). Unlike sermons (like Deuteronomy), or prayers (like Dan. 9), or hymns (like Exod. 15), or epistles (like Romans), in Old Testament narrative the theological message presented by the author is generally implicit, rather than explicit in the account. To be sure, the narrator often has his characters mouth his own orthodox theology, but they often express heterodox ideas as well.[38] So one must always ask whether the narrator's and the characters' perspectives on issues are the same.[39]

In the end the inspired narrator's view must be allowed to prevail. When one is seeking to draw out the theology of a narrative text, it is crucial to understand the author's underlying theological perspectives. Second Kings 4:1–7 occurs within the context of what scholars identify as the "Deuteronomistic History," which extends from Joshua through Kings. The designation is rooted in the fact that these writings reflect the theological perspectives and often echo the theological language of Deuteronomy. Accordingly, we will not go far wrong if we find in our text illustrations of truths found in Deuteronomy, where Moses' theology is explicitly and overtly declared. But the principle applies to all narrative texts. The theology of each biblical author is informed and formed by antecedent texts and traditions, and the narrative compositions become vehicles for communicating the inherited theology. However, in the absence

---

37. For a superb exploration of the depth of theological and ethical instruction available in Old Testament narrative, see now Gordon J. Wenham, *Story as Torah: Reading the Old Testament Ethically* (Edinburgh: T. & T. Clark, 2000).
38. As in the speech at the dedication of the golden calf in Exodus 32:4, "These are your gods, O Israel, who brought you up out of the land of Egypt!"
39. First Samuel 15 presents a challenge for interpreters. Theologians typically appeal to Samuel's words in verse 15 to defend the doctrine of divine immutability, "And also the Glory of Israel will not lie or regret (נחם, NIV "change his mind"), for he is not a man, that he should regret (נחם)." However, in the very same chapter, another character, Yahweh no less, declares, "I regret (נחם) that I have made Saul king" (v. 11), and at the end the narrator expresses his own view, "And Yahweh regretted (נחם) that he had made Saul king over Israel."

of overt theologizing (our text mentions God only in the phrase "man of God"), the narrators' theology is determined by asking critical questions of the passage:

1. What does this passage tell us about God?
2. What does it tell us about the world and society in general?
3. What does it tell us about the human condition, the nature of sin, the destiny of humankind?
4. What does it tell us about the way God relates to human beings?
5. What does it tell us about an appropriate ethical and spiritual response to the work of God in one's life?

Applying these kinds of questions to 2 Kings 4:1–7, we discover a series of theological truths that have permanent relevance for the people of God, and cry out for proclamation in our churches:

1. When faith in God is lost, social disintegration follows.[40]
2. Bad things do happen to good people. Disaster is not necessarily a symptom of personal sin, but simply a consequence of the fallenness of the entire human race, hence a gracious (if unwelcome) reminder that we are utterly dependent upon God.
3. Yahweh, the God of Israel, has all the resources of heaven and earth available to him; he is not limited by natural physical, chemical, and biological laws.
4. Security is found in trusting God, not Baal or any other gods of this world.
5. God typically exercises his providential care through human agents.
6. The role of prophet (spokesperson for God) requires an intimate personal and professional relationship with him.

Delivering the Message of Narrative Texts

Having explored how the preacher may discover the eternal message of God from biblical narrative texts, we turn to a brief consideration of how

---

40. The widow's plight should have been prevented if the safety nets provided for in the Pentateuch had been in place. The book of Judges provides a plethora of illustrations of the social degeneracy that attends the loss of faith in God.

that message may be communicated. Ezra 7:10 provides us with the first principle of communication: This great preacher of the restored community of Israel in Jerusalem set his heart/mind to study, to apply, and to teach the Torah in Israel. Preachers must embody the message they proclaim. One of the reasons congregations are bored with our preaching is because it comes across as second hand, inauthentic. If we would preach the message of 2 Kings 4:1–7 we must realize that just as the widow looked to Elijah for sustenance, so people look to us, and expect us to deliver bread, not stones. If we would preach this passage with power and transforming conviction, we must demonstrate in our personal lives before the congregation what it means to find our security in God, rather than the fertility religions of our age. Nothing rings as hollow as a sermon from the lips of one who has not had a personal encounter with God through the study of the text. Contrariwise, no preaching is more convincing than that which is embodied in the preacher himself. Having said this, how does one preach the message of Old Testament narrative? I offer a few suggestions. Some are unique to this genre of Scripture; others apply generally to all preaching that is biblical.

First, read more, rather than less, of the biblical text. Evangelicals must rediscover that in the reading of the Scriptures worshipers hear the voice of God. Despite our lofty creedal statements and our affirmations of the inerrancy, infallibility, and authority of the Scriptures, the relative absence of the Scriptures is one of the marks of contemporary evangelical worship. At best the Scriptures are read piecemeal and impatiently so that we might get on with the sermon, which suggests to the congregation that our interpretation of Scripture is much more important for them that the sacred word of God itself. At worst, we do not open the Scriptures at all. In our efforts to be contemporary and relevant, we dismiss the reading of the Scriptures as a fossil whose vitality and usefulness has died long ago, whether advertently or inadvertently. In the process we displace the voice of God with the foolish babbling of mortals, and the possibility of true worship is foreclosed. And then we wonder why there is such a famine for the word of God in the land (Amos 8:11–14). We may begin to put things right by devoting more time to reading the Scriptures, and to reading large blocks of Scripture at a time. However, as everyone knows, there is oral reading and there is oral reading. Pastors and lay people need to develop skill in the expository reading of Scripture for themselves and for the members of the congregation who will be engaged in this task. This means paying proper attention to tone and inflection, pronunciation, the grouping of phrases, emphasis, pitch, etc.[41] We also need to develop creative ways of communicating Scripture, such as dramatic readings.[42]

Second, develop the sermon around the theological overflow that derives from the passage. In our own study we pay careful attention to grammatical and syntactical details to discover the mind of God through the selected passage, but the people do not need to gag on these details; they need a living word from God. This means that the themes developed in the sermon must *both* derive from the text and address the needs of the congregation. When dealing with didactic, prophetic, or psalm texts, the sermon outline may often parallel the exegetical outline. However, this is more difficult, though not impossible, in sermons based on narrative texts. A sermon based on 2 Kings 4:1–7 could easily follow the main points of the exegetical outline proposed above, and look something like this:

Theme: My God shall supply all your needs (2 Kings 4:1–7; cf. Phil 4:19)
   A. The nature of our need (2 Kings 4:1–2)[43]
   B. The prescription for our need (vv. 3–4)[44]
   C. The resolution of our need (vv. 5–7)

In universalizing the widow's problem we will need to guard against promoting a "health, happiness, and success" gospel, which is little more than a modern version of the ancient fertility religion. Instead of creating the impression that God is a divine genie ready to gratify every Aladdin

---

41. For a helpful guide to effective reading of Scripture see T. McComiskey, *Reading Scripture in Public: A Guide for Preachers and Lay Leaders* (Grand Rapids: Baker, 1991). To the helpful set of questions to assist us in evaluating our reading he offers on page 19, we could add, "Did I read in such a way that the characters in the narrative came alive as real credible people?"
42. Using the biblical text as a base, I have reproduced the book of Ruth as a dramatic reading for six readers, which I have members of the congregation read to launch a five-part sermon series on the book of Ruth.
43. In addition to discussing the woman's specific problem, in developing this point one should examine the use of the verb זעק, "to cry out," elsewhere when people find themselves in a desperate need of help/salvation, for example, Exodus 2:23, where the cry is simply an outcry without address, and repeatedly in Judges, where the cry is addressed directly to God. Here it is addressed to the prophet as the recognized agent of God. The fact the crisis is created by death, the fundamental human problem, deserves development in the sermon.
44. With his question Elisha forces the woman to admit that she has no resources in and of herself to solve her problem.

who rubs his lamp, we need to highlight the fact that the God of Israel, who was incarnate in the Son, rather than the gods of this world, is the only answer for the deepest human needs, and that trusting faith is the link between the resources of heaven and the needs of God's people. It is not difficult to keep the audience's attention as one fleshes out for them the historical and cultural background to this fascinating episode. The challenge is to translate the details into timeless principles.

In some texts we get so carried away by the literary artistry of the author, especially the skill with which he exploits dialogue in the development of the characters, that we forget that biblical narratives are really theological statements with hands and feet. Although in many instances the author seems to take great delight in telling the story (as in the case of Ehud and Eglon), and many passages were intended to be enjoyed, we must remember that the authors were consciously writing Scripture, and that ultimately these narratives must transform the readers as they find themselves in the same sorry predicament as the biblical characters and encounter the living God who speaks through these narratives. In the final analysis, the subject of the entire history of salvation is God, and the metanarrative of biblical revelation is nothing if it is not about the grace and the glory of God who reveals himself in history, and whose record of revelation is preserved in the Scriptures.

Conclusion

When we study narrative texts with this kind of seriousness, we will begin not only to appreciate more fully the literary artistry of the biblical authors and drawn in by the pathos of the characters, but also to be gripped by the depth and timelessness of their theological message. The God who spoke to and through Israel in ancient times spoke climactically in his Son, the climax of the biblical story.[45] And, he continues to speak in these days through the inspired record of those events, the narratives of Scripture. Preachers and pastors are vested with the awesome privilege of telling and retelling the old, old story in new and fresh ways, but unless we grasp the message the authors of the stories were intent on communicating, our proclamation may be no more than popular psychology or ethics in spiritual

---

45. For an excellent discussion of this matter see Christopher J. H. Wright, *Knowing Jesus Through the Old Testament* (Downers Grove, Ill.: InterVarsity, 1991).

dress. The dress may be impressive, but unless we commit ourselves to the paradigm modeled by Ezra (study, apply, teach), the message that is communicated will be devoid of both integrity and authority. Preaching from biblical narratives offers unlimited opportunity for engaging both the past and the present, and for discovering anew the glory and grace of God in the history of his people and in the life of the church.

20

PREACHING FROM HISTORICAL NARRATIVE TEXTS OF THE OLD TESTAMENT

Walter C. Kaiser Jr.

THE RECOGNITION[1] AND ANALYSIS OF biblical historical narrative as a separate and identifiable genre is one of the most helpful recent discoveries of biblical research.[2] In some ways, it is the culmination and one of the more important results of a plethora of critical studies offered in the last two hundred years.

The earliest efforts in this field were given over to uncovering whatever remnants of historical truth could be reconstructed from the text as it existed in its present form.[3] The criteria for this endeavor, unfortunately, were rarely drawn from contemporaneous ancient Near Eastern documents, but instead from texts that were designed by nineteenth and twentieth-century scholars using criteria that had been borrowed from critical studies of classical or even modern texts. As a result, the criteria were shown to be ineffective when used on epigraphic material that had lain buried in the ground, often since the times of their composition.

---

1. It is a joy to honor Eugene Merrill for his effective teaching career with this chapter.
2. In three previous essays, I have elaborated on several aspects of narrative preaching: Walter C. Kaiser Jr., "I Will Remember the Deeds of the Lord: The Meaning of Narrative," in *An Introduction to Biblical Hermeneutics: The Search for Meaning*, ed. Walter C. Kaiser Jr. and Moisés Silva (Grand Rapids: Zondervan, 1994), 69–84; idem, "Narrative," in *Cracking the Old Testament Codes: A Guide to Interpreting the Literary Genres of the Old Testament*, ed. D. Brent Sandy and Ronald L. Giese Jr. (Nashville: Broadman & Holman, 1995), 69–88; and idem, *The Old Testament Documents: Are They Reliable and Relevant?* (Downers Grove, Ill.: InterVarsity, 2001), 173–82. Also see my essay "Teaching and Preaching from Narrative Texts of the Old Testament," in my *Preaching and Teaching from the Old Testament* (Grand Rapids: Baker, 2003), 63–82.
3. For more elaboration on this point, see Kaiser, *The Old Testament Documents*, 53–54, 133–38.

It was left to the German scholar Hermann Gunkel to introduce the discussion of the artistic aspects of the text.[4] Gunkel introduced this topic in his introduction to the commentary on Genesis, but he gave little or no attention to this literary form of the text in the commentary itself.

Yairah Amit[5] credits Franz Rosenzweig[6] and Martin Buber[7] as being the pioneers in the use of poetics in biblical studies beginning in the 1920s and 1930s. Here was the beginning of literary genre studies, even though both Rosenzweig and Buber focused merely on selected stylistic features, such as the notion that *Leitwort,* the "lead word," or "leading word," "leads" or guides the reader through the writer's text. The point was, however, that for the first time, a connection was being observed between the content and the form in which a text was embodied.

Amit[8] located the "turning point" that began to give us a more comprehensive view of the literary forms of a text in the new science of literature called the *"Werkinterpretation,"* or the "New Criticism." Amit thought that Meir Weiss's 1962 book in Hebrew titled *The Bible Within: The Method of Total Interpretation* (which deals mainly with poetry rather than narrative)[9] and the article he published in the journal *Molad* titled "The Poetics of Biblical Narrative: Researching Biblical Narrative according to the Latest Methods of Literary Criticism,"[10] set the stage for all the work that was to follow on literary genres. What was happening was a movement away from a predominantly historical and diachronic approach to the narratives of the Bible and toward a more synchronic literary approach.

As Amit admits, "The synchronic approach which examines the story as we find it and pays no attention to its history, was given a strong boost in an innovative and provocative article by Menahem Perry and Meir

---

4. Hermann Gunkel, *Genesis,* trans. M. E. Biddle (Göttingen: Vandenhoeck & Ruprecht, 1910; English trans., Macon, Ga.: Mercer University Press, 1997).
5. Yairah Amit, *Reading Biblical Narratives: Literary Criticism and the Hebrew Bible,* trans. Yael Lotan (Minneapolis: Fortress, 2001), 11.
6. Franz Rosenzweig, "The Secret of Biblical Narrative Form," in *Scripture and Translation: Martin Buber and Franz Rosenzweig,* trans. L. Rosenwald with E. Fox (Berlin: Schocken, 1936; English trans., Bloomington, Ind.: Indiana University Press, 1994), 129–42.
7. Martin Buber, "Leitwort Style in Pentateuch Narrative," in *Scripture and Translation,* 114–28.
8. Amit, *Reading Biblical Narratives,* 11–12.
9. An English translation can be found in Meir Weiss, *The Bible Within: The Method of Total Interpretation,* trans. B. Schwartz (Jerusalem: Magnes Press, 1984).
10. Meir Weiss, "The Poetics of Biblical Narrative: Researching the Biblical Narrative According to the Latest Methods of Literary Criticism," *Molad* 2 (1963): 402–6.

Sternberg. . . ."[11] This bifurcation of the historical base from the literary form was an unfortunate development from an evangelical standpoint, for it was to lead to further complications. Almost immediately, Perry and Sternberg were challenged as to why they limited their analysis of the text to 2 Samuel 11, for had they gone on to the sequel in chapter twelve, they would have seen that the posture of the text was not ironic, but one of moral rebuke.[12] This discussion would also lead to problems about where it is that a literary unit began and ended. What demarcated the wholeness of that literary unit? What literary devices marked off its boundaries?

But there were more problems than these literary ones: why was the story worth preserving and repeating in later generations if it had little or no factual basis in time and space? What set this story off from the millions of other stories that could have been told at this point, but obviously did not make the text of the canon?

This young and innovative area of study began to attract more attention. Noteworthy among the many contributions was a most readable offering by Robert Alter.[13] But it probably was Ronald Allen's essay in Don Wardlow's book titled *Preaching Biblically*[14] that may have been one of the first to call our attention to the fact that the way a literary genre shaped a biblical passage needed to be reflected in the way the sermon was developed, organized, and delivered. Soon after Allen's essay came Thomas G. Long's *Preaching and the Literary Forms of the Bible*.[15]

What was now being observed, but had not been fully appreciated prior to these new applications of the New Criticism, was that even contemporary readers automatically adjusted the rules of interpretation as they moved from one genre to another; for example, in reading a modern newspaper.

---

11. Amit, *Reading Biblical Narratives*, 12, referring to M. Perry and M. Sternberg, *Ha-Sifrut* 1 (1968): 263–92 [Hebrew].
12. See the rebuttals of Boaz Arpali, "Caution, a Biblical Story! Comments on the Story of David and Bathsheba and on the Problems of Biblical Narrative," *Ha-Sifrut* 2 (1970): 580–97 [Hebrew]; and those of Uriel Simon, "An Ironic Approach to a Bible Story: On the Interpretation of the Story of David and Bathsheba," *Ha-Sifrut* 2 (1970): 598–607 [Hebrew].
13. Robert Alter, *The Art of Biblical Narrative* (New York: Basic Books, 1981). Also noteworthy was Adele Berlin, *Poetics and Interpretation of Biblical Narrative* (Sheffield: Almond Press, 1983) and Shimon Bar-Efrat, *Narrative Art in the Bible* (Sheffield: Almond Press, 1989). See David M. Gunn and Danna Nolan Fewell, *Narrative in the Hebrew Bible* (New York: Oxford University Press, 1993).
14. Ronald J. Allen, "Shaping Sermons by the Language of the Text," *Preaching Biblically*, ed. Don Wardlow (Philadelphia: Westminster, 1983), 25–59.
15. Thomas G. Long, *Preaching and the Literary Forms of the Bible* (Philadelphia: Fortress, 1990).

One simply does not read the editorial page the same way that one reads the comic strips or the advisements in that same newspaper. Each genre in the newspaper had its own special set of guidelines that required that we automatically adjust our way of handling each text without a lot of formal application of sets of staid rules and regulations, which are consciously recalled.

In the same way, the biblical texts carry with them special literary devices that signals to the reader or listener that a particular set of conditions existed for interpreting and understanding what was being communicated through that form. Thus, parables are not to be read as if they are narratives, psalms, or laments. Neither are prophetic materials to be read as if they are miracle genre or torah genre. Each genre carries its own clues for the reader and listener, and each expects that enough has been offered to help the reader come to a proper understanding of its own point of view.[16]

Narrative Criticism

Whereas the New Criticism finds the literary text sufficient in and of itself, apart from any considerations of the text's background or its author's assertions or intentions, Narrative Criticism tends to stress the final and present form of the text in its wholeness and coherence. But in the end, both New Criticism and Narrative Criticism end up saying that the text has its own integrity apart from any considerations as to how the text came to be written or any of the historical reality that was in or behind the story. The goal now is to analyze the literary features of narrative—period!

In a way, this is a refreshing change for conservative readers and interpreters of the text, who had been assailed for almost two hundred years with the meager results of trying to get *behind* the text and ascertain its legitimate historical remnants. As it turns out, very little history was left and even fewer scholars agreed with any other scholar on what had been established historically as a result of all of its literary criticism.

Nevertheless, these new literary approaches to the Bible have proven to possess some useful results for the reader and proclaimer of the Bible.[17]

---

16. On the use of genres for teaching and preaching, see Kaiser, *Preaching and Teaching from the Old Testament*.
17. I was stimulated in developing this list of useful results, though from an evangelical bias, by my working in Richard G. Bowman's article, "Narrative Criticism: Human Purpose in Conflict with Divine Presence," in *Judges and Method: New Approaches in Biblical Studies,* ed. Gale A. Yee (Minneapolis: Fortress, 1995), 18–19.

Foremost among these gains is the fact that narrative criticism focuses on the present form of the text. All too frequently, many preachers, especially when dealing with biblical narrative, tend to take isolated pieces of text scattered throughout the Bible and build from there their own point of view or a viewpoint that is found somewhere else in the Bible, but not in any of the texts the preacher or teacher is currently using.

This new criticism teaches us once again to focus on the narrative itself. All personal points of view, speculations of one sort or another, or even creative reconstructions must give way to those literary signals and dynamics found in the story itself. It is the text that is before us that should occupy our attention rather than a hypothetical text, in the liberal tradition, that was believed to have underlain the present text brought together from a multitude of primitive sources and somewhat crudely joined together by a redactor. Likewise, from the evangelical tradition, it is the text that is before us, and not one that we are reminded of in the later New Testament texts, or in some theological tractate of the much later Christian era.

Another advantage that is gained by this method is that our efforts are placed primarily on understanding the entirety of the story before us, despite what may appear to be inconsistencies or contradictions in the narrative. Rather than exploiting these troublesome features into some sort of ideological reading, as a deconstructionist would, we must try to explain even these aberrant portions in a holistic and constructive way that shows how possible sense could come from these parts rather than deconstructive nonsense.

A third gain that can come from using narrative techniques, and which has recently been emphasized, is that we begin to use the Bible's own literary conventions that are endemic to Hebrew literature rather than imposing categories that we have learned from other literary traditions. These literary conventions and techniques may be studied in the abstract, or the uninstructed reader of the Bible may instinctively pick them up by merely reading these biblical stories over and over again.

The last positive gain from narrative criticism is that by drawing our meanings from the text itself, we are protected against importing meanings and thereby overinterpreting the Bible. The importation and inclusion of texts and materials external to the text of the story itself radically alters the center of gravity in a text and becomes almost an instant signal that an exegetical and homiletical disaster is impending.

Again, this is not to say that every gain in narrative or new criticism is positive, for it is not. In addition to usually rejecting, or merely refusing to discuss or acknowledge, the historical background and the facticity of the events covered in the narratives, these new approaches are almost uniformly agreed on one other point: no one must appeal to the author's assertions or truth intentions in order to determine what a text means anymore. This tended to leave the reader in charge of his or her own interpretation of the text since there is no longer any way to determine which meaning is a valid meaning for that text. Of course, that also complements the relativistic views of the postmodern ethos.

Despite all these positive and negative cautions, there is much to be learned from carefully observing the narrative genre for all teachers and preachers. It is to this task that we now turn.

The Elements of Narrative

In order to have a narrative, one needs at the very minimum a story and a storyteller.[18] While some stories use the first person "I" and thereby blend the narrator and central character in the story, most biblical texts prefer to use the third person, thereby allowing the text much freedom in introducing a variety of perspectives as the story goes from one place or time to another.

Involved in this package of elements are the following literary devices: scene, plot, point of view, characterization, setting, dialogue, *Leitwort* or lead word, structure and rhetorical tropes. Most of these are used in the construction of most narratives. Therefore, in order to teach and preach on the stories of the Bible, one must either be aware of these matters instinctively, because of constant contact that has made one automatically aware of them, or they must be formally studied.

So where do we begin as we attempt to understand a biblical narrative? Should we start with the scene or with the plot, for arguments have been made for both of these narrative elements. "In the Old Testament prose," J. P. Fokkelmann announced, "the scene is about the most important unit

---

18. That was the obvious conclusion of Robert Scholes and Robert Kellogg, *The Nature of Narrative* (London: Oxford University Press, 1966), 240. Scholes and Kellogg affirm that a narrative "requires a story and a story-teller."

in the architecture of the narrative."[19] Steven D. Mathewson, with the backing of Jean Louis Ska, declared that "The place to start your analysis is the plot, since Old Testament stories focus more on action than the development of particular characters."[20] So where do we begin?

The Plot

It is the plot that gives structure to the story, but it refers to the sequence of events more in terms of their causes and their consequences. That is to say, a story's sequencing involves its having a beginning, a middle and an end,[21] exhibiting the "classical pyramid"[22] shape, or what others call the "pediment"[23] shape. Thus, the story moves towards a resolution or climax of some sort.

While plot does help us to get at one of the possible structures of the story, its use for sermon building will tend to force all narrative sermons into an anticipated grid: (1) exposition, (2) crisis, conflict, or complication, (3) climax or change, (4) resolution or unraveling, and (5) ending or dénouement. This certainly fits most narratives, but it does not allow for the uniqueness of each narrative.

The Scene

Therefore, it is better to begin with the scene, for each scene depicts something that took place at a particular time, place, or with a particular character. The scenic structuring seems to be a better way of unfolding the plot as it moves from time to time, place to place, or from character to character. This will keep us fresh and unique in our approaches to each biblical story rather than structuring the story in a predictable pediment or pyramid outline every time.

---

19. J. P. Fokkelmann, *Narrative Art in Genesis: Specimens of Stylistic and Structural Analysis* (Amsterdam: Van Gorcum, 1975), 9.
20. Stephen D. Mathewson, *The Art of Preaching Old Testament Narrative* (Grand Rapids: Baker, 2002), 44. See Jean Louis Ska, *"Our Fathers Have Told Us": Introduction to the Analysis of Hebrew Literature* (Roma: Editrice Pontificio Instituto Biblico, 1990), 17.
21. It was Aristotle who said every story "has beginning, middle and end." *Poetics* 7.26–27.
22. Shimon Bar-Efrat, "Some Observations on the Analysis of Structure in Biblical Narrative," *VT* 30 (1980): 165.
23. Amit, *Reading Biblical Narratives,* 47–49. She analyzes this by saying that the three stages of complication or crisis, change (which is at the peak or heart of the story), and unraveling, that form the pyramid, also have an introduction she calls exposition and a conclusion she calls the ending.

Many narrative critics appeal to the story of Naboth's Vineyard in 1 Kings 21 as an example of a scenic structure. The scenes take place in:

- 21:2–3—The Vineyard
- 21:4–10—The King's Palace
- 21:11–14—Naboth: Seated in a Prominent Place
- 21:15–16—The King's Palace
- 21:17–27—The Vineyard

The story does begin with an expository note in 1 Kings 21:1: " Some time later there was an incident involving a vineyard belonging to Naboth the Jezreelite." However, it is also clear that there are five scenes built around the change in place location. As Amit[24] points out, the five scenes are arranged in concentric order with the first and fifth location corresponding to each other as does the second and the fourth scene location. The middle of the five scenes forms the heart of the series so that we are offered an A, B, x, B, A pattern. Amit would use this fivefold pediment structure on 1 Kings 21:

1. An Introduction sets out the situation (v. 1).
2. The Complication: The king wants the vineyard (vv. 2–10).
3. The Change: The killing of Naboth (vv. 11–14).
4. The Resolution: The king will not inherit the vineyard (vv. 15–24).
5. The Conclusion: The king's remorse and his son's fate (vv. 25–29).

Notice also that both the method of using plot and the method of using scenes are not only equally legitimate, but in this case render very much the same analysis. Nevertheless, a slight preference can still be given to using scenes as a more formal criterion over using plots. Notice the slight variation that can be observed in the division of the verses in the two outlines given for 1 Kings 21.

The Point of View

Now that the narrator's basic structure for the story has been discovered mainly through the use of scenes, but backed up by the uncovering of the

---

24. Ibid., 53–58.

plot, the interpreter must press on to ask what is the writer's main thrust and point of view in telling this story. Unfortunately, most good storytellers refrain from attaching a moral or a tag-line to their story that makes the point they wished to say in straightforward prose. For most stories, that would be like admitting defeat—as if the story by itself was not clear enough. Consequently, writers like to have one of the main characters give the punch line, as it were, that shares with the reading or listening audience why it was so important to tell this story. Only in rare instances where the narrator is telling the story from a third-person perspective does he or she ever get involved by directly stating what it is that gave the story its poignancy.

The point of view gives to the reader or listener the distinctive key that unlocks the whole passage, for it is this piece of information that tells us precisely what is the topic or subject being talked about in this text. In this way, the teacher or preacher can be assured that the topic or subject being addressed is not one of the speaker's own devising or imposition on the text.

For example, I have been using for years as my parade example of a point of view being encapsulated in a quotation put into the mouth of one of the main characters the episode of the Zarephath widow woman found in 1 Kings 17. The writer has her sum up the four scenes from the early days of the prophet Elijah with these words: "Now I know that you are a man of God and that the word of the LORD from your mouth is the truth" (1 Kings 17:24). From this clue, I preached from the following sermon title: "Finding that the Word of the Lord is dependable/the truth!"

Fixing the point of view in a verse, or a portion of a verse, because of the prominence that the writer gives to it by means of such things as quotations, shields the interpreter from imposing a psychological, ideological, historical, or later theological viewpoint on the text. It is to be remembered that, while narrative is not direct speech, that is, as we find it in prose, nevertheless, as indirect speech we are still hearing from a spokesperson who claims to have stood in the council of God and heard by revelation the particular point of view that he had in mind when he recorded this text.

Of course, there always are a number of supporting roles that are sublimated to the main point of view, but these support and supplement the main point being made in the passage.

The Characterization

Now that the structure and the focus of the text have been established, all pointing as to *how* the narrative was put together, we can turn to the question of *what* it is that the narrative sets forth. These data are best seen in the way the story depicts character. It is in the main characters of the story, their actions, speeches, and the narrator's comments about their character that provide an idea of what the substance and content of the story is all about.

Unfortunately, the Old Testament is exceedingly sparse in its descriptions of its characters. One gains only the briefest of descriptors of each of the characters. A gentilic designation (an Amalekite, Hittite, or the like), a physical one ("a head taller than any of the others [Saul, 1 Sam. 9:2]), or a professional one (a prophet, a prostitute, or a shepherd), is found scattered throughout most of the Old Testament stories. However, enough is given for the purposes of the story.

Missing almost completely are any psychological descriptions. The text will, however, let us know that Jacob is a "deceiver," and Nabal is a "fool." What a great contrast to the stories of the Greek classical period or the typical Russian descriptions and analyses of character!

If character is so infrequently used, how then are we to determine character in the Old Testament? The answer is that we rely mainly on the actions, but especially the dialogues of the participants. The way a person acts and the way she speaks becomes a major clue as to what sort of person each one really is.

Some characters remain the same throughout the entire story; thus they are called *static characters*. When characters show change and development, they are called *dynamic characters*. Accordingly, David shows a lot of change and development over the years of his life. But we know so little about the judge Shamgar that he can only be seen and depicted as a static character.

The one character that is a part of every narrative in the Old Testament, whether he is there by way of implication or explicitly present, is God. The interpreter and preacher, therefore, must always have her or his attention centered on God's part on the narrative. In fact, to downplay God's part in the story and to focus only on the human side of the story would be to miss the point and to bifurcate the divine and human worlds. Thus, we must always ask ourselves, "What is God doing in this scene?" "How does God's action bring out the purpose noted in the focal point of this text?" To leave

God out of the proclamation of any text is to fall into the trap of being reductionistic, which often leads to developing one's own set of moralisms that are then foisted on this text despite the author's clear statement of purpose to do otherwise.

The Setting

It is important to make sure that we understand that the plot and the characters in each Old Testament story have a setting in real space and real time. Shimeon Bar-Efrat is insistent on this point, He declares:

> A narrative cannot exist without time, to which it has a twofold relationship: it unfolds within time, and time passes within it. The narrative needs the time which is outside it in order to unravel itself by stages before the reader. . . . The narrative also requires internal time, because the characters and incidents exist within time.[25]

The result is that we have the *external* time it takes to tell a story, which is known as "the time of narration," and the *internal* time, which is the time that expired in the story, also known as "narrated time."

But why should we make such a comparison between the time of narration and narrative time? Ska answers succinctly: "The ratio between the two makes it possible for the reader to detect the necessary choices of the narrator and the effects he wanted to produce."[26] Bar-Efrat agrees:

> By studying the relation between narration time and narrated time the relative weight of the various sections of the narrative will be clarified, as well as their proportions with regard to one another and the narrative as a whole, thereby disclosing the focal points of the narrative.[27]

Steven Mathewson illustrates this point effectively when he points to Genesis 38. At first, the narrated time in Genesis 38:1–11 amounts to some

---

25. Shimeon Bar-Efrat, *Narrative Art in the Bible,* trans. D. Shefer-Vanson (Sheffield: Almond Press, 1989), 141.
26. Ska, *"Our Fathers Have Told Us,"* 8.
27. Bar-Efrat, *Narrative Art in the Bible,* 143.

eighteen or twenty years and contains only 32 percent of the story. But verse 12 introduces Genesis 38:12–30 with a standard phrase that slows the time down considerably. "Now after a long time," the narrator began, as he went on to linger in verses 12–23 on Judah's sexual affair with the disguised Tamar. Thus, verses 1–11 serve as a background to the narrative, but it is clear where the writer wanted emphasis. Then in verses 24–30, the pace picks up again. Nevertheless, the narrated time in verse 12–30 was about nine months, yet it occupies some 68 percent of the story.[28]

Yairah Amit summarizes the case by concluding that

> the use of time in biblical stories is calculated and deliberate. The control that the omniscient and omnipresent God has over the world is above all manifested in the control of time. . . . The management of time is not merely a matter of correlation or lack of correlation between the time of narration and the narrated time; it is a central value in biblical literature as a whole.[29]

But setting also deals with place and space as well as time. Therefore it is necessary to note, especially in historical narratives of the Bible, the special aspects found therein. Some scholars downplay the element of space, or deny its usefulness in this discussion.[30] But Amit points to the large amount of text that is given over to describing the tabernacle, not just once, as God commanded it to be built in seven chapters, but it is followed with the actual construction of the same in another six chapters, making a total of thirteen chapters or one third of the whole book of Exodus.

It is true that parables are detached from time and space because they are invented stories that make a point. Thus, Nathan the prophet begins his confrontation with King David by saying: "There were two men [unnamed and without further delineation] in a certain town [also nameless and without any identifying features], one rich and the other poor" (2 Sam. 12:1). But in historical narrative, the writer usually will not fail to give us geographical and topographical indications. Even though we may not at this late date be able to identify any or all of these sites, the very use of these space and place indicators gives us a feel for the authenticity and reliability

---

28. Mathewson, *The Art of Preaching Old Testament Narrative*, 54–56.
29. Amit, *Reading Biblical Narratives*, 114.
30. Amit cites Hermann Gunkel, *Genesis*, xxxviii. Cf. Bar-Efrat, *Narrative Art in the Bible*, 196.

of the story. Again Amit was right on target when she affirmed that the "use of place-names is therefore a regular feature with a specific function: to serve the biblical author's historiographical needs."[31]

Enough of the narrative elements have been traced thus far for our purposes here. This is enough to help the communicator of each of these historical narratives elicit from the text's own structure a sure and tried way to make the same point that the writer was trying to get across. The more difficult part of our task will be to go on to make applications and to give legitimate significances to the central points that are being raised in the text.

Application or Significances

It is time to see how all of these constituent parts of a narrative analysis come together. It is one thing to take the text apart, but it is another to bring it all together and show how it can help the preacher be more effective.

First of all, by now it is clear that the title or topic for a sermon should be obtained from the focal point or point of view embedded within the text itself. That is probably the best place to begin. This will put us in touch with the main topic from the very start of our work.

This assumes that we have already marked out the scope of the section that has been chosen for the message. Often the author of the pericope will have marked off the extent of this portion by certain rhetorical devices. For example, the author may bracket off the section by using an *inclusio,* that is, a repetition of a key concept, phrase or word, at the beginning and the end of the section. Or, the author may have used a *Leitwort;* that is, a leading word or a keyword that tells us that the unit belongs together. Also, the plot will trace where a narrative begins, reaches its climax, and where it ends. But the interpreter must always see each pericope in terms of the author's purpose for writing the whole book and the sections as he has indicated them in the text.

Next, note each of the scenes in the narrative that has been chosen for the sermon. Determine what the theme line in each scene is. Then determine what interrogative, common to all the scenes, is answered by each of

---

31. Amit, *Reading Biblical Narratives,* 119.

the scenes in the same way. Using the title or subject obtained from the focal point of the passage, apply that title to each scene to see if it answers: Who? What? Why? Where? When? or How?

Once the common interrogative has been found, then identify the homiletical keyword. This homiletical keyword has three characteristics and all three must be present. It is a noun, because it must name something. But it must also be an abstract noun, for rather than dealing with the passage from a concrete position, we must deal with it abstractly so we can derive principles from it that will be transferable into applications and contemporary significances.

The message should be concluded with two to four paragraphs that invite distinctively specific actions that uniquely come from this passage and its principal teachings. Care must be taken not to drift into generalities that fit hundreds of other texts or that calls only for cerebral and cognitive types of responses. Instead, the call must be for decisive actions that result in real changes for me, others, and my world.

Illustrating Preaching from Historical Narrative

First Samuel 23:1–29 is a complete historical narrative from a period when David was exposed to Saul's jealous desire to kill him. The focal point of this text occurs several times. David asks in verse 23:1, "Shall I go and attack the Philistines?" (cf. v. 4). He asks later, "Will the citizens of Keilah surrender me and my men to Saul?" (v. 11). Accordingly, we may state our topic: *Seeking Direction and the Will of God*.

We must next decide where the scenes divide. It would appear that there are four main scenes: (1) Judah, 1 Samuel 23:1–2; (2) down to Keilah, verses 3–5; (3) in Keilah, verses 6–13; (4) at Horesh in the Desert of Ziph, verses 14–29.

Now I must ask myself, in seeking direction and the will of God, does this passage tell me *why* I should seek God's direction? Does it tell *how* I should do so, *when, or where*? Does it answer the question *Who or what* should seek God's direction?

I believe the best interrogative in this text is *when?* This then leads to the homiletical keyword of *times*. Now I will have a transitional sentence that says: There are *four* (count the scenes) *times* (my homiletical keyword) *when* (my interrogative) believers should seek for direction and the will of God (our focal point and subject for the passage). The outline that follows then will be:

I. When We Seek Direction for Ourselves (1 Sam. 23:1–2)
   A. Where There Is a Need
   B. When We Are Confused
II. When We Seek Assurance for Others (1 Sam. 23:3–5)
   A. When There Is Doubt or Discouragement
   B. When There Is Improper or Unshared Focus
III. When We Need to Discriminate between What Could Be and What Will Be (1 Sam. 23:6–13)
   A. When Others Misinterpret the Providence of God
   B. When the Conditions of Obedience Have Been Met
IV. When We Need Deliverance from Harm (1 Sam. 23:14–29)
   A. Refreshed by a Friend
   B. Betrayed by Schemers

Instructed by this incident, David, under the inspiration of the Holy Spirit, composed Psalm 54. Here David appeals to the name and power of God over against all of the usual forms of help to deliver him from those seeking to take his life. After David had prayed in verses 1–3, the fruit of that prayer can be seen in verses 4–7. God in his "faithfulness," or more literally, "according to his truth," must accomplish the annihilation of the ungodly enemies of the cross. Here the measure for the action of God is his truth. David and we are allowed to rejoice as a result of this victory over our enemies only if we refresh ourselves in a holy manner in the manifestation of God's justice. But if we too are infected with evil desires, all is turned into a wrong and evil conclusion.

The specific calls for distinctive sets of actions are that we ought to pray for direction for ourselves when we are genuinely perplexed. There will also be times when we need to pray that others, especially those we lead, will also have the assurance they need to act with us. But in those extremely difficult times, there is a wisdom that only God can give. The future is not unknown and untried by him, for he knows at once all that could have been as well as what will be. He alone can give the deliverance we seek. No wonder, then, that our Lord's disciples asked him to teach them how to pray. Prayer is not an art that is caught, but a discipline that is taught. We are never shut up or blocked by trouble as long as God has an open ear and invites us to come to him.

Conclusion

Historical narrative is one of the great genres for preaching, for most can come to love history when it is told well and long to hear a story that is memorable. The amazing aspect of 1 Samuel 23 is that the Lord knew both what could have taken place, had David not acted, and what would take place. And he revealed both scenarios to David. Here is a clear example of divine sovereignty and human responsibility in a beautifully balanced setting. And even when Saul was about to close in on David, God providentially intervened at the last moment by calling Saul away to face the Philistines just as he had David trapped. Saul came within a hair's breadth of changing history to suit his own fancies, but for God.

Here also is a good example of how the geographical and historical references create both the reader's interest and more vivid curiosity about real people in real life situations. The use of dialogue brings out both character and the fast movement of the story. But even more amazing, as with all biblical narrative, is the dominating part played by God in this text. He not only answers prayer, but he knows the future perfectly, both the could-have-beens and the what-will-be.

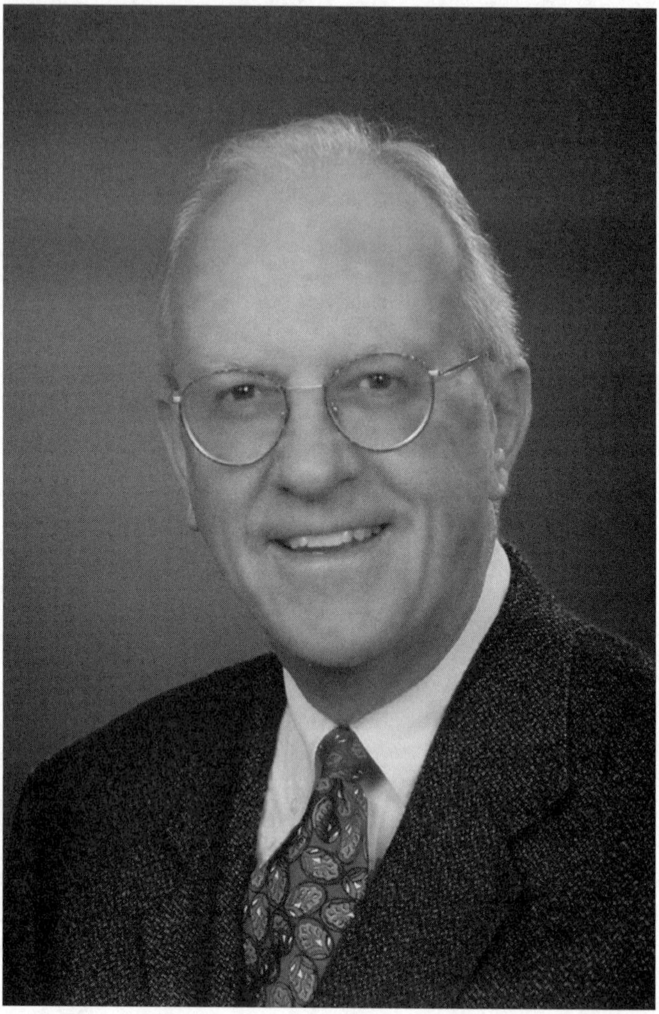

EUGENE H. MERRILL
A Brief Personal History

Michael A. Grisanti

EUGENE HAINES MERRILL WAS BORN IN his parents' home in the tiny village of Anson, Maine, on September 12, 1934. Four siblings eventually joined Gene in the Merrill household. Gene's father operated a linotype machine for newspapers and moved the family several times during Gene's early years. During World War II, his father began working at the shipyards in Bath, Maine, to help in the war effort. After the war, Gene's father moved the family to Lakeport, New Hampshire. During Gene's junior-high years at Lakeport, he began his involvement in theatrical productions. Before his sophomore year in high school, the family moved to Bangor, Maine. Gene graduated from Bangor High School in 1953, where he had been involved in Chorus, Student Council, French and Latin Clubs, and had several roles in various dramatic productions. As a senior at Bangor High, Gene won the graduation-essay contest. A note next to his yearbook photo reads, "Gene has contributed a lot to the speech and dramatic activities. He is always willing to give his time to benefit others." That desire to help others characterized his coming years of life and ministry as well.

Although Gene's parents never made a habit of attending church, they often sent the children to Sunday school. Not long before his fifteenth birthday, Gene attended a youth camp in Vermont where he made a decision to accept Christ as his personal Savior. Just six days after his fifteenth birthday, he was baptized in a lake by a local pastor. In the following years, his mother and siblings followed him in this life-changing step of faith.

During high school, Gene decided he wanted to attend a Christian college. The emphasis on the arts at Bob Jones University captured his attention through an article he read in *Time* magazine. In the fall of 1953 he began his college education and initially pursued a major in interpretative speech. In the midst of his freshman year, Gene was called to the ministry, which changed his ultimate plans. Instead of dropping his speech major, he added a second major, Bible. During his four years at BJU, Gene worked to pay for his tuition, participated in several Shakespearean productions, was involved in debate, radio, and television work, and was also active in various ministry opportunities on the weekends. His fellow students elected him as president of the senior class

During the summer between his junior and senior years at BJU, Gene ministered on the small Long Island, in the Bahamas. After graduation in May of 1957, Gene accepted a position as assistant pastor in charge of youth at a church in Portsmouth, New Hampshire. During the next year Gene realized that he was not cut out for youth work. He did enjoy teaching and, with his pastor's recommendation, he returned to his alma mater for graduate work, completing his M.A. (in Bible) in 1960. He worked as a graduate assistant and continued his involvement in drama, radio, and television. During that time he met, dated, and eventually became engaged to Janet Hippensteel. They were married in December 1960. The following fall Gene and Janet returned to Greenville, South Carolina. Gene began working on his Ph.D. in Old Testament Interpretation at Bob Jones, and Janet began teaching in Greenville County schools. After he completed his doctorate in 1963, both Gene and Janet joined the faculty at BJU. Over the next three years, in addition to their teaching ministries, Gene and Janet took various courses at Columbia University. Gene also had the opportunity to serve as a visiting scholar at Union Theological Seminary during this time. In 1966 the Merrills moved to New York City, where Janet could fulfill the residence requirements for her doctorate at Columbia University. During these years Gene taught fifth-grade boys at Barnard School for Boys in the Bronx, taught English at Northeastern Bible College in New Jersey, and served in various churches in that region, often as an interim pastor. He also began a second M.A. (in Jewish Studies) at New York University. In 1968 Gene and Janet moved to western Massachusetts, where both taught at Berkshire Christian College for the next seven years. Gene taught Old Testament and speech. He continued preaching in churches and serving as an interim pastor as needed. Their only child, Sonya Leigh, was born in 1970.

During this time Gene would travel to New York City each week to take courses for a doctorate at Columbia University in Middle East languages and culture. By the end of the school year in 1975, Gene had completed all his course work under the tutelage of his major advisor and professor, Moshe Held.

After considering various teaching opportunities, in 1975 the Merrills moved to Dallas, Texas, where Gene began his teaching ministry at Dallas Theological Seminary. During his almost three decades at Dallas Seminary, Gene has remained active in the ministries of First Baptist Church, Dallas, where he was recently honored for twenty years of teaching the same Sunday school class. While teaching at D.T.S., Gene has also lectured, taught, and preached numerous times in Puerto Rico, Brazil, Great Britain, Germany, Russia, Ukraine, Canada, India, Israel, Jordan, and all over the United States. He is now the Distinguished Professor of Old Testament at Dallas Seminary.

Bibliographical Overview

After Gene completed his first doctoral dissertation, he continually made contributions to biblical scholarship publications. Since 1963, he has written more than 150 book reviews, more than 150 articles, essays, encyclopedia entries, seven books, and has been involved in at least five significant cooperative projects. He has been involved in editing at least three other books or collections of books and served as a translator/co-translator in three biblical text projects. Gene's writing career can be divided into three general periods: Bob Jones years, New England years, and Dallas Theological Seminary years.[1]

Bob Jones Years (1963–1966)

Three years after finishing his doctoral dissertation, "An Investigation of the Person and Work of the Old Testament Prophet of God," Gene completed the first edition of *An Historical Survey of the Old Testament* (1966). He also began writing journal articles. Issues related to Old Testament introduction and Israelite history captured much of his attention.

---

1. Only the titles of key works written by Gene find mention below. Complete bibliographic information is located at the end of this chapter.

New England Years (1966–1975)

While teaching, primarily at Berkshire Christian College, and working on his master's degree at New York University and his master's and doctorate at Columbia University, Gene wrote sixteen articles and published his N.Y.U. master's thesis, *Qumran and Predestination: A Theological Study of the Thanksgiving Hymns* in the Studies on the Texts of the Desert of Judah series. These ten years proved instrumental in broadening Gene's understanding of the languages and culture of the ancient Near East. His work in Jewish studies, cognate languages, and especially the book of Isaiah as it relates to a Babylonian backdrop paved the way for productive involvement in the study of Old Testament theology and the history of Israel, two pursuits that would capture much of his attention in the coming years.

Dallas Theological Seminary Years (1975–Present)

At D.T.S., Gene has written abundantly. Along with his teaching schedule and writing various articles and essays, he completed his second dissertation in 1984, "The Language and Literary Characteristics of Isaiah 40–55 as Anti-Babylonian Polemic," at Columbia University.

In the ensuing years Gene wrote a number of biblical commentaries. He wrote five commentary sections in the *Bible Knowledge Commentary* on Numbers; 1 Samuel; 2 Samuel; 1 Chronicles; and 2 Chronicles (1985), a basic commentary on Chronicles for the Bible Study Commentary series (1988), an exegetical commentary on Haggai, Zechariah, and Malachi (1994), and a theological-exegetical commentary on Deuteronomy (1994).

In the area of biblical history, Gene completed his superb history of Israel, *Kingdom of Priests: A History of Old Testament Israel* (1987) and revised his well-used *An Historical Survey of the Old Testament* (1991).

In addition to various articles and essays, Gene's major contributions to biblical theology are seen in his four essays in *A Biblical Theology of the Old Testament* (1991), covering the Pentateuch, Chronicles, Ezra, Nehemiah, Esther, Ezekiel, and Daniel; his entries in *Evangelical Dictionary of Biblical Theology* (1996); and his programmatic essay in the *New International Dictionary of Old Testament Theology and Exegesis*, entitled "Old Testament History: A Theological Perspective."

His most recent work is an Old Testament survey he coauthored with Charles Dyer, the *Old Testament Explorer* (2001, as part of the Swindoll Leadership Library).

Although the above sketch suggests that Gene's primary interest has been in expositional or exegetical projects, those who know Gene realize that his primary interests lie in the area of Old Testament history and biblical theology. Whatever contribution the present volume makes in Old Testament history represents a token of gratitude for and a celebration of Gene's investment in this realm of biblical scholarship.

Impact on Students

As one of Gene's students, I have enjoyed the privilege of getting to know him as a scholar, teacher, and a friend. He contributed to my thinking in many ways before I arrived on the campus of D.T.S. for my doctoral studies. In that regard, I would like to use some descriptive terms to summarize Gene's impact on my life and many others who have benefited from his teaching and writing.[2]

Clarity

Gene's students and friends have come to greatly appreciate his ability to express his ideas with great clarity. None of us walk away from his classes, essays, articles, and books wondering what he is trying to say. He models the importance of giving attention to effective communication.

Concern for Students

In the midst of his busy schedule, he had time for his students and colleagues and their questions. Those of us who now teach understand how challenging that can be, as we ourselves consistently try to show interest in and compassion for our students in the midst of various demands.

---

2. This material is revised from a letter I wrote for inclusion in a scrapbook presented to Gene in the fall of 2002 in celebration of twenty years of consistently teaching a Sunday school class at First Baptist Church in Dallas, Texas.

Commitment to Scripture

Gene always wants to go wherever Scripture will take him. Even though he maintains an anchored commitment to a conservative understanding of God's Word, he is willing to ask the tough questions and consider answers that may not be part of the traditional understanding up to that time. He has consistently sought to maintain a balance between the creative possibilities raised by various texts and his desire to honor key theological truths.

Servant's Heart

Although he is an accomplished scholar and writer, his desire is to serve our blessed Lord and lift up His name through his life and ministry. His academic degrees and literary contributions, although abundant, are not accomplishments that he makes prominent before others. His faithful and consistent ministry in the local church setting also betrays his desire to minister to those around him, from all walks of life.

Select Bibliography

Note: The following bibliography provides a selection of works written by Gene. Under each category the works are listed in chronological order. Except for the books and unpublished materials categories, which have a complete listing, I have selected works that demonstrate the chronological span of Gene's writing ministry, the breadth of his research, and his key areas of interest.

Books

Qumran and Predestination: A Theological Study of the Thanksgiving Hymns. Leiden: E. J. Brill, 1975.
Kingdom of Priests: A History of Old Testament Israel. Grand Rapids: Baker, 1987.
1, 2 Chronicles. Grand Rapids: Zondervan, 1988.
An Historical Survey of the Old Testament. 2d ed. Grand Rapids: Baker, 1991.
Haggai, Zechariah, Malachi. Chicago: Moody, 1994.

Deuteronomy. NAC. Nashville: Broadman & Holman, 1994.
Old Testament Explorer, with Charles H. Dyer. Nashville: Word, 2001.

Essays

"Numbers," "1 Samuel," "2 Samuel," "1 Chronicles," and "2 Chronicles." In *Bible Knowledge Commentary,* edited by John F. Walvoord and Roy B. Zuck. Wheaton, Ill.: Victor, 1985.

"Pilgrimage and Procession: Motifs of Israel's Return." In *Israel's Apostasy and Restoration: Essays in Honor of Roland K. Harrison,* edited by Avraham Gileadi. Grand Rapids: Baker, 1988.

"The Unfading Word: Isaiah and the Incomparability of Israel's God." In *The Church at the Dawn of the 21st Century,* edited by Paige Patterson, John Pretlove, and Luis Pantoja Jr. Dallas: Criswell, 1989.

"A Theology of the Pentateuch." "A Theology of Chronicles." "A Theology of Ezra, Nehemiah, and Esther." "A Theology of Ezekiel and Daniel." In *A Biblical Theology of the Old Testament,* edited by Roy B. Zuck. Chicago: Moody, 1991.

"Deuteronomy, New Testament Faith, and the Christian Life." In *Integrity of Heart, Skillfulness of Hands: Biblical and Leadership Studies in Honor of Donald K. Campbell,* edited by Charles H. Dyer and Roy B. Zuck. Grand Rapids: Baker, 1994.

"History." In *Cracking Old Testament Codes,* edited by D. Brent Sandy and Ronald L. Giese Jr. Nashville: Broadman & Holman, 1995.

"'What Is Man?' A Study of Old Testament Anthropology." In *Genetic Engineering: A Christian Response,* edited by Timothy J. Demy and Gary P. Stewart. Grand Rapids: Kregel, 1999.

"Government in the Old Testament and Its Relevance to Modern Politics." In *Politics and Public Policy: A Christian Response,* edited by Timothy J. Demy and Gary P. Stewart. Grand Rapids: Kregel, 2000.

Contributor

Baker Encyclopedia of the Bible. 2 vols. Edited by Walter A. Elwell. Grand Rapids: Baker, 1988.

Evangelical Dictionary of Biblical Theology. Edited by Walter A. Elwell. Grand Rapids: Baker, 1996.

"Old Testament History: A Theological Perspective." In *New International Dictionary of Old Testament Theology and Exegesis,* edited by Willem VanGemeren. 5 vols. Grand Rapids: Zondervan, 1997. Gene also served as one of the associate editors and wrote sixty-seven lexical entries.

Journal Articles

"Can We Trust Old Testament Chronology and Dating?" *Advent Christian Witness* 13, no. 1 (1964): 10–11, 14.

"Who Are Today's Prophets?" *Christianity Today* 15, no. 12 (1971): 8–10.

"Name Terms of the Old Testament Prophet of God." *JETS* 14 (1971): 239–48.

"The Aphel Causative: Does It Exist in Ugaritic." *JNSL* 3 (1974): 40–49.

"Rashi, Nicholas de Lyra, and Christian Exegesis." *WTJ* 38 (1975): 66–79.

"Fixed Dates in Patriarchal Chronology." *BSac* 137 (1980): 241–51.

"Paul's Use of 'About Four Hundred and Fifty Years' in Acts 13:20." *BSac* 138 (1981): 246–57.

"Palestinian Archaeology and the Date of the Conquest: Do Tells Tell Tales?" *GTJ* 3 (1982): 107–21.

"Ebla and Biblical Historical Inerrancy." *BSac* 140 (1983): 302–21.

"Covenant and the Kingdom: Genesis 1–3 as Foundation for Biblical Theology." *CTR* 1 (1987): 295–308.

"Isaiah 40–55 as Anti-Babylonian Polemic." *GTJ* 8 (1987): 3–18.

"The 'Accession Year' and Davidic Chronology." *JANES* 19 (1989): 101–12.

"The Late Bronze/Early Iron Age Transition and the Emergence of Israel." *BSac* 152 (1995): 145–62.

"Internal Evidence for the Inerrancy of the Pentateuch." *CTJ* 2 (1998): 102–22.

"Remembering: A Central Theme in Biblical Worship." *JETS* 43 (2000): 27–36.

"Deuteronomy and History: Anticipation or Reflection?" *Faith and Mission* 18 (2000): 57–76.

Bible Translation and Study Notes

Translator of "Jeremiah" in the *New King James Version* (1982)
Translator of "Deuteronomy" in the *New Living Translation* (1996)
Translator of "Deuteronomy," "Haggai," "Zechariah," and "Malachi" in the *NET Bible* (2001)
Translator of "Deuteronomy" in the *Holman Christian Standard Bible* (forthcoming)
Study Notes on "Chronicles," and "Daniel," in the *Nelson Study Bible: New King James Version* (1997)
Study Notes on "Deuteronomy," "Haggai," "Zechariah," and "Malachi" in the *NET Bible* (2001)

Unpublished Materials

"An Investigation of the Person and Work of the Old Testament Prophet of God." Unpublished doctoral dissertation, Bob Jones University, Greenville, South Carolina, 1963.
"The Language and Literary Characteristics of Isaiah 40–55 as Anti-Babylonian Polemic." Unpublished doctoral dissertation, Columbia University, New York, New York, 1984.

Subject Index

A

Abimelech, 277–80
Abraham, 67, 70, 108, 218–19, 230, 232, 331; date of birth for, 219; movements of, 218
Agricultural-Resettlement Model, 149–52
Ahab of Israel, 62, 89, 91, 194
Ahasuerus of Persia, 385–88, 390, 391–92
Ahaz of Judah, 60
Ahijah, 373–74
Ai, 143, 144, 264–68
Alt, Albrecht, 222
Amarna letters, 162, 219, 269–71
Amenhotep II of Egypt, 244–48, 250, 254
Amorites, 218, 221
anthropology, 133–35
antilegomena, 395
ʿApiru, 269–71. *See also* Habiru.
Apostles' Creed, 100
Aramean wave, 218
archaeology, 30, 49–50, 74–96, 140–42; abuse of, 93–95; demographics based on, 284; Jerusalem, 161–63; "new," 84–85; of Exodus–Judges era, 256–82; of patriarchal era, 220–24; of United Monarchy era, 160–69
Artaxerxes of Persia, 303
artifacts; literary, 87–95; nonliterary, 86–87
Ashkelon, 234
Assyria, 180, 194–95, 291–92; Eponym Lists, 89–90; King Lists, 132–33
authorial intent, 360–79
Avaris, 249, 260
Azekah, 91

B

Baal, worship of, 158
Baal-Berith, temple of, 277–78
Babylonia, 301–2
Bacon, Francis, 121
Barak, 272–73
Beit Mirsim, Tell, 153
Beitin, 265–67
Beth-haraphid, 92
Bethel, 71, 265–67, 332
Bilhah, 230
Black Obelisk, 91
Boaz, 58–59
Bronze Age; Early, 265; Late, 93, 157, 163; Middle, 232
Bronze Age I; Late, 142, 143, 220–21; Middle, 220–21
Bronze Age II; Late, 142, 143, 153; Middle, 150

C

Cambyses of Persia, 309
Canaan, 93–94, 139, 234, 270
Canaanites, 59, 64
caravans, 218–19
casual (life records) history, 29–30
Chaldeans, 205
characterization, 421–23, 448–49
chiasmus, 383–84
Cicero, 28
conquest of Canaan, 93–94, 139, 142–55, 263–69, 416
context, 56–58
covenants, 40, 94–95
Creation, contextualized description of, 57–58

critical method. *See* historical.
cuneiform tablets, 89
Cyrus of Persia, 210, 303

D

Dan, Tell, 90, 166, 249, 275–77
Daniel, 208–9
Darius of Persia, 303, 309–10
David of Israel, 73, 90, 166, 167, 186, 291–96, 366, 369–70, 373, 374–76, 450; census by, 289; idealization of, 62
Debir, 153
Deborah, 272–73
deconstruction, 187
deliberative (written) history, 30
demographics, 284–87
density coefficient, 286
Descartes, René, 121
Deuteronomistic history, 169–77, 183–86
dialogue in narrative, 423–24
discourse criticism, 360–79
Divided Monarchy, 179–200; chronology for, 182–83; historicity of, 188–997; literary sources for, 180–83; record of, 192–99; study of the, 183–88; use of numbers, 296–9
Dream Stele, 247
dynamic characters in narrative, 448

E

Early-Date Exodus/Conquest Model, 142, 152–54
Ebla, 49–50, 328
Echoing, 70–71
Ed-Duweir, Tell. *See* Lachish.
Eglon, 66, 271–72, 419–20, 422–23, 426
Egypt, 233–34; Eighteenth Dynasty, 238–39, 262; inscriptions, 233–34; Nineteenth Dynasty, 237–38; Twelfth Dynasty, 260–62
Ehud, 66, 69, 419–20, 422–23, 426
Eighteenth Dynasty of Egypt, 262; as date of Exodus, 238–39
Ekron, 195
El, 221
El Tekeh, 195
el-Dabʿa, Tell, 249
El-Maqatir, 266–68, 267f

ʿElep, 298
Elephantine Island, 209
Eli, 280
Elohim, 61, 122, 184, 337n
Empty Land Myth, 210
Eponym Chronicle, 89–90, 91. *See also* king lists.
es-Sultan, Tell, 143
Esther, 210–11, 380–406; characterization in, 388–89; coincidences in, 392–95; God's presence in, 395–403; irony in, 390–91; literary structure of, 381–88; reversal in, 389
Et-Tell, 143, 265, 266n
Evil-Merodach of Babylon, 207
execration texts, 233–34
exilic period, 201–14, 300–303
Exodus, 138–39, 257–62, 326–28; date of, 94, 142–45, 152–54, 236–55; modern-day models, 154–55; paradigm of, 108–9; pharaohs of, 239–53
external time, 449
extrabiblical evidence, 39–40, 77, 82, 209, 271
Ezekiel, 207–8
Ezra, 211–12, 304–6

F

fiction, 55
Flood, the, 65, 68
foreshadowing, 71–72

G

Gedaliah, 301–2
genealogy, 117–21, 416; and anthropology, 133–35; in Genesis 12–50, 130–35; linear, 117–19; Near Eastern, 132–33; segmented, 119
Genesis, 234, 323–39; genealogy and genealogical history in, 117–21, 130–35; 12–50, historicity in, 130–35
genre, and history, 227–29
Gezer, 89, 164
Gideon, 61
God of Israel. *See Yahweh.*
Gog, 207–8
Governors within united monarchy, 168
Gunkel, Hermann, 222

H

Habiru, 145, 148–49, 245, 247. *See also* Apiru.
Hagar, 332
Haggai, Prophet, 211, 300–20
Haman, 385–88, 390, 391–92, 393–94
Hammurabi of Babylon, 93; Code of, 135, 230; dynasty, 132–33
Hannah, 72
Harran, 232
Hazor, 89, 164, 167, 232, 234; conquest of, 268–69, 272–73
Hegai, 393
Heilsgeschichte, 101
Hellenistic era, 201
Herod's temple, 313–14
Herodotus, 28
Hexateuch, 146, 147
Hezekiah of Judah, 91, 109, 195
historical; -critical method, 77–80, 106, 116, 120–26, 131; distance, 33–34; evidence, 34–36; fact, 105–7, narrative preaching, 439–54
historical minimalism. *See* minimalism, historical.
Historicity, 42–44, 54–56; biblical, modern challenges to, 44–52; of the Divided Monarchy, 188–99; in Genesis 12–50, 130–35; and large numbers, 297–99; of the patriarchal narratives, 219–25; tribal, 134
Historie, 101
historiography, 27, 31–33, 56–57, 80–82, 109, 117
history, 26–29, 97–98, 108–9, 226; biblical, 38–44, 75–83, 99–105, 109–10, 228–29; casual, 29–30; critical view of, 227–28; deliberative, 30; factual, 27–29, 31–33; fiction and, 54–73; genealogical, 119–21; genre and, 227–29; material remains of, 30; selectivity of, 33, 61–64; theology and, 97–111; sources for, 29–31, 40–42
historicized fiction, 55
Hittite treaties, 40, 94–95, 172, 251
Hobbes, Thomas, 121
Hormah, 348
humor, in book of Esther, 380–406

Hyksos, 249, 257–61

I

Iggeret, 176
inquiry, role of, 35
inscriptions; Black Obelisk, 91; cuneiform, 89–90; Egyptian, 233–34; Kuntillet ʿAjrud, 95; Kurkh Stele, 91; Lachish, 92; Mari–33, 232; Memphis Stele, 245; Merenptah, 88, 271, 273–75; Mesha, 90–91; Mesopotamian, 230–33; Moabite Stone, 90–91; Murashu, 209; Nuzi, 93; Rosetta Stone, 237; royal, 291–96; Taylor Prism, 91–92; Tell Dan, 90, 166; treaty texts, 94–95
internal time within narrative, 449
intertextuality, 71–73
Iron Age, 265
Iron Age I, 149, 153, 157–58, 280; Early, 220
Iron Age II, 150
irony, in book of Esther, 380–406
Isaiah, Prophet, 109
Ishmael, 302
Israel; as scholarly construct, 47; divided monarchy of, 179–200; origins of, 142–54, 156; united monarchy of, 160–78; wilderness journeys of, 340–59, 416
Israel Stele. *See* Merenptah.
Issachar, 63–64

J

Jacob, 70–71, 230, 231, 332
Jael, 62–63
Jebel Sin Bisher, 351–52
Jehu of Israel, 89, 91
Jephthah, 144
Jeremiah, Prophet, 207
Jericho, 143; conquest of, 144, 262–64; Eglon's palace at, 271–72
Jerusalem; evidence for, 161–63; population of, 284–86, 288; siege of, 92, 206
Jezreel Valley, 145–46
Joram of Israel, 90
Joseph, 257
Joshua, 59, 93–94
Joshua the high priest, 305

Subject Index

Josiah of Judah, 67–68
Judah, 59, 90, 206, 300–1
Judges, 269–81; narratives, 416

K

king lists, 132–33, 182
Kuntillet ʿAjrud, 95
Kurkh Stele, 91

L

Laban, 231
Labashi-Marduk of Babylon, 207
Lachish, 92, 195
Laish. *See* Dan, Tell.
La Peyrère, Isaac de, 121
Late-Date Exodus/Conquest, 143–45
Leitmotif, 419
Leitwort, 419, 440

M

macrostructure, 71–73
Malachi, (prophet), 213
Mardikh, Tell, 49–50
Mari, 135, 232
maximalists, 45, 102–4, 188, 220–21
Medes, 204–5
medialists, 102
Megiddo, 67–68, 89, 164–66, 167
Memphis Stele, 245
Mendenhall hypothesis of scribal confusion, 297–99
Merenptah, 88, 237–38, 271, 273–75
Mesha Inscription, 90–91
Mesopotamia inscriptions, 230–33
midrashic detail, 109–10
minimalism; historical, 45–52, 85–86, 88, 99–102, 188–92, 202; patriarchal narratives and, 223–25
Moab, 90, 193
Moabite Stone, 90–91
Mordecai, 385–88, 391–92, 393–94, 402
Moses, 71; historiography of, 126–30; revelation of Yahweh to, 325
Murashu Archives, 209

N

Nabonidus of Babylon, 207
Nahor, 232

Narrative Criticism, 442–44
narrative texts; analysis of, 426–33; arrangement of, 64–69, 417–34; context of, 56–57, 424–26; elements of, 444–51; interpreting, 433–34; literary dimension of, 54–73; message of, 411–37; nature of, 415–24; purpose of, 412–15; shaping, 448–49.
Nathan, (prophet), 366, 372–73, 450
Near East, genealogy, 132–33; inscriptions, 230–34. *See also* inscriptions.
Nebuchadnezzar of Babylon, 198–99, 205
Neco of Egypt, 67–68
Nehemiah, 212–13, 303; building activities of, 162n
Neo-Babylonian Empire, 204–10
Neriglissar, 207
New Criticism, 442
New Documentary Hypothesis, 122
Nineteenth Dynasty of Egypt, 237–38
Noah, 65, 68
Noth, Martin, 222
Numbers; book of, 33, 340–59; structure of, 345–49; literary units of, 343–45; source-critical division, 341–43
numbers, use of, 283–99
Nuzi, 93, 230–32

O

Old Testament; as history, 116–17; as literature, 116, 187–88; nature of, 75–76; preaching from, 409–38; as theology, 98–99, 116
Omri of Israel, 193–94
Osorkon IV, 196
Ostraca, 92

P

Palestine, 217, 287–89
paneled structuring, 69–70
parable, 32, 32n
parallelism, 72–73
patriarchal narratives, 115–37; dating, 217–35; background of, 217–19; historicity of, 219–25; maximalist analysis of, 220; orthodox analysis of, 219–20; tradition-historical analysis of, 222–23; versions

of, 122–26; Yahweh in, 323–39. *See also* narrative texts.
Peaceful-Infiltration Model, 145–48
Peasant-Revolt Model, 148–49
Pedaiah, 305
Pentateuch, 40, 100, 146, 147; grammar of, 173–74; sources for, 122–23
Per-Ramesses, 248–49
Persian court chronicle, 398
Persian Empire, 201, 210–13
perspective, 57–61
Peru-nefer, 260–61
Pithom, 258–60
plot, 445
point of view, 59–61, 402–3, 420–21, 446–47
population levels; United Monarchy and, 163–64; Jerusalem, 167, 284–86, 288
postexilic Israel, 201–14, 300–320
poststructuralism, 81
preaching from narrative texts, 409–54
probability, 35–36
Ptolemy's Canon, 182
Purim, 398–99

Q
Qantir, 249
Qarqar, Battle of, 62, 91
quote prominence analysis, 362–68

R
Ramesses of Egypt, 143, 157, 237–38, 248; archaeology of, 249–50; city of, 260–62
Ramesses II of Egypt, 193, 236, 248, 261; death, 252; campaigns of, 250–51; monument building by, 252; political relations of, 251; tomb of, 253
reader-response hermeneutics, 81
reality, reconstruction of, 141–42, 155–56
recapitulation, 64–65
Reformation, 121
Renaissance, 121
repetition, 69–71, 419
Restoration, 303–18
revelation, 40–42
Rosetta Stone, 237
royal inscriptions, 291–96
Ruth, 58–59

S
Samson, 67, 71–72, 73
Samuel, (prophet), 366, 371–72
Samuel–Kings, 107, 175–77
Sarah, 108, 230, 331
Saul of Israel, 366
Scriptural testimony, 289
Scythians, 207
second temple studies, 201–2
Sefer, 176
selectivity, 33, 61–64, 76–77, 417–19
Senegal, 134
Sennacherib of Assyria, 91–92, 109, 194–96
Seti I of Egypt, 248; tomb of, 253, 254
setting of narrative, 449–51
Shalmaneser III of Assyria, 91
Shealtiel, 305
Shechem, 234, 277–80
Shenazzar, 305
Sheshbazzar, 304–6. *See also* Zerubbabel of Judah.
Sheshonq I of Egypt, 165–66, 193
Shiloh, fall of, 280–81
Shishak of Egypt, 165–66, 177, 193. *See also* Ramesses II of Egypt.
Sidon, 91
significances, 451–52
Sinai, Mount, 350–54
Sinuhe, 234
Sisera, 62–63
six-chambered gates, 164–66
Six-Day War, 147
skepticism, 35–36, 45–49, 77–80, 85–86, 121–22, 131
slave, cost of, 235
So of Egypt, 196
social sciences, 169; biblical texts and, 202–3; Divided Monarchy and, 186–87
Solomon, 62, 89, 141–42, 167, 291–96, 366, 376–77, 416–17
Spinoza, Benjamin de, 121
statehood, ancient concept of, 163–64
static characters in narrative, 448
Stepped Stone Structure, 167
Syria, 217

T

Taylor Prism, 91–92
temporal overlay, 65–69
tentative reality, 155–56
Thutmose of Egypt, 237, 242
Thutmose II of Egypt, 240–42
Thutmose III of Egypt, 242–45
Thutmose IV of Egypt, 247
Timnah, 141–42
tôlᵉdôt formula, 127, 228
tradition-historical model, 145–48, 222
treaty texts, 94–95
truth claims, 31–33, 42–43
Twelfth Dynasty of Egypt, 260–62
Tyre, 91

U

United Monarchy, 360–79; literary issues, 169–77; remains of, 160–69

V

Victory Stele, 237
Von Rad, Gerhard, 222

W

water supplies and population, 284–85
Wayyiqtol, 65–69
Wellhausen, Julius, 122–26, 131, 217, 223
Werkinterpretation, 440
Wilderness narratives, 340–59, 416
Wisdom Literature, 398
Wolof tribal genealogies, 134

Y

Yahweh, 61, 122, 184; as actor and speaker, 364–65, 423; meaning of, 326–28; origins of, 323–26; patriarchs' knowledge of, 323–39; quotes of, 368–71; Samaria's, 95; use of, 327–35

Z

Zechariah, Prophet, 211, 307, 319–20
Zedekiah of Judah, 301
Zerubbabel of Judah, 304–6, 311, 317–18

Author Index

A

Aharoni, Y., 342–43
Ahlström, Gösta W., 47
Albertz, R., 203
Albrektson, Bertil, 58
Albright, William F., 183, 265
Allen, L., 207–8
Allen, Ronald J., 290, 441
Alt, Albrecht, 145, 146
Alter, Robert, 55, 441
Amit, Yairah, 440–41, 446, 450, 451
Ashley, Timothy R., 343
Astour, Michael C., 269–70
Austel, Hermann, 160–78
Averbeck, Richard E., 115–37
Avishur, Y., 190

B

Bar-Efrat, Shimon 449
Barr, James, 226
Barstad, H. M., 210
Barton, John, 139
Bebbington, David, 37
Bedford, P. R., 211
Ben-Tor, Amnon, 273
Berg, Sandra B., 394–95, 402, 403–4, 405
Bergen, Robert D., 360–79
Berquist, Jon L., 202
Bienkowski, Piotr, 271
Bietak, Manfred, 249, 261
Biran, Avraham, 276
Blenkinsopp, J., 213
Block, Daniel I., 207–8, 409–38
Blum, Erhard, 124, 125, 129
Breasted, J. H., 252
Brettler, M. Z., 189

Briant, P., 204
Bright, John, 9, 38–39, 213
Broshi, Magen, 285–86, 287–89
Brueggemann, Walter, 369
Buber, Martin, 440
Bullock, C. Hassell, 97–111
Bush, Frederic W., 211

C

Carter, C. E., 212
Cassuto, Umberto, 327
Childs, Brevard, 103–4, 325
Chisholm, Robert B., Jr., 54–73, 402–3
Clines, David J. A., 187, 403
Coats, G. W., 341
Cole, R. Dennis, 340–59
Collins, John J., 226
Coote, Robert B., 45–46, 47, 48
Cross, F. M., 170, 184
Curtis, Byron G., 300–20

D

Dandamaev, M., 204
Davies, G. Henton, 101
Davies, Philip R., 47, 49, 175–76, 188–89
Davies, W. D., 204
De Pury, Albert, 170
De Vaulx, J., 342
De Vaux, Roland, 327
Deist, Ferdinand, 226
Dequecker, L, 213
Dever, William G., 48, 51–52, 74–75, 163–64, 168, 224, 225, 233
Dillard, Raymond B., 62
Dillmann, A., 342
Dilthey, Wilhelm, 36

E

Eichrodt, Walther, 102
Elayi, J., 204
Eskenazi, T. C., 202–3
Exum, J. C., 187

F

Fewell, D. N., 186
Finkelstein, Israel, 149–50, 164–65, 280–81, 287–88, 289
Finkelstein, L., 204
Flanagan, J. W., 191
Fleming, Daniel, 135
Flinders Petrie, W. M., 193, 273
Fokkelmann, J. P., 444–45
Fouts, David, 57, 283–99
Fox, James, 134
Fox, Michael V., 397, 400
Frei, Peter, 202
Fretheim, Terence, 337
Fritz, Volkmar, 147

G

Garstang, John, 263–64, 271–72
Glueck, Nelson, 141–42
Goedicke, Hans, 196
Goldingay, John, 97, 105–6, 108–9, 190, 208–9
Goldstein, J., 209
Gordis, Robert, 397, 398
Gottwald, Norman, 148
Grayson, A. Kirk, 292–93
Green, A. R., 196
Grisanti, Michael, 10, 11, 457–65
Gunkel, Hermann, 440
Gunn, D. M., 186

H

Hallo, William F., 50
Halpern, Baruch, 31–32, 167–68, 190
Hamilton, Victor P., 203
Harel, M., 351–52
Harris, James, 252
Hasel, Gerhard, 106
Hayes, John, 38–39
Heinzerling, Rüdinger, 298
Heltzer, M., 190

Hendel, Ronald, 220–21
Herberg, Will, 43–44
Herodotus, 309
Herrmann, S., 189–90
Hertzberg, H. W., 375
Hess, Richard S., 51–52
Hill, A. E., 213
Hoerth, Alfred J., 140, 152
Hoffmeier, James K., 51–52, 154, 341
Hoglund, K., 211
Holladay, John, Jr., 163, 258–60
Howard, David M., Jr., 10, 11, 22–53, 173, 186, 191, 400, 401, 411
Hummel, Horace, 404
Hurwitz, Avi, 51–52, 175–76

I

Irvine, Judith, 134

J

Jacob, Benno, 327
Jacob, Edmond, 98
Johnston, Gordon H., 380–406
Josephus, 313
Judd, E. P., 202–3

K

Kaiser, Walter C., Jr., 9, 39, 43–44, 103, 140, 152, 326–27, 411, 439–54
Kaufmann, Yehezkel, 404
Kenyon, Kathleen, 262–64, 271
Kitchen, Kenneth A., 134–35, 162, 196, 225, 229, 234
Knauf, E. A., 171, 185
Kropat, A., 176
Kuhrt, Amélie, 210

L

Laniak, T. S., 211
Leibowitz, N., 327
Lemaire, André, 166
Lemche, Niels Peter, 45, 47, 50, 189, 218, 228
Lewis, C. S., 52
Livingston, David P., 266
Long, Thomas G., 441
Long, V. Philips, 41, 51–52, 103, 107, 187
Longman, Tremper, III, 62, 187

Author Index

Lot, Ferdinand, 37–38

M
McCarter, Kyle, 220–21
McKenzie, S. L., 184
Malamat, Abraham, 135
Mandelbaum, Maurice, 36
Martens, Elmer, 97–98
Mathewson, Steven D., 445, 449–50
Mendenhall, George E., 148, 297–98
Merrill, Eugene H., 9, 39, 74–96, 102–3, 140, 147, 152, 155, 201, 213, 235, 280, 411, 457–62
Milgrom, J., 344, 354
Millard, A. R., 227, 229
Miller, J. Maxwell, 38–39, 48, 186
Mitchell, T. C., 208
Mittmann, Siegfried, 213
Moberly, R. W. L., 328, 335
Moore, G. F., 54
Morrison, Martha, 231
Motyer, Alec, 326
Muilenburg, J., 101

N
Niebuhr, Gustav, 75
Norin, S., 191
Noth, Martin, 38–39, 169–70, 222

O
Oded, B., 208

P
Parke-Taylor, G. H., 324
Partlow, Jonathon, 403
Paton, Lewis Bayles, 398–99
Patterson, Richard D., 179–200
Payne, J. B., 183
Pettinato, Giovanni, 328–29
Porten, B., 209
Provan, Iain W., 51–52

R
Rainey, A. F., 51–52
Rasmussen, Carl G., 138–59
Rea, John, 257–58
Redford, D., 341
Rendtorff, Rolf, 124, 125, 129

Robinson, Edward, 264–66
Rohl, D., 193
Römer, Thomas, 170
Rooker, Mark F., 217–35
Rosenzweig, Franz, 440–41
Ross, Allen P., 323–39
Ross, J. F., 329
Rowley, H. H., 238
Ryle, Herbert, 325

S
Sailhamer, John, 99, 103–4
Sapin, J., 204
Scolnic, Benjamin E., 298
Segal, M. H., 327, 338
Sellin, Ernest, 266
Shafer, R. J., 35
Shanks, H., 190
Shea, William H., 236–55
Shiloh, Yigal, 286, 287–88
Shryock, Andrew, 134
Silverman, M., 209
Ska, Jean Louis, 449
Snell, D. C., 208
Soggin, Alberto, 38–39
Speiser, E. A., 224, 325
Steiner, R. C., 212
Sternberg, Meir, 31–32
Stolper, M. W., 212
Strange, John, 46

T
Talmon, Shemaryahu, 398
Thiele, Edwin R., 142, 183
Thompson, Thomas L., 46, 47, 189, 223–25
Timm, Stefan, 210
Tollefson, K. D., 203
Toombs, Lawrence, 279–80

U
Ussishkin, David, 164–65

V
Van Seters, John, 46, 124, 125, 129, 132, 223–25
VanderKam, James C., 213
Von Rad, Gerhard, 80, 99–101, 325

W

Waldbaum, J. C., 208
Walton, John H., 109
Warner, S. M., 226
Weeks, Kent, 252
Weiland, Forrest S., 394
Wellhausen, Julius, 44–45, 122–23, 129
Wenham, Gordon, 327–28, 331–32, 345–47
Westermann, Claus, 125–26, 325–26
Whitelam, Keith W., 45–46, 47, 48, 49
Whybray, R. N., 189
Wiebe, John, 397
Wilkinson, John, 284–85
Williamson, H. G. M., 203, 213
Wilson, Robert R., 125, 132, 133
Wiseman, D. J., 203, 206
Wood, Bryant G., 157, 256–82
Wood, Leon J., 9, 39, 140, 152

Y

Yamauchi, Edwin M., 191, 201–14
Youngblood, R., 369
Younger, K. Lawson, Jr., 51–52, 57, 63

Z

Zadok, R., 204

Scripture Index

Genesis, 34, 39, 109–10, 125, 173, 177, 226, 228, 236, 323, 339, 409
Genesis–Deuteronomy, 30, 34, 40, 100, 121, 124, 126, 128, 146, 173, 178, 186, 221, 228, 231, 324, 410, 460
1 . . . . 68–69, 330
1–11 . . . . 117, 123
1:2, 6, 7–8 57–58
2:4 . . . . 68–69, 118, 127–28, 330
2:19 68–69
3 330
4 330
4:1 330
4:26 . . . 324–28, 333, 335
5 . . . . 117, 119, 416
6:9 118
6:11–20 65
7:2–3, 7–24 65
7:17–24 68
8:1–5 68
8:2–5 65
10 . . . . 119, 416
10:32 128
11 416
11:9 118
11:10–30 119
11:27–32 218
11:27–50 424
11:30 . . . . 120, 417
11:31 135
11:31–32 232
12 335
12–50 . . . . 116, 117, 120, 126–137
12:1 120
12:3 128
12:6 233
12:6–8 120
12:8 . . . . 325, 334
12:10–20 70
12:10–13:2 108
13:3, 18 120
13:16 417
13:18 233
14 234
14:13 135
14:13–14 120
14:14 249
14:22 . . . . 130, 332
15:2 . . . . 130, 332
15:3 231
15:5 . . . . 296, 417
15:7 . . . . 130, 331
15:8 130
15:13–16 248
16 230
16:1–16 332
16:2, 5 130
16:11 . . . . 130, 332
16:16 . . . . 230, 332
17 . . . . 65, 325
17:1 336
17:1–8 70
18:1 120
18:14 . . . . 130, 331
18:19 332
19–20 65
19:37–38 130
20:1 120
20:1–18 70
21 417
21:5 219
21:10 230
21:22–34 120
22 418
22:1–17 70
22:3 67
22:8 333
22:14 . . . . 130, 333
22:17 296
22:19 120
22:20–24 119
23:1–6 120
24:1–4 120
24:10 135
24:15 119
25:12–18 119
25:19 118
25:26 219
26:7–10 70
26:25 233
26:26–33 120
26:33 130
27 . . . . 232, 423
27:20 393
27:42 422
28:3 336
28:13–15, 18–19, 20 . . 71
28:16 332
29:1–3 120
29:4–5 135
29:21–30 221
30 230
31:17–24 120
31:44–53 30
32:28 71
32:32 130
33:18–34:2 120
35:1–8 120
35:3 71
35:10–15 71
35:11 336
35:16–21 120
35:20 130
35:47 336
36 . . . . 119, 416

Scripture Index

37:1 120	6:2–4 324	19:1 350
37:2 118	6:2–5 323	19:6 128
37:12–17 120	6:2–8 130	20–23 94–95
37:25 219	6:3 . . . . 325, 327, 329,	20:1 172
37:28 235	333, 336–38	20:2 331
38 449–50	6:4 337	20:3–5 357
38:29–30 119	6:6–8 160	21:32 235
39:2, 5, 21, 23 330	6:7 337	23:10–12 175
41 110	6:14–27 416	25–31 . . . . 126, 127
41:57–42:2 108	6:20 329	32 346
46:5–7 120	7–11 110	32–34 . . . . 126, 409
46:8–27 119	7:8–11:10 108	32:13–14 120
46:27 295	7:17–21 110	34 335
47:1–6 120	8:27 350	34:5–7 334
47:9, 28 219	9:8–12 242	34:6–7 335
47:11 . . . . . 152, 248, 260	11:1–10 110	39:32–43 127
47:26 130	12–17 352	40 127
47:27 . . . . . 152, 248, 260	12:2 346	
48–49 . . . . 221, 232	12:29–36 346	Leviticus, 139, 151, 159,
48:1 119	12:37 . . . . . 152, 248, 260,	410
48:3 336	349	1–8 127
48:15 128	12:40 . . . . . 219, 248, 260	1:1–4 136
49:10 370	13–19 347	18:18 221
49:25 336	13:19 262	26 425
	13:20 349	26:33 371
Exodus, 139, 151, 159,	14 418	
236, 327, 410, 413	14–15 . . . . 244, 252	Numbers, 139, 151, 159,
1–19 409	14:2 349	296, 348, 356, 359, 410,
1:1–7 119	14:6–7 252	460
1:8–12 257	14:13–31 346	1–10 358
1:8–22 108	14:18 243	1–21 352
1:11 . . 152, 236, 239, 244,	14:21–29 108	2 295
248, 257, 258, 260	14:21–31 349	3 295
1:13 258	14:23–28 59–60	9:1–2 343
1:13–2:14 262	14:30 241	9:15–23 343
2–3 131	15 433	9:18–23 . . . . 344, 359
2:17–19 71–72	15:4 . . . . 59–60, 349	10–17 409
2:24 120	15:13–18 160	10–21 416
3 336	15:20 346	10:12 350
3–18 126	15:22 349	11–12 347
3:6 . . . . 120, 126	15:23 349	11–25 358
3:12 61	15:23–26 346	11:4–34 346
3:13–14 336	15:27 . . . . 346, 349	11:34 350
3:14 325	16–17 416	11:35 350
3:14–15 130	16:1–15 350	12:1–15 346
3:15 126	16:1–36 346	12:16 350
3:18 351	16:35 346	13:3 351
3:22 108	17:1 350	13:25–14:38 348
4:11 58	17:8–16 346	13:26 351
4:29–12:36 262	19 41	14:3–45 348
5:3 351	19–24 126	14:8 335
6 . . . . 324–29, 336	19:1–20:21 346	20–21 347

20:1 353	33:41–42 ...... 342, 353	9:7–10:11 409
20:2–13 347	33:42–43 353	10 352
20:22 353	33:42–49 347	10:6 352
21:1–3 348	33:43–44 ...... 342, 353	10:7 353
21:4 353	33:44 .... 347, 353	10:12 174
21:10 353	33:45 353	10:16 174
21:11 .... 353, 354	33:45–46 354	11:1, 13, 18, 22 174
21:12–20 343	33:45–49 342	12:5 .... 185, 371
21:14 ...... 30, 127, 136	33:46–49 354	12:5, 11, 14,
21:21–35 143	33:49 347	16, 18, 21 371
21:25 167	33:50 356	14:23–25 371
21:30 354	33:50–51 342	15:20 371
22–24 409	33:50–56 ..... 341, 348,	16:2, 6–7, 11 371
22:1 354	354, 355	17:14–15 174
26 295	33:51 356	19:1 94
26:59 329	33:52 355	21:15–17 221
31–36 340	33:52–53 .... 355, 356	26:3–5 120
32 359	33:53 355	26:5–10 ..... 100–1, 222
33 ....340–59, 344,	33:54 .... 355, 357	27 174
352, 359, 416	33:55–56 ...... 355, 358	27:15 185
33:1–4 342	34 359	28 .... 186, 425
33:2 344	34:1–12 341	28:63–64 371
33:2–40 347	34:1–15 359	30:6 174
33:3 349		31:9–13 311
33:3–4 341	Deuteronomy, 94–95, 123,	33 232
33:3–17 346	139, 151, 159, 173, 174,	34:3 271
33:5–8 .... 342, 349	178, 186, 410, 421, 432,	
33:5–37 347	433, 460	Joshua, 35, 46, 48, 57, 139,
33:6 347	Deuteronomy–2 Kings,	145, 151, 159, 340
33:8 347	124, 169, 171, 184	Joshua–2 Kings, 171, 413
33:8–9 .... 342, 349	1–3 409	Joshua–Esther, 30, 409,
33:9 347	1–4 352	410
33:9–10 349	1:2 352	1–11 ..... 144, 146, 156
33:10–11 .... 342, 349	1:8 120	1:6–9 312
33:11–17 350	4 409	2:1–21 262
33:12–14 342	4:6–7 415	2:5 263
33:13 345	4:10 172	2:6 264
33:14 347	4:15–20 185	2:15 263
33:15–17 342	5 409	3 41
33:17–18 .... 342, 350	5:5 172	3:16 264
33:18–25 351	5:6–8 185	4 .... 30, 41
33:18–30 342	5:14–15 175	6 262
33:24 358	6:4–5 .... 174, 185	6–8 144
33:25–32 352	6:10–11 94	6:5 .... 263, 264
33:30–33 342	6:12–24 100–101	6:17–18 264
33:32–34 353	7:1 295	6:20 .... 263, 264
33:34–37 ...... 342, 353	7:7–8 415	6:24 .... 143, 264
33:37 347	7:7–11 120	7 267
33:37–41 353	7:27 295	7–8 264
33:38–39 347	8 409	7:2 .... 265, 267
33:38–40 342	8:17 422	7:3, 5 268
33:40 348	9:1–24 415	8 267

8:9 . . . . 265, 267	3:14 . . . . 272, 423	17–21 73
8:11 268	3:15 423	17:1 72
8:12 . . . . 265, 267	3:15–16, 20–22 422	17:6 425
8:14 268	3:15–17 . . . . 66, 69	18:1 425
8:28 . . . . 143, 268	3:17 422	18:7, 27 . . . . . . 249, 276
8:29 268	3:18 422	18:28 276
9 144	3:19 422	18:31 . . . . 275, 277
10:2 268	3:19–20 . . . . 418, 422	19:1 425
11:1–11 268	3:22–25 422	20:29–45 64–65
11:4–6, 9 59–60	3:28 . . . . 422, 423	21:25 425
11:11 143	3:29 272	
11:20, 23 356	3:31 . . . . 416, 426	Ruth
12 416	4–5 . . 59–60, 62–63, 270,	2:3 393
12:9 265	272, 426	3:6–7 59
13:1–7 139	4:1 425	3:8 58–59
15:1–62 157	4:2 272	4:11–12 133
15:48–52 153	4:3 272	4:12 119
17:16–18 59–60	4:13–15 272	4:18–22 . . . . 119, 133, 416
18:11–28 63–64	4:21 62–63	
19:1–9 63–64	4:21–22 63	1 Samuel, 52, 53, 72–73,
19:10–48 63	4:24 272	107, 175, 176, 178, 432,
19:49–51 63–64	4:28–30 63	460
23 169	5:17 275	1 72
23–24 232	6 418	1–4 280
23:11–13 358	6–9 . . . . 298, 426	1–1 Kings 11 360–79
24:2–4 120	6:1 425	1:1 72
24:2–13 101	6:15 61	1:6 58
24:12–13 94	6:16 60	1:9 72–73
24:26 279	6:17, 20, 22, 24, 25–34,	1:17 73
	36–40 61	3 70
Judges, 54, 72–73, 145,	9 . . . . 277, 280	6:9 393
146, 151, 159, 425	9:4, 6, 20, 27 277	8–1 Kings 11 362–66, 377
1 . . . . 139, 269, 425	9:35–40, 45 279	9–31 421
1:1–2:5 67	9:46, 47 277	9:2 448
1:1–3:6 425	9:46–49 278	10:1–8 367
1:11–15 426	9:49 277	11:15 371
1:19 59–60	10:1–5 . . . . 416, 426	12 169
1:27–36 63–64	10:6 425	12:6–17 . . . . 367, 368,
2–16 425	10:6–12:7 426	371–72
2:1–5 59–60	11:26 144	14:47, 52 295
2:6–3:6 66	12–2 Kings 25 181	16–17 417
2:10–23 159	12:8–15 . . . . 416, 426	18:7 295
2:11 425	13 72	23 452–54
2:11–23 169	13–16 426	24:10–16 367
2:11–3:6 425	13:1 425	
2:19 426	13:2 72	2 Samuel, 33, 52, 53, 73,
3–16 423	14:5–6, 8–9 71–72	107, 175, 176, 178, 432,
3:7 425	15:9–19 71–72	460
3:7–11 426	16:1–3 67	1:6 393
3:7–16:31 . . . . . 425, 426	16:4–21 70	1:19–27 367
3:12 . . . . 423, 425	17 72	5:9 167
3:12–30 271, 422–23, 426	17–18 275	7 107

7:1–16 184	9:3–9 . . 367, 368, 370–71, 378	18:7–8 195
7:1–17 107		18:13–16 195
7:4–16 . 367, 368, 368–70, 373, 374, 377	9:15 . . . . 89, 167	18:13–19:7 91–92
	9:15–19 164	18:13–20:19 109
7:18–29 367	9:18 219	18:14–16 194
8:1 294	9:24 167	18:17–19:36 195
8:1–18 290	10 294	18:17–19:37 194
8:2–14 295	10:10, 12, 20, 27 294	19:8–37 194
8:4–5 291	11:31–39 367, 368, 373–74	19:9 195
8:6 293	14:8 186	19:34 186
8:13–14 291	14:16, 23 185	20:5–6 186
8:14, 15 293	14:25 192	20:12–15 205
11 441	14:25–28 . . . . . . 166, 192	21:7–9 186
12:7–12 . . . . 367, 368, 372–73	15:3–5 186	22:2 186
	15:11–14 185	23:8–9, 13, 15, 19–20 185
12:8 58	16:3–4 185	
12:11 450	16:21–28 193	23:29–30 . . . . 67–68, 205
22:1 375	16:31 194	24:10–17 198
22:2–51 . . . . 367, 368, 374–75	17 447	24:14–16 301
	17–2 Kings 13 424	24:20–25:12 92
24 . . . . 286, 289	17:16–23 185	25:1–21 198
24:9 289	17:24 447	25:8–21 371
	18:36 120	25:11–12 301
1 Kings, 29, 33, 43, 52, 107, 173, 175, 176, 177, 178, 190, 216, 421, 432	21 446	25:27–30 170
	21:3–6 185	
	21:28–29 90	1 Chronicles, 29, 33, 43, 107, 175, 176, 177, 178, 432, 460
2:1–9 367	22:43 185	
4 168		
4–5 294	2 Kings, 29, 33, 43, 52, 107, 173, 175, 176, 177, 178, 190, 216, 421, 432	3 305
4–11 416		3:18, 19 305
4:1 432		17:1–15 107
4:1–7 . . . . . . 427, 428–31	1:9–15 69–70	18:1–17 290
4:20 294	3:4–27 90–91	21 . . . . 286, 288, 289
4:21–5:16 291	4:1–7 . . . . . 418, 421, 433, 434, 435, 436	21:5 289
4:24 219		29:17–19 120
4:24–25 295	4:7–19 156	29:29 293
4:26 291	4:21–34 219	
4:29 . . . . 293, 294	7:2 57–58	2 Chronicles, 29, 33, 43, 107, 175, 176, 177, 178, 432, 460
4:32 291	8–19 186	
4:34 293	9:15–18 219	
5:3, 4 295	12:3 185	8:4 219
5:10 293	13:22–23 120	9:27 . . . . 291, 294
5:12 295	14:3 186	9:29 293
5:13, 15 291	14:4 185	10–36 181
6:1 . . . . 142, 144, 152, 219, 236, 238, 240, 243, 245, 246, 254	15:4 185	12:1–12 192
	16:2 186	12:4 192
	16:4 185	17:1–18 181
8:2 311	17:4 196	19:1–20:30 181
8:11, 22 377	17:7–23 169	26:6–15 181
8:23–53 . . . . 367, 368, 376–77	17:23 371	28:5, 19 60
	18–23 123	28:15 271
8:54 377	18:3 186	28:23 60

29:3–32:8 181	1:3–22 396	9:29–32 384
30:6 120	2:1–18 384	10 384
32:1–22 194	2:19–23 .... 384, 385	
34:3–7 181	2:20 389	Job–Song of Songs, 410
35:1–25 181	3:1–7 .... 384, 385	
35:23–24 67–68	3:1–15 .... 382, 384	Psalms, 432
36:6–7 199	3:1–9:19 382	18 375–76
36:17–21 92	3:7–15 .... 385, 396	19:1 41
36:23 303	3:8–15 384	54 453
	3:10, 11 390	78 110
Ezra, 29, 43, 175, 177, 208,	3:12–15 ...... 384, 386	78:60 281
211, 304, 305, 315, 319,	4:1–3 .... 384, 387	86:15 335
438, 460	4:1–17 .... 382, 384	103:8 335
1 306	4:3 .... 396, 397	104:3 57–58
1–6 305–6	4:4–17 .... 384, 385	105 109–10
1:2–4 303	4:7 393	136:15 .... 241, 244, 252
1:8 304	4:12–17 389	145:8 335
1:11 304	4:13–14 403	148:4 57–58
2 .... 212, 306	4:14 .... 394, 397	
2–6 306	4:15–16 389	Proverbs
2:2 .... 304, 306	4:16 ...... 396, 397 4:17	25:1 136
4:8, 17 212	389	
5:1 .... 307, 319	5:1–8 ....384, 385,	Ecclesiastes
5:7–17 310	388, 396, 403	9:11 393
5:14–15 .... 304, 306	5:1–14 382	
5:14–16 306	5:9–14 .... 384, 385, 392	Isaiah–Malachi, 410, 432
5:16 305	5:9–6:14 384	
6:2–12 303	6:1–11 .... 384, 387, 388,	Isaiah
6:14 .... 307, 319	389, 391, 392	6 409
6:14–15 303	6:6–11 390	7:1–16 182
7:10 .... 410, 435	6:12–14 385	9:1–7 370
7:11–26 303	6:12–7:10 382	11:1–16 370
7:12–26 212	6:13 393	16:5 370
7:27–9:15 420	7:1–10 ....384, 385,	36–37 194
	388, 396	36–39 .... 109, 182, 409
Nehemiah, 43, 211, 460	7:9–10 .... 384, 385, 390	36:1–39:8 91–92
1–7 420	8:1–14 .... 384, 385	39:1–4 205
5:15 213	8:1–17 .... 382, 384	40–55 460
7 212	8:2, 8 390	40–66 109
8:8 10	8:9–14 .... 385, 386	52:6 337
9 178	8:15–17 ... 384, 385, 387	55:3 370
9:7–8 120	8:17 .... 387, 390	
9:17 335	9:1 389	Jeremiah, 207, 421
11:25 167	9:1–19 ....382, 384,	1 409
12:4 319	385, 390	1:1 307
12:12–21 319	9:6–10:3 381	7:1–8 182
12:31–13:31 420	9:9 399	7:12–14 281
	9:20–28 .... 384, 385	22:24 318
Esther, 34, 210, 380–406,	9:20–32 ...... 390, 396	23:5–6 370
413, 460	9:20–10:3 . 382, 384, 385	26–28, 409
1 .... 384, 390	9:22 .... 390, 399	26:6, 9 281
1–2 ...... 382, 384, 385	9:25 390	27–29 182

29:5–7 301
30:8 370
33:15–26 370
34:7 197
36–43, 409
37–39 182
39:10 301
41, 43 302
51:59–52:34 409
52 182
52:3–27 92
52:30 302

Lamentations
1:1 301

Ezekiel, 207, 460
1–3 409
1:1–2 182
16:46–57 167
24:1–2 182
33:21–22 409
34:23–24 370
37:24–25 370
38 208

Daniel, 208, 460
1–8 409
1:1–2 182
1:1–7 198
4 207
5 208

Hosea
1, 3 409
3:5 370
10:14 182

Joel
2:13 335

Amos
7:10–17 409
8:11–14 435
9:11 370

Jonah 409
4:2 335
4:11 288

Micah
5–6 298

Nahum
1:3 335

Haggai, 212, 213, 300,
       304, 320, 460
1:1 .... 305, 307, 320
1:2 310
1:3 307
1:4 .... 306, 310
1:5–6 311
1:6 316
1:8 311
1:9 .... 306, 311
1:12 ....307, 311
1:12–15 307
1:13 ......307, 308, 311
1:15 .... 311, 320
1:21 305
2:1 .... 306, 320
2:1–9 317
2:2 305
2:3 313
2:4 308
2:4–5 312
2:6–9 313
2:10 .... 306, 320
2:10–19 316
2:11–14 307
2:12–13 314
2:13 307
2:14 ......307, 315, 316
2:16–17 316
2:18–19 317
2:19 316
2:20 .... 307, 320
2:21 318
2:23 317

Zechariah, 213, 460
1–8 320
1:1 .... 319, 320
1:7 320
2:4 319
7:1 320
12:7–8 370

Malachi, 213, 460

Matthew–Luke, 33

Matthew–John, 30, 409

Matthew, 30
1 416
1:1 370
1:12 318
28:1–15 32–33

Mark 30

Luke 43
1:1–4 .... 28–29, 136
1:32 370
3:27 318

Luke–Acts, 30

John, 30, 43, 415
2:19, 21 314
20:30 33
20:30–31 .... 29, 416
20:31 415
21:25 .... 29, 33

Acts, 409
7:14 295
13:22–23 370
20:27 409

Romans, 433
1:3 370

1 Corinthians
15 .... 31, 42

Ephesians
6:12 60

Philippians
4:19 436

2 Timothy
2:8 370
3:16 41
3:16–17 .... 52, 433

Hebrews
1:1–2 40–41
11:10 314
12:28 314

Revelation
21:3, 22 314
22:16 370